THE GREAT MUTINY

Christopher Hibbert

THE GREAT MUTINY
India 1857

THE VIKING PRESS
NEW YORK

Published in 1978 by The Viking Press
625 Madison Avenue, New York, N.Y. 10022

LIBRARY OF CONGRESS CATALOGING IN PUBLICATION DATA
Hibbert, Christopher, 1924-
The Great Mutiny.
Bibliography: p.
Includes index.
1. India—History—Sepoy Rebellion, 1857-1858.
I. Title.
DS478.H488   954.03'17   78-15825
ISBN 0-670-34983-6

Pages 11–15 constitute an extension of this copyright page.

Printed in the United States of America
Set in Monotype Times

FOR NICK AND MARY

Contents

List of Plates

ILLUSTRATIONS ACKNOWLEDGEMENTS

The author and publishers are grateful to the following for permission to reproduce photographs: India Office Library for nos. 1, 2, 5, 6, 9, 17, 18, 19, 23, 24, 25, 31, 45, 49, 50, 52; National Army Museum for nos. 3, 4, 8, 11, 33, 34, 35, 36, 38, 39, 40, 43, 51; Radio Times Hulton Picture Library for nos. 7, 10, 14, 15, 16, 22, 30, 32, 37, 41, 42, 44, 46, 53, 54, 55; The Mansell Collection for nos. 12, 13, 47; Lieutenant-Colonel J. C. Inglis for no. 29; Mr Neil Lothian for nos. 27, 28, 48.

Author's Note
and Acknowledgements

This is a narrative history of the Indian uprising of 1857 incorporating as much hitherto unpublished material as I have been able to find. In order to recount in a single book events which Kaye and Malleson in their six volumes took 3,750 pages to describe, certain of these events have been treated rather cursorily so that others could be enlivened by the kind of detail that evokes the sight and sound of this most tragic episode in nineteenth-century Indian history. For the same reason little space has been given either to the analysis of military or political problems or to the discussion of the Mutiny as an early stage in India's struggle for independence.

Compared to the vast amount of material composed for and by the English, the Indian documentation of the Mutiny is extremely scanty. I am, however, profoundly grateful to the many Indians who went out of their way to help me when I was working in their country. I am particularly indebted to Shri Ravi Vyas, Shri Zamir Ansari, Shri Sudhir Bansal and to Dr Atma Ram Gulati who translated various documents for me from Hindi and Urdu. I am also most grateful to Shri S. Tirmizi, Deputy Director, National Archives of India, New Delhi; to Shri R. L. Madan, the Archivist, and his staff in the National Archives; to Dr K. P. Srivastava and the staff of the Uttar Pradesh State Archives in Lucknow; to Shri T. K. Mukherjee, Director of Archives, Government of West Bengal; and to Shri G. C. Joshi, Regional Archives Officer, Allahabad. For helping to make arrangements for me to see these Archives I would like to thank Shri G. Vethakkan, First Secretary, Education, High Commission of India in London; Sir Michael Walker, formerly British High Commissioner in Delhi; Lord Allen of Kilmahew; Major Ian Dowdall-Brown of the British High Commission; and Mr Stanley Hodgson of the British Council. I am also indebted to Dr Nazir Ahmad Chaudhry, Director of Archives in the Government of the Punjab; and Mr A. R. Murray of the British Embassy, Islamabad.

The principal collection of Mutiny papers is in the India Office Library where I have received most generous help from Mrs Rosemary Seton. There is a further large collection of papers at the Centre of South Asian Studies in the University of Cambridge where I was kindly assisted by

Miss Mary Thatcher. I am most grateful also to Mr D. S. Porter of the Department of Western Manuscripts at the Bodleian Library; to Mr A. E. B. Owen of Cambridge University Library; to Mr Patrick Cadell of the Department of Manuscripts, National Library of Scotland; to Mr D. K. Smurthwaite of the National Army Museum; to Mr J. C. Andrews and Miss Glover of the Ministry of Defence Whitehall Library; to Dr T. A. Heathcote, Curator of the Royal Military Academy Sandhurst Collection; to Major Kenneth Warburton and Father F. Turner, S.J. of Stonyhurst College; to Dr J. M. Fewster of the Department of Palaeography and Diplomatic, University of Durham; to Mrs M. A. Welch of the Manuscripts Department, University of Nottingham Library; to Mr E. J. Priestley of the Merseyside County Museums, Liverpool; to Mr James Campbell and Miss Montgomery of Worcester College, Oxford; to Colonel J. R. Baker, Secretary of the Rifle Brigade Museum Trust, Winchester; and to Major M. K. Beedle of the Regimental Headquarters, The Staffordshire Regiment, Lichfield.

I am also indebted to Mrs Mollie Travis and the Trustees of the Broadlands Archives; Miss Joan Wilson, the Duke of Wellington's archivist; and to the archivists and their staffs at the County Record Offices of West Sussex, North Yorkshire, Hertfordshire, Northamptonshire, Hampshire, Cambridgeshire, Lincolnshire, Kent, Northumberland, Warwickshire, Norfolk, Suffolk, Gloucestershire and Berkshire. I am equally grateful to Mr R. F. Atkins, Director of the Sheffield City Libraries; Mr J. M. Collinson, Archivist at the Leeds City Libraries; and Miss Judith Dale, Wolseley Librarian, Hove Area Library.

I am grateful to Her Majesty the Queen for gracious permission to quote from Queen Victoria's and the Prince Consort's correspondence in the Broadlands Papers.

A great number of family papers, letters, diaries and memoirs have been lent to me, and I want especially to thank Mrs Keith Arden for the papers of her husband's grandfather, Colonel William Radcliffe Peel Wallace; Miss Doris Ashton for the diaries of her grandmother, Edith Sharpley; Mrs Rosalind Aspinall for the Mayne family papers; Mrs Christina Back for the letters of her grandfather, Captain Henry Calthorpe Gardner; Mrs C. C. Baines for the memoirs of her husband's grandfather, General Arthur Maister; Brigadier R. A. Barron for the letters of his great-grandfather, Charles Henry Ewart; Lady Berners for the letters of her great-grandmother, Mrs Warwick Walter Wells; Major-General H. M. C. Bond for letters from his great-great-uncle, Robert Henry Ponsonby; Mr Kenneth D. H. Bond for the memoirs of his great-grandmother, Phoebe Jane Watts; Colonel R. P. Bridge for the papers of his aunt, Frances Carew; Mrs Collin Brown for papers of the Metcalfe, Bayley and Brown families; Commander Michael Chichester for the letters of his grandfather, Major-General Hugh Chichester; Colonel Henry Clowes for the letters of his great-uncle, George Clowes;

Sir Patrick Coghill for the letters of his great-uncle, Colonel Kendal Coghill; Miss Helen Davidson for a letter from her great-uncle, Richard Stairforth; Miss Mary Dodd for the memoirs of her great-grandmother, Sarah Fagan; Mrs Elizabeth Douglas for the letters of her great-grandfather, Ralph Assheton Nowell; Mr F. V. Eyles for a letter from Lieutenant Gerard Noel Money; Colonel C. G. Gordon for the diaries of his grandfather, General John Gordon; Miss Betty Green for the papers of her great-grandfather, Robert Parker Campbell; Miss Enid Hadow for the letters of Dr Gilbert Hadow; Mr Laurence Hardy for the memoirs of Lieutenant Frederick Hardy; Lieutenant-Colonel John Inglis for the papers of Sir John and Lady Inglis; Mrs Sheila Kidd and Mrs Ruby Bloomfield Walton for the papers of Mrs Walton's grandfather, Major Godfrey Colpoys Bloomfield; Mrs Phoebe Kerr for the reminiscences of her grandfather, David Foggo; Miss Sheila Lightfoot for the letters of her grandfather, J. G. Lightfoot; Mrs A. R. H. Macdonald for letters from her great-uncle, Lieutenant Williams Mountsteven; Mr Jack P. Mackie for the letters of Major James Bailie; Mr M. A. McLaggan for the letters of his wife's great-great-uncle, Major-General Sir C. R. H. Nicholl; Mr Ross Mangles for the papers of his grandfather, Ross Lowis Mangles; Miss Monica Morris for the papers of her father, Lieutenant-Colonel H. A. Morris; Lieutenant-Colonel H. R. Nicholl for the diaries of his grandfather, Major-General Sir C. R. H. Nicholl; Mr J. L. Northridge for a letter from Lord Lawrence; Mr F. C. G. Page for the diary of Colonel Montagu Hall; Mr L. Potiphar for the diary of his grandfather, Private F. Potiphar; Mrs Violet Rhodes James for the papers of her grandmother, Mrs Juxon Henry Jones; Mr David Shirreff for the papers of his great-great-grandfather, Major Francis Shirreff; Dr R. H. B. Snow for the memoirs of his grandfather, Lieutenant-General Richard Barter; Mrs Grace Stansfield for the papers of her husband's great-uncle, Major-General Henry Hamer Stansfield; Lady Tegart for the memoirs of her grandfather, Major Henry Henderson; Mrs E. M. L. Thomson for the diaries of her great-grandmother, Charlotte Isabella Lindsay Dampier; Mrs Georgina Thompson for the diary of her grandfather, Dr E. M. Wrench; Miss I. M. Vincent for the diary of her grandmother, Mrs George Wilson Boileau; Mrs Anne Walters for the papers of her great-grandfather, Major-General Frederick Parkinson Lester; Mr Edward Poore-Saurin-Watts for the papers of Major Robert Poore; Mrs B. Walker-Heneage-Vivian for letters from her father-in-law, Major Clement Walker-Heneage; Mrs Elizabeth Weller for the letters of her great-grandmother, Matilda Spry; Mr Christopher Willis for the reminiscences of his great-grandmother, Esther Anne Nicholson; Mrs David Young for the letters of her great-uncle, Sir Archdale Wilson; Mrs Malcolm Young for the letters of her great-great-aunt, Emma Young. I am also grateful to Lieutenant-General Frank Wilson for a copy of the diary of Mrs William Brydon.

For lending me other family records and rare books I am most grateful to Mr S. Bamford; Mr K. C. Brown; Miss R. E. Butter; the Hon. Mrs Désirée Butterwick; Miss Margot Collins; Group Captain A. R. F. de Salis and Lieutenant-Colonel E. W. F. de Salis; Miss Frances Dempster; Lieutenant-Colonel Ronald Dinwiddie; Mr J. P. Entract; Mr Charles Hawthorne; Mr A. C. S. Irwin; Mrs A. C. Kay; Mr Hubert Le Mesurier; Mr Neil Lothian; Mr Colin Munro; Commander John Ouvry; Mrs Philip Pickering; Dr Brian Rogers; Lieutenant-Colonel J. Dow Sainter; Mr K. G. Sutton; Major-General F. L. Tottenham; Colonel R. J. Trett; and the Hon. William Wallace.

For drawing my attention to sources which I might otherwise have missed and for their help in a variety of other ways I am deeply indebted to Mrs Mary Ameer Ali; Mr Charles Balch; Miss Daphne Barker; Mrs Yvonne Barraud; Major M. J. Barthorp; Miss June Beckett; Mr R. F. Cooke; Mr P. J. de Courcy Bennett; Mr P. S. A. Berridge; Miss Elizabeth Bolton; Mr Philip Brown; the Hon. Mrs Nona Byrne: Miss Olive Chamberlain; Miss Stella Charman; Mr E. D. M. Cleaver; Captain John Colchester; Mr William Conroy; Mrs S. H. Crow; Mr E. M. O'R. Dickey; Mr G. Ferguson; Lieutenant-Colonel L. S. Ford; Mr Hubert Gough; Mrs Cecile Hardwick; Miss Cynthia Harnett; Miss Eileen Harvey; Major Anthony Hibbert; Miss Beryl A. S. Hodder; Mrs G. L. Hobbs; Mrs Dorothy Horner; Mrs Noel Horsey; Miss Nesta Inglis; Mrs Gwendoline Jacks; Miss Sheila Kaufman; Mr W. J. Kemp; Mr B. J. Kirchner; Mrs Y. Lewis; Lieutenant-Colonel William Logan-Home; Dr James N. M. Maclean; Miss M. A. Marshall; Mr F. J. McCarthy; Lieutenant-Colonel A. E. E. Mercer; Mrs Helen Henshaw; Mr C. G. Mitchell; Mr Christopher Price; Mr Michael Prior; Mrs Edward Ray; Miss Elizabeth Rose; Major Richard Rose; Mrs Audrey Seccombe; Mr Gerald Sharp; Miss Eve Sheldon Williams; Mr Frank T. B. Snow; Mr Theon Wilkinson; Miss M. E. Worsley; and Mr D. C. Yates.

I want also to thank Miss Marion Oakeshott of the British Council; Sir Robin Macworth-Young, the Queen's Librarian; Mr Richard Collier; Mr Michael Edwardes; Mr Roger Mortimer; Mr David Higham; Mr Paul Scott, and Professor Eric Stokes; and to record a special debt of gratitude to Lieutenant-Colonel Frank Wilson who has kindly made his collection of books on India freely available to me.

I am extremely grateful to the Marquess of Anglesey who has most generously put at my disposal all the notes which he assembled for the second volume of his history of the British cavalry.

Mrs Joan St George Saunders has kindly worked for me in the British Library, the Public Record Office and the Royal Commission on Historical Manuscripts; Miss Caroline Francis and Miss Voky Steel have copied documents for me at Nottingham; and Miss Mary Cosh has worked for me in Scotland.

For their help in several other ways I am most grateful to Mrs John Rae; Mrs Maurice Hill; Mrs John Street; Miss Belle St George; Mrs I. C. Howard; and Shri Jaleh Uddin.

Finally I would like to say how deeply I am indebted to Dr James Maclean of the University of Edinburgh for having read the book in proof and for having made several valuable suggestions for its improvement; to Professor Victor G. Kiernan for having helped me with the glossary; and to my wife for having compiled the index.

C.H.

A Glossary of Indian words and terms will be found on page 395. The spelling of Indian words follows that usually adopted at the time of the Mutiny. Modern or alternative spellings are given in the Index.

A Chronological Table of the principal events described in the book will be found on page 399.

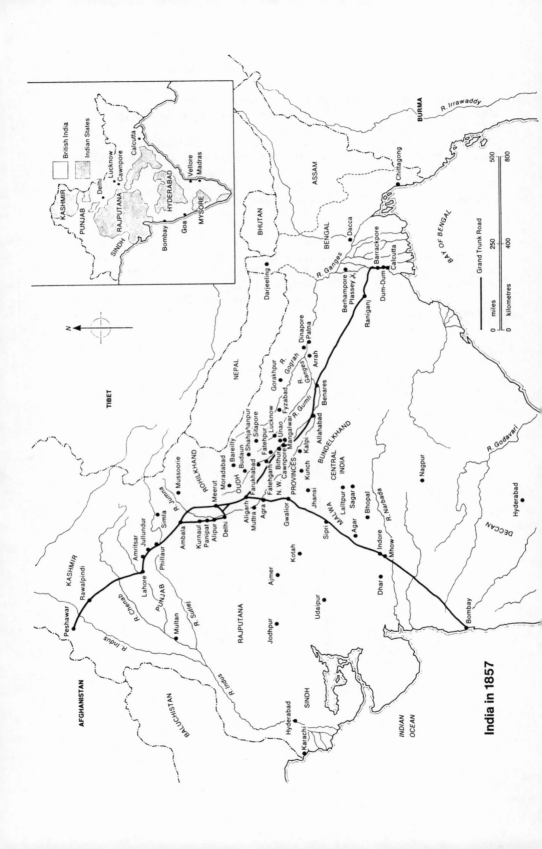

India in 1857

Preface

They called themselves 'Kings of the World', the 'Shadows of God'; and in their vast domains these grandiose titles of the Moghul Emperors of India seemed appropriate. Descendants of the Mongol warlord, Jenghiz Khan, and of the ferocious conqueror, Tamerlane, they were the richest rulers on earth, as powerful as the Caesars. The first of them, Babur, born in 1483, had marched south from Samarkand, through the rugged passes of the Hindu Kush, to Kabul; from Kabul his armies moved farther south to Delhi; and in Delhi he established the great empire in India which his heirs were to rule for five generations. In the time of his grandson, Akbar, a charter was granted by Queen Elizabeth I of England to the 'Company and Merchants of London trading with the East Indies'. Thirteen years later, in 1613, his great-grandson, Jahangir, granted this Company permission to establish a permanent trading station on the Indian coast north of Bombay.

So the English came to India as merchants. And, as their ambassador at the Moghul court warned the Company's directors in London, they must never 'seek plantation by the sword', like their predecessors, the Portuguese and the Dutch, but 'at sea and in quiet trade'. So long as they did so, he assured them, they would prosper. And so they did.

In 1707, however, the last of the great Moghuls, Aurangzeb, died at Ahmednagar, leaving seventeen sons, grandsons and great-grandsons to squabble over their inheritance. The empire began to disintegrate; foreign invaders marched in to seize what lands they could; former Moghul governors, dispossessed Hindu nobles and soldiers of fortune founded independent principalities. And the East India Company, enlisting soldiers for the defence of its now valuable trade in these troubled times, became a military as well as a mercantile power. When war broke out between France and England in Europe, this new military power was soon in conflict with the French who had themselves established trading posts in India and enlisted soldiers to protect them. An army, raised by the Company and commanded by a former clerk in its Madras office, Robert Clive, defeated the French and their Indian protégés; and at Plassey in 1757 Clive won a victory which effectively made the British masters of that rich part of the subcontinent known as Bengal.

During the rest of that century the East India Company extended its power and influence, defeating those princes who challenged its expansion, entering into alliances and treaties of protection with others who were prepared to see their own power decreased, reducing some to the state of Company pensioners, as Bahadur Shah II, the so-called King of Delhi, humiliated descendant of the Moghul Emperors, was to be reduced in the next century. In 1773 the Houses of Parliament, long disturbed by the virtually uncontrolled empire being established by the East India Company in India, passed a Regulating Act which made the Company responsible for governing the territories it controlled, and appointed one of its senior officials, Warren Hastings, Governor-General of Bengal with supervisory authority over the other two Presidencies, Madras and Bombay. In 1784 Parliament, increasingly alarmed by the Company's omnipotence and the behaviour of its servants, passed a new India Act which brought them more firmly under the control of the British Government. The Board of Directors still appointed the Company's officials in India; but these officials were now under the ultimate authority of a Minister of the Crown, known as the President of the Board of Control. The Governor-General in Calcutta, in whose appointment the Government in London was to have the final say, was also brought more securely under the control of the Cabinet and was forbidden 'to pursue schemes of conquest and extension of dominion in India'.

The East India Company, in fact, became the agent of the British Government in India. Gone were the days when its ill-paid employees made vast fortunes by trading on their own account: they were now officials of a centralized bureaucracy whose reputation for integrity became widely respected. This reputation was much increased after 1833 when the Company, compensated with an annuity of £630,000 charged on the territorial revenues of India, was ordered to 'close their commercial business, and make sale of all their merchandise, stores and effects'; and it was further enhanced in 1853 when appointments to the Company's service – in effect to the Indian civil service – were opened to public competition.

In addition to its responsibility as the British Government's representative in the civil administration of India, the Company was also responsible for the armies which each of the Presidencies – Bengal Madras and Bombay – separately maintained. These armies were manned by native infantrymen, known as sepoys, and by native cavalrymen, *sowars*. There were also native officers in each regiment, but the most senior amongst them was subordinate to the most junior British officer and could not give orders even to the British sergeant-major. As well as these regiments of the East India Company's armies, there were also stationed in India various regiments of the British Army, known in the reign of Queen Victoria as Queen's Regiments and serving for the period of their overseas duty under the orders of the Commander-in-Chief, India. At one time there had been one British to every three Indian soldiers in India. In 1856, however, the ratio had fallen to one in more than six. This was later seen as one of the main causes of the troubles soon to come.

PART ONE

1

Sahibs and Memsahibs

*· Life in British India before the Mutiny · the Metcalfes and
the Cannings · days and nights in camp, cantonment and
on the march · servants and officers' wives · 'treatment of the Natives,
high and low' ·*

On the west bank of the River Jumna, two miles upstream from the
high, red sandstone walls of the King of Delhi's palace, there once
stood the magnificent house of Sir Thomas Metcalfe, British representative at the King's court. It was planned as a house suitable both
to its owner's important position in India and as a repository for his
fine furniture and marble statues, his oil paintings and engravings, his
25,000 books and extensive collection of relics of Napoleon Bona-
parte. It contained a vast banqueting hall twenty-four feet in height
as well as a dining-room not much less imposing, a drawing-room, a
library, a study, a billiard-room, and a Napoleon Gallery, the centre-
piece of which was Canova's bust of the Emperor. Upstairs there
were numerous bedrooms; below the ground floor a spacious
*tykhana** and swimming-pool; surrounding all four sides of the
house was a classical stone colonnade and a wide veranda. Outside,
tended by innumerable gardeners, were neat lawns and paths and
rows of tubs containing English annuals, lines of cypress trees, gar-
denias and rose trees, groups of palms and strangely perfumed
creepers overhanging an artificial lake. Close to the house there was
a brick dais on which, when receptions were given, the bands of
native regiments played English airs beside a 'gorgeous marquee of
Kashmir shawls with silver poles and Persian carpets'.[1]

A meticulous, fastidious man who could not bear to see women
eat cheese, who considered that if they *must* eat mangoes and oranges
they might at least have the modesty to do so in the privacy of their
own bathrooms, Sir Thomas had designed both house and garden

* For the meaning of unfamiliar Indian words see the glossary on page
395.

with the utmost care and had been gratified to see it completed exactly as he had pictured it.

In the late 1840s his daughter, Emily, having finished her schooling in England, came to live with him there and later set down her memories of his well-ordered daily life, characteristic of that lived by other rich Sahibs all over India. Sir Thomas rose at five o'clock precisely and, after eating a light breakfast in his dressing-gown on the veranda, walked up and down while delivering orders to silent, submissive servants. At seven he went to bathe in the swimming-pool; then, having dressed, he attended prayers in his oratory before eating his main breakfast, promptly at eight. After breakfast he would quietly smoke for half an hour, servants placing the hookah behind his chair on an embroidered carpet. He would then retire to his study to write letters until ten o'clock when his carriage was brought beneath the portico by the coachman. He walked to his carriage between rows of servants, one holding his hat, another his gloves, others his handkerchief, his gold-headed cane and his dispatch-box. These various articles were then placed in their ordained positions in the carriage which promptly drove off, two grooms standing at the back.

He returned from his office at half past two for dinner at three. After dinner he sat reading for a time before going down to the billiard-room. A game of billiards was followed by two hours spent on the terrace contemplating the river. Then it was time for a light supper and an evening hookah. Immediately the clock struck eight he stood up and went to bed, undoing his neckcloth and throwing it, together with his well-tailored coat, on to the floor to be picked up by the appropriate servant. If this or any other servant did not perform his duties to the master's entire satisfaction, Sir Thomas would send for a pair of white kid gloves which were presented to him on a silver salver. These he would draw on with becoming dignity, then firmly pinch the culprit's ear.[2]

Undemanding as Sir Thomas Metcalfe's daily round appeared to his daughter, there were many other English officials in India who worked for as few hours a day as he. The Governor-General, however, was not one of them.

Lord Dalhousie, a man of firm, decided views and of masterful disposition, had been sworn in as Governor-General of India at Calcutta in January 1848. From the beginning he had displayed a capacity for work which had become more remarkable with each

passing month, sitting down at his desk at half past nine in the morning and never quitting it 'even while he ate his lunch, till half past
five in the afternoon'.[3] After eight years, during which the reforms
he tenaciously supported were pushed through against all opposition,
his health was broken; he returned home to England at the age of
forty-three already a dying man. He left behind him so awesome a
reputation that a member of the Government House staff noticed
over a year later that people still did 'not mention his name without
lowering their voices and looking nervously over their shoulders'.[4]

His successor was Lord Canning whose capacity for unremitting
work was quite as exceptional as Dalhousie's, but whose opinions
were both less rigid and more humane. The son of George Canning –
whose early death as Prime Minister had so grieved King George IV
that his Majesty had arranged for his widow to be created a viscoun-
tess with remainder to his heirs male – Lord Canning had gone from
Eton to Christ Church where he had taken a first class degree in
classics and a second in mathematics. Three years later he had married
the Honourable Charlotte Stuart, eldest daughter of Lord Stuart de
Rothesay. Entering Parliament the following year, he had rapidly
made a name for himself in the governments of Peel, Lord Aberdeen
and Palmerston. He was still in his early forties when, in 1855,
Palmerston offered him the Governor-Generalship of India.

Canning was a handsome man, ambitious and determined, warm
and amusing in private but reserved with those whom he did not
know well, sometimes aloof, even cold. Lord Granville who claimed
to be one of his 'greatest friends' admitted that this reserve prevented
there being any deep intimacy between them. 'One great characteristic of Canning was his truthfulness,' Granville wrote, 'and inaccuracy
of any kind was what he was most severe upon in others.'[5]

When he was asked to succeed Lord Dalhousie, Canning did not
at first feel drawn to accept the appointment. He knew that the
generous salary of £25,000 a year was augmented by the East India
Company, still the British Government's agent for the military and
civil administration of India. The Company provided a large house
in Calcutta as well as a house at Fort William, paid the salaries of
various servants and met the cost of the ball which was customarily
held at Government House on the Queen's birthday. But the expenses
of the appointment were necessarily heavy; and, although Government House had some fine rooms, it was, as Canning was to discover,
'miserably furnished', with 'private apartments incapable of ever
being made really comfortable', and without a single water closet.[6]

Moreover, the climate of Calcutta was such as to make any man hesitate before accepting responsible and arduous employment there.

Lady Canning did not much want to go to India either. She was a beautiful woman of thirty-eight, amusing and popular, very much at home in London society. But in the end, so people said, it was she who persuaded her husband to go, fearing that if he did not he would fall more deeply in love with another woman to whom he was already too dangerously attached.[7]

On her arrival in Calcutta, Charlotte Canning found Government House even more uncomfortable than she had expected. The garden, well stocked with oleanders, hibiscus, jasmine and roses, was certainly most pleasant. Nor could it be denied that the outward appearance of the house was very fine. Designed by a nephew of the great architect James Wyatt – a captain in the Bengal Engineers who based his plans on those drawn by Robert Adam for Kedleston Hall in Derbyshire – Government House was an imposing, classical, three-storeyed, umber-coloured building, the ground-floor rooms shaded, like those of Metcalfe House, by a columned veranda. But inside, so Lady Canning discovered, it was possible to keep tolerably cool only by shutting up 'every chink of window' at half past seven in the morning, by pulling down the Venetian blinds, and hanging up mats of the fibrous roots of scented grass (which she learned to call tatties) across all the outer doors.[8] As her husband wrote,

any attempt to go out, even in a carriage, makes one gasp and dissolve immediately, and an open window or door lets in a flood as though one were passing through the mouth of a foundry. At 5 p.m. windows and Venetians and doors are thrown open, and in comes the strong wind, blowing one's papers off the table (which is performed by the punkah at other times) and making the chandeliers swing, and their glass drops jingle, all night long. But even at night (if one gets out of the draught, which we never do, for we dine in a gale which blows up the corner of the tablecloth and sends the bills of fare and lists of the tunes across the table, unless a fork is put on them) one becomes what Shelburne would call natando in sudor in an instant.[9]

Those of Lord Canning's staff who were new to India found the heat equally oppressive. Lieutenant-Colonel Lord Dunkellin, the Military Secretary, told Lady Clanricarde,

the thing that annoys me most is the very little fresh air that one is able to get . . . as all day one lives shut up in a room with the blinds down close to the windows to prevent the glare and heat of the sun from coming in, and no one dreams of going out unless on some particular business before 5.0 or 5.30 at the earliest . . . The only time for calling or paying a visit is between half past eleven and two – after that hour to try and pay a visit unless specially bidden would be the height of impropriety, as was firmly pointed out to me on proposing in my innocence one day to go and see if someone was at home. It appears that in old times Indian ladies were in the habit after 'tiffin' of *loosing* themselves (I mean their garments) and rolling upon their beds in search of sleep to work off the heavy meal with which they had just gorged themselves, and tho' modish dames are not now quite so greedy or quite so comatose in their nature, still it is considered proper to give them an opportunity of becoming so in case they should feel so disposed.[10]

With the advent of the summer rains, there came further tribulations. Cockroaches as big as mice ran along the floors like pairs of miniature coach-horses; bats flew into the bedrooms; lizards crawled up the walls; red ants became so numerous that the legs of tables had to be placed in saucers of water; other insects were denied access to wine glasses by silver covers. Both the Governor-General and Lady Canning had two servants each behind their chairs to flick away the flies with horse-tails. Another servant's sole duty was to go round the house wiping the damp from the writing-tables. But even so, writing paper became unusable; books became mouldy and discoloured; Lord Canning's dispatch-box 'assumed the appearance of a bottle of curious old port – white and fungus-y'; shoes got furry with mildew in a day; hat linings erupted in distasteful lumps; rotting gloves had to be thrown away by the dozen.

Charlotte Canning found the lack of privacy as disconcerting as the damp and heat. Dark servants glided into the room and stood in attitudes of silent submission for minutes on end 'without one realizing that one was no longer alone'. 'I am not sure,' she wrote home, 'that I do not regret creaking footmen. These gliding people come and stand by one, and will wait an hour with their eyes fixed on one, and their hands joined as if to say their prayers, if you do not see them; and one is quite startled to find them patiently waiting when one looks round.'

Lady Canning also found her social obligations rather tiresome:

The plan here is for everyone to come very early, long before they are asked, and no one to go till the greatest lady gets up to take leave, then all the others come up and bow in a flock, and off they go, and are all cleared away in two minutes, the ADCs handing the ladies. The ADCs also receive the ladies and hand them in, but some shy ones still touchingly cling to their husbands, their natural protectors, and look very

absurd dragged up by two men ... People always sit in armchairs at
dinner all over India ... The arms shut in one's crinolines and petticoats
and one feels quite buried in them with one's elbows unnaturally hunched
up ... But this all explains why dinner-tables, for fifty or sixty people, are
far longer than in England[11] ... These dinners are very wearisome.
Neither C. nor I can get at all the people. Not a man has ever voluntarily
spoken to me since I came to India ... and the ladies look terribly afraid
of me ... The Indian families – I don't mean half-caste or Indian blood,
but people who are of the families always connected with India and who
have only been sent home to be educated ... are more insipid and dull
than words can express – and generally very underbred.[12]

Much more distressing than all the new people, customs and conditions to which Lady Canning was obliged to accustom herself, was her
husband's inability to spare her much of his time. A most conscientious and thorough man, determined to master all the strange and
complicated problems that confronted him, he began work in his
first-floor study at six o'clock; he then hastened over his breakfast to
get back to his desk which he rarely left until the evening when he
would go for a hurried walk by himself, round and round the path in
the garden, not for pleasure but merely for exercise. Even so, he felt
that he was not giving enough time to his work, that the numerous
matters on which he was expected to pronounce judgement were not
being examined with the thoroughness which they ought to receive.
'The shortest perusal of the history of each case,' he lamented, 'leaves
little leisure for going deeply into any.'[13]

There were, as Charlotte Canning had good reason to suppose,
scarcely any Englishmen in India who were required to work as hard
as her husband. Certainly few army officers did.

Lieutenant Frank Ashley Cubitt, a young officer in the 5th Fusiliers,
found life at the musketry depot at Dum-Dum extraordinarily easy.
He got up early, as nearly everyone in India did, and went out for a
walk or a ride before attending the short morning parade:

Then a bath, reading the newspapers, and breakfast. After that a stroll
into the jungle behind us with a gun to shoot any curious plumage bird
which I was fond of stuffing afterwards ... Between twelve and two we
spent making calls on Dum Dum society which was partly civilian, partly
military ... After calling we had tiffin, then a siesta till five or six when
the evening walk or ride was taken, all the station's beauty turning out
and making a pleasant time of it. Dinner at seven and then, dancing and
merriment at some friend's house ... or going to the mess to play

billiards or to read the English papers . . . or staying at home to play cards.[14]

Home for unmarried subalterns like Cubitt was usually a brick-built bungalow, coated with white plaster and approached by a flight of steps leading up to a veranda which extended down the sides as well as across the front. One of a long line of many others all much alike, it would stand in a large compound of three or four acres, enclosed by an earth mound and a ditch or a straggling hedge of prickly pear and cactus. Parts of some compounds were cultivated as flower gardens, other parts as kitchen gardens, or as orchards for growing those fruits which, to a young man fresh from England, seemed a poor substitute for the apples of Kent or the plums of Norfolk – 'the mango with a flavour like turpentine; the banana with a flavour like an over-ripe pear; the guava which has a taste of strawberries; and the custard-apple which has no perceptible taste at all'.[15] In some corner of the compound there would be a well from which yoked bullocks drew skinfuls of water. The full skins were tipped out by the gardener into channels leading to the flower beds where jasmine, tuberoses and oleanders grew, surrounded by paths which were generally covered with sea shells which not only drained the water quickly away after heavy rain but were commonly believed to deter the slithering passage of snakes.[16]

In a typical bungalow the front door led directly into an untidy sitting-room.

The furniture, which is scattered about in most unadmired disorder, is in the last stage of dilapidation. Every article in an Anglo–Indian household bears witness to the fact that Englishmen regard themselves but as sojourners in the locality where fate and the quartermaster-general may have placed them. A large, rickety table in the centre of the room is strewn with three or four empty soda-water bottles, a half-emptied bottle of brandy, a corkscrew, glasses, playing-cards, chessmen, a Hindustanee dictionary, an inkstand, a revolver, a bundle of letters, a box of cigars, the supplement of *Bell's Life* and a few odd volumes from the regimental book club. Then there are eight or ten chairs, a good half of which might well claim to be invalided on the score of wounds and long service; a couch with broken springs; a Japanese cabinet, bought as a bargain when the old major was sold up; and an easy cane chair of colossal dimensions, the arms of which are prolonged and flattened, so as to accommodate the occupant with a resting-place for his feet. In one corner stand a couple of hog-spears; a regulation sword; a buggy-whip; a hunting-crop; a double-barrelled rifle and a shot-gun . . . On nails

driven into the plaster hangs a list of the men in the company to which
the young fellow is attached; a caricature of the paymaster; a framed
photograph of the cricket eleven of the public school where he was
educated; and, if he be of humorous turn, the last letter of admonition
and reproof received from the colonel of his regiment.[17]

On one side of the young man's sitting-room was a room used
either as a bedroom by a fellow-officer who shared the bungalow with
him or as a lumber-room. On the other side was his own bedroom
containing a worm-eaten bedstead enclosed by white gauze mosquito
curtains. Instead of a mattress, which would certainly be too hot and
might well breed fleas, two cotton quilts were stretched over the
knotted ropes of the bed. Beside it was a brass basin on an iron stand,
a number of metal trunks, a few basket chairs, one or two photographs of his family in morocco frames, and, as in the sitting-room,
a punkah. This essential apparatus, a frame of wood and canvas, was
suspended from the ceiling and attached – by a cord passing through
the wall – to the big toe of the servant whose duty it was to keep it in
motion by kicking out his leg and so fanning the air above his master's
head. Leading out of the bedroom was a bathroom paved with bricks,
some of which formed a square over a drain. In this square space the
naked Sahib stood while servants splashed him with water from a
succession of porous red clay jars which had been left to cool in the
shade of the windward wall.

Even the most junior officer was attended by a whole tribe of
servants who normally lived with their families in a range of whitewashed baked mud huts at the back of the compound. Lieutenant
Cubitt had thirteen: a bearer, a groom, a sweeper, a water-carrier, a
laundryman, 'several punkah-wallahs, a gardener who also acted as
a private policeman at night . . . and a khitmutgar', a butler who 'did
credit to [his master's] selection, arranging for ice, fresh fish and
other luxuries to be brought in daily by a coolie from Calcutta'.[18]

Other officers also employed a tailor who could usually be seen
sewing and stitching as he squatted down in the shade of the veranda;
and, if they were married, an ayah to relate the gossip of the station
while she was brushing the memsahib's hair or to act as nurse to the
children.

Dr Gilbert Hadow, a medical officer recently commissioned and
with no money other than his pay, discovered on arrival in India that
he could not possibly manage with less than eight servants. In addition to a tailor and a laundryman, he had to have a *bhisti* to carry
water for bathing and drinking and for keeping down the dust; a

khidmatgar to clean the cutlery and to wait on him both at his own table and at the table of his host when he dined out; a man to act as valet, to shampoo his hair, clean his boots, make his bed and attend to the lamps; and two under-servants to run errands and do duty as punkah-wallahs throughout the day and night. When he was on duty at the hospital, Dr Hadow had, in addition, a man with a large hand-punkah to fan him on his rounds; a second man to carry his instrument tray; a third to bring up a brass jug of water, a basin and towel; a fourth to carry the portable desk and the stout volume in which the patients' illnesses and treatments were registered; and a fifth to turn the pages.[19]

Most native servants were treated quite reasonably by their masters, but many were not. In his privately printed memoirs Henry Ouvry of the 9th Lancers more than once records administering 'a good thrashing' to careless servants who were liable to be 'cut half a month's wages as well'.[20] Frank Brown, a spice merchant, told his nephew that the stories circulated in England of the maltreatment of native servants were not exaggerated. Brown knew one man who kept an orderly 'purposely to thrash' the others.[21] William Howard Russell, the Irish journalist, who was in India in 1858, was 'very much shocked to see ... two native servants, covered with plasters and bandages, and bloody, who were lying on their charpoys moaning'. 'They were so-and-so's servants,' Russell was informed, 'who had just been "licked" by him.' Even when native servants were not beaten, Russell observed, 'the tones in which they are spoken to have rarely one note of kindness, often many of anger in them'.[22]

Officers newly arrived in India – known to the old hands as 'griffins' – took some time to grow accustomed to the attention which native servants were expected to bestow upon their masters, to being shaved in bed when still half asleep, to be 'fussed over' – as Lieutenant Henry Campion was – by attendants who wanted to fasten their braces or even wipe their whiskers dry after washing, to having huge umbrellas opened over their heads whenever they left their tents, to being surrounded by ministering hands when having a bath.[23] 'If one's washing they hand one the soap and then stand each with a towel ready to slip it into one's hand directly it is wanted,' Robert Poore wrote home to his family in England. 'When you begin to dress each man stands with something ready to put into your hand the instant you feel inclined for it.'[24] 'You have to have all these servants, though,' another officer explained, 'for they will not do one another's work; a syce would never lose caste by sweeping the floor or a *khansaman* do the work of a *mally*. Besides, they are used to the climate and we can do nothing in this fearful heat.'[25]

In the hot months military activity virtually ceased while those who could escaped to the hills. Sometimes, however, a summer's march might be necessary; and then servants became 'absolutely essential'. The march, beginning in the early hours of the morning, would usually end about nine o'clock when the temperature rose to well over one hundred degrees. Tents would then be pitched for the day by servants roundly cursed in a mixture of Hindustani, English and gibberish for their slowness and inefficiency. Vivian Majendie, a young artillery officer, described how, having sworn at or beaten all the servants who had occasion to come into contact with him, he normally strolled into the mess-tent as soon as it had been erected, tired, hot and excessively irritable though not in the least hungry. There he found, laid out on a rickety camp-table, 'a repast so terribly substantial' as to throw him 'into a yet more profuse perspiration: a tough spatch-cock; curry made principally of the necks and skins of chickens; some doubtful eggs; and a dishful of gigantic things called "beef-chops"'. 'During breakfast,' Majendie continued, 'our coolies stand behind us with huge fans . . . And afterwards calling for a light for our cheroots, we return to our tents, there to lie down panting on our beds . . . to be tormented by flies . . . or prickly heat . . . How shall I ever forget these long hot mornings when one's only amuse-ment – if amusement it can be called – was watching the thermometer gradually working its way up to 114° or 116° [or even 125°], or gazing listessly out at the quiet camp, where not a human being, except a sun-dried nigger perhaps, was to be seen, and over which swept the terrible furnace-wind of Hindustan with its clouds of parched dust, pungent as dry snuff? . . . The great scorching sun beat down upon us with a heat which was almost past endurance and all nature seemed to have fallen into a death-like lethargy.'

It is high noon now. The men in their tents are lying with nothing on but a shirt, or a pair of trousers, gasping for breath, prostrate and sicken-ing beneath the fearful heat; the horses stand at their picket lines with drooping heads and protruding under-lips, too lazy almost to whisk away the flies which buzz around them and settle on them as if they were so much carrion; while hard by sit the syces fast asleep, having dropped in despair the piece of harness which they are supposed to be cleaning, and given up as futile all attempts to appear busy. Under a neighbouring tope of trees are six elephants, equally lazy and sleepy, and goaded nearly to madness by insects; every now and then taking up a quantity of sand with their trunks, they throw it over their backs to drive away the flies . . . now standing on three legs, now on four, swaying to and fro, flapping their great ragged ears, putting their trunks into their mouths and pulling them out again . . . There are some crows sitting on a tree, with their beaks wide open gasping for breath; and a flock of goats have made up their minds that it is much too hot to browse, and following the example of the herdsman . . . have got beneath the shade of some trees and gone to sleep . . .[26]

About one o'clock the *khansaman* would lay out tiffin, comprising as at breakfast, in Majendie's experience, 'the most substantial and least tempting food' which could be imagined; and, after turning up their noses at everything on the table, the officers would return to their tents, their cheroots and that same listless state in which they had passed the morning. About four o'clock the syces began to wake up; soldiers appeared at the doors of their tents; elephants were led away to bathe in some nearby tank; horses were also taken to water; pariah dogs got up to stretch their skinny legs; and women milk-sellers walked about the camp in their white cotton robes and brightly coloured shawls, their smooth, strong, braceleted arms supporting burnished brass pots, their anklets jingling as they softly cried, '*Dudh! Dudh!*'[27]

Dinner-time came at last; and although it was usually as substantial and unwelcome as breakfast and tiffin, the beer – in which, to the astonishment of the 'griffin', the older officers drank each other's health in inconceivable quantities – was always swallowed with the greatest pleasure and relief. After dinner men and officers stumbled back to their tents once more, to lie sweating sleeplessly in the heat, disturbed by the howls of pariah dogs, the yelling of jackals, the gurgling groans of camels, the beating of native drums, the squeals and kicking of horses, and the droning chanting of Indian servants, who in spite of all edicts on the subject could not be prevented from singing.

Occasionally there was a dust storm. The sky would suddenly darken, a light breeze would come up, then black dense clouds of dust would come tearing down, 'seeming to threaten to swallow you up', as William Mountsteven said, sweeping through the most tightly closed crevices, and leaving a thick, gritty coating on everything 'till even the sheets on your bed are brown, and you could easily write your name upon the pillow'.[28] Or perhaps there would be a whirlwind which would catch up all the clothes that the dhobies had been wash-ing and whirl them into what Lieutenant Cubitt described as 'an inverted cone of sticks and straw and linen dancing along with half a dozen men rushing frantically after it', picking up all the rubbish in its course, tearing up tents and scattering grain, then abruptly collapsing in a silent heap as if thrown down from above.[29] Or there might be a sudden storm such as the one Dr Hadow described as coming up just before sunset one May evening and lasting

for upwards of three hours. Many tents were torn to shreds; many more blown down and some carried right away. The ground was more than ankle deep in water, and the worst part of the business was the mess fires were put out and the dinner washed away. The loaves of bread turned to huge lumps of poultice, and, as Taylor's tent still stood, we all huddled into it and sat shivering and eating lumps of cold poultice with some anchovy paste he produced and drinking rum by way of dining.[30]

After such storms the air would resound with the croaking of frogs; masses of insects flitted about, white ants, moths, cockchafers and fireflies, beetles, crickets and millions of *bheerbahutis*, creatures which looked like shreds of red velvet. 'Everything was sodden. You yourself were damp and out of sorts',[31] and India seemed to many a homesick, disgruntled Englishman, 'a detestable country'. Its people were 'savages'; its food inedible; its climate horrible; the whole 'damned place' seemed full of revolting insects that ate huge holes in new, expensive uniforms, of soggy peaches that tasted like turnips and cantankerous camels that smelled like drains.[32]

The morning bugle awakened those who had been able to sleep at about half past three; and, while soldiers were turned out of bed by their sergeants, servants entered the officers' tents to pull on their masters' stockings. The camp was soon in an uproar of noise as tents were struck and folded up, horses saddled, camels and elephants loaded with the baggage which had recently been removed from their backs, and men, tripping and cursing over boxes and tent pegs in the dark, hurried away to fall in with their companies. Another day's march had begun.

Then often, as the sun came up, the miseries and discomforts of the night were forgotten and everything began to look 'as nice and green' as it did to Lieutenant Nicholl of the Rifle Brigade on a march in July to Fyzabad: the whole countryside was 'like one vast cricket field surrounded by trees' which were 'really splendid', particularly the tamarinds, the finest trees he had ever seen, their feathery foliage as soft as ostrich plumes.[33] Others noted the fertile fields of sugar cane, corn, tobacco and rice; the mango groves; the cavalcades of merchants riding camels laden with goods from Kashmir; the mosques, and the Hindu temples. The passing troops observed with pleasure, too, quiet villages where women in white dresses, their shapely brown arms bare to the shoulder, suckled babies as they talked to each other under the trees; or gathered round wells with bright brass pots; or stood quite naked in tanks of water from sacred rivers, muttering prayers or laughing as they dipped their children in the water and pulled them out by their ankles.[34]

If a multiplicity of servants helped to ease the daily life of Englishmen at military stations in India, their wives and daughters were even more indulged. 'If they drop a handkerchief they just lower their voices and say "Boy!" in a very gentle tone and then creeps in some wizened, skinny brownie, looking like a superannuated thread-paper, who twiddles after them for a little while and then creeps out again as softly as a black cat.'[35]

The lady's day might begin with an early morning ride followed by a leisurely tour of her house to ensure that the servants were attending to their appropriate duties and that nothing had been illicitly removed from the store-cupboards; or she might walk over to a meeting of the Mutton Club to discuss the sharing of a slaughtered sheep, or go out to inspect the garden. She would take her parasol as a matter of course for her skin had always to be carefully protected; pale complexions were essential to those with pretensions to good looks; the 'merest touch of the tarbrush' was 'sufficient to create a stigma'.[36] She might then settle down to write one of those long letters which were regularly dispatched to friends and relations in England; or she might read a book, a novel from the library perhaps or, if she were of more serious bent, a book of sermons. Alternatively she might attend to her book of pressed wild flowers or her collection of insects.

Collections of coleoptera were quite fashionable for a time, and several ladies, finding on their arrival in India that their fellow Anglo–Indians could not tell them the names of any beetles or butterflies and that Indians (putting on enormous spectacles, pursing their lips, tilting their heads to one side as though really interested in the problem) asserted that this was a particularly rare species till now unnamed, formed sudden resolves to be naturalists. But the making of a collection was always a difficulty; for one could not go hunting beetles oneself – one's husband would have been sadly distressed at such undignified conduct – which meant that one had to delegate this duty to servants; who, in spite of professing enthusiastic interest in their mistress's hobby, were dreadfully stupid, continually producing with an air of triumph cockroaches and other horrors, instead of the beautiful winged insects, metallic-glistening and many-coloured that whirred past one's lamp in the evening.[37]

After tiffin most ladies went to rest during the hot afternoon, rising in the early evening to dress for the essential parade of carriages in the Mall (or whatever the area selected for this ritual happened to be called), the visit to the bandstand, the formal dinner, or the per-formances at the theatre, which usually consisted of three or four short one-act plays as these not only provided more parts for the officers and ladies who wanted to take part but also, so it was sup-posed, proved less tedious than one longer play for the not entirely voluntary audience.

The arrival of a new young lady in the station was likely to cause the utmost excitement amongst officers and wives alike. 'No sooner is it known that Miss So-and-So is coming to the station than every-one begins to speculate who she will accept,' wrote Dr Hadow. 'For it is taken as a matter of course that all the bachelors will propose without loss of time, as the geese generally do in fact without waiting to see if the lady is likely to suit them or without thinking anything about relatives or antecedents. . . . There is something very absurd in the race for a wife out here.'[38] But, at least, the race, while it lasted, 'helped to relieve the boring sameness of the days'.[39]

Occasional relief might also be provided by the local rajah or nawab offering some sort of entertainment, an animal fight maybe, or a dinner which might prove amusing, even though the natives were quite ignorant, of course, about the correct method of serving a meal, putting lobsters and fruit together in one dish, sausages and sugared almonds in another, and 'gracing their tables with silver plate and glittering ormolu, side by side with dishes of the most domestic character', 'to the unsmotherable amusement of the guests'.[40] Break-fast at the Rajah of Patiala's palace, for instance, was served (on an admittedly snow-white cloth) 'in an odd assortment of silver plate, delf and china ware', and consisted of 'cakes, biscuits, tea, coffee, wine, fish fried and boiled, curries of many kinds, roast fowl . . . champagne, Worcester sauce, pale ale, claret, hock, bottled porter, pickled salmon, *pâté de foie gras* and sausages'.[41]

A tour of a prince's palace might well prove to be equally comic, for in order to display his attachment to Western taste, some rooms would be furnished with 'pianos by the dozen; harps; babies' cots; four-post bedsteads; ladies' wardrobes; marble-topped round tables; billiard-tables, with caverns for pockets, and a prevailing irregularity of service, engendered by the curling up of the wood'.[42] In the Nawab of Fatehgarh's palace the rooms were 'more like a shop in the China bazaar in Calcutta than anything else, full of lumber, mixed with articles of value. Tables were spread all down the centre of the room, covered with the most heterogeneous articles: round the room were glass cases full of clocks, watches, sundials, compasses, guns, pistols and swords.'[43] There were certain English ladies who never saw the inside of a palace, since they did not choose to mix with natives of any class, all of whom were beneath ordinary notice. One of these ladies, asked what she had seen of the country and its people since coming to India, replied, 'Oh, nothing thank goodness. I know nothing at all about them. Nor I don't wish to. Really I think the less one knows of them the better.'[44] She would have agreed with the sentiments of an Englishman who, before leaving on a hunting expedition, was asked if he was not going to wait for the local rajah who had offered to accompany the party. 'I should think not,' the man replied. 'We don't want the beastly niggers with us.' The next day the rajah and a friend called at his tent. 'They entered as gentlemen,' one of the party commented, 'and made the usual salutation. With the exception of myself, I do not think one of our party even rose from his chair.'[45]

Even senior and experienced civil servants, who prided themselves on their understanding of the native mind, were occasionally guilty of the most obtuse insensitivity. The Rajah of Patiala was once asked to visit Sir John Lawrence, Chief Commissioner for the Punjab, at Ambala on a Sunday. The rajah arrived with his band playing and his *zomboruks* firing. He was asked not to make such a noisy display on the Christian sabbath. But, he protested, he would be disgraced in the eyes of his relations and all neighbouring states if his visits were not accompanied by the proper ceremonies. When asked why the Rajah had been asked on a Sunday when it must surely have been recognized that this difficulty would arise, a British official grudgingly admitted, 'Ah, well! Yes, *that* was wrong.'[46]

A hundred years before, the insensitivity, disdain and lack of curiosity which characterized so many English residents in India would have been barely conceivable. But the Age of Reason had been followed by an age in which the Englishman assumed – as Brigadier-General John Jacob, a famous leader of Indian cavalry, assumed – that the British were masters of India because they were 'superior beings by nature to the Asiatic'.[47] Their superiority, both in science and religion, induced them to look down upon dark-skinned heathens steeped in idolatry and upon a country whose inhabitants ascribed most illnesses to evil spirits, where a Mohammedan could declare that he would not hold the evidence of all the telescopes in the world against the humblest of the prophets named in the Koran, and where no Hindu had ever dissected a human body for the purpose of teaching anatomy until as late as 1836.[48]

There were, of course, many Englishmen and women still to be found who loved India, admired the Indians, endeavoured to understand them and to learn about their history, art, language and customs. But there were many other unwilling residents who disliked the place from the beginning, and who, resentful of having to live there, embittered and unhappy, grew to hate it. Their feelings found expression in an autobiographical novel written by Matthew Arnold's brother, William Delafield Arnold, who, after an education at his father's school, Rugby, and Christ Church, Oxford, obtained a commission in the 58th Native Infantry, later becoming an Assistant Commissioner in the Punjab:

You see, a man ten thousand miles off can't come back [home] the first fine morning he wants to [a character in the book writes to a friend]. He very soon finds he has got a bad bargain, but also one which he must stick to . . . [He is] ashamed, too, to regret his own act. People think, or pretend to think, that he is very happy and so on . . . You would hate India; everybody does. The best men . . . who work hard . . . hate it; idle, good-for-nothing dogs like myself hate it. Perhaps the worst like it best; they can get drunk here, and that is about all they want; but even they hate a country where beer and wine is expensive.[49]

Admittedly there were men who did not regard India 'as a more or less profitable investment', and looked forward to the day when Indians would be given a liberal share in all the duties of administration, when the highest office to which a native might aspire would not be limited to that of Deputy Collector in the executive and that of Sadr Amin in the judicial branch of the administration. There were also numerous officials, lonely representatives of British power, who were completely trusted and respected in the vast districts for which they were responsible. Indeed, without respect and a general feeling that their rule was not unjust, it would have been impossible for the relatively few British in India to control an empire of well over a hundred million people. But at the same time there were numerous English men and women in India who dismissed the ruins of Kanauj as 'nothing but old bricks and rubbish'; who gave picnic breakfasts in mosques and danced quadrilles to the music of regimental bands

on the marble terrace beside Mumtaz Mahal's tomb at Agra; who did
not hesitate to use their whips to force their way through an Indian
crowd; who were as appalled by the audacity of 'these damned
niggers' presuming to enter their carriages on the railways as they
were by the thought that these same 'blackies' might one day be
admitted to white men's clubs as members rather than as servants.[50]
'I have been saying for years,' Frank Brown, long a resident in India,
wrote home in 1857, 'that if a man who left this country thirty years
ago were now to visit it he would scarcely credit the changes he would
universally witness in the treatment of the Natives, high and low. The
English were not then absolute masters everywhere. Now they are,
restraint is cast away . . . and [they display] a supercilious arrogance
and contempt of the people.'[51] Edmund Verney, a young naval officer
noticed this, too. 'The English residents generally appear to be very
prejudiced against the natives, and show this in their behaviour,' he
told his father. '[Even] when a kindness is done to a native by an
Englishman, it is often accompanied by a contemptuous thought
which appears only too clearly in the countenance. The terms in
which I have heard even clergymen and others, who would desire to
do good to the Hindoos, speak of them, convinces me that this is the
case.'[52] William Howard Russell concluded:

The fact is, I fear, that the favourites of heaven, the civilizers of the
world . . . are naturally the most intolerant in the world . . . 'By Jove!
Sir,' exclaims the major, who has by this time got to the walnut stage of
argument, to which he has arrived by gradations of sherry, port, ale,
and madeira, 'By Jove! Those niggers are such a confounded lazy sensual
set, cramming themselves with ghee and sweetmeats, and smoking their
cursed chillums all day and all night, that you might as well think to train
pigs.'[53]

2

Soldiers and Sepoys

*· Military stations and bazaars · British soldiers and Indian sepoys ·
discontent of native regiments · Dalhousie's unpopular reforms ·
threats to religion · the new cartridges · lack of understanding
between officers and native troops ·*

'You can have no idea of the size of the station here,' Lieutenant
Gordon of the 6th Native Infantry wrote home to his parents on
arrival at Cawnpore where the military quarter, known as the cantonments, stretched for six miles along the south bank of the Ganges. At
Cawnpore, as at most other large military stations, there were
numerous public buildings in addition to the barracks of the European regiments and the huts of the sepoys. As well as the officers'
messes, the theatre, library and billiard-rooms, there were assembly
rooms, where entertainments were occasionally given in honour of
passing notabilities, a racquets-court, a Freemasons' Lodge and a
race-course in rather better trim than those to be found elsewhere in
India which often had 'at least three blades of auburn grass on every
square foot of ground, and [had] the further advantage of being perforated with rat-holes'. There were also several capacious ice-houses
for the storage of frozen water which was collected in the winter in
shallow earthen pans and furnished the residents 'with the luxury so
indispensable to their comfort during the hot season'. Inevitably
there was an Anglican church – built in the style usually known as
'disappointed Gothic' – chapels for Roman Catholics and for the
members of various nonconformist congregations, a mission hall of
the Society for the Propagation of the Gospel, and a 'well-stocked
burial ground'.[1]

The lines of the European, or Queen's, regiments were separate
from those of the native regiments of the East India Company; and
the native city was quite separate from both. The spacious European
station was 'laid out in large rectangles formed by wide roads', the
native city in contrast being 'an aggregate of houses perforated by

tortuous paths, so that a plan of it would resemble a section of worm-eaten wood . . . The handful of Europeans [occupied] four times the space of the city which [contained] tens of thousands of Hindoos and Mussulmen'.[2]

The soldiers had their own bazaars crowded with shopkeepers and silversmiths; dealers in tobacco and bhang; rice-merchants and leather-workers; barbers and carriers; prostitutes and thieves; vendors of sweetmeats, of fish and game, of fruit and beer and spirits; half-naked girls sitting on the ground in the posture of tailors, sifting flour; and butchers, squatting beside great carcasses of meat, holding knives between their toes. It was in these bazaars that the British soldiers spent most of the spare time they did not spend sleeping in bed.[3]

Trooper Charles Quevillart of the 7th Dragoon Guards, who had hitherto seen little of the world outside his native Norwich, was astonished by the size and bustle of the bazaar when he arrived at Karachi. There were not only Indians there but Arabs, Jews and Eurasians, sepoys and Englishmen, Chinese with pigtails and Parsees in white dresses and shining oilskin caps. They talked with a 'babel-like confusion of tongues', the speech of the Indians sounding like 'the rattling of pebbles in an iron pot'. Once Quevillart saw a naked black man, with a red handkerchief tied round his head and his body covered in grease, go berserk in the crowd, slashing to right and left with a tulwar until overcome and killed by an outraged mob. But usually the crowds in the narrow lanes and alleyways were perfectly good-natured and affable, as well as marvellously entertaining, presenting 'an astounding mélange of Parsee merchants in monstrous chariots with outriders, Arab horse dealers, native ladies and children fantastically bedizened in carriages drawn by oxen, buffaloes drawing hackeries, water-carriers yelling, coolies squabbling'. The shopkeepers made no display of their wares but sat cross-legged on mats outside their shops and stalls, casting up their accounts and fanning themselves with hand-punkahs. On being asked to sell something they invariably produced their worst stock first, asked three times its value and settled down with a kind of gloomy relish to the customary bargaining which was carried on to the accompaniment of loud shouts from the passers-by and the banging of tom-toms. Inside their shops, Quevillart complained, the flies were so numerous that it was 'utterly impossible to discern a particle' of what the shops contained, while the stench was intolerable. 'Every inhabitant makes a common sewer in front of his dwelling,' he noticed, 'and the narrow passes are blocked up with dung heaps in which recline pariah dogs . . . The houses are built of mud, wood and brick, simply mere hovels.'[4]

Quevillart did not exaggerate. In these Indian bazaars which commonly contained over twenty times as many people as the military quarters which had brought them into existence, masses of huts, shops and houses were huddled together 'on no general plan, and without any regard at all to sanitary conditions', in the words of an official report. 'There are generally no public necessaries. There are often open cesspits among the houses', the practice being to dig the mud for the huts close by and then to use the hole made by the digging as a rubbish dump and cesspit.[5] Quevillart was particularly intrigued by a narrow street of mud huts at the far end of the bazaar known as the 'Lol-Bibbees Bazaar'. This was the prostitutes' quarter. The women there wore pantaloons, their breasts exposed, rings and bangles all over their arms and legs. Some of the younger ones were quite attractive, but

Oh, Jemima! The sight of the older women was simply disgusting, for they were one and all deplorably ugly and little was left for the imagination as a yard of calico would have furnished a dozen of them with a full dress. Some had breasts hanging as low as their waists and I noticed one party with appendages so long that she was enabled to suckle her child by throwing them over her shoulders.[6]

Nevertheless, British soldiers often frequented the 'Lol-Bibbees Bazaar' as Quevillart soon discovered; and venereal diseases were rife, about a quarter of the patients in British military hospitals suffering from them, mainly from syphilis. In the 1830s there had been a lock-hospital for prostitutes on all military stations in India, but in the 1850s, this being considered most improper, the last of the lock-hospitals had been closed and venereal diseases had much increased.[7] It was because of this that Queen's regiments had begun to make arrangements to supply healthy girls of their own for men who would otherwise have gone to the bazaar. In the 7th Dragoon Guards a dozen clean girls were 'attached to the Regiment by the Quartermaster-General's Department'. 'They are to be well housed in the cantonments,' Quevillart wrote, 'and are not to leave the station without the sanction of the General. Their regulated scale of pay is four annas [a quarter of a rupee] for private soldiers, and to others according to their rank. They are women of low caste, furnished by the Honourable East India Company's agent at the rate of five rupees [about 10s.] per head, and a pleasant little sample of women they are.'[8]

Much as they enjoyed these women, the soldiers were even fonder of drink. Immediately on his arrival in camp, Quevillart was sent to the regimental stores to collect his bedding. On his way there he saw some men carrying two huge barrels of stout back to their barracks from the native canteen. By the time he himself returned to the barracks with his bedding – having paused on his way to buy two pints of goat's milk from the camp milkman who swindled him in giving change – the men were all helplessly drunk, twenty of them lying unconscious by the empty barrels in one of which another lay stupefied amidst the dregs.[9] Many other soldiers described drunken escapades in the lines and bazaars. 'The native police, under the superintendence of a European Inspector, would make haste to the scene of the disturbance and endeavour to put a stop to it,' Corporal Alexander Morton recorded. 'If a row was continued the native police carried nets which they threw over the drunkards' heads, knocked them off their feet and rolled them up.'[10]

There was never any 'want of grog' in India, wrote Sergeant Pearman of the 3rd Light Dragoons in his memoirs.

The canteen was open all days . . . and you could buy [over] three pints of [spirits] for one rupee or two shillings, and this arrack or rum was over-proof . . . In the canteen you could have as much as you liked to drink [but] carry none away to barracks [though] we had plenty of men who made 'bishops', a sort of bladder to fit into their shirt, inside their trousers, to hold about eight drams and smuggle it out . . . There was men dying every day from the effects of drink [which] . . . did more for death than the fever . . . At the time the *batta* money was served out there were about thirty men in hospital from drink. The Regimental Sergeant-Major died, Sergeant-Major Kelly died; Sergeant Jones and many of the privates died . . . Drink was the rage in India.[11]

The trouble was there was not enough to occupy the men in their long leisure hours, Quevillart thought. After the morning parade, breakfast 'of smoking hot grilled beefsteaks, tremendously peppered', was served out at eight o'clock. Then there was nothing to do until one o'clock when it was time to go to dinner which, since the British cooks could not stand the heat and smoke of the cook-house, comprised curried meat and potatoes with rice, indifferently prepared by 'a native cook and two coolies whom each man had to pay at the rate of 12 annas a month'. During those five morning hours and throughout the long afternoon the men 'turned into bed and slept the time along', or drank their cheap arrack which they called 'Billy Stink', or, setting out lines with baited hooks, caught crows which were then 'pitched against each other in mortal combat' with bits of coloured cloth tied round their necks to facilitate the gambling.[12]

In some well-organized regiments there were coffee-rooms with chess-sets, backgammon and draught boards, as well as libraries from which the men could 'take the books to their own beds where they could lay and read', or, since many could not read themselves, get their more literate comrades to read to them.[13] In the cooler weather they might go out shooting, play football or cricket or a game known as long bullets, 'the great game for soldiers in India', which was rather like golf, though played with the hand not a club.[14] In the evenings there were occasional dances to which 'all the females of the station were invited – half-caste and all, so long as they were the wife of a soldier'.[15] Most of these wives were well known to all the men, having, as likely as not, had several husbands in the same regiment. For since widows received pensions for only a very short period, they were naturally anxious to marry a new husband as soon as possible after the previous one died. General Sir Neville Lyttelton recorded the story of one particularly hasty re-marriage:

> In India burials follow death very rapidly, and in one instance at all events a widow's re-engagement was equally hasty. She attended her husband's funeral the day after he died, and on the same day the Colour Sergeant of the company proposed to her. She burst into tears, and the NCO, thinking perhaps that he had been too hasty, said he would come again in two or three days. 'Oh, it isn't that,' said the bereaved one, 'but on the way back from the cemetery I accepted the Corporal of the firing party', by no means such a good match.[16]

Only about twelve in a hundred men in a regiment were allowed official wives – for which they received no more than five rupees a month if she were European, two and a half if native[17] – so that most soldiers either had to be or chose to remain bachelors. 'But you didn't need a wife,' one of them said, 'so far as comfort went.'[18] Less pampered certainly than their officers, they nevertheless had numerous native servants to perform the tasks that in England they would have had to do for themselves. In addition to the sweepers who cleaned the barracks and dealt with the latrines, there were numerous native tradesmen for whose services the British soldier could well afford to pay.

> We employ the barber [wrote Trooper Hyom of the 10th Hussars], giving him at the rate of 6d per month each man, and they shave you almost when you are asleep. The Dhobie or washerman we also employ

at the rate of 1s 3d per month and you have a clean shirt and sometimes two every day besides trousers, jackets, etc., all as white as snow . . . I always employed one shoemaker . . . and used to give him 1s 6d for my Bluchers and 5s for Wellington boots . . . You also get the Native Tailor to work for you at so much per day, 6d to 9d being the average price.[19]

These natives, treated usually with a kind of amused contempt, were obliged to grow as accustomed to insults and blows as the servants of many officers were. Sergeant Pearman recalled, as a typical example, how a British soldier hurled a boot at one of the black men who came into the barrack-rooms of a morning with large earthen vessels on their heads, calling out, 'Hot coffee, Sahib'. The vessel broke and the steaming coffee ran down the poor man's body.[20]

Yet, bored as they were most of the time in cantonments, the British soldiers did discover occasional enchantments. Quevillart recorded, for instance, the fascination of the troupes of acrobats and sword swallowers, jugglers and snake charmers who used to come into the lines, astonishing the troops with their skill and versatility. He saw men and women who could pluck glass eyes from their sockets with their fingernails, revealing their real eyes beneath; who could climb to the top of unsupported ladders, wriggling their way up through the steps; who could swallow balls of cotton, a hundred yards in length, then, piercing their sides with a knife, draw the cotton through the wound and wind it round a stick; who, while whirling through the air in a dervish-like dance, could take wet paint off a sharp sword-point with their eyelashes. There was one young woman, naked to the waist to show that there was no deception, who could run a long, wide, twin-edged dagger down her throat to 'the very hilt and, after walking round the circle, draw it up'.[21]

On most evenings Quevillart would stroll across to the lines of the 98th Regiment to listen to their band. There were crowds of natives there; small naked children with shaven heads; bigger children with rolls of cotton round their loins and turbans on their heads; their fathers, servants of the English officers, in long shirts down to their knees and with cummerbunds round their waists. 'Almost every man and many of the women had painted caste marks on their foreheads, some with a round patch the size of a sixpence between their eyes, others with one, two or three diverging lines, drawn upwards from the top of the nose to the forehead, of white, red or yellow ochre.'[22]

One evening while Quevillart was listening to the band of the 98th an officer's evangelical wife came up to talk to him and to warn him of the evils of drink, ending her peroration, 'Let us show by our lives to the heathens around us that as Christians we have been washed of our sins and called to be sons and daughters of God Almighty, soldiers of the Cross.' Quevillart was about to speak up on behalf of himself and his regiment, to assure the lady that the 7th Dragoons were as sober a set of God-fearing men as had ever been created, when he saw several of the most ruffianly men of his regiment approaching from the direction of the 'lower quarter of the bazaar improperly dressed and considerably the worse for liquor'; he thought it as well to return immediately to his barracks.[23]

Quevillart drew a picture of these barracks in his journal. It shows a long, bare, comfortless room – with rows of punkahs above two lines of closely spaced beds and with saddles and bridles hanging from the ceiling – badly designed and overcrowded, much the same as hundreds of others all over India. The floors of some of these barracks were of stone or brick but many others were of rammed earth covered with watered cow dung, a composition considered better than anything else for keeping away fleas and bugs.[24] Open windows, which were screened in hot weather by tatties, gave on to a veranda which, in turn, in many recently built barracks, was enclosed by an outer veranda. These double verandas had been designed to make the interiors cooler; but, in fact, they succeeded only in rendering them more airless and providing the quartermaster with extra sleeping space. There being so few quarters for married men, the inner verandas were often filled with wives and children, one family screened from the next by blankets hanging from the ceiling. The inner verandas were also used for the accommodation of urine tubs which were removed when full by native sweepers who, in pushing their bamboo rods through the handles, usually contrived to spill a good deal of the contents on to the floor, thus adding to the foul smell from the nearby open latrines which pervaded the area. When a report on the Indian Army's sanitary conditions was eventually published in 1859, no medical man was surprised that the sickness among white troops in India was about twice what it was at home, or that 'fevers, dysenteries, diseases of the liver and epidemic cholera' were so common.[25]

The living quarters of the native soldiers, although exceedingly primitive, were far less unpleasant than those of the British. Most native troops in all three of the East India Company's armies were married, and were permitted to live on the station with their wives and children, their widowed mothers, aged grandmothers and any other relations for whom they cared to provide. Each man was allotted a small piece of ground on which he was expected to build his own hut, a simple edifice of bamboo, matting and mud, thatched with straw. A married man's hut was usually about fifteen feet long, nine feet high and eleven wide; a single man's about two-thirds that size. Grants were made towards the cost of construction which, in any case, was rarely more than two rupees.[26]

Sanitary conditions in the native lines were little better than they were in the bazaar; and in most stations the huts were built much closer together than they need have been. But for most of the year the men slept in the open air in front of their huts on charpoys, and their general health was a good deal better than that of the white troops.[27]

The sepoys were also of more imposing physique than the European soldiers since there was never a shortage of recruits, and commanding officers were able to choose only the strongest, tallest and most presentable-looking men, while medical officers felt justified in rejecting all those with physical defects. In the Bengal Army most soldiers, both Muslim and Hindu, were enlisted in Oudh, the large province in what is now Uttar Pradesh, whose capital was Lucknow. They were generally taller than the white soldiers, few being less than five feet eight inches. Three out of four were Hindus, and of these most were high-caste Brahmins or Rajputs, the profession of arms being considered by Hindus worthy and honourable, like the calling of a poet.[28]

Their pay of seven rupees a month was scarcely a third of that earned by European troops, but even so – though reduced by various fees and deductions – it was far more than they could have hoped to earn as civilians. Admittedly they were frequently in debt, for not only did numerous relations consider themselves entitled to their support, but also there were certain Hindu *dustoors* which could not be ignored. Europeans might consider the laying out of two or three hundred rupees on a marriage as an unwarranted extravagance for a private soldier. To a self-respecting Hindu, however, it was a *dustoor* imposed by a tradition as compelling to him as a law. In debt or not, when they returned to their villages – where many of their fathers were landholders – they were treated as men of consequence to whom every respect was due.[29]

A high proportion of these Hindus were vegetarians, eating little other than chupatties, dhal, and rice; and while the smoking of opium and the consumption of *ganja* and bhang were common, the higher classes of Hindus never drank intoxicating spirits, believing that, like the eating of meat and fish, it was a defiling practice to be left to Mohammedans, to low-caste Hindus and to the 'so-called Christian dummers' who were often Eurasians of partly Portuguese stock.[30]

Although it was virtually impossible to gain promotion by merit, a native soldier did at least have the satisfaction of knowing that, provided he could read and write and had a record of good conduct, he would be promoted when his turn eventually came, even though he might have to wait twenty years before he became a havildar, was unlikely to be commissioned until he was within a year or two of being pensioned off, and would never rise higher in rank than the most junior European subaltern, however young and inexperienced the subaltern might be.

This system of promotion by seniority – even if it sometimes resulted in native soldiers becoming officers only when they were, in General Jacob's words, 'worn-out imbeciles unfit for command'[31]– did not appear to worry the sepoys any more unduly than did their debts. Nor did their uniforms of thick, unyielding European cloth. They never looked, nor ever felt, entirely comfortable in these uniforms. 'I found it very disagreeable wearing the red coat,' Sita Ram Pande recorded, remembering his early days in the 26th Bengal Native Infantry. 'It was open in front, but was very tight under the arms. The shako was very heavy and hurt my head, though of course it was very smart. I grew accustomed to all this after a time. Yet I always found it a great relief when I could wear my own loose dress.'[32]

The sepoys rarely wore their uniforms when not on parade. As soon as they returned to their huts, they would discard their tunics and trousers, and, having indulged in those ritual ablutions imposed upon them by their faith, put on instead a dhoti or a pair of linen trousers before sitting down to eat the meal prepared for them by their families. The sepoy might then, like the British soldier, settle down to sleep, or to smoke, or to indulge with his neighbours in the gossip of which they never tired, or play with his children, or make love with his wife, or go over to the gymnasium with which every native regiment – in significant distinction to every British regiment in India – was supplied. To most observers, indeed, the sepoy seemed, as he seemed to an English officer in the Bengal Artillery, 'perfectly happy with his lot, a cheerful, good-natured fellow, simple and trustworthy'.[33] He might have some odd ideas and strange habits, to be sure; but then the Englishman's taste for beef and brandy must seem strange, even disgusting to the sepoy. This did not prevent them feeling a respect, even affection for each other. Another officer wrote:

You might see the sepoy, watchful and tender as a woman, beside the sick-bed of the English officer, or playing with the pale-faced children beneath the veranda of his captain's bungalow. There was not an English gentlewoman in the country who did not feel measureless security in the thought that a guard of sepoys watched her house or who would not have travelled, under such an escort, across the whole length and breadth of the land.[34]

Although apparently content with their present lot, the sepoys did, however, have fears for their future. And these fears were shared by the people in the towns and villages from which they came. Lord Dalhousie's reforms, while considered sensible and just by most of their British masters, were not seen in the same light by most Indians. Throughout Dalhousie's years in office intensive efforts had been made to establish the rights of landholders to the property which they claimed to own and the amount of money which ought to be received from it. Several great landowners had been dispossessed of large parts of their estates. Thousands of lesser landlords had been dispossessed entirely. And many, relatively poor, who let out small parcels of land while ploughing other pieces themselves – the kind of men from amongst whom most sepoys were recruited – had also been deprived of the lands which they had inherited. So they, too, felt deeply aggrieved by the Government's reforms, apprehensive as to what further deprivations their British rulers might have in mind. Nor were the peasants as pleased with the reforms as the Government had expected. They preferred their own old ways to the strange ones being imposed upon them by the foreigners. As one of them told an English inquirer, they did not understand the new rules and regulations; they did not trust the new law courts whose native officials were notoriously corrupt and whose procedure was quite incomprehensible; they would much rather have been governed by their former native masters, unpredictable and violent though they sometimes were. 'The truth, Sir, is seldom told in [the English] courts,' a Brahmin told William Sleeman, whom Dalhousie sent on a tour through one of those few remaining semi-independent states in India to help him decide whether the incompetence of its government justified him in annexing it. 'There they think of nothing but the number of witnesses, as if all were alike. Here, Sir, we look to the quality. When a man suffers wrong, the wrongdoer is summoned before the elders, or most respectable men of his village; and if he denies the charge, and refuses redress, he is told to bathe, put his hand on the peepul tree, and declare his innocence . . . A man dares not, Sir, put his hand upon that sacred tree and deny the truth. The gods sit in it and know all things; and the offender dreads their vengeance.'[35]

The policies which Dalhousie had adopted towards the Indian princes had proved equally unpopular, and had not only made the princes feel insecure and resentful but had also undermined their subjects' confidence in British justice. Believing that the rule of all Indian princes was likely to be corrupt and was certainly an affront to English standards of justice, Dalhousie had annexed their territories whenever these could be shown to be seriously misgoverned or their ruler did not have an heir of whom the Government approved. It had long been recognized by Hindus that a father could adopt an heir if he had no natural son. It was a particularly treasured right amongst them because no part of their faith was more firmly held than that a man was saved from punishment after death by a son's sacrifices and prayers which could be performed as efficaciously by an adopted as by a natural heir.

This threat to the Hindu custom of adoption was seen by Indians as part of a concerted attack upon their religions as a whole. Muslims shared with Hindus this fear for their religion. Indeed, the Commissioner of Patna reported that there was a 'full belief' among even 'intelligent natives', especially 'the better class' of Mohammedans, 'that the Government was immediately about to attempt the forcible conversion of its subjects'. The Lieutenant-Governor of Bengal considered that the suspicion had taken such deep root that he must issue a proclamation denying it, which, far from subduing the people's fears, served merely to aggravate them.[36]

There had been no such widespread fear in the eighteenth century. The British had been far more tolerant then. Their officials had contributed to Mohammedan processions; they had administered Hindu temple funds and supervised pilgrimages to holy places; their officers had piled their swords, next to their soldiers' muskets, round the altar at the Hindu festival of *Dasehra,* to be blessed by the priests. It had been perfectly well understood that the obligations and restrictions that caste imposed upon a Hindu soldier's behaviour were all-important to him, that he would have to throw away his food if the shadow of a European officer passed over it, that it would be better to die of thirst – as some soldiers did die[37] – than to accept a drink from a polluted hand or vessel. But since then all had changed. Indian culture was less inclined to be respected than to be mocked by British officials who agreed with Lord Macaulay that it consisted of nothing better than 'medical doctrines that would disgrace an English farrier – Astronomy, which would [be laughed at by] girls at an English boarding school – History, abounding with kings thirty feet high, and reigns thirty thousand years long – and Geography, made up of seas of treacle and butter'.[38]

Rarely scrupling to pull down temples that might stand in their way, the British had brought the so-called wonders of science to India, the electric telegraph, the railway and those steam-engines which, so some villagers told Sita Ram Pande, were driven by the force of demons trying to escape from the iron box in which the *Firinghis* (the foreigners) had imprisoned them – demons who were, perhaps, precursors of those devils that, as ancient prophecies foretold, were to rule the world in an accursed age soon to dawn.[39] The railways, the electric telegraph and the steam-vessel would bring all men closer, the British said; but that in itself was a threat. For bringing men closer might eventually put an end to caste; and without caste how could a man be rewarded for his acts in a previous incarnation?[40]

There were more obvious threats to religion than railways. Missionaries, prohibited from working in India in the eighteenth century, now spoke openly of the day when all men would embrace Christianity and turn against their heathen gods; and, though it was claimed that the missionaries were not paid by the Government – as the chaplains who cared for the British soldiers and civilians were – their activities were approved of, and in many cases supported by, the Government. So what really was the difference?

Moreover, as the Indians went on to argue, there were plenty of British officers and officials who behaved as though they were missionaries themselves. Colonel S. G. Wheler, commanding officer of the 34th Native Infantry, openly admitted in 1857 that he had endeavoured to convert sepoys and others to Christianity, that he conceived this to be the aim of every Christian, that it was certainly his own object in life, that he always hoped that 'the Lord would make him the happy instrument of converting his neighbour to God or, in other words, of rescuing him from eternal destruction'.[41] Colonel Wheler, in Lord Canning's opinion, was 'not fit to be trusted with a regiment'.[42] But he continued to command it; and his opinions were far from uncommon amongst army officers, many of whom shared his views that the entire Bible, the Old Testament as much as the New, was the inspired word of God. Even in the 7th Dragoon Guards, so Trooper Quevillart recorded in his journal, 'a religious mania sprang up and reigned supreme'. 'The adjutant and sergeant-major having become quite sanctimonious and attending religious meetings every morning . . . In consequence a vast number of men . . . also muster strongly at these meetings.'[43] If the number of conversions amongst the men in native regiments was negligible, no one denied that Colonel Wheler and the adjutant of the 7th Dragoon Guards were far from being alone in their anxiety to see many more.

Proselytizing civilians were even more common. Herbert Edwardes, Commissioner of Peshawar, who believed that India had been given to England rather than to Portugal or France because England had made 'the greatest effort to preserve the Christian religion in its purest apostolic form', had no doubt of his evangelical mission.[44] Nor had Robert Tucker, judge at Fatehpur, who set up large stone columns, inscribed with the Ten Commandments in Hindu and Urdu, English and Persian on each side of the high road leading to Fatehpur, and who 'used two or three times a week to read the Bible in Hindoo-stanee to large numbers of natives who were assembled in the compound to hear him'.[45]

'The missionary is truly the regenerator of India,' announced one of many similar and widely circulated tracts. 'The land is being leavened, and Hindooism is everywhere being undermined. Great will some day, in God's appointed time, be the fall of it. The time appears to have come when earnest consideration should be given to the question whether or not all men should embrace the same system of religion.'[46]

The Government's determination to convert Indians to Christianity seemed evident too in a variety of small ways. In certain areas *patwaris*, sent to mission schools to learn the Hindi script, were presented on the completion of their course with copies of the New Testament. In other areas the Christian gospel was preached to prisoners in the local gaol.[47] Indeed, it was widely rumoured that the Government were making a special effort to interfere with religion in gaols where the prisoners were at their mercy. Ostensibly for the purpose of more convenient administration, the practice of allowing each prisoner to prepare his own food in accordance with Hindu doctrine was discontinued in favour of communal cooking by Brahmin cooks, a regulation which ignored the fact that there were various groups of Brahmins who could not eat food prepared by cooks who did not belong to their own group. Ostensibly for the purpose of cleanliness, Muslim prisoners were required to shave off their beards, symbols of their faith. And ostensibly because they could be used as weapons, brass *lotas* had to be replaced with earthenware drinking vessels which were much less easy to cleanse were they to be touched by polluted lips.

The order about earthenware *lotas* was worse than an order in a modern gaol that everyone must use the same toothbrush; it was not only physically disgusting, it was sacrilegious. It was regarded as religious persecution; the gaols were being used to destroy caste and interfere with the cycle of rebirth. Townspeople sided with the prisoners; there were riots in at least two places in Bihar. This was in 1855.[48]

In hospitals, too, Indian susceptibilities were ignored in the accommodation of patients. 'Sick men or women, high or low, "purdah nisheen" (those who never go out in public) and others' were all required to share the same wards, Hedayet Ali, a Sikh subahdar, complained. 'People imagined in their ignorance that it was the intention of the British to take away the dignity and honour of all.'[49]

While the virtues of Christianity were praised by missionaries in gaols, the evils of the native religions were condemned and lamented outside them. 'There is something very oppressive in being surrounded by heathen and Mohammedan darkness, in seeing idol-worship all around,' wrote Honoria Lawrence, wife of the Chief Commissioner of Oudh. 'When we see the deep and debasing hold these principles have on the people, it is difficult to believe they can ever be freed from it.'[50]

Some primitive practices, suttee, for example, had been forbidden by law, to the satisfaction of the more progressive and enlightened, like Rajah Ram Mohan Roy and Dwarakanath Tagore, but to the dismay of the orthodox. The orthodox were similarly outraged when Hindu widows, no longer permitted to burn themselves to death on their husbands' funeral pyres, were allowed to remarry. Perhaps even more obnoxious, both to the old-fashioned Hindu and the Muslim, was an earlier law which enabled a son who had changed his religion to inherit his father's property. This was inevitably interpreted as an attempt to remove at least one possible obstacle to a child's conversion to Christianity.

The fear of forcible conversion to Christianity became stronger than ever in the army in 1856 with the passing of the General Service Enlistment Act. This stipulated that all recruits to the seventy-two battalions of the Bengal Army be required to accept service on the same conditions as men enlisted into the Bombay and Madras Armies, and that they must agree to serve overseas if required to do so. Previously only six battalions of the Bengal Army had been available for foreign service, it being considered impossible for a faithful Hindu to go to sea as he could not, in a wooden ship, have his own fire to cook his food which his faith obliged him to do himself; nor could he properly perform the prescribed rituals of daily ablution even if water butts, filled by men of the same caste and never approached by others, had been available.[51] Hindu sepoys who had gone overseas or crossed the Indus were likely to be spurned by their comrades when they returned home. After the Afghan War 'none of the Hindoos in Hindostan would eat with their comrades who went to Afghanistan', wrote Subahdar Hedayet Ali, 'nor would they even allow them to touch their cooking utensils. They looked upon them all as outcasts, and treated them accordingly.'[52]

It was emphasized by the authorities that the General Service Enlistment Act did not apply to men already serving in the Army, only to recruits. But it was felt that the provisions of the Act might one day be extended to cover all sepoys whatever their length of service and that, in any case, the honoured career of a soldier was now open only to those prepared to be false to the faith of their fathers.[53]

There were yet other causes of the sepoys' growing discontent. It was announced at this time that those found unfit for active service would no longer be allowed to retire on invalid pensions but must be employed on cantonment duty. An exasperating parsimony also led to the announcement that sepoys would in future have to pay postage on their letters instead of being allowed to send them free under the frank of their commanding officer. But these grievances were both paltry compared with the alarm aroused by rumours about a new rifle cartridge which was gradually being introduced into the Bengal Army.

The army was then mainly equipped with a smooth-bore musket which was quicker to load than the few rifles at that time in use but was less accurate over long ranges. After lengthy experiments at Enfield in England a new rifle had been developed which effectively combined long-distance accuracy with a less protracted method of loading. It had consequently been decided to bring this Enfield rifle into general use throughout the army.

Rifles of the old pattern had two grooves in their bores. They were loaded by ramming a charge of powder down the muzzle followed by a bullet which, to ease its way down the rifling, was wrapped in a patch of cloth lubricated with a mixture of wax and vegetable oil. The new rifle had three grooves, and the powder and bullet were made up together in a single cartridge – like the cartridge for a musket. To load the rifle, the end of the cartridge containing the powder had to be bitten or nipped off so that the charge would ignite; the cartridge was then pushed down the rifled bore of the muzzle. To make its passage easier, the paper of which the cartridge was composed was heavily greased. The grease was tallow which, so experiments had shown, lasted longer as a lubricant than the wax and vegetable oil used with the bullets for the old rifle. But the problem with tallow, as the Adjutant-General of the Bengal Army had realized, was that,whereas it was entirely unobjectionable to European troops, it was certainly not so to native troops for if it contained beef fat it would be degrading to Hindus and if it contained pig fat it would be offensive to Mohammedans. It was suggested, therefore, that the new cartridges should be issued only to British troops in India. The suggestion was ignored. Some cartridges greased with tallow had been sent out from England in 1853 to test the suitability of the new lubrication to the climate. These found their way into the hands of Indian soldiers before being returned to England in 1855. At that time no outcry had been raised against them. Since then, however, the greased paper having proved suitable for the climate, further cartridges had been sent out from England; and manufacture of them had begun in India where no specification for the composition of the tallow was given to the contractors. Since beef and pig fat were the cheapest animal fats available, the sepoys' suspicion that these were used instead of mutton or goat fat was far from unreasonable.

So far none of the new cartridges had been issued. But consignments of Enfield rifles had reached the various musketry depots in India where detachments from selected native regiments were, at the beginning of 1857, being given preliminary training in their use. There had been no objections yet; but suspicions about the cartridges which would have to be used with the new rifles were deepening, and rumours were spreading fast.

All the sepoys' fears, suspicions and grievances might even so have been overcome, had there remained the same sympathy and understanding between them and their officers as had existed in the earlier years of the century and in the century before. Sita Ram Pande recalled:

In those days the sahibs could speak our language much better than they do now, and they mixed more with us. Although officers today have to pass the language examination, and have to read books, they do not understand our language ... The only language they learn is that of the lower orders, which they pick up from their servants, and which is unsuitable to be used in polite conversation. The sahibs often used to give nautches for the regiment, and they attended all the men's games. They also took us with them when they went out hunting, or at least all those of us who wanted to go ... Nowadays they seldom attend nautches because their padre sahibs have told them it is wrong. These padre sahibs have done, and are still doing, many things to estrange the British officers from the sepoys. When I was a sepoy the captain of my company would have some of the men at his house all day long and he talked with them. Of course, many went with the intention of gaining something ... but far more of us went because we liked the sahib who always treated us as if we were his children ... I know that many officers nowadays only speak to their men when obliged to do so, and they show that the business is irksome and try to get rid of the sepoys as quickly as possible. One sahib told us that he never knew what to say to us. The sahibs always knew what to say, and how to say it, when I was a young soldier.[54]

In a few native regiments, indeed, the British officers did not merely ignore their men when they could but actually abused them on parade, swearing at them in 'the most insulting language imaginable'. According to a British resident in India

the sepoy is [regarded as] an inferior creature. He is sworn at. He is treated roughly. He is spoken of as a 'nigger'. He is addressed as 'suar' or pig, an epithet most approbrious to a respectable native, especially the Mussulman, and which cuts him to the quick. The old [officers] are less guilty ... But the younger men seem to regard it as an excellent joke, as an evidence of spirit and a praiseworthy sense of superiority over the sepoy to treat him as an inferior animal.[55]

The lack of understanding between the British officers and the sepoy was aggravated by regimental life in India being considered by many officers as a kind of purgatory to be endured while waiting to pass on to a higher calling. There were far from enough suitable civilians to fill the growing number of responsible posts in the East India Company's Civil Service; and for many of these posts a man with a military training might well be considered better suited than a civilian, so that regiments were frequently being asked to supply officers for the civil service as well as for the army staff. Since the pay was so much higher – and the chances of promotion so much greater than in his regiment where a capable man might still be a captain at fifty – officers were naturally anxious to accept the civil appointments offered them. And the native regiments became so short of officers in consequence that many of them regularly had seven or eight absent from their full complement of twenty-four.[56] 'Every young officer who comes out now,' one cavalry colonel complained, 'says "my father is a Director [of the East India Company]" and so [on] and so [on], "directly I have passed my examination I shall be off and care nothing for the regiment." And no wonder when the threat of being sent back to one's regiment is held out as a punishment for mis-conduct or misbehaviour.'[57] Sita Ram Pande said:

> Any clever officer was always taken away from his regiment, and he never came back for years . . . When he did come back he knew very little about the men . . . I have known four Commanding Officers come to a regiment within a year, and three Adjutants and two Quartermasters . . . It takes us a long time to learn the ways of a sahib and once the men have got used to him it is wrong to have him removed.[58]

In his young days at the beginning of the century, in contrast to the 1850s, the colonel of Sita Ram's regiment was a familiar figure to everyone, responsible for discipline, not forbidden, as he subsequently was, to award a punishment more severe than five days' drill without obtaining higher authority. He was 'well known all around' as well as in the regiment, Sita Ram said; and 'the villagers came from as far as thirty miles away to inform him where the game was' when he wanted to organize a tiger hunt to which he would, perhaps, invite a local landholder.[59] Contemporaries of his, who appear in other memoirs of the time, wrestled with their men or fenced with them or took them out hawking. One colonel is described as sending a non-commissioned officer ahead of him on the march to discover the best chess players in the village nearest his camping-ground.[60] Another, who knew 'how to treat the sepoys in their own way', who was not one 'of your pipe-clay rigid disciplinarians who would utterly extinguish the native in the soldier', could make his men roar with laughter or shake in their shoes as he pleased.[61] Like most British officers in India then he had a native mistress, and made no attempt to interfere with her ancient faith which he was prepared to respect until God saw fit to change it. It was not until the 1830s and 1840s, when marriage to white women

58

became more common, that living with a native mistress was considered to be rather disreputable. By then it was 'fashionable to admire what came from England and to eschew everything "black"; increasingly the figure of fun became, not the griffin ... but the peppery colonel with his hookah, his mulligatawny and his Indian mistress'.[62]

3

Chupatties and Lotus Flowers

· The 'chupatty movement' – growing unrest · the sepoys' grievances exacerbated – early mutinies · trouble at Dum-Dum in January 1857 · at Barrackpore in February – and at Berhampore · spreading disquiet · the Mangal Pande affair at Barrackpore, 29 March · General Anson at Ambala, April ·

'There is a most mysterious affair going on through the whole of India at present,' Dr Gilbert Hadow wrote home to his sister towards the end of March 1857. 'No one seems to know the meaning of it . . . It is not known where it originated, by whom or for what purpose, whether it is supposed to be connected with any religious ceremony or whether it has to do with some secret society. The Indian papers are full of surmises as to what it means . . . It is called "the chupatty movement".'[1]

One morning that month Mark Thornhill, Magistrate of Muttra, found four of these chupatties, 'dirty little cakes of the coarsest flour, about the size and thickness of a biscuit', laid on the table in his office. He discovered that a man had come out of the jungle with them, had given them to the watchman with instructions to make four like them and to take these to the watchman of the next village who was to be told to do the same.[2] Other officials reported that the number of chupatties was five and that that number had been sent on to the watchmen of five neighbouring villages who in turn had each been told to send five others on to five other villages. By this means, it was said, chupatties were travelling all over the North-Western Provinces at the rate of about a hundred miles in twenty-four hours. George Harvey, Commissioner for the Agra Division, thought that they were being distributed over a distance of between 160 and 200 miles in a single night.[3]

Some believed that the distribution of chupatties was a magical rite to avert some impending catastrophe; others that it was a practice adopted to appease gods responsible for epidemics of cholera; yet others that it was a call to the people to resist the imposition of Christianity. There was a widespread belief among the natives that the British Government themselves were responsible for it, that the distribution was intended as a warning of the Government's determination to join everyone in India together, to make them eat the same food and to force them to become Christians. But 'no one could say why such a curious method had been adopted' for conveying this determination to them.[4] Certainly the village watchmen did not know why they had to run through the night with chupatties in their turbans, though they obviously felt some calamity would befall them if they should break the chain. The native police were as mystified as anyone. Mainuddin Hassan Khan, a *thannadar* in Delhi, was 'astonished' by the reports to which he nevertheless attached the utmost importance, since the distribution of chupatties 'undoubtedly created a feeling of great alarm in the native mind throughout Hindustan'. Asked by the joint magistrate at Delhi to report privately what he believed to be the origin of the matter, he could offer no explanation other than that his father had once told him that upon 'the downfall of the Mahratta power, a sprig of millet and a morsel of bread had passed from village to village, and that it was more than probable that the distribution of this bread was significant of some great disturbance which would follow immediately'.[5]

There were rumours that lotus flowers, leaves of brinjal and bits of goats' flesh were also being passed from hand to hand within the sepoy regiments; that an ominous slogan '*Sub lal hogea hai*' ('Everything will become red') was being whispered everywhere; that magical symbols, their meaning unknown even to those who scrawled them, had appeared on the walls of many towns; that protective amulets were being sold in the hundreds in bazaars; and that fakirs and *maulvis* were moving about the countryside, gathering crowds of villagers around them, warning them of the designs of the *Firinghis,* urging them to stand firm, to resist all pressures, and to fight for their faith. Certainly agents of dispossessed princes, agitators and troublemakers were at work, reminding the sepoys that the British were not invincible, as had been shown in the Afghan War; telling them that, since the Crimean War, Russia had conquered and annexed England, and that the total population of England was less than 100,000, so that – even if the Russians let them – the English could not reinforce their regiments in India; assuring them that Queen Victoria had sent out Lord Canning with the express purpose of converting them to Christianity; warning them that, now nearly all India was British, they would in future only be needed to fight overseas where their caste would be broken; aggravating their fears and suspicions. The word was spread that the new cartridge was meant to defile the sepoy and destroy his caste; that muskets were also being defiled by being packed in cows' fat; that civilians were to be polluted as well as soldiers by the dust of ground cow-bones which was being secretly mixed with the flour on sale in the markets; that one day when the sepoys were assembled on their parade-grounds mines would explode beneath them and blow them all up; that the widows of British soldiers killed in the Crimean War were being shipped out to India where the principal zemindars would be compelled to marry them, thus ensuring that their estates would eventually fall into Christian hands.[6]

Most British officers in native regiments refused to believe that their own men could possibly be misled by such stupid, idle talk. But there were a few who could not share the general confidence. Sir Charles Napier, who had resigned as Commander-in-Chief soon after the annexation of the Punjab in 1849, had been convinced that the sepoys of the Bengal Army were dangerously unsettled. The annexation had been a great blow to the sepoys from Oudh who were then in the Punjab because they had received extra pay while serving outside the Company's territories; but now that the Punjab belonged to the Company this extra pay was withheld. Some of it which they had already received was, in fact, declared repayable. Such had been the resentment at this unfair order that twenty-four battalions had seemed on the verge of refusing their pay altogether and one, the 66th, after ninety-five of the men had been tried for mutiny, had been disbanded, its number and colours being given to a regiment of Gurkhas. Worse than this, Sikhs from the Punjab had now been enlisted in native regiments, much to the disgust and anger of the sepoys of Oudh who not only considered Sikhs unclean and complained that they smelled horribly because of their habit of using curds to dress their long hair, but who also felt that their own special relationship with the East India Company was coming to an end. Having quarrelled with the Governor-General over the methods adopted to deal with the sepoys' complaints, Sir Charles Napier had resigned, protesting that the whole army was on the verge of mutiny, a view by which Dalhousie had professed himself utterly astonished and from which he recorded his 'entire dissent'.[7]

Mutinies in the army were not uncommon, though, nor were they considered by Indians the fearful crime which they were thought to be by Englishmen. The word used in Hindustani, '*ghadr*', does not convey the meaning that 'mutiny' conveys to English ears; it has no more pejorative sense than 'faithlessness' or 'ingratitude'.

So long as the Colonel was the father and mother of his regiment and had the power to deal with most grievances, this was what mutiny was – but as the Colonel's power diminished, as the decisions which mattered to the sepoy were more and more taken by distant people whom he had never seen, the word came less and less to represent what the sepoy felt he was doing. Even if his officers listened, no one at headquarters seemed to take much notice; it must sometimes have seemed that if he was to get anyone to pay attention, his only course was to refuse duty. He learnt in the army that in this, as in so many other things, the English had strange ideas, and as a rule he remembered to behave as they expected. But the lesson was foreign and sometimes he forgot it.[8]

He had forgotten it at Vellore in 1806 when fourteen British officers and over a hundred British soldiers were killed following the announcement of obnoxious orders – subsequently withdrawn – that sepoys must not display painted marks on their faces and must in future wear leather stocks and hats with leather cockades instead of turbans. These orders flagrantly ignored the sepoy's dislike of hats as being the headgear usually adopted by untouchables converted to Christianity, as well as his dread of leather, and his need to wear a mark on his forehead as a sign of his sect and of his recently having performed the ceremonies of his religion.

The sepoy had also forgotten the lesson at Barrackpore in 1824 when a whole catalogue of grievances, aggravated by a fear that the sepoys might be ordered to travel by sea, resulted in another mutiny, more deaths, more executions, and the disbandment of another regiment, the 47th, whose number was struck off the army list. Since then there had been other mutinies less publicized, some actually concealed from the public by the authorities.[9]

Most officers continued to insist, however, that a general mutiny of the Bengal Army was inconceivable. They admitted that there were *some* regiments in which discipline was so appallingly lax that sentries relieved each other when and how they pleased, that men quit the ranks without leave and scoured the countryside in quest of plunder; but such things could not possibly happen in *their* regiments: whatever happened to others, *their* men – their *baba-logues*, their 'babies', as some commanding officers paternalistically called them – would remain staunch.[10] It was true, too, that some officers had received warnings from their native servants that there would soon be a 'general rising in the country, in which the sepoy army was to take the lead'.[11] Colonel Sydney Cotton had been told this.[12] So had Colonel Montagu Hall.[13] So, too, had Captain Charles Skinner whose orderly had urged him to go home on leave to England, for there was to be a 'massacre of Firinghis'.[14]

But 'no one gave credit to such stories'. It would all 'come to nothing'; an insurrection in India was 'out of the question'.[15] A few civilians confessed that they would have felt rather more secure had there been more British officers serving with native regiments and more European troops in India. As it was, the country, whose population was about 150 million in 1856, had an army of 300,000 men of whom less than 14,000 were Europeans. There were, in addition, some 23,000 men of the Queen's Army stationed in India, but many of these were in the Punjab, the recently annexed province of warlike people across whose frontiers were the unruly tribesmen of Afghanistan. There was only one British battalion in the seven hundred miles between Lucknow and Calcutta.[16]

And it was near Calcutta, in the arsenal at Dum-Dum, that the first symptoms of mutiny were discerned.

One day in January 1857 a low-caste labourer at Dum-Dum asked a sepoy for a drink of water from his *lota*. The sepoy, being a Brahmin, had naturally refused: his caste would not allow him to grant such a request; he had just scoured his *lota*; the man would defile it by his touch. 'You will soon lose your caste altogether,' the labourer told him. 'For the Europeans are going to make you bite cartridges soaked in cow and pork fat. And then where will your caste be?'[17]

News of the labourer's vindictive warning had soon spread throughout the lines; and Captain J. A. Wright, the sepoy's European officer, had thought it advisable to report the incident to the General commanding the Division, and to add:

There appears to be a very unpleasant feeling existing among the native soldiers who are here for instruction, regarding the grease used in preparing the cartridges, some evil disposed persons having spread a report that it consists of a mixture of the fat of pigs and cows . . . Some of the depot men, in conversing with me on the subject last night, said that the report has spread throughout India, and that when they go to their homes their friends will refuse to eat with them. I assured them (believing it to be the case) that the grease used is composed of mutton fat and wax; to which they replied, 'It may be so, but our friends will not believe it. Let us obtain the ingredients from the bazaar and make it up ourselves. We shall then know what is used, and be able to assure our fellow-soldiers and others that there is nothing in it prohibited by our caste.'[18]

The officer commanding the Division, to whom this letter was passed, was Major-General J. B. Hearsey whose father was believed to be half-Indian and whose wife, the daughter of his own half-brother, was certainly so. Hearsey's knowledge of Indian history was 'prodigious', Lady Canning had discovered, and 'for a *short* time' he was 'not a bore'; but the 'tremendous noise and laugh of this enormous strong old man [were] too much for long'. He was such a 'great boaster and talker' that it was surprising to discover what 'sense and coolness' he could show.[19] He certainly displayed good sense now. Understanding native beliefs and prejudices far better than most of his fellow-officers, General Hearsey took Captain Wright's warning seriously. He sent it on at once to the Deputy Adjutant-General with his own recommendation that the men should be allowed to grease their own cartridges with a substance that did not offend them. Having passed through those tortuous channels which were the designated route for military communications of a like nature, the recommendation was eventually accepted. By then, however, there had been trouble elsewhere.

At an evening parade of the 2nd Native Infantry on 4 February at Barrackpore, the sepoys had demonstrated their deep mistrust of the new cartridges and had made it clear that, even if they were allowed to use their own greasing materials, they would still not be happy about them because of the suspect feel of the paper. A court of inquiry into their insubordinate behaviour at this parade was held at Barrackpore two days later when the various witnesses called all voiced their misgivings. The evidence of the first witness was characteristic:

Question: Were you on parade on the evening of the 4th instant when the new cartridges were shown to the men of the regiment?

Answer: I was.

Question: Did you make any objection to the materials of which those cartridges were composed?

Answer: I felt some suspicion in regard to the paper [which] might affect my caste.

Question: What reason have you to suppose that there is anything in the paper which would injure your caste?

Answer: Because it is a new description of paper with which the cartridges are made up and which I have not seen before.

Question: Have you seen or heard from anyone that the paper is composed of anything which is objectionable to your caste?

Answer: I heard a report that there was some fat in the paper. It was a
bazaar report . . . My suspicion of the paper proceeds from
its being stiff and like cloth in the mode of tearing it. It seems
to us different from the old paper.[20]

While the court was sitting, further evidence came to light of the
sepoys' unrest. On the evening of 6 February, Captain A. S. Allen of
the 34th Native Infantry was sitting on his veranda when a sepoy
stealthily approached him and asked him if he could speak to him in
private about a family matter. After Allen had dismissed his servant
and they were alone the sepoy told him that there was 'a plot amongst
the men of the different regiments' at Barrackpore. They were determined to rise up against their officers and to burn their bungalows as
a protest against being forced to give up their caste and become
Christians. There was a story going round the station that a European
regiment with artillery was being sent from Dinapore to coerce the
sepoys at Barrackpore; but this would be useless, as, having defied
their officers, the mutineers were going to march off to Calcutta and
seize Fort William.[21]

A *jemadar* of the 34th Native Infantry also gave warnings of an
imminent revolt. Two or three sepoys of the regiment had approached
him during the night and had asked him to accompany them to the
parade-ground. There he had found about three hundred men from
different regiments gathered together. 'They had their heads tied up
with cloths,' the *jemadar* reported, 'leaving only a small part of the
face exposed. They asked me to join them, and I asked what I was to
join them in. They replied that they were willing to die for their
religion and that . . . they would plunder the station and kill all the
Europeans and go where they liked.'[22]

Sending these statements on to Calcutta with warnings of the
'mutinous spirit' that seemed to have 'taken deep root among the
sepoys' at Barrackpore and was a 'mine ready for explosion',[23]
General Hearsey also forwarded the findings of the court of inquiry:

The Court accordingly met and was attended by my son, Lieutenant
John Hearsey, a College-passed officer who is now residing with me, and
has been instructed in the Musketry School at Hythe when lately in
England on sick furlough. Lieutenant Hearsey took with him to the
Court one of these Enfield rifles and materials for making up the
cartridges, to show to the native officers . . . The rifle was much admired
but they still objected to the glazed paper . . . In short their suspicions are

fairly roused on the subject of cow and pig fat and it will be quite impossible to allay them, unfounded though they may be . . . It is my intention to have the brigade paraded tomorrow, and myself explain the absurdity of the notion that Government entertains the most distant intention of interfering with their religion or caste.[24]

General Hearsey delivered his speech to the assembled sepoys on 9 February, impressing upon the men, in his fluent Hindustani, that their objections to the new cartridges were completely groundless and that it was absurd 'for one moment to believe that they were *to be forced* to become Christians': coercion was contrary to the tenets of Christianity itself, only those who 'of their own good-will and accord desire to become Christians' being accepted into the faith.[25]

The men would have liked to believe him. But their apprehensions were only partially dispelled; and a detachment of the 34th Native Infantry which was sent on special duty from Barrackpore to Berhampore later on in February deepened the growing alarm among the sepoys of the 19th Native Infantry at Berhampore.

The commanding officer of the 19th was Lieutenant-Colonel W. St L. Mitchell, a hot-tempered and self-confident man who, like so many other officers in native regiments, refused to believe his men capable of disloyalty. 'I have now been nearly sixteen months in command of the 19th Regt N.I.,' he wrote on 16 February. 'And I consider the men as a body are quiet, orderly and obedient, and some of my native officers very superior to the generality of native officers.'[26]

General Hearsey derided such ill-founded confidence. 'You will perceive in all this business the native officers were of no use,' he impressed upon the authorities in Calcutta. '*In fact, they were afraid of their men*, and dare not act. All they do is to hold themselves aloof, and expect by so doing they will escape censure as not *actively* implicated. This has always occurred on such occasions,' added Hearsey (who, by his tact and good sense, had repressed an incipient mutiny at Wazirabad in 1849), 'and will continue to do so to the end of our sovereignty in India.'[27]

Colonel Mitchell was not a man of either tact or good sense. On hearing, to his horrified astonishment, that his men were expressing the same unwillingness to handle the cartridges as the 34th had done, he stormed down to the parade-ground where he harangued the men so angrily that they were convinced, as they said in a subsequent petition to General Hearsey, that 'the cartridges were greased, otherwise he would not have spoken so'. 'If you will not take the cartridges,' the Colonel threatened them, according to their own account (which Mitchell denied), 'I will take you to Burma where, through hardship, you will all die.'[28]

Seeing the men remain sullenly disobedient, Mitchell strode back to his quarters where, soon afterwards, the sound of shouting reached his ears. Rising from the bed on which he had thrown himself in exasperated exhaustion after ordering a general parade for the next morning, he called up the cavalry and artillery to the lines; then, returning there himself, once more harangued the men who appeared so provoked by his anger and so agitated by the appearance of the artillery and cavalry that his native officers begged him to desist. He left the parade-ground defeated for the second time.[29]

While the 19th at Berhampore returned rather shamefacedly to their duties, evidently anxious to atone for their disobedience but still determined not to use the cartridges, the 34th at Barrackpore were paraded for another speech by General Hearsey who again assured them that they had no need to fear for their religion or their caste, that the cartridge paper of which they complained had exactly the same smooth surface and shiny appearance as a letter which he had just received from an Indian prince and which he produced for their inspection. The speech was received in gloomy silence; and Hearsey had no reason to suppose that the mine of which he had warned Calcutta was any less likely to explode.

Feelings of disquiet and foreboding were now spreading fast across the country. Mrs Elizabeth Sneyd, on her way to look after her daughter who was ill at Fatehpur, was obliged to stay the night at Cawnpore. She went to book rooms for herself and her ayah at the principal hotel which she found had almost entirely been taken over by a native prince whose armed retainers were crowded together in the compound. She could obtain nothing better than 'a most dirty room' normally occupied by the hotel-keeper's clerk, nor anything to eat other than 'the stale remnants of the natives' dinner'. In the courtyard were several sepoys who usually saluted politely whenever they saw European ladies. 'These men,' Mrs Sneyd wrote, 'did nothing but point and laugh at me amongst themselves while talking a great deal together in an undertone, keeping seated on the ground the whole time.' She felt frightened; but, like so many other English women in India at this time, she 'tried to show a brave face'.[30]

Mrs Peppé, who was on her way to Darjeeling from Gorakhpur with her children, also did her best to conceal her fear. She was travelling by boat. At night when the boatmen and servants went ashore, the boat was moored to a post driven into the bank. 'Almost at every stoppage the servants brought my mother strange stories of how unsettled the whole of India had become,' William Peppé, at that time a child of six, remembered. 'She tried to keep up a brave heart, hoping all was well with her husband.' One evening a young Indian stepped on board and, without invitation, sat down cross-legged in front of Mrs Peppé. Was she not afraid to travel alone through India at such a time, he asked her. 'Afraid? Afraid of what? Who would want to do me and my little ones any harm? I have lived all my life here, and my children also.' She continued calmly knitting until the man had gone; then, having watched him out of sight, she called urgently to the boatmen to hurry over their meal and come aboard again. She sensed, like General Hearsey, that danger was close, as though a mine were soon to explode.[31]

The explosion came on Sunday 29 March. The General was in his quarters that day when a lieutenant, 'his hands and his clothes partly covered with blood', dashed in to tell him that there was a riot in the native lines. Calling for his two sons, both officers of native infantry regiments, Hearsey left immediately for the parade-ground of the 34th. Here a sepoy, Mangal Pande, evidently under the influence of some intoxicating drug, was rampaging about with a loaded musket in front of the quarter-guard, dressed in his regimental jacket but barefoot and with a dhoti instead of trousers, calling upon the bugler to sound the assembly, and shouting, 'Come out, you *bhainchutes*, the Europeans are here! Why aren't you getting ready? It's for our religion! From biting these cartridges we shall become infidels. Get ready! Turn out all of you! You have incited me to do this and now, you *bhainchutes*, you will not follow me!'

The English Sergeant-Major, Hewson, summoned by a native officer, ran over to the *jemadar* in command of the quarter-guard to demand why he did not arrest the man. 'What can I do?' the *jemadar* replied helplessly. 'The *naick* is gone to the adjutant. The havildar is gone to the field officer. Am I to take him myself?' The Sergeant-Major answered by telling him to fall in his guard with loaded weapons. 'Some of the men grumbled,' Hewson later reported; 'and he never insisted on the men loading or falling in.'[32] By then the Adjutant, Lieutenant Baugh, had arrived on the scene. Galloping up to the quarter-guard with shouts of, 'Where is he? Where is he?' Baugh was brought up short by an urgent warning from Hewson who called out, 'Ride to the right, Sir, for your life. The sepoy will fire at you!' At that moment Mangal Pande opened fire, hitting the Adjutant's horse, and bringing both animal and rider to the ground. But Baugh immediately jumped to his feet, fired his pistol at the sepoy, missed him, then, throwing his pistol at his face, charged towards him, followed by the Sergeant-Major. The sepoy stood his ground, drawing out his tulwar with which he slashed at Baugh, cutting him on the shoulder and neck, while Hewson was knocked down from behind with a blow from a sepoy's musket. Both Adjutant and Sergeant-Major would, no doubt, have been killed had not a Muslim sepoy, Shaikh Paltu, dashed forward to hold Mangal Pande round the waist while the two wounded Englishmen made good their escape.

In coming to their rescue, Shaikh Paltu was entirely on his own. Assailed by other sepoys, both Hindu and Muslim, who threw stones and shoes at his back, he called on the guard to help him hold Mangal Pande, but they shouted back that if he did not let him go they would shoot him. So, wounded himself by now, Shaikh Paltu was obliged to loosen his grip. He backed away from Mangal Pande in one direction, while Baugh and Hewson, belaboured in their withdrawal with the butt ends of the guards' muskets, withdrew in another.

Colonel S. G. Wheler, the proselytizing commanding officer of the 34th, now appeared on the scene. He ordered the guard to arrest Mangal Pande. They declined to do so. 'I felt it was useless going on any further in the matter,' Colonel Wheler lamely testified at the subsequent court of inquiry. 'A native in undress mentioned to me that the sepoy was a Brahmin and no one would hurt him. I considered it quite useless and a useless sacrifice of life to order a European officer, with the guard, to seize him . . . I then left the ground and reported the matter to the Brigadier.'[33]

The Brigadier, Charles Grant, was equally incapable of dealing with the problem when he at length appeared. And it was not until the Hearseys came galloping on to the parade-ground that order was restored. As soon as he saw what had happened, the General demanded why the mutinous sepoy had not been arrested. It was explained to him that the guard would not obey orders. 'We'll see about that,' said Hearsey, and rode off towards the guard.

'His musket is loaded,' someone warned him. The General answered, 'Damn his musket!'

'Father, he is taking aim at you!' called out his elder son.

'If I fall, John, rush upon him and put him to death.'

Having given this order, Hearsey rode up to the quarter-guard and, shaking his revolver at the *jemadar*, said, 'Listen to me. The first man who refuses to march when I give the word is a dead man. Quick march!'

The guard obeyed him. But as they approached, so Hearsey reported, Mangal Pande

turned his musket muzzle towards his own breast hurriedly, touching the trigger with his toe. The muzzle must have swerved, for the bullet made a deep graze, ripping up the muscles of his chest, shoulder and neck, and he fell prostrate. We were on him at once ... His regimental jacket and clothes were on fire and smoking. I bid the *jemadar* and the sepoys to put the fire out which they did ... I then went, accompanied by Major Ross and my two sons amongst the crowd of sepoys ... and reassured them that no person should be permitted to interfere with their religion and caste prejudices whilst I commanded them. [I also told them that] they had not done their duty in allowing their fellow-soldier, Mungul Pandy, to behave in the murderous manner he had done. They answered in one voice, 'He is mad, he has taken bhang to excess.' I replied, 'Could you not have seized him, and if he resisted have shot him or maimed him? Would you not have done so to a mad elephant or a mad dog ... ?' They said, 'He had loaded his musket.' 'What,' I replied, 'are you afraid of a loaded musket?' They were silent. I bid them go quietly to their lines, and they did so, immediately obeying my orders.[34]

Mangal Pande did not die of his self-inflicted wound and was brought to trial less than a week later. It transpired that he was twenty-six years old and had been in the army for seven years during which his conduct had been good.

'Were you under the influence of any drugs?' he was asked.

'Yes, I have been taking bhang and opium of late,' he readily admitted. 'I was not aware at the time of what I was doing.'

But when asked – as he frequently was asked – to give the names of the persons who, as he had said, had incited him to mutiny, he refused to do so, answering the question, 'Did you act on Sunday last by your own free will, or were you instructed by others?' with the words, 'Of my own will.' And when called upon for his defence, he merely repeated, 'I did not know what I was doing. I did not know who I wounded and who I did not. What more shall I say? I have nothing more to say. I have no evidence.'[35]

So Mangal Pande, whose common caste name was soon to be adopted by the European troops as an epithet for all mutineers, was condemned to death. And the 34th Native Infantry returned, if not to normal, to an uneasy quiet. Its officers were officially asked for their opinion of the regiment. Captain Aubert said that he had recently 'observed a great want of respect on the part of the men towards their officers . . . the men did not stand up and salute'. Baugh, the adjutant, whom his fellow-officers seem not to have much liked and who was not popular with the men, agreed that the sepoys had of late been 'greatly wanting in respect towards the officers', that they 'performed their duty in such a sullen and sluggish manner' that the sergeant-major had one day remarked to him that he 'did not know what had come over the regiment'. On being asked whether he would accompany the regiment on active service with full reliance upon the loyalty and good conduct of the native officers and men, Baugh replied, 'certainly not'.[36]

Other officers in the regiment, however – despite all that had happened – had no such doubts as to its loyalty. Captain Allen had noticed 'no falling off of respect'. Lieutenant Bunbury, when asked whether *he* would accompany the regiment on field service with confidence in its loyalty, answered, 'Certainly I would.' And Captain Drury firmly believed that, with the exception of a few men whom he could not name, 'the general feeling of the regiment [was] very good indeed'.[37]

These were not exceptional opinions either in the 34th Native Infantry or in the 19th. Later on that year European officers were to express the opinion that all the men of both regiments ought to have been blown from the artillery's guns.[38] But at the time, even the comparatively mild punishment inflicted upon them was considered by many officers unjustifiably severe. The 19th were marched from Berhampore to Barrackpore and there, under the guns of two field batteries, were ordered to pile their arms. Obediently they obeyed, accepted their final instalment of pay and marched off the parade-ground to return to their homes, taking their uniforms with them, cheering General Hearsey for not having treated them more severely, 'several old native officers breaking down and crying like children'.[39] After a delay of six weeks, during which claims for leniency or exculpation were meticulously examined in Calcutta, the punishment of the 34th was also decided upon. Mangal Pande having been executed on 8 April and the *jemadar*, who had commanded the quarter-guard, on 21 April, it was decided that the rest of the men, including those who had attacked their wounded officers, should merely be disarmed and disbanded for fear lest a severer punishment should lead to a more serious mutiny. Although this punishment was much more lenient than some of their officers had expected, the sepoys of the 34th took it less quietly than the 19th, throwing their caps on the ground and trampling on them before leaving the parade-ground 'with looks that suggested they would cause further trouble when they could'.[40]

Already there *had* been further trouble at the musketry depot at Ambala where the Commander-in-Chief had arrived on a tour of inspection escorted by the 36th Native Infantry.

The Hon. George Anson, Commander-in-Chief in India, was then fifty-nine years old. A son of the first Viscount Anson and brother of the first Earl of Lichfield, he had served with the Scots Guards at Waterloo. Soon afterwards he had entered Parliament as Member for South Staffordshire, and had never been in action since. Having attained the rank of major-general in 1853, he was offered command of a division in the Bengal Army; in the following year he assumed command of the Madras Army, and early in 1856 became Commander-in-Chief. A handsome man of great charm and many accomplishments, he had never been called upon to show any notable gifts in the exalted rank which he had attained. He had reached that rank, indeed, more through his family connections and numerous friendships, his affability and knowledge of the world than through any obvious talents as a soldier. A member of the Jockey Club and a power in the higher circles of the Turf, he had won the 1842 Derby with a horse he had bought for £120. As much in demand in England as an arbiter of social disputes and affairs of honour as the Marquess of Hartington was to be, he caused great surprise when he chose to leave the country for India where he arrived with the reputation of being the best whist player in Europe, the husband of a 'lovely young wife', indeed 'the finest gentleman, the handsomest and most fortunate man of the day'.[41] In India he aroused a good deal of resentment by his obvious prejudice against the Indian Army, choosing all his aides-de-camp from Queen's regiments and openly admitting that he never saw an Indian soldier 'without turning away in disgust at his unsoldierlike appearance'. But although he proved rather 'a disappointment' in Calcutta, Lord Canning had to admit that it 'would be very difficult to quarrel with anyone so imperturbably good tempered, and so thoroughly a gentleman'.[42]

On approaching the Ambala musketry depot, Anson's escort of the 36th Native Infantry was met by two native officers of the same regiment who, already stationed there, came out to greet them. Far from being accorded the kind of welcome they expected, the two

native officers were reviled as traitors to the cause, as Christian per-
verts, as being unclean from their use of the new cartridges. Appalled
by these accusations, they ran back to Ambala to tell Captain E. M.
Martineau, the commander of the depot, what had happened.
Martineau, understanding and sympathetic, immediately set about
trying to discover how serious was the unrest in the 36th. Much
disturbed by what the men told him, he reported his fears to the staff
at Simla where they received scant attention. Repeating them later,
Martineau warned:

Feeling is as bad as can be and matters have gone so far that I can
hardly devise any suitable remedy. We make a grand mistake in supposing that because we dress, arm and drill Hindustani soldiers as Europeans,
they become one bit European in their feelings and ideas. I see them on
parade for say two hours daily, but what do I know of them for the other
22? What do they talk about in their lines, what do they plot? . . . For all
I can tell I might as well be in Siberia.

I know that at the present moment an unusual agitation is pervading
the ranks of the entire native army, but what it will exactly result in, I am
afraid to say. I can detect the near approach of the storm, I can hear the
moaning of the hurricane, but I can't say how, when or where it will break
forth . . . I don't think they know themselves what they will do, or that
they have any plan of action except of resistance to invasion of their
religion, and their faith.

But, good God! Here are all the elements of combustion at hand,
100,000 men, sullen, distrustful, fierce, with all their deepest and inmost
sympathies, as well as worst passions, roused, and we thinking to cajole
them into good humour by patting them on the back, saying what a fool
you are for making such a fuss about nothing. They no longer believe us,
they have passed out of restraint and will be off at a gallop before long.
If a flare-up from any cause takes place at one station, it will spread and
become universal.[43]

General Anson was totally disinclined to take such a gloomy view
or to suppose that most of the sepoys in northern India were so convinced that their caste and faith were threatened as to be on the verge
of violence. Through an interpreter he spoke to the troops of Ambala
in an effort to allay their fears; but, while they professed to Captain
Martineau that they believed the General to be sincere in what he told
them, the feeling in the army and amongst their families was such that
they would be outcast and ostracized if they were to use the cartridges.
So, rather than risk a mutiny, Anson eventually decided that, for the
moment at least, firing practice at Ambala and the other two musketry
depots would be suspended. At the same time he asked for a

report on the paper used in the manufacture of the Enfield cartridges, expressing to Calcutta his own opinion that they were indeed covered with a huge quantity of grease.[44] Calcutta did not agree that the firing practice should be suspended. A new drill had been devised: the men would not in future be required to bite the cartridges; they could tear the ends off with their fingers. So, objections to them having been removed, there was no longer any reason why the Enfield cartridges should not be used. And used they were, according to the revised drill, for the first time at Ambala on 17 April.

But the new drill did not remove the men's objections. Assured though they were that the cartridges contained no proscribed materials, they still did not trust the feel of them. Besides, having grown so accustomed to biting the old cartridges, who could be sure in his excitement in action he might not inadvertently bite a new one?

Soon after that first firing practice at Ambala fires broke out in the lines, and the bungalows of European officers and the huts of those native soldiers who had used the new cartridges were burned to the ground. A Sikh attached to the depot reported that these fires were the portent of worse to come: the men had sworn to burn down every building on the station. It was a threat which was soon to be fulfilled elsewhere.

4

Mutiny at Meerut

· Brigadier Wilson at Meerut · Colonel Carmichael-Smyth and the firing-parade of the 3rd Light Cavalry, 24 April 1857 · disgrace of the 3rd Cavalry · the outbreak and murders at Meerut, 10 May 1857 ·

At the beginning of May 1857, Brigadier Archdale Wilson, the 'tall, soldierly-looking' station commander at Meerut, returned to duty from the hills where he had been convalescing after an attack of small-pox. A kindly, quiet, though sharp-tempered man of fifty-three, one of the thirteen sons of a Norfolk parson and a nephew of Lord Berners, Wilson was already looking forward to retirement in East Anglia. After a brief education at Norwich Grammar School and the military college of the East India Company at Addiscombe, he had received his commission as second lieutenant in the Bengal Artillery at the age of fifteen, had arrived in India five months later and now, after nearly forty years' service there, was more than ready to go home. As he told his 'dear old woman', whom he had left behind in the hills, the summit of his ambition was a small cottage in Norfolk and '£600 a year with peace and quietness'. That 'would be heaven'. Instead, he had come back to the blazing heat of Meerut where his garden had been shrivelled by the sun, the geraniums had all gone out of flower, and only a few withered fuchsias were left in the baked earth. His horses had 'all grown as fat as butter'; and, worst of all, there seemed to be a fuss which he had not got to the bottom of yet over 'some mutinous fellows in the 3rd Light Cavalry'. It was the new cartridges, so Wilson learned, that had caused all the trouble.[1]

The new Enfield rifle which was to fire these cartridges had been issued at Meerut at the beginning of January 1857 to one of the two European regiments there, the 60th Rifles, which had later also been issued with ten rounds of ammunition per man. But when the skirmishers of a native regiment, the 3rd Light Cavalry, were ordered to attend a parade on 24 April to learn the new firing-drill, the European officers of the regiment were warned that the sepoys would refuse to defile themselves by touching the cartridges. Informed by two Muslim *naiks* that these cartridges had been greased with both beef and pork fat, the men took a solemn oath to have nothing to do with them unless every other regiment agreed to handle them, the Muslims amongst them swearing on the Koran, the Hindus by the holy water of the Ganges. The men were assured that the blank cartridges to be used on parade were not the new sort but the ones to which they had long been accustomed; even so, they would not be required to bite the ends off with their teeth but to tear them off by hand. But they remained unappeased. They had heard that the new cartridges had arrived at Meerut, for a low-caste *sowar* of the 3rd, the orderly of the Havildar-Major, claimed that he had already been shown the new drill and, in practising it, had fired off two of them. How could the men distinguish between these new cartridges and the old ones? In any case, even if the usual cartridges were to be used, these were now said to be manufactured with a new kind of paper impregnated with a defiling fat.

Protesting that they could not touch the offensive material, for if they did so, they would lose their caste and therefore be unable to return to their homes, the men approached their native officers who, in turn, went to warn a sympathetic European officer of their attitude. This officer, Captain H. C. Craigie, wrote an abrupt note to the acting Adjutant, telling him to go to the Colonel at once, as there was 'a commotion throughout the native troops about cartridges'. '*This is a most serious matter,*' Craigie added, underlining the words, '*and we may have the whole regiment in mutiny in half an hour if this is not attended to. Pray don't lose a moment* ... We have none of the objectionable cartridges, but the men say that if they fire any kind of cartridge at present they lay themselves open to the imputation from their comrades and from other regiments of having fired the objectionable ones.'[2]

The Colonel to whom this warning was addressed was George Monro Carmichael-Smyth. He was the youngest of the eight children of James Carmichael who had added Smyth to the family name under the terms of the will of a rich grandfather. Although of a well-known Anglo–Indian family, he had not had a particularly distinguished career, having achieved neither rapid promotion in his regiment nor the rewards of service outside it. At the age of fifty-three, one of his few claims to fame was his shared authorship of an original if partisan and didactic *History of the Reigning Family at Lahore.* An aloof and argumentative man, he was not well liked by either his officers or his men.[3]

While on leave at Mussoorie earlier on in the month he had heard that there had been disturbances at the musketry depot at Ambala following the use of the new cartridges; and he had met a man who had told him that a havildar, talking of the trouble at Berhampore, had observed, 'I have been thirty-six years in the service . . . but I still would join in a mutiny, and what is more I can tell you the whole army will mutiny.'[4] So impressed was Carmichael-Smyth by these words that on the very day of his return to Meerut he repeated them in a letter to Colonel Curzon, Military Secretary to the Commander-in-Chief. Yet that same day he also confirmed the holding of the parade for the new firing-drill by the skirmishers of his regiment the following morning, believing, so he later wrote, that once the men were told that they were to tear off the ends of the cartridges, not bite them, they 'would be much pleased to hear of it'.[5]

A young Cornet in his regiment, John MacNabb, did not agree with him. MacNabb was only eighteen and had not been with the regiment long; but, in the words of an older officer who had befriended him, he was 'a very fine young fellow, full of bright youth and vigour'.[6] Certainly he held a more realistic view of the firing-parade than did his Colonel. MacNabb told his mother:

There was no necessity to have a parade at all or to make any fuss of the sort just now. No other Colonel thought of doing such a thing, as they knew at this unsettled time their men would refuse to be the first to fire these cartridges . . . The men themselves humbly petitioned the Colonel to put the parade off till this disturbance in India had gone over, in fact pointing out to him what he ought to have seen himself. He . . . sent for the [acting] Adjutant and asked him what he advised. Fancy a Colonel asking his Adjutant. He ought to be able to make his own mind up . . . if he is fit to command a regiment.[7]

The acting Adjutant, 'always severe to the men', in MacNabb's opinion, 'said that it would be like being afraid of them' if the parade were to be cancelled. Carmichael-Smyth concurred with this opinion. Accordingly, on the morning of Friday 24 April, ninety men of the 3rd Light Cavalry marched out on to the parade-ground. The acting Adjutant ordered them to take three cartridges each. They refused to do so. The Havildar-Major was then instructed to load and fire his carbine. This he did, demonstrating the new motions of the drill.

I then ordered the cartridges to be served out to the ninety men on parade [Carmichael-Smyth subsequently reported]. The first man to whom a cartridge was offered said he would get a bad name if he took it. I said to him, 'You see the Havildar-Major has taken one and fired one.' He replied, 'Oh, the Havildar-Major!' in a manner to signify that his position obliged him to do it, adding, 'If all the men will take the cartridges, I will.' He assigned no reason for not taking it, but still refused to do as I ordered him. I then ordered one to be given to [another man] but he also refused, saying, 'If all the regiment[s] will take cartridges I will.' After this I ordered each man in succession to take cartridges but with the exception of five men [three Muslims and two Hindus] they all refused to do so. None of them assigned any reason for refusing, beyond saying that they would get a bad name.[8]

The five non-commissioned officers who had accepted the cartridges were then dismissed; and, after further explanations and orders by the Colonel had proved unavailing, the remaining eighty-five men were taken off duty and confined to their lines.

'The men of course had *no* real excuse for not doing what they were ordered,' commented Cornet MacNabb who thought that the men would not have disobeyed the orders 'if they had been left alone, instead of being paraded, and addressed, and all that humbug'. He added:

Another mistake was that instead of serving out the cartridges the night before as usual, they were not given them till they got on parade, which of course made them doubt if they were the old ones . . . But the real case is that they hate Smyth, and if almost any other officer had gone down they would have fired them off [even though] they did not want to be the first regiment that fired . . . Craigie told me that, from what he knows of the men in his own troop, and in the Regiment, he would have guaranteed that they fired them five minutes after he had spoken to them. Craigie was told this by his men by whom he is beloved.[9]

The day after the abortive firing-parade a court of inquiry, consisting of seven native officers, with one British captain as superintending officer and another as interpreter, assembled to take the evidence of various witnesses including that of a labourer from the magazine who affirmed that the cartridges offered to the men were, in fact, exactly the same as those in use for the past thirty-three years. At this court the native troopers gave much the same answers to questions concerning their reasons for refusing them as had been given at the court of inquiry at Barrackpore.[10]

On receiving the findings of the Meerut court of inquiry, a court-martial of all eighty-five men was recommended by the Judge Advocate-General and approved by the Commander-in-Chief. At their subsequent trial, by the votes of all but one of the fifteen native officers who were members of the court, the accused were convicted and sentenced to imprisonment with hard labour for ten years. A recommendation for mercy, on the grounds that the men, previously of good character, had been misled by rumours, was rejected by the Commander of the Meerut Division, Major-General W. H. Hewitt, who held that this only made their offence more culpable. The sentence of imprisonment was therefore confirmed with a remission of five years for eleven men who had been less than five years in the service.[11]

On Saturday 9 May 1857 all the troops at Meerut – the 3rd Light Cavalry, the 11th and 20th Native Infantry, the first battalion of the 60th Rifles, the 6th Dragoon Guards, a troop of horse artillery, a company of foot artillery and a light field battery – were assembled on the European infantry parade-ground. They were paraded to form three sides of a square; and through the open side the convicted men were marched and halted. The European troops were armed, their guns and rifles loaded. There were about 1,700 of them in all, rather less than the total number of sepoys. Under a dark sky, troubled by storm-clouds, the sentences were read out; then the eighty-five men were stripped of their uniforms; their boots were removed and their ankles shackled. Most accepted this treatment resignedly; but others shouted and cursed, threatening the European troops with fierce reprisals, execrating their fellow-sepoys for doing nothing to help them. When the last shackle had been hammered home they were marched off under a guard of the 60th to the New Gaol. 'And as they passed our regiment, carrying their boots which had been taken off for the purpose of fixing the fetters,' so Lieutenant Hugh Gough, a young officer of the 3rd Light Cavalry, recorded, 'a number of them threw them at the Colonel, cursing him loudly in Hindustani, and calling to their comrades to remember them. There was a good deal of murmuring in our ranks, and had it not been for the presence of the British troops it is impossible to say what might have taken place.'[12] Later that day Gough and one or two of his fellow-officers visited the gaol where the men were imprisoned, and he felt deeply moved by their plight. 'Old soldiers, with many medals gained in desperately-fought battles for their English masters, wept bitterly, lamenting their sad fate, and imploring [us] to save them from their future,' Gough wrote. 'Young soldiers, too, joined in; and I have seldom, if ever, in all my life, experienced a more touching scene.'[13]

To be stripped of their uniforms was disgrace enough, but to be forced to suffer the added humiliation of being publicly fettered like common criminals was more, they said, than they ought to have been asked to bear. A worse punishment could not have been hit upon, MacNabb decided.

It is much worse to them than death . . . They will never see their wives and families, they are degraded, and one poor old man who has been 40 years in the regiment, and would have got his pension, is now thrown back the *whole* of his service . . . It is a great pity that it has happened in my regiment, 'The old and steady 3rd', and brought on us in such a useless manner. It is the *first* disgrace the regiment has ever had . . . Some of our officers went down to the Gaol to see them and pay their wages. They say it was heartrending. Yet they accused no one, but thanked them for coming to see them . . . When they were being paid, one man said, 'Oh, give it to my wife,' another, 'Oh, give it to my brother. What good is it to me. I am a dead man now.'[14]

There were many Europeans far senior to MacNabb who agreed with him that the sentences were unreasonably harsh and felt that the men should never have been subjected to the humiliation of shackling. The Commander-in-Chief expressed his regret that such an 'unusual procedure' had been considered advisable.[15] The Governor-General roundly condemned so unnecessarily provocative an addition to the sentence of imprisonment which seems to have been carried out at the instigation of the Deputy Judge Advocate-General.[16]

Soon after his return from the gaol, Hugh Gough was sitting on the veranda of his bungalow when a native officer of the regiment called to see him on the pretence of discussing the troop's accounts. It soon transpired that his real mission was to inform Gough that a mutiny of the native troops at Meerut would take place the next day, Sunday 10 May, when their comrades would be delivered from imprisonment. Gough took the warning seriously.[17] Almost every night since the arrest of the eighty-five men of his regiment there had been fires in one part of Meerut or another. Burning arrows had been shot into thatched roofs; houses and stores had been set alight; violent arguments had erupted in the bazaar.

Gough went immediately to Carmichael-Smyth to pass this information on to him. But the Colonel 'treated the communication with contempt', reproving him for 'listening to such idle words'.

Later that evening Gough met the Brigadier, Archdale Wilson, and told him the same story, 'but he also was incredulous'.[18] So was Major-General W. H. Hewitt, Commander of the Meerut Division, who went so far as to assure the Commander-in-Chief that the native troops at Meerut were 'behaving steady and soldierlike'.[19]

Known as 'Bloody Bill', Hewitt was sixty-seven years old. He had served in India for over half a century, and in all that time does not appear to have ever gone home on leave to England.[20] He was extremely fat, of a kindly, lazy, placid disposition, 'a dear old boy' in one junior officer's opinion;[21] but it was supposed by everyone that he had long since passed the age when he ought to have retired, and by some, that he was rapidly approaching his dotage. Brigadier Wilson condemned him as 'a fearful old dolt . . . an exasperating idiot'.[22] But Wilson agreed with Hewitt that the reports of a threatened mutiny at Meerut were not to be taken seriously. He had just written to his wife to tell her so. He had rather expected that a few of the eighty-five men who had refused to handle the cartridges would have been sentenced to death as an example, but he was 'not sorry it was otherwise'. 'So ends this business,' he had added. 'I hope we shall have no more of it here.'[23]

The next morning, Sunday 10 May, Hugh Gough and John MacNabb drove to church together. Forty years later Gough could still recall the scene vividly – the undress summer uniform of frock-coat and white overalls which they were both wearing; MacNabb's smart alpaca coat, trimmed with lace; and Gough's teasing remark about the lace which, being the wrong sort, would be sure to catch Colonel Carmichael-Smyth's sharp, reproving eye.[24] In church the two young officers sat next to H. H. Greathed, the Commissioner of Meerut, and his wife; and after the service they spoke to Mrs Greathed for a few moments about the events of the previous day. She had been to dinner the evening before with Lieutenant-Colonel W. N. Custance of the Dragoon Guards. They had talked of the placards which servants had reported having seen in the city 'calling upon all true Mussulmans to rise and slaughter the English'.[25] But all seemed quiet enough now. Gough left the Greatheds to attend to his ponies and to play with his pet bear and leopard. MacNabb went to spend the morning with friends in the Artillery. It was a stiflingly hot day. So hot was it, in fact, that the evening church-parade, usually held at half past six, was postponed until seven o'clock; and many officers' wives were thankful that they did not have to get up and dress as early as usual. At about six o'clock, however, they were beginning to stir.

Hugh Gough, too, was starting to get dressed. He was Orderly Officer of the day, and would soon have to be on parade. He was still in his shirt-sleeves when a servant came rushing into his bedroom to tell him that the Native Infantry lines were on fire. He dashed outside, half dressed, to see clouds of smoke billowing up into the evening sky from the burning bungalows, and heard the sharp cracking sound of musketry fire. His syce was already running towards the veranda steps, holding a bunch of lucerne grass in one hand and the reins of Gough's black charger in the other. As the horse took a munch of the grass, Gough jumped on to his back and galloped down towards the parade-ground of the 20th Native Infantry.[26]

Several officers of this regiment had been sitting quietly talking in their Commanding Officer's bungalow when they had been called down to the men's lines where about seventy badmashes from the bazaar were clamouring outside the regimental magazine. Some sepoys, it was said, had assured the prostitutes in the bazaar – who were taunting them with their failure to rescue their imprisoned comrades – that they need not worry, for the native troops were going to mutiny that very evening; and a rumour had since got about that the European soldiers had been ordered to disarm all the native regiments. By the time the officers arrived in the lines both the sepoys and the rabble of the bazaar appeared dangerously close to violence. The senior officer present ordered the grenadier company to disperse the mob around the regimental magazine. But the sepoys, paying no attention to his command, slunk away from him; and when a *sowar* of the 3rd Light Cavalry galloped into their lines, shouting that the Europeans were coming and that if they intended to act they must do so at once, they rushed upon the bells of arms, breaking into them, seizing weapons for themselves and for the badmashes who followed after them. Soon the lines were in uproar, with sepoys and badmashes firing off their weapons in every direction. The Colonel of the 11th Native Infantry galloped across 'to see what all the noise was about'. His horse was shot; and then he, too, was shot; and within minutes his own regiment, in which he had 'the old traditional faith', was also in uproar, groups of wildly shouting sepoys ransacking their bells of arms and shooting at all Europeans in sight. Other sepoys, holding their fire, urged their officers to escape while they could. A few officers stayed to remonstrate, knocking the '*loaded and cocked*' muskets down with their fists. But now most realized their men were beyond control and 'made up their minds to be off'. One or two walked away slowly, refusing to run from their own men; but the majority hurried off as fast as they could to seek hiding-places for themselves or to protect their women and children. Six of them, led by the Commanding Officer of the 20th, sought shelter in a servants' latrine in the compound of Colonel Carmichael-Smyth's bungalow. Three of these attempted to escape from here, going their separate ways; but all of them were killed, either shot by sepoys or cut down by badmashes from the bazaar. The other three stayed where they were until they heard the sound of European troops on the march when they rushed out to join them and were saved.

Not many British officers in native regiments were so fortunate. Colonel Carmichael-Smyth managed to escape from his bungalow, and to warn the Commissioner and the General of the outbreak; then, as Field Officer of the week, he joined Brigadier Wilson on the artillery parade-ground. But the two officers whom he was entertaining to dinner that evening, the Surgeon-Major and the Veterinary Surgeon, tried to get away in a buggy and were both shot, the latter fatally. Several other officers were murdered by ruffians from the bazaar, including John MacNabb whose mangled body could only be identified by his friend, Hugh Gough, because of its height and the curious silk braid on the alpaca coat.[27]

Mrs Muter, the wife of a captain in the 60th Rifles, had driven to church as usual; and, while waiting for the service to begin, she had sat in her pony carriage outside the church door, her back to the cantonments, watching the sun sinking 'in a blaze of fiery heat' beneath the baked plain, unaware of the horrifying scenes behind her. It was not until she was on her way home that she realized her life was in danger. But the throngs of shouting natives were so busy throwing stones at two wounded European artillerymen that they paid no attention to her carriage which she drove past them as fast as the ponies would take it. At her bungalow she found her frightened servants clustered round the door. The *khansaman*, protesting that he could no longer be responsible for the safety of her silver, begged her to take it back into her own charge and to run away with it and hide, a proposal which, so she proudly claimed, she 'regarded as an insult'. She did, however, allow the *khansaman* and the nightwatchman to escort her to the quarter-guard where they left her, with several other women, under the protection of some European soldiers before returning to her bungalow to break open various cases which had been packed and sealed for an intended departure to the hills.[28]

Mrs Craigie and the sister of Lieutenant A. R. D. Mackenzie also managed to escape. They had left for evening service together rather later than Mrs Muter; but they had never reached the church, the terrified coachman turning back at sight of the mob. As they passed the bazaar on their hasty return journey, a soldier of the 6th Dragoon Guards came running out of a side street, pursued by a yelling mob. The ladies courageously stopped the carriage to pull the soldier in, before rattling off again followed by badmashes who slashed at the hood of the carriage with their tulwars.

The escape of these ladies and Mrs Muter was exceptional. Mrs Chambers, the pregnant wife of the Adjutant of the 11th Native Infantry, was murdered and mutilated by a Muslim butcher from the bazaar. Mrs Macdonald, whose husband had been shot as he tried to calm the sepoys of the 21st, was hidden by her children's ayah and her dhobi in a *bhisti*'s hut. Here she and the children were given native clothes in which to disguise themselves; and, led by the *chowkidar*, were then hurried away towards the Artillery School. But on their way they were stopped by a mob who demanded to examine them. The *chowkidar* bravely protested that the woman was his sister-in-law, but the covering was pulled from her face, and, while her children were rushed away by the other faithful servants, she was cut to the ground where, like her friend Mrs Chambers, her body was savagely mutilated. Mrs Dawson, wife of a veterinary surgeon, was in bed with smallpox when a mob surrounded her bungalow. Her husband came on to the balcony to protect her; but, after he was shot, flaming torches were thrown at her until her clothes caught fire and she was burned to death. Mrs Courtney, who helped to run the Meerut hotel, was protected for a time in her flight by some friendly *sowars* of the 3rd Light Cavalry; but later her coachman was knocked off his box and she and her children were killed. Another woman, never certainly identified, was seen being dragged along in a *palka-ghari* while a *sowar*, riding beside the carriage, stabbed her repeatedly, though she was already dead.[29]

Although even now in some parts of the cantonments officers were still being saluted by their men, elsewhere the rioting was by this time completely out of hand. Badmashes, still pouring out of the bazaar, were burning and plundering the lines in the wake of the sepoys, attacking isolated groups of Europeans, arming themselves with whatever weapons they could lay their hands on. A party of sepoys had gone off to release their comrades from the New Gaol; others later went to release the prisoners – over eight hundred of them – from the Old Gaol. In the bazaar areas European soldiers, mostly artillery-men and riflemen making their way to or from a popular rendezvous which sold ginger-beer and was known as 'the pop-shop', were set upon by the mob with sticks and stones and knives. A few managed to escape, but many more were killed. At the same time native shop-keepers were attacked and their premises looted, while Muslim fanatics smashed the contents of wine stores. Most of the native police either stood idly by, or joined in the plunder themselves. Later, bands of marauders, carrying knives and flaming torches, descended upon the city from the surrounding villages.[30]

There was little that any of the British officers could do to quell the violence which before morning had resulted in the deaths of about fifty European men, women and children.[31] As he approached the parade-ground of the 20th Native Infantry, Hugh Gough had pulled up his horse 'in wonder and horror'. The thatch of the mud barracks was ablaze; the sepoys were 'dancing and leaping frantically about, calling and yelling to each other, and blazing away into the air and in all directions'. Catching sight of Gough they shouted at the native officer and *sowars* with him to get out of the way as they dashed towards him firing their muskets. Gough pulled his charger round and, as musket balls whizzed round his head, galloped off to his own troop which he found also in a state of wildest excitement.

Most of them were mounted and galloping to and fro [Gough recorded]; the lines were being burnt and there was a general rush to the magazine, where the men helped themselves to the ammunition – regardless of its being the 'unclean cartridges'. As for any efforts on my part to bring them to a sense of their duties or of obedience to my orders they were absolutely useless . . . After a time the disregard of my authority changed to open mutiny; there were loud shouts of *'Maro! Maro!'* ('Kill him! Kill him!') and a few men, chiefly recruits, fired pistol shots at me, mostly at random, although one shot so far took effect as to pierce the cantle of my saddle . . . Seeing all was lost, and that my power as their officer was absolutely gone, and acting on the earnest, in fact forcible, solicitation of the better disposed (for they took my horse's head and forced me to leave) [I] decided to make the best of my way to the European lines. [I] left at a gallop, being for a time pursued with shouts and execrations.

The only way open to him was through the native bazaar where the speed of his horse saved him from being cut down by angry men who slashed at him with tulwars and lathies and pelted him with stones.

Accompanied now by a European quartermaster-sergeant and still escorted by a loyal native officer and two *sowars*, he charged off to the civil lines beyond the cantonment to the rescue of Mr and Mrs

Greathed. The Greatheds' servants met him at the door and assured him that their master and mistress had no need of his protection, having driven away some time before.[32] The Greatheds were, in fact, on the roof of their house, having been persuaded to hide there by their faithful servants who had promised to keep everyone away. Soon after Gough's hasty departure, the mob arrived at the door, demanding that the Commissioner should be delivered up to them. 'I attacked the mob with great ferocity like a terrible lion,' claimed one old pensioner whose tributes to his own valour rival those of Benvenuto Cellini himself. 'By the favour of God I fought many actions with the mutineers ... The above is but a short account of my doings. If I were to describe them in detail it would be immense.'[33] Despite the pensioner's heroic resistance, the mob soon pushed the servants aside, pouring into the house, plundering, smashing what they could not carry away, and setting fire to the remnants. As the fire took hold, threatening the lives of the Greatheds, one of the servants approached the leaders of the mob and offered to betray his master and mistress. He took the leaders off towards a haystack where he said the Greatheds were concealed. As soon as the mob had departed, the Greatheds came down from their hiding-place and passed through the smoke-filled house to the garden where other servants successfully concealed them throughout a night disturbed by constant alarms and threats of discovery.[34]

On leaving the Greatheds' house, Hugh Gough had ridden away to the artillery lines where the native officer, who till then had accompanied him faithfully, told him that he and the two *sowars* must now go their own way, as 'whether for life or death, they must return to the regiment'. They saluted him, turned gravely round and trotted off.[35]

His fellow-officers in the 3rd Light Cavalry, Captain Craigie and Lieutenant Mackenzie, were also, for a time, protected by their own men. Mackenzie had been quietly reading in his bungalow when his bearer rushed in to tell him that a hullabaloo had broken out in the lines. Hurriedly putting on his uniform and sword, he had jumped on his horse and had ridden off towards the noise of firing. Scarcely had he turned out of the compound gate, however, than he met the English quartermaster-sergeant of the regiment who came running towards him, shouting, 'O, God, Sir! The troopers are coming to cut us up!'

'Let us stick together then,' Mackenzie had replied. 'Two are better than one.' The sergeant, thinking otherwise, ran off across the compound, pursued by a mob of badmashes and by Mackenzie's *chowki-dar* who thrust at him with a spear, cutting open his lip. The sergeant turned, shot the man dead, leaped over the garden wall and dashed into a nearby bungalow from which he emerged a moment later with two other officers of his regiment. Both the officers and the sergeant managed to mount horses, but were prevented from escaping by a large body of mutineers until one of the officers' servants, a low-caste sweeper, led them to a gap in the compound wall through which they galloped off, leaving the sweeper to be hacked to death by the enraged sepoys.

While the sergeant made good his escape, Mackenzie had also been attacked by sepoys whom, he felt sure, would have sealed his fate had not Captain Craigie come to his assistance. Craigie, 'an excellent linguist' who had 'great influence among them', eventually persuaded about fifty *sowars* to ride with him, Mackenzie and Lieutenant Melville-Clarke to the New Gaol in an attempt to prevent the release of the imprisoned sepoys.

The roads were full of excited natives, who actually roared approbation as we rode through them [Mackenzie recalled], for they evidently did not distinguish in the dusk the British officers, and took the whole party for a band of mutineers. We three officers led, and as we neared the jail our pace increased, till from a smart trot we broke into a gallop . . . The telegraph lines were cut, and a slack wire, which I did not see as it swung across the road, caught me full on the chest and bowled me over into the dust . . . Fortunately I was not hurt, and regaining my horse I remounted . . . and in a few minutes we reached the jail, only to find that we were too late. The prisoners were already swarming out of it; their shackles being knocked off by blacksmiths, before our eyes; and the jail guard of native infantry on our riding up to it, answered our questions by firing at us . . . There was nothing to be done but ride back to the cantonments [which now] seemed one mass of flames.[36]

While Craigie galloped off to the European lines with a group of loyal *sowars* and the regimental colours, Mackenzie, with a dozen or so volunteers, tore back to Craigie's house to protect his sister and Craigie's wife who had now returned there from the church. The house was the only one in the row not yet in flames. Inside it the two ladies had collected together three double-barrelled guns, bullets, caps and a powder-flask; but they had not loaded the guns, not knowing how to do so. Before loading them himself, Mackenzie took his sister and Mrs Craigie to the door of the house and, calling to the troopers who had ridden back with him from the gaol, he 'commanded them to their charge . . . Like madmen they threw themselves off their horses and prostrated themselves before the ladies, seizing their feet, and placing them on their heads, as they vowed with tears and sobs to protect their lives with their own.'

'Greatly reassured by this burst of evidently genuine emotion', Mackenzie then loaded the guns, placing one of them by itself against the wall and giving the ladies to understand that in the last resort it was to be used on them, a knowledge that 'comforted and strengthened them'. Through the windows flashed the brilliant light of the burning houses as the hiss and crackle of flaming timbers mingled with the frequent sharp reports of fire-arms and the yells of the mob. A man in the crowd caught sight of Mackenzie as he came out on to the upper veranda; and, shouting to his companions to help him kill the *Firinghi* and burn his house, he and several others rushed forward to the boundary wall with lighted brands. They recoiled at the sight of Mackenzie's levelled gun; but, a larger crowd gathering, Mackenzie decided that they must leave the house and seek refuge in a stone-built Hindu temple in the grounds. So, rejoined by Captain Craigie they fled towards it, concealing themselves as best they could under the cover of dark blankets.

Looking apprehensively through the slits on either side of the single narrow doorway, they remained in the shrine for several hours, the men occasionally going outside to talk to the troopers whose loyalty now seemed to be wavering under the influence of a havildar-major, who, so a young sepoy whispered to Mackenzie, was urging them to kill the foreigners and join the rest of the regiment in mutiny. Eventually the havildar-major and some others rode off; but soon afterwards one of Craigie's servants, a Hindu bearer, ran up to warn his master that a crowd of badmashes were swarming in at the garden gate. He implored Mackenzie to give him a gun to fire at them. Craigie handed a gun to the man who made off with it into the darkness. A moment later there was the sound of a shot followed by yells and groans, and the bearer returned to say that he had fired at the mob, killed the leader (later identified as a Muslim butcher) and so driven the rest off. Mackenzie recorded:

It was now about midnight . . . The uproar was quietening down; and we determined on making our escape, if possible. So . . . we harnessed Craigie's horses to his carriage; placed the ladies inside . . . ; made a native boy who usually rode postillion . . . mount one of the horses; and set off, Craigie and I riding with drawn swords beside the carriage . . . A knot of the troopers, evidently wavering in their intentions, occupied the avenue before us, loudly talking and gesticulating. The postillion hesitated; but, on our threatening to run him through the body if he did not at once gallop on, he ... lashed his horses and in a moment we had charged through ... and were racing along the avenue at full speed.[37]

If the junior officers had been powerless in the face of the mutiny at Meerut, so had their superiors. As soon as Brigadier Wilson learned of the outbreak, he sent messages to the Artillery and to the Dragoon Guards to join him on the parade-ground of the 60th Rifles. But it was some time before General Hewitt arrived; and when the elderly gentleman did appear he seemed confused and uncertain what to do, while Wilson did not feel justified in giving further orders once the Divisional Commander had appeared. No warning of the outbreak could be sent to Delhi since the telegraph line from Meerut had, significantly, already been cut by four o'clock. And although the line to Agra had remained open long enough for the Postmaster's sister to send a message to her aunt telling her not to pay a proposed visit to Meerut as the sepoys had risen in revolt, when a second, official, telegram was dispatched to Agra the line was cut after the transmission of the opening sentence.[38]

Wilson's initial orders to the Artillery and the Dragoon Guards were, at least, promptly obeyed, or even anticipated. Those of the Dragoon Guards who had horses were soon dressed, armed, saddled and mounted. The Artillery quickly got out their guns. At the same time the 60th Rifles hastily threw off their white drill uniforms and paraded in their green service dress. Captain Muter of the 60th, the senior officer of the regiment present, dispatched the first available company to secure the treasury from its native – and, as he presumed, unreliable – guard, though when the riflemen arrived they found the sepoys still in position and the treasure untouched. But after these first operations had been carried out there were long delays while rolls were called and ammunition distributed; and it was not until about eight o'clock that the troops were drawn up and ready to move off. The moon was not yet up; dense smoke from the burning buildings obscured the light of the flames; it was impossible to see any concentration of mutineers. The 60th were ordered to fire in the direction of the smoke from the bungalows, and the artillery discharged a few rounds, almost at random, into a tope of trees where it was supposed some sepoys might lie concealed. But no move was made to concentrate nearer the bridge which crossed the ravine known as the Abu

Nullah and led on to the Delhi road. And it was towards Delhi – though Wilson did not know this yet – that most of the mutinous troops from Meerut were to make their way.

During the next few months Wilson and Hewitt were to be harshly attacked for not having pursued the troops to Delhi as one young officer, Captain Rosser of the Dragoon Guards, evidently sought permission to do. But Wilson claimed that he had no reason to suppose that the mutineers would leave the city in that direction. It was more likely, he thought, that they would disperse to their various homes, as many of them did, some in uniform, others not. In any case, he and Hewitt protested that they could not abandon Meerut to the badmashes. And even if the mutineers were to be pursued, how could the Europeans hope to catch them up and destroy them, wholly unprepared as they were for a long night march? In any case, the 6th Dragoon Guards were quite unsuited to such a difficult operation. The regiment, which had been sent home from the Crimea the year before, was only about half its proper strength, while half its horses were not yet fully broken. Most of its men were young recruits who had been at Meerut for less than two months and had no experience of the Indian hot weather.[39]

So the European troops remained where they were, while the mutineers – harried by a few ringleaders whom Lieutenant Möller of the 11th Native Infantry heard shouting, 'Quick, brothers, quick! Delhi! Delhi!' – moved towards the old Moghul capital, forty miles to the south.[40]

5

Rebels and Fugitives

Bahadur Shah II, King of Delhi, was then eighty-two years old. As a young man he had been renowned for his athleticism, his skill in archery and horsemanship, his sure aim in shooting birds on the wing from the back of an elephant. But his later years had been largely devoted to literary composition, to manuscript illustration and miniature painting. Although he enjoyed watching cock-fights and partridge-contests, he was fond of animals, devoted to his favourite elderly elephant, and derived infinite pleasure from the pet doves and nightingales to whose cooing and chirping he listened with delight in the gardens which he had himself laid out below the palace wall on the bank of the Jumna river. Interested in architecture and music, he also dabbled in the art of cookery and invented a kind of sweetmeat whose ingredients included strong pepper and *karela*. He never drank wine and abstained from all drugs, even opium, though he derived pleasure from his hookah and from chewing pan and had a passion for mangoes. His one eccentricity was rumoured to be 'a fixed belief that he could transform himself into a fly or a gnat and that he could in this guise convey himself to other countries and learn what was going on there'.[1]

His father, Akbar Shah, was a Sufi who had married a Rajput; and from his parents he inherited that tolerance and understanding of Hinduism which had marked the policies of his renowned ancestor, the Moghul Emperor, Akbar the Great. He refrained from eating beef; he visited Hindu temples wearing a mark on his forehead and the Brahmanic thread round his neck; he showed his approval of Hindu festivals by watching them from a high tower in the palace; he appointed several Hindus to important offices in his household. 'It is still remembered,' wrote Zakoullah, the historian, who knew him well, 'that whenever the Hindus waited on him and complained against any of the Mussulmans, he warned the latter saying, "If you, Mussulmans, are to me like one eye, truly the Hindus are dear to me like the other eye."' Nor did he condemn those who were converted to Christianity. When a member of his court became a Christian he welcomed him back, silencing those who criticized the man's action with the words, 'There is no cause for shame in what he has done.'[2]

Bahadur Shah's family could trace their ancestry to that most powerful Tartar conqueror, Tamerlane, who had invaded India in 1398. But Bahadur Shah himself had no power. A pensioner of the British, he lived in his vast palace in some comfort, surrounded by an enormous number of relations of varying degrees of consanguinity and with real or pretended rights to his protection. Some of the closer relations lived in comfort like himself; but others inhabited houses and tenements within the palace walls which were no better than hovels, some having to make do with huts of plaited straw in corners of dark and crumbling courtyards.

The King was still allowed to maintain a cultured court whose officials, with titles appropriate to a far grander past, obeyed the rules of an antiquated procedure. His British masters still treated him with great courtesy, maintaining the fiction of his sovereignty. But they denied his real status as a king by no longer offering him *nazrs*, those ceremonial gifts which had once been presented to him four times a year. They no longer troubled to ensure that his face appeared on coins. Nor were they willing to increase his allowance of Rs. 100,000 (about £10,000) a month which, large as it was, was far from enough to maintain either his palace or his dependants. Nor would they agree to recognize as his heir his beloved favourite son, Mirza Jiwan Bakht, a bright and handsome though sickly-looking youth, the beloved child of a favourite young wife, Zinat Mahal. Yet for all his present impotence and insignificance, the King's name was revered by millions of Indians, Hindus and Muslims alike, who looked up to him, a symbol of ancient legitimacy, as their natural leader in any national cause, the Sovereign of the World.[3]

At about seven o'clock on the morning of 11 May 1857 the King's physician, Hakim Ahsanullah Khan, was summoned to his master's room. 'Look!' the King said to him, 'the cavalry are coming in by the road of the *Zer Jharokha*!' The physician, a thin man with a white straggling beard, joined the King by the window and, looking out, saw about twenty *sowars* trotting towards the palace beneath a stone lattice-work balcony on which the Moghul emperors had once shown themselves to their people. The *sowars*, most of them in uniform, a few in Indian clothes, rode beneath the windows of the King's apartments and shouted up to him, 'Help, O King! We pray for assistance in our fight for the faith!' The King, surprised by their arrival, made no reply, but sent instead for Captain Douglas, commander of his bodyguard. Douglas hurried along from his apartments to speak to the *sowars* from a balcony 'outside the oratory by the marble parapet' near the King's apartments, telling them to go away, that their presence was an annoyance to his Majesty, that they were to proceed to an old palace on the banks of the Jumna outside the city wall and then their case would be considered. They turned as if to obey him; but, riding south along the river bank, they turned instead into the city through the Rajghat Gate.[4]

Some time later another much larger body of cavalry, followed by running infantry, approached the bridge of boats, passed the toll-post and the body of the toll-collector who had been murdered by the earlier party and trotted across the bridge towards the King's palace. Looking out of his office window, Sir Thomas Metcalfe's nephew Theophilus, Joint Magistrate at Delhi, saw these troops coming across the bridge and realized immediately that they were the mutineers from Meerut. He had come down to his office early that morning to hand over his work to his successor. He had not been well lately, suffering from severe inflammation of the eyes, and had obtained six months' sick leave. He was due to depart that evening for Kashmir where his only child was already staying with his sister. But immediately on arrival at his office he had been told of the uprising at Meerut; and on seeing the second party of mutineers arrive at Delhi, he jumped into his buggy to drive to the Calcutta Gate through which the road from the bridge of boats led into the city. On his way he stopped near the Magazine to arrange for guns to be trained on the bridge over which the mutineers were still crossing; but there were no cattle there to move the guns, so he drove on in his buggy to the Calcutta Gate where he found several other Europeans standing behind the Gate which had already been closed and barricaded.

The leading mutineers hammered on the gate, then trotted away along the sandy bed of the river beneath the walls of the palace to find another entrance into the city. Simon Fraser, the Commissioner, told Metcalfe to drive round to make sure that the small water gate at the far end of the palace wall had been closed; but when he was half-way there Metcalfe met a large body of mutineers galloping out of the great gate of the palace, shouting and brandishing swords. Beyond them, on the open ground in front of the palace, was a huge crowd of people all dressed in white 'as if expecting a gala day'. Driving the buggy as fast as he could past the mutineers, one of whom slashed the hood with his tulwar, Metcalfe sent it full tilt into the mob, jumped out and elbowed his way through to a group of mounted policemen. He ordered the police to charge the mutineers. They declined to stir. So Metcalfe, a powerful as well as a decisive man, knocked one of them off his horse and jumped into the saddle himself. Throwing off his coat and pulling off his trousers so as to be less easily identified, he galloped off into the heart of the city to find their superior officer. On his arrival at the *Kotwali* in his shirt and under-drawers he was told that all the officials who had been with him at the Calcutta Gate had been either murdered or severely wounded and that the whole city was in revolt. Borrowing a native dress and a sword, he decided to make for the Kashmir Gate and to try to reach the cantonments; but on his way, a rock hurled at him from a window struck the upper part of his spine and brought him crashing un-conscious to the ground.[5]

The report that Metcalfe had received of the attacks on the other officials was true. Captain Douglas and Simon Fraser were both dead. So was John Ross Hutchinson, the Collector, who had been hacked to death near the palace. So were the compositors in the offices of the *Delhi Gazette*. So were a missionary's daughter and another girl, a friend of hers, who tried to hide in a cupboard. So were a woman and her two daughters who were shot by a sepoy. The mother was killed first and one of the girls cried out, 'Oh! They have shot Mama!' before running away with her sister towards some bushes where they too were killed.[6] The manager of the Delhi and London Bank, who had climbed on to the roof of his house, was cut to death there with his children and his brave wife who was said to have killed two of their assailants with a hog-spear before being killed herself. Fifty other Europeans and Eurasians, nearly all of them women or children, were taken prisoner.

We were all confined in one room, very dark [recorded one of them, a Eurasian woman, Mrs Aldwell, who had succeeded in persuading her captives that she and her family were Muslims], and in consequence of the sepoys, and every one who took a fancy to do so, coming and fright-ening the children, we were obliged frequently to close the one door that we had, which then left us without light or air . . . Some of the King's special servants attended by a small number of infantry sepoys, came and called out that the Christians were to come out of the building and that the five Mahomedans were to remain . . . The women and children began crying . . . but they went out . . . and a rope was thrown round to encircle the whole group . . . and in this manner they were taken out . . . and . . . brought under the Pipul tree in the courtyard and there murdered with swords by the King's private servants. None of the sepoys took part in killing them. The privilege, for so it was considered, of murdering them was particularly reserved for the King's own servants, as it was believed by them, that the killing of an infidel would ensure them a place in paradise.[7]

In another quarter of the city, in the Kashmir bazaar, an English merchant, James Morley, returned to the house which he shared with his friend William Clark to find the garden full of smashed furniture, broken plates and books and bundles of burning clothes. Of his wife and three children there was no sign. Nor could he find Mr and Mrs Clark or their little boy. But when he went round to the side where the servants' huts were he heard the sound of someone crying near the cowshed. Here he found his old dhobi who told him what had happened.

Oh, Sahib, when you had gone away the Memsahibs and the children all sat together very frightened, for we could hear a great noise and the firing of guns. And Clark Sahib got out his fowling piece and loaded it . . . Soon a large crowd with sticks, swords and spears came into the compound. Clark Sahib stood on the steps and said, 'What do you want?' They only abused him and said they would kill every Feringhee . . . The people all rushed in . . . The servants all ran way. Only I remained behind. Mr Clark said, 'Take everything but do not kill us.' They then abused him and looked at Mrs Clark, and said, 'Is this your wife?' And laughed at him. They began to break and loot everything. My Memsahib had taken three babes into the *ghosulkhana* and shut the door. Mr Clark had stood with his gun behind him. But they saw it and said, 'Give it to us.' Then one man went to Mrs Clark and spoke bad words to her. Clark Sahib called out in a terrible voice, '*You soour!*' and shot him dead. He then wounded another man with the other barrel and commenced fighting with his gun like a *lattee*. I knew that now they would murder everyone. I ran to get my Memsahib out of the *ghosulkhana*, but there were people all round the house. They hit me and told me to go away or they would murder me, too. I went into the garden and sat behind a hedge. I heard a great crying, and they threw things out of the house and broke the panes of glass in the doors. They then said, 'Let us go and loot.' And they all went away.[8]

Inside the house all the furniture had been destroyed, hacked to pieces; and the contents of food cupboards, jams and jellies and biscuits were lying in heaps. 'There was an overpowering smell from the brandy and wine that had run out from the broken bottles.' Morley lingered in the outer room, looking round it, shrinking from going farther. At length he stepped into the next room. The Clarks' son was 'pinned to the wall with his head hanging down'. The bodies of his parents lay side by side on the floor. The old dhobi went into one of the bedrooms and stood wringing his hands and crying by the door that led into the *ghosulkhana*. Morley could not bring himself to follow him. He sat down on the floor with his head on his knees.[9]

Two miles north of the city, beyond the high ground known as the Ridge, was the military camp. Here the day had begun with an early morning parade of the entire Delhi garrison under the personal command of Brigadier Graves. The three native infantry regiments, the 38th, 54th and 74th, and the battery of native artillery listened as the general order about the execution of Mangal Pande at Barrackpore was read out to them. Captain Robert Tytler of the 38th was 'struck forcibly by something extraordinary' that occurred during the parade: as sentence on Pande was made known there was 'a murmur of disapprobation throughout the whole regiment', the men hissing and shuffling their feet. It lasted for only a few seconds, but Tytler was shocked by it, 'never having witnessed anything like it before'. Still disturbed by the incident, he went home for breakfast. His wife, Harriet, had the meal with him, their two small children having had theirs already with the Breton maid. There were musk melons on the table. Outside on the veranda the household tailor sat stitching quietly. It seemed to be a morning like any other.[10]

Breakfast in the regimental messes was served as usual, the officers talking together until nearly eight o'clock when they went back to their bungalows. Lieutenant Edward Vibart of the 54th had returned to his when the orderly havildar of his company came running up to report that the regiment had received orders to march down instantly to the city as some troopers of the 3rd Light Cavalry from Meerut were 'creating disturbances'. Putting on his uniform as quickly as possible, Vibart ordered his pony to be saddled, then galloped off to the parade-ground where he found the regiment falling in and his commanding officer, Colonel Ripley, 'who appeared much excited', giving orders to the various companies. Vibart's company and the Grenadiers were told to proceed under command of Major Paterson to the artillery lines to escort two guns to the city, while the remaining companies, with Colonel Ripley at their head, marched off with the band towards the Kashmir Gate.

At the same time Captain Tytler and Captain Gardner of the 38th were told to take their companies to a house near a new powder magazine on a ridge overlooking the river to make sure that no more mutineers crossed over from Meerut. Having grabbed more cart- ridges from the storemen than they were meant to receive, the men marched off in a 'very excited manner, shouting vehemently every now and then' despite their officers' protestations. On reaching their objective the men who were not posted as sentries to watch the river piled their arms and went into the house where they produced water- melons and sweetmeats which they insisted on sharing with the two English captains. Captain Tytler recorded:

Captain Gardner remarked to me how lucky it was that our men seemed so well disposed, as we were convinced that there was something serious going on in the city [where] every now and then fires could be seen breaking out ... We now remarked that our men were forming small groups in the heat of the sun. I ordered them to come in and not expose themselves thus. They said, 'We like being in the sun.' [In one of the rooms] a native, from his appearance a soldier, was haranguing the men and saying that every power or government existed its allotted time, and that it was nothing extraordinary that that of the English had come to an end, according to what had been predicted in their native books. Before I could make a prisoner of him ... the men of the two companies with a tremendous shout took up their arms and ran off to the city exclaiming, '*Prethiviraj ke jai*! Victory to the Sovereign of the World!'[11]

The men of the 54th with Colonel Ripley at their head had already reached the Kashmir Gate. Inside the Gate was a fortified enclosure known as the Main Guard which was always garrisoned by a detach- ment of fifty sepoys under a European officer, the detachment this week consisting of men of the 38th Native Infantry under Lieutenant Procter. As Colonel Ripley's regiment marched to the sound of music through the Kashmir Gate, the officers were fired on by the *sowars* of the 3rd Light Cavalry from Meerut and four of them fell dead. The survivors ordered their men to return the fire, but the sepoys merely fired their weapons into the air, then joined the *sowars* in attacking their colonel and the other European officers with their bayonets.

Two officers managed to escape down a side street. Here they were attacked by the populace hurling bricks at them but finally managed to evade their pursuers through a gap in the city walls. Two others barricaded themselves with the sergeant-major in a house, the door of which was soon battered down; the sergeant-major was killed, and though one of the officers managed to get away, he lost sight of the other in the crowd. Lieutenant Procter of the 38th also ordered his men to fire on the mutineers, but they refused to do so, jeering at Procter in his helplessness; the time had now come, they said, for revenge on the *Firinghis* who had tried to undermine their religion.[12]

Leaving Procter to argue with his men, Captain William Wallace of the 74th, the Field Officer of the Week, galloped out of the Kashmir Gate to demand more reinforcements from the cantonments. Passing Paterson and Vibart on the way, he implored them 'for God's sake' to make haste with the guns as their fellow-officers of the 54th were being murdered in the Main Guard.

At this moment the body of our unfortunate Colonel was carried out, literally hacked to pieces [Vibart recalled]. Such a fearful sight I never beheld. The poor man was still alive, and, though scarcely able to articulate, I distinctly gathered from the few words he gasped out, that we had no chance against the cavalry troopers, as our own men had turned against us . . . I now entered the Main Guard, and found everything in confusion. On looking out into the open space in front of the church, a few cavalry troopers in their French-grey uniforms were seen galloping back in the direction of the King's palace . . . But as for the men of my own regiment . . . they had all vanished . . . The lifeless body of Captain Burrowes was lying close by the gate of the churchyard . . . Other bodies were observed scattered about the place . . . Since then I have witnessed many painful sights, but I shall never forget my feelings that day as I saw our poor fellows being brought in, their faces distorted with all the agonies of a violent death, and hacked about in every conceivable way . . . But we had no time to indulge in sad reflections, for reports now reached us that, besides the 3rd Cavalry troopers, the 11th and 20th had also arrived from Meerut, and were on their way to attack us . . . A consultation was held to decide what was best to be done. At length it was determined to hold the Main Guard, and for this purpose the two guns were placed in position at the gate which commanded the approach from the palace and swept the open ground in front.[13]

So far, the two companies which had arrived with the guns appeared to be reliable; while Lieutenant Procter's men, though unwilling to obey his orders, as yet showed no inclination to join the mutineers inside the city. But Vibart thought that they remained where they were only because they believed the European troops would arrive any moment from Meerut. They kept asking when these troops were likely to be in Delhi; and the European officers replied with an assumed confidence which became less convincing as the morning wore on.

By the early afternoon, however, they were feeling more hopeful. At about one o'clock they were joined by nearly one hundred and fifty men of the 74th Native Infantry under Major Abbot and two more guns under Lieutenant Aislabie. Then there arrived some two hundred men of the 54th who came into the Guard with their regimental colours, explaining that they had been seized with panic when the cavalry troopers from Meerut had fired on their officers, and had separated in all directions but had now managed to reform. It soon appeared, though, that neither these men nor any of the others would remain loyal any longer than it suited them to do so. They obeyed orders reluctantly or not at all; and when an officer asked one of them why the troops at Meerut had mutinied, he replied insubordinately, 'Why not? The Commander-in-Chief is up at Simla, eating his dinners and pays no heed to our complaints.' Concerned that they might be set upon at any moment if European troops did not come to their assistance, Vibart and his friends were even more perturbed when various English families, who had escaped massacre in the city, came into the Main Guard for protection.

They could offer them little comfort. Indeed they could give help to no one. When the nearby church of St James's was plundered by a wild and screaming mob that bore away all its contents down to the chairs, stools and hassocks and rang the bells in mockery before cutting them loose so that they fell through the tower to the floor, they were obliged to stand by, not a single sepoy being willing to obey their orders. Pleas for help from Mr Galloway who, with a borrowed sword in his hand, was attempting to defend the Government Treasury, had to be ignored. He was killed. Nor were the officers at the Main Guard able to offer any help to Lieutenant Willoughby, the Commissary of Ordnance, who was responsible for the protection of the Magazine.[14]

George Willoughby, a shy, reserved, rather fat young officer, had been at the Magazine since early morning and, from a small bastion on the river face, had seen the mutineers from Meerut marching across the bridge of boats. His native guard refused to obey his orders; but helped by his assistants, Lieutenants Forrest and Raynor, two sergeants and four civilian clerks, he barricaded the outer gates of the Magazine and placed guns inside them loaded with double charges of grape. He then laid a train of powder from the store to a tree which stood in the yard of the Magazine, so that, if the defence failed, a good deal of the immense store of ammunition which was in the Magazine could be blown up. Scully, one of the civilian clerks, volunteered to stand by this tree and to fire the train when Willoughby gave the signal.

Hardly had the above arrangements been completed when the guards from the palace came and demanded possession of the Magazine in the name of the King of Delhi [Lieutenant Forrest reported]. To this no reply was made, and immediately after the Subadar of the native infantry guard on duty came and informed Willoughby and myself that the King had sent down word to the mutineers that he would without delay send them down scaling ladders from the palace for the purpose of scaling the wall; and shortly afterwards they arrived. On these being erected against the walls, the whole of our native establishment deserted us by climbing up the sloped sheds on the inside, and descending the ladders on the outside. We opened a fire of grape on them and kept it up as long as a single round remained. Every shot went crashing through them and told well.

After firing the last round, Buckley, another of the civilian clerks, was shot through the right arm; and Lieutenant Forrest was hit by two musket balls in his left hand.

It was at this critical moment that Lieutenant Willoughby gave the signal for firing the Magazine . . . In an instant, and with an explosion that shook the city and was heard distinctly at Meerut, the Magazine blew up. The wall was thrown flat upon the ground, and it is said that some hundreds of the enemy were buried under the ruins or blown into the air.[15]

Scully, the clerk who had fired the train, was also killed in the explosion. But the others, by some extraordinary chance, all survived; and covered in dust and powder, found their way to the Main Guard. They were not, however, to find shelter there for long. Soon after their arrival an order came from the Brigadier withdrawing Major Abbot's men and Lieutenant Aislabie's two guns. And as Abbot's men, followed by the guns, approached the gateway, some sepoys of the 38th rushed at the gate and closed it. They then discharged a volley into the midst of a group of officers; and, as though this were the signal for general mutiny, the other sepoys inside the enclosure began to open fire on officers and civilian families alike.[16] Edward Vibart recalled:

Scarcely knowing what I was doing, I made for the ramp which leads from the courtyard to the bastion above . . . Everyone appeared to be doing the same. Twice I was knocked over as we all frantically rushed up the slope, the bullets whistling past us like hail, and flattening themselves against the parapet with a frightful hiss.

Several officers were shot in the back before they reached the bastion. Others, having clambered to the top, immediately jumped out through the embrasures below, then began to scramble up the counterscarp. The rest, responding to the despairing cries of women who had taken shelter in the officers' quarters above the gateway, turned back to find 'some ladies in a state bordering on distraction and the [three daughters of Mrs Forrest] weeping over their mother who had been shot through the shoulder'.

'To take the ladies into the ditch and scale the counterscarp seemed an impossibility'; but the roar of a gun in the courtyard below, followed by the whistle of a round shot passing over their heads, forced them to make the attempt. Some of the officers, tying their belts together to serve as ropes, jumped into the ditch first to break the fall of the ladies who were to follow them. Most of the ladies jumped without hesitation; but one, Mrs Forster, fat and elderly, began to scream, refusing to move. A second shot from the gun cracked into the parapet, showering splinters over the officers who stopped pleading with Mrs Forster to jump and gave her a push, sending her tumbling headlong into the ditch.[17]

From the bottom of the ditch the counterscarp rose steeply, almost perpendicularly. Even if it were possible for the ladies to clamber up it, their ascent would be so slow that they must surely be shot in the back before reaching the summit. Already sepoys with their muskets could be seen peering over the rampart. The fugitives took shelter by pressing hard against the inner wall of the ditch so that it was impossible for the sepoys above to depress their muskets sufficiently to shoot them. After a while the sepoys disappeared, running away to join their comrades in plundering the Treasury.

The attempt on the counterscarp now began. Time and again the women almost reached the top when the earth, crumbling away beneath their feet, sent them rolling back into the ditch. 'Despair, however, gave us superhuman energy,' Vibart said, 'till at length we all succeeded in gaining the summit. We now quickly ran down the short glacis, and plunged into some thick shrubbery that grew at the bottom. Here we stopped to take breath; but the sound of voices proceeding from the high road, which ran close by, induced us to hurry off again as fast as possible.'

Mrs Forster could not keep up with the others. Stunned by her heavy fall and by a bullet wound in her forehead, she lagged behind and seemed about to collapse when two of the strongest of the officers attempted to carry her. But the enormous weight of her now half-conscious body, and the thorny bushes in the thick undergrowth, were too much for them. They felt obliged to abandon her and hurried on to catch up with the others who were now making for Metcalfe House. Stumbling over the rough ground and through thorny shrubs which tore the women's dresses to shreds, sweat streaming down their faces, not daring to look behind them, they eventually reached the long drive to the house. A crowd of people stood in the grounds in the rapidly gathering darkness; but they were not molested; and on approaching the house they were welcomed by some of Sir Theophilus's servants. The *Khidmatgar* took them inside, conducted them down a narrow flight of steps into a dark cellar where he left them, promising to bring them food and drink. Some of them were so exhausted that, despite their danger, they lay down on the hard, damp floor and fell fast asleep.[18]

A few other Europeans had already made remarkable escapes from the city. The four children of Captain William Wallace were spirited away by a faithful *khansaman* and found their way to Meerut. The merchant, James Morley, whose family had been killed in his house in the Kashmir bazaar, put on a petticoat and veil belonging to the wife of his old dhobi and, following the dhobi as he drove a bullock laden with old clothes through one of the city gates, managed to reach the Kurnaul road.

People were to be seen going along it laden with plunder [Morley wrote]. One gang surrounded us and said that the old man was very cunning and was taking away some rich goods. He, however, said at once, 'Search my bundle,' which they did, and, finding nothing, let us go. I then told the old man whenever a gang came near us to call out to tell them to go and loot the Feringhees, and to make jokes about what had occurred. This he used to do and it averted all suspicion from us . . . On the third day . . . I got tired of my disguise and was indeed ashamed of it, so, as I thought no one would harm us so far from Delhi, I put on a suit of the dhobee's clothes. We were often insulted, hooted and abused by the villagers, but they did not offer me any violence. I saw the body of a European woman lying shockingly mutilated by the roadside, and it made me sick to see a vulture come flying along with a shrill cry. I saw another body of one of our countrymen. It was that of a lad about sixteen. I buried him, but it was a shallow grave, poor fellow . . . On the sixth day after leaving Delhi I arrived at Kurnaul.[20]

Sir Theophilus Metcalfe, recovering consciousness from the blow that had knocked him from his horse, made his way to a well-disposed *thannadar* who conducted him in native clothes to the house of a zemindar outside the city. The zemindar, who had never spoken to an Englishman before, agreed to hide him on the roof of his zenana where Metcalfe remained for three days until it was considered safer for him to be moved to a cave in a *kunker* pit. While hiding here, armed with a pistol and a tulwar which the zemindar had given him, Metcalfe heard three men whispering together outside. 'Here is where he is hiding,' said one of them, and Metcalfe recognized the voice of his office orderly. Dashing out into the sunlight which dazzled him after the darkness of the cave, Metcalfe killed the nearest man; and, the other two running off, he made his escape to the palace of the Nawab of Jugaur. The Nawab, who refused to see him, agreed to shelter him for a time, but then sent him on his way with an escort of soldiers, protesting that he would be attacked by the King of Delhi if he harboured him any longer. Distrusting the Nawab's soldiers, Metcalfe stole away from them, rode into a nearby village and jumping off the old pony with which he had been provided, lay down in the middle of a group of sleeping villagers, covering his face. When the Nawab's soldiers approached and roused one of the recumbent figures asking which way the Englishman had gone, the man sat up angrily, said there was no Englishman about, and returned to his interrupted slumber. The soldiers rode off, and Metcalfe made good his escape to Kurnaul.[21]

Other fugitives from Delhi had also by now reached Kurnaul. Amongst these were George Wagentreiber and his family. Wagentreiber, whose house was outside the city walls, had left for his office at the *Delhi Gazette* as usual that morning. But, unable to pass through the Kashmir Gate, which had by then been shut by the officers at the Main Guard, he returned home 'in a towering passion' to find that most of his servants had fled and that his wife, in attempting to prevent their departure, had also 'worked herself up into a frenzy'. Mrs Wagentreiber was the youngest daughter of one of the fourteen wives of Colonel James Skinner, the distinguished half-caste leader of irregular cavalry.[22] A dark-skinned lady who had spent her early years in purdah, Elizabeth Wagentreiber not only looked like an Indian but well understood the ways of her mother's people. Had she not done so, neither she nor her husband and baby daughter would have survived the ordeals which they were now to undergo.

When her husband returned from the Kashmir Gate, he sent a note across to a neighbour, Dr Balfour, suggesting that he come across to the Wagentreibers' house which had a tiled roof and would be a safer refuge than the Doctor's thatched bungalow. But Balfour replied that there was no cause for alarm and that it would not be advisable to display any signs of anxiety. Since fires could now be clearly seen in the city from which the sounds of gunfire and explosions regularly reached them, Wagentreiber considered Dr Balfour's complacency unjustified. So, waiting only to collect a few provisions and fire-arms, he drove out with his wife and daughter and a fourteen-year-old stepdaughter towards the cantonments pursued by a crowd of beggar boys who pelted the carriage with stones, shouting at its occupants to stop and salaam them. Passing a group of sepoys, Wagentreiber called out to ask where the Brigadier and officers were, only to receive in reply the insolent suggestion, 'Go and find them!' Unable to find them anywhere in the lines, Wagentreiber drove back to his house at the gate of which he met another neighbour, Mr Murphy, the Deputy Collector of Customs, who told him that most of the Europeans who lived in the area had collected at his house where they proposed to make a stand. So the Wagentreibers went to the Murphys' house. But the sight of a large body of sepoys swarming out of the Lahore Gate induced them to change their minds about making a stand, and they retreated hurriedly to the Flagstaff Tower where the Brigadier was now said to be.[23]

Also making for the tower were the two half-caste signallers from the wooden cabin farther down the road. These signallers, William Brendish and J. W. Pilkington, had crossed the river the day before to try to discover what had gone wrong with the electric telegraph wires to Meerut. They had been unable to find any fault; so early that morning their superior, Charles Todd, had set out to discover the fault for himself. He had not returned; but Brendish soon had little doubt what had happened to him as crowds of shopkeepers swarmed past the cabin door and a wounded British officer shouted, 'For God's sake, get inside and close your doors!' Brendish immediately obeyed and, as the lines to the north were still open, tapped out a message, on his own authority: 'We must leave office. All the bungalows are being burnt down by the sepoys from Meerut. They came in this morning . . . Mr Todd is dead I think. He went out this morning and has not returned . . . We are off.'[24] Brendish and Pilkington, taking Mrs Todd and her baby with them, then hurried away to the Flagstaff Tower.

At the tower all was confusion. The ladies and children, accompanied by various native servants, were huddled together inside the building in a cramped space less than eighteen feet in diameter, some of them with wet handkerchiefs tied round their heads as a protection against the stifling heat, one or two lying unconscious by the open door. Outside, the men stood with loaded guns, watching apprehensively as the Brigadier addressed the few sepoys who had not yet joined the mutineers, reminding them of their past service, enjoining them to be true to their oath and salt. As they listened some of the men spat 'in a disgusting and disrespectful manner', and one called out, 'Don't listen to the *boorao*!'[25]

While the Brigadier was speaking, a swirling cloud of dust could be seen on the road leading up to the tower from the city; and soon, through it, could be discerned the shapes of men crowding up the hill with sticks and knives. As they approached, one of the Europeans moved purposefully towards the two remaining guns of the Delhi brigade which had been placed in position to defend the tower. The crowd hesitated and drew back. At that moment a puff of white smoke, followed by a huge coronet of red dust, rose above the city walls; a few seconds elapsed, then came the deadened *thud* of the earth-shaking explosion of the Magazine, an ominous sound which was greeted by the sepoys with shouts of '*Deen! Deen! Deen!*'[26]

The sepoys were still outside the Flagstaff Tower, however, though 'standing in groups in a most sulky mood', when Captain Tytler came up with eighty or so men of the 38th whom he and Captain Gardner had managed to dissuade from running off with their comrades into the city. Looking about him Tytler was relieved beyond measure to see that his family were there with Mrs Gardner, and decided that 'an immediate retreat was absolutely necessary, particularly after hearing that the cavalry mutineers had left the city and were approaching cantonments'. He noted the 'smiles and scornful looks of defiance and exultation' on the faces of the sepoys standing beside the tower, contrasting them with the 'resigned Christian fortitude' of the Europeans. But although the Europeans were evidently prepared to defend the position to the last, and some of the women were helping to pass muskets and ammunition up the staircase to the top of the tower, Tytler felt sure that if a stand were to be made there the same fate would befall them as had already befallen the officers of the 54th, whose mangled bodies, sent out of the Main Guard for the sake of the ladies there, were now lying in a cart near the two guns, 'covered by pretty ladies' dresses'.[27] His mind made up, Tytler went to the Brigadier to suggest an immediate retreat, pointing out that the sepoys of the 38th he had brought with him were the best of the regiment and could be trusted to help them. The Brigadier told him to go back to his men and to make quite sure of their feelings.

I begged of our sepoys not to deceive us but to tell me would they cover our retreat [Tytler wrote]. They solemnly declared they would . . . Most of the men came up to me and put their hands respectfully on my head, whilst with the most solemn oaths they swore they would protect us . . . They begged that I should take personal command of them, and that the two guns now with us should be kept [with them] . . . I hurried back and reported the result to the Brigadier, begging of him as it was nearly evening that we had not one moment to lose.[28]

But several of the Brigadier's other advisers did not agree with Tytler, protesting that the sepoys, only too anxious to get the Europeans away from the safety of the fort, would surely fall on them at once if they abandoned it. While the arguments continued, Dr Batson of the 74th, who had the ability, unusual among British officers, to speak Hindustani as fluently as English, volunteered to carry a letter to Meerut to obtain the assistance of European troops. The Brigadier granted permission. Batson then took leave of his wife and three daughters, and returned to his house where he coloured his face, hands and feet, assumed the garb of a fakir and set out for the river. But unable to disguise the blueness of his eyes, he was soon recognized for what he was, attacked and stripped naked. He escaped with his life only because, whenever approached by unfriendly-looking Muslims, he fell to the ground and 'commenced uttering the most profound praises in behalf of the Prophet Mahomed'. He did not, however, have to make similar abasements before Hindus, all of whom he encountered 'expressed the most merciful feelings towards the Ferunghees'.[29]

While waiting for the return of Dr Batson – who was to spend twenty-five days wandering about in villages and topes – Brigadier Graves, 'overwhelmed as he was with anxiety, fatigue and the responsibility of his painful position', could not make up his mind what to do. Three times he sent Tytler back to his men to get the assurance they had already given; and it was not until Tytler came back to report for the fourth time that the men could be trusted that the Brigadier said wearily, 'Well, what is to be done?'

'Put all the ladies and children in every available cart,' Tytler replied. 'The guns to follow with the infantry close behind them. The latter I will take command of.'

The Brigadier accepted the advice. But the column of retreating Europeans had no sooner reached the bottom of the Ridge than two sepoys of the 38th, who had been on duty at the Magazine and were now 'scorched in a frightful manner', came up and joined their comrades. The English, they said, had deliberately blown up the Magazine in order to destroy the whole of the 38th guard. They were the only two who had escaped. Tytler denied the story. No Englishman, he protested, would ever destroy his own guard on purpose; but the two men replied, 'No, we saw it ourselves. It is true. We were all blown up.' And from the mutters that Tytler heard in the ranks about tasting the blood of Englishmen in revenge, he knew that the story was believed.

Some of the men began to move off there and then. Others made the excuse that their vows to protect the Europeans were no longer binding since the two guns which they had asked to be kept with them had gone on ahead and were now out of sight. Tytler promised to fetch the guns back; and, borrowing the Brigade Major's horse, he galloped after them. But the men with the guns refused to obey his orders, and before he could return to his men the retreat had become a general flight. In the turmoil Tytler found his wife and children in a carriage with the Breton maid and Mrs Gardner. He thought he could never forget the look of entreaty on his wife's face as she pleaded with him to get into the carriage to protect them. But he felt it his duty to get back to his men; and when Mrs Gardner asked him 'in agony' what had become of her husband, he hesitated no longer. He told them to hurry on towards Kurnaul and was proud that Harriet, acquiescing in his decision, 'did not even murmur'.

Galloping back past a turmoil of carriages, horses and running, shouting men, Tytler passed an officer being sick in the back of a tumbril and a major of the 74th who told him 'in a friendly voice' to show less zeal and look after his family. On reaching the bridge which crossed the canal near the cantonments, he caught sight of Gardner alternately 'running and walking, quite faint and exhausted'. At the same time crowds of natives were pouring into the cantonments 'like fiends', while a number of *sowars*, leaving their companions to plunder the houses on the road, were hurrying to overtake the slower-moving stragglers at the rear of the retreating mass of Europeans. Calling out to Gardner that there was no disgrace now in attempting to save their families, Tytler told him to jump up behind him on the horse.

Together they galloped off, pursued by several Goojurs wielding heavy sticks. Having fought the Goojurs off, they finally caught up with the carriage carrying their wives and the children; and as Gardner jumped on to the back of the carriage, Tytler got on to the coach-box, telling the syce who had been driving to ride the horse. But the delay enabled the Goojurs to catch up with them. They knocked the syce off the horse which they led away. Tytler managed to pull the syce up into the already overladen carriage which rattled off again towards Kurnaul until, the weight proving too much, one of the front wheels broke and fell off. After walking for a little way with the children in their arms, they managed to find places in another carriage, 'an old rickety, veritable apology for a carriage' which 'threatened to fall to pieces' and indeed soon did: its axle tree bent, the screw-nuts worked loose, one of the back wheels rolled off, and no sooner had it been replaced than the two front springs collapsed. Commandeering an empty magazine cart on its way from Kurnaul to Delhi, Tytler and Gardner pushed the drivers off, turned the bullocks about, and in this slow conveyance they passed through Panipat. Just beyond Panipat they were fortunate in finding a more serviceable carriage which conveyed them safely to Kurnaul. On the way they passed a party of sepoys from their regiment who were returning from rifle practice at Ambala. The sepoys did not molest them but, as they marched past, 'screeched out like demons'.[30]

The Wagentreibers were also by now on their way to Kurnaul. They had not waited for the Brigadier to order a general withdrawal from the Flagstaff Tower. As soon as the cart carrying the bodies of the officers killed at the Main Guard was driven up to the tower, Elizabeth Wagentreiber told her husband it was time to be off. Five miles out of Delhi on the Kurnaul road, concealed in a grove of tall, thick mango trees, was the house of the Nawab Zea-ood-deen Khan, a rich and influential landowner for whom George Wagentreiber had performed some service in the past. Here they stopped to ask for shelter. The Nawab was away; but his servants admitted them, promising to do what they could to help. The coachman was sent back towards Delhi with Wagentreiber's signet ring as a token of his good faith, to try to fetch money and food; and, while waiting for his return, Wagentreiber took his daughter and stepdaughter on to the roof of the house, leaving his dark-skinned wife in the large, untidy garden to deal with any sepoys who might come looking for them. Near the well in the garden was the *chowkidar*'s hut; and by this Elizabeth Wagentreiber sat down to wait, pulling the back of her skirt over her head so that it looked like a *chudder*, telling the frightened *chowkidar* to light a fire and to bring out his cooking pots. The *chowkidar* kept muttering in agitated protest that for sheltering the *Firinghis* all the servants could be killed. But she silenced him by telling him that he would be well rewarded if all went well, and that if the sepoys came he was merely to say that there were no *Firinghis* in the house which they could search if they wished. 'The Sahib has loaded guns,' she added, 'and is watching from the roof. If you betray us he will shoot you first. I have only to raise my hand as a signal for him to fire and I will do so without hesitation if you do not obey me, so beware.'

Twice a group of sepoys came into the compound to ask the *chowkidar* if he had seen any of the *Firinghis* from Delhi. The *chowkidar* said he had seen some during the afternoon, but that they had all gone now. And, seeing him busily cooking and all the windows and doors of the house open, the sepoys turned away satisfied. But then the Nawab's gardener appeared. He had been to Delhi, he said, to get orders from his master. These orders were that no Europeans were to be sheltered in his house. So, fearing that it would be dangerous to stay longer, the Wagentreibers left, Elizabeth driving the carriage, George sitting on the box, his stepdaughter holding the baby and ready to hand up the loaded pistols should they be needed. The carriage rattled out of the gates in the bright moonlight and was soon 'tearing madly up the road to Kurnaul'.

It was to be a fearful journey. Chased for a time by a crowd of men with clubs and sticks, the Wagentreibers were then attacked by a gang of dacoits wielding spears and lathies and uttering 'weird and wild' screams like jackals. Wagentreiber shot two of these dacoits as the terrified horses dragged the carriage careering down the road and his wife struggled to prevent it from toppling over into the ditch. Farther down the road they were attacked by another gang of dacoits who rushed upon them with clubs and swords. One of them managed to jump on to the carriage and to cut Wagentreiber about the head before being shot dead; another brought his club down with tremendous force on Elizabeth's arm, but she held on to the reins, uttering not a sound. They then came up with the party of sepoys of the

38th Native Infantry which the Tytlers had already met. The sepoys called on them to stop. But not trusting them they rattled past until they saw ahead of them a band of Goojurs drawn up across the road; and, doubtful that they could force their way through, they decided to turn back and to throw themselves upon the mercy of the sepoys.

The havildar in command of the sepoys seemed friendly. He asked them what they were doing, pretending to be in ignorance of what had happened at Delhi and eventually promising to protect them from the Goojurs who had now caught up with them. The Goojurs seemed willing to leave the Wagentreibers alone; but at that moment the dacoits also appeared and their leader, taking the havildar aside, whispered something which 'turned the tide completely'. The sepoys were immediately called off by the havildar and told not to interfere.

Mrs Wagentreiber pleaded with them, begging them to remember that, as the daughter of the celebrated Colonel James Skinner whose memory was revered in native regiments – she was entitled to the protection of all true soldiers, or at least to an honourable death at their hands and not at those of 'such cowardly ruffians' as the dacoits, in whose direction she pointed disdainfully with her whip. At the mention of Skinner's name, the havildar's attitude changed again. He said that it was his regiment who had had the privilege of escorting the great man's remains to Delhi: he could not offer his daughter the protection of his men as an escort, but he would see that she got away safely from the dacoits.

So once more the carriage drove off, and the Wagentreibers were able to make their way to a *chowki* where a wizened old Brahmin promised them shelter and rest. As he led them through the village, two young men came up to ask him where he was taking them. The old man laughed and, pointing ahead, said that he was going to give them comfortable charpoys to lie on and that he hoped their sleep would be 'sound and long'. Understanding the words and their implication, Mrs Wagentreiber quickly turned the family back.

Returning to the *chowki* they found another old man who salaamed reverentially, taking off his turban and laying it at Mrs Wagentreiber's feet as a tribute due to one of the daughters of the great 'Sekunder Sahib'. He was, he said, the headman of one of 'Sekunder's' villages: he would go with them on their way; no one would harm them while he was with them; but the people were very angry with her husband for having shot and killed one of their pursuers, so the Sahib must get inside the carriage with the girl and the baby while he himself would ride next to the Memsahib on the box. Soon after setting off they caught up with Brigadier Graves and a party of other Europeans who had escaped from Delhi, and with them they reached Kurnaul.[31]

Several other fugitives from the cantonments managed to effect their escape through the kindness of natives. Mrs Wood, the wife of a doctor in the 38th Native Infantry, and her friend, Mrs Peile, whose husband was a lieutenant in the same regiment, met with many acts of selfless generosity. Dr Wood had been so severely wounded at the Main Guard, where his jaw had been shot away, that he could not speak and could scarcely move; but, with the help of various villagers, his wife and her friend managed to bring him to safety in Kurnaul. Their flight was beset with danger and difficulties. They were robbed of their horses, and subsequently of all their other possessions, by a band of marauders one of whom, Mrs Wood was horrified to notice, was holding his club in a hand encased in a smart white kid glove. During their six days' wandering they were often insulted and threatened in villages whose inhabitants refused them food and shelter. Yet in others they were hidden and cared for by kindly people who did all they could to help them. At one place a zemindar took them in, provided them with bread and milk, and with charpoys to rest on; at another, men offered to carry Dr Wood through the night to Gossowlte where they were 'very kindly used, one man taking pity' on them and cooking them 'most delicious curry'.[32]

Mrs Peile's husband, who caught up with them before they reached Kurnaul, also received much kindly help, as well as cruel interference, on his way from Delhi. For several weeks before the outbreak, Lieutenant Peile had been ill in bed; and, being a man always strictly observant of the rules and conventions of the service, had remained in his bungalow until two o'clock on the afternoon of 11 May, fearing that he 'might incur censure' by leaving his house while on the sick list. It eventually occurred to him that 'in such emergencies the services of every European officer would be acceptable', so he wrote to the Brigade Major with a request that the Brigadier might be informed of his desire to do his duty. He then went outside to see what he could do while waiting for an answer. Hearing that Colonel Ripley of the 54th, who had been so savagely wounded in the Main Guard, had been brought back to the cantonments, he went to him, bathed his wounds and, in accordance with instructions received from the

Flagstaff Tower, had him carried there on a charpoy by the hospital bearers.

After the order to retreat from the tower had been given, in the hope that some at least of his men might even now be 'brought back to a proper sense of their duty', Peile returned to the cantonments where, as he recounted, he found several officers assembled

with no fixed attention as to their future movements ... By degrees nearly all these left, leaving Lieutenant-Colonel Knyvett, Ensign Gambier and myself alone. Thinking it useless to remain longer, as our lives were evidently in danger, but still wishing if possible to save our colours, I consulted with Ensign Gambier, who consented to accompany me on horseback taking them with us. I obtained the consent of Colonel Knyvett to their removal, but on demanding them from the sentry over them, he refused to deliver them up unless the Colonel himself verbally gave the order. On turning round however to ask the Colonel to do so, to my astonishment I found he had quitted the guard-house and I never saw him after. Ensign Gambier thinking, I conclude, that further persuasion was useless, left also, and I have since heard joined the Colonel somewhere outside.

Although now on his own, Lieutenant Peile remained set on retrieving the colours which, after a good deal of argument, were handed over to him. But on leaving the guard-house with them, he discovered to his 'horror and disgust' that his syce had decamped with his horse, 'taking a large quantity of cheroots with him'. Unable in his debilitated state to carry the standard on foot, Peile returned it to the guard-house and decided at last to follow the example of his Colonel and make off. He had taken but a few steps when a trooper took a shot at him. The ball passed harmlessly through his helmet; and, turning round, he shot the man dead. Another sepoy then levelled his musket at him. He was saved on this occasion by a man from his own regiment who knocked the musket aside and ran the would-be assassin through with his bayonet, 'at the same time calling him by a name' which Peile in the narrative of his adventures did not think it 'necessary to repeat'.

Peile, abandoning the dignified demeanour which he had for so long maintained, now ran away, falling over 'several times from sheer weakness and fatigue', receiving two more shots through his helmet and one through the flap of his coat. Eventually he hid under some brushwood where he was discovered by a group of Goojurs who, having stripped him of all his clothes apart from a flannel waistcoat and a pair of socks, were so convinced that he had money concealed somewhere about his person that they half-strangled him with the sleeve of his shirt in a vain attempt to extract information as to its hiding-place.

Recovering consciousness he set off barefoot for Alipur, where, after close interrogation by about two hundred people, he was given water, sweetmeats, 'some old native clothes, a pair of shoes and an old pugree'. Sent on his way, he was denied shelter at a nearby village but was offered chupatties and water outside it; then, meeting a friendly Brahmin, he was conducted to the local zemindar who provided him with a charpoy 'and the best food procurable'. Asleep in the zemindar's house he was woken by two *sowars* of the 3rd Light Cavalry who rushed in with drawn sabres, threatening to kill him. Finding, however, that their intended victim could not stand up, they sat down by his bedside instead, called for hookahs, and informed him that they were two of the eighty-five men who had been imprisoned at Meerut, displaying the marks of the shackles to prove it. They 'finished off by relating with *goût* how they had butchered several Europeans' at Delhi and intended to butcher two more – the Brigadier and Brigade Major, Peile presumed – when they found them.

Falling asleep again on the *sowars'* departure, Peile was once more awakened, this time by a warning that there were fifty armed sepoys in the next village searching for refugees. Guided by the friendly old zemindar, he set off immediately in the opposite direction to hide until the sepoys had passed on. 'The next morning all was reported safe, and I therefore came out of my retreat,' Peile continued his narrative, 'and wandered over the village, a man at large, accompanied by a whole host of men, women and children following me to obtain a look at the Feringhee refugee.' In this way time passed on until Sunday when he was brought news of a wounded doctor with two women fugitives, one of whom, he felt sure, must be his wife. He determined to try to find them, against the advice of the zemindar who, giving him new clothes and money, parted from him with tears in his eyes.

Returning to the Kurnaul road, Peile made his way to a large village where he was offered food and water and 'a situation by the head man at a salary of 100 rupees per mensem as an assistant to him in his dacoity excursions'. Accepting the refreshment but declining the employment in as polite a manner as it was offered him, Peile went on his way, having failed to obtain any information about his wife. Soon afterwards, however, he came across a man who not only knew where she was but promised to take him to her.

After a short distance he made me strip [Peile concluded his account], but found only the rupee which . . . the zemindar . . . had given me. This he returned to me. A little later I was again molested by some other people, who took me into their village, stripped me naked in the presence of a large crowd of men, women and children, but they also only found the one rupee which was again returned to me. My companion and I then went on our road, and soon after he conducted me to [a village] where to my great delight [I found] . . . my wife and Dr and Mrs Wood.[33]

After their brief sleep in the cellar, Lieutenant Vibart and the other fugitives in Metcalfe House – five men, two women, three girls and a native servant who seemed unwilling to leave them – decided they must get away before the sepoys came to plunder it. Taking some bread, meat and a bottle of water with them, they emerged into the darkness and made their way towards the river Jumna whose waters, trickling in narrow channels at this time of year, had receded far from the banks, leaving a swampy marsh a quarter of a mile broad on either side. As they trudged north through the muddy sand, each man helping one of the women, they saw to their left the whole extent of the cantonments in a blaze of light and behind them flames leaping up from Metcalfe House which they had left only just in time.[34] The noise of firing continued at intervals; and every now and then the night breeze brought to their ears the sound of shouts and frantic yells.

To get away to the north they had to cross the canal which was close to the northern end of the cantonments; but so occupied were the mutineers with plundering the bungalows that the fugitives waded across without being seen, the water coming up to their chests. Mrs Forrest's youngest daughter, a girl of nine, was carried on Vibart's shoulders. Beyond the canal a vast plain of stubble fields covered with thistles stretched before them in the moonlight without a single landmark to guide them. Through this they stumbled wearily in their wet clothes, Lieutenant Forrest lagging behind in great pain from the hand which had been wounded in defence of the Magazine, and badly bruised from the recoil of a howitzer. His wife, also suffering from a wound in her shoulder, walked steadily on, uttering no complaint.

About three miles from the cantonments, unable to proceed any farther, they took shelter in a small patch of scrub. Scarcely had they lain down here, however, than a party of sepoys coming from the direction of Meerut suddenly appeared less than a hundred yards away, making directly for the scrub where they lay concealed. The men, walking in Indian file, passed within a few feet of their hiding-place, seeming not to notice them, until one of them caught sight of a bottle of water which had been left lying in the open. He stooped to pick it up, whispering to his companions who then peered into the bushes, muttering to each other that there were people hiding there. Vibart cocked the double-barrelled gun which, apart from three flimsy regimental swords of an old infantry pattern, was the only weapon his party possessed. He watched the sepoys, holding his breath, clearly seeing the gold regulation necklace of the native officer who led them. After a brief interval, to Vibart's astonishment, the sepoys moved off, seated themselves leisurely on the ground a hundred yards away, and made no attempt to follow the Europeans when they sprang from the bushes and ran off in the opposite direction.

Morning came and the fugitives trudged on, resting for a time in the shade of some tamarisk trees where they were startled by the unseen approach of a villager who stood looking at them for a few moments, then walked on without speaking. Forrest, so worn out now that he asked the others to go on and leave him to die in peace, was with the greatest difficulty persuaded to get up. But they had not gone much farther when it was obvious that the women, who had to put the skirts of their dresses over their heads to protect them from the blazing sun, could not continue in the dreadful heat. Once more they lay down to rest; and, while two of the men went off to find water the remainder of the party were approached and surrounded by about forty villagers who, though appearing at first with their spears and lathies to be far from friendly, eventually brought them milk and chupatties and told them that there were three other *Sahib-logue* who had wandered into their village.[35]

These three fugitives were Mr Marshall, an Englishman who kept a shop in Delhi, Colonel Knyvett of the 38th Native Infantry and the young ensign, Gambier, who had escaped with Knyvett from the lines of their regiment while Lieutenant Peile was arguing with the sentry about the colours in the guard-house. Gambier claimed to have seized one of the colours and to have reached the guard-house door, where it had been snatched from his hands by one of the sepoys. Finding Knyvett outside, he had said, 'Colonel, we must be off'; and, since the Colonel 'seemed to oppose the idea', he had grabbed him by the wrist and dragged him away across the parade-ground, beyond which they had both fallen exhausted under a tree, thankful to have escaped being hit in the back by the sepoys who had taken a few ill-aimed shots at them. In the morning they had hidden in a 'broken down mud hut' where they had been given food by some Brahmins who had led them – together with Marshall who had joined them on the way – to the village near which they had been hiding when Vibart's party found them.[36]

The enlarged band of fugitives, now thirteen in all, moved slowly on again until the sun sank once more through a haze of reddish dust. Helped across the Jumna by some of the villagers, they lay down to sleep on the far bank, waking up aching with cold, then stumbling on again through the night, one of the men barefoot, having given his shoes to a Forrest girl who had lost hers in the river.

In the morning they found shelter in a tope of mango trees where a crowd of about a hundred villagers gathered to watch them as they ate some dhal and chupatties which they paid for with the last of their rupees. While they were eating, a fakir clothed in a long yellow robe, his face smeared with paint and ashes, entered the tope and, sitting down near by, beckoned to the villagers to gather round him. They obeyed his call and listened intently, occasionally casting glances at the *Firinghis*. When the fakir had departed, they urged the fugitives to be on their way again as the sepoys were out looking for them. So on they went into the burning plain (now swept by a scorching wind), little caring any more where they went or what was to become of them.

They had not got far when they were surrounded by a band of Goojurs armed with spears and bludgeons, 'fierce-looking men who gave a fearful shout and rushed upon [them] with demoniacal gestures', howling and dancing in a manner that seemed ludicrous when Colonel Knyvett described it afterwards but 'was certainly no laughing matter then'. The Goojurs disarmed them, stripped them of their rings and studs, watches and buttons, and such clothes as took their fancy. Vibart 'trembled with foreboding' as he 'saw the unfortunate ladies in the grasp of these savages. One of them had her clothes literally torn off her back, whilst the others were treated with similar barbarity'; and all of them, so Ensign Gambier recorded, were deprived even of their stays. 'At last, when they had appropriated everything . . . the entire band retreated a short distance and commenced quarrelling over the spoil.'[37]

Spared their lives at least, the fugitives made their way with bare and lacerated feet to the village of Khekra, so tortured by thirst that on passing a stagnant puddle they fell to their knees and drank the filthy contents. At Khekra, so Ensign Gambier afterwards wrote to Mrs Knyvett:

We were led in triumph, as it were, into an open space by a bazaar where charpoys were brought out and we gladly rested ourselves. Chupattis were handed over the heads of the assembled multitude who closed round us, gaping in perpetual wonderment and cracking coarse jokes on our condition and chances of life, making it impossible to realize that a few days ago these were British subjects who would have salaamed and joined hands and kissed our feet and crouched in abject humility to us . . . From our comparatively comfortable position we were ejected by a she-fiend (a disgrace to your sex, My dear Mrs Knyvett). The very men of the village shrunk in awe from the horrid hag as, with foulest language, extended skinny arms, and frantic gestures, she rushed out from an adjoining house, the personification of malice, tipped over our charpoys one after the other, and cleared the space in a twinkling. Defend me from ever meeting such a woman again! We sneaked off . . . and were taken to a fakir's hut [where] we were the object of attraction to hundreds of curious eyes, as if we were the last imported rarity into the Surrey Zoologicals . . . A large sheet was spread for us to lie on – 'to catch our blood,' so the Colonel said, 'when they sacrificed us . . . after we had been fattened up for a day or two' . . . I assure you that the Colonel prevented us from forgetting how to laugh, whether he indulged in the gloomiest suggestions as to our fate [or] described some of our adventures with that irresistibly comic effect which made us sometimes shake with laughter [even when] the knife, as it were, was at our throats.[38]

After resting on the sheet provided for them at Khekra, the fugitives were conducted to another small hut on the outskirts of the village. Here, they were told, they could spend the night. But the atmosphere of the hut was so close and stifling that they chose to spend the night outside in the open where, so Colonel Knyvett forecast, they would all be murdered before morning. When daylight came they were advised to get back into the hut as, if the sepoys saw them, they would surely all be killed. They accordingly re-entered the hovel whose door was fastened behind them. There they spent the entire day, suffocated by the heat and pestered by swarms of flies so thick that the air was darkened by them. Food and water were brought to them; and the barber-surgeon of the village cleaned Mrs Forrest's wound, extracting bits of the fabric of her dress which had been carried into it and pouring boiling ghee through it before binding it up.

As darkness fell they emerged from the hovel again; and as they lay on the ground a fakir treated them to an extempore song about the virtues of the great and mighty *Sahib-logue*, while another whispered in Mrs Forrest's ear 'the comforting intelligence' that they were all to be 'polished off' during the night. The next day they succeeded in finding a native to take a message to Meerut thirty miles away; but the messenger had not long departed when they were told they must move immediately to a *bagh* about two miles distant, as their hiding-place had been discovered by sepoys who had sworn to seize them and to carry them back prisoners to Delhi. So the bedraggled party got to their feet yet again and moved on, joined now by two English sergeants' wives, each with a baby, who had been wandering about since the outbreak at Delhi four days before.

While they were in the *bagh* a messenger arrived from Hurchundpore, a walled town five miles farther down the road to Meerut. Here an old German Jew named Cohen had lived nearly all his life. He had become quite native in his habits and was much respected by the people of the town. He offered the fugitives his protection and hospitality. Eagerly they accepted it; and on arrival in Hurchundpore were welcomed by Mr Cohen whose family provided them with tea, baths, clean clothes and shirts, with petticoats for the ladies and cloth to cut into more, with comfortable rooms, and an excellent dinner followed by a bottle of cognac.[39]

Their plea for help dispatched from Khekra had arrived at Meerut while General Hewitt was at dinner in one of the European barracks. Considering it impossible to assist fugitives so near Delhi, the General had cast it aside and it had fallen under the table. Someone had picked it up and informed Lieutenant Mackenzie of its contents. Mackenzie had at once requested permission to ride out with some of his men and attempt to bring the fugitives in. The General had acceded to his request on condition that another officer went with him. Hugh Gough had volunteered to go; and the two officers had set off together with some forty native troopers who, on their arrival in Hurchundpore, were mistaken by the inhabitants for troops of the King of Delhi. '*Badsháh ká fouj! Badsháh Delhi ka fouj aya!*' the people shouted. 'The King's troops! The King of Delhi's troops have come!' Hearing these shouts the fugitives, for some reason they could not afterwards explain, threw off the clean clothes with which Mr Cohen had supplied them and stood 'in the filthy garments of the previous day, ready to meet the worst. In the midst of all this excitement two

European officers were observed riding up the street'. They were greeted by the fugitives with 'a frantic delight' which Gough found it 'impossible to describe'. 'They hung about us,' he said, 'embraced us and called us their saviours.'[40]

Escorted by Gough and Mackenzie, the fugitives left for Meerut before dawn next morning. Passing by the charred and blackened ruins of the houses that had been burned by the mutineers, they arrived safely at the artillery barracks where the survivors of the uprising, now joined by various refugees from outlying stations, had been assembled for their safety. Here they found Lieutenant Osborn who, stripped of all his clothes with the exception of a pith helmet by marauding Goojurs, had been cared for by a native woman and carried into Meerut on a charpoy by some kindly-disposed villagers. But they did not find George Willoughby who was reported to have been murdered whilst resisting robbery. Nor was Mrs Fraser reunited with her husband. 'Poor Mrs Fraser! She had hitherto born up with the certain expectation of meeting him . . . It was very unfortunate. An officer stood by the cart, of course not knowing who she was, and in reply to her eager question stated the melancholy fact of his death.'[41]

6

The Mutiny Spreads

· *Alleged incompetence of senior officers · British troops march
on Delhi · their revenge – punishment of mutineers · Wilson joins forces
with Barnard, 7 June 1857 · battle of Badli-ki-Serai, 8 June · spread
of disturbances · plight of British officials · John Lawrence holds
the Punjab · murder of prisoners at Peshawar and Ajnala · mutiny at
Dinapore, 25 July · siege of Arrah, 27 July to 3 August ·
Vincent Eyre captures Kunwar Singh's stronghold at Jagdishpur,
13 August · anarchy in North-Western Provinces · mutiny at Gwalior,
14 June · escape of the women to Agra ·*

The more alert and intelligent of the younger officers in India very
much doubted whether their seniors had the capacity to deal with the
danger now threatening the Empire's existence. Lieutenant Frederick
Roberts, one day to become Field Marshal Lord Roberts, Commander-in-Chief, expressed common enough opinions when he told his
family that outside the Punjab, where the best man in the country
ruled with firm hands, India was at the mercy of 'idiot after idiot'.
The Government in Calcutta was quite 'imbecile'; some of the older
officers were 'perfect children – quite unable to take care of themselves'; the ladies were 'the only people who had behaved properly'
in the crisis; many of their husbands had been 'positively disgusting'.
Roberts wrote from Amritsar:

Oh, my dear Mother, you would not believe Englishmen could ever
have been guilty of such imbecility as has almost invariably been displayed during this crisis; some few have shone, but they are exceptions
... Perfectly ridiculous, an army going to pieces in this way ... You
would scarcely believe how paralysed everything is ... We have a most
dilatory, undecided Commander-in-Chief.[1]

The Commander-in-Chief, General Anson, was still far away in the
north at the end of the third week in May. When news of the massacres at Meerut and Delhi first reached him, he had been at Simla,
looking forward to a few days' shooting in the hills. He realized the
importance of sending as many troops as could be spared to Delhi,

recognizing that the moral effects of the fall of Delhi were incalculable, and that the longer the mutineers remained in possession of it the more likely it was that there would be uprisings elsewhere. But the Adjutant-General, the Quartermaster-General, the Commissary-General and the general in command of the Medical Department all assured him that it was quite impossible to move any useful number of troops in that direction for the time being, since the permanent transport establishments of the army had been abolished for reasons of economy some years before. While Anson was waiting for these staff officers to make their due and proper arrangements, Sir John Lawrence, the Chief Commissioner in the Punjab, urged him at least to disarm the native regiments at Ambala which were becoming increasingly disobedient and restless. This was wholly unnecessary and unjustified, the officers of these regiments assured Anson: wholesale mutiny was still unthinkable; besides, the men had been given assurances that they would not be disarmed and nothing but harm would come of the promise being broken. So the regiments remained armed while a proclamation was read to them reiterating the Government's denials that any interference with their religion was intended.

At Meerut, Brigadier Wilson was finding General Hewitt as exasperating as Lawrence found the slow, complacently hidebound military officers in the Punjab. 'Hewitt is a dreadful old fool, a sad stumbling block,' Wilson told his wife. 'He thinks of nothing but preserving his old carcass from harm.' He had certainly made Meerut almost impregnable and seemed to consider that his duties ended there. The thought that he might have done more to prevent the fall of Delhi by pursuing the Meerut mutineers seems never to have occurred to him. 'My force is very anxious to be doing something,' Wilson continued. 'We are all fretting at being kept here . . . and if we do not receive instructions soon, I think I shall move in the direction of Delhi. The responsibility of doing so without orders, though, is very great.' Wilson was also held back by the belief that even if he did act on his own responsibility, and even if he could overcome the difficulties of moving with 'no cattle except fifteen elephants and a few bullocks', he might well find all the troubles over long before he reached Delhi. As late as 20 May he still had 'every hope' that all would 'in a very short time be again quiet and settled'. 'The general opinion is', so he assured his wife, 'that the mutineers, failing to get any native chiefs to join them, are dispersing and sneaking away whenever they can, and that when we arrive before Delhi we shall find they have all vanished.'[2]

The Commander-in-Chief was less optimistic; yet, even so, it was not until 25 May that, badgered by Lord Canning and Sir John Lawrence – neither of whom fully appreciated his problems of transport and supplies – he felt able to leave for Bagpat where he had ordered General Hewitt's Meerut force to meet him before they marched on to Delhi together. But Anson got no farther than Kurnaul. Already ill when he left Simla, he contracted cholera on the journey south and died on 27 May.

His successor, General Sir Henry Barnard, was 'a dear old gentleman' in more than one officer's opinion, 'always chatty and jolly'. He was said to be 'too fond of giving away to the opinion of others, yet he had endeared himself to all who came in contact with him by his gentlemanly conduct and desire to please everyone when it lay in his power'.[3] The son of a clergyman, he had been commissioned into the Grenadier Guards in 1814 and since then had spent most of his career in staff appointments, recently as Chief of Staff to General Simpson, Lord Raglan's successor in the Crimea. As though determined to prove that he was a far more forceful commander than his predecessor, General Barnard pushed on fast towards the rendezvous with Hewitt and Wilson, marching at speed through the dust and the fierce May heat, pausing only and then reluctantly to punish natives convicted of having taken part in the recent atrocities.

His subordinates, however, bent on vengeance, were far more anxious than he to punish the natives and were none too scrupulous in determining guilt. 'We burnt every village and hanged all the villagers who had treated our fugitives badly until every tree was covered with scoundrels hanging from every branch,' wrote Lieutenant Kendal Coghill who had earlier confessed himself 'in such a rage at the slack notice taken of these mutinies' and had expressed his opinion that it would have been far better to blow mutinous regiments from guns rather than disband them.[4]

Holy men suffered with the rest. 'For these were the gentry,' as Captain Barter, Adjutant of the 75th, explained, 'who acted as go-betweens to the native regiments and by their teaching spread and encouraged disaffection.' So 'the meditative dodge' did not save them. Barter saw one of them being led away with a rope round his neck by some officers and men of his regiment and 'without loss of time hanged to the branch of a [pipal] tree'. Another day Barter heard the

hum of voices, like the sound of some huge bee-hive disturbed. There was a rush of many feet and in an incredibly short space of time every village within reach of camp was in a blaze. Several officers joined in this performance, and amongst others our paymaster. There was a parade of all hands in the evening and a lecture read to us by Colonel [Hope] Grant of the 9th Lancers, for, as usual when things are done without consideration, more harm is done than good, and the villages belonged to a native lady or 'Rana' who had been most kind in aiding our fugitives to escape from Delhi. No doubt, though, but some of the villagers had committed atrocities for nine of them were hung from a large tree by the roadside after the parade.[5]

The trials – when trials were held – were often mere formalities. Officers were heard to swear that they would hang the prisoners whether or not they were found to be guilty; and, after being condemned to death as a matter of course, prisoners, mutineers, rebellious villagers and escaped convicts from the gaols were sometimes tortured before their execution by private soldiers whose officers did not interfere.[6] The bravery and resignation with which the prisoners died struck all who witnessed their executions. They did not struggle or attempt to grab the rope when the carts were driven away from beneath the trees. 'Often and often have I seen natives executed, of all ages, of every caste, and every position in society,' wrote Robert Dunlop, a Deputy Commissioner in the Punjab. 'Yet never have I seen one of them misbehave. They died with a stoicism that in Europe would excite astonishment and admiration.'[7] They died in 'most perfect apathy', an English private soldier said. Very occasionally they would make some provocative remark such as, 'I die contented, having seen English ladies molested and torn to pieces in the public bazaar.'[8] Or they might address a few casual words of farewell to a face they recognized amongst the spectators. E. A. Thurburn reported that a native officer in his regiment who was hanged as a mutineer called out to him, 'When you write to the adjutant remember me very kindly to him.' Then 'springing from the platform he launched himself into eternity with the greatest nonchalance and coolness'.[9] Captain Charles Gordon, who watched scores of natives being hanged, never saw one 'care twopence about it'.[10]

The spectators soon grew indifferent themselves to the sight of men hanged, so accustomed did they become to it, and so well persuaded after what had happened at Meerut and Delhi that 'these cursed women slayers', these 'black-faced curs', these 'fiendish niggers' deserved no mercy.[11] 'I don't consider niggers in the same light as I would a white man,' one officer told his brother. 'To be gracious or merciful to these cruel brutes, these cowardly monsters, is nothing more nor less than to be absurd in their own eyes whilst you certainly don't advance your cause.'[12] Another officer, believing that 'kindness would be interpreted for funk', advocated the extermination of the entire population of Delhi.[13]

Robert Dunlop trusted that the behaviour of the rebels would give all those who did not know India a proper insight into

the weak and childish but cruel and treacherous native character . . . It is a patent fact that the proud contempt which the Anglo-Saxon bears to the Asiatic has proved, to a great extent, the salvation of our Indian Empire. Nearly all men come to the country fully prepared to accord equal rights and privileges to its dusky inhabitants; but . . . experience leads to a common conviction of their debasement.[14]

Dunlop gave an example of the effect which the atrocities committed by the rebels had had on the mind of one former well-wisher, a portly old major whose 'merry black eyes, mildness of manner and uniform kindness to the natives had given him, among the sepoys of his own regiment, the name of the "Rajah Sahib".' This man became so 'frenzied by the loss of near and dear relatives' that he now 'looked with horror on the entire race, and advocated a retribution which would have overwhelmed the avengers as well as their victims'.[15]

Captain William Wallace shared this major's feelings. Although his own family had escaped, he considered it his duty to take up by the cartload those whom he suspected of being rebels, 'to tie them up to a convenient tree and leave them hanging. All they asked for was a pipe.' Wallace said he 'never felt any remorse. They were such brutes.'[16]

So familiar did the sight of hanging corpses become, in fact, that after a time men took no notice of them any more. Lieutenant John Fairweather recalled attending an auction of some rebels' goods.

I fancied a man behind me was pressing rather rudely against me. I dug him with my elbows but he seemed to return my dig. I then turned round rather angrily towards the man and found it was the body of a rebel that had been hanged on a tree . . . It gave me a bit of a shock, but such scenes were so common that a swinging corpse forming part of a crowd at an auction seemed to affect no one.[17]

Only those with the strongest stomachs, however, could remain unaffected when prisoners were blown away from the mouths of cannon, a punishment inflicted in the days of the Moghul emperors and subsequently adopted by the British in India. This was 'a frightful sight', Dr John Sylvester thought; and for the victims a peculiarly horrible punishment since, though hanging in itself was sufficient to make paradise very uncertain, death by mutilation after defilement made its attainment even less likely. The victim was lashed to a gun, the small of his back or the pit of his stomach against the muzzle, then 'smeared with the blood of someone murdered by a member of his race if such could be procured'.[18] When the gun was fired the man's body was dismembered. Usually the head, scarcely disfigured, would fly off through the smoke, then fall to the earth, slightly blackened, followed by the arms and legs. The trunk would be shattered, giving off 'a beastly smell', and pieces of flesh and intestines and gouts of blood would be splashed not only over the gunners but also over any spectators who stood too close. Vultures would hover overhead and with grisly dexterity catch lumps of flesh in their beaks. 'The pent-up feelings of the bystanders found vent in a sort of loud gasp like *Ah-h*!' wrote an artillery officer who was required to supervise such an execution. 'Then many of them came across the ditch to inspect the remains of the legs, and the horrible affair was over.'[19]

After a time even this frightful punishment was witnessed without horror. 'So great is the disgust we all feel for the atrocities committed by the rebels,' wrote one observer, 'that we had no room in our hearts for any feeling of pity; perfect callousness was depicted on every European's face; a look of grim satisfaction could even be seen in the countenances of the gunners serving the guns.'[20]

While the men of Barnard's column were punishing captured rebels with indiscriminate severity on the march to Delhi, Hewitt and Wilson were also on the move at last, Hewitt 'in a state of helpless imbecility', according to a junior officer who had occasion to speak to him. Wilson suffered agonies from the heat and dust, lying down with a wet towel round his head when the force halted for a rest, and sleeping in his boots as he had done for the past three weeks.[21] At the village of Ghazi-ud-din-Nagar their troops came up with the enemy who had been sent out from Delhi to impede their advance. But the British gunners cleared the way for a charge by the 60th Rifles and a pursuit by the Carabiniers, and the sepoys were soon retreating towards Delhi. His men were 'so knocked up by the sun and want of water', Wilson explained, they could not pursue the enemy as closely as he wished. And the next day the sepoys returned to the attack with reinforcements. But once again they were driven back by the artillery;

and Wilson, enabled to continue his advance, joined forces with General Barnard at Alipur on 7 June.

The next day a third engagement was fought at Badli-ki-Serai, a group of buildings five miles north-west of Delhi, where the mutineers opened up a ferocious cannonade upon the advancing British troops. 'Papa says he was never in a hotter fire – even at Chillianwalla,' Charles Ewart of the 2nd Bengal Fusiliers, son of the Assistant Adjutant-General, reported to his mother. 'They fired musketry, round shot, shell and every other thing they possibly could . . . He says his horse stopped at every ditch it came across and the shot went whizzing about him like hail.'[22] 'I heard many officers who have been in action before say that they were never under such fire as the rebels poured into us,' Lieutenant Hugh Chichester of the Bengal Artillery confirmed. 'Nearly every shot they fired told on us . . . They had no end of heavy guns in position, and made some excellent long and straight shooting, the grape rattling in amongst [us] like a hailstorm.'[23] Here, as later, British officers were amazed by the 'wonderful range and accuracy' the mutineers 'got out of their guns'. It was such a 'most extraordinary thing', in fact, that some officers put it all down to 'astonishing luck rather than skill, for the firing of shells and the cutting of fuses [were] much too scientific for natives to understand'.[24]

Despite their highly proficient gunnery, however, the rebels were driven back from Badli-ki-Serai. And by nightfall the British were again in possession of the high ground looking down upon Delhi from which they had been driven a month before, contemplating a scene of utter desolation, 'the walls of the houses blackened by the smoke of their burned roofs. Each compound had its flower and kitchen gardens dried up and withered for want of the usual daily watering, but here and there a flower sprang up and blossomed in the trampled beds, only making desolation more desolate.'[25]

Throughout the North-Western Provinces now, the disturbances were spreading fast. The 9th Native Infantry mutinied at Aligarh and went off to join the rebels at Delhi; the 10th mutinied at Fatehgarh and most of the men dispersed to their homes. There were mutinies also at Shajahanpur, at Bareilly, at Rohini, at Azangarh, at Budaun, at Moradabad, and, in Rajputana, at Nusseerabad and Neemuch. In a few places civil rebellion preceded the mutiny, the people attacking British-owned factories, churches and mission-schools, and destroying the bankers' and *mahajans'* books of account, before the soldiers rebelled.[26] At most places, the mutineers rose first, encouraging the badmashes to join them. But in almost every case the officers and their wives were taken by surprise, believing to the last that whatever happened in other regiments, their men would remain staunch. 'They're all niggers alike,' one officer said.' But I can trust *my* fellows.'[27] The sepoys themselves often continued to protest their loyalty until the very day of their outbreak and were often sincere in their protestations. For there seems to have been no organization, no concerted action, no preconceived plan. One intelligent Brahmin sepoy explained to an officer, 'Sir, there is one knave, and nine fools; the knave compromises the others, and then tells them it is too late to draw back.'[28] In many cases groups of sympathetic sepoys protected their officers from harm, knocking down the muskets of others who would have shot them, or fetching carriages in which they could escape.

Three sepoys caught hold of me, and said they would try and save me [one officer wrote]. They threw off my hat, tore off my trousers . . . covered me as well as they could with my horsecloth . . . and, putting me between the two, the third walked in front; and what between knocking up one man's musket, whose bayonet was just at my back, and declaring I was one of their wives, we got through all the sentries and crossed the river. They then wanted me to make the best of my way off, saying that the chances were ten to one that my wife was killed by that time, but I told them plainly I would not try to escape without her. [So they took me to] our house where they set me down, and one man said, 'Now I will go and bring your wife to you if she is still alive.' So off he went and after about twenty minutes of the most agonizing suspense dear Mary and I met again. I must say the three sepoys with us behaved splendidly.[29]

Deprived of the means to support their authority, several government officials deserted their posts, as did the magistrate at Muzaffarnagar who closed the public offices as soon as he heard of the rising at Meerut and went to hide in the jungle, leaving the town and the surrounding villages to be plundered by marauders. At Simla there were disgraceful scenes when an unfounded rumour spread abroad that a battalion of Gurkhas had mutinied and were about to rob and murder the *Firinghis*. The Europeans fled headlong from the station, many of the men abandoning the women as they rushed for safety followed by bearers carrying their baggage. Emma Young described how she, with various friends and their children, rushed out of the town and scrambled down a water-course to hide under some shrubs. Advised to seek safety in one of the town's banks they ran back there to find it full of ladies, ayahs and children, all lying on the ground or walking about the verandas. There were more than 100 European gentlemen, tradesmen, clerks, etc., all armed, and it was thought that this number with the two guns would have been sufficient to defend the place. But General Penny was quite incapable of maintaining order, and was evidently in the greatest possible fright himself. He allowed many to get intoxicated; and, if the Gurkhas had chosen to come [which they had no intention of doing], they could easily have murdered us all. It was a most disgraceful scene and made one ashamed of one's countrymen.[30]

Most government officials, however, behaved calmly and bravely, going about their official business as if in a time of profound tranquillity. They displayed no apprehension at having to rely for their safety upon a few policemen of doubtful loyalty; they made preparations to defend their houses (though many of them, like the Deputy Commissioner of Mullaon, knew 'as much of entrenching as an owl');[31] and they rode off only when their lives depended upon immediate flight. In some cases they chose to die at their posts rather than submit to threats from people over whom they had been placed to rule – as did Robert Tucker, the Judge at Fatehpur who said that he would go out to meet the enemy with his bible in one hand and who was murdered on the roof of his cutcherry after he had killed over a dozen of his assailants with the pistol that he carried in the other.[32]

William Edwards, Magistrate and Collector of Budaun, having sent his wife and child away to a place of safety, found himself 'the sole European officer in charge of the district, with a lawless population of over a million people'. His only assistant was a Muslim Deputy-Collector who had been with him less than a month; he had 'every reason to distrust' the sepoys of the Treasury Guard; his police were 'little more to be depended on'; his applications for military aid from Bareilly, thirty miles away, had been met with refusals, 'as none could be spared'. Yet even when the sepoys at Bareilly mutinied and a large number of them, having massacred the Europeans and released nearly four thousand convicts from the huge gaol in the town, advanced on Budaun, Edwards determined not to desert his post. 'I went into my room,' he wrote, 'and prayed earnestly that God would protect and guide me, and enable me to do my duty.'

His problems were further increased when an indigo planter and his son, a customs official and a Eurasian clerk with his wife and family all fled to his house, seeming 'quite paralysed' with fear, refusing to believe that their 'safety was far more endangered by remaining together and attracting attention than by separating', protesting that 'their only hope was in sticking close to the magistrate for protection'.

At about half past five on the morning of 2 June the sepoy guards at the Budaun Treasury, having heard of the mutiny at Bareilly, broke out into mutiny themselves. They persuaded the police to throw away their badges and join them. Then, assisted by the mutineers from Bareilly, they smashed open the doors of the gaol from which three hundred yelling prisoners poured out to march down towards Edwards's house. 'I felt my work was then over,' Edwards wrote, 'and that it was now time to try and provide for my own safety.' He mounted his wife's horse and galloped away in the direction of Moradabad, followed by the other Europeans and two faithful servants, an Afghan and a Sikh, the Eurasian family flying off into the fields.

On their way to Moradabad, Edwards and his party were warned by a Muslim zemindar that the countryside was swarming with rebels, and that they would never make their escape in that direction. He would shelter Mr Edwards, he said; but he could not risk offering shelter to the others. And as the others would not leave him, and he felt he could not desert them, Edwards moved on with them to 'a miserable village called Kukorah', the sky behind him lit by flames from the burning bungalows of Budaun. After resting for a few hours in Kukorah the fugitives rode down to the Ganges, crossed the river under fire from a crowd of people on the far bank, and began a wandering search for safety that did not end for three months.

Pursued by rebels they passed through villages where men whose homes had been plundered crowded around them asking eagerly, 'When will your raj return? When will your raj return?' Offered an escort by 'a native gentleman of influence' they narrowly escaped being shot by his brother who 'quite intoxicated with opium, and very insolent and excited in his manner', threatened them with a double-barrelled gun. When found and attacked by their pursuers, their escort ran away, leaving the customs official to be hacked to death and his mutilated body to be eaten by dogs. Edwards and the two indigo planters managed to escape and, disguised as natives, to reach Farukhabad where the planters left him to go on to Fatehgarh where they were both murdered when the regiment there mutinied. Edwards, with the Collector of Farrukhabad, his wife and four children, then found shelter in a filthy cattle shed at Kussowrah under the protection of a friendly and influential zemindar, Hurdeo Buksh.

Here two of the children died before the rest of the party were able to get away by boat to Cawnpore on the last day of August.[33]

William Tayler, the humorous though pugnacious Commissioner of Patna, saved the town from insurrection by the prompt arrest of the leading *maulvis* of the Wahabis, around whom Muslim rebels would be likely to collect, and by the enlistment of the help of other natives upon whose loyalty he felt able to rely. Farther north in the Punjab, whose Chief Commissioner was the resolute Sir John Lawrence, equally prompt and decisive action was taken by Lawrence's officials – Robert Montgomery, the Judicial Commissioner, Herbert Edwardes, Commissioner of Peshawar, and Edwardes's deputy, Lieutenant-Colonel John Nicholson – all of whom had been energetically engaged upon the rapid, not to say ruthless, modernization of the Punjab since its annexation. Within days of the news from Delhi being received at Lahore, every important place in the Punjab had been secured; the arsenals had been saved; commanding positions occupied; and such effective arrangements had been made for the safeguarding of the treasure of the various districts that throughout the crisis only £10,000 was lost in the entire area. Suspect native regiments were immediately disarmed; sepoys who deserted and endeavoured to reach Delhi were closely pursued and dispersed; those suspected of being the leaders of mutiny were shot or blown from guns. No regard was paid to the pleas of British officers, whose belief in the staunchness of their men was ignored. Some of these officers, so dismayed by the disgrace of their regiments, flung their swords and spurs upon the piles of muskets and sabres which their men had been required to surrender, feeling, as one of them confessed after a disarming parade and the break-up of his regiment, that they had 'lost a dear friend whose existence was essential to their happiness'.[34] One commanding officer, Colonel Sandeman of the 33rd who had been with the regiment for more than thirty-two years, protested that he would answer with his life for every single one of his men; and, when the order to disarm was firmly repeated, 'the poor old fellow burst into tears'.[35] Another commanding officer, Colonel Spottiswoode of the 55th, some of whose men mutinied, was so distressed by the thought that the rest would now be disarmed, that he committed suicide rather than witness the dishonouring of the regiment he loved.[36]

Most officers in the Queen's regiments, however, thoroughly approved of the drastic measures adopted in the Punjab whose officials had always believed in showing a bold front and taking the initiative at once. One of those who warmly applauded the commissioners' resolute actions was Captain Bailie of the 87th Fusiliers whose regiment was at Peshawar, the important post on the Afghanistan border where eight native regiments were also stationed. Here Bailie witnessed the execution by blowing away from guns of forty sepoys. 'It was a horrible sight,' he told his father, 'but a very satisfactory one ... The pieces were blown about in all directions ... Since then we have hung a good many – a dozen or half a dozen at a time and blown away a few more.'[37]

The danger of an uprising in the Punjab was not entirely averted, though, by the prompt action of its administrators, as it was scarcely to be expected that all the disarmed sepoys would remain quietly within their lines in a frontier area where arms were abundant. As Sir John Lawrence told a friend, 'We are all here in a nice quandary.'[38] British officers placed their pistols beside their plates at meals and on the pews in front of them at church. Several of the disarmed sepoys tried to escape from Peshawar. And the men of the 51st made a sudden rush at a batch of new recruits in an unsuccessful attempt to grab their arms before racing out of the cantonments. They were pursued not only by police and British troops but also by the men of the frontier tribes who had been offered thirty rupees a head for any deserter they brought back to camp. Major Bailie saw these tribesmen 'beating the fellows up like quail and knocking them over out of the cornfields', then bringing them into camp, vociferously demanding receipts for dead and wounded bodies. One of the sepoys made a sudden spring for his captor's tulwar, snatched it from him, cut him down, then lunged at a British officer before being shot by a pay sergeant of the 87th. By this time one hundred and ninety-two sepoys of the 51st were collected in the middle of the road; and the Brigadier was begged by various British officers to authorize a court martial. Bailie told his wife:

before he could change his mind (as he was half-inclined to do), the Major, myself, Osborne and two subalterns, all 87th, sat down, wrote a few lines, got the Brigadier's signature in confirmation – turned out the 87th and then and there shot the whole 192 of them. I will say this for the wretches, they took it all in the most unconcerned way possible – marching steadily – halting – fronting opposite our firing parties – just as if they were only at drill. I fancy the 51st must be pretty well disposed of – about 100 more shot one way or another at the first start, then another 100 or so in the pursuit, then our 192, and a lot of prisoners that the villagers were bringing in all last night.[39]

'It was not a time for tenderness – for mercy – even for justice,' commented Sir John Kaye. Certainly justice was a rare quality in these months in the Punjab. At Ajnala near Amritsar, 282 sepoys of the 26th Native Infantry who had mutinied at Lahore and subsequently surrendered in the belief that they were to be given a fair trial, were executed summarily by the Deputy-Commissioner of the district, Frederic Cooper, a proud Christian of the 'true English stamp and mould'. They were brought out of the tahsil in batches of ten to be shot by Cooper's Sikhs. While the first two hundred or so were being killed, the remainder were kept locked up in one of the bastions of the tahsil. When the door was opened to bring these others out, so Cooper wrote in his account of the discharge of his 'tremendous responsibility', 'Behold! Unconsciously the tragedy of Holwell's Black Hole had been re-enacted ... Forty-five bodies, dead from fright, exhaustion, fatigue, heat and partial suffocation, were dragged out.' These bodies, together with those of the survivors who were shot, were tipped down a deep, dry well near the police station on top of their comrades already deposited there by the village sweepers.[40]

Both Lawrence and Montgomery congratulated Cooper on his 'energy and spirit'. His action would be a feather in his cap as long as he lived, Montgomery said, adding that any stragglers who might be picked up were to be sent to Lahore: 'You have had slaughter enough. We want a few for the troops here and also for evidence.'[41]

Although William Tayler had been able to save Patna from insurrection, elsewhere in Bihar there were widespread mutinies and savage fighting. A few miles from Patna the native regiments at Dinapore were known to be seriously disaffected; yet General Lloyd, the old, gouty man in command there, assuming a confidence that did not disguise his nervousness, assured Tayler that there was no need to disarm them. When the need made itself obvious, he merely removed their percussion caps, then, while the European troops were having dinner, he ordered the sepoys on to the parade-ground where they were required also to surrender the contents of their cap-cases. They responded by opening fire on their officers, and then running away, helping themselves on the way to their confiscated percussion caps.[42]

We had just had tiffin [wrote one of their officers] and I was playing at billiards when there was a tremendous row, and all the officers rushed from the Mess ... I ran about 100 yards into the square as I expected to see the sepoys show their ugly faces directly ... The 7th and 8th Native

Regiments had left their lines and were all standing and shouting with their muskets in their hands by the Magazine; the 40th were close to us outside their lines, wavering if they should go or not. However when we showed ourselves they fired at us. Fortunately no one was hit, although the bullets came near and hit the trees . . . The Adjutant [of the 40th], a very fat man of the name of Burns, stood firm, and put his hand on his heart, and said 'Fire you brutes!' They would not however fire while he stood there; but the other officers finding the fire too hot retreated, and then Burns did the same, the men blazing away at them all. By a miracle no one was hit though the bullets were flying all round . . . The 10th Queen's and the artillery went [towards the 40th] at the double, and then all the sepoys of this regiment ran off as hard as they could go to join the 7th and 8th.[43]

The successful defection of these three native regiments at Dinapore encouraged a Rajput noble, the generous and well-liked Kunwar Singh, to join them with his retainers. And, hearing this, Lloyd persuaded himself that Dinapore would soon be under heavy attack. He consequently declined to listen to any pleas for help from other threatened places beyond its walls.

One of these places was Arrah, a small town not far from Dinapore, where six officials, subsequently joined by three railway engineers, had determined to remain at their posts, having sent their wives and children to the protection of the 10th Queen's Regiment at Dinapore. These six, the Judge, the Collector, the Magistrate, the Assistant Magistrate, the Civil Surgeon, and the Sub-Deputy Opium Agent, all moved into the Judge's house which they left by day to carry on their public business as usual, and by night to patrol the town in turn, accompanied by an increased force of native police and watchmen. Towards the middle of June, it was suggested that for greater security the whole party should move to a two-storeyed building, originally destined for a billiard-room, which one of the railway engineers, Vicars Boyle, defying the sarcastic comments of his colleagues, had fortified by bricking up the veranda arches and placing numerous sandbags against the walls. Objections were made to this move on the grounds that a retreat from the Judge's house would 'probably have led to panic in the town' and that the proposed fortress was 'singularly uncalculated for defence against superior numbers', being overlooked by the engineer's large house and hemmed in by trees, outhouses and garden walls. But when the native troops at Dinapore mutinied and made for Arrah, the British there realized that they had no alternative now but to defend themselves in the building in which Vicars Boyle had one day hoped to play billiards. So, dispatching a few dozen cases of port and sherry to augment the large supply of rice, grain, biscuits, water, brandy and beer already stored there, they installed themselves in their little fortress where they were joined by the Muslim Deputy-Collector, his young servant, another native servant, six Eurasian volunteers, and, thanks to the foresight of William Tayler, fifty Sikhs whose loyalty the others were obliged to take on trust.

No sooner had they bricked themselves up in the building than the mutineers arrived in Arrah, looted the Treasury of 70,000 rupees which had not been removed for fear of provoking the sepoy guard, broke open the gaol and, joined by prisoners, gaol guards, and hundreds of badmashes, charged down upon the *Firinghi* stronghold, 'shouting like demons and firing as fast as they could'.

This first attack was held off. The sepoys retreated, leaving their dead in front of the building, together with a wounded man who for two days weakly fought to keep off the kites and crows until he died. For the rest of that day the mutineers kept up a continuous fire with musket and cannon from behind the surrounding trees and garden walls. The fire was maintained spasmodically throughout the night, covering the defenders with plaster and brick dust, but otherwise doing little damage, the gunners being prevented from taking proper aim by the Europeans' best marksmen 'blazing away at them from the top' of their fortress. Day after day the firing continued as the mutineers, having failed to smoke the defenders out by setting fire to a pile of chillies, slowly approached the building by digging a deep mine. A party of Sikhs ran out one night to grab the mining-tools; and with these a counter-mine was sunk. But the mutineers continued their digging, and the Europeans feared that 'it was only a matter of time before [they] were all blown sky-high'.[44] One of the survivors recorded their plight:

Feverish, jaded, bitten by mosquitoes and flies . . . in fear of being struck down by cholera from the effluvia arising from four dead horses which, when living, had been tied up to be ready in case flight were practicable . . . each man rose at dawn from his couch on the floor (Sikhs and Europeans slept cheek by jowl) after having taken his share of watching during the night. He next generally proceeded to a corner where tea was preparing by means of a patent lamp . . . We had dug a well inside the house so there was at least plenty of water . . . A few biscuits, some parched grain and a cheroot completed the breakfast; then the enemy's firing generally commenced for the day . . .

Dinner at three o'clock was an improvement on the former meal – rice and dhal with a little chutney . . . The dining-room, a sort of pit formed by a small staircase, the lower end of which had been bricked up, was for some time thought the securest place in the house; till one day the diners were astonished by the appearance of a brass piano castor, which had been fired from one of the cannon, and came smashing through the thin wall . . . Providentially no one was hurt, the usual occupant of the stair being that day late for dinner.[45]

There was, in fact, only one casualty, a Sikh who was mortally wounded by a musket ball which fractured his skull and lodged in the back of his brain. The Judge 'got a nasty wound in the face by the recoil of his own gun'. But he went on fighting. So did the Sikh *jemadar*, a huge, good-natured man who laughingly commented, 'No harm done!' after every unsuccessful cannon-shot, and who was wounded in the hand while contemptuously hurling brickbats at the sepoys from the roof.

The Sikhs behaved splendidly, John Halls, the Civil Surgeon, wrote, answering the mutineers' offer of 500 rupees for every European they brought out with 'sarcastic remarks and musket bullets'. They both designed and carried out 'some of the most important measures for the safety of the garrison'; and not only enabled the enemy's mining-tools to be turned against them by their stealthy sallies at night but also procured some sheep to enliven the garrison's boring diet. Yet Halls confessed that, bravely as they and the rest of the garrison fought, he had never thought that they could possibly survive unless relief arrived within one or two days. Listening during the night to the mutineers' horrible shouts of '*Maro! Maro! Kill! Kill!*' he waited apprehensively for the expected assault.[46]

The relieving force was slow in coming, for General Lloyd, like Hewitt at Meerut, remained reluctant to spare men for operations outside his own station even when the danger there was past. And it had taken strongly worded remonstrances from William Tayler, Commissioner of Patna, to make him change his mind. Eventually a detachment of two hundred British soldiers and Sikhs were sent by steamer to rescue the garrison at Arrah; but the steamer ran aground in the night, and Lloyd decided to recall the men with whom he had so unwillingly parted. Hearing of the General's decision, Tayler, accompanied by a junior civil servant, Ross Mangles, rode over to Dinapore to 'pitch into the old muff'.[47] When they arrived, however, the General had been persuaded not to recall the men but to send a further one hundred and fifty British soldiers and Sikhs, under command of Captain Dunbar, to reinforce the stranded detachment and to push on with it to Arrah. Ross Mangles, a friend of Herwald Wake, the Magistrate at Arrah, volunteered to go with Dunbar, and a few days later wrote to tell his mother what happened. The combined force were within five miles of Arrah when they saw, by the light of a bright moon, a party of horsemen on the road in front. The horsemen galloped off at the Europeans' approach; the march continued undisturbed; at eleven o'clock the moon went down.

We were passing a thick mango grove to our right when all of a sudden, without any warning, the whole place was lighted up by a tremendous volley poured at us at about 30 or 40 yards distance [Mangles recorded]. It is impossible to say how many men fired into us – some say 500, some 1,500. The next thing I remember was finding myself alone lying in the middle of the road with a crack on the head and my hat gone . . . When I recovered there were several men lying by me but not a living soul could I see. There was lots to hear though, for the bullets from right to left were whistling over my head. I was just thinking where our men could be and which way I could run when I saw the sepoys advancing out of the grove with their bayonets within a dozen yards of me. I fired my double barrel right and left into them, and then ran towards our men whom I could hear shouting on the left under a tremendous fire. Everything was now in a most dreadful confusion. The men were all scattered in groups, firing in every direction and killing each other. At last a Captain Jones, a very fine fellow (our commander was never seen again after the first volley) got hold of a bugler and got the men together in a sort of hollow . . . where we all laid down in a square. I was in the middle with the doctor helping him to tie up the wounds of the poor fellows and bring them water. The firing was all this time going on. The enemy could see us as we were all dressed in white, whilst they were nearly naked and behind trees and walls. However, the men fired about at random. At last the poor doctor was knocked over, badly wounded. It was dreadful to hear the poor wounded fellows asking for help . . . We held a consultation and determined to retreat . . . The whole distance, 18 miles, we walked under a most tremendous fire, the ditches, the jungle, the houses, and in fact every place along the road was lined with sepoys. We kept up a fire as we went along but . . . we could see no enemy, only puffs of smoke. We tried to charge, but there was nobody to charge . . . Dozens of poor fellows were knocked over within a yard of me . . . The last 5 miles I carried a wounded man who begged me not to leave him . . . I got the poor fellow safe over the nulla. I swam out, got a boat, put him in and went over with a lot of others . . . The men threw away their muskets to pull the boats or swim over and were shot down like sheep . . . Out of the 400 fellows that started for Arrah nearly 200 were killed, and of the remainder I do not think there were more than 60 to 80 who were not wounded . . . This has been the most disastrous affair that has happened out here ... Most dreadful mismanagement throughout.[48]

Sorely afflicted by an attack of gout, and bitterly cursed by his soldiers' wives – who ran down to the river's edge to welcome the steamer back only to see it run past its moorings to the hospital[49] – General Lloyd made no further efforts to help the garrison at Arrah. But a more enterprising officer decided to assume personal responsibility for the relief. This was Major Vincent Eyre, an elderly artillery officer who had consistently refused offers of employment in the Civil Service, preferring to stay with his regiment, though failing to receive the promotion which his character and talents deserved. Eyre was on his way from Calcutta to Allahabad with his battery when he heard at Buxar of the plight of the garrison at Arrah. Persuading Captain L'Estrange, who was at Buxar with a detachment of one hundred and sixty men of the 5th Fusiliers, to join him, he immediately marched to Arrah on his own responsibility.

Defeating the mutineers at Gujraganj, where they had hoped to check his advance, he sent them flying from Arrah, relieved the grateful garrison, pursued the rebels towards Jagdishpur, and, proclaiming martial law, hanged thirty wounded prisoners as well as various native officials who had entered Kunwar Singh's service. Reinforced, he attached Kunwar Singh's stronghold at Jagdishpur; captured it; blew up all the main buildings in the village; and, while the old Rajput escaped to fight again, distributed the vast stores of grain that had been collected for the rebel army to the peasants from whom it had been exacted. Eyre, having thus quelled the insurrection in western Bihar, took his battery off to Allahabad in obedience to his original orders.[50]

As British authority collapsed, whole areas in the North-Western Provinces were given over to anarchy. Many *talukdars* remained passively loyal to the Company; others made vain attempts to halt the tide of insurrection; one or two *maulvis* declared that rebellion was a sin; several native officials declined to leave their posts; most Christian converts stayed on the side of their masters. But these were very few among the tens of thousands who for the moment felt no regret at the collapse of a power which had collected such heavy taxes, which had protected the *baniyas* in the prosecution of their extortionate transactions. If a majority of them were content to stay in their villages, there were many others prepared to follow dispossessed landowners who set out to recover ancestral estates or to join the retinues of rajahs who announced the resumption of their authority as vassals of the Emperor.

Taking full advantage of the disorder, mobs of badmashes, mutinous native policemen, independent bands of rebellious sepoys and escaped convicts roamed around in search of plunder as they incited the peasants to turn against the *Firinghis,* while Muslim fanatics marched about under green flags calling for the revival of the supremacy of Islam. Rajputs and Jats fought against each other in the renewal of smouldering feuds. Goojurs fell upon mail carts and robbed peaceful villagers. Sepoys quarrelled with each other and came to blows over the division of their spoils. Various natives set themselves up as local rulers like Khan Bahadur Khan, a pensioner of the British Government, at Bareilly, and the Nawab of Farrukhabad at Fatehgarh. But they could exercise little control and any of their orders which were disliked were ignored.

British officers and civilian officials attempting to escape to safety with their families through this turbulent countryside were liable to be shot on sight. A large party of Europeans, including four small children, fleeing from Mohamdi were within half a mile of Aurangabad when their pursuers caught up with them and within ten minutes had killed all but two of them, stripping their bodies naked. Another party, trying to escape by river from Fatehpur, were overtaken by two boatloads of sepoys who opened fire on them. The women and children were urged to jump into the water 'rather than fall into the hands of their inhuman enemies'. Most of them did so. Some were shot there by sepoys or by rebel villagers on the banks; others were borne away in the stream and drowned; the rest, together with the few men who had survived, were led off as prisoners towards Cawnpore.[51]

As at Delhi, several of the fugitives managed to escape with the help of friendly Indians or faithful servants. Mrs Blake, widow of Major Blake of the 2nd Native Infantry who had been shot through the chest by his men, was shepherded to safety past jeering crowds by their *khidmatgar* who risked his life for hers.[52] Esther Anne Nicholson, a seventeen-year-old girl living with her father, an opium agent, at Gorakhpur, was dragged out of danger by twelve peasants who put their shoulders to a 'very primitive sort of covered wagon, like a huge Noah's ark', which had been made by her father and into which were crammed her two younger sisters, her baby brother, her aunt and two cousins.[53] Sarah Fagan, wife of a captain in the Engineers who lived in a house remote from the barracks at Jullundur, was still there with her sister-in-law, her five youngest children and their English nurse when her husband's men mutinied. On the first sounds of the firing she went out boldly

to the havildar of the guard which had been placed over the treasure chest of the Engineers' department in the compound. Giving him his proper titles, an act of courtesy too often neglected by the English, she told him there were only women and children in the house and she placed their lives in his hands. He said to her, 'Go in and shut all the doors and windows, stop the punkahs and put out all the lights and do not suffer a single person to enter the house, and I will answer for your safety with my life.' He could not save the treasure which the guard under him plundered, but he fulfilled his pledge to her.[54]

Mrs Irwin, the wife of a lieutenant whose regiment mutinied at Lalitpur, wrote of the compassion of a Brahmin who offered her water from his *lota*, inviting her to drink from it; of the kindness of the people in a village where she was given 'lovely milk to drink' and fresh chupatties to eat and where a boy sang a song to her about his hope that the *Firinghis* would be allowed to live; of a munshi who sheltered her in his house and provided her with charpoy, punkah, tatties, a bath and library of 'awfully learned books'; of a woman who behaved very kindly to her when she was captured and imprisoned by retainers of the Rajah of Banpur, smuggling into her place of confinement bits of dried fish which she secreted in her *ghurrah*.[55]

The women who escaped from Gwalior had many similar acts of kindness to record.

Stationed at Gwalior was a force of well-trained troops known as the Gwalior Contingent. They were officered by Europeans in the pay of the Maharajah Sindhia who had declared his belief in the indestructible foundations of British power. At nine o'clock on the night of 14 June, in response to a prolonged high bugle note, the Maharajah's sepoys poured out of their huts and, armed with muskets, rushed up and down the lines 'like madmen'. Their officers, most of whom were in bed, got up, hastily dressed and rode out towards them. The commanding officer of the 2nd Infantry was shot immediately; another officer was killed soon afterwards. Major Shirreff, commanding the 4th Infantry, endeavoured to persuade his men, to whom he was much attached, that their fears of being disarmed by European troops were utterly unfounded, protesting that he would 'cast in his lot with them whatever happened'. To 'show his confidence in them he moved up along the parade to the Quarter-Guard surrounded by them'. As he approached the Guard the sergeant-major's bungalow was set on fire; and, realizing the futility of reasoning with the men, now more excited than ever, Shirreff began to retrace his steps, holding the hand of one of his faithful subahdars. 'The subahdar was repeatedly warned to leave him unless he wished to share his fate. At length he did so and ran off towards his own hut.' After the subahdar had gone, one of the sepoys crowding round Shirreff said to another – alluding, it was supposed. to an oath they had taken not even to spare their own families if their religion was endangered – 'Don't you see your father before you? Shoot him!' The sepoy fired immediately, and, as Shirreff fell to the ground, other sepoys also discharged their muskets at him. Two British sergeants who had come into the lines to the Major's assistance were shot as they ran away.[56]

Soon it sounded, so another officer's wife recorded, 'as if the fiends of hell had been let loose. There were noises of burning houses, breaking open boxes, smashing windows and china . . . the striking of gongs . . . the throwing down of doors.'[57] The European men were hunted down and fourteen of them were killed, including the surgeon and the chaplain.

Mrs Stewart [wife of a captain in the artillery] got into a buggy with her children, and Mrs Hawkins [wife of Captain Hawkins, also an artillery officer], who had had a baby only two days before, was carried away on a bed – her children by her side, and a sergeant's wife carrying the baby [so Mrs Shirreff was told by a friend of her husband]. In this way they might have escaped, but Captain Hawkins, who had always said that in the event of a mutiny he would put himself and his family under the protection of his men, insisted upon their returning . . . They were met by some men of the 4th Regiment who told Captain Hawkins to get off his horse. On his hesitating they pulled him off. He remonstrated with them, asking why they should kill him. Mrs Stewart [whose husband had been badly wounded in the neck] jumped out of the buggy and threw her arms round Captain Hawkins. Two shots were fired and they both fell dead. Then Mrs Hawkins's baby and the nurse were killed. Then two of Mrs Stewart's children. Then another of Mrs Hawkins's children, then another afterwards . . . Poor Stewart in the meantime lay wounded till the morning when some men came up and he asked them about his wife and family. They told him that they were all killed. He said, 'Then you had better kill me, too', upon which he was shot.[58]

Mrs Stewart was one of the few women to be killed. For the sepoys at Gwalior said 'they had only to kill the men, not the memsahibs'.

Mrs Murray, wife of Captain Murray of the 4th Infantry, and Mrs Meade, wife of Captain Meade of Meade's Irregular Cavalry, escaped with their children across the Morar River, wading through the water to the Maharajah's palace where 'his Highness was sitting on the ground, with a number of his sirdars, by the light of a tall native lamp. It was a strange sight; the garden full of his Highness's cavalry and artillery; the alarmed looks of the people, including the Maharajah who . . . wrung his hands in despair.'[59]

Mrs Webb, a sergeant's pregnant wife, hid in an empty house for the night with her husband, her father and her stepmother. She was only seventeen years old but she already had a child of three who was also with her. At dawn a group of sepoys appeared outside the house shouting to them to come out. 'I was the first and my stepmother the next to come out,' Mrs Webb recorded. 'Then my husband stepped out, throwing off his coat and waistcoat, and stood in his shirt-sleeves facing the crowd . . . and last of all came my dear old father. After a few moments a shot was fired. This struck my husband in the shoulder; then another struck him full in the chest, and he fell back dead. The next shot was well aimed, for it struck my father in the heart.'

'Speechless with horror and petrified with grief,' Mrs Webb gazed down upon her dead husband and father, as the crowd silently approached. Abruptly coming to her senses, she picked up her child and, followed by her stepmother, began to walk away quickly down the road towards the telegraph office. The crowd, still silent, made no move to detain her. Outside the telegraph office men were cutting the wires and pulling down the poles. By the steps lay the corpse of an official of the Commissioner's Office.

The sight of it quickened our footsteps [Mrs Webb remembered], and a cowering desire to hide came over me. Awful fear had taken hold of me . . . For a time I forgot my dead in thoughts of safety. On the way we had to wade through a stream and I forgot to remove my shoes, and they remained embedded in the mud. I had to walk bare-footed. The heat was at its height . . . A village *chokidar* met us and offered to show us the way to the [Maharajah's palace]. He took us through bypaths and fields where we fortunately met a vegetable woman whom I had known and often dealt with. After a few questions, she turned sharply to the *chokidar* and said, 'Why are you taking them the wrong way? Come with me.'

We seemed to have travelled miles when we arrived near a large well, surrounded by natives drawing water. We got a drink there. It might have been ten or eleven o'clock. While standing there some mutinous *sowars* rode up and questioned us, 'Where are the Sahibs?' I replied,

'Killed.' And they turned in the direction they had come from. The poor vegetable woman had disappeared also – through fear I suppose. We hastened to go on . . . Not a native addressed us. At last we saw we were approaching Scindia's palace.

At the palace they waited with other women and children for the bullock carts which were to take them on to Agra. After two hours' delay the carts arrived, and they moved on again. On the second day of the journey they were joined by Mrs Quick, 'an enormous woman', wife of a staff-sergeant. 'When questioned about her husband she merely replied that she had not seen him for some hours before the outbreak. The fact was that he had deserted her and fled to Agra days before. The sepoys were good to her and sent her to join us.'

The convoy got as far as the Chambal River where the bullock drivers returned to Gwalior and the women and children climbed into the ferry boat. The boatmen rowed steadily for a time, but then they all jumped out and began pulling at the plugs to sink the boats. The women, beating them off with the oars, contrived to get the boat into water shallow enough to wade through. They reached the far bank and trudged on, through burning sands under a scorching sun. Mrs Quick's face turned black and she fell down unconscious. Some of the other women opened her dress, finding a tin box of jewellery hanging round her neck as well as a box of bank receipts and a quantity of silver spoons. They did their best to revive her; but it was too late to save her. She died just before some elephants arrived, sent by the Maharajah to take them on to the safety of the fort at Agra.[60]

Also making for Agra was Mark Thornhill, Magistrate of Muttra, who had an extraordinary and revealing story to relate.

7

A Magistrate in Rajputana

Adventures of Mark Thornhill, magistrate of Muttra · looting of the Treasury at Muttra, 30 May 1857 · mutiny of the Bhurtpore army, 31 May · Thornhill's attempts to restore order at Muttra and surrounding villages · mutiny of his forces · his retreat to Agra ·

Mark Thornhill's district of Muttra adjoined the state of Bhurtpore whose territories had been taken over by the British Government on the death of the Rajah until his son came of age.[1] Captain Nixon, one of the British Agent's assistants in Bhurtpore, had proposed making use of the young Rajah's army to help suppress the mutineers and had been authorized to march it to Delhi by way of Muttra. On its arrival in Muttra, Thornhill was not impressed by its appearance. The men's uniforms of swallow-tailed coats and black caps were of a pattern not seen since the beginning of the century. They wore dhoties instead of trousers; their shoes looked like slippers. Their weapons were as antiquated as their clothes, their muskets having flint locks and their cannon, all of a different size, being mounted on carriages which would have fallen to pieces had it not been for the ropes coiled round their wheels. The men all looked dirty and marched – or ambled – along with no attempt to keep in step.

The army command was composed of various chiefs, none of whom was prepared to take orders from any other and all of whom held civil appointments in the Rajah's administration as well as military ones in his army. They were all related to him in some way and, although punctiliously polite to each other at durbars, were constantly quarrelling in private, particularly over the disparate salaries which the Rajah allowed them. Durbars had to be held regularly because Captain Nixon could issue no orders without the approval of the leading chiefs who had in turn to consult those less exalted. Hours would, therefore, be spent in discussions which, as often as not, ended without any firm decision being made. Thornhill attended one durbar held under an immense canopy erected in front of the state tent. Chairs were arranged in a semi-circle, Captain Nixon sitting in the centre with two men wielding silver-handled fans behind him, the British officials occupying the seats on his right, the chiefs on his left. Nothing of importance was discussed, most of the time being spent in offering and accepting compliments. Thornhill's attention was largely directed towards the behaviour of two exceptionally fat chiefs sharing a single chair into which one would endeavour to settle himself more comfortably while the other, obliged to lean forward when addressed, was temporarily incapable of resisting his encroachments.

The Bhurtpore army chiefs, from the beginning most unwilling to march against the rebels, became increasingly reluctant to proceed farther once their men had shambled out of Muttra. Reasons were constantly given for the necessity of an immediate return to Bhurtpore, it even being alleged that the army was in imminent danger of dying of thirst as all the wells had run dry – until Thornhill discovered that the real trouble was that the soldiers had refused to draw water, insisting that the villagers must do it for them. After many halts and false starts, the chiefs grudgingly agreed to move on again when assured that large reinforcements were on the way from the army of the Rajah of Ulwar. These reinforcements did arrive but they were immediately followed by the news that the sepoy guard at the Treasury in Muttra had mutinied.

The Treasury at Muttra contained over half a million silver rupees and about £10,000 worth of copper coins. Doubtful of the integrity of the guard, Thornhill had more than once requested permission to send this treasure in to Agra; and, in anticipation of being given authority to do so, he had had the money packed in boxes and had collected carts for their conveyance. Thornhill's requests had at first been ignored; and when at length permission had arrived for him to move the treasure it was too late. The officer in charge of the transport party, Lieutenant Burlton, had given the order for the bullock carts to move off; but the native officer had stood his ground and asked him insolently, 'Where?'

'To Agra, of course.'

'No, no, not to Agra,' the native officer had shouted back, turning to the guard. 'To Delhi!'

'You traitor!' cried Burlton; but no sooner were the words out of his mouth than he fell dead, shot through the heart by a sepoy who had crept up behind him and discharged his musket into his back. This was the signal for the guard to break their ranks and rush into the office, firing their muskets and forcing the Europeans and Eurasians inside to leap through the open windows, jump off the veranda and run for their lives across the office grounds towards a belt of trees at the end of the garden. The sepoys then set fire to the building and marched off with the treasure towards Delhi, throwing handfuls of copper coins to the crowds of onlookers who had gathered to watch the exciting proceedings, pausing on their way to release the prisoners from the gaol and to set fire to the nearby house of a retired English sergeant.

After their departure a mob of city badmashes, rowdy villagers and convicts rushed into the still burning Treasury where they discovered some silver and copper coins that had been overlooked by the sepoys. Quarrelling over possession of these, they fell to blows with swords and clubs; several of them were killed while others were injured by falling roof beams and masonry. Undeterred, the mob then ransacked the room in which the records of the Treasury were stored on stone shelves, tearing up documents, scattering papers in every direction, throwing them on to the smouldering embers, displaying their utter detestation of the alien tax-gatherers. Having disposed of the Treasury, they then turned to the *Firinghis'* houses, plundering and smashing in a process of loot and destruction which had now become only too familiar. They would then have attacked the city of Muttra itself had not the news reached them that the Magistrate was returning with a large force of English soldiers, an ill-founded rumour which sent them scuttling off to their homes where much of the property which they had plundered was hurriedly hidden in straw stacks and dry wells.

Hearing of the mutiny of the sepoy guard at Muttra, the Bhurtpore army decided to follow its example. Taking their antiquated weapons with them, they wandered back to their homes. The British officers and officials with the army decided to continue the march to Delhi; but Thornhill thought that he ought now to try to return to his district. So, accompanied by Joyce, the head clerk, and a small native escort, he retraced his steps to Muttra.

It was a hazardous, exhausting journey. They kept to the by-lanes, avoiding villages by riding across the fields, their horses negotiating with difficulty the steep banks of the water-courses and at night stumbling in the deep ruts of the sandy paths, clouds of dust blotting out the stars. Although the air resounded with the firing of matchlocks, one village arousing another, the countryside was deserted; the *kadam* trees by the banks of the black mud lakes had 'an aspect of decay that would fit them for the margin of the Styx'. Occasionally they were obliged to pass close to a village whose inhabitants, armed with clubs and spears, would gaze at them in menacing defiance over the mud walls. Once they were fired on and chased by a mob brandishing sticks. Passing at night through the streets of the town of Raal, the puggrees round their hats twisted into turbans, they were challenged more than once; but their native escort concluded their replies with the customary invocations to the sacred river, 'Glory to the Ganges! Holy Ganges!', and they were allowed to proceed. It was the festival of *Dasehra;* and the streets were, in contrast to those of the unfriendly villages, full of gaily attired people and lit by a profusion of little lamps and the glow of fires from ovens cooking sweetmeats. They moved in the shadows and, unmolested, reached the far side of the town and the road to Muttra.

On the outskirts of Muttra the black form of a watchman loomed out of the darkness on the top of his mound. He told them that the sepoy guard, having looted the Treasury, had marched out of the town without doing any further damage apart from setting fire to the house of the Baptist missionary. At this news the remaining members of the native escort, who had been growing more and more surly every hour, threatening to desert as the rest had done, became more respectful, believing that, as the mutineers had gone, the English might soon come back.

Yet the closer Thornhill approached the town the more alarming its appearance became. The hedge, erected by the customs to impede the smuggling of salt and opium, appeared to be on fire; and through the trees they could see cascades of flying sparks which suggested to Thornhill the idea of burning rafters. Two men from the escort, sent ahead to reconnoitre Thornhill's house, returned to report that the doors and windows had been torn out and the contents ransacked. The servants had fled and the gardens were strewn with fragments of clothes and pieces of broken furniture. All the other houses of Europeans had been similarly plundered; and of some nothing was left but bare walls blackened by smoke.

Thornhill and Joyce made their way to the house of the Seths, rich bankers who, if only from self-interest, might be expected to favour a return to order under British rule. The street leading up to the house was barricaded and guarded by men hired to keep off the mob. But the two Englishmen were allowed to pass and were admitted to the vast mansion. It was a comfortless place to European eyes for, despite its immense size and palatial exterior, it was little more than a huge collection of small rooms overlooking courtyards and almost entirely empty of furniture. Apart from curtains and awnings there were no decorations to be seen, nor any pictures, nor any books other than the first volume of a magnificent manuscript of the Koran, each letter bordered in gold, once the property of a Muslim prince from whom it had been stolen in some long-forgotten war. But the Seths' horde of jewels and precious metals appeared limitless. Their vaults were filled with gold and silver; their women, who were kept in strict seclusion, could occasionally be glimpsed wearing emerald necklaces, each stone the size of a large marble; their cupboards and chests were filled with huge pearls, rubies and diamonds, one of which measured an inch and a half across.

The meal provided by the Seths for their visitors was as disappointing as their house. It consisted of rice and chupatties saturated with oil and warm milk which, simmered over an open fire, had acquired in the process 'an overpowering flavour of smoke'. Later 'they procured us some tea, very bad', Thornhill recorded, 'and an immense tea-pot of solid silver, but the establishment did not contain a kettle, and we had to make the tea with some water brought up in a brass bowl'. Anxious to make amends for their inability to entertain European visitors, the hosts sent out for china and cutlery from a local shop, while their manager gave an account of recent happenings in the town, though, in strict conformity with Indian etiquette, leaving the communication of details to his subordinates.

Early the next morning Thornhill and Joyce, accompanied by a party of horsemen, drove off to their former office. As they drew near it they found the road thickly littered with fragments of paper which prepared them for the shock of discovering that nothing was left of the building but the bare black walls which were scored with the marks of pickaxes and crowbars. The floors were covered with the charred remains of the fallen roof. In a ditch at the end of the grounds they discovered the skeleton of Lieutenant Burlton. A dog, heedless of their approach, continued to gnaw at the bones until, pelted with clods of earth, it slunk away, snarling and baring its teeth. It had not yet touched the hands which were still intact at the end of the upraised, fleshless arms, giving to the skeleton 'an air of ghastly masquerade'. Having buried the body, the two Englishmen climbed back into the carriage and drove around the station, appalled by the scenes of desolation on every side, the blackened walls, the charred remains of wood and thatch, the broken furniture and smashed china and glass, the scraps of clothing lying amidst the bright flowers of the gardens, the shattered pews and pulpit outside the church, the splintered door frames on the cracked pavements.

On returning to the Seths' house, Thornhill was pleased to find that their hosts had done all they could to make it more comfortable for their guests. A large room had been prepared for them; servants had been dispatched to procure tablecloths, knives and forks, china plates and tea-cups. Instead of the oil-drenched chupatties of the night before, there were eggs for breakfast with fish and rice.

When the table had been cleared, Thornhill sat down to write some letters; but he had no sooner started work than he was disturbed by the sound of a great commotion outside, by the shouts of running men and the firing of matchlocks. Seizing his gun he dashed out on to the terrace which was already filled with servants looking down across the river. On the far bank were crowds of villagers, waving their arms and crying out for help against the inhabitants of a larger village who were, at that very moment, attacking them. Little reassured by Thornhill's shouted promise that, although he could do nothing to help them at the moment, he would punish their assailants as soon as order was restored, the villagers remained on the bank, renewing their cries for assistance until a great pyramid of flame from behind the trees beyond them announced the burning of their plundered homes.

Having lost all authority outside the city, Thornhill was now, so the Seths warned him, in danger of losing his life inside it. They begged him not to leave the house again, for he would certainly be murdered if he did. Indeed, his very presence was a danger to them all, as they had been warned that if the Englishmen remained in their house any longer it would be burned to the ground. Disregarding their pleas, Thornhill decided that it would be 'better to meet the danger than to live in constant apprehension of it'. So, towards sunset each evening, he and Joyce made it their practice to drive out into the streets, their guns in their hands and at full cock. The crowds in the streets were 'nearly all armed' and 'very disrespectful', but no attempt was made to attack them.

An attempt was made, however, to burn down the Seths' house by throwing a fireball into a courtyard used for storing timber and straw. Convinced by this that he must immediately take measures both to protect the city from outside attacks and to make his authority respected within it, Thornhill summoned a meeting of the principal inhabitants. All those who were summoned came. They were shown up to the terrace, made their salaams to Thornhill and Joyce who were seated at one end under a canopy, then sat cross-legged on the white cloth which had been spread over the stone floor. They all pledged their loyalty to the Government. But after they had gone Thornhill heard that some of them dispatched letters to the King of Delhi informing him of the unprotected state of the city and suggesting that his Majesty should send troops to take possession of it.

For the moment, though, there was the more immediate danger that the villagers from the surrounding districts would fulfil their threat of attacking and plundering the city. As anxious as Thornhill to prevent this, the leading inhabitants, who had previously taken precautions only to defend their own houses, reluctantly agreed to find men to defend the gates in their respective districts and to lend their support to the enlistment of additional policemen with whose help Thornhill was able to disarm the city mob. Having secured the city as best he could, Thornhill decided to overawe the unruly villages beyond the walls by marching out with whatever men he could collect for such a purpose. He hoped that by burning down those villages that seemed least able to resist him he might intimidate others which he thought it 'prudent to avoid'. Provoked by this, however, several villages joined forces under the leadership of one Debi Singh, who assumed the title of Rajah, took to wearing a yellow dress, among Hindus a symbol of royalty, and assembled a force which it was beyond the power of Thornhill to subdue.

At this time there arrived in Muttra an English officer with a small force of loyal native troops; and with these reinforcements Thornhill felt strong enough to attack Debi Singh who was captured as he ran for hiding in a field of sugar cane. With his capture order was restored to the immediate area. But elsewhere there was anarchy; and Thornhill, as he moved from village to village with his small native army, began to realize that the real condition of the country was

very different from what it was supposed to be by [his superiors] at Agra ... Village fought against village ... caste against caste ... The distant villages set the English government at open defiance; the nearer ones, afraid of our cannon, were more cautious in expressing their feelings. They were profuse, indeed, in their declarations of loyalty, and avoided all acts of open disobedience, but they persistently evaded the payment of their revenues. It was the belief of the government, and also of the English generally that the natives were attached to our rule; and more-over that, weary of the present anarchy, they longed for the re-establishment of order. My present experience did not confirm this belief. No one regretted the loss of our rule; and, with the exception of the *baniyas* who suffered by it, all classes enjoyed the confusion.

One wealthy landowner told Thornhill that the recent few weeks had been the happiest of his life. He had gone about in state and done exactly as he liked, punishing those whom he wished to punish, rewarding those who had pleased him. He had not objected to the English Government at first; but lately it had meddled in everything and upset all his people's ancient customs. 'Besides,' he added, 'what with the heavy land revenue, the school rates, and all the other new cesses, taxation had become pretty well unbearable.'

The peasants on his land were inclined to agree with him. Thornhill noted that they

voluntarily returned to that condition of semi-serfdom from which it was the especial boast of our Government that it had freed them. At the same time there was re-established suttee, domestic slavery, and all those other barbarous customs, the abolition of which we had justly regarded as the chief glory of our rule, and as our best title to the gratitude of the people. It was evident that in its most humane and philanthropic efforts our Government had not been in harmony with the sentiments of the country.

Thornhill himself confessed that he could to a certain extent enter into the feelings of the people. He derived a perverse pleasure from contemplating the change in the appearance of the countryside which had reverted to the wild picturesqueness associated with the feudal ages, with fortifications in every village, and grandees resuming their ancient state and surrounding themselves with troops of attendants and hosts of armed retainers, with cavalcades of horses and gaily caparisoned camels, with crowds of followers carrying swords and spears and clothed as though for a carnival. But now and then Thornhill would come across a corpse lying in a mango grove or thrown down a well, and he would recognize the darker side of this renascent India; and, recalled to his duty as Magistrate of Muttra, he would be brought once more to face the terrible problems that confronted him, the impossibility of placing implicit trust in the ragged army that was his sole instrument of authority.

This army, the so-called Kotah Contingent, had been sent from Agra to Muttra, ostensibly to restore order, but in reality because the officials at Agra were far from convinced of its loyalty. Watching it on the march, Thornhill also could not but wonder how long it would obey the orders of Captain Dennys, its English commander.

Dennys rode with the advance guard; behind him came the cavalry in their loose scarlet coats and white turbans; these were followed by the infantry, trudging along in uniforms of a British pattern but with dhoties wrapped around their loins beneath the thick material of their awkwardly bulging trousers. Then came the artillery, consisting of two guns, each mounted on a dark blue carriage drawn by six horses and followed by other similar carriages filled with ammunition on which sat glum native artillerymen in uniforms of the same drab colour as the carts. Behind the carts were more infantry, then a long line of camels laden with tents and sacks, trunks and cooking pots, each animal connected to the next by a cord linking the nostrils of the one to the tail of the other. It was insufferably hot, the wind blowing as though from the mouth of a furnace, the clouds of dust so thick that the sky was obscured and even the trees by the roadside were but dimly visible. To protect themselves from the fiery wind, the men enveloped their heads in the wrapping of their enormous turbans, thus giving themselves, so Thornhill thought, the appearance of wanderers through some Arctic waste.

Reposing little confidence in this surly column, Thornhill was not in the least dismayed when he learned that it had been recalled to Agra. Nor was he surprised to learn that soon after its arrival there it had mutinied. Nor yet was he comforted by a troop of cavalry sent as replacements which arrived as he was asleep in bed and which woke him up by firing pistols in the air. This troop also soon mutinied. So, left without any means of supporting his authority, he decided to leave for the fort at Agra which after a perilous night ride he reached in safety, passing on his way lines of silent men in clanking chains, looming out of the darkness like phantoms from another world, some of the five thousand prisoners released from the Agra gaol.

8

Agra and Calcutta

Nowhere in India are there more fine examples of Moghul architecture than in Agra, the city on the Jumna, 140 miles south of Delhi, where stand the mausoleum built by the beautiful Empress, Nur Mahal, for the body of her father; the domes and minarets of the Taj Mahal; and the pinnacles and turrets of the marble palace of Shah Jahan. This massive fortified palace towers above one of the ravines which have been scored by centuries of rain into the bank of the river. Its walls and gateways were erected in what is known in the West as the sixteenth century by the Moghul Emperor, Akbar. Its interior buildings, constructed a century later, are mostly the work of his grandson, Shah Jahan, who raised the nearby Taj Mahal as a memorial to his beloved wife. From the river the defences, battlements, embrasures and projecting bastions rise, tier upon tier, to protect the immense red sandstone wall of the fort whose outline is varied by lofty towers and turrets and whose summit is crowned with pavilions of white marble and with roofs and cupolas of burnished gold. The upper part of the sandstone wall is pierced by windows behind which are dark and winding staircases, gloomy vaults and narrow passages. Above them are the courtyards and summer houses, the pavilions, the labyrinthine warren of gardens, cloisters, cells, storehouses, offices, barracks, mosaic-floored courts, imposing halls and mean hovels that compose the vast and intricate plan of a Moghul palace.

Most of the Europeans in Agra had expected John Russell Colvin, the Lieutenant-Governor of the North-Western Provinces whose offices were in Agra, to order a withdrawal of the Christian population to the fort as soon as news was received of the uprising at

Meerut. This, indeed, was what Colvin had first intended to do. But, though a brave and capable man, he was neither self-reliant nor decisive. Conscientious and kind, he had been considered an excellent administrator in times of peace; but when the crisis came he looked to other men to guide him and gave way to the most commanding. At a special meeting of Europeans called the day after the massacre at Delhi, he appeared quite incapable of controlling the noisy assembly as men voiced opposing views, and officers who had not been asked to the meeting burst into the room to offer their advice. The general feeling was that it would be a sign of weakness to withdraw to the fort: the outbreaks of mutiny were merely localized military revolts, the rural disturbances the work of irresponsible mobs. Their own servants remained for the moment obedient and deferential. So they imagined the rest of the population, apart from a few troublemakers, would also stay quiet.[1]

The leading advocate of their views was Robert Drummond, Magistrate at Agra, an energetic, resolute man, stubborn, unpopular and overbearing. He argued that it would be folly to exhibit any sign of fear. The population of Agra could effectively be overawed by the British going quietly about their business as though nothing unusual had occurred elsewhere. The police might be increased, and a corps of volunteers might be raised; but any further action would defeat its own purpose.[2]

Colvin gave way, evidently persuaded that Drummond was right. He sent several telegrams to Calcutta, assuring the Governor-General's office that the troubles in the North-Western Provinces would soon be over, and contented himself for the time being with holding a parade of the British and native troops at Agra. The parade was not a success. Colvin first addressed the British troops, exhorting them not to distrust their native comrades but at the same time reminding them of the Delhi massacre, which naturally inclined them to distrust them all the more. Turning to the sepoys he assured them of his confidence in their loyalty which prompted their officers to call for a cheer. The sepoys responded by uttering a yell and 'looked with a devilish scowl at the Europeans'.[3] The confidence which their officers reposed in their loyalty was, however, by no means shaken. And when Lieutenant Henry Henderson, Assistant Executive Engineer of Agra, presumed to express doubts about the dependability of the native infantry there he caused an uproar in the mess of the 44th. The Colonel turned on him 'in an awful rage" telling him 'he had a great mind' to put him under arrest.[4]

Despite their confidence, real or assumed, that the disturbances would soon be over, the British at Agra could not but feel concern when inexplicable fires kept breaking out in the city and rumours spread of the secret meetings of conspirators. On 23 May, after reports had been received of the mutiny of the 9th Native Infantry, panic seized the British and native Christian communities. Carts, packed with furniture and women and children, raced towards the fort; people rushed through the streets, shouting that the mutineers were crossing the bridge. Edith Sharpley, the ten-year-old daughter of an army officer – who, with her two sisters, was living with an older brother and a cousin at Agra so that she could attend a school there kept by an American couple – was standing on a bench in a classroom at the school, pointing out places on a map, when 'suddenly there were rapid footsteps and several gentlemen, all armed' burst into the room. Her cousin was among them. He picked Edith up, called for her two elder sisters to follow and ran from the room. On the way home

we encountered a native who appeared to be a Hindu priest running towards us [Edith recalled years later]. His long flowing hair was covered with ashes and flying loose all over his body. He was shouting curses on the Europeans and brandishing a naked sword. As soon as my cousin saw him he put me down on the ground and told us three sisters to get behind him. He then drew his own sword and we all walked forward. The priest walked by, pretending not to see us.

After this the Europeans in Agra moved at night into those houses which were the most defensible. 'We were all drilled in various ways,' Edith Sharpley said. 'Every woman had to learn how to load muskets. The children were taught to get the caps, powder and bullets to take to the women when they wanted them.' They had dinner at five o'clock so that the servants could get home before dark. One evening after dinner a native on horseback rode up to the high wall of the garden where Edith and her sisters were playing, pointed a revolver over it and fired a shot. The men in the house chased after him, but he escaped.[5]

Despite the growing alarm in Agra and the spreading mutinies outside it, Robert Drummond continued to insist that there must be no rush to the fort; the British must display to the natives a calm and confident bearing. He proposed to Colvin that the native regiments at Agra should be disarmed as a precaution; and this was done. But when Colonel Fraser, the bluff but kindly Chief Engineer, suggested that women and children should be removed to the fort together with the valuable property of private individuals and the Government, Drummond persuaded Colvin to turn the suggestion down.[6] Mrs Vansittart – whose husband considered 'this rebellion much more serious than the generality of people' but was reluctant to say so as it would only have caused him 'to be run down as an alarmist' – considered the senior officials and army officers at Agra to be 'nincompoops', almost to a man. Colonel Fraser appeared at meetings 'looking gloomy, stupid and cross'; Brigadier Polwhele, the senior army officer, brave though incompetent, was a 'silly, scatterbrained old man'; while as for 'silly Mr Colvin', he was 'frightened' and 'panic-stricken', 'ridiculed by the natives and not respected by the Europeans'. 'Safe himself in Government House', he left 'everybody else in danger'.[7]

Colvin, in fact, was nearing breakdown; and at the beginning of July, after the threatened approach of mutineers had led him at last to authorize the removal of the women and children to the fort, he was obliged temporarily to hand over the Government to a provisional Council. The Council unfortunately was no more effective than Colvin had been. Brigadier Polwhele, its senior member, was urged to take his men out to attack the approaching mutineers. Polwhele did not consider his force strong enough to do so. Persuaded to change his mind, he led his men out to Sacheta where, the force opposed to him being far too large for him to disperse, he was obliged to retreat to Agra under heavy, well-directed fire, pursued by enemy cavalry.

The soldiers returned to the fort, exhausted, dirty, angry, humiliated, and in many cases wounded. 'We all crowded round them with glasses of water which they eagerly drank,' Edith Sharpley remembered. 'An officer caught me up in his arms, saying, "You are far too small a little girl to do this work. You will be trampled on." Then he carried me to where the water was kept and made me stand there.'[8]

Everyone in the fort was utterly dispirited, except apparently Brigadier Polwhele, who came back 'quite unconcerned at the humiliation his arms had sustained, repaired to his comfortable quarters, ate his dinner, and, quite satisfied that he had thoroughly performed his duty, went to bed'.[9]

While he slept mobs roamed through his former cantonments, burning bungalows and destroying the property which had so ill-advisedly been left in them. At the same time badmashes ran through the city, murdering every Christian who had not fled to the fort with one exception – an eccentric, drunken Eurasian clerk from the Accountants' office who, without surprise or alarm, welcomed the mob warmly into his house, offered them all a drink, then joined them in smashing up his own furniture.[10]

When Mark Thornhill, the Magistrate from Muttra, arrived at Agra with Joyce, his head clerk, he was kept waiting for a long time beneath the high wall of the fort in the darkness and pouring rain, before anyone would let him in. Joyce's shouts were answered by the sleepy voice of a man who told them it was against the rules to open the gates at night: they would have to wait outside until dawn. Thornhill then called up, asking for his brother, who was somewhere inside the fort, to be woken up and told that Mark was here. Minute after minute passed before the brother, whose quarters were on the far side of the fort, could be found. Eventually he appeared to say that the main gate could not be opened. They would have to go round to the south side. After a time they found the entrance there and were admitted into a large, untidy enclosure full of surly British soldiers, who looked as though they had not slept for days, and some other Europeans, not in uniform and equally unwelcoming, who peered at the newcomers suspiciously.

Thornhill's brother congratulated them on their safe arrival and told them to dismount as horses were not allowed within the defences. Leaving their horses tied to stakes in the enclosure, they walked towards the great gateway. Passing over a bridge and through a maze of courts, passages, archways and tunnels, they entered at last 'what seemed the courtyard of a castle, but a castle only elsewhere to be seen in dreams or read of in fairy tales'. Lofty walls enclosed it; galleries supported by slender columns ran around it; towers and windows, balconies and small cupolas of white marble loomed above it. Leaving this courtyard through a tall stone arch, they were taken into a long tunnel which led on to a steeply inclined stone ramp that, in turn, took them out on to a large open space surrounded by low buildings of intricately carved stone. Passing through yet another archway, Thornhill entered a garden shaded by trees of the thickest foliage and crossed by paths of shining white stone. In the middle of the garden was a huge marble basin filled with water. Terraces and pavilions of the same brilliant whiteness, topped by gilded cupolas and golden domes, surrounded it on every side. The sun had just risen; the gold shone; the marble glistened. It seemed to Thornhill 'like a scene from the *Arabian Nights*'. Behind a curtained door-way, his wife and children were waiting to welcome him.[11]

Thornhill soon discovered, however, that conditions in the fort were far less peaceful and comfortable than his first impressions of the beautiful palace had led him to hope. It was excessively crowded, over six thousand people having taken shelter there, soldiers, civilian officials and their families, native servants, half-castes, Italian monks, nuns, Swiss missionaries, American salesmen, even rope-dancers and acrobats from a travelling French circus.[12] Edith Sharpley was shar-ing a tiny room with three other girls and her mother. There was no window, so permission was obtained to knock a hole in the wall which was discovered to be seven feet thick. Later, Edith's married sister and her baby came to share the room as the cubby-hole where they had been sleeping had been filled with bricks to support the cannon on the roof above.[13] The Thornhills' small room contained not only the families of both brothers and the children's ayahs but also so much furniture that there was scarcely space to move. So, clearing the jumble of boxes and bedsteads from the small room above it, Thornhill decided to occupy that; and, having done so, went in search of water to wash. He found a well, but there was no bucket. Wandering off in search of one, he came upon an English sergeant standing by a cart full of large tin cans such as those sup-plied to soldiers. He asked the sergeant who could give him permis-sion to buy one. The sergeant did not know, and added with a genial smile that in Thornhill's place he would not waste time finding out. Thornhill took the hint and helped himself to two tins from the cart which, next time he passed it, was quite empty.[14]

Soon after Thornhill's return to his family's cramped room there was a sound of firing followed by a man rushing past with the alarming news that the fort was being attacked and that everyone was to assemble on the ramparts. Thornhill and his brother seized their guns and rushed out; but on reaching the ramparts and peering through the loopholes of the high battlements they could see nothing more than pleasant views of the distant countryside. Dashing off to a nearby bastion, they climbed out on to an embrasure from which they could look down into the enclosure beneath, where a crowd of English soldiers and civilians were shooting between the stakes into the ravine beyond. The enemy, it was said, lay concealed there, pre-paring to assault the fort. The fire was not returned, however. The ravine displayed no signs of life. And before long it became clear that the men were firing not at mutinous sepoys but at a donkey grazing in a hollow and at a flock of vultures gorging themselves on the carcasses of dead sheep. Despite the rattle of musketry fire and the shouts of the musketeers, neither the donkey nor the vultures were in the least disturbed. For the shots went nowhere near them, a circumstance explained by an emissary from the enclosure who told the puzzled spectators on the bastion above that the soldiers and their companions were all extremely drunk. 'Presently an order came from the General to stop the firing. It did not receive much attention. Those who were tired of the amusement, left off. The rest continued it till the afternoon.'[15]

Breakfast for the Thornhills that morning consisted of no more than a little rice and lentils and a small piece of cold meat. But even this frugal meal sadly depleted the small store which the Thornhills had been able to bring into the fort with them. Through the kindness of a family in a neighbouring room, who had managed to bring in a bag of flour, subsequent meals were made rather more substantial by the addition of unleavened cakes. Yet it was some time before a central supply of food was organized; for there appeared to be little sign of any competent authority in the fort.

The notification that rations would be available in the fort was announced by a native orderly who did not divulge, or perhaps did not know, where the issue would take place. After traversing a vast number of courts and lanes which took him to the far side of the fort, Thornhill came upon a large building outside which sat an English officer who asked each arrival the number of his dependents and then issued him with an order for the appropriate amount of rice, flour, sugar and lentils. Inside the building several grain-sellers sat before the heaps of provisions which they weighed out laboriously on small wooden scales, accompanying the operation with a droning chant which Thornhill, after his long night ride, found 'very soporific'.[16]

For the occupants of the fort, the days passed in acute discomfort. Heaps of rotting rubbish accumulated in the open spaces. In one courtyard there was a decomposing sheep which no one troubled to bury; in another a litter of carts and gun-carriages; in another piles of rubbish which the now heavy rains were washing into an open well. The nights were as suffocatingly hot as the days. Clothes drenched with sweat were hung up in the morning sun and within two minutes were as dry as the marble walls. In search of fresh air, people climbed to the roofs of the buildings to sit by the embrasures of the battlements. As darkness fell, flames could be discerned on the distant horizon where village fought against village and the homes of the vanquished were set on fire. Nearer the fort spurts of flame shot up from the cantonments showing that the destruction of the station was not yet complete.

There was no sign of the rebel army. But few of the Europeans had confidence that when it appeared the defences of the fort would be strong enough to resist it. Half the cannon were unmounted; the powder magazines had not been made bomb-proof; the stores of provisions were hopelessly inadequate to feed the thousands of people within the walls; no steps whatever had been taken to deal with the problems of sanitation, and already there had been two deaths from cholera. Even if the garrison survived hunger and disease it would remain in great danger from mining. For on the north side the houses of the city approached so close to the fort that the enemy might easily dig without being seen; and beneath the fort there were innumerable subterranean passages that were believed to extend under the ditch and to have exits in the city.[17]

To Thornhill it seemed that the authorities were 'paralysed. The gates were kept closed, the sentries mounted guard, and the other ordinary routine duties were performed. Beyond this, things were left to themselves; the works for defence were not pushed on, nor was the filth removed, nor any attempt made to ascertain the real position of the mutineer army.'[18]

There were constant disputes inside the fort about every conceivable subject on which it was possible to disagree, from the formation of a militia to the times of church services on Sundays. One of the fiercest disputes arose over the defences of the fort which were much weakened by the proximity of houses to the walls. These would provide ample shelter for assailants, and Colonel Fraser proposed that they should be demolished. Their owners, however, naturally objected and enlisted the sympathy of some of the higher civil officials, who accordingly opposed Fraser's plans. Sides were taken, and heated quarrels ensued. It was eventually agreed that the demolition should be carried out and that the owners would receive compensation, though not in money, since there was none, but in promissory notes, redeemable with interest on the restoration of order. This arrangement pleased no one. Why should these owners be promised compensation, complained the English residents and Christians of Agra whose houses had been destroyed by the mob, when they themselves had received none? The owners were equally resentful. How could they be sure that order ever would be restored and that their compensation would ever be paid? The complaints grew even more strident when, in order to placate the feelings of the Muslims in the city, it was proposed to spare a mosque in the very middle of the area to be blown up. In the end the mosque was destroyed; but the recently erected house of a commissariat contractor – 'a favourite with the military' – was, to the fury of the civilians, spared in all its pure whiteness among the grey rubble of the demolished suburb, a constant irritant to all the civilians in the fort.[19]

The discontent was increased by rumours, 'at first whispered, soon openly spoken, that, in real fact, of authorities there were none. Mr Colvin's mind, it was said, had given way, and the General become imbecile.' The reputation of the General was not enhanced when a group of natives presented themselves at the gate of the fort, explaining that they were servants of some of the English gentlemen inside and asking to be permitted to join their masters. On being recognized and admitted, they declared that the entire rebel army had marched away. They were not at first believed, and were accused of being spies. But soon afterwards others came, repeating the same story; and at length a column was sent out to reconnoitre. The officer in command returned to report that, after traversing the whole of the city and most of the cantonments, he had found not a trace of a single rebel. The fort at Agra had been guarding its gates against an imaginary enemy.[20]

Soon after this the General was relieved of his command. John Colvin sent for him, and, without divulging its contents, handed him a dispatch containing the order for his dismissal. The General took it with a friendly smile, 'not the least anticipating its contents. He read it, turned very pale, and appeared as if about to faint; he recovered himself, and behaved with much dignity. He rose, handed back the letter to Mr Colvin, bowed and left the room.'[21]

Colvin himself, however, was no more capable of dealing with the problems of the fort than the General had been. On receipt of an extraordinarily ill-timed letter from Calcutta, reprimanding him for his delay in sending the administration report for the previous year, he was so upset that instead of laying it aside to be answered at a more convenient time – if such a time should ever come – he demanded a full report to be prepared at once; and when this could not be done, because the records had all been burned, he began to dictate a complicated explanation. After a few sentences, though, 'he became confused, hesitated, then broke down altogether', pitiably aware that his once acute powers of exposition had now quite deserted him.[22]

Mark Thornhill had occasion to call upon him at about this time.

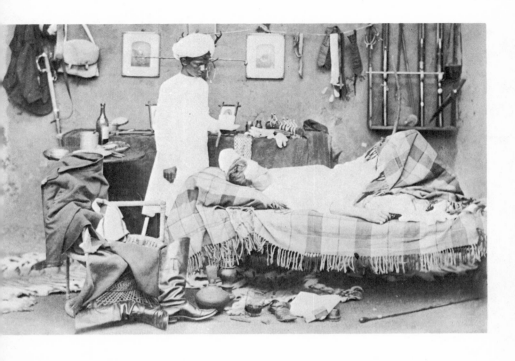

1. and 2. A British officer and his servants in his bungalow

3. Officers in camp
from a drawing by Captain G. F. Atkinson

4. Sepoys preparing for firing practice
from a drawing by Captain G. F. Atkinson

5. The wing of Government House, Calcutta,
which contained the Cannings' private apartments

6. Lord Canning

7. Sir Archdale Wilson

8. Officers returning to their regiment in a mail-cart
from a drawing by Captain G. F. Atkinson

9. The Red Fort, Delhi

10. The tree in Delhi beneath which the European
and Eurasian prisoners were massacred

11. A group of mutineers

12. Nana Sahib from J. W. Shepherd's
*Personal Narrative of the Outbreak
and Massacre at Cawnpore*

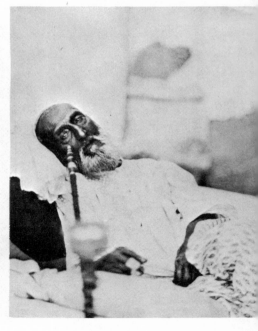

13. Bahadur Shah, King of Delhi

14. Sir James Outram

15. Sir Henry Havelock

16. Major-General James Neill

17. The remains of General Wheeler's entrenchment at Cawnpore
from a watercolour by Captain D. Sarsfield Greene, R.A.

18. The House of the Ladies at Cawnpore
a watercolour by Captain D. Sarsfield Greene, R.A.

He found him in a large hall overlooking the river. A servant drew aside one of the curtains that were hung before the arches of the colonnade. Thornhill stepped into a room half filled with furniture and books that lay piled in heaps on the floor and against the walls. Seated at the end of the room were three officers, one of whom rose to escort Thornhill into a hall with an arched roof and walls of enormous thickness. Speckles of sunlight, faintly tinged with blue from the sky above and the river beneath, filtered through the delicate marble tracery of the single window. In an armchair, surrounded by furniture and books which lay on the floor in the same confusion as in the outer room, sat Mr Colvin, his head bent over an open volume on the large table in front of him. The officer announced Thornhill's name. Thornhill approached the table. Colvin raised his head. Politely he asked his visitor to sit down, and asked what it was that Thornhill had come to tell him.

For some little while he listened attentively [Thornhill recorded], then gradually his eyes fell on the book before him, though he did not appear to be reading. When I had finished speaking he remained still in the same attitude, and so for some minutes we continued, Mr Colvin bending over his book, motionless as a figure of wax, I seated beside him. I had just quitted a noisy scene at one of the barracks, where the state of things in the fort had been angrily debated. After that noisy assemblage, the silence and stillness of this apartment were very impressive. No sound from without penetrated the massive walls, there was no movement within. The subdued light, the shadows in the deep recesses, added to the feeling of repose. Presently Mr Colvin raised his head – he seemed by an effort to collect his thoughts – and began to speak about the subject of my visit. That disposed of he chatted a little on ordinary topics, and I took my leave. At the doorway I turned to bow, and I saw that he had again bent over his book, and his attitude and features had assumed their former expression of weariness and abstraction.[23]

Since both the Lieutenant-Governor and the General were so obviously incapable of bringing order out of the chaos of the fort, Colonel Cotton took over the command; and gradually, under his direction and that of some equally energetic officers, conditions began to improve. Every room and cell in the fort was numbered, and its occupants listed; rations were more efficiently divided and distributed; defences were strengthened; rotas of duty set out; and an expedition was dispatched to Aligarh, a town forty miles from Agra on the road to Meerut.[24]

The British soldiers, many of them displaying symptoms of cholera, left the fort accompanied by several civilian volunteers in a fearful thunderstorm. On their way to Aligarh they were attacked by a band of Muslim fanatics.

When the Ghazees charged, an old mollah, or priest, sat by the bank chanting the Koran to encourage the warriors; as the combat thickened, his voice rose louder; at length he worked himself up into an ecstasy of fanaticism. He closed the volume, seized a sword, and exclaiming, 'I too will be a martyr!' he rushed on our soldiers, one of whom ran him through with his bayonet.[25]

The other fanatics were no more successful. They charged the British soldiers with the utmost desperation, shouting war cries and waving their swords above their heads. But nearly all of them were shot before they had delivered a single blow. It was an easy victory for the expeditionary force; yet when they returned to the fort at Agra little of importance had been achieved. Communications with Meerut had not been opened up; nor had the countryside been quietened; Europeans foolhardy enough to ride too far from the walls of the fort continued to be attacked by natives. Still, the fresh air had improved the soldiers' health. They returned to the fort 'looking a good deal less sickly than they had done when they left it'.[26]

Life at Agra now became rather like that on board ship during a long voyage. 'There was the same monotony, the same sociability, the same gossip and quarrelling.'[27] During the day, while the polished marble of the pavements reflected an almost blinding glare, millions of flies swarmed in the courtyards and buzzed against the screens of reed and thatch which were erected to exclude them from the small, stiflingly hot rooms. Overhead vast numbers of kites and vultures circled in great sweeping curves, ascending and descending in long spirals. It was said that these carrion birds 'possessed the instinct of approaching death'. At night swarms of fleas crawled and flitted out of the cracks in the masonry.[28]

Most people got up very early to go for a walk along the ramparts or, if they had horses or vehicles, to drive or ride outside the gates, though never venturing far afield. Few remained out after seven o'clock when the burning heat drove them indoors to spend another day in listless apathy, or, on Sundays, to attend a service 'in one of Akbar's fine audience halls'.[29] After dinner, the mats and curtains were rolled up from the windows, and as twilight began to fall, people emerged once more to stroll about in the courts and along the battlements, many of them, even the smallest children, wearing black mourning bands round their arms, looking down upon the river, so swollen by the rains it looked more like a broad, long lake, at the flat roofs of the dull-coloured houses in the city, the green expanse of grass and crops and groves of trees that stretched towards the horizon, and, amidst a shapeless mass of mouldering masonry and the ruins of ancient palaces, the magnificent white freshness of the Taj Mahal. It was over a mile away, yet the atmosphere was so clear at this time of day that every detail of its architecture was distinctly visible, the cupolas clustering around the central dome, the coloured mosaics adorning the marble walls, even the delicate marble traceries of the windows.

As darkness fell and the ayahs led the children away to bed, chairs and tables were brought out on to the terraces. Charcoal fires were lit, kettles put on to boil, and invitations were issued to guests who arrived bringing their own little packets of tea or, more rarely, sugar. Conversation was languid and intermittent. For long periods there was silence as the people, wondering what the future held, sat gazing at the beauty of the moonlight as it fell upon the dark trees and the white marble or, when there was no moon, at the lights thrown by the coloured lamps that stood upon each table. At nine o'clock a gun fired, and most took this as a signal to go to bed.[30]

If the soldiers and civilians in Agra had done little to convince the people of the North-Western Provinces that the British were capable of restoring their rule in India, the continuing determined and ruthless action of the officials in the Punjab had made a deep impression on the natives north of the Sutlej. As he rode down to the disarming of the sepoys at Peshawar, Herbert Edwardes noted that 'very few chiefs and yeomen of the country' attended him, and he remembered thinking that, to judge from their faces, 'they came to see which way the tide would turn. As we rode back friends were as thick as summer flies, and levies began from that moment to come in'.[31]

So many recruits were enlisted, in fact, that the Chief Commissioner was eventually able to raise 34,000 new troops, and to send to Delhi seven battalions of Punjabi infantry, three regiments of Punjabi cavalry, as well as a Punjabi corps of sappers and miners and two siege trains. Lawrence, feeling safe enough now in the Punjab, also dispatched to Delhi six battalions of European infantry, a regiment of European cavalry and a large force of European artillery. So persuaded was he, indeed, of the importance of recapturing Delhi that he even contemplated sending there the European troops at Peshawar and asking Dost Mahomed, the Amir of Afghanistan, to occupy the valley on the understanding that if he proved a faithful ally the territory should be ceded to him in perpetuity. This proposal horrified both Edwardes and Nicholson; and when the Governor-General was asked to consider it he agreed with Edwardes that if territory, no matter how distant, were to be abandoned at this stage, 'it would be impossible that faith in the permanency of our rule in India should not be shaken. The encouragement to join the league against us would be irresistible.'[32]

In Calcutta, Lord and Lady Canning were endeavouring to maintain an appearance of calm amongst people who behaved as though they were threatened with imminent slaughter. Lady Canning continued to take her evening drive with a small escort. Lord Canning, agreeing with his wife that they 'ought not to appear in a state of mourning for this temporary outbreak', insisted that the ball at Government House, customarily held on the Queen's birthday, should take place as usual and that the offer of the European guard of honour to remain in the basement until the festivities were over should not be accepted: no alteration would be made to the usual practice of leaving house and guests under the protection of Indian soldiers. As it happened the ball was 'a very fair one'. 'The respectable and serious made a point of coming, and a number of natives', though most of the Armenians and half-castes stayed away, being 'thoroughly frightened';[33] and one English lady, perturbed by a rumour that villainous Indians would take advantage of the ball to murder all the leading members of the community, declined the invitation and hired two British sailors to stay in her house for the night to protect her, 'but they got tipsy, and frightened her more than imaginary enemies'.[34]

Other ladies were given due cause for disquiet. Mrs Sneyd complained that her servants, formerly 'so obsequious and cringing in manner' were now 'insufferably insolent', frequently taunting her with the threat that the British would soon be thrown out of India. Mrs Sneyd complained:

When I insisted upon our rooms being properly swept and cleaned instead of being left in a dirty and neglected state, even our lowest servants would [make remarks about the end of British rule]. And my ayah would often stand before the looking-glass, throwing herself into a variety of attitudes while admiring herself and dancing with a shawl fantastically thrown over her shoulders like the nautch girls instead of dressing me when I wanted her, and this she did in my presence with the taunt I have before mentioned: 'Ah! *Your* rule will soon come to an end, and we shall have our *own* King!'[35]

Yet the Cannings considered the reactions of the people in Calcutta to such danger as they might meet both undignified and provocative. One evening at dinner at Government House 'a very shaky lady' startled the other guests by saying before she sat down, 'I hope we shall arise safely.' And another guest, 'boiling over with indignation at not being allowed to go up-country with her husband', according to Lady Canning, declared that 'she was not a common woman, but she had a revolver and knew how to use it'.[36]

Canning, exasperated by men going about with loaded revolvers and placing their families aboard ships in the river, wrote:

All I can say is that in my life I never came across such a set of old women – some of them with swords by their sides – as those who fetch and carry the news of this town among the clubs and gossiping 'tiffin' rooms of their acquaintance. Men, soldiers, whose authority on matters relating to the Army and the Sepoys is readily credited, and whose words are caught up by Newspapers' caterers, are spreading not reports only – but opinion as to the state of things present and future, which makes me ashamed for Englishmen.[37]

Equally exasperated by those who demanded fierce vengeance, Canning told Queen Victoria:

There is a rabid and indiscriminate vindictiveness abroad, even among many who ought to set a better example, which it is impossible to contemplate without a feeling of shame for one's own countrymen . . . Not one man in ten seems to think that the hanging and shooting of forty thousand or fifty thousand men can be otherwise than practicable and right.[38]

He later wrote to Sir Henry George Ward, Governor of Ceylon, who had dispatched all his European troops to Bengal:

The rabid unreasoning spirit of blood and vengeance . . . is activating the European community: not the common herd and the Press alone, but men of experience and sober character; and rather those who have been sitting quietly under their punkahs in Calcutta, and have felt nothing of the convulsion (unless in their pockets) than those who have been actors and sufferers in it . . . For the present the Englishmen in Bengal if polled would, I firmly believe, carry by acclamation the hanging or shooting of every man who has ever been a sepoy.[39]

When the Calcutta Masonic Fraternity, the European Trades' Association, and the Armenian and French communities all offered their services as volunteers for the protection of the city, he declined to enlist them; and when persuaded to change his mind, made no secret of the fact that he did not consider their services would be of much use. Resenting his attitude towards them, the 'ditchers' – as the European merchants were known to the civil servants, since so few of them ever bothered to travel beyond the old defensive line, the Maratha Ditch – were loud in their abuse of Canning who was 'far too ready to play down the seriousness of the situation' and 'far too inclined to be lenient with the mutineers'. This was the opinion, too, of many soldiers and civil servants. 'Lord Canning ought to be turned out of India,' wrote Mrs Juxon Henry Jones, the wife of a surgeon attached to the 3rd Native Infantry, expressing a widespread opinion. 'He is behaving so ridiculously and so leniently that the rebels are not punished. It is disgraceful.'[40] Leopold Berkeley, an Assistant Commissioner, agreed with her: Canning's policies were 'ridiculous'; the sepoys 'should all be shot like dogs'.[41]

Canning caused further offence when he issued an order which became known as the Gagging Act, requiring all printers of newspapers to obtain licences from the Government, and providing for the suppression of publications deemed subversive. The European community quite agreed that native journals which had been advocating the cause of the mutineers ought to be suppressed; but that English journalists, who had been calling for more rigorous suppression of the mutiny, should also be subject to similar restraint seemed to them outrageous. They were equally outraged when Canning decreed that licences would also be necessary in future for anyone who wanted to carry arms.

Yet Canning refused to be intimidated. He took what measures he thought necessary for the maintenance of British rule, authorizing the disarming of native regiments when there were good grounds for belief in their disloyalty, giving extraordinary powers to civil and military officers for the summary trial and punishment of all disturbers of the peace, and arresting the King of Oudh whose dependents were suspected of plotting rebellion in his name. But he refused to give way to those who badgered him to deal more harshly with the rebels.

As long as I have any breath in my body [he told Lord Granville], I will pursue no other policy than that which I have been following, not only for the reason of expediency but because it is just. I will not govern in anger. Justice, and that as stern and inflexible as law and might can make it, I will deal out. But I will never allow an angry or indiscriminate act or word to proceed from the Government of India as long as I am responsible for it.[42]

In this spirit he firmly refused to agree to accept a petition, signed by a number of important residents of Calcutta, suggesting that martial law should be proclaimed throughout Bengal; and he passed a resolution, which became known as the Clemency Order, intended to ensure that captured sepoys should not be punished without regard to the gravity of their offences. Such compassion seemed to most Europeans in Calcutta not merely misplaced but absurd, even iniquitous. They petitioned the Queen for the recall of 'Clemency' Canning as he was now called. Such a man, they protested, was no fit person to deal with the monsters who had perpetrated the horrors witnessed at Meerut and Delhi. But the Queen was not impressed by the petition. She knew that Canning was well aware of the dangers of racial animosity and she recognized that stern justice for the rebels had to be tempered with understanding of their fears. 'I think that the greatest care ought to be taken not to interfere with their religion,' she told Lady Canning, 'as once a cry of that kind is raised among a fanatical people – very strictly attached to their religion – there is no knowing what it may lead to and where it may end'.[43]

9

Nana Sahib

'All well at Cawnpore,' the Governor-General was informed during the third week in May. 'Calm and expert policy will soon reassure the public mind . . . The plague is, in truth, stayed . . . A very few days will see the end of it.'[1]

The officer who dispatched these reassuring messages was Major-General Sir Hugh Massy Wheeler, a short, spare, grey-haired man of sixty-seven, 'not imposing in appearance except by virtue of a thoroughly military gait'.[2] Born in Ireland, the son of a captain in the East India Company's service who had married a daughter of the first Lord Massy, Wheeler had received his commission at the age of fourteen after a brief education at Bath Grammar School and had spent nearly all his subsequent life in India. He loved the country; he loved his soldiers, whose language he spoke as well as they did themselves; he had married an Indian woman. He could not believe that there would be any serious trouble with the regiments at Cawnpore. There were four native regiments there, the 1st, 53rd and 56th Native Infantry and the 2nd Cavalry. Including a company of native artillery they were about 3,000 strong. They outnumbered the European troops about ten to one; and many of the white soldiers were invalids. Yet this disparity of numbers seems to have concerned the British officers and civilians as little as it did the General himself. Lieutenant-Colonel Ewart of the 1st Native Infantry expressed his trust in the faithfulness of his men.[3] Mrs Charles Hillersdon, wife of the Magistrate, wrote on 15 May that Cawnpore was 'quiet and the regiments staunch'.[4] If there were to be any local trouble it was felt that General Wheeler was well qualified to deal with it. He was well liked and respected; he had had a distinguished career in India, and had been expected to succeed General Anson as Commander-in-Chief. He had been in command of the Cawnpore division for almost a year.

Cawnpore was an important post on the trunk road between Delhi and Benares with a population of about 60,000 people. It stood on the western bank of the Ganges which, when the rains filled up its bed, was more than a mile across and even now in the dry season was over five hundred yards wide. Navigable for light craft down to the sea a thousand miles away at Calcutta and for three hundred miles upstream, the river was crossed at Cawnpore by a bridge of boats which, as an artillery officer stationed there recorded, 'served to conduct a ceaseless throng over into Oude. Merchants, travellers, fakirs, camels, bullocks, horses went and came incessantly. Moored inshore were multitudes of vessels looking with their thatched roofs like a floating village . . . The native city was densely packed as all the human hives of the East.'[5]

The city contained no fine buildings to be compared with those of Delhi and Benares, Lucknow and Agra, as it had no comparable past, having developed in the late eighteenth and early nineteenth centuries as an East India Company garrison. But it was now a highly prosperous trading centre, its wide main street, the Chandni Chowk, or Street of Silver, being filled with the shops of silk merchants and saddlers, goldsmiths and silversmiths, and scores of leather workers producing the best and cheapest shoes and horse harnesses in India. It was also a city with a less enviable reputation as a sanctuary for vagrants and rascals of all kinds. And it was these badmashes who were deemed responsible for the increasing unrest in Cawnpore which the military authorities were obliged to notice as May drew to a close.

On the morning of 20 May, General Wheeler still felt that all was well, but by the evening, after hearing of disturbances in the city and outbreaks of fire in the infantry lines, he was constrained to report that there was 'a good deal of excitement and alarm'. And the next day he went so far as to write to Calcutta: 'reports just received of a crisis approaching here'.[6] By 22 May, however, the danger appeared to have receded and by 3 June, although the city was 'in excitement', he felt that all was secure once again. Indeed, he felt sufficiently confident of his position to send two officers and fifty men from his small force to Lucknow where the Commissioner had 'expressed some uneasiness'. This left him weak, he confessed, but he trusted to holding his own until more Europeans arrived.[7]

This confidence was not shared now by most other people in Cawnpore. Mrs Hillersdon, worried by 'all sorts of dreadful rumours going about', wished to God she was 'out of this horrid country'.[8] Mrs Ewart would never have believed she would be expected to endure 'such nights of anxiety'.[9] The Eurasian wife of the English sergeant-major of the 53rd was told in the bazaar, 'You will not be alive another week.'[10] A deputation of civilians, Europeans, Eurasians and Indian Christians called upon General Wheeler to tell him of their fears. He assured them that there was 'no immediate cause for apprehension', but he advised them to arm themselves just in case, and told them that, in the unlikely event of an uprising, shelter would be provided in the military barracks.[11]

W. J. Shepherd, the half-caste head assistant in the Commissariat Office, did not like the idea of seeking shelter in the barracks. Supposing his family would be safer if they went into hiding in the city, he set about making arrangements to rent two houses there in the name of friends and to have Indian dresses made for his wife and children. Other civilians tried to hire boats to get away by river, or to escape by road to Allahabad. But they were told that the shallows in the river forbade all passage and the roads leading out of the city were infested with robbers and rebels. So, whether or not they trusted in the protection afforded by them, the civilian families decided that they would have to make for the barracks if danger threatened. And when rumours of an imminent uprising spread through the colony, it was to the barracks that they fled in panic. Captain Fletcher Hayes saw them there the next morning and confessed that in all the years he had been in India he had

never witnessed so frightful a scene of confusion, fright and bad management as the European barracks presented. Four guns were in position loaded, with European artillerymen in night caps . . . looking like melodramatic buccaneers. People of all kinds, of every colour, sect and profession were crowding into the barracks . . . Buggies, palki-gharees, vehicles of all sorts, drove up and discharged cargoes of writers, tradesmen and a miscellaneous mob . . . all in terror of the imaginary foe. Ladies sitting down at the rough mess tables, women suckling infants, ayahs and children in all directions and – officers too.

Hayes saw quite enough to convince him that if an insurrection did take place, the British would have no one to thank but themselves, because they had 'now shown to the Natives how very easily [they could] become frightened and, when frightened, utterly helpless'.[12]

The fear of the people in the barracks was certainly not allayed by any confidence in the defenders' ability to protect them. In addition to various outhouses, there were two main buildings, one with a thatched, the other with a *pukka* roof, each designed to accommodate a hundred men and both with far more than that number of people crowded into them. They stood in an exposed position on the plain to the east of the city about a mile from the river bank. Close by them were some other, half-finished barrack buildings, constructed of red brick not yet coated with the white plaster which was universally applied to all such military buildings in India and still encased in flimsy bamboo scaffolding. Around them a trench and a low mud wall about four feet high were still in the process of slow construction.

It was suggested to Wheeler that it would be far better to take up a defensive position within the sturdy walls of the Magazine. But he declined to do so for fear lest, by removing the sepoy guard already there, he would provoke the collision which he was so anxious to avoid. Besides, he felt sure that even if the sepoys did mutiny, they would march to Delhi rather than trouble themselves with the Europeans at Cawnpore. The withdrawal to the barracks entrenchment would only be a temporary expedient; then, 'in a few – a very few days', Cawnpore would be safe. Wheeler admitted that he had been afraid there might be some sort of uprising on the Muslim festival of the *Eed,* and, that being also the Queen's birthday, he had thought it as well to cancel the firing of the usual salute in case the noise of the guns should be misinterpreted by the natives. Yet the feast had passed off without any serious disturbances. There *had* been an unpleasant incident when a cashiered subaltern drunkenly fired an ill-aimed shot at a patrol of the 2nd Cavalry who had challenged him as he staggered out of his bungalow in the dark; but at the young man's trial it had been held that his state of intoxication excused his conduct and that his fire-arm had gone off by mistake. The sepoys of the 2nd Cavalry 'muttered angrily that possibly their own muskets might go off by mistake before very long'; and one of them complained to W. J. Shepherd that 'if we natives had fired upon a European we should have been hanged'.[13]

Nevertheless, General Wheeler, despite occasional reservations and warnings, continued to propound the belief that 'all [was still] well at Cawnpore', and that any unpleasantness there might be in the future would not last long. He did not think it necessary to supply his entrenchment on the plain with provisions for more than twenty-five days, though the regimental officers, having 'no very lively confidence in Sir Hugh as a caterer, sent in large contributions of liquor and hermetically sealed tins from their mess-stores'.[14] It was just as well that they did so, for the contractors instructed to supply the entrenchment were not the most honest of men, and while an appropriate quantity of grain was laid in for the horses, the supplies of dhal, ghee, salt, rice, sugar and flour were to prove woefully inadequate.[15]

In the opinion of many officers, however, what was far more reprehensible than either the General's choice of defensive position or his insufficient stocking of it was his reliance for help on the local magnate, Dhondu Pant, Maharajah of Bithur, who arrived at Cawnpore with three hundred men, cavalry and infantry, and protestations of support for the English cause.

Dhondu Pant, known as Nana Sahib, was then about thirty-five years old. He was one of the adopted sons of the last Peshwa of Bithur, Baji Rao II, a Mahratta monarch who had been dethroned by the British and granted a pension in exchange for his former dominions. Although he had been refused permission to live at Benares or Muttra as he wished to do, and had been obliged to pay certain taxes which he considered derogatory to a prince of his rank, Baji Rao had otherwise been treated generously by the Company and had been enabled to live in princely style at Bithur on his annual pension of eight lakhs of rupees, the equivalent of about £80,000. When he died in 1851, however, having lived far longer than his 'feeble constitution' and 'debauched habits' had led the Company to expect, his pension had been stopped at once, in accordance with the terms upon which it had been granted him. His adopted son, naturally displeased that the family income had been so suddenly curtailed, had done all he could to persuade the British to allow him to continue to receive the pension if not in whole at least in part. The British Commissioner was sympathetic, pointing out that, while Nana Sahib had considerably reduced his household expenses, his commitments to his adoptive father's numerous dependants were such that his expenditure was necessarily heavy; that a native of his rank 'would never under the most pinching circumstances convert the family jewels and plate into money'; and that he 'shared the common belief' that it 'would be derogatory to his position' to sell the 'large stud of horses, elephants, camels and other animals' which he had inherited.

But the Governor-General did not agree. The late Peshwa had received an enormous income during his lifetime, the equivalent of more than £2,500,000. His family had 'no claim whatever on the consideration of the British Government'. The property which he left was probably much larger than it was avowed to be, and that was large enough in all conscience. Undeterred by this rebuff, Nana Sahib appealed to the Court of Directors in London, only to be told that his application was 'wholly inadmissible'. He then sent an emissary to London, a clever, attractive, sly and ingratiating young man named Azimullah who, as a starving child, had been found a place in the Cawnpore Free School, had become first a *khansaman,* then a teacher, and finally confidential agent to Nana Sahib. But although a great success in London drawing-rooms – where his dark good looks and agreeable manners, his pleasantly accented, fluent English and rather insolent charm intrigued more than one lady whose loving letters to him were later discovered in his master's palace[16] – Azimullah failed completely in the main purpose of his mission. The Court of Directors remained adamant in their refusal to continue the pension, a refusal which so rankled with Nana Sahib that he could not forbear mentioning it to his every British visitor, urging those of sufficient influence to intercede with the authorities on his behalf, and even, if they were returning to England, to 'take the earliest opportunity some day quietly after dinner . . . of representing to Her Majesty the exact state' of his unfortunate case.[17]

Nana Sahib did not strike his visitors as being in unfortunate circumstances. His palace was well-furnished, lit by sparkling chandeliers, decorated with fine looking-glasses and luxurious carpets and, so rumour had it, provided with secret galleries of pictures, 'horribly unfit for any human eye', painted by both European and native artists who had done their best to gratify their patron's lascivious taste. His wardrobe was abundantly stocked with magnificent kincobs and precious Cashmere shawls; and on gala days he would appear 'crowned with a tiara of pearls and diamonds and girt with old Baji Rao's sword of state, which report valued at three lakhs of rupees'.[18] He had a large well-kept garden around his fine palace, an extravagantly stocked menagerie, an 'aviary full of birds', an extensive collection of guns by celebrated European makers, and an equally impressive collection 'of swords and daggers of every country and age'. He enjoyed showing these collections to his many European visitors who described him as a generous host, providing sumptuous entertainments for his guests, although in his presentation of

European meals evidently not very scrupulous in laying out the best china and plate.

I sat down to a table twenty feet long . . . which was covered with a damask tablecloth of European manufacture [wrote one of his English guests], but instead of a dinner napkin there was a bedroom towel. The soup – for the steward had everything ready – was served up in a trifle dish which had formed part of a dessert service belonging to the 9th Lancers – at all events the arms of that regiment were upon it; but the plate into which I ladled it with a broken teacup was of the old willow pattern. The *pilao* which followed the soup was served upon a huge plated dish, but the plate from which I ate it was of the very commonest description. The knife was a bone-handled affair. The spoon and fork were of silver . . . The plated dishes containing side dishes were odd ones . . . The pudding was brought in upon a soup plate of blue and gold pattern and the cheese was placed before me on a glass dish belonging to a dessert service. The cool claret I drank out of a richly cut champagne glass and the beer out of an American tumbler of the very worst quality.[19]

Although a generous host, Nana Sahib was not a notably attentive one. He did not treat his guests with 'the semi-barbarous discourtesy evinced by some native hosts, who [passed] the evening seated among a group of courtiers, scrutinizing the dancers through a lorgnette, and apparently regarding the whole proceeding as a ballet arranged for their individual amusement'.[20] Occasionally he would invite a guest to play billiards with him, indulgently allowing his opponent to win the game which he could play himself remarkably well. But more often he remained aloof from the entertainments he provided, leaving it to one of his adoptive brothers to represent him. In any case, he did not speak English very well: English-language newspapers, including the *Delhi Gazette* and the *Englishman* were delivered to the palace, but he was obliged to employ a Eurasian to explain their contents to him.[21] He was not, in fact, so his European visitors thought, particularly intelligent, nor, in the opinion of an English doctor who attended him, in the least interesting.[22] He was supposed to be extremely fond of food and of dancing girls with eyes 'rubbed round with lamp black and sensual lips rosy with the juice of betel-juice', predilections which his stout, sleek, softly elegant and moustached appearance seemed to confirm.[23] He was not, though, a complacently contented man. Perpetually irritated by the termination of his father's pension, he was additionally annoyed that, while the British at Cawnpore politely referred to him as the Maharajah of Bithur, this was a courtesy title not officially recognized at Calcutta where his right to a salute as the heir of the Peshwa was also denied him. Nor was he allowed to stamp letters with his father's seal as he wished to do. Such slights to his pride rankled with him always, and led him to refuse all invitations to entertainments offered to him by the leading officials of Cawnpore.[24] Indeed, Nana Sahib rarely travelled far from his palace at Bithur. But during the spring of 1857 he had been to Lucknow where he had met the Financial Commissioner, Martin Gubbins, who regarded him far less favourably than did his British acquaintances at Cawnpore.

His manner was arrogant and presuming [Gubbins wrote]. To make a show of dignity and importance, he brought six or seven followers with him into the room, for whom chairs were demanded. He appeared to be of middle age and height, and, as Hindoos of rank generally are in India, corpulent. Mahrattas of pure descent are usually fair in complexion. But the Nana is darker than they generally are.[25]

Nana Sahib left Lucknow in a great hurry, protesting that events at Cawnpore rendered his return a matter of urgency. Gubbins, considering this 'exceedingly suspicious', conveyed his distrust of 'the so-called Maharaja' to the Commissioner, Sir Henry Lawrence, who wrote to General Wheeler a note of warning. Wheeler, however, ignored the warning. He had no reason to distrust the man himself who was always perfectly agreeable with him and who was of the same caste as his wife. When Nana Sahib returned to Cawnpore with his large retinue of colourfully dressed horsemen armed with lances and old cavalry swords, and foot soldiers carrying long matchlocks and brass blunderbusses, he was invited to take charge of the Government Treasury in the suburb of Nawabganj.[26]

'Here we are just as we were a week ago . . . in the barracks all night and nearly all day,' a young officer wrote home to his mother while Nana Sahib's retinue were occupying the Treasury. 'There is no doubt that our power has never been in such danger . . . Always hitherto we have been fighting against open enemies, now we cannot tell who are friends, who enemies.'[27]

The wall around the entrenchment was still not finished and, in any case, was built of such dry, crumbly earth that it was not much protection even from a bullet. An attempt had been made to replace the roof of the thatched barracks with tiles, but this work was not completed yet either. Officers left their families in this exposed and seemingly indefensible position at night to return to their regiments with the deepest foreboding, well aware now of the restless state of their men, wondering how long the uncertainty would last and what would follow it.

It was, then, almost with a sense of relief that they learned on 5 June that the *sowars* of the 2nd Cavalry had sent their families away to the slums of the city as an obvious preliminary to mutiny. And that night the mutiny broke out at last. The 2nd Cavalry rode off to Nawabganj where, helped by Nana Sahib's men, they broke into the Treasury, killing their Subahdar-Major who tried to prevent them; then they unlocked the doors of the gaol, set fire to various other buildings and made for the Magazine. The 1st Native Infantry soon followed them, ignoring the pleas of Colonel Ewart, addressed to them in Hindustani, not to commit 'so great a wickedness', but allowing both him and the other officers to escape unharmed into the entrenchment.

For the moment the 53rd and 56th remained unaffected by the uproar. Their adjutants managed to get them on parade; and there they stood until daylight when they were dismissed to cook their breakfasts. While they were getting their breakfasts ready, some messengers from the mutineers came up to ask why they were not joining in the plunder. The temptation was too much for the 56th to resist, though most of the 53rd for the moment waveringly stood their ground until General Wheeler, hoping to frighten them into good behaviour, ordered a battery to open fire on them. As though incredulous that they should be so unjustly treated, the 53rd did not break at once, but after the third shot they scattered and, with the exception of about eighty men who steadfastly declined to join the mutiny, ran away towards the other regiments.

Already a deputation of mutineers had called upon Nana Sahib who seems to have soon made up his mind that he had no longer anything to gain by appearing to support the British. He was afterwards to write that he had 'joined the rebels from helplessness'; but while he was certainly unable now to act independently and was obviously afraid of what the future might bring, the sepoys' need of a leader of high rank undoubtedly appealed to his ambition and caught his imagination. So that when the leader of the deputation said to him, 'Maharaja, a kingdom awaits you if you join our enterprise, but death if you side with our enemies', Nana Sahib quickly replied, 'What have I to do with the British? . . . I only pretended to help them. At heart I am their mortal enemy . . . I am altogether yours.'[28]

The deputation then asked him to lead the mutineers to Delhi.

Nana Sahib agreed to do so, laying his hands on the sepoys' heads and swearing to be faithful to them. The next morning the four regiments took the Delhi road. They had got no farther than Kalianpur, however, when Nana Sahib was persuaded by his advisers – principally, it seems, by Azimullah, the agent who had represented his interests in London – that he ought not to be going to Delhi where he, a highly distinguished Brahmin, would be subordinate to the decrepit Mohammedan Emperor. It would be far wiser, he was urged, to remain at Cawnpore where the four mutinous regiments would rally round his name, soon defeat the few *Firinghis* in their pitiable entrenchment, and elevate him to that position in the world which the Peshwa Baji Rao II had once enjoyed. So the mutineers were called back from Kalianpur; and on the morning of 6 June, General Wheeler was informed that his entrenchment would shortly be under attack.[29]

Wheeler was far from ready to resist attack. Two days before, he had faced the fact that mutiny at Cawnpore was inevitable, but he had still been convinced that the mutineers would make for Delhi. Now that they had turned on him instead, how could he hope to survive unless help came quickly? There were over three thousand of them, supported by the Nana's men and by most of the native population. They were well trained, well armed and well supplied, and every day there were reports of landholders from the surrounding districts coming into Cawnpore with scores of matchlock-men to reinforce the Nana's forces, whereas the numbers inside the entrenchment were less than a thousand and of these nearly four hundred were women and children. There were about two hundred European soldiers, many of them invalids; a hundred European officers from the native regiments; a hundred civilians, and a few native officers, sepoys and servants who had chosen to remain with their masters. They were at least well supplied with muskets and ammunition, there being up to ten loaded muskets available for every man capable of firing one should an assault be made on the entrenchment. There were, however, only a few light guns, most of them nine-pounders, and all of them had to be fired from positions dangerously exposed to musket-shot.[30]

For a time after the delivery of Nana Sahib's warning, there was no sign of the threatened attack, for the mutineers were too occupied in plundering the city, where the houses of Europeans were first looted and then burned, and rich merchants as well as poor native Christians were abused and attacked by the mob. Few of the British and Eurasian civilians, who had preferred to hide in the city rather than flee to the crowded entrenchment, escaped detection. Some were dragged from their hiding-places and murdered in the streets; others taken to Nana Sahib's headquarters. One of these was Edward Greenway, a rich merchant, who had offered a home to the cashiered officer who had drunkenly shot at the 2nd Cavalry patrol. The officer had defended his host's large house 'until the last cartridge had been expended and had then walked in among the assailants, and bade them cut his throat: an invitation to which they eagerly responded'. The mutineers had then secured Greenway, his Eurasian wife, his sister and children, and marched them off to Nana Sahib who ordered them to be confined in the hope of obtaining a ransom. Other captives were executed immediately. One Portuguese merchant, who had done a great deal of business with Nana Sahib in the past, refusing to believe that he could possibly be in danger, declined to leave his shop. He was therefore dragged away to his former patron who 'turned away his face' and allowed him to be cut to pieces.[31]

Looking across the dull, sandy plain towards the city, the Europeans in the entrenchments could see the flames leaping towards the morning sky on either side of the Ganges Canal. Then, at about ten o'clock, crowds of sepoys could be seen running across the canal bridges; and 'exactly at half past ten', so Shepherd, the Commissariat Office clerk, calculated, the first of Nana Sahib's guns opened fire.[32]

Nana Sahib did not expect the men in the entrenchment to hold out for long. He confidently predicted, indeed, that they would surrender before nightfall; and he remained all day in the saddle waiting for them to give in. But darkness fell; there was no sign that they were prepared to capitulate; and Nana Sahib dismounted and lay down to sleep on a piece of carpet beside the battery which he had decided to command in person. In the morning the guns were moved closer to the entrenchment to ensure a more accurate fire, and Nana Sahib moved into Duncan's Hotel, which was about three-quarters of a mile to the north-west of the entrenchment, and there began to plan his future regime as the new Peshwa. First his army was reorganized with Subadhar Tika Singh, who had led the mutineers of the 2nd Cavalry to Nawabganj, as General and Commander-in-Chief, though there was another leader in the rebel camp who was soon to prove himself a far more capable general than Tika Singh. This was Ramchandra Panduranga who assumed the name Tatya Tope. The pseudonym, so the Political Assistant for Bundelkhand was told by an Indian informant, was 'a Dekhan title', the latter word meaning captain or commanding officer. 'He is a stout man,' the report continued, 'of middling stature . . . with fair complexion and whiskers . . . He always wears a white turban . . . He served the Nana Sahib first as an aide-de-camp and afterwards up to the outbreak as "chef de cuisine", when he was employed to raise troops.'[33]

'He was far from good-looking,' added an Englishman who saw him at Bithur. 'The forehead was low, the nose rather broad at the nostrils, and his teeth irregular and discoloured. His eyes were expressive and full of cunning, like those of most Asiatics; but he did not strike me as a man of eminent ability.'[34] In this the Englishman was wrong. Tatya Tope was to distinguish himself as one of the most talented of all the rebel leaders.

Once the rebel army was reorganized, order was imposed upon the city by the appointment of Nana Sahib's adoptive brother, Baba Bhat, as chief of the judiciary. Baba Bhat, described as 'a dirty-looking fellow, wearing green spectacles across his nose, with an unwieldy turban on his head', dispensed justice perched on the corner of a billiard-table in a small house near the Post Office, surrounded by 'a host of scribes, smartly dressed . . . ready to catch a word that might fall from his "Excellency's" lips'.[35] Despite his eccentric appearance Baba Bhat was a shrewd judge and an extremely severe one, passing sentences much more harsh than those which would have been delivered in the time of the Company's rule, reviving Hindu criminal law and punishing prisoners with mutilation. He was assisted in his work by an efficient *kotwal* who had previously worked for the Company's police and had replaced two less capable appointees, one of whom had been dismissed after being seen mounted on a horse with a famous courtesan. A Superintendent of Supplies was also appointed and given authority to imprison those unwilling to do business with him.[36]

From documents later discovered at Gwalior it appears that Nana Sahib's ambitions were not limited to the establishment of his rule at Cawnpore. He evidently envisaged, or amused himself by imagining, his holding sway over huge tracts of India and being able to demand such large tributes from rulers of countries beyond her borders that his advisers would be able to receive salaries commensurate with that of his Prime Minister, who was to receive 1,200,000 rupees a year.[37] But before all this could be achieved, of course, General Wheeler had to be disposed of; and in this endeavour Nana Sahib's army was not making much headway. To some observers, in fact, many of his soldiers were not much interested in the siege. They 'did just as they pleased, manned the attacking batteries . . . or not as they deemed fit, the greater portion taking their ease, lounging in the bazaars and on the banks of the canal, and plundering the provisions as they were brought into the city'.[38] All the same, those who did remain in the batteries and fired their muskets at the entrenchment caused fearful damage and suffering there.

At first, Nana Sahib's guns being too distant from their target for accurate bombardment, most of the round-shot flew far wide of the barracks; but, even so, for the women and children sheltering there, the strange, frightening, 'dreadful whizzing' noise and the occasional crash and roar of tumbling masonry were too fearful to bear in silence. Lieutenant Mowbray Thomson, a young officer of the 56th Native Infantry, who looked like 'an undergraduate in his first term', remembered that all through the first day's bombardment the shrieks of the women and children were 'terrific'; but after that ordeal of initiation, 'they never uttered a sound except when groaning from the horrible mutilations they had to endure'.[39]

The mutilations were, indeed, horrifying. Captain Jenkins, shot through the jaw, 'lived for two or three days in excruciating agony,' Thomson reported, 'and then died from exhaustion, as it was quite impossible, without the aid of instruments, to get the wretched nutriment we possessed into his throat'. Mrs Williams, whose husband Colonel Williams soon died from apoplexy, was also shot in the face and lingered two days in frightful suffering and disfigurement, all the time attended by her daughter who was herself suffering from a bullet wound through the shoulder blade. A private soldier in the 32nd was killed by a bullet which then passed through his wife's arms and wounded one of the twin babies she was carrying. Thomson later saw this poor woman, Mrs White, lying on her back with a baby at each breast, unable to support them in their suckling. The General's son, Lieutenant Godfrey Wheeler, his 'favourite darling son', as his father called him, was sitting on a sofa, recovering from a wound while one of his two sisters fanned his face, when a round-shot came hurtling over the mud wall and knocked his head clean off. No less than three of his fellow officers were later killed in the same way.[40] Mr Shepherd was in one of the barracks when an '18-pounder cannon ball passed through the window, took off the solar hat [of a clerk in the Collector's Office] and, hitting an inner wall, bounded into the corner and fell with tremendous force upon the legs of a native wet nurse: she had an officer's baby in her lap which was not hurt at all, but both the legs of the woman were broken below the knee, and she died within an hour from loss of blood and pain'. Shepherd's own baby was killed by a bullet that struck her in the neck, wounding her mother's arm. She lived for thirty-six hours; then, wrapping her up in some old clothes, Shepherd buried her in a shallow grave which he scratched out in the dry earth with a Persian knife. The dead were not usually buried. As Shepherd recorded:

A very respectable-looking European lady, with grey hair, about fifty or fifty-five years of age . . . came into our room in the barracks very quietly and laid herself down. We thought she was asleep, but a little while after she was heard to moan pitifully. Some one got up to see what was the matter with her. She turned a little on one side and brought up something that looked like the lungs of a goat, and died shortly after. They say she had burst her heart. The fright had been too great for her. We made many enquiries as to who were her friends and relatives, but none came to claim her. At last, at sunset, the fatigue party took the corpse and put it in the well outside the trenches

where all the dead bodies were tipped at nightfall, and where 250 were to be dropped before the siege was over.[41] The room which Shepherd had found for himself and his family was already packed to the walls when the grey-haired lady appeared; but soon after her death two young women came in, each carrying two hysterical children whose perpetual screaming was described by Shepherd, in great pain from a wound in his back, as 'distracting beyond description'. Shepherd's family had been driven from the first room they had found when round-shot came flying through the smashed door and covered them with pieces of shattered masonry as they crowded in the corners. They fled from their next place of shelter when

a sudden alarm prevailed that the building was on fire which caused so great a panic, especially among the ladies, that, though no fire was seen, nearly all rushed out with their little ones and ran into the other building . . . The fear of the shots, which were as usual flying all round, was entirely overcome for the moment by this sudden and new alarm. The gentlemen were unable to restrain this flight, and were compelled in a manner to give support to the ladies . . . On reaching the other barrack, a fearful scene was presented to my sight [wrote Shepherd]. The side rooms were crowded to suffocation, and a great many were left unwillingly under the thatch in the middle. Something struck the roof with a tremendous crash, and an immense ball darted down, killing a handsome looking youngster, who was held by the hand by his mother, and wounding one or two besides . . . For a moment a fearful silence prevailed, then the heartrending shrieks of the mother (an officer's wife) burst upon us . . . It would be impossible to describe the horrible consternation and fright, or the wild alarm and dismay that was visible upon the features of all around . . . I saw several familiar faces there, but the following occurrence is most vivid in my recollection. Captain Jeppings, the Deputy Paymaster, was one of those under the door arches with his wife and children. He was quite calm and collected, endeavouring to encourage the ladies with him. He knelt down and offered up a . . . prayer to God. After which he wrote something on the wall with a pencil [the names of his family and the friends who were with them] and appeared quite resigned . . . Suddenly another piercing shriek of a female was heard and all turned round to know the cause. Two soldiers' wives were seen hastily moving out of a corner in the side room and pointing to something under a bed. Quick as lightning a sergeant, having a pair of pistols in his belt, rushed forward and dragged out a most hideous loathsome figure of a native (blackened and scorched all over as if burnt with fire) and, pulling him away to the veranda, instantly shot him through the head . . . All agreed that from his appearance he had something to do with setting fire to the other barrack.[42]

Finding the other barrack was not on fire after all, they rushed back there. Soon afterwards the thatched roof of the barrack they had left caught fire, consuming everything beneath it, including the few medical supplies which had been brought into the entrenchment and the jackets of the soldiers of the 32nd who were seen poking about in the ashes afterwards, looking for their lost medals.[43]

Driven from the ruins of the room they had occupied before the panic caused by fear of fire, the Shepherds ran to find shelter elsewhere. Unable to find a room whose occupants considered they had space enough to receive them, they were forced to spend a whole day 'clinging to the walls and crouching in corners to avoid the shots'. At last they found a room 'with more than sufficient unoccupied space' to receive them all. They had no sooner thanked God and taken possession of it, however, than 'an old grey-headed officer who had apparently been asleep got up, and in the most rude manner' ordered them to get out. They begged to be allowed to remain, at least 'until the fury of the enemy's battery' abated a little. But he would not listen to them, threatening personal violence unless they left immediately.[44] So they went out on to the ruins of the veranda again, 'looking all around in utter despair', until they found temporary shelter in a room recently abandoned as uninhabitable. Later they discovered less uncomfortable quarters in one of the side rooms of the thatched barrack which the rebels had abandoned as a target since the outbreak of the fire which had destroyed the main part of the roof. This was a relatively quiet part of the entrenchment now, and soon, therefore, an excessively crowded one; but it did not remain either for long, as some native prisoners succeeded in escaping over the wall one night and informed their comrades outside which were the best targets to attack.[45] The prisoners, it was generally agreed, ought to have been left under the guard of a previous warder, the formidable Bridget Widdowson, wife of a private in the 32nd, who had watched over them sternly, sword in hand, and had ensured that there should be no possibility of their escape while in her charge by tying them all together with ropes round their waists.[46]

This intrepid woman was one of several celebrated heroines of the siege of Cawnpore. Mowbray Thomson also singled out for praise a Mrs Fraser who, regardless of her own privations and hunger, did all she could to soothe those more badly hurt or less courageous than herself.[47] Shepherd wrote of the

noble behaviour under distress of some of the soldiers' wives and daughters ... I have seen them patiently attending upon their wounded and suffering husbands and fathers unremittingly night and day, exposed to all sorts of dangers, themselves labouring under sickness, surrounded by young children whose cries and wants at any other time would be enough to send the best of mothers mad.

Shepherd's own surviving daughter, 'a sweet child' of five, made his 'heart bleed often to the core' by sitting in the corner, 'the very picture of patience', her eyes suffused with tears, struggling not to complain of her hunger or thirst, doing her best not to make things more difficult for her parents whom, she knew, could do nothing to help her. One day she whispered to her ayah how thirsty she was; and the old woman, 'without mentioning a word to anyone', crawled out to the well, 'braving the storm of shots which were as usual flying on all sides', to bring back some water for the little girl in her *lota*.[48]

Not all behaved heroically, of course. Mowbray Thomson cited the example of 'one officer of high rank and in the prime of life' who never once came out of his shelter in the barracks to help in the defences.[49] Shepherd was appalled by the conduct of some of the soldiers of the 32nd, who repeatedly tried to snatch away from him the precious earthen vessel in which he stored water for his family. Other soldiers of the 32nd bullied the native Christian drummers into helping them draw water from the well which they sold for eight or ten shillings a bucket. One day Shepherd found a private of the 32nd brandishing a bayonet and swearing at Shepherd's meek and sickly young brother in an attempt to force him to serve as his assistant at the well. Shepherd remonstrated with the man who became more violent than ever, threatening to run the boy through with his bayonet and 'make an example of him'. Since none of the twenty or so people standing around was prepared to come to his help, Shepherd thought it as well to advise his brother to go off with the dangerous-looking soldiers. The boy agreed but was saved before he got to the well by the intervention of Mr Twoomry, a masterful apothecary.[50]

There was only one well within the entrenchment, and as it was in an exposed position, it was extremely dangerous to draw water there by day. Even at night the creaking of the tackle would usually call forth a storm of musketry. It was not long before the machinery, like the brick framework, was shot away; and thereafter it was necessary to haul the bucket up by hand from a depth of over sixty feet. John Mackillop of the Civil Service, in his own estimation 'not a fighting man', appointed himself 'Captain of the Well'. He survived in the office for a week until killed by grape-shot in the groin. Before dying he expressed the wish that a lady to whom he had promised a drink should not be disappointed.[51]

Parched with thirst, children could be seen sucking pieces of old water bags, putting scraps of canvas and bits of leather straps into their mouths in an effort to squeeze the last drop of moisture past their lips. Hunger, too, assailed them. In the early days of the siege, private soldiers could be seen leaving the room used as a food store with bottles of champagne, tins of herrings and salmon, pots of jam, bottles of rum and sweetmeats. But soon there were so few provisions left that daily rations were limited to half a pint of split peas and flour cooked with water into a kind of porridge and handed round in tin pots. Men risked their lives to drag back dead bullocks inside the entrenchment; dogs were considered a luxury; and so prized was horseflesh that when a *sowar* came within possible range of the mud wall it was the horse that received the first shot rather than the rider. Even the oldest hacks were considered suitable for consumption. After one ancient animal had been recovered, 'lump, thump, whack went nondescript pieces of flesh into the fire'. The head 'with some mysteries of the body' was stewed, made into soup, then dispatched to the outposts where it was delivered without explanation and accepted without question. Captain Halliday thought it sufficiently appetizing to take some back to his wife in the barracks and was shot dead on the way.[52]

Life in the outposts 'assumed the horrors of a nightmare'. The earth wall, supported in places by sandbags, afforded scant protection to the defenders who, throughout the siege, could snatch only brief, troubled moments of sleep behind them while piles of civilian hats, shakos and musket barrels were exposed to view on the parapet to give an impression of strength. As well as the outposts there were the unfinished barracks to man, for some sections of these were occupied by rebels. In the adjoining sections a few of 'the railway gentlemen', civil engineers employed on the East Indian Railroad, held out for three days 'without any military superintendence whatever and distinguished themselves greatly'.[53] After the three days an officer came to their help; and as the importance of the post began to be realized, other officers and civilians, engineers, telegraph clerks, opium-agents and surveyors were dispatched to it together with a surgeon 'who never lacked ample employment'.[54]

The fifty-nine trained artillerymen who had entered the entrenchment had all been killed or wounded by the end of the first week, and had to be replaced by infantry officers and civilian volunteers. The guns which they were required to work were by now scarcely serviceable. Some had been knocked off their carriages; others had had their sides driven in; one had lost its muzzle. Only two could be made to carry grape, owing to the irregularity of the bore; and these had to be loaded in a most eccentric manner – with women's stockings filled with the contents of tapped shot-cases. All of them were too light for their purposes; and Lieutenant Delafosse, exasperated by the little damage inflicted by his six-pound balls, rammed three of them at once down the barrel of his gun, filled the chinks up with grape, and told his men to stand back while he fired off his portentous charge. To his delight, not only did it not burst the muzzle but it silenced the rebel's guns which had been firing at him.[55] But although the guns were fired with such difficulty and the enemy's guns, which raiding parties often rushed out by night to spike, were soon replaced from Nana Sahib's seemingly inexhaustible supply, there were only two occasions when there appeared to be some danger that the rebels would break over the earth walls. Mowbray Thomson thought that, had they been more enterprising, the entrenchment could not have held out for twenty-four hours. As it was, the mutineers seemed rarely prepared to leave the cover of the surrounding buildings and then only 'under the influence of infuriating doses of bhang'.[56]

The first attack was made on 11 June. Two days before, green flags had been set up calling the Mohammedans to battle, and a flag of the Hindus, *Mahavir Jhanda*, had also been flown. But on that occasion a respected *maulvi*, after standing by the flag for some time praying for victory with his beads in his hand, had not considered the day auspicious.[57] On the 11th, however, the defenders could see 'some thousands of armed men spread about under every cover available', firing away 'as fast as they could load'. Shot and bullets came pouring into the entrenchment 'tearing away tents and the pillars of the barracks on every side'. Men and women in the shattered buildings fell to their knees in prayer, expecting that this storm of fire was bound to be followed by an assault. A few wrote their names on the wall, as Captain Jeppings had done, wanting to leave behind them some sort of memorial. But no assault came. Nor did an assault follow another fearful bombardment on 21 June when 'a very quiet mob', some in uniform, others not, were seen collecting all round the entrenchment in such numbers that Shepherd thought 'at the lowest computation they could not have been less than six thousand'. Many of them approached the earth wall, pushing in front of them big bales of cotton to serve as cover while they advanced. But this attack also was not pressed home. The rebels retreated, leaving behind them the bales of cotton which the defenders went out to collect when it was dark, using them to block up holes in the crumbling defences.[58]

So the siege continued. The stench in the entrenchment was fearful now, even though the vultures and adjutant birds soon ate the flesh of the animals that were not cut up for cooking. The temperature in the day sometimes rose to one hundred and thirty-eight degrees, and men looking across the baked and dusty plain fancied they saw cool forest scenery and water shimmering under the heat.[59] One woman ran out on to the open plain with a child in each hand, evidently hoping to end their miserable lives; but she was chased and dragged back by a private soldier.[60] A missionary of the Propagation Society went mad 'and used to walk about stark naked', after his mother, whom he had brought out on to the veranda to escape for a moment the fetid atmosphere of the barracks, was severely wounded.[61] 'And as the days passed,' so Lieutenant Thomson said, 'faces that had been beautiful became chiselled with deep furrows. Some were slowly sinking into the settled vacancy of look which marked insanity.' Everyone was 'tattered in clothing, begrimed with dirt, emaciated in countenance'.[62]

Every day there were new deaths to report. Lieutenant Jervis of the

Engineers – who scorned to run past gaps where the enemy's fire was always strong and listened impassively to shouts of 'Run, Jervis, run!' – was shot through the heart. Mr Heberden of the Railway Service was shot through the lips as he was giving a lady a drink of water. Charles Hillersdon was talking to his wife who had recently had a baby 'when a round shot . . . completely disembowelled him. His wife only survived him two or three days. She was killed by a number of falling bricks . . . causing concussion of the brain.' A native servant was shot through the head as he hurried towards an outpost with his master's gruel before it had time to cool.[63]

The privation and suffering were too much for General Wheeler who, looking 'very feeble and aged', issued orders as he sat on a mattress in the corner of his small room. His wife and two daughters sat in another corner together with Mr Roache the Post Master who had been acting as his aide-de-camp since the death of his son. Wheeler had tried to get several messages to Lucknow, but the native messengers had either deserted to the enemy, been captured by them or had taken the opportunity of going home. Shepherd offered to disguise himself as an Indian and act as a spy and messenger for the General. His offer was accepted. But having been given too much rum to fortify him at the time of his departure, he was rather drunk when he left and soon fell into the hands of the enemy.[64] A message from Cawnpore did eventually reach Lucknow but the Commissioner there felt that since the enemy commanded the river he could do nothing to help. 'Pray do not think me selfish,' Sir Henry Lawrence added. 'I would run much risk could I see commensurate prospect of success. In the present scheme I see none.'[65]

So the defenders of the entrenchment at Cawnpore had to pursue their fight unaided. Moncrieff, the station chaplain, continued to make his rounds, reading prayers from post to post where men listened to him with heads bent and hands over the muzzles of their rifles. The Roman Catholic priest, Joseph Moones, well fed by Irish soldiers who gave him tasty bits from their scanty rations, also continued with his ministrations until he died. Captain Moore, a tall, fair-haired blue-eyed Irish officer of the 32nd, who had taken over the direction of the defence after all his superiors had been incapacitated, endeavoured to ensure that all its links were as strong as he could make them. He continued to lead sorties, sallying out across the dusty plain with parties of volunteers, forcing back the rebels who rarely stood to fight, shooting some, bayoneting others, but taking no prisoners now. Lieutenant Delafosse still stood by his guns which were almost all blown up; the carriage of one, catching fire, threatened to ignite the powder in the battery. Helped by two private soldiers he threw himself beneath the burning gun and put out the fire by pulling down the fiery splinters and scattering earth on the flames, while the enemy's shot flew past his head at the rate of six a minute. Babies were born and some, for the moment, survived, to die with their mothers later. Several women, unable to bear the stench of the barracks any longer, got into craters in the compound where many died of the heat. The native servants were reduced to eating the grain which had been laid in for the horses, although the eighty sepoys who had chosen to stay with their officers had been sent out of the entrenchment to make their best way home.[66]

Scarcely a day had passed since the siege began when Nana Sahib had not been joined by a party of matchlock-men and lancers brought into Cawnpore by some landholder from the outlying districts. He had also been joined by a wealthy Muslim citizen of Cawnpore, Mohammed Ali Khan, better known as Nane Nawab, who was placed in charge of the battery near the Racquets Court. The Nawab established his headquarters in the gallery of the Court; and the surrounding area became a favourite resort of the Muslim troops and of Cawnpore's most celebrated courtesan, Azizun, who could often be seen there entertaining her admirers and providing them 'with milk, etc., on the public road'.[67]

Nana Sahib himself had now moved from Duncan's Hotel to live in a large tent in the grounds of a former charitable institution known as the Savada House, which was situated to the south of the entrenchment beside the road to Allahabad. Here many of the Muslim leaders congregated including Tika Singh whose soldiers, having completed their spells of duty in the batteries, walked up to the sweet and sherbert stalls by the canal or lay down to rest with a pipe of opium in the shade of the trees. Neither they nor the troops in the other batteries pursued the siege with noticeable vigour, and by the end of the third week in June their leaders decided to bring the operations to a close. A spy who had entered the entrenchment in the guise of a water-carrier reported that the British, short of food and much reduced in numbers, might be willing to surrender. So an emissary was dispatched to General Wheeler with a short letter written by Azimullah and addressed to 'the subjects of Her Most Gracious Majesty, Queen Victoria'.

The envoy chosen was recognized as Mrs Greenway by Lieutenant

Thomson who noticed that her ears were torn where the rings had been pulled out of them. Others identified her as Mrs Jacobi, also a Eurasian woman, the sister-in-law of Henry Jacobi, a watchmaker. Whoever she was, she arrived outside the entrenchments in a palanquin, was admitted through the wall by the sentries, and handed to General Wheeler the message from Azimullah which read: 'All those who are in no way connected with the acts of Lord Dalhousie, and are willing to lay down their arms, shall receive a safe passage to Allahabad.'[68]

Irritated by the tone of the note, both General Wheeler and the younger officers were for rejecting it outright. But Captain Moore prudently pointed out that once the wet weather, now overdue, set in, it would be impossible to hold out much longer, even if the defenders' responsibility towards the women and children justified intransigence. The rains would wash away the wall, flood the trenches and dampen the powder. In any case, there was hardly any food left.

Persuaded by Captain Moore's arguments, General Wheeler agreed to surrender; and accordingly the next morning Moore met Azimullah outside the entrenchments and agreed to hand over the position, provided the defenders were allowed to march out under arms; that carriages were provided for the wounded, the women and children; and that a sufficient number of boats were collected and provisioned for the journey downstream to Allahabad.

To all this the rebel leaders agreed; and, after Nana Sahib had waived an unreasonable demand that the entrenchment should be evacuated that very night, a deputation of officers was escorted on elephants down to the river to see the arrangements which were being made for their departure. They were not much reassured by what they found. The chosen point of embarkation was the Satichaura Ghat, a dreary-looking landing place at the mouth of a dried-up ravine whose precipitous banks were surmounted by broken fences and patches of prickly pear. On one side of the ravine was a temple with steps leading down into the shallow water of the Ganges; on the other, the mud hovels of the village from which the ghat took its name. Lying on the sandy bed of the river were a few dilapidated boats with roofs of broken thatch. At the instigation of the officers the roofs of these boats were patched up by a force of hastily enlisted workmen; the bottoms were floored with bamboo; and the paltry stores of food and water were supplemented by a more generous allowance of flour and milk.

Satisfied that the arrangements for the journey to Allahabad were at least adequate, the officers returned to the entrenchment where the bedraggled garrison had been celebrating the end of the siege, apparently having 'at once forgotten their past sufferings'.[69] 'The soldiers were singing and dancing and they tried to get up a little fun for the children,' wrote Amelia Horne, the stepdaughter of the agent of the North Western Dak Company at Cawnpore. 'A cask was converted into a drum and belaboured with a stick; one man whistled a jig, while the others started to dance. The children, though very much broken down and emaciated, yet gathered round the dancers and tried to show their appreciation of the entertainment got up for them.'[70]

On the return of the officers from the river, the people in the entrenchment gathered together the few possessions they felt able to take with them and prepared to walk down to the landing place. Some chose to take Bibles or prayer-books; others to conceal in their clothing what jewellery, silver or other valuables they had managed to save from their burned and looted homes; many felt in duty bound to take with them the objects which had been entrusted to them by the dying as bequests for families in England; the able-bodied men stuffed their pockets with ammunition 'until they were walking magazines'.[71] Led by Captain Moore and an advance-guard of the 32nd Regiment, the exodus began; the men able to walk going on foot, some of them barefoot and many without shirts which had long since been torn up for bandages; the wounded and the women and children riding in bullock carts and on elephants which they were 'obliged to climb up by their tails, as the mahouts would not allow the animals to sit down'.[72]

Major and Mrs Vibart, the elderly parents of Edward Vibart who had made good his escape from Delhi, brought up the rear and were helped on their way by some mutineers from Major Vibart's regiment who carried their belongings, attending them 'with the most profuse demonstrations of respect'.[73] Other rebels came up to ask after their officers against whom they had so recently been fighting and 'appeared much distressed at hearing of their death'. Colonel Williams's former bearer approached Mrs Williams, who was wounded in the lip, and, pitying her two daughters who were 'in wretched plight, scorched and blistered by the sun', he heard with deep sorrow that his master had died. 'My mistress asked about the property left in the house,' the bearer testified, 'and enquired about all the servants, and especially after the cook. She then told me to go and fetch him, as she wanted him to go down to Allahabad with her;

and told me to go to her son in the Hills, and inform him of all that had occurred . . . and to show him the spot where the Colonel was buried.'[74]

Crowds of people swarmed out of the city to watch the sorry procession go by, looking, mostly in silence, at the dirty, half-dressed memsahibs clinging to the ropes on the elephants; at the wounded figures in the palanquins, their limbs bound up with strips of petticoat and stockings; at the thin children in the bullock carts. They allowed them to pass without molestation, with the single exception of a sepoy who tried unsuccessfully to grab a soldier's musket. As the last of the garrison left the entrenchment, hundreds of natives ran over the earth walls to see what was left worth taking. But, so a disappointed camel-driver said, there was nothing there except 'three useless brass guns that had been split, two leather bottles of liquid butter, a sack of fine flour and the bodies of eleven Europeans. They were on quilts on the ground, some of them still breathing, though dying from severe gun-shot wounds.' So the would-be plunderers left the site and the vultures and jackals moved in.[75]

The head of the slow-moving column reached the ravine, wound its way down towards the sandy bed and made for the boats at the landing place. Standing knee-deep in the water, the men began to help the women and children and their wounded friends into the boats. 'But no sooner were we in the boats,' Lieutenant Delafosse reported, 'and had laid down our muskets and taken off our coats in order to work easier than . . . two guns that had been hidden were run out and opened on us immediately, whilst sepoys came from all directions and kept up a brisk fire.'[76]

The troopers who had helped the Vibarts down to the river discharged their carbines at the nearest boat; and from the high banks above the stream, from the houses in a nearby village, from behind a pile of timber awaiting shipment from the ghat, and from the opposite shore, volley after volley of musketry and grape-shot were fired towards the river as the boatmen, having placed pieces of red hot charcoal in their straw roofs, leaped out of the boats and ran for safety up the temple steps. The Europeans who still had guns in their hands fired at the fleeing boatmen, at the retreating *sowars* of Vibart's regiment and at the positions from which hundreds of concealed rebels seemed to be shooting at them.[77] As some of the boats leaped into flame, desperate efforts were made to push the keels of others off the sandbanks on which they were stuck fast. Around them women and children crouched down in the water, or waded out towards the middle of the stream where the water reached up to their chins, or tried to find shelter behind the tall, overhanging prows, while their husbands, fathers and friends struggled to help them or to make their escape downstream. Moncrieff, the chaplain, opened his prayer-book and had begun to read from it when he was killed. A man near him was clubbed to death in the mud by boatmen as he scrambled for the safety of an open drain. As scores of other men fell dead in the water or on the sand at the river's edge, a squadron of troopers came down towards the burning boats from the direction of the temple. A group of them made for General Wheeler whom the half-caste wife of a bandsmen of the 56th saw cut down by a sword-blow across the neck. 'My son was killed near him,' this woman recorded. 'I saw it . . . Some were stabbed with bayonets; others cut down . . . We saw it; we did; and tell you only what we saw . . . Children were stabbed and thrown into the river. The schoolgirls were burnt to death. I saw their clothes and hair catch fire. In the water, a few paces off, by the next boat, we saw the youngest daughter of Colonel Williams. A sepoy was going to kill her with his bayonet. She said, "My father was always kind to sepoys." He turned away, and just then a villager struck her on the head with his club, and she fell into the water.'[78]

The cavalry waded into the river with drawn swords and cut down those who were still alive, while the infantry boarded the boats to loot [recorded Amelia Horne]. One unfortunate, a Mr Kirkpatrick, in trying to ward off the blows from a sabre with his arms, had both arms chopped off. I saw him about half an hour later lying in the water still alive!

The air resounded with the shrieks of the women and children, and agonized prayers to God for mercy. The water was red with blood, and the smoke from the heavy firing of the cannon and muskets and the fire from the burning boats lay like dense clouds all around us . . . My poor little sister . . . moaned piteously, crying out the while: 'Oh, Amy, don't leave me!' A few yards away I saw the boat containing my poor mother slowly burning, and I cowered on the deck overwhelmed with grief, not knowing what horrible fate the next moment had in store for me. My heart beat like a sledge hammer, and my temples throbbed with pain; but there I sat holding my little sister's hand, while the bullets fell like hail around me, praying fervently to God for mercy.[79]

When the firing ceased the men were separated from the women and children and were all shot. One boat, however, of lighter draught than the others, its thatched roof unburned, began to drift down-stream through the thick black smoke and the slowly reddening water. Twelve men, 'beating the water for dear life', swam after it.

One of them was Lieutenant Thomson who, realizing that he could do nothing to save either the wounded being burned to death in the boats or those who had been able to throw themselves out into the water, threw away his father's Ghuznee medal and his mother's portrait and struck out to save himself. He and a few others managed to reach the boat and haul themselves aboard.

A second boat got away from the ghat, and, while drifting, was struck by a round shot below the water-mark, and was rapidly filling when she came alongside and we took off the survivors [Mowbray Thomson recorded]. Now the crowded state of our poor ark left little room for working her. Her rudder was shot away, we had no oars, for these had all been thrown overboard by the traitorous boatmen, and the only implements that could be brought into use were a spar or two and such pieces of wood as we could in safety tear from the sides. Grape and round shot flew about us from either bank of the river, and shells burst constantly on the sandbanks ... Mrs Swinton, who was a relative of Lieutenant Jervis of the Engineers, was standing up in the stern, and, having been struck by a round shot, fell overboard and sank immediately. Her poor little boy, six years old, came up to me and said, 'Mamma has fallen overboard.' I endeavoured to comfort him, and told him Mamma would not suffer any more pain ... He cried out, 'Oh, why are they firing on us? Did they not promise to leave off?' I never saw the child after that ... The wounded and the dead were entangled together in the bottom of the boat: to extricate the corpses was a work of extreme difficulty, though imperatively necessary from the dreaded consequences of the intense heat, and the importance of lightening the boat as much as possible ... A bullet struck the side of my head, and I fell into the boat, stunned by the wound. 'We were just going to throw you overboard,' was the greeting I had from some of the men when I revived ... Shortly after midday we got out of range of their great guns ... But they chased us the whole day firing volleys of musketry [and] arrows with lighted charcoal attached to them to ignite the thatched roof [which], in consequence, we were obliged to throw overboard ... At 5 p.m. we stranded [and] when we did succeed in getting adrift, the work of pushing away from the sand-banks was incessant; and we spent as much of the night out of the boat as in it. There was no moon, however, and although they did not cease firing at us until after midnight, they did us little damage.[80]

The next day most of the people in the boat were either killed or wounded; but escaping from a party of sixty rebels sent to destroy them in a boat which grounded on a sandbank, the survivors managed to reach Surajpur where their own boat grounded once more. Major Vibart, the senior officer present, wounded in both arms, ordered a party to wade ashore to keep their pursuers at bay while he and a few others attempted to ease the boat into deeper water. The landing party succeeded in driving off the sepoys, but when they returned to the river the boat was gone, and they never saw it or its occupants again. Left to make their way to Allahabad on foot, the officers and men who had landed struck away across country, fighting off the rebels sent out to kill them, apprehensively passing alligators basking by the river's edge, losing many of their number until there were only four of them left, two Irish private soldiers, both wounded and both 'altogether destitute of clothing of any kind', Lieutenant Delafosse also naked apart from 'a piece of sheeting round his loins', and Mowbray Thomson. Thanks to the protection of a local rajah, Dirigbijah Singh, these four eventually reached safety, though one of the soldiers died soon afterwards and Lieutenant Delafosse went out of his mind for a time, harbouring the pleasant delusion that he had been presented with £30,000 and had inherited vast estates in Scotland to which he invited everyone he saw.[81]

At the Satichaura Ghat in Cawnpore, the women and children who had survived the massacre, about 125 of them, were pulled out of the river and collected together on the sand by some of the Nana's men. Most were barefoot; many were wounded; some, who had pieces of jewellery snatched from them, had bleeding fingers and ears. Once they were all assembled orders were given to molest them no more. They were allowed to accept the skin bags offered to them by a party of water-carriers whose pity was aroused by their plight.

'Their clothes had blood on them,' testified a witness of their removal to the Savada House where Nana Sahib had had his headquarters. 'Two were badly hurt and had their heads bound up with handkerchiefs. Some were . . . covered with mud . . . Some had their dresses torn . . . There were no men in the party, but only some boys of twelve or thirteen years of age.'[82]

Seven of them, four British and three Eurasian, were carried off by troopers of the 2nd Cavalry. But when Nana Sahib, whose responsibility for the massacre at the Satichaura Ghat has never been established, heard of their abduction he ordered that they should be returned. And, with the exception of two of the Eurasian girls, they were all sent back. One of those retained by their captors was General Wheeler's youngest daughter, a girl of eighteen, whose supposed fate was enacted in theatres and described in magazines and books all over the world. She had, it was said, killed her captor, a young trooper named Ali Khan, as well as his entire family, then thrown herself down a well. In fact, so it appears, she had agreed to become a Muslim and to marry him. Many years later a Roman Catholic priest in Cawnpore came upon an old lady in the bazaar who told him on her deathbed that she was Miss Wheeler. She said she had married the sepoy who had saved her from massacre, that he had been good to her and that she did not want to get in touch with the British authorities.[83] The other Eurasian girl was Amelia Horne who was also eighteen. She was, she claimed, forcibly converted to Mohammedanism and married to a mutineer who eventually allowed her to escape to Allahabad after she had signed a paper exculpating him.[84]

The other women in the Savada House were soon joined by several of those who had escaped in the boat from the ghat. The boat had been captured at Nazafgarh where Major Vibart had sent Lieutenant Thomson's party ashore to fight off their pursuers. It had been dragged back to Cawnpore with a load of about sixty men, most of them wounded, twenty-five women and four children. According to a native spy

the Sahibs were seated on the ground; and two companies [of Nana Sahib's troops] stood with their muskets ready to fire. Then said one of the Memsahibs, the doctor's wife [Mrs Boyes], 'I will not leave my husband. If he must die, I will die with him.' So she ran and sat down behind her husband, clasping him round the waist. Directly she said this, the other Memsahibs said, 'We also will die with our husbands.' And they all sat down, each by her husband. Then their husbands said, 'Go back.' But they would not. Whereupon the . . . soldiers . . . pulled them away forcibly. But they could not pull away the doctor's wife, who there remained. Then the Padre . . . requested leave to read prayers before they died . . . The Padre's hands were loosened so far as to enable him to take a small book from his pocket, which he read. But all this time one of the Sahibs, who was shot in the arm, kept crying out to the sepoys: 'If you mean to kill us, why don't you set about it quickly and have the work done?' After the Padre had read a few prayers, he shut the book, and the Sahibs shook hands all round. Then the sepoys fired. One Sahib rolled one way, one another, as they sat. But they were not dead. So they went in and finished them off with swords.[85]

The women and children were then taken to the Savada House, and thence to a smaller house near by, a house originally built by a British officer for his mistress and known as Bibighar. Here, on 10 July, they were joined by some officers' wives who had escaped from Fatehgarh and had been captured at Nawabganj. There were in all now just over two hundred women and children crammed inside the few rooms at Bibighar, or, as it was to become known in India, the House of the Ladies. There was no furniture or bedding in the house. Bamboo matting was provided for the captives to lie on; chupatties and dhal for them to eat, and some milk for the children. The food was served in earthenware pans and saucers by a party of low-caste sweepers under the orders of a tall, fair-skinned native woman, Hussani Khanum, who had been a prostitute's maid and was nick-named, 'The Begum'. Every day 'The Begum' escorted two of the ladies to grind corn in the stables attached to a big, yellow-painted hotel about a quarter of a mile from Bibighar. In this hotel Nana Sahib now held his court.[86]

At the end of the previous month Nana Sahib had held a review to celebrate the successful termination of the siege of the entrenchment. As well as several batteries of artillery and detachments from various regiments which had mutinied and largely dispersed, there were six complete infantry and two cavalry regiments on the parade-ground when their leader appeared to a twenty-one gun salute. He announced that, in celebration of the army's triumph, he would shortly distribute 100,000 rupees to the brave troops who had brought that victory about, whereupon the salute of guns was repeated.

Two days later the guns fired yet again when the Nana proceeded to Bithur to be installed on his father's throne as Peshwa and to have the consecration mark fixed to his forehead. That evening Cawnpore was illuminated and a proclamation announced to the people that 'by the kindness of God' all the Christians who had been at Delhi and 'at other places' had been 'destroyed and sent to hell by the pious and sagacious troops, firm in their religion'; and that, as 'the yellow-faced and narrow-minded people' had been conquered at Cawnpore, it was the duty of all subjects of the new government 'to rejoice at the delightful intelligence', to carry on their work, and to be 'as obedient to the present government as they had been to the former one'.[87]

Confident in the satisfactory establishment of his new rule, Nana Sahib was reported to be much enjoying himself at his gaily-painted hotel, lavishing money on a favourite courtesan, and laughing at the hilarious antics of a comedian who, during the noisy entertainments which were held each night, imitated the stiff, proud walk of an English officer. There was, however, a slightly disturbing cloud in Nana Sahib's blue sky. There were reports of sickness and death in the nearby House of the Ladies where his hostages were dying of cholera and dysentery at a most worrying rate: in the space of just over a week twenty-five of them were brought out dead in addition to a Hindu nurse. If they continued to die off at such a rate there would soon be none left. So orders were given for the captives to be brought out in turns twice a day on to the veranda to breathe some fresh air, and to be attended to by a doctor. But no sooner had Nana Sahib been reassured that the fast rate of the death roll in the House of the Ladies had been slowed than disturbing news reached him from the south. Scouts dispatched on camels in the direction of Allahabad came galloping back with reports that a strong British army was fast approaching Cawnpore by forced marches.[88]

10

Enter Henry Havelock

· Henry Havelock · James Neill · mutiny of the 6th Native Infantry
at Allahabad, 6 June 1857 · arrival of Neill at Allahabad, 11 June – his
ruthless methods · Havelock leaves Allahabad for Cawnpore, 7 July ·
his victorious campaign and arrival at Cawnpore · murder of
Nana Sahib's hostages · defeat of Nana Sahib, 16 July ·
Neill's revenge · the executions at Cawnpore ·
rebels' alleged atrocities – cries for vengeance ·

The British Army now approaching Cawnpore was commanded by
Brigadier-General Henry Havelock. Early impressions of Havelock
could be misleading. There were those who found him rather absurd,
'an old fossil dug up and only fit to be turned into pipe clay'.[1]
Scarcely more than five feet in height, he walked as though he wore
iron ramrods in the back of his jacket and never dined without his
sword together with such a quantity of medals, like rows of five-
shilling pieces, that Lady Canning thought he looked 'almost
ridiculous', 'as if he carried his money tied up in a bunch on his
shoulders'.[2] But she, like most others, soon grew to respect him. He
was, she said, deemed by many to be too outdated for words; 'but all
the same we believe he will do well. No doubt he is fussy and tiresome, but his little, old, stiff figure looks as fit and active for use as
if he were made of steel.'[3]

He was sixty-two years old. His hair and moustache were white;
his brown, leathery face deeply lined; his firmly set mouth fringed by
a beard of extremely old-fashioned cut. Born in Sunderland, the son
of a rich, opinionated shipbuilder who had moved south to a large
country house in Kent which he was obliged to sell when his business
failed, Henry Havelock had not wanted to be a soldier but a lawyer.
After leaving Charterhouse he had for a time trained in a special
pleader's office; but, having quarrelled with his father, who refused to
continue paying his allowance, he was obliged to accept the offer of a
commission in the army made to him by his elder brother, an officer

whose conduct at Waterloo had so aroused the admiration of General von Alten that he had been promised a commission for anyone he cared to name.

Once in the army, Havelock displayed an eager determination to succeed in it, so exasperating his fellow subalterns who found him laboriously studying the campaigns of Napoleon and Frederick the Great that they would throw his books out of the window and jump on his head. And when his father lost the little money he had salvaged from the wreck of the shipbuilding business – a misfortune which persuaded Henry he would have to go out to serve in India where poor officers stood a better chance of promotion – he immediately enrolled at the Oriental Institute in Leicester Square so as to become proficient in Persian and Hindustani.

In India his diligent studies were continued, and his reputation for earnestness and industry increased. When other young men in his regiment amused themselves with racing, drinking and nautch girls, he preferred the company of Baptist missionaries under whose influence he was persuaded that it was his 'solemn Christian duty to devote his time and attention to the spiritual welfare of his men', to hold religious meetings, to preach sermons, to give Bible lessons, to take part in the singing of hymns, to persist in his attempts to win friends for Jesus 'in the very teeth of ridicule and opposition'. Aloof, argumentative, ambitious and censorious, he concealed a deep need of affection behind a manner at once reticent and ruminative. Promotion came to him slowly, for he was repeatedly passed over 'by three sots and two fools'. But in a series of campaigns in which he displayed coolness and great courage, he gained the reputation of a reliable soldier. Yet he had never achieved his main ambition, which was to command an army in the field.

Now his chance had come. 'May God give me wisdom to fulfil the expectations of Government,' he wrote to his wife, the daughter of a Baptist missionary, 'and to restore tranquillity to the disturbed districts.' He was only too well aware of the divine protection he would require in leading so small an army against so far more numerous a force at a time of year when European troops usually spent most of their days sweltering in the heat on their beds. But he was comforted by the belief that he had been 'chosen by the Almighty to perform a Christian duty'. Indeed, he believed that if the Government had been less unwilling to allow missionaries to teach the Bible to sepoys the notion that they were to be forcibly converted to Christianity could never have spread so fast. Now that the notion had

spread, however, there must be no weakness in the face of its consequences. He expressed the strong opinion that there 'must be no
more disbandments for mutiny. Mutineers must be attacked and anni-
hilated; and if there are few in any regiments, and not immediately
announced to be shot or hanged, the whole regiment must be deemed
guilty and given up to prompt military execution.'[4]

Similar views had already been expressed by Colonel James Neill
of the 1st Madras Fusiliers, whom Havelock now met on his journey
north from Calcutta at Allahabad. Neill was also a God-fearing man
who believed himself capable of higher command than had yet been
entrusted to him. Stern and hard-swearing, strong and masterful, he
was not only admired by senior officers who saw in him, as Lord
Canning did, the kind of forthright, determined man whom the crisis
demanded, but he was also loved by those who were asked to join his
personal staff when he was called with his regiment from Madras to
Bengal. 'He was the finest-looking man I ever saw,' wrote one of
them, Lieutenant George Blake, 'great shaggy moustache and eye-
brows, and he feared nobody . . . He was the sternest and, at the same
time, kindest and best-hearted of men.'[5] Neill's aide-de-camp,
Captain Gordon of the 6th Native Infantry, who had been hidden in a
hut by the men of his company when the rest of his regiment mutinied, also considered the Colonel 'really one of the kindest and most
considerate men' he had ever known. 'He enters with his whole heart
into the miseries and distresses of individuals,' Gordon added. 'I
wouldn't miss being with him on any account whatever . . . He is
worth half a dozen Havelocks.'[6]

Neill himself was inclined to agree with this verdict; and, when
Havelock arrived at Allahabad, he made no secret of his belief that it
was he rather than 'Mr Pomposity', as his staff referred to Havelock,
who ought to have been placed in command of the movable column
that was to march on Cawnpore. Neill had certainly performed the
tasks that had so far been given to him with notable dispatch, if not
with faultless efficiency. He had delighted the army by promptly
arresting the stationmaster at Calcutta who had declined to delay the
departure of a train on which Neill had hoped to send up some of his
Fusiliers to Benares, the Hindus' most sacred city, where many state
prisoners were held and where several members of the Moghul royal
family lived in discontented idleness. At Benares, Neill had insisted
on the immediate disarming of the 37th and had taken over command
from Brigadier Ponsonby who had appeared to be losing control of
himself when the regiment panicked in the middle of the ill-conducted

parade and seemed about to fire on the European troops. Order had soon been restored by Neill, who declared his belief that 'the Word of God gives no authority to the modern tenderness for human life'. Under his directions, so it appears, artillery had opened up on the frightened sepoys, as well as upon a regiment of Sikhs and some irregular cavalry who, fearing that they too were going to be attacked, started firing themselves.[7] After the parade, gallows were immediately erected; and scores of natives suspected of rebellious intent were subsequently hanged on them, including 'some boys, who, perhaps in mere sport, had flaunted rebel colours and gone about beating tom-toms'.[8] Hanging parties also went out into the surrounding districts, 'and amateur executioners were not wanting to the occasion. One gentleman boasted of the numbers he had finished off, quite "in an artistic manner", with mango trees for gibbets and elephants for drops, the victims of this wild justice being strung up, as though for pastime, in "the form of a figure of eight".'[9]

Neill had restored order with equal promptness and severity at Allahabad where the 6th Native Infantry, a previously loyal regiment, in terror at his approach, had murdered most of their officers including seven young cadets just arrived from England; and, joined by hundreds of the town's inhabitants, had then broken open the gaol, plundered the shops, torn down the telegraph wires, destroyed the railway lines and sheds, bombarded the railway engines which they had not dared to approach, and massacred those native Christians who had not run off for the fort.[10] The fort itself, which was garrisoned by about a hundred European volunteers, a few invalid artillerymen, a company of sepoys of the 6th and a detachment of Sikhs, might also have fallen had not Captain Brayser of the Sikhs, formerly a private soldier and once a gardener, persuaded his men to assist in the disarming of the sepoys. By the time that Neill arrived, however, the Sikhs had discovered huge stores of liquor in the cellars of the fort where everything, as a missionary said, was as badly managed as could be.[11] The Sikhs had poured as much of the liquor as they could down their own throats before selling the rest to the European volunteers who were soon so drunk that they could not stand up, let alone fire their muskets. 'Thank God,' said the sentry who opened the gate for Neill, 'you'll save us yet.'[12]

Neill lost no time. Although utterly exhausted and so weak that he could swallow nothing except water and champagne and had to be carried on a litter into the batteries, he issued orders for the bombardment of the town and for the retaking of the bridge which the rebels had captured; he bought up or destroyed all the liquor in the fort; he asked Brayser to persuade the Sikhs that they would have better chances of plunder if they camped outside the walls, and he sent out fighting patrols to intimidate the surrounding countryside into submission. Eagerly responding to his orders, European volunteers and Sikhs descended upon the town, burning houses and slaughtering the inhabitants, old men, women and children as well as those more likely to be active rebels who were submitted to the travesty of a trial. 'The gallows and trees adjoining it had each day the fresh fruits of rebellion displayed upon them,' admitted E. A. Thurburn who was appointed Deputy Judge Advocate General. 'Hundreds of natives in this manner perished and some on slight proofs of criminality.'[13] 'Every day ten or a dozen niggers are hanged,' Lieutenant Pearson of the 84th told his mother.[14] Their corpses hung 'by twos and threes from branch and signpost all over the town . . . For three months did eight dead-carts daily go their rounds from sunrise to sunset, to take down corpses which hung at the cross-roads, and the market-places, poisoning the air of the city, and to throw their loathsome burdens into the Ganges.'[15]

'God grant I may have acted with justice,' Neill wrote on 17 June. 'I know I have with severity, but under all the circumstances I trust for forgiveness.'[16] The next day cholera broke out in the fort. There were no medicines to treat the symptoms or alleviate the pain, no punkahs to cool the sufferers in the appalling heat. Twenty-eight men died within two days. The screams of the sick were so terrifying that two women occupying a room over the hospital were said to have died of fright.[17]

To a request that he should move quickly on from Benares to Allahabad, Neill had curtly telegraphed, 'Can't move. Wanted here.' Now he found himself unable to proceed to Cawnpore. Not only was cholera rife, but the native contractors, as justifiably terrified by the Europeans as they had been by marauders during the recent riots, could not be found to furnish the necessary supplies. Moreover, 1,600 bullocks collected for the transport of these supplies had been driven off by the mutineers. But after insistent efforts, by the time Havelock joined him at Allahabad, Neill had been able to dispatch to Cawnpore three hundred men of the Madras Fusiliers under Major Renaud, accompanied by four hundred Sikhs, a small force of irregular cavalry and two guns. Renaud had been instructed to encourage the inhabitants to return to their villages, and to 'instil confidence into all of the restoration of British authority'. Yet 'all places *en route* close to the road where the rebels had been succoured' were to be attacked and destroyed. Signal examples were to be made of Mubgoon, where all the men were to be slaughtered, and of Fatehpur where all the leading insurgents were to be hanged and the head of the Deputy Collector was to be 'cut off and stuck up on one of the principal Mahomedan buildings in the town'.[18]

Havelock was quite as busy and just as frustrated as Neill, knowing that, in spite of all his efforts, his impatient critics were blaming him for being 'so slow in getting on to Cawnpore', complaining that Neill would not have been 'such a dawdler'.[19] It was not until a week after his arrival at Allahabad that he felt able to move on, leaving Neill in command there and sending on a message to Renaud to halt where he was, to burn no more villages unless they were actually occupied by insurgents.[20] And even then Havelock had not received all the summer clothing for which he had asked: most of his men as they marched out of the city in the stifling heat of the overcast afternoon of 7 July, watched by crowds of sullen, resentful Muslims, were still wearing their heavy woollen tunics. It was a pitifully small force – an assorted collection of about a thousand British troops from four different infantry regiments, less than 150 Sikhs, six guns, a detachment of native irregulars, and no more than twenty volunteer cavalry composed of officers whose regiments had mutinied, shopkeepers whose premises had been burned, and indigo-planters whose workmen had run away, 'in short of all who were willing to join'. All the force's forage caps, including the General's, were covered with white cotton to protect the neck, except those of the Madras Fusiliers, a regiment of tough, hard-drinking Europeans, several of them gentlemen whose debts or misbehaviour had led them to consider service in the ranks in 'Neill's Blue Caps' preferable to more public disgrace. The 'Blue Caps' and a few others carried the new Enfield rifle; the rest had to make do with muskets. Behind the column followed the inevitable, seemingly endless, straggling crowd of animals and carts, servants and camp-followers, both men and women, that always accompanied an Indian army on the march.

Many of the troops seemed quite as surly as the citizens of Allahabad. Before their departure, Havelock had submitted them to one of those Napoleonic addresses which Captain Gordon for one found so tiresome. 'Soldiers!' the General began in ringing tones. 'There is work before us. We are bound on an expedition whose object is to restore the supremacy of British rule and avenge the fate of British men and women . . .' There was some scattered cheering; but when

Colonel Hamilton of the 78th Highlanders turned in his saddle and shouted, 'Hurrah!' in an effort to elicit a more encouraging response, the silence was broken only by muttering.

'Your men like better to cheer when the bugle sounds "Charge" than when it sounds "General Parade",' Havelock commented to Hamilton as he rode past him. This brought forth a rather more encouraging sound from the Highlanders, and Havelock smiled as though much pleased. But those close to him knew how worried he was that now, when at last he had an army to command, it was such a small and dispirited one.[21]

As usual after an hour or two, the camp-followers lagged far behind the leading troops. The trudging human figures, the bumping carts and the surly-looking camels stretched for miles across the plain over which rose clouds of thick yellow dust. During the afternoon, when the dark clouds overhead burst and the rain came pouring down, the line of march became so distended that as darkness fell, Havelock called a halt. The men, who had covered little more than eight miles, took shelter in a steaming mango grove while waiting for their tents to come up, grumbling at the middle-aged artillery men from the Invalid Depot at Chuner who had been allowed to ride in tumbrils.[22]

The following morning, bugles called them from their tents at four. That day they marched another eight miles; about twelve the next; another twelve on 10 July, tramping past swamps and the blackened ruins of huts now further defaced by weather stains and mould, the unpleasant smell of neem trees in their nostrils, hearing the croaking of frogs, the hum of insects and the shrill piping of the cicadas above the noise of the march. The going was very slow; but even so, many of the men, and most of the young recruits, could not keep up with the rest. 'In a way,' one officer commented, 'it was a good thing that we knew by now Cawnpore had fallen. I don't think we would have been any good if we had had to hurry to save it.'[23]

On both sides of the line of march were scenes of devastation, every building or object which indicated the spread of British civilization having been destroyed, even the milestones lying smashed by the roadside or tossed into the paddy fields. Hanging from the trees, their legs eaten away by pigs, were scores of bodies strung up by the men of Renaud's column whose commander had been 'rather inclined to hang all black creation'.[24]

Havelock's weary army subjected the native population to less indiscriminate punishment. Occasionally a village supposed to be harbouring rebels was shelled. But otherwise 'the few niggers seen were generally ignored'; and when an officer's servant attempted to steal the wares of a sweetmeat seller, J. W. Sherer, the Magistrate from Fatehpur who was accompanying the force, tied the culprit to a tree and beat him with his cane.[25]

On the fifth day the pace of the march quickened, for Havelock's spies reported that Renaud's column was threatened by a huge force under Nana Sahib advancing down the Grand Trunk Road. So, after exhausting marches by day as well as night, the army overtook Renaud, and came upon the enemy near Fatehpur. The rebels were occupying a strong position amidst walled enclosures and mango groves in front of the town. But Havelock's infantry marched forward with determination, while his artillery splashed through a swamp to open up on the enemy flank. Within ten minutes the enemy, who had started the battle in such confidence, were in utter confusion, dismayed by the long range of the Enfield rifles and the accurate, steady fire of Captain Maude's artillerymen. As they began to retreat Colonel Bannatyne Fraser Tytler, the Assistant Quarter-Master General, rode up to Maude, calling out, 'Knock over that chap on the elephant!' as he pointed to a rebel leader riding off the field. Maude laid a gun himself, sent a ball bowling across the field under the elephant's tail and the rider flying through the air.

'As we moved forward,' Havelock wrote in his dispatch, 'the enemy's guns continued to fall into our hands, and then in succession the rebels were driven from the garden enclosures, from a strong barricade on the road, from the town wall, into, and through, out of, and beyond the town.'

Four hours later the fighting was all over, and the men fell down to sleep in the shade, many of them too tired to eat. Though several had collapsed and died of heat-stroke, not one had been killed by the enemy. It was a brilliant victory; and Havelock was blissfully proud of himself, of being the victorious instrument of Almighty God in 'a most righteous cause, the cause of justice, humanity, truth and good government in India'.

'One of the prayers oft repeated throughout my life since my school days has been answered,' he told his wife. 'I have lived to command in a successful action . . . I captured in four hours eleven guns and scattered the enemy's whole force to the winds . . . But away with vain glory! Thanks to Almighty God who gave me the victory . . . I now march to retake Cawnpore.'[26]

So, while the Sikhs were sent back to Neill at Allahabad – after faithfully executing their welcome orders to plunder Fatehpur as a punishment for its inhabitants' rebellion – the army moved on down the Cawnpore road, past abandoned tents and ammunition, blackened, empty villages and vultures tearing flesh from the sides of dead bullocks. They were checked at Aong where the rebels fought bravely; and several of Havelock's men were killed. But they were not delayed for long. They pushed on to the Panda Nudi, an unfordable river, where the rebels were prepared to blow up the stone bridge. Exhausted as they were by the long march and the fighting at Aong, the men responded readily when, while lying down waiting for their breakfast, they were ordered to get to their feet and march down in the burning sun towards the river. Again they were successful. More enemy guns were captured; and the rebels retreated from the bridge under which their mines, not yet in position, exploded without causing much damage. The way to Cawnpore was now open.[27]

The next day was hotter than ever. Havelock's force started out before dawn after a night in which few of the men could sleep, pestered as they had been by flies in the still and stifling air. With nothing to eat except biscuits – for the meat which they had been too tired to eat the night before had now rotted – they marched for sixteen miles, several men collapsing by the roadside once the burning sun was up, the others grimly stamping on, thinking of the two hundred women and children held, so they had been told, as hostages by Nana Sahib: 'By God's help, men,' Havelock had said, 'we shall save them, or every man of us die in the attempt. I am trying you sorely, men, but I know the stuff you are made of. Think of our women and the tender infants in the power of those devils incarnate!'[28]

Nana Sahib's headquarters were crowded with leading rebels, some proposing a retreat to Bithur, others suggesting a move towards Fatehgarh, yet others arguing for a withdrawal south of Cawnpore and for a further stand there. The last plan was at length adopted; but then there was the problem of the hostages to be discussed. It was pointed out that they could prove to be dangerous witnesses against the rebels; that to dispose of them now might save lives later because the British, intent on releasing them, would not risk another battle with Nana Sahib's forces once they knew their women were dead. The proposal to kill the hostages seems to have been strongly condemned by the women of Nana Sahib's household who. threatened to throw themselves out of a high window if any further murders were committed and who, in the meantime, refused all food and drink.

Despite their protestations, however, the execution of all the hostages was decided upon. First three Englishmen from Fatehgarh, who had been placed in the house a few days previously, together with the merchant Greenway, Greenway's son, and a boy of fourteen, were brought out and shot dead by a squad of sepoys. Then it was announced that the women would also be shot. But the sepoy guard protested; they would not kill the memsahibs. And when the order came to shoot the prisoners, they appear to have put their muskets through the windows of the various rooms and fired them into the ceilings. Exasperated by their behaviour, 'the Begum' went to fetch some less fastidious men who would not shrink from the necessary task of executing Christians. She returned with five, two Hindu peasants, two Mohammedan butchers, and a man wearing the red uniform of Nana Sahib's bodyguard who was said to be her lover. These men entered the house from which shrieks of terror and screams of pain were presently heard. One of the butchers came out with a broken sword, went over to the hotel and returned with a new one. By nightfall the screaming had stopped but groans continued long after the executioners had left and the doors had been closed.[29]

'The hotel where Nana had his quarters was within fifty yards of this house,' J. W. Sherer wrote in his official report, 'and I am credibly informed that he ordered a nautch and passed the evening with singing and dancing. Early next morning orders were given for the Beebeegurgh to be cleared.'[30]

'The bodies were dragged out, most of them by the hair of the head,' according to one witness. 'Those who had clothes worth taking were stripped. Some of the women were alive. I cannot say how many; but three could speak. They prayed for the sake of God that an end might be put to their sufferings.'[31]

Most of the dead bodies were thrown into a well, and so, Sherer thought, were some of those still living. Sherer also believed that, when the well was full, the rest of the corpses were dropped into the Ganges.[32]

General Havelock found Nana Sahib's men, five thousand strong, drawn up in a crescent outside Cawnpore, evidently expecting a frontal attack. He decided, however, that he 'would not oblige them', but, 'like old Frederick at Leuthen', attack them on their left flank. This involved a long march through mango groves and ploughed fields in the intense heat of the afternoon. It was 'one of the most severe marches ever made in India', a gunner officer thought. 'The sun struck down with fearful force. At every step a man reeled out of the ranks and threw himself fainting by the side of the road – the calls for water incessant all along the line.'[33]

The men had not gone far when they came under heavy fire, the crashes of the shot through the trees being accompanied in the distance by a sepoy band playing what sounded like – and was no doubt intended to be – *Auld Lang Syne*. At the turning point, the infantry wheeled into line, then lay down while Maude's cannon endeavoured to silence the enemy fire. But his guns were too light; the rebels' pieces too well sheltered; and the Highlanders were ordered to charge. It was the first of several charges bravely carried out that day, as Havelock, who to Major North seemed as 'gifted with ubiquity as scornful of danger', rode about the field, giving orders, shouting encouragement: 'Well done, 78th! Another charge like that wins the day! . . . Well done, gentlemen volunteers, I am proud to command you! . . . Come, who'll take this village, the Highlanders or the 64th? . . . The longer you look at it, men, the less you will like it. Rise up. The brigade will advance!'

As though vying with each other to earn their General's approbation, the regiments sprang forward in turn and gradually drove the enemy back. For a time the rebels rallied under the urgent commands of their leaders. But a final, desperate charge, in which Havelock's son and aide-de-camp took a prominent part, broke the rebels' line. Nana Sahib galloped away towards Bithur, while thousands of people from Cawnpore fled from the city into the surrounding countryside to avoid the vengeance of the British soldiers.[34]

In response to a telegram from the Commander-in-Chief, James Neill, now promoted Brigadier-General, handed over his command at Allahabad and arrived at Cawnpore on 20 July, passing over Havelock's battlefields where his aide-de-camp was obliged to hold a handkerchief to his nose, though 'the smell appeared to have no effect upon the General'.[35] Neill was under the impression that the authorities in Calcutta had lost confidence in Havelock and wanted Neill's superior talents to be available to guide him. The meeting between the two men was, therefore, far from cordial. Havelock knew that Neill, who had been writing to the Commander-in-Chief with advice as to how the operations ought to be conducted, had resented being left behind at Allahabad and would certainly not take kindly to being left at Cawnpore when the army moved across the Ganges for Lucknow. 'Now General Neill,' he said to him as soon as they were alone together, 'let us understand one another. You have no power or authority here whilst I am here, and you are not to issue a single order.'[36]

Fortunately the two men did not remain in Cawnpore together for long. Five days after Neill's arrival Havelock left to join the army which, earlier on that week, had been laboriously transported across the now wide and rapid Ganges in a steamer which had constantly broken down in the torrential rain. Neill would complain of being required to stay behind to organize everything, Havelock warned Calcutta, but there was no other officer to whom the task could be entrusted. Complain Neill did. He also privately expressed the opinion that the 'old gentleman', as he called Havelock, was not up to the difficult task that confronted him, that he was jealous of Neill as his heir-at-law, liking him 'no more than heirs-at-law usually were liked'.[37]

Left to himself in Cawnpore, Neill made up his mind to punish with the most savage ferocity people who were presumed to be responsible for the murder of the women and children in the House of the Ladies. He had inspected the house, 'a most dismal-looking little place', with Captain Gordon who was 'at a loss to describe the horrors of that human slaughter-house'. Ladies' and children's clothes of all descriptions were strewn about, petticoats, skirts, slippers, stays, straw hats and bonnets, and 'all of them covered with blood'. There were the boards of prayer books from which the leaves had been torn out, scattered papers, the remains of a few coarse chupatties and some earthenware saucers, tresses and plaits of hair. The floor was covered with clotted blood, 'looking like Russian leather'.

All the way to the well was marked by a regular track along which the bodies had been dragged, and the thorny bushes had entangled in them scraps of clothing and long hairs. One of the large trees . . . had evidently had children's brains dashed out against its trunk . . . and an eye glazed and withered could be plainly made out . . . smashed into the coarse bark.[38]

Officers and men paraded through the scene of 'these most *atrocious, fiendish* of murders' day after day, picking up strands of hair to send home to England.[39] Some became almost hysterical with rage and pity. The '*poor poor* creatures', wrote Major Bingham as though in tears after looking down the well where the mangled bodies could be vaguely discerned in the gloom. 'It was a sight I wish I had never seen, but once seen never to be forgotten.'[40] Every soldier who visited Bibighar felt the same. For to the mid-nineteenth century British

210

mind this ruthless murder of women and children was a crime of unspeakable, blasphemous enormity. Englishmen regarded women in a light quite different from that in which Indians did, as creatures not merely of another sex but almost – if they were not mere drudges – of another form of creation, as (in T. H. Huxley's phrase) 'angels above them'.

Neill, who confessed that he could not control his feelings, was determined that the people of Cawnpore should never be allowed to forget the appalling, unforgivable crime which their countrymen had committed. While Havelock had been there, efforts had been made to stop the enraged soldiers taking indiscriminate revenge upon the people; and orders had been issued for the hanging, in their uniforms, of all troops found guilty of plundering.[41] But now that Havelock had gone, Neill provided for what he took to be a punishment 'suited to the occasion', though he knew it would be 'objectionable to the Brahminized infatuated elderly gentlemen' in Calcutta. He determined

that every stain of that innocent blood shall be cleared up and wiped out, previous to their execution, by such miscreants as may be hereafter apprehended, who took an active part in the mutiny, to be selected according to their rank, caste, and degree of guilt . . . The task will be made as revolting to . . . each miscreant's feelings as possible, and the Provost-Marshall will use the lash in forcing anyone objecting to complete his task. After properly cleaning up his portion the culprit is to be immediately hanged, and for this purpose a gallows will be erected close at hand.[42]

In obedience to Neill's requirement that the task should be made as revolting as possible, the victim, before being hanged, was to be made to kneel down and to lick clean a square foot of the floor, which would previously be moistened with water by natives of the lowest caste. Even this punishment, which was witnessed on three occasions by a corporal of the 78th, was not considered cruel enough by some officers who added to its horrors. 'We made the Nana Sahib's (the Fiend's) Collector prisoner,' wrote Major Bingham. 'We broke his caste. We stuffed pork, beef and everything which could possibly break his caste down his throat, tied him as tight as we could by the arms and told the guard to be *gentle* with him . . . The guard treated him *gently*. I only wonder he lived to be hung which I had the pleasure of witnessing.'[43]

After watching the punishment of another victim, 'a fat soubadar of the 1st Native Infantry', Captain Gordon recorded in his diary:

When he became a little dilatory at his work he was brightened up by several good cuts across the back from a cat which a European soldier was standing alongside with for that purpose. This was repeated several times and he roared like a bull. He was then led out and hanged on a tree close to the back of the house and his body buried at the side of the road. I talked to him in *polite* terms the whole way down from the camp to the house . . . General Neill is determined that every sepoy caught is to have a similar punishment until all the blood is effaced. Alas! It will take several hundreds of them to do that.[44]

Humiliating as the executions at Cawnpore were made to be, most victims accepted them with dignity and some remained defiant to the end. Trooper Potiphar of the 9th Lancers recorded the degradation and executions of a *sowar* and a sepoy of the 10th Native Infantry:

Upon arriving in sight of the Gallows I was surprised to see the villain of a Sepoy salaam the Gallows by bowing his head and touching his forehead with his hand. He was now taken into what is called the Slaughter House and the Bloody Mat was brought out. The Provost Marshall and his men got ready to carry out operations. The mat being wetted so as to moisten the dried blood and the two men came forward each with the lash in hand. The culprits were now ordered to kneel and to lick up the blood, at the same moment the lash fell heavily. This is carried on for about 10 minutes, that is if the prisoner took all things quiet, if not the lash was again plied freely. He is then brought to the Gallows. These men were dareing brutes and no dought by the way they took death had been guilty of some atrocious deeds. The man of the 10th before being hung spoke to the crowd, which was immense of both natives and Europeans. He made use of the words that he was satisfied to die and we need not think we were going to beat the Sepoys because they would yet beat us. They were then swung into eternity and when dead were buried a few yards from the Gallows. The graves were being dug before their eyes before being hung.[45]

'No doubt this is strange law,' Neill commented, 'but it suits the occasion well, and I hope I shall not be interfered with until the room is thoroughly cleansed in this way . . . I will hold my own with the blessing and help of God. I cannot help seeing that His finger is in all this.'[46]

The 'strange law' – which operated against those who had no direct connection with the murders, as well as those few who might have had and could be found – continued in force for over three months. During this time piteous messages – such as 'Dear Jesus, send us help today, and deliver us not into the hands of our enemies' – were inscribed on the walls in order to increase the fury of the soldiers who were marched through Bibighar, on their arrival in Cawnpore, to witness the scene of their countrywomen's massacre.[47] The floors of the house were left as Neill had found them. Private Wickins of the 90th Light Infantry, who passed through Cawnpore in October, said the buildings still presented 'a most horrid spectacle':

There were little children's socks and shoes and dresses of every description all covered with the blood and brains of the innocent. Even the trees in the neighbourhood bore evidence of the fiendish cruelty of the Asians, and outside the building, strewed upon the ground in many places, there was a quantity of females' hair, and I would have preserved some of it, but it was too rotten owing to its being exposed to the weather.[48]

Private Metcalfe of the 32nd said that the Highlanders knelt down on being taken into the building and 'took a Highland oath that for every one of our poor creatures who were thus slain, 100 of the enemy should bite the dust, and I need not add that they kept their vow'.[49]

Officers, too, took this oath. Garnet Wolseley, a captain in the 90th, who confessed on arrival in Calcutta that his sword was 'thirsty for the blood of these cursed women slayers', told his brother that after walking through 'that slaughter house at Cawnpore where all the marks of the late atrocities were still fresh', he made the vow that 'most soldiers made there – of vengeance and of having blood for blood, not drop for drop, but barrels and barrels of the filth which flows in these niggers' veins for every drop of blood which marked the floors and walls of that fearful house'.[50] Wolseley subsequently asked his company for a volunteer to execute a mutineer said to be implicated in the Cawnpore massacre. A similar request had been made in the Crimea where not a single man would agree to act as hangman though offered a discharge home and twenty pounds bonus. On this occasion, however, every man in the company stepped forward to offer his services.[51]

In another regiment a man was heard to say that, learning of the 'foul atrocities the devils had committed', he would 'hang a Pandy as soon as look at him'.[52] The rebels certainly were guilty of atrocities. Robert Poore, for instance, saw the body of an English sergeant whose skin had been burned by a torch before being 'cut about in a most fearful manner',[53] and many other officers testified to having come across the severed limbs of white bodies, both male and female, adults' as well as children's. But most of the appalling crimes rumoured to have happened, and reported as facts in letters to England, bore scant relation to the truth. Magistrates and Special Commissioners who endeavoured to discover reliable evidence of widespread torture and rape failed to do so. A. M. Cocks, Special Commissioner at Aligargh, for instance, reported that he had heard of one mutineer who, before his execution, boasted of having dishonoured an Englishwoman; but having made inquiries into this and other allegations, Cocks had not been able to verify the truth of the claim and certainly 'nothing like it occurred' at Aligargh.[54]

Lady Canning commented:

A child who was said to have been killed slowly, bit by bit cut off, was certainly killed at once with a tulwar, and so it is in each place . . . People on the spot say the stories going about are not true of *that* place but happened elsewhere, and so on. Those who have gone from place to place never find evidence of the horrible treatment everyone here believes. Only the massacres are really certain.[55]

Yet letters written by officers to their families were full of the most lurid details of rapes and violations and of what Lieutenant Arthur Moffat Lang called 'perpetual lying reports about massacres in churches and other places'.[56] Major Bailie reported to his father that English ladies had been sold by auction in the bazaars; that children had been roasted alive before the eyes of their mothers down whose throats bits of flesh were forced before they, too, were killed.[57] George Blake said that an officer who fell into enemy hands had a finger and toe cut off every day.[58] Kendal Coghill told his family that at Meerut an officer's wife had been dragged from church, stripped and her breasts cut off. At Delhi, ladies had been publicly dishonoured in the streets before being massacred. At Allahabad, twenty-eight officers had been murdered in the mess, their arms and legs cut off to be arranged in dishes like joints of beef; and their mess orderly had also been killed and cut up into pieces which were then crammed down his children's throats. At Cawnpore children had been found nailed to the walls with bayonets and 'put alive into boxes and set fire to – others were spitted on bayonets and twisted round in the air, and to make the tortures more exquisite all this was done in the presence of the mothers who were compelled to look on . . . in a state of nudity'.[59]

Believing these myths the rage of British officers and civilian officials knew no bounds. Garnet Wolseley looked forward to the wholesale destruction of 'the black-faced curs' who had been guilty of such dastardly crimes.[60] Henry Ouvry – who like many others 'got a lock of hair belonging to a lady who was murdered' at Cawnpore and burst into tears at the sight of the well there – observed, 'If I can weep I can kill also, as I have already done, and if it pleases God to spare me I have not done yet.'[61] Dr Wise hoped that a bloody revenge would be taken. 'An awful example must be made,' he wrote. 'No mercy shown to any prisoners. Death to all who have arms . . . When this crisis is over [the Hindu] must be treated as a servant and kept in his place, not treated and supported as a pampered dependant.'[62] Captain Wade thought it ridiculous to talk of 'showing mercy to these fiends'; he himself would 'willingly go through another campaign to see them destroyed root and branch'.[63] A staff officer in Calcutta wrote to Havelock's Assistant Adjutant-General:

> Of course, you will take a bloody revenge . . . The troops ought to be let loose on Bithoor. Neither man, woman or child of the beast's [Nana's] family left alive, and not one stone standing on another. This is the most horrible business [ever] perpetrated in India . . . It would be to doubt the everlasting justice of God to suppose that so black a villain should not meet his deserts, and I hope the troops will take it in hand.[64]

Missionaries and chaplains endorsed the cries for vengeance. The rebels had 'imbrued their hands in the innocent blood of helpless women and children . . . and that very blood was appealing to heaven for vengeance,' the Rev John Rotton wrote. 'The Lord could not otherwise than be avenged on such a nation as this.'[65] When an officer dared to hint that there was no reliable evidence for many of the alleged atrocities, that some women had certainly been mutilated but none had been raped, he was angrily shouted down.[66] Ralph Nowell wrote home to his mother, 'It is only in a few instances that I ever heard talk of any *real* atrocities – and then rarely or never committed by the sepoys.'[67] But few officers dared make such comments in the mess. When one of John Sylvester's fellow officers named Gale 'tried to palliate the atrocities of Nana Sahib', Sylvester wondered how on earth 'an Englishman could talk such cowardly balderdash'. 'We had a violent demonstration after mess last evening about niggers and their deserts,' wrote Sylvester of another occasion. 'Gale left the table evidently disgusted. I cannot understand any Englishman sympathizing with niggers.'[68]

At the trials of arrested rebels Sylvester had no cause to complain about the attitude displayed towards the defendants, some of whom, R. H. Clifford said, were obliged to face their accusers with cloths tied round their mouths so that they could not answer the charges.[69]

There were certain magistrates who endeavoured to be fair. Allen Hume, magistrate at Etawan, who was a son of the radical politician Joseph Hume, acted bravely in the capture of mutineers in his district. Yet, having brought them to justice, he ensured that they received as impartial a trial as the circumstances allowed. He hanged only seven convicted mutineers and those by methods which caused the least suffering; and he refused to be intimidated by those who venomously attacked him for his 'excess of leniency'.[70] Hume, however, was an exception. A more characteristic example was the Magistrate known as 'Hanging' Power who proudly boasted that he had hanged one hundred mutineers in three days near Fatehgarh and who claimed that he would have liked to have hanged the widow of an English officer who had suffered the misfortune of becoming pregnant by her captor, the Nawab of Farrukhabad.[71]

Power's methods of wholesale hanging met with widespread approval throughout India. Indeed, there were many who wished there were more magistrates like him. Robert Henry Ponsonby, who confessed to his sister to being 'rather bloodthirsty' and ready to use his pistol 'without any provocation', was 'very sorry' that only thirty or forty men had been hanged in his district. Others professed themselves sorry that even the pretence of a trial was considered necessary before a hanging could take place. Often, of course, formal trials *were* dispensed with.[72] Robert Dunlop, Magistrate at Meerut – a leading proponent of the belief that 'the slightest mawkish sentimentality' would be fatal – recorded with satisfaction that at Basaud 'all men able to carry arms were shot down or put to the sword and their residences burnt. The only prisoners taken, some fifteen in number, were ordered out of the camp, and executed in the evening by order of the Military Commandant.'[73] Even men who made a pretence of following the usual judicial procedures found means of hanging natives they thought ought to be hanged. George Ricketts, Deputy Commissioner at Ludhiana, told his son that having convicted two men of treasonable correspondence he reported the case to two different authorities. One of these ordered him 'to hang A and let off B', the other told him 'to hang B and let off A'. So he hanged them both.[74]

At Cawnpore in July 1857 some men seemed so eager to hang rebels whom they suspected of being involved in the massacre there that 'they appeared for the moment to forget there were many men and women threatened with a similar fate at Lucknow'.[75]

11

Lawrence at Lucknow

· Sir Henry Lawrence – the 'bitter feuds' at Lucknow · uprising of the 48th Native Infantry, April 1857 · mutiny of the regiments at Lucknow, 30 May · preparations for the defence of the Residency · mutiny of police, 11 June – misadventures of the fugitives · disaster at Chinhat, 30 June – the Residency surrounded ·

The Residency at Lucknow was a large, imposing building which successive Residents had been enlarging in a variety of contrasting styles since its original construction in 1780. It stood on rising ground above the river Gumti, looking down upon a sprawling city that covered an area of some twelve square miles and contained more than 600,000 people. On the same side of the river, to the west beyond an iron bridge, stood another large building which also enjoyed a commanding position. This was an old, tumble-down fort known as the Machi Bhawan. To the east, on both sides of the city walls, was a conglomeration of palaces and public buildings, mosques and tombs, 'a vision . . . of domes azure and golden, cupolas, colonnades, long façades of fair perspective in pillar and column' – the Chattar Manzil, the Kaiser Bagh, the Moti Mahal, the Shah Najif, the Sikandar Bagh and the Bara Imambara. Beyond these, south of the canal that encircled the city on that side, were the Martinière, an extraordinarily eccentric hotch-potch of an edifice which, built by a French adventurer, was now a school for European and Eurasian children, and the Dilkusha, the Heart's Delight, a royal palace in whose park peacocks strutted between herds of deer and antelope. The Residency was surrounded by numerous other buildings constructed for British officials and soldiers, a banqueting hall, a church, offices, stores, stables and private houses. The area was entered through an archway with a guard-house known as the Baillie Guard Gate after a former Resident who had built it at the beginning of the century.[1]

At the time of the uprisings at Meerut and Delhi, the Residency was occupied by Sir Henry Lawrence, Chief Commissioner of Oudh.

Recently promoted Brigadier-General with 'full military powers', Lawrence was then fifty-one years old, though – tall, thin and haggard – he looked much older.[2]

His face bore the traces of many years' toil beneath an Indian sun and the still deeper marks of a never-ending conflict with self. His eyes, overhung by massive, craggy brows, looked out with an expression in which melancholy was strangely blended with humour: his thin wasted cheeks were scored down their whole length by deep lines; and a long ragged beard added to his look of age.[3]

The son of a tough and forthright colonel who had spent most of his life in India, Lawrence had been born in Ceylon and had returned home as a child to attend a rigorous boarding school in Ireland kept by a clergyman uncle. A quiet, reserved boy, he did not enjoy playing games and showed no promise as a scholar. He was mainly remarkable for a sternly unremitting, self-righteous honesty. 'Anything mean or shabby always roused his ire,' recorded a fellow pupil at Addiscombe to which he was dispatched at the age of fourteen, 'and then the curl of his lip and the look of scorn he could put on were the most bitter and intense I ever witnessed ... I do not remember his ever being sent to the black hole, or getting into any serious scrape. He seemed even then to have organized a course for himself, and was neither to be coaxed nor driven out of it.'[4]

He had no taste for pleasure or frivolity. Once, after returning home from a dance with his sister, he made the characteristic remark, 'What a wretched unprofitable evening! Not a Christian to speak to. All the women decked out with flowers on their heads, and their bodies half naked.' No one was surprised when, on arriving in India as a second lieutenant in the Bengal Artillery, he fell immediately under the influence of the chaplain at the Artillery's headquarters at Dum-Dum where a small band of similarly-minded officers looked upon the more dissolute of their companions with scornful disdain. Assiduous in the pursuit of professional knowledge and in learning native languages, he was determined to fit himself for staff employment; and in 1837 his industry was rewarded by his being appointed Assistant Revenue Surveyor of the North-Western Provinces. Soon afterwards he married his cousin, the Rev George Marshall's remarkable daughter, Honoria; and encouraged by her help and affection, began not only to prosper in his career, but also to develop a warmth of nature which had previously lain hidden behind that reserve which few men had been able to penetrate. Thereafter he distinguished himself in the Kabul campaign and in the Punjab where he was appointed

Resident at Lahore in 1847. The next year he was knighted. Disagreeing with the policies both of Lord Dalhousie and of his own younger brother, John Lawrence, his colleague on the Punjab Board of Administration, Sir Henry was obliged to resign his office, much 'fretted', as he confessed, to be 'so cavalierly elbowed out of the Punjab' for which he had worked so hard. Already broken in health by worry, disappointment, and the criticism of his colleagues, he was further distressed by the death of his beloved wife, and was about to return home with his daughter when Canning's offer of the Chief Commissionership of Oudh reached him. He accepted at once, arriving in Lucknow on 20 March 1857.[5]

The situation he found there was profoundly disturbing. The annexation of the Kingdom of Oudh, of which Lucknow was the capital, had been deeply resented not only by the deposed King whose family were constantly complaining of the treatment to which they were now subjected, but also by the *talukdars* who were being deprived of all the lands and villages to which they could not prove a legal title. Nor did the peasants and the zemindars display any of the expected gratitude to their new masters for having relieved them from the misrule of the old, corrupt, decrepit dynasty. The province was overrun by former dependants of the King's court now reduced to penury; by tradesmen and craftsmen whose exotic manufactures were no longer so readily saleable; by disbanded soldiers of the King's army; and by vagabonds turning to crime in order to buy opium upon which the British had imposed so heavy a tax that it had become an almost unobtainable luxury.[6] Equally disturbing was the effect that the annexation had had upon the sepoys. William Sleeman had warned Dalhousie that annexation would lead to mutiny in the Bengal army, for Oudh was 'the great nursery of the sepoys'.[7] And in that nursery the sepoys had formerly been a privileged class, with far more hope of having their grievances listened to attentively in Lucknow than their civilian relations. Now all that was changed. 'I used to be a great man when I went home,' lamented one Oudh soldier who would have been accompanied by a servant to carry his bags. 'The rest of the village rose when I approached. Now the lowest puff their pipes in my face.'[8]

The annexation might not have raised such protests had the British officials in Lucknow been more tactful and conciliatory men. But Coverley Jackson, who had been appointed officiating Chief Commissioner when Sir James Outram, the former Resident, had been obliged by illness to go home, was a man of most violent temper

and hasty judgement, one of whose first acts was to take possession
of a palace belonging to the royal family.[9] The Financial Commissioner, Martin Gubbins, was equally short-tempered and even more
stubborn. Ommanney, the Judicial Commissioner, was, in Sir Henry
Lawrence's words, 'not a wise man, jealous of interference, and yet
fond of interfering'.[10]

In fact, Sir Henry Lawrence found that most of the principal
officers were 'at bitter feud' both with Jackson and with each other.
Jackson, who was 'universally disliked',[11] remained eight days to help
his successor settle in; and during that time Lawrence discovered that
'when thwarted he could not restrain himself and lost his judgement'.
He felt obliged to tell Jackson that he was 'very wrong in some of his
acts and in more of his expressions'. Sir Henry hoped that he would
be able to get on better with Martin Gubbins, who might well prove
'troublesome' having such strong views, but who had been 'so
tremendously mauled by Mr Jackson that he hailed' with pleasure the
new Chief Commissioner's arrival.[12] But in this Lawrence was to be
disappointed.

Lawrence set to work with a will, well aware how much there was to
be done and how little time there was in which to do it. More sympathetic and understanding in his dealings with Indians than many of
his colleagues, he opened the doors of the Residency to both native
nobles and traders for the first time since the annexation, holding
'large durbars for both classes (separately)' and encouraging 'the individual members of each class' to come to him daily. For 'in preserving tranquillity, the chiefs and people of substance' could be 'most
usefully employed', many having as much to lose as the British themselves.

Ten men may in an hour quell a row which, after a day's delay, may
take weeks to put down [Lawrence wrote]. Time is everything just now.
Time, firmness, promptness, conciliation, and prudence . . . A firm and
cheerful aspect must be maintained. There must be no bustle, no appearance of alarm, still less of panic. But at the same time there must be the
utmost watchfulness and promptness. Everywhere the first germ of
insurrection must be put down instantly.[13]

Lawrence was particularly concerned about the military disposi-
tions at Lucknow. The position of the troops was 'as bad as bad can
be – all scattered over several miles, the Infantry in one direction, the
Cavalry another, the Artillery in a third, the magazine in a fourth and
almost unprotected'.[14] The barracks of the 32nd Foot, the only
European regiment in Lucknow, were outside the city, about a mile

and a half to the east of the Residency and a good deal farther away than that from the lines of the native regiments which were known to be unsettled and on edge, likely to rise at the first provocation. Early in April that provocation came.

Dr Walter Wells, surgeon of the 48th Native Infantry, having occasion to visit the medicine store of the hospital, and feeling at the time indisposed, thoughtlessly took a few sips from a bottle containing a carminative. This action, which rendered the medicine obnoxious to all his Hindu patients, was reported by the native apothecary to the sepoys who complained loudly of the insult to their caste. The commanding officer, Colonel Palmer, sternly rebuked the Doctor and smashed the bottle in the presence of his men. But the sepoys were not satisfied, and were determined to be revenged upon the Doctor whose wife, Frances Wells, told her father how they did so:

We were in bed and sound asleep when the women came screaming that the house was on fire, and on rushing out [we found] the thatch was in flames. Never shall I forget the horror I experienced. I tore my children out of bed and in my *nightgown* ran over to the Dashwoods' house, but had I not met one of the officers who relieved me of the children I think I should have fainted by the way. At 12 o'clock the whole of the roof fell in and there is nothing left of our house but the walls ... My woman went outside to drink water and saw 10 sepoys placing lighted straws on the thatch, instantly screamed out and the men ran off but the thatch being old and dry caught in a second ... The whole place was light as day, and although feeling in a dreadful state I could hardly help laughing at some of the odd things that happened. One young man ran over with my brooches, rings, stays and tea caddy. I am told the sight our store room presents is most extraordinary ... currants, salmon, potatoes etc., all baked ... Dear Papa, it makes me tremble to think of it. I can write no more.[15]

Soon after the burning of the Wellses' bungalow there was trouble with the men of the 7th Oudh Irregular Infantry who, refusing to bite their cartridges, threatened to murder their officers.[16] Lawrence marched towards them with all the European troops he could muster; and they, catching sight of a port fire lit by a British gunner, broke ranks in terror. Most of them ran away; the rest laid down their arms. But although the fugitives returned to their lines the next morning, it was obvious that there would be further disturbances before long.

Martin Gubbins strongly – some said vehemently – urged Lawrence to bring up a party of British soldiers from the 32nd to protect the Residency in case of attack. But Lawrence was reluctant to do so for fear lest by displaying alarm a new crisis might be precipitated; and it was not until Gubbins was backed by several army officers in Lucknow that the Chief Commissioner gave way, authorizing part of the 32nd to come up to the Residency area with the women and children of the regiment and the rest to move three miles north of the city to keep watch on the native lines at Mariaon.

Lawrence also gave orders for the occupation and strengthening of the Machi Bhawan, that large dilapidated fort to the west of the Residency beyond the iron bridge. Here quantities of supplies were stored, guns were mounted and numerous cannon, cast long ago for the kings of Oudh, were displayed along the walls, more as a gesture of British determination to resist attack than in the hope that they could ever be brought into effective use. While work at the Machi Bhawan was still in progress, preparations were also made to turn the Residency and its surrounding buildings into a defensive position. Trenches were dug by coolies and prisoners in irons, gun emplacements erected, walls strengthened, windows blocked up, provisions brought in and ammunition stored in makeshift magazines.

Such precautions seemed to many Europeans in Lucknow unnecessary, even absurd. Martin Gubbins – who was busy turning his large house into a formidable defensive position, eventually employing seventy-five native servants in building bastions and digging ditches – complained that others were taking the crisis far too lightly. Although ordered to sleep at night in the Residency, several of the wives of officers of the 32nd still drove through the city to see their husbands during the daytime. Occasionally they were insulted and often scowled at but they saw no reason to discontinue the practice. Admittedly 'there were a great many ill-looking men about' and several posters had been stuck up in the town calling upon true Mohammedans to rise up and destroy the *Firinghis*. It was also true that there had been some disturbances in the sepoy lines, and a few buildings had been burned. But any suggestion that a serious outbreak was imminent was derided both by the officers' wives and by their husbands. Nor, from all appearances at least, did the Chief Commissioner believe Lucknow to be in any immediate danger. He made it clear to guests at the Residency that the preparations for defence were merely a sensible precaution. At his dinner-table he discouraged talk of dissension and mutiny, and would not yet allow the demolition of buildings whose proximity to the Residency defences profoundly worried those who considered only the military implications.[17]

When Martin Gubbins, in that provocatively combative way of his, argued that all the native regiments ought to be disarmed, Lawrence disagreed. He was Chief Commissioner of Oudh not just of Lucknow, he reminded Gubbins, who was 'almost insubordinately urgent' in his suggestions.[18] If he disarmed the regiments in and around the city, the others in the outlying districts might well mutiny in protest. Gubbins strongly doubted it; but in this instance he did not gain his way. Lawrence – who could be as obstinate as any of his subordinates when convinced, after thought and prayer, that he was right – remained adamant. Even when one of his staff, Captain T. F. Wilson, on the evidence of a reliable sepoy warned him that the firing of the nine o'clock gun on the night of Saturday 30 May was to be the signal for a general mutiny, he chose to discredit the report. That evening he went out as arranged to dine at his house at Mariaon. At nine o'clock the firing of the gun was followed by a prolonged silence. Sir Henry, with a smile, called across the table, 'Wilson, your friends are not punctual!'

A moment later the dinner-table was violently disturbed as sounds of shouting and musketry from the native cantonments reached the ears of the guests. Sir Henry leaped to his feet and dashed out on to the moonlit steps where he impatiently waited for his horse while the native officer on duty drew up the guard of sixty sepoys in a line in front of him. The native officer then marched up to Captain Wilson, saluted and asked, 'Am I to load?'

I turned to Sir Henry and repeated the question [Wilson recorded]. He said, 'Oh yes, let him load.' The order was at once given and the ramrods fell with that peculiar dull sound on the leaden bullets . . . As the men brought up their muskets, Sir Henry cried out, 'I am going to drive those scoundrels out of cantonment. Take care while I am away that you all remain at your posts . . .' Whether through the effect of this speech and Sir Henry's bearing, I know not, but the guard remained steadily at its post, and with the bungalows blazing and shots firing all round, they allowed no one to enter the house, and the residence of Sir Henry was the only one that night in the cantonment that was not either pillaged or burnt.[19]

While his guard stood resolute, Sir Henry galloped off into the cantonments to order a force from the 32nd to patrol the road that led to the city so as to prevent the mutineers joining forces with the badmashes as they had done at Meerut. This precaution proved unnecessary, however, as the sepoys were for the moment fully occupied with arson and plunder in their own lines. They first rushed upon the officers' mess which, found to be empty, was set alight. They then stormed down the lines into the officers' bungalows, murdering an officer who had been hidden under a bed by a few of his more faithful men, and shooting Brigadier Handscomb, commander of the Oudh brigade, who rode out to reason with them.

From the roof of the Residency three miles to the south, the conflagration was clearly visible. The chaplain, the Rev Henry Polehampton, had said prayers as usual; and all the ladies had retired to their rooms when the noise of musketry fire had brought them all on to the landings. Mr Polehampton had advised them to assemble on the roof where they would be safer from attack as the only approach was by a spiral staircase. When the last of the ladies had reached the top of the staircase, the chaplain offered further prayers for their salvation and 'for those engaged in the strife', while 'column after column of bright flames shot up from the cantonments'. Towards midnight Mrs Inglis, wife of Colonel John Inglis of the 32nd, received a message from her husband. The others crowded round her as she read the news that all was 'over for the present'.[20]

It was not, however, a long respite. In the morning Lawrence marched out with a force of European infantry and artillery towards the race-course where a number of mutineers from the 71st were assembled. He opened fire on them with his guns, driving them off. But in their flight they were joined by most of the 7th Cavalry so that pursuit was impossible. No more than sixty prisoners were taken; and although about five or six hundred men of the three infantry regiments at Lucknow remained loyal to their British masters, the rest went over to the mutineers.

Mutiny was followed by riot. On the afternoon of that Sunday, thousands of Muslims assembled outside their mosques and marched through the city under the standard of the Prophet, while troublemakers poured out into the streets attacking Christians, grain-merchants and shopkeepers, breaking into their premises, looting and ransacking, smashing earthenware pots, tearing down mat doors, slitting open sacks of flour and beans and kicking their contents across the ground. Later it was reported that the head of a half-grown buffalo had been placed upside down over a gateway near the King's palace with a garland of small white flowers around its horns, an ominous sign which the Europeans did not understand; and that men had been seen carrying dolls dressed up as European soldiers, the heads of which, 'much to the amusement of the mob', had been struck off with sword cuts.[21]

Such reports caused a momentary panic in the Residency area. During the afternoon ladies and their children came scurrying over to the Residency from the Ommanneys', the Gubbinses', Dr Fayrer's and other nearby houses, believing that they were under threat of assault. 'Such a scene of confusion, talking and rushing about' Mrs Case, wife of Colonel Case of the 32nd, had 'never witnessed. The alarm turned out a false one and most of the ladies returned to the different houses.' But several remained in the Residency including Mrs Inglis and her three children who, given a corner of Mrs Case's room, were much alarmed when 'told not to crowd too much together, as the building was not very strong and would not stand so great a pressure'.[22]

The next few days were quieter and it began to be hoped that perhaps the worst was already over. The Lucknow police remained faithful, and crime in the city was kept in check. Natives caught threatening Europeans or arrested as spies were summarily punished. A fakir who abused a British sentry, drawing a finger menacingly across his throat, was placed in irons and given a hundred and fifty strokes of the lash; and a man caught tampering with the guns in one of the entrenchments was hanged on the gallows which had been erected near the Machi Bhawan for the execution of the captured mutineers. Some merchants temporarily closed down their businesses; and some native servants began to complain to their masters that shopkeepers would not serve them unless for ready money. But it was not yet difficult to buy supplies in the city, and prudent families began to lay in stocks of flour and sugar, arrowroot, ghee, rice and dhal, beer, wine, tobacco, candles and soap.[23]

Preparations for the defence of the Residency area continued unabated. Captain R. P. Anderson of the 25th Native Infantry, whose house was in an exposed position on the Cawnpore road, pulled down his garden wall behind which a besieging force might have sheltered, and erected a wooden stockade in its place. On the near side of this stockade he dug a ditch; alongside this he threw up a mound of earth to a height of about five feet; and then dug another ditch, driving sharply-pointed bamboo stakes into its bottom.[24] Other houses around the perimeter which it had been deemed practicable to defend were fortified in a similar way. Martin Gubbins, assisted by an Indian architect whom he had befriended, worked harder than ever on his own house, turning it 'into a fort which would not have disgraced Marshal Vauban himself'. Emptying his library shelves to fill up holes in his defences, he subsequently found that a volume of

19. The Satichaura Ghat, Cawnpore

20. The massacre in the river at Cawnpore
from Charles Ball's *History of the Indian Mutiny*

21. View of Lucknow
from Charles Ball's *History of the Indian Mutiny*

22. Sir Henry Lawrence

23. L. E. R. Rees in Indian dress

24. Sir Mountstuart Jackson

25. Lieutenant and Mrs George Willoughby

26. View of the Residency, Lucknow
from C. H. Mecham's *Sketches and Incidents of the Siege of Lucknow*

27. The wrecked billiard room of the Residency
from C. H. Mecham's *Sketches and Incidents of the Siege of Lucknow*

28. Martin Gubbins's house
from C. H. Mecham's *Sketches and Incidents of the Siege of Lucknow*

29. Sir John Inglis

30. Ruins of the Baillie Guard Gate and the Banqueting Hall, Lucknow

31. The Chattar Manzil on the banks of the Gumti
with the King of Oudh's boat in the foreground

32. Wounded officers at Simla

33. Wounded men

34. Reinforcements on their way to Delhi by camel,
with a doolie in the foreground

35. Troops in a bullock cart

Lardner's Encyclopaedia could stop a musket ball after passing through 120 pages, and that a quarto copy of Finden's *Illustrations of Byron*, although completely destroyed by its impact, successfully blocked the flight of a three-pound shot.[25] Captain Fletcher Hayes, Sir Henry Lawrence's erudite Military Secretary, sacrificed for the barricades his 'splendid library . . . of priceless Oriental manuscripts; the standard literary and scientific works of every nation of Europe; dictionaries of every language spoken on earth' as well as 'valuable pieces of furniture'.[26]

To assist in the defence of the fortified houses volunteers were enrolled and drilled by sergeants of the 32nd. They came in all shapes and sizes, Captain Anderson wrote – tall, thin British officials of the Bengal Civil Service; small, fat European clerks; Italian and French merchants who had formerly been in business in the city. There were also several doctors, of whom there were now so many in Lucknow that there was not enough medical work for them to do.[27] Some of these doctors were expert shots. Dr Fayrer was 'first-rate';[28] and Dr Hadow, equipped with an Enfield rifle, was to claim nineteen certain victims.[29] But as for the rest of the volunteers, Anderson despaired of their ever becoming even remotely well trained. They were really 'quite hopeless'; the laughing-stock of the regular soldiers. 'One evening, on account of some noise in the street, I had to turn out the volunteers,' Anderson remembered. 'And whilst under arms I observed that one man was absent. I went to hunt him up, and found him dancing madly about the room, in a bewildered state. He could not find his musket; and then he upset all his percussion caps; and moreover, he could not find his cartridges.' Another man, whenever on sentry go, persisted in challenging Anderson each time he saw him, though he would turn his back on strangers, and, lazily shouldering his musket, lead them to the guard-room where he would call out conversationally, 'Sergeant, somebody's come!' Perhaps it was this volunteer whom Anderson heard one night asking how on earth one presented arms. The answer came in the unmistakably Italian voice of one of the merchants, Signor Barsatelli, 'Never mind, Sir, make a *leetle* noise. Who's to see in the dark.' Barsatelli himself, who had come to Lucknow to sell Florentine alabaster, was an extraordinary figure, always theatrically over armed and overdressed as though preparing himself for a dramatic role in one of the earlier battles of the Risorgimento. But for all his grandiose appearance and his constantly expressed expectation of imminent death, he was to prove himself one of the bravest of all

Anderson's soldiers. 'Nothing could keep the Signor from the steady performance of his duty. There he stood, with a musket in one hand and a double-barrelled rifle in the other; at his side a huge cavalry sword and pendant; over his breast hung his ammunition pouch, resembling an Italian hand-organ.' Indeed, most of Anderson's volunteers were to become steady and reliable soldiers as time went on, learning to be alert and confident and to fire their weapons 'pretty well'.[30]

The regular soldiers of the 32nd were also to behave well in time, although for the first few weeks there was a great deal of drunkenness and much plundering of tempting cellars including that of M. Deprat, a French merchant, who lost nearly all his brandy and champagne, though not his claret and Sauternes which the soldiers did not fancy.[31]

Sir Henry Lawrence was indefatigable, appearing 'to live in his saddle', rising at dawn to ride about the compound, giving encouragement and advice, supervising the placing of guns including an eight-inch howitzer which was found buried in the grounds and dragged into position by elephants, often having 'his bedding spread out near the Baillie Guard Gate, not to sleep but to meditate undisturbed'.[32] He was looking more haggard and worn than ever now. But he still endeavoured to appear confident and cheerful, making such efforts to keep up the spirits of the people in the Residency with whom he sat down to dinner every night that Mrs Wells described him as 'a most affable old gentleman',[33] though these attempts at cheeriness, Mrs Brydon, the wife of Dr William Brydon – the lone survivor of the retreat from Kabul – suspected were 'as trying to him as they were to us'.[34] Conscious of his growing weakness, Sir Henry telegraphed to Lord Canning suggesting that if he became unfit to carry on, Major Banks, Commissioner of the Lucknow Division, should succeed him as Chief Commissioner and that command of the troops should be given to Colonel John Inglis of the 32nd, 'a delightful man to have in command', in J. W. Sherer's opinion, 'pleasant-tempered, agreeably mannered, attending to anything asked, giving it if possible, saying at once why it could not be given if he thought it undesirable'.[35] 'This is no time for punctilio as regards seniority,' Lawrence wrote, anticipating opposition to these appointments. 'They are the right men, in fact the only men for their places.' Soon afterwards he felt compelled to delegate his authority to a provisional council of which Martin Gubbins became president.[36]

One of Gubbins's first acts was to persuade the other members of the council to agree to the disarming of a company of sepoys which, although it had not yet mutinied, had not openly declared its loyalty to the Company. But as soon as he heard of this measure, Lawrence resumed his authority, dispatched messengers after the disarmed sepoys with orders to tell them that any who wished to return would be welcomed back. About a hundred and fifty did come back on this assurance, and most of them remained loyal till the end of the siege. Lawrence also invited all pensioned sepoys to return to their colours, an invitation which was too eagerly accepted by some old men who hobbled in, limbless on crutches or with sightless eyes, in the hope of service or reward. Eighty old pensioners were, however, regarded capable of further service, issued with weapons and trusted to use them in defence of their former masters.

As more and more families, having escaped from outlying stations, came into Lucknow, life in the Residency and its surrounding buildings became increasingly uncomfortable. 'There is not one hole or corner where one can enjoy an instant's privacy,' Mrs Case complained in her journal. 'The coming and going, the talking, the bustle and noise, inside as well as outside, the constant alarming reports, and at times the depressed expression on some of the countenances baffle all description.'[37] It was also suffocatingly hot; yet Mrs Ogilvie, a doctor's wife, insisting that hot air was better than no air, had all the windows kept open so that a scorching wind and swarms of mosquitoes and 'great, *cold*, clammy flies' rendered the crowded rooms almost unbearable.

Despite the sweltering heat, the ladies were glad to have so much to occupy them outside their rooms. Every morning they went down with pudding or soup, tea, sugar and oddments of clothes to the women of the 32nd and various families of fugitives who were occupying the cooler but no less packed *tykhana*. They would then seek some shady place to make clothes for the refugees since work was 'such a comfort'. At half past nine in the evening Mr Polehampton read prayers in Mrs Ogilvie's room; then they would all go to bed, hearing throughout the hot night the sentry's intermittent call, 'All's well!' Mrs Inglis slept on the roof watching the distant fires which she imagined to be the rebels' signals. At dawn she would look down on the city as the sun rose on the gilded mosques, minarets and towers and, like Mrs Case, be lost in wonder at the 'fairy scene, truly beautiful beyond description'. But nearer at hand, in the Residency garden, the scene was less tranquil. Trenches scarred the flower beds and lawns; men were asleep untidily around the guns; prisoners and coolies continued to work on the defences.[38]

The quiet was no longer reassuring. On 11 June the cavalry of the military police refused to obey orders and rode out of the city, followed the next morning by the infantry. Captain Gould Weston, their Superintendent, set off after them, caught up with them, and, entirely on his own, endeavoured to persuade them to return with him to the city. One of them raised his musket to put an end to his harangue, but another knocked the muzzle to the ground, protesting, 'Who would kill such a brave man as this?'[39]

On Weston's forlorn return to Lucknow, Mrs Inglis asked her husband if he thought they could possibly hold out now. 'Our position is a bad one,' he told her gloomily, 'and we shall have a hard struggle.' Mrs Inglis commented resignedly that she was glad to know what to expect as it enabled her to prepare for the worst. The next day was Sunday. A service was held in the church as usual before breakfast. The officiating chaplain preached on the subject of Judgement Day. His congregation returned to their uncomfortable lodgings in low spirits. After breakfast at the Gubbinses' the master of the house read prayers and another sermon, and in the evening he led his guests back to church once more. The chaplain, Mrs Brydon noted in her journal, 'preached on the same subject – Judgement Day'. It was the last time the church was used, being requisitioned the next week as a storehouse for grain; and 'not all its congregation were sorry'. Thereafter Sunday services were held in the chaplains' houses; and this, Private Henry Metcalfe of the 32nd commented, 'was about the only way in which we could tell the day of the week, for every day was such a sameness that they all appeared alike to us'.[40]

That week the rains came. On the morning of 22 June there was a heavy shower and a good deal of thunder; in the afternoon it was hotter than ever; but three days later cascades poured from a leaden sky, driving Mrs Inglis from the roof of the Residency. She climbed down the spiral staircase, unaware as yet that she was sickening for smallpox but feeling wretchedly ill, weak and depressed.[41]

Her depression was shared by almost everyone. Colonel Case wrote every day to his wife whom he had but recently married, and his letters were 'beautiful, so full of Christian confidence and manly, soldier-like courage'. But she knew that in his heart he could not really feel such hope. She had heard that the rebels were concentrated only fourteen miles away, and that the hundredth anniversary of the battle of Plassey, 23 June, had been the day fixed by native prophecy for the *Firinghis* to be driven out of India. That day had passed; but since then bad news had arrived from Cawnpore, and there seemed no chance of early relief. 'All our servants have deserted us,' wrote Katherine Bartrum, wife of a surgeon with the Bengal Artillery, on 27 June, 'and now our trials have begun in earnest; from morning till night we can get no food cooked, and we have not the means of doing it for ourselves. How we are to manage now I cannot tell.'[42]

Mrs Bartrum had been living at Gouda at the beginning of the month with her husband, Robert, and their baby. 'We are becoming alarmed,' she had written on the morning of 6 June. 'The police sowars show symptoms of rising. For many nights we have scarcely dared to close our eyes. I keep a sword under my pillow and dear R has his pistol loaded ready to start up at the slightest sound.' That afternoon a messenger arrived from Secrora 'saying that Sir Herbert Lawrence had desired that the ladies and children from the out-stations should be sent into Lucknow immediately for better security'. Two hours later they started on elephants for Secrora where Robert had to leave her. 'I begged him to go on with us,' she recorded, 'but he could not leave the regiment, though his heart ached at giving his wife and child into the care of a guard of sepoys in whom he could feel little confidence.'[43]

Despite Dr Bartrum's apprehension, four days later his wife and baby arrived in Lucknow where they were installed at first in the Begum Kothi, 'a most uninviting-looking place, so dirty'. Mrs Bartrum shared a room with fifteen other women and children, all of them packed closely together so that each might derive some benefit from the makeshift punkah which an enterprising woman had managed to have fixed during the day. The room swarmed with flies that settled so thickly on the food that Mrs Bartrum could not tell what it was, 'for it only looked like a black and living mass'. She felt quite desolate without her husband, from whom she had never before been parted, and after breakfast – 'which arrived when it suited our attendant to bring it' – she just lay on her charpoy trying to keep cool, thinking of her beloved Robert, attending to the occasional wants of her baby and waiting for nightfall when she and the others gathered round a candle stuck in a bottle and drank tea as they talked of 'happy times in England where our childhood had been spent'.[44]

Unfortunate as Mrs Bartrum considered herself, others were much more so. Mrs Inglis discovered in one of the rooms of the Residency

a 'very nice-looking girl about eighteen' who had arrived from Sitapore with her little boy 'and two bad wounds in her side. Of her
husband's fate she was ignorant.' Another woman who had escaped
to Lucknow with two babies, one of which was dead, had seen her
husband's brains blown out. Several refugees from Secrora came in
carrying the corpse of a woman whose body had been fearfully
mangled.[45]

Madeline Jackson, the seventeen-year-old niece of Coverley Jackson,
Sir Henry Lawrence's predecessor, had been staying at Sitapore with
the Commissioner, George Christian, and his wife when the sepoys
mutinied there. 'Mr Christian was shot and Mrs Christian sat down
crying . . . and the poor baby they took on a spear and threw into the
river.' Several other Europeans were murdered; but Madeline and her
brother, Mountstuart, managed to escape into the jungle through 'an
extraordinary whistling sound' which Madeline did not realize until
her brother told her so was made by the musket balls of the pursuing
sepoys. She ran into a thorn-bush in which her white muslin dress
became entangled; and she could not free herself until Mountstuart
threw himself on the bush to tear it off her, the colour leaving his face
as the thorns ran into him. She then lost her hat and her shoes came
off in a river, but 'at least the firing stopped' as the sepoys lost track
of them. When they were able to rest, Mountstuart gave Madeline his
boots, binding leaves round his own feet with strips of handkerchief.
A villager took pity on them and gave Madeline a white sheet to
wrap round her tattered dress so that she might pass more easily for
an Indian. Other villagers gave them food. 'And, of course, we had no
money – one never carries it about in India', Madeline commented.
'So we gave them our pistol.'
    Night fell. They tried to find their way to Lucknow by the stars, but
stumbled into a hostile village where men with swords stole Mountstuart's watch and cuff-links. One of the men offered to guide
Mountstuart to Lucknow. But Madeline was told that she must stay
behind: she could not walk so far. Another of the men assured her
that he would make her his wife. Presently they managed to escape
again, and, deeper in the jungle, they came across some other English
people, Lieutenant Burnes, Sergeant-Major Morton and the Christians' three-year-old daughter, Sophy.
    Together they found their way to Mithauli, a fort belonging to a
Rajah, Loni Singh, who agreed to shelter them for a time in a more
remote fort at Katchiani where they were joined by Captain and Mrs

Orr and their child, fugitives from the massacre at Aurangabad. The heat and mosquitoes were 'dreadful', Madeline Jackson recorded. 'We fanned ourselves with little native fans. I used to fan myself and little Sophy most of the night, in my sleep, too, I think. I had a lump on my hand for a long time . . . The poor men used to walk up and down for exercise like tigers in a den.'

After a few days the rajah told them that a band of mutineers was coming to look for them: he could no longer shelter them and they must fend for themselves in the jungle. Suffering from fever, they left the fort and survived in the jungle for a time until Loni Singh, convinced that British rule in India was over, sent his retainers out to find them and to bring them captive into Lucknow. So, the men chained, the women bundled into carts, the prisoners were taken to the city. 'We were all prepared for death,' Madeline Jackson wrote. 'I could not bear the uncertainty and asked Mrs Orr how they would kill us. She only said I would know soon and that it would not take long.'

A dense crowd gathered to watch them pass the gate of the Kaiser Bagh, staring at them, some taunting them, pressing so closely round the carts that the cavalcade was brought to a halt. Madeline's hand was crushed between a soldier's gun and the wall of the gateway; and, for the first time, she broke down, sobbing loudly, 'awfully ashamed' of herself for her weakness. On entering the room where they were to be confined, her brother Mountstuart, who had seemed close to death on the road, fell fainting to the floor; Mrs Orr shrieked for water; Sophy Christian appeared to be dying; Lieutenant Burnes, who had raged in wild protest as the fetters were riveted round his wrists, was now silently insane.[46]

By now there was not a single representative of the British Government at any of the outlying stations in Oudh. The downfall of authority had been followed by a general uprising of the *talukdars* who, helped by their retainers, ejected the families to whom their former estates had been allocated and took the opportunity of attacking their rivals and enemies. Few of them actively supported the mutineers. But the rebels in Oudh were strong enough without them, so numerous indeed that, as Lawrence was informed, they were advancing to attack Lucknow. Gubbins, basing his advice on faulty information about the strength of the enemy force and writing derisively 'What stuff!' on an intelligence report which suggested that it was larger than he supposed it to be, heatedly urged Lawrence to march out to disperse them. When his advice was rejected he cried out angrily, 'Well, Sir Henry, we shall all be branded at the bar of history as cowards!' Eventually, against his better judgement, Lawrence gave way to his Financial Commissioner's pressing representations.[47]

So, on 30 June, a force of about six hundred men, half of them Europeans, marched out of Lucknow towards Chinhat. From the beginning the expedition was characterized by a succession of disasters. Orders had been given for the march to begin at dawn; but the sun had long since risen before the leading ranks moved off. Lawrence's instructions for providing the men with breakfast were not carried out; many of them had been drinking heavily the night before; some of them were still drunk, and nearly all were tired out by hours of continuous duty.[48]

Three miles outside Lucknow the force was halted. Lawrence, who had chosen to command it himself though scarcely qualified to do so, went forward to reconnoitre; and, finding no enemy in sight, he decided to withdraw. But before his orders could be carried out he was informed by some 'native travellers' that the main body of the rebels at Chinhat had fallen back; if he attacked now he would have only the advance guard to deal with. So, although it was insufferably hot and the *bhisties* had deserted, Lawrence decided to go on, provided the men of the 32nd – the British soldiers upon whom he would mainly have to rely – felt up to it. He sent his aide-de-camp back to ask them. Colonel Case of the 32nd, 'as nice an officer and as good as ever drew a sword', in the opinion of one of his men,[49] protested that the regiment was certainly not fit for an attack. But the reply given by the regiment's former commander, now Lawrence's second-in-camp, John Inglis, was, 'Of course they could advance – *if* ordered.'[50]

The 32nd were, therefore, given the command to advance. Slowly they came forward, but were soon halted under a ferocious fire from the enemy who lay well concealed in the groves of trees in front of Chinhat. There were well over five thousand rebels there under a skilful commander, Barhat Ahmad, who, after a prolonged artillery duel, deceived Lawrence into believing that his men were in retreat. A British staff officer came riding up to the guns crying out, 'That's it! There they go! Keep it up!' But far from retreating, the rebels were merely changing front and were soon advancing steadily and in dense masses on the right. Within an hour the British force was in full retreat. The native cavalry fled from the field; the native gunners deserted to the enemy; the bearers dropped their dhoolies and ran away in confusion. Only the native infantry remained loyal, some of them actually picking up wounded British soldiers rather than their own wounded in their evident anxiety to gain the esteem of their officers who had been inclined to suspect them of 'being tainted with the general disaffection'.[51]

Colonel Case fell mortally wounded; then his men, too, fled in confusion; and the retreat became a rout as Barhat Ahmad's horse artillery pursued the running soldiers with repeated discharges of grape and his cavalry harassed the stragglers. The cavalry appeared to be commanded by a European, a Russian it was supposed, 'a handsome-looking man, well-built, fair, about 25 years of age, with light mustachios and wearing the undress uniform of a European cavalry officer, with a blue and gold-laced cap on his head'.[52]

Scores of the British soldiers he was pursuing fell dead. Many others, 'desperately wounded and unable to rise, whom no one could or would assist, were seen fighting like bulldogs held at bay, till they also at last fell dead', wrote a Calcutta merchant, L. E. R. Rees, who had come to Lucknow on business and had offered his services as a volunteer. 'None asked for mercy, for none expected it . . . Dr Darby [whose wife and baby, born under a gun-carriage in Wheeler's entrenchment, were both massacred at Cawnpore] called out in vain to [the rest of the men to stop running away] for God's sake; and Lieutenant Webb, his face black with gunpowder and the peak of his cap shot off, made himself hoarse with shouting to the men to halt.'[53]

'My God, my God!' someone heard Lawrence mutter. 'And I brought them to this.'[54] He handed over command to Colonel Inglis, and rode back with his staff into Lucknow to try to organize artillery support for his defeated troops.

There were many acts of heroism during the retreat.

I saw one fine young fellow wounded in the leg [wrote Private Metcalfe of the 32nd]. He coolly sat down on the road, faced the enemy, and all we could do or say to him would not urge him to try and come with us. He said, 'No, you fellows push on, leave me here to blaze away at these fellows. I shan't last long and I would never be able to reach Lucknow now.' He remained, and was very soon disposed of poor fellow . . . A bonny young man was being conveyed back on a gun carriage after being wounded. I saw his brother being struck down with a bullet and without the least warning he jumped off the limber and joined his brother to be killed with him. Another man, maddened by the heat and fatigue, charged single-handed into the ranks of the enemy and was soon put to rest.[55]

In the Residency Mrs Inglis, though still suffering from smallpox, could not bear to remain in bed any longer. She got up and went to the window to watch the soldiers returning. 'They were straggling in by twos and threes,' she wrote, 'some riding, some on guns, some supported by their comrades. All seemed thoroughly exhausted. I could see the flashes of the muskets, and on the opposite side of the river could distinguish large bodies of the enemy through the trees.'[56]

Mrs Case came into the room and said, 'Oh, Mrs Inglis, go to bed. I have just heard that Colonel Inglis and William [Mrs Case's husband] are both safe.' 'A few minutes afterwards John came in,' Mrs Inglis continued. 'He was crying; and, after kissing me, turned to Mrs Case and said, "Poor Case!" Never shall I forget the shock his words gave me, or the cry of agony from the poor widow.'[57]

Below their window, other women and their children were offering cups of water to the thirsty stragglers as they came over the iron bridge; while in the city behind them, people were 'flying in all directions up the streets as far from the Residency as possible. Horses without riders galloped up and down; elephants and camels were hurried away by their drivers; and the boats on the river shoved off far away from the English encampment'.[58] For a time Lucknow appeared deserted, but not for long. As the last of the defeated soldiers came across the bridge, thousands of mutineers could be seen closing in on the Residency area from every side, occupying the surrounding buildings, siting guns, making loopholes for snipers. Horsemen came splashing through the Gumti fords and galloping through the streets. And in the prison opposite the Baillie Guard Gate, convicts who the day before had been carrying beams and baskets of mud towards the Residency defences were now clambering by ropes down the walls.[59]

By nightfall the Residency was completely surrounded by the rebels whose watch-fires burned on every side and whose guns flashed and roared in the darkness. The siege of Lucknow had begun.

12

The Siege of Lucknow

*Machi Bhawan blown up – death of Lawrence, 4 July 1857 ·
the horrors and privations of the siege · intermittent attacks ·
behaviour of the garrison · arrival of the spy, Angad, on 22 September
to report Havelock's approach ·*

After the disaster at Chinhat it was realized that the defended position around the Residency was now far too extended and that the troops in the Machi Bhawan would have to be withdrawn, the guns there spiked and the old fort blown up. Lawrence had envisaged the possibility of this withdrawal at the beginning of June when he had written to Colonel Inglis, 'I am *decidedly* of opinion we ought to have only *one* position, and that, though we should hold . . . the Machi Bhawan as long as we can, all arrangements should be made with reference to a sudden concentration at the Residency.'[1] This sudden concentration could no longer be delayed.

Colonel Palmer, in command at the Machi Bhawan, was given his instructions by a makeshift semaphore from the Residency roof. He led his men out of the Machi Bhawan at midnight on 1 July. They were accompanied by a rattling cavalcade of carts full of women and children, sick and wounded. But fortunately the mutineers had left the area to join plundering forays in the city, and there was no opposition to the withdrawal until they reached the Baillie Guard Gate which was locked. They had arrived earlier than expected and the man with the key could not be found. A shout of 'Open the gate!' was mistaken for 'Open with grape!' and the British gunners were just about to fire when an officer prevented them.[2]

Soon after the last man had passed through the gate, the Machi Bhawan blew up with so thunderous a roar that all the doors of the Residency flew open, and two women fell out of bed.

It was such a tremendous shock [wrote Mrs Brydon], that we all sprang up not knowing what had happened, but thinking that the sepoys had really blown up our defences and forced their way in. Our room was so thick with dust that when we had lighted a candle we could scarcely see one another. The bricks and mortar had fallen from the ceiling, and the poor little children were screaming with terror.[3]

Looking in the direction of the explosion Dr Hadow saw 'an immense column of thick smoke, jet black, standing in the air for some minutes where the old fort had been . . . Then quietly dropping it fell over us as if to crush the city . . . In its place we saw nothing but a heap of ruins.'[4]

There were, however, no casualties. Even a drunken Irish soldier who could not be found when the roll was called came in the next day uninjured. He had been blown into the air by the force of the explosion; but, falling to the ground, he had resumed his drunken sleep and on waking had strolled over to the Residency, picking up two stray bullocks on the way.[5]

Later that morning Sir Henry Lawrence was working in his room when a shell crashed through the window and landed at his feet. He was urged to move to a less exposed room; but 'the dear old man answered that sailors always consider the safest place in a ship to be that where the shot had last made a hole'. When pressed, however, he gave way, saying that he would change his quarters the following day. The move was never made. On the morning of 2 July he was resting on his bed, having made his customary rounds of inspection, when another shell exploded in the room, filling the air with smoke, masonry and brick dust. Captain Wilson called out, 'Sir Henry are you hurt?' There was no reply. The question was repeated twice; and at length Sir Henry murmured softly 'I am killed.' As the dust gradually cleared, Wilson 'saw that the white coverlet of the bed was crimson with blood'. Sir Henry was taken to another room where Dr Fayrer and Dr Hadow examined the wounds in the left thigh and abdomen which they saw at once were mortal. Amputation of the leg was considered impossible; so a tourniquet was applied and 'the agony which this caused was fearful to behold'.[6]

'How long have I got to live?' Lawrence asked. Forty-eight hours, Fayrer replied. And the forecast proved precisely correct. During that time Lawrence 'remained perfectly sensible' for most of the time, Fayrer recorded, speaking 'fast and freely' as round shot battered the walls of the house to which the dying man had been removed. Much to Martin Gubbins's annoyance and chagrin, Lawrence appointed Major Banks, Commander of the Lucknow Division, as his successor, and entrusted the command of the troops to Colonel Inglis. He spoke often of his friends and children, of his dead wife and native servants, and of his colleagues, asking for forgiveness from anyone whom he thought he might have offended. Several times he said that he wanted no other memorial on his tomb than 'Here lies Henry Lawrence who tried to do his duty. May the Lord have mercy on his soul.'

The soldiers who were summoned to carry his body out to his grave bent down one after the other to kiss him on the forehead.[7]

For the next next few days the thirty-seven acres of the Residency area were the scene of 'the wildest confusion'. Artillery bullocks wandered about in search of food and stumbled into wells; horses, maddened by thirst, bit and kicked each other. Soldiers took advantage of the chaos to plunder the Commissariat; several native servants robbed their masters before running off, though many others remained faithful until the end of the siege and some risked their lives to help complete the fortifications for which they were rewarded with lavish rates of pay.[8]

The line of fortifications and defended houses was about a mile in circumference and according to every recognized principle of military science was indefensible.[9] Yet to attempt its defence there were scarcely more than one thousand and seven hundred men. Of these seven hundred and eighty were British soldiers, including officers and surgeons, fifty were Christian (mostly Eurasian) drummers, one hundred and sixty were European civilian volunteers and seven hundred and twenty were native troops. There were also about seven hundred Indian camp-followers and servants, some five hundred women and children, and rather more than fifty pupils from the Martinière.[10]

At first the defenders were constantly frightened that the mutineers, about eight thousand in number supported by military police and several hundred *talukdars'* retainers, would overrun their position. For they were now under intensive bombardment from guns which fired all manner of missiles, from bits of iron to huge blocks of wood, copper coins, carriage springs, bunches of telegraph wire, stink-pots, 'which made a fearful hissing noise and great stench', and even bullocks' horns. The blocks of wood caused much wry amusement among the tougher men of the 32nd who would cry out as one of them flew over the walls, 'Here comes a barrel of beer at last!' or 'Ah, they know we are short of firewood!' The enemy were not short of round-shot, though; and by the middle of July houses were not only pock-marked with bullet-holes but with the larger craters formed by shot which, here and there, could be seen firmly lodged in the masonry.[11]

Although it was said that the enemy's artillery was commanded by 'a practised officer, most probably a European', since several pale-faced figures wearing European clothes were supposed to have been discerned in their ranks[12] – one of them being rather uncertainly identified as a Captain Rolton, a man born in Lucknow who had 'adopted native habits, customs and ideas . . . whose daughters were married to Mussulmans and whose sons served . . . in the late King's army'[13] – in fact the guns seemed to have been fired largely at random. This was not so of the arrows which were shot, complete with burning oil and wicks and with great accuracy, at grain stacks and wood stores. Nor was it true of the musket fire which accounted for most of the fifteen or twenty deaths a day that occurred during the first week of the siege, and which was also directed at the Union Jack flying defiantly from the Residency flagpole and constantly patched and repaired. But certainly there was no concentration of artillery fire which could have led to a breach in any weak part of the defences.

On 1 July the defenders were subjected to what Mrs Inglis described as a 'most terrific bombardment of cannon fire and musketry'. Miss Palmer, the Colonel's daughter, ignoring warnings that it was not safe to do so, had remained on the second storey of the Residency where one of her legs was taken off by a round-shot. Her companions on the ground floor sat 'trembling, hardly able to breathe', feeling sure the enemy would get in 'when the most terrible death awaited' them. Some of them knelt down to pray by the side of a bed where Mrs Case read the Litany. Afterwards, when the firing had died down, they discussed what they should do if the mutineers did get in. 'Some of the ladies', according to Mrs Case, kept 'laudanum and prussic acid always near them', though she herself could 'scarcely think it right to have recourse to such means', and Dr Fayrer refused to supply them. Mrs Inglis agreed with her. As wife of the senior officer present, she was asked if suicide were justifiable to save them from a fate worse than death. She replied that 'it could not be right' and if the time of trial came, 'God who sent it would put it into [their hearts] how to act'. At one time, she added, her husband had talked of blowing them all up should it be necessary to save them from dishonour or a worse death. 'It was strange how calmly we talked on these subjects.'[14]

Indeed, as time went on, most of the European women in Lucknow began to accept their situation with a kind of resigned forbearance. There were some, of course, who felt 'utterly unable at first to cope without their husbands and servants'. Mrs Bartrum, for instance, was quite bewildered. She was given her ration of sea biscuits, flour, salt, rice, peas and meat; but she had no idea how to cook them, and had to rely on a native servant who put all the ingredients together into an ancient copper saucepan from which he produced a grotesque stew, 'perfectly green'. The days were bad enough, Mrs Bartrum complained, but the nights were much worse: she could only find a coolie to pull the punkah by paying him highly, and then he was 'so tiresome' because he kept going to sleep and she grew so tired of jumping out of bed to wake him up that often she was obliged to fan her baby herself. Even the incompetent Mrs Bartrum, however, eventually learned to perform those menial tasks which she had formerly considered quite impossible. She got up at dawn; went outside to look for bits of wood which, with great difficulty, she cut up with a dinner knife; then lit a fire to boil water for breakfast and for washing her clothes.[15]

Other women proved themselves capable from the beginning. Mrs Brydon and Mrs Gubbins organized a roster so that the men on duty at their posts were regularly provided throughout the night with tea and brandy. After her husband had read the prayers and psalms for the day, Mrs Inglis went out to gather firewood – a precious and rare commodity, since the main stocks had been used for the ramparts – risking being killed by a stray shot or bullet from which few parts of the compound were ever safe.[16] Mrs Boileau busily occupied herself in turning the bits of flannel she could lay her hands on into shirts and blouses which were much in demand, many of the men having no change of clothing and their single shirt in rags.[17] One 'gallant civilian', whose clothes had been torn to shreds in his flight through the jungle, was provided with a green baize suit cut from the cloth of the Residency billiard-table.[18] An officer – thankful during the early weeks that his white uniform had been recently dyed khaki as 'washerwomen were conspicuous by their absence' – decided before the siege was over that he did well to exchange his ragged trousers for a pair a lady made for him out of a bombazine dress. Another officer, so Captain Wilson said, 'wore a shirt made out of a floor cloth'. The officers' wives were little better dressed. One of these, an odd Scotch woman who shocked the others by cleaning her teeth in public, outraged them even more by appearing in garments that were worse than diaphanous. 'What an eccentric woman she is; dressing transparently,' commented a disapproving observer. 'Certainly most of us had scanty wardrobes (satirical), but we managed to cover ourselves. She could be seen through.'[19]

Many of the women undertook nursing duties in the Banqueting Hall which had been turned into a hospital, changing the patients' bandages, fanning them, giving them ice-water. There was not as much danger here as there was elsewhere from the rebels' round-shot, as it had been made known to the enemy that the Banqueting Hall was also the prison of various captured princes of the royal house of Oudh who sat gloomily silent, displaying flashes of pleasure when Inglis presented them with a cigar, a poor substitute, even so, for the opium which they craved.[20] But if not a dangerous place, the Banqueting Hall was a most unpleasant one. The windows had been barricaded, so the atmosphere was stifling, the hot gusts of air that occasionally blew through the open doors facing the Residency and the Baillie Guard wall at the back seeming to increase rather than to relieve the oppressive sultriness. Lying in rows along the floor, on beds and sofas, on mattresses and cloaks, were the wounded who had survived the retreat from Chinhat or who had been injured since. Every day new casualties were brought in, but room could always be found for them, since amputation was almost invariably followed by death and by the middle of July there were, on average, about ten deaths of Europeans a day. 'The natives we don't count,' said L. E. R. Rees. 'We feel their loss is nothing very great; but it pains us all to hear of a poor European being knocked over.'[21]

Not all the deaths were caused by enemy fire. As early as the first week of July two children died of cholera which thereafter claimed victims regularly, Captain Mansfield of the 32nd dying, as others did, 'in just a few hours'. His friend Captain Alexander was seriously injured while examining a mortar which blew up in his face, turning him into 'a dreadful figure, black as ebony and covered with blisters which afterwards suppurated'. Nearly everyone suffered from boils or gastritis, skin rashes and persistent colds; and many contracted scurvy which swelled the head, loosened the teeth and led to the slightest bumps producing extensive black bruises. Colonel Inglis, who did not sleep with his clothes off for over three months, looked to Mrs Case 'as though he would not be able to stand the wear and tear much longer'; his hair had 'turned quite grey'. Mrs Bruère, who had been pulled through a hole in the back of her house by some kindly sepoys while others were threatening to murder her at the front, was so shocked by the death of her 'portly, elderly husband' that she went 'right out of her senses'. So did Captain Graham who shot himself in his bed.[22]

After paying a visit to the hospital in the middle of July, Rees wrote of the 'squalor and disagreeable, fetid smell which pervaded the long hall of the sick' despite the constant fumigations and the best endeavours of the surgeons, the apothecary, the native servants, the women who acted as nurses and the pupils from the Martinière, dirty, hungry-looking boys who were employed in driving away the insects from the prostrate bodies of the patients.[23] 'Everywhere wounded officers and men were lying on couches, covered with blood and often with vermin . . . Everywhere cries of agony were heard, piteous exclamations for water or assistance.'[24]

It was not surprising, one of the doctors' wives thought, that there was so much sickness, for the air outside the hospital was almost as pestilential as it was inside it. The latrines which had been dug before the siege began were soon full, and as most of the sweepers had run off, there was no one to empty them. To the smell from these was added the stench from corpses and the carcasses of animals left rotting in the heat. The greatest care was taken to ensure that wounded animals were driven out of the compound. When Captain Anderson's horse broke its leg, its master and some volunteers in his post crawled out on hands and knees, risking their lives to force it to hop on three legs outside the entrenchment, some pulling on its head-rope, others pricking its rump with bayonets. 'All we dreaded,' Anderson explained, 'was the animals dying and our having no means of removing them.'[25] When horses or bullocks did die within the entrenchments, fatigue parties were sent out as soon as possible to bury them. And more than one survivor of the siege remembered burying these putrid horses at night in the teeming rain as the most disagreeable of all the duties which he was obliged to undertake.[26] One night the heavy rains caused the collapse of a huge stack of chaff-straw fodder which had been eaten away at the bottom by bullocks. When the stack fell eight bullocks were buried and suffocated; and Captain Birch, accompanied by a former secretary to the Chief Commissioner, had to go out to bury the carcasses. Birch thought that he would never 'forget that night's work. We had to dig out the eight suffocated bullocks, drag them to their place of internment, dig their graves and cover them up.'[27] Yet, careful as the garrison were to bury the rotting corpses, many could not be reached; and these caused as much distress to the besieged as the pouring rain and the swarms of flies which followed them everywhere, even into their mouths when eating.

Weakened by the sickly air, the Lucknow garrison were weakened, too, by their inadequate diet. At the beginning the stores had been considered plentiful enough for each man to receive, amongst other items, a pound of meat and a pound of flour a day, women being allowed three-quarters of this ration and children half.[28] These amounts were gradually reduced until the men were getting no more than four ounces of flour a day and the children two. 'Our fare is not particularly good,' Rees wrote in the middle of July, 'beef and chupatees with a few extras. Still I fare better than many. I at least have enough.' A fortnight later, however, he was complaining:

Our grand diet consists of coarse, exceedingly coarse *attah* (ground corn with all the husks unsifted), *mash dhal* (a nasty black slippery kind of lentils), and bitter salt, with, every other day, a small piece of coarse beef, half of it bones. The whole of this, when passed under the hands of my *chef-de-cuisine*, a filthy, black fellow who cooks for three or four others, and whom I am obliged to pay 20 rupees a month, results in an abomination which a Spartan dog would turn up his nose at.[29]

What annoyed Rees most of all was that some civilians still had ample stocks of food, while one at least – he referred to Martin Gubbins – enjoyed 'even luxuries'. Others were recklessly open-handed. Rees's friend Deprat, for instance, whose cellar was plundered by English soldiers, shared with his companions all the delicacies he had left, giving away 'with his usual generosity *saucissons aux truffes*, hermetically sealed provisions, cigars, wine and brandy to whoever wanted any'.[30]

There were, however, precious few delicacies like these in Lucknow. Mrs Inglis, who meticulously weighed and issued rations to her dependants each morning, wrote at the beginning of July of a general lack of bread, butter, milk, sugar and vegetables, though she usually managed to find a little arrowroot for the mother of any sick child who approached her. It was, indeed, the children who suffered the most. The milk of several nursing mothers dried up 'through grief and fretting', while small children sickened and wasted 'for want of proper nourishment'. In August the widow of a civilian who had been shot through the lungs at his post approached Mrs Inglis for a little milk for her dying child; but by then three of Mrs Inglis's goats – which she had brought up from the cantonments in May and had carefully tended ever since – had been requisitioned by the butchers, and she had no milk to spare. 'It went to my heart to refuse her,' she wrote. 'But at this time I had only just enough for my own children, and baby could not have lived without it. I think [the mother] understood that I would have given her some if I could.'[31]

Reduced though they were to living on the kind of mash of which Rees complained, or, in outposts like Anderson's where there were no cooks, on biscuits and sardines, what most of the soldiers and volunteers missed far more than good food was decent tobacco. When tea and coffee ran out they managed to make 'a tolerably good substitute' for these by roasting grain. But they found no palatable alternative to tobacco. They tried to smoke green leaves and became ill in consequence. They filled their pipes with tea leaves and dried guavas. They picked up wet and crumpled stubs of cheroots as though they had come upon priceless treasure. They stole precious stocks from men for whom, when under attack, they were prepared to risk their lives. They sold valued possessions – Rees sold his gold watch and chain – so as to be able to bid for cigars that might be offered at the auctions regularly held of dead men's effects.[32]

The prices realized at these auctions were extraordinary and continually increasing. Sir Henry Lawrence's property, sold at auction in August, fetched 'fabulous prices', Mrs Inglis recorded: 'brandy, £14–£16 a dozen. Beer, £5–£7 a dozen. Hermetically sealed provisions from £7 a tin. A bottle of honey £4. Cakes of chocolate, £3–£4. Sugar, had there been any, would have commanded any price.' 'Money has ceased to be of any value and people are giving unheard of prices for stores of any kind,' confirmed Mrs Case who said someone paid '£7 for one of Sir Henry's hams and £1. 5s. for a tin of soup'. She had heard of people paying twenty pounds for a dozen bottles of brandy, five pounds for a small box of vermicelli, and offering twenty-five rupees (fifty shillings) for two pounds of sugar – an offer which was refused. Soap was so scarce that 'little square pieces' sold for seven rupees each. In September cigars were selling for three rupees each; tea was sixteen shillings a pound; brandy fetched anything up to one hundred and eighty rupees a dozen and beer seventy rupees a dozen; ham sold for ninety rupees and a bottle of pickles for twenty. By October brandy had gone up to fifty-four rupees a bottle; fifteen cheroots sold for fifty-one rupees; twenty-five rupees were given for a set of old cooking utensils.

Clothes fetched equally enormous prices. In July shirts were selling at twenty rupees each, flannel waistcoats at twenty-five rupees, and three pairs of worn socks were sold for twenty rupees. In September,

Captain Mansfield's 'old flannel shirt' was knocked down at auction for fifty-five rupees; 'three old flannel shirts and three ragged waistcoats realized 105 rupees'; and at an auction in October a tweed coat and a pair of pantaloons were sold for no less than one hundred and one rupees. It was considered indelicate to sell ladies' clothes at auction; but servants went about with the dresses and bonnets of their dead mistresses for sale in boxes.[33] At the auctions of men's clothes there was an atmosphere of gruesome jocularity, potential buyers picking over the lots and parading themselves about in garments either much too large or much too small for them, trying not to think – as Rees could not help thinking – that 'probably the next auction would be over their *own* clothes'. When they returned to their outposts, however, their momentary gaiety was soon dispelled as they contemplated the crumbling walls of the houses in which they were compelled to fight or die.[34]

There were days of hope. Rumours reached them of dissent amongst the rebel forces in the city from which there came occasionally 'the most frightful cries and screams', or of relief forces rapidly approaching which would induce Captain Boileau to lead his men in singing, 'Cheer, boys, cheer!' One evening there were such loud cheers from the garrison that everyone ran out of the Residency, feeling certain that reinforcements had arrived. Colonel Palmer rushed up to Mrs Inglis, congratulating her on her deliverance, and excitedly picked up one of her children. Wounded men in the hospital staggered out of bed, protesting that they must 'help the fellows coming in'. The ladies in the brigade mess dashed up to the top of the roof to watch the troops advance. But when the excitement was at its height, Colonel Inglis declared in an angry voice, 'It's the most absurd thing I ever heard!' He told the people who had run out of the Residency to go back to their meal, and looked so annoyed that no one dared to speak to him. At length he told them that an officer on the look-out tower had heard firing in the distance where the natives were celebrating some national event – in fact firing a salute to the newly chosen ruler of Oudh – and had 'jumped to the wrong conclusion'.[35]

Thereafter people were less inclined to believe hopeful reports than rumours of reverses or disaster, particularly after news arrived of the murders at Cawnpore. The wife of a drummer of the 48th spoke with horror of little children being cut up into pieces and their bodies stuck on poles, of an Englishman being 'tortured terribly and asked "How he would like his mutton chops and bread and butter now?"' Three days later there was a partial eclipse of the sun which was interpreted by the native servants as indicating that the Devil's Wind had not yet ceased to blow: there would be further massacres, horrors, famine.[36]

On such days, as the rain poured remorselessly down and 'everything looked most miserable', some men 'gave up even the least glimmering of hope ... and delivered themselves up to a sullen, obstinate, silent despair. Thus, hopeless of life, and hoping only to be killed, their existence became almost a burden to them, and [they] cast envious glances at the poor fellows carried to their graves every evening.'[37] Colonel Inglis 'found it impossible to make these men careful. They seemed to be quite reckless', walking slowly and quite upright past gaps in the defences which were constantly watched by enemy snipers.[38]

Other soldiers, who got drunk as often as they could lay their hands on any liquor, became almost mutinous. Private Metcalfe told the story of an Irish soldier reprimanded for not challenging him by 'one of the most indefatigable officers in the garrison', Lieutenant McCabe, who 'was continually bobbing about as the soldiers termed it', knocking over any 'damned swab' of a Eurasian volunteer who thought praying was more important than fighting.

'Why the devil didn't you challenge me?' McCabe asked the Irish sentry angrily.

'Because I knew it was you, sir, and that you would be coming this way.'

'You should have fired, sir. You are not supposed to know anyone outside your post, especially at night, sir.'

'Then, by Jesus Christ, the next time you come the same way at night I will accommodate you. I will shoot you right enough.'

McCabe 'took no further notice, and did not trouble the same sentry again'.[39]

Yet whenever the enemy threatened to make one of their intermittent attacks, everyone would dash to his post and stand firm ready to receive them. Often these threatened attacks never materialized. There would be heavy cannon fire, and musket balls would hammer and dance on the walls 'like peas in a frying-pan'; there would be shouts of command, brigade calls and the noise of war clarions, but not a man would appear. The volunteers would peer into the darkness, listening for the sounds of bodies creeping through the long grass, fancying they saw figures which would then disappear, mistaking the moonlit leaves of a castor-oil tree for the folds of turbans, and opening fire at phantoms. On other occasions, however, the rebels would come on, 'swarming as thick as bees', 'a sea of heads and glittering weapons', as grape struck against the defenders' batteries and earth-works, musket balls flew over them in showers, bugles sounded the advance, and elephants trumpeted dragging forward the heavy guns. Then the men in the threatened posts would be hard put to it to resist their assailants; and frequently only did so by subterfuge, by shout-ing at the tops of their voices to give the impression that they were much more numerous than they really were, 'as if they had a whole regiment with them'.[40]

During one of these attacks, several of the enemy succeeded in forcing their way through the stockade around Anderson's house and in getting as far as the mound in front of the inner ditch. 'Come on, come on!' their leader urged. 'The place is ours! It is *taken*!' Three separate, fierce assaults were made on the house and although each was driven off, Anderson was beset by the fear that, even if his men could withstand another attack, the outposts on either side of him might not be able to do so.

We well knew what we had to expect if we were defeated [Anderson wrote], and therefore, each individual fought for his very life. Each loop-hole displayed a steady flash of musketry, as defeat would have been certain death to every soul in the garrison . . . We dreaded that the other posts might have been further pressed than we were. At intervals I heard the cry, 'More men this way!' and off would rush two or three (all we could possibly spare) . . . and then the same cry was repeated in an opposite direction . . . During this time even the poor wounded men ran out of the hospitals, and those who had wounds in their legs threw away their crutches and deliberately knelt down and fired as fast as they could; others, who could do little else, loaded the muskets.[41]

'It was, indeed, heart-rending to see these poor fellows staggering along to the scenes of action,' wrote Rees of another occasion when the wounded were drawn from their beds by the fear of being over-run.

Pale, trembling with weakness, several of them were bleeding from their wounds which reopened by the exertions they made. One unfor-tunate wretch, with only one arm, was seen hanging to the parapet of the hospital entrenchments with his musket, but the momentary strength which the fear of his being butchered in his bed and the desire of revenge had given him, was too much for him. He died in the course of the day.[42]

Crouching in their room while these attacks were going on, the women expected every moment to hear the shouts of murderous sepoys outside; and, during one attack, Mrs Case could not help thinking what would be the feelings of any lady suddenly transported from quiet, peaceful England to this room, around which the bullets are whizzing, the round shot falling, and now and then a loud explosion, as if a mine were blowing up which I think is almost worse than all the . . . fire of the musketry. It is an awful time . . . The nights are dreadful. One looks forward so anxiously for the first ray of daylight. Then the day arrives with no news of our relief. One's heart sickens at all this delay, and knowing nothing of what is going on outside the gates.[43]

One night Mrs Case 'really thought for a moment that [the mutineers] had got in'. She knelt down by her bed with Mrs Inglis to say a prayer. 'It was frightful to hear the shells whizzing over our heads . . . The firing did not continue very long, and then succeeded a complete and death-like silence which was even more painful. Mrs Inglis remained at the door for some time to see if anyone might pass from whom she could hear what was really going on.' At length Colonel Inglis appeared and told them that it was all over; they could go to bed. So they finished their prayers and did so, only to be roused by news of more deaths. Mrs Reed came into their room to tell them that her husband had died in the night and that one of her children had got cholera. 'How sad and depressing all this is, day after day . . . Nobody could imagine all these horrors unless they witnessed them.'[44]

Without their faith, many felt sure, they could not have survived them. Mrs Brydon often thought of 'a pet saying' of her mother's: 'Providence is a rich provider.' Despite the fact that God did not appear to be providing much for her at the moment, she always felt this saying to be 'most true, more and more so in times of trouble'.[45]

Taking comfort from their religion, and from such rare pleasures as a green tree which still stood in the Residency grounds, and the cooing of some doves that appeared untroubled by the fighting, most of the besieged eventually came to accept their plight and probable death with a resigned submission to God's will. 'Balls fall at our feet, and we continue the conversation without a remark,' Rees commented. 'Bullets graze over our very hair and we never speak of them. Narrow escapes are so very common that even women and children cease to notice them.'[46] Women, in fact, so Martin Gubbins said, became so used to the sound of shot whizzing over their heads and thudding into masonry that they were far better than men at differentiating between the weight of the missiles. A man would say, 'There goes a 21-pounder!' 'No, that was an 18-pounder' a woman would contradict him; and she it was who would be proved right.[47]

Children, too, became almost indifferent to danger and expert in recognizing the strange sounds and terms of warfare. Johnny Inglis's 'quick ears detected immediately where a bullet fell', his mother recorded. 'And he would run and pick it up whilst it was still warm.' He and the other children spent much of their time playing war games, throwing earth against a wall in imitation of shells bursting, making tunnels like the mines which they knew the sepoys were burrowing beneath them, dragging about sardine tins filled with stones which they pretended were ammunition wagons, bombarding broken dolls with bits of fallen masonry, calling out to each other, 'That's clean through his lungs!' or 'That wants more elevation'. One day Anderson heard a little boy, no more than four or five years old, call to his companion, '*You* fire round-shot at me, and *I'll* return shell from my battery!'[48]

There were certain adults who also appeared to consider the siege a kind of game, and to derive a thrill from its dangers and even its discomforts. There was a Private Cuney of the 32nd who, followed by a faithful sepoy who evidently adored him, went out night after night to raid the enemy positions, to kill men and spike guns. Frequently placed in the guard-room for disobedience, he was let out when there was fighting to be done. Wounded more than once, he left his bed rather than miss a sortie, during the course of one of which he was killed.[49] Captain Fulton who was also accompanied everywhere by a native soldier, a muscular Sikh with a barrel of powder on his back, took an equally zestful pride in his daring skill and seemed to derive the same sort of pleasure in exercising it. 'He was a superb engineer,' Captain Birch recorded, remembering the expertise with which he placed just the right amount of powder in exactly the right places around the columns and corners of enemy-held buildings which he contrived to blow up without endangering the garrison's defences.

As soon as the train was laid the order was given to 'withdraw the escort'. I generally sent it away with the native officer, leaving only sentries to warn us of a rush of the enemy. Then came the second order, 'withdraw the sentries', and with them I used to rush in, leaving Captain Fulton all alone in the enemy's country to fire the train. He returned at full speed and simultaneously came the blow-up. I never knew him fail.[50]

One day Fulton was in a trench with Birch 'when he turned his face with a smile on it and said, "They are just going to fire." And sure enough they did. The shot took away the whole of the back of Captain Fulton's head, his face like a mask still on his neck.'[51]

Scarcely a day passed without a death as shocking. A friend of Dr Hadow was killed one morning while having breakfast: 'A round-shot came through two brick walls, and when the dust cleared away we found him lying in a crushed heap on the floor just as if a suit of clothes had been thrown down there, he was so entirely without shape.'[52] 21 July was a particularly bitter day for Mrs Brydon. The chaplain, Polehampton, was killed that day. So was 'good, kind Major Banks, shot through the temple'. Mrs Brydon had just finished preparing the Major's body for his wife to see when she was told that her 'own dearest husband' had been hit, shot through the loins. 'When I got to him I found him on a couch and Dr Fayrer dressing his wound,' she recalled . . . 'I am so thankful to be able to attend to him myself. He is in great pain, they suppose from a nerve being touched, and can't turn himself. From my heart I grieve for poor Mrs Banks who has lost the one that was everything to her and their darling little girl.'[53]

No one, Dr Gilbert Hadow thought, could look without pity at these orphaned children, many of whom 'were so soon to follow their parents to the grave'. 'You saw the little things drooping and dying from day to day,' he wrote. 'This was the saddest part of all.'[54] Mrs Brydon's diary is full of references to her own and other young children's sufferings:

July 25 . . . Poor little Helen Grant died yesterday of cholera . . . Baby still ailing and so thin. Mary Anne drooping sadly, quite lost her appetite . . . very feverish . . . *July 31* . . . A little girl had three of her toes much injured by a bullet . . . *August 17* . . . Mrs Green (48th) died last night and Mrs Levin's baby the night before. Major Bird's baby was buried this evening . . . *August 30* . . . A sergeant's wife and baby both died today . . . *September 4* . . . Another little girl died yesterday . . .[55]

Mrs Boileau poignantly recorded the last days of her own baby daughter:

September 1st. My darling Ina very ill, with ulcerated sores and diarrhoea . . . so wasted and so thin . . . I fear she can never get over this. God help me . . . *September 2nd*. Baby is no better. She cannot bear being moved . . . Dr Partridge gives me hope of her, though, and may God yet spare her to me in His infinite mercy. I get a little milk for her and break up a hard ration biscuit in it . . . *September 5th*. Baby much the same . . . *September 9th*. Baby seems better today. She sat up of her own accord and talked and laughed in her own old pretty way. God grant she may be really better. *September 10th*. Baby is better. I brought her outside and she began to talk of the horses . . . *September 11th*. . . . My darling is not so well today. Her throat seems sore and she swallows with much difficulty. Oh, how shall I bear to lose her . . . The Doctor tells me she is very ill . . . *September 12th*. I know my pet lamb is going from me. Bessie [Fayrer] came over for some hours to try to comfort me, but the only one who could comfort is, alas, I know not where. Oh, George darling, thank God you are spared the agony that I am going through . . . *September 13th*. My little darling was taken from me at five o'clock after such a night of agony and painful watching as I pray God I may never spend again. I cannot write it . . . Sergeant Court made her a little coffin . . . I put her into it with my own hands . . . At twelve o'clock she was carried away to that wretched mournful churchyard . . . Oh, God Almighty comfort me . . .[56]

Another mother was sitting down sewing with her baby and ten-year-old daughter when a round-shot came crashing through the wall and tore off the little girl's head. The distraught mother lost her milk; and the baby eventually died of starvation. Nowhere within the Residency defences was safe from attack; and death was likely to come at any time, as it came to Mrs Leguere who was shot through the lungs while drinking a cup of tea, and Mrs Dorin who was shot dead while getting into bed.[57]

The artillery suffered particularly heavy casualties; and before the siege was over every single one of their officers had been killed. They were replaced by civilian volunteers and officers of the native infantry, most of whom, through constant practice with the guns, became nearly as skilful as the men whose duties they had taken over. The position could never have been held, in fact, without the help of the native infantry, as Inglis himself conceded.[58] Rees complained of the Sikhs, who had 'behaved so shamefully at Chinhutt, sulkily sitting down, doing nothing, sneering at our efforts'.[59] But most other sur-vivors wrote of the native soldiers with admiration and gratitude. Mrs Inglis was much touched by the generosity of the Sikhs (who gave her son chupatties, though 'they could not have had much to eat themselves, poor men'), and by the devotion of the men of the 13th Native Infantry who reverently carried their colonel to his grave, 'the greatest mark of respect and affection they could show him, as it is against their caste to touch a dead body'.[60]

Both Gubbins and Anderson wrote of the steadfast manner in

which their sepoys resisted all the enemy's blandishments, their offers of higher pay and better rations.

> They would say to our men, 'Leave the infidels and come out. We'll give you good food and plenty of it,' [wrote Anderson]. Our sepoys would reply, 'We have eaten the Company's salt. We cannot break faith with our masters like you have.' This answer exasperated the mutineers who would say, 'You are as bad as they are. You have become vile Christians. But never mind, we are off to kill all the men of your reinforcements; and when we return we will pay you off. We will not spare a single man.'[61]

On 20 September almost three months had passed since the disastrous battle at Chinhat. Relief seemed as far away as ever, and survival now remote. All the buildings, shattered by round-shot, had been further damaged by the torrential rains; and some had been cut away by the persistent fire of musketry alone. Anderson's veranda had long since collapsed, and his upper storey, under constant battering from the enemy guns, had had to be abandoned for lack of cover. Two walls of the Residency had fallen down and a gust of wind was all that was necessary to bring down the shaky north-east wing. Six men of the 32nd, which had taken over all but the ground floor of the building, had been buried in the ruins. Two men had been saved by rescuers who risked their own lives to pour brandy down their throats as they endeavoured to dig them out under heavy fire; but the other four were suffocated. The Gubbinses' house had also been subjected to such heavy cannonading by twenty-one-pound shots which passed right through the outer walls that the upper north rooms had had to be abandoned, and some of the ladies who had previously found shelter in the house had been forced to leave to find quarters elsewhere, some at the Ommanneys', others at the Brigade Mess. With the enemy repeatedly mining beneath them, and constantly threatening to storm across the shattered defences, these ladies did not feel they would survive in their new quarters for long.[62] 'Everyone is getting very dispirited,' Mrs Bartrum recorded in her diary. 'No news of relief. They say we are forgotten and that reinforcements will never appear . . . This hope deferred does indeed make the heart sick.'[63]

Contact had been made with General Havelock, but his reply to the most recent letter smuggled out to him by a sepoy pensioner named Angad Tewari had not been reassuring. Havelock had warned Inglis that he would not be able to reach Lucknow for twenty-five days, and had added, 'Do not negotiate, but rather perish sword in hand.'[64] On 16 September Angad, who was promised five thousand rupees if he succeeded in his mission, was sent out again with a letter which he concealed in a quill in his rectum. 'No one really expected that he would get through or, if he did, that he would bring back any messages of comfort.'[65]

Just before midnight on 22 September, however, Angad came rushing through the lines, fired on by rebel sentries. He had exciting news to impart: Havelock had crossed the Ganges and would be at Lucknow within a few days.[66]

13

The First Relief of Lucknow

Havelock's campaign · his victory at Unao, 29 July 1857 ·
his decision to withdraw, 30 July · Neill's reaction – Havelock
presses on · victory of Bashiratganj, 5 August · his withdrawal to
Cawnpore, 13 August · defeats rebels at Bithur, 16 August ·
Sir James Outram appointed to command · arrives at Cawnpore,
5 September – waives right to command ·
march resumed, 19 September – Lucknow relieved, 25 September ·

Two months before, when Havelock crossed the Ganges at Cawnpore, he had been only too conscious of the difficulties he would have to overcome. Behind him was the fast-flowing river, five times as wide as the Thames at London Bridge. In front were the unfriendly villages of Oudh, occupied by an unknown number of armed rebels and of mutinous sepoys rallying once more to the banner of Nana Sahib and ready to cut across his rear as soon as he advanced towards the army besieging Lucknow. His own force of 1,200 British troops, 300 Sikhs and ten guns, 'imperfectly equipped and manned', was pitifully small. 'The enterprise is a desperate one,' Major North concluded, 'and it will be seen whether a force so weak as ours can do more than make the attempt.'[1] Havelock himself described his difficulties to the acting Commander-in-Chief, Sir Patrick Grant, as 'excessive', the chances of relieving Lucknow 'hourly multiplying' against him.[2]

He encountered his first obstacle on 29 July at a village near the small town of Unao not many miles from the river's bank. Here a large force of sepoys were entrenched in fortified enclosures and in the loopholed houses of the village. They were protected on their right by a swamp, on their left by flooded meadows, so that the turning movement which had proved so successful at Cawnpore was impossible. There would have to be a frontal attack. The Highlanders and Madras Fusiliers ran forward into a fire which became so fierce as they approached the village that the 64th had to be sent to their support. The village was set alight, but the sepoys held their ground until all their guns had been captured. And when they retired at last, 'a very large force of infantry, cavalry and guns' was reported to be advancing to their support. Havelock went forward to meet them, choosing a good position from which Maude's guns could fire at them when they came within range. The enemy's guns opened fire first, but within minutes of replying Maude's guns and the Enfield rifles of the Madras Fusiliers had scattered the sepoy force to the edges of the swamp, making it impossible for them to deploy into line.

After a short halt, during which the wounded and sick were put into carts and the dead buried, the army moved on again, the captured guns being left behind and spiked since there was no transport to carry them off. But within a few miles the advance was blocked once more by a rebel force occupying the walled and moated town of Bashiratganj. Havelock planned to annihilate them there by sending the 64th around the town to cut off their single line of retreat, a narrow causeway across the swamp behind, while the Highlanders and Madras Fusiliers assaulted the gate in front. The plan might well have succeeded if the 64th had fulfilled their role with more determination; but, as at Cawnpore, they were excessively cautious, and the enemy were already streaming across the causeway when the 64th reached it.[3]

The General, who was loudly cheered in camp that night, was not displeased with the progress of his little army. 'Soldiers!' he addressed them in an Order of the Day composed in that grandiloquent style to which they were growing accustomed, 'Soldiers! Your General thanks you for your exertions today. You have stormed two fortified villages, and captured nineteen guns. But he is not satisfied with *all* of you,' he felt constrained to add, remembering the conduct of the 64th. 'Some of you fought as if the cholera had seized your minds as well as your bodies. There were men among you, however, whom he must praise to the skies.'[4]

Satisfied though he was with the conduct of most of his force, Havelock could not but doubt the wisdom of taking it further against an enemy so numerous and so determined. Sickness and wounds had greatly reduced his own numbers, while there were no litters or carts left for casualties that might occur in the future. He had no tents, and far too few guns. He had no means of crossing the water obstacles ahead of him, and his communications were liable at any moment to be cut by Nana Sahib. So, though he knew he would be severely criticized and that the men were willing to go on, he made up his mind to retire. He 'felt the Lord Jesus [was] at [his] side' when he

came to his decision. But, conscious of a need for earthly coun-
sellors, he sent for Colonel Tytler who agreed with him; and when
dispatches arrived announcing the mutiny of the regiments at
Dinapore – which meant that the reinforcements which might have
been sent to him from there would now be held back – he had no
further doubts. Despite the protests of officers who maintained that
to retreat now would be to lose all the moral superiority which their
past victories had given him, he gave the order to retire.[5]

When Neill heard what Havelock had done he was so horrified,
angry and indignant that he protested immediately with the utmost
intemperance:

I deeply regret that you have fallen back one foot. The effect on our
prestige is very bad indeed . . . Your camp was not pitched yesterday
before all manner of reports were rife in the city . . . That you had returned to get more guns, having lost all you took away with you; in fact
the belief amongst all is that you have been *defeated* and *forced* back. It
has been most unfortunate your not bringing any guns captured from the
enemy. The natives will not believe that you have captured one. The
effect of your retrograde movement will be very injurious to our cause
everywhere . . . When the iron guns are sent to you, also the half-battery
and the company of the 84th escorting it, you ought to advance again and
not halt until you have rescued, if possible, the garrison at Lucknow.
Return here sharp, for there is much to be done.[6]

Having read this letter, 'the most extraordinary [he had] ever
perused . . . perhaps the most astounding words ever addressed by a
subordinate officer to his commander' – Havelock was furious. He
had already received a most intemperate complaint from Neill who
protested that 'no use whatever' had been made of his services, that
he had been tied 'hand and foot'.[7] Havelock replied to this second
letter immediately:

There must be an end to these proceedings at once . . . I do not want
and will not receive any advice from an officer under my command, be his
experience what it may. Understand this distinctly; and that a consideration of the obstruction that would arise to the public service at this
moment alone prevents me from taking the stronger step of placing you
under arrest. You now stand warned. Attempt no further dictation . . .
I alone am responsible for the course which I have pursued.

He had his reasons for falling back, and he would communicate them
to nobody.[8]

In fact, Havelock did discuss his problems with his staff, not only with Tytler, but also with his son Harry and the enterprising field engineer, Captain Crommelin, though certainly with no one else. 'We are still in the dark about the General's intentions,' wrote Lieutenant W. T. Groom on 3 August. 'Everybody is frightfully disgusted at his conduct; but . . . doubtless . . . he has very good reasons for his apparent want of energy.'[9]

In fact Havelock had already changed his mind about withdrawing and had decided to adopt the course suggested in Neill's letter. The next morning, after the company of the 84th and the half-battery had reached him together with a warning that he could expect no reinforcements other than these, he set out once again for Lucknow after delivering to his men a characteristic speech of encouragement and exhortation. Ahead of him on the road was the spy, Angad, carrying about his person a message to the Residency written by Tytler in tiny letters, some of them in Greek: 'We shall push on as speedily as possible. We hope to reach you in four days at furthest. You must aid us in every way, even to cutting your way out if we can't force our way in. We are only a small force.'[10]

It was, in fact, far too small a force for the task which he had set it. Once again he drove the enemy out of Bashiratganj by the same method he had adopted there before; but he had no cavalry to pursue the retreating sepoys who withdrew only to make another stand. With his force further reduced by cholera – and, so Tytler said, 'cowed by the numbers opposed to them' – Havelock felt unable after all to go forward to renew his attack through a countryside up in arms against him, especially as the Gwalior Contingent had now mutinied and was within fifty miles of Cawnpore. His son Harry, difficult, arrogant and cantankerous, vehemently opposed the idea of another retreat, voting for an advance 'at all hazards'. But both Tytler and Crommelin took Harry 'to task severely'; and at length his father said, 'I agree with Tytler.' So, its commander having taken what he described as 'the most painful decision' he had ever had to form in his life, the force gloomily withdrew to its old camping-ground at Mangalwar. Here Havelock, anxious not to be cut off from Cawnpore, spent his time supervising the building of causeways and bridges of boats across the now slightly sunken Ganges.

Inglis continued to call to him for help from Lucknow; so did the authorities at Agra. But there was nothing he could do for either of them. When, however, Neill wrote from Cawnpore to warn him that the town was threatened by four thousand mutineers at Bithur, he felt bound to accede to his request to support him. Yet rather than let it be supposed that he had abandoned Oudh in fear of his enemies there, he decided to inflict yet another defeat upon them first.[11]

So once again his little army marched down the road towards Bashiratganj. Once again his artillery fired their guns with devastating accuracy, though under so heavy a fire that Lieutenant Crump had never known the like; within five minutes every man at the gun Crump was laying was wounded with grape. And once again the Highlanders charged, cheering grimly, through the swamp. 'Oh if you could have seen the Highlanders,' Harry Havelock told his cousin, 'a handful – 120 men – overwhelmed almost with shot, shell and grape – up to their middles in swamp – rush with a cheer on two guns behind entrenchments and defended by not less than 2,000 sepoys and wrest them from them without a second's check – you would have been proud of your countrymen for ever.'[12]

With their help Havelock won his victory; and, as the last of the rebels ran away through Bashiratganj and across the causeway behind it, he returned to Cawnpore. He arrived there on 13 August. But although all his men were badly in need of rest, and so many of them were suffering from cholera that the doctors warned him that at the present rate there would be none left in six weeks, he felt unable to leave them in peace for long. Three days later, he marched them north under a scorching sun to face the rebels at Bithur.

The enemy, 'the flower of the mutinous soldiery', as Havelock afterwards described them, were occupying a position outside the town beyond a plain covered with sugar cane and castor-oil plants. Defended by breastworks, redoubts and batteries, sited by Tatya Tope, it was 'one of the strongest positions' that Havelock had ever seen. Yet 'after a severe struggle', so he recorded in his subsequent dispatch, 'the enemy were driven back, their guns captured and infantry chased off the field in full retreat'.

Havelock's traditionally dramatic Order of the Day paid tribute to the brave troops, their ranks 'thinned by sickness and the sword', whose exertions had brought about his victory. They had stumbled to their feet to cheer him as he rode down the lines before leading them back to Cawnpore in a rainstorm so torrential that they had had to halt and turn their hunched backs to its force. 'Don't cheer me, my men,' he had said. 'You did it all yourselves.' Now he returned their compliment:

May the hopes of treachery and rebellion be ever thus blasted! And if conquest can now be achieved under these most trying of circumstances, what will be the triumph and retribution of the time when the armies from China, from the Cape, and England shall sweep through the land? Soldiers! in that moment, your labours, your privations, your sufferings and your valour will not be forgotten by a grateful country![13]

On his return to Cawnpore from Bithur, Havelock was handed a copy of the Government *Gazette* dated 4 August which contained this announcement: 'Major-General Sir James Outram, K.C.B., of the Bombay Army, to command the Dinapore and Cawnpore Divisions which are to be combined in one command.'

There was no explanatory letter from the Commander-in-Chief, no expression of thanks to Havelock for his past services. No slight was intended to Havelock who had never held the Cawnpore Division, to which his rank did not entitle him, and who recognized that Outram, also appointed Chief Commissioner of Oudh in succession to Sir Henry Lawrence, was a senior general whose services the Government were naturally anxious to employ. Yet he could not help feeling bitterly disappointed that his independent command was at an end and that Neill and his friends were given good reason for supposing that Havelock had been superseded as a punishment for his withdrawal from Bashiratganj. He was comforted, however, by the thought that his successor was a man with whom he could work far more happily than with Neill.[14]

James Outram was a man of great talent and generosity. Eight years younger than Havelock, he had had a more distinguished career, as both soldier and administrator. In November 1854, at the age of fifty-one, he had been promoted Major-General and Resident of Oudh; and a year later, with the local rank of Lieutenant-General, he had been given command of the army for the Persian War in the conduct of which his reputation had been further enhanced.[15] Lady Canning had not taken to him when she had met him in Calcutta. He was, she thought, 'a very common looking little dark Jewish bearded man, with a desponding slow hesitating manner, very unlike descriptions'.[16] But when he arrived at Cawnpore on 15 September there were few officers more respected in the army and none more popular. 'We all like Sir J. Outram extremely,' one young officer wrote. 'He is a first-rate officer, very clever and amusing. His conversation you can listen to any time.'[17]

He is very pleasant and friendly [another officer confirmed]. When I called on him one day I found him in his shirt sleeves and a pair of old military pantaloons sitting on his bed smoking a cheroot. He was not by any means a handsome man, broad and powerful looking with frizzly dark hair ... I had hardly seated myself when he offered me a cigar which I thankfully accepted, they are scarce enough in camp ... The General never ceased smoking and he was most liberal with them. He also gave dinner parties daily to which we were all asked in turn.[18]

His popularity was much increased when it became known that he had waived his right to command, that he had sent a telegram to Havelock assuring him that he would leave to his subordinate the glory of relieving Lucknow for which Havelock had 'already so nobly struggled' and that, should Havelock wish to make use of his military services, he would willingly serve under him as a volunteer.[19]

Havelock's staff acknowledged the unselfishness of Outram's decision, which was expected to lose him the chance of obtaining a baronetcy and a pension as well as the largest share of the prize money on the fall of Lucknow. But they doubted that he would be able to stand silently by when Havelock took decisions with which he could not agree. These misgivings seemed justified even before Outram's arrival in Cawnpore. For when Havelock proposed that the two brigades in his new force, to be commanded respectively by Colonels Neill and Hamilton, should be called wings rather than brigades Outram replied that while, of course, he would leave him unfettered in his arrangements, he would suggest for Havelock's consideration that they ought to be constituted as brigades 'with a Brigade-Major to each Brigadier, and with a field hospital to each Brigade'.[20]

After his arrival on 5 September Outram's suggestions as to alterations in Havelock's arrangements became less diffident. He had been in the camp only a few hours when he caused Havelock's orders for crossing the river to be countermanded. Soon afterwards he overruled Havelock who had decided that the army would march without tents: no, said Outram, tents really ought to be taken. In fact, Havelock's son complained, Outram continued to

direct every detail whenever he pleased just as though he had never resigned the command in the first place which now meant that no one in the force knew who actually was commanding and consequently instead of the prompt and unhesitating obedience and execution of orders which had resulted from my father's acknowledged and proverbially decisive system of command – short, precise and clear – there arose a hesitancy, tardiness and inexactness of execution which put everything into confusion.[21]

The 'confusion resulting from orders and counter orders' became so intolerable, indeed, that Major Havelock urged his father either to ask for 'an uncontrolled and undivided command or to resign back into Sir James's hands that which was no gift but merely the establishment, under the name of an act of unparalleled generosity (and possibly with the very highest motives and intentions), of an anarchy'. Havelock himself was well aware of the difficulties resulting from his not being in full control. But he did not want to cause any trouble between himself and Outram whom he liked and admired; and so he allowed matters to go on as they were, hoping that Outram would soon recognize the impracticability of the present system. Unwilling to let matters drag on as they were, however, young Havelock wrote out his own letter of resignation from the staff, asking to be allowed to join the volunteer cavalry, and taking the opportunity to point out that, so long as Major-General Outram continued 'to interfere in every detail connected with the movements of the force', a vital military principle of undivided command was being violated.

Harry Havelock showed the letter to his father before sending it off. The General read it, smiled, and said, 'No, Harry, we won't send this but I'll write to him.' He then composed a letter to Outram mentioning a point on which they had disagreed and requesting to have Sir James's orders on it, evidently hoping that the reference to his requiring orders would awaken Outram to the fact that he did not know whether he was in command of the army or not.

The letter was far too delicate, though, in Harry Havelock's opinion. He doubted that Sir James properly understood what his father was trying to imply. 'For a few hours' Outram, who protested that he had no intention of interfering at all, refrained from doing so; but the next day 'he was again issuing directions on all sides'. And, according to Harry Havelock, who came to the conclusion that Outram had resigned the command 'so that he might get the Victoria Cross',[23] General Havelock never afterwards recovered his former self-confidence.

His false position preyed upon him night and day . . . In place of being prompt, deciding and unhesitating he appeared to vacillate and falter, often when asked for orders saying 'You had better go to Sir James first' . . . He did not complain of it, as he never complained of anything, but it rankled in his mind continually and soon began to tell on his health and spirits . . . He sacrificed his fame as a soldier to his desire to avoid the appearance of returning Sir James's professed generosity (which I will not undertake to say was not *bona fide* in *intention*, at the same time as it was fatally mischievous in practice) with coldness and ingratitude.[24]

The army, now numbering just over 3,000 men, which Havelock nominally commanded, began to cross the Ganges on 19 September.

On that day the spy, Angad, came into camp and was directed to the house occupied by General Neill.

A man walked into the room where we were having breakfast [recorded Neill's aide-de-camp], and laid a little bit of dirty mud on the table less than a small acorn, and said it was a letter from Lucknow. It had no address so the General told me to open it. So I scraped off the mud and cut off a little bit of quill sealed at both ends and pulled out a slip of paper written in Greek . . . and read as follows: 'My dear General . . . I hope to be able to hold on to the 20th–25th . . . [But] I must be frank and tell you that my force is daily diminishing from the enemy's fire and our defences grow daily weaker. Should the enemy make any really determined effort to storm this place I shall find it difficult to repulse them . . .'[25]

The contents of this letter were made known to Havelock's men who, after a night of torrential rain, began their advance into Oudh on 21 September, their thoughts 'occupied all the time' with the women and children in Lucknow. They had covered less than six miles when they came upon the enemy at Mangalwar. The rebel leaders, by now accustomed to Havelock's favourite flanking movement, had drawn up their men to counteract it. They could not, however, resist the impetus of his attack; and soon the volunteer cavalry were galloping away in pursuit of the retreating sepoys, slashing at them with their sabres, killing over a hundred of them. Sir James Outram rode with them, disdaining to draw his sword, striking about him with a gold-headed Malacca cane. Havelock also joined in the charge for a time but, not wanting to get too far ahead, rode back towards Maude's guns 'his horse bleeding copiously from four or five tulwar cuts'. 'As the poor beast commenced to stagger,' Maude said, 'the General [who had never been so much as scratched in any of the battles in which he had fought in his long career] quickly dismounted saying to me, with a proud but melancholy intonation, "That makes the sixth horse I have had killed under me."'[26]

From Mangalwar, Havelock led the army on the now only too familiar route through Unao and Bashiratganj. Beyond Bashiratganj it began to pour with rain once more, and the men sloshed through the mud. The fields on either side of the raised road were deep under water. They came up to the Sai River which they had expected to cross by boat; but the enemy's retreat had been so precipitate that the bridge was still there without a sepoy in sight. Most of the army crossed the river that night; and as they lay down to sleep they could hear, sixteen miles away, the faint, intermittent boom of the guns in Lucknow.

The next morning the march was resumed in sunshine; and as they approached Lucknow, the roar of the guns began to die away and the men knew that the enemy were turning their attention from the Residency to the force now attempting its relief. But still there were no sepoys to be seen. Then, two miles south of the city wall, they came upon the Alambagh, a group of buildings in a walled park shaded by many trees. Here a cavalry patrol, sent forward to reconnoitre, returned to report that the enemy were drawn up in vast numbers south of Lucknow, their left on the Alambagh, and their centre and right protected by hillocks rising above the swampy ground on either side of the road. Havelock decided to turn their right and sent Colonel Hamilton's brigade off through the ditches and soggy fields to his left. At the same time the artillery, struggling to get their horses and guns through trenches filled with water, pushed forward to reply to the enemy's heavy fire; while Neill's brigade, having held the front until Hamilton's movement was completed, moved forward into the attack. The Alambagh was soon stormed and overrun; and the cavalry, led by Outram, galloped forward to capture five guns and drive the enemy as far as the canal beneath the walls of Lucknow. Withdrawing to the Alambagh, the whole force spent the night on a nearby ridge while the rain poured down in sheets until the ground was ankle-deep in mud. The next morning tents were pitched; and, while the men ate and slept, the generals debated the problem of Lucknow.

It was universally acknowledged that to follow the most direct route to the Residency, across the canal bridge and then through streets closely overlooked by loopholed houses, would be madness. It had always been Havelock's plan to avoid this kind of suicidal street fighting by making a wide detour to the right across the Gumti and then coming down on the Residency from the north. But, as a cavalry patrol discovered, this route crossed land so flooded by the recent rains that it would be impossible to get artillery across it. Outram, therefore, suggested an advance to the canal bridge where the army could turn right through the southern and eastern outskirts of the city and then left by the Kaiser Bagh to approach the Residency by the Baillie Guard Gate.

Although he always set great store by his artillery, Havelock still felt it would be a better plan to make the wider detour and thus be in a position to approach the iron bridge with fewer casualties than were likely to be incurred on Outram's route. But Outram was adamant; and when Harry Havelock went to his father to ask for orders for the staff, the General said he was 'to take them from General Outram'. Outram did not demur. He gave Major Havelock his orders for the attack which Havelock noted down, then wrote out in full and read out to Outram clause by clause.[27]

The next morning was bright and sunny; the men were given a good breakfast, and at eight o'clock the army was ready to move off. Outram led the way with Neill's brigade towards the canal bridge under heavy fire from guns and muskets concealed in the long grass and sugar cane on either side of the road. General Havelock was to follow him with Hamilton's brigade; but as there was a delay since the men were not ready, a message had to be sent forward to tell Outram to halt. So Neill's infantry were forced to lie down for ten minutes, while 'the bullets fell among them like a shower of hail', as a civilian volunteer reported; 'the round-shot and grape literally tore up the road, cutting the brave fellows to pieces'. Casualties were heavy; and Outram was slightly wounded in the arm.

Casualties were even heavier when the time came to advance and take the bridge which was defended by five guns and hundreds of sharpshooters in the buildings on either side. Outram turned to the right with part of Neill's brigade to try to bring a flanking fire upon the enemy from the canal bank, while the skirmishers of the Madras Fusiliers were sent to the left, and Maude was left to silence the guns from the front. But the road was too narrow for the deployment of more than two guns; and Maude's casualties were such that he had to call upon volunteers from the infantry to help him. When Major Havelock and Tytler came up with the leading men of Hamilton's brigade, Maude called out in exasperation, 'Do something, in the name of heaven!'

Both Havelock and Tytler recognized immediately that Maude's task was quite impossible, and that only an infantry charge could save him. So Harry Havelock rode up to Neill and urged him to order an assault by the Madras Fusiliers. 'I am not in command,' replied Neill. 'I cannot take the responsibility. And Outram must turn up soon.'

Extremely angry, though making no reply, Havelock turned his horse and galloped off, pretending to seek instructions from his father. No sooner was he out of sight, however, than he wheeled his horse about, rode back to Neill and said, 'You are to carry the bridge at once, Sir.'

The order to the Madras Fusiliers was given. Immediately one of their officers, together with Havelock, Tytler, and a few men both of the Fusiliers and of the 84th dashed forward before the rest were ready. They were met by a hail of shot which killed Tytler's horse, wounded the officer and all but one of the men, yet left Havelock still sitting in the saddle with a hole in his hat and a lock of hair cut off by a ball that grazed his forehead. He waited there, waving his sword, until the rest of the men came up, then went headlong with them across the bridge into Lucknow.

The rest of the brigade rushed after them, making better progress through the long narrow lanes than they had expected until they came under a ferocious fire from the Kaiser Bagh. From there on, the advance through twisting streets, beneath garden walls and towering buildings was painfully slow and costly. Every house seemed occupied; round every corner was the muzzle of a gun. Few officers knew where they were or in which direction they had to go. It was 'a scene of great confusion', wrote one of them, with 'guns and infantry mixed up, soldiers wandering in search of their companions, and the wounded in the *doolies* carried here and there without orders'.

General Havelock, a horse shot under him for the seventh time, and Sir James Outram, more agitated than Captain Gordon had ever seen him, kept looking at a map of the city as they discussed what moves they should now make. Outram suggested halting for a few hours to allow the rearguard and stragglers to close up; by then perhaps they might have found a less contested route to the Baillie Guard Gate. But Havelock, misunderstanding his proposal and believing that he wanted to call off the attack until the morning, strongly opposed him, representing the vital necessity of 'reinforcing the garrison lest it should be attacked and surprised in the darkness'. 'There is the street,' Havelock said, pointing ahead of him. 'We see the worst. We shall be slated, but we can push through and get it over.' The men were ready to go on; the Residency was little more than half a mile away.

Outram suddenly lost his temper, snapping at Havelock, 'Let us go on, then, in God's name!' Afterwards, he much regretted his loss of control, believing that it might have been better officially to have resumed command, and to have tried to save some of the many lives that were now certain to be lost. But it was too late to hold back now. The Highlanders were sent forward first, followed by the Sikhs, and were met by a fearful fire from the rebels who stood on every roof, discharging their muskets, hurling down bricks and stones and even spitting at the figures below. In a long wide street 'with sheets of fire shooting out from the houses' they stumbled over trenches cut through the pavement as they attempted to reply to the incessant fire of the rebels, shouting at each other and occasionally cheering above the skirl of the bagpipes.

Harry Havelock was badly wounded. So was Tytler. Neill, calling out to one of his officers, 'Hot work this, Blake', was shot through the head and killed by a mutineer who 'fired a rifle held at arm's length'. But the survivors pressed on through what Captain Gordon described as 'a perfect storm of grape' and 'showers of musket balls' from the houses on either side. 'I was in such a state of excitement with the cheering of the men who were running as hard as they could and yelling that I scarcely knew what happened,' Gordon added. 'It was worth living any length of time to have such an experience.'

At last through the smoke the Residency came into view. Men could be seen jumping up excitedly on the ramparts to either side of the Baillie Guard Gate whose doors were now 'completely riddled with round shot and musket balls'.[28]

Beyond the Baillie Guard Gate the whole of that day, 25 September 1857, had been spent in intense excitement and anxiety. The thunder of the guns and the crackle of rifle and musketry fire had drawn closer and closer, while large numbers of rebels could be seen running over the bridges and swimming across the river. Others were clearly visible standing on the roofs of the houses firing into the street at the figures of the advancing troops which, though recognized with delight down by the river earlier on in the day, were now hidden by the buildings of the city. At about six o'clock 'a tremendous noise of cheering' could be heard from the Baillie Guard Gate as scores of people ran forward to welcome the relieving forces. At the sight of the bearded Highlanders and Sikhs tossing children high in the air and kissing them as they put them down again, many women burst into tears. 'God bless you, Missus,' one of the Highlanders said to Mrs Boileau. 'We're glad we've come in time to save you and the youngsters.' She and other women offered them water or cups of weak, milkless, unsugared tea. Men walked up to shake them by the hand, to thank them for coming.[29]

Inglis's orderly rushed into his quarters and out again carrying his master's sword which had not been used since Chinhat. A few moments later Inglis himself appeared accompanied by 'a short, quiet-looking, grey-haired man' wearing a smart blue coat buttoned up to the chin which made Captain Birch realize that the old garrison, who 'had long deserted red and blue', must have looked more like buccaneers than British soldiers to the relieving force.[30] 'We hardly expected you in before tomorrow,' Inglis said to General Havelock, who replied, 'When I saw your battered gate I determined to be in before nightfall.'[31] Havelock then shook hands with Mrs Inglis and said he feared that she and her family must have suffered very much. 'I could hardly answer him,' she wrote. 'I longed to be with John alone; and he shared my feelings, for ere long he returned to me, and never shall I forget his heartfelt kiss as he said, "Thank God for this!" Yes, we were safe, and my darling husband spared to me.'[32]

In a nearby room Captain Birch was talking to Sir James Outram 'who did not seem pleased with the conduct of operations and said that losses had been very severe; he feared 800 killed'. When asked for orders, 'he bowed, and said, "General Havelock commands today"'.[33] He then left to set up his headquarters at Dr Fayrer's house where one of the first questions he was asked by Mrs Boileau was, 'Is Queen Victoria still alive?'[34]

Others, less concerned for the moment with bulletins from Windsor, asked for news of Delhi.

PART TWO

14

The King of Delhi

· *Bahadur Shah at Delhi* · *conditions in the city, May to
September, 1857* · *the King's sons – sepoys' depredations* ·
arrival of Bakht Khan, 2 July – growing disorder ·

On the day after the mutinous sepoys from Meerut had been admitted
into Delhi, the King had held a durbar in the *Diwan-i-Khas* for the first
time in fifteen years. The arrival of the mutineers had taken him by
surprise, and he had not welcomed their coming. He was both
alarmed by the likely consequences of their revolt and dismayed by
their riotous behaviour as they poured into the palace courtyards,
shouting, firing their muskets and carbines, siting guns, blowing
bugles at unfounded reports of a European attack on the city, and
settling down in the *Diwan-i-Khas* as though in camp. Yet, unable to
get rid of them – and sharing their distrust of the English and their
fear that their religion might, indeed, be threatened – the King did not
refuse them his support.

The King . . . told his attendants . . . to call the Indian officers forward
[a royal *vakil* later testified]. The officers of the cavalry came forward,
mounted as they were, and explained that they had been required to bite
the cartridges [which] were greased with beef and pork fat, that they had
killed the Europeans at Meerut and had come to claim his protection.
The King replied, 'I did not call for you. You have acted very wickedly.'
However, the troops in large numbers came into the *Diwan-i-Khas* and
said, 'Unless you, the King, join us, we are dead men and we must in
that case just do what we can for ourselves.' The King then seated himself
in a chair and the soldiers – officers and men – came forward one by one
and bowed their heads before him, asking him to place his hand on them.
The King did so and after a little while he went to his own apartments.[1]

Soon after this, sitting on the Silver Throne which had been
specially brought up from the vaults, he accepted tribute from the
officers of his new army and listened to their promises of allegiance.
He then appointed several of the royal princes to high command in

the army, conferring the office of commander-in-chief upon the eldest of his thirteen sons, Mirza Moghul, and appointing his grandson, the effeminate and heavily scented nineteen-year-old Mirza Abu Bakr, a colonel of cavalry.[2] Then, after letters had been prepared for dispatch to various rajahs urging them to march at once upon Delhi with all their forces to join the King's army,[3] Hakim Ahsanullah Khan was ordered to hold a council of the leading men of the city and to provide for supplies of food for the soldiers already there so as to prevent further plundering. Later a Military and Civil Management Committee was established with ten members, six military and four civilian. But this committee exercised little authority, for the mutineers could not be persuaded to obey its decrees.[4]

For fear of being looted of all their stocks, the owners of grain stores and grocers' shops had long since closed and locked their doors. The courtyards of the palace were consequently full of people shouting for food or complaining that their shops or houses had been broken into.

When one of the sepoys went to a shop for supplies [recorded Syed Mubarak Shah, a police official in the city], he would call out, 'give me a seer of sweetmeats for a *pice*', on which the poor merchant would answer: 'Ah, Maharaj, a seer of sweetmeats for one *pice*! No one has ever asked for so much! Jemadar Sahib, such a thing is quite improper in your Excellency.' On which the sepoy by way of reply generally raised his musket and shot the poor man. No one asked who had done the deed. No one listened to any complaint. Each sepoy was then a King in his own estimation.[5]

The King ordered his son, the Commander-in-Chief, to take a company of infantry into the city and to issue a proclamation that all shopkeepers who did not open their shops immediately would be imprisoned, and that all convicted looters would have their noses and ears cut off. This proclamation having little effect on the shopkeepers, the King himself was persuaded to parade through the streets on an elephant, accompanied by one of his younger sons and an imposing array of soldiers. He spoke in a kindly tone to the shopkeepers who were induced to open their stores for a time, though many of them quickly shut their doors again once the parade had returned to the palace.

At the palace the King found the crowds in the courtyards larger and more rowdy than ever, the troopers from Meerut now adding to the turmoil by loudly complaining that the men of the regiments which had mutinied at Delhi had looted the treasure from the Delhi

Collectorate and were refusing to share it with them. Exasperated by the noise and importunity, the King told the Princes to clear all the regiments, with one exception, out of the city and to encamp them outside the gates and along the sandy river bed beneath the palace walls.[6]

While the Princes were endeavouring, with indifferent success, to enforce this order, the King made a speech to the native officers present, calling on them to remember that the *Diwan-i-Khas* was a sacrosanct enclosure which had never before been forcibly entered by armed men, that their unruly behaviour was 'most unbecoming in the reign of a Mahommedan King who was a bright light in the history of the world and at whose feet all other Kings waited with bended knee'.[7]

But the King's speech made little impression; and, dismissed from his presence, the officers soon returned to renew their complaints, some of them, according to one account, going so far as to address his Majesty

with such disrespectful terms as '*Ari, Badshah! Ari, Buddha!* Look here, King! I say, old fellow!' 'Listen!' cried one, catching him by the hand. 'Listen to me!' said another, touching the old king's beard. Angered at their behaviour, yet unable to prevent their insolence, he found relief alone in bewailing to his servants his misfortunes and his fate.[8]

Given though he was to these periodic bouts of despair, the King was far more resilient and capable than his age and frailty led some observers to suppose. It seemed, indeed, for a time that he was convinced – as many members of his family were convinced – that it was his fate to lead his people in defence of their religion against the foreigners whom, as his verses show, he had never really trusted. According to the munshi, Mohan Lal, although he had given no encouragement to the mutineers at first, and had sent a camel-driver to the Lieutenant-Governor at Agra informing him of their arrival, he now 'took an interest in encouraging the rebellion'.[9] He issued detailed orders to his officers and court officials on all manner of subjects and visited some part of the city's defences almost every day after saying prayers for victory. Furthermore, by issuing a proclamation calling upon 'all Hindoos and Mussulmans [to] unite in this struggle', and by forbidding the killing of cows on the festival of the '*Id*, he helped to disappoint British hopes of a religious conflict in the city.[10]

He was well aware of the extent of his problems. By the end of May tens of thousands of sepoys had entered Delhi; and though most were camped outside the walls, many more had quartered themselves in shops and houses and around the Chandni Chowk between the Lahore Gate and the Palace, much to the annoyance of the citizens whom they displaced.[11] As well as outraging the citizens by their depredations, the sepoys were constantly quarrelling with each other over the plunder they had acquired. This was often in such quantities that crowds of them could be seen outside goldsmiths' shops waiting to have the coins and bullion melted down into ornaments which they could conveniently wear under their clothes. They were also constantly pestering their officers – who, in turn, pestered the palace – for money.[12]

The King had little to give them; and when he approached the leading merchants of the city for help in meeting the daily expenses of the troops, he had little more success than he had had with the rajahs whom he had summoned to join him.

Even when paid, the sepoys did not follow their commanders into battle with any enthusiasm, particularly when led by Mirza Moghul, the Commander-in-Chief, whose talents they derided.[13] According to Syed Mubarak Shah, 'hundreds, yes thousands of sepoys . . . would take a quantity of cartridges and go beyond the walls in the direction of the batteries, sit down and bury them in the sand, then returning to their comrades would say, "My brothers, my ammunition is all expended. I am going back to the city for more and will return immediately." '[14]

In fact, as their enemy's accounts clearly show, the sepoys frequently left the safety of their defences to attack the British outposts on the Ridge; but they certainly did not often do so under the leadership of Mirza Moghul who showed no enthusiasm when urged to attack the entrenchments at Meerut. He would unhesitatingly go out and exterminate the British, Mirza Moghul said, if supported by various other leaders who were in fact as reluctant to fight as he was himself. Losing patience with him, the King ordered his grandson, Mirza Abu Bakr, to take command of a field army; but the young man proved himself as unadventurous and unheroic a general as Mirza Moghul. Stationing himself on the roof of a house to observe his artillery open operations with an initial bombardment, he soon 'hastily descended from the roof' when an enemy shell exploded near by, 'mounted his horse, and galloped off with his escort of *sowars* far into the rear of the position, not heeding the cries of his troops. A general stampede then took place.'[15]

Soon after this the King wrote a long pained letter to Mirza Moghul:

My son, let it be known that when the sepoys first came to me, I told them plainly that I possessed neither soldiers nor money to help them but that I would not hold my life dear if it were of any use to them . . . They promised to lay down their own lives in the attempt to carry out my orders and in showing me allegiance . . . [so they were permitted to frequent] the *Diwan-i-Khas*, the *Diwan-i-Am*, the *Mahtab Bagh* and other places inside the Palace and to stay there as they liked, [though] they were ignorant and unacquainted with court etiquette . . . By now [many] days have passed but the sepoys continue to indulge in their own vicious habits . . . They are still not carrying out my commands. I ordered them to encamp outside the city . . . but I find that one regiment is residing at the Delhi Gate, a second at the Ajmer Gate and a third at the Lahore Gate right inside the city walls . . . And they come riding on horseback into the [Palace courtyards] improperly dressed, without turbans . . . even though whenever an officer of the British Government came into the Palace, he dismounted from his horse at the Gate of the *Diwan-i-Am* and proceeded on foot . . . Moreover I find that the sepoys have plundered the bazaars . . . by day and night. On the false pretence that an Englishman is lurking inside, they dash into people's private dwellings and plunder them. They break open the locks and take away the shutters and doors and plunder the goods inside most shamelessly . . . If the sepoys do not strive sincerely to obey the orders of the King . . . then we shall partake ourself to the [shrine of] Qutab Sahib and sit there as a fakir . . . My son, you must not take this lightly. On account of old age and feebleness I cannot bear all the loads on my own shoulders. It is no easy matter to rule a people and at the same time to keep an army under control.[16]

Native spies in the pay of the English were constantly stealing out of the city to provide the King's enemies with reports of his tribulations and difficulties, his being 'very angry with the army', his shortage of money, his people's growing discontent, their praying 'for the success of the English'.[17] Many of the reports were wildly exaggerated – and were known to be so by the English commanders who circulated them only as a means of raising the spirits of their own force[18] – but life in Delhi was certainly turbulent. The administration had not collapsed in chaos as English officials in Calcutta sometimes liked to suggest. The police courts still functioned, if in a rather arbitrary fashion; and the city's newspapers continued publication.[19] Yet the diary of Munshi Jivanlal, a well-educated inhabitant of Delhi who had helped to administer the pensions paid by the British

Government to the King's family, shows how widespread discontent and unrest in the city were:

May 20 – Information received that an English force was approaching. On hearing this news the cavalry and infantry were dismayed; men began to run about seeking advice from one another. In a little while it was rumoured that the information was bare of the garment of truthfulness. Scouts who had been sent out returned stark naked, having been plundered by the Gujars ... At three o'clock Hakim Ahsanullah Khan complained that soldiers were looting in the city, and requested that they should be expelled ... Two Europeans were discovered and murdered by the mutineers.

May 21 – ... The King issued a proclamation by beat of drum that Hindus and Mahommedans must not quarrel. The Hindus had closed all their houses for fear of their lives ... The house of Sobha Chand was plundered on the charge that he was in league with the English ... The demand for gold increasing, many of the soldiers were duped by the city *budmashes* who, leading them to one of the *Mohallas,* invited them to sit down while they brought them gold mohurs. Then taking the money to buy the gold, they decamped ... The soldiers revenged themselves upon the innocent people of the *Mohalla* ...

May 27 – It was discovered today that the guns in the bastion had been spiked, while others had been filled with stones, gravel and ends of string. Great excitement prevailed as it was clear that the English had some powerful friends in the city ... A body of Gujars attempted to carry off gunpowder and ammunition from one of the magazines.

May 28 – An order was issued today to pay the mutineers ... Deductions were made on account of the sums already paid to them ... A great uproar ensued ...

May 31 – Bodies of cavalry arrived from the Hindun and impressed every man of every class, high and low, on whom they could lay hands, for transport service. The city was in great uproar. Many rose to resist such oppression by force of arms. Two or three European Christians and Jews were found to-day, taken to the *Kotwali* and killed in the customary manner.

June 14 – A man accused of sympathizing with the English was shot, and his body suspended from a tree. Thirteen bakers residing at the Kabut Gate were dragged from their houses and killed, on being suspected of supplying bread to the English.

June 17 – The King threatened to take poison unless greater discipline was enforced and the oppressions discontinued ... [20]

But greater discipline was not, for the moment, enforced; the oppressions were not discontinued; princes and senior officers still illegally exacted money from merchants and bankers in the name of the King; and the disorder in the city was aggravated by the increased cannonading from the British camp, which killed many people within the walls, and by the coming of the heavy rains. The rains induced the officers of the army to seek permission to leave their camps outside the walls. The King granted them permission, so the troops came back into the city, occupying as barracks the Civil Courts and the Mohammedan College as well as numerous houses. On 23 June, the centenary of the battle of Plassey, a gun constructed in the reign of Shah Jahan was mounted on the walls, a he-goat was tied to the mouth, twenty-five seers of sweetmeats were placed inside the barrel, and a necklace of flowers was hung around the muzzle. Then several Brahmins and astrologers were summoned and directed to consult their almanacks as to whether the mutineers would be victorious. After due deliberation they replied that 'great disturbances would last for a year . . . Beyond this the astrologers would say nothing'.[21]

A few days after the astrologers had delivered themselves of this brief, disturbing report, a large force of reinforcements, including seven hundred cavalry, four regiments of foot, and nine guns with two European non-commissioned officers, arrived outside the city from Bareilly.[22] They were commanded by Muhammad Bakht Khan, a proud and sturdy man with a barrel-like chest, a large stomach and very fat thighs, who had served in the army for forty years and had been the senior native officer in a battery of field artillery during the first Afghan War. A man of commanding personality and uncertain provenance, he claimed to be of royal birth, at one time asking the King to confirm that he was of the same family as himself, at another representing himself as being related to the royal family of Oudh.[23] British officers who had known him in the past described him as 'a big fat man, obsequious, fond of the society of Europeans . . . A most intelligent character, but a more dreadful hypocrite never stepped on earth.'[24]

The King, at any rate, though offended by his coarse manners, seems to have accepted him as a welcome alternative to the members of his own family as leader of his army. He grasped his hand in token of friendship; and replied to his protestations of royal descent that he was 'assuredly of a noble family' and that confirmation of his claim to be related to the Moghul Emperors was really not necessary as 'a greater man than the General did not exist'.[25] When Bakht Khan asked to be given acting command of the army, the King, grateful that he had brought so much money with him from the looted Bareilly treasury, readily acceded to the request; and when the newly created Lord Governor-General informed the King that if any of the princes attempted to plunder the city he would cut off their noses and ears, his Majesty replied, 'You have full authority. Do whatever seems good unto you.'[26]

Bakht Khan exercised his authority with great zest. He announced that soldiers would no longer be allowed into the *Diwan-i-Khas* or to loiter in the palace gardens; that men without turbans would not be admitted to the royal levees; that the troops would be paraded every morning at a fixed hour; that the Lord Governor-General would personally inspect them and regularly visit the Magazine and the Artillery Park.[27] Bakht Khan also issued orders that any soldier found plundering was to be arrested and severely punished by the severing of an arm. At the same time he informed the *Kotwal* that if there *were* any further plundering the police would be held responsible and the *Kotwal*, as their chief, would be hanged. He also announced that anyone suspected of communicating with the English would receive no mercy; and as though in earnest of this threat, five butchers carrying out meat towards the English camp on a charpoy had their throats cut.[28] The princes strongly resented the interloper's pretensions, complaining to the King that he always made sure that the troops he had brought with him were well supplied with provisions, even at the expense of the rest of the army. But the King would not listen to their grumbling, censuring them instead 'for their bad behaviour' and ordering them 'to disgorge the money they had forcibly taken from the bankers, otherwise their allowances would be stopped'.[29] The King even permitted the General to whisper into his ear at durbars, though when the princes took strong exception to this 'and openly charged him with bad manners in thus violating the customs of good society', the General, evidently unwilling to be considered unaware of court etiquette, thought it as well to apologize and to flatter the princes so that the matter was dropped.[30]

Yet while Bakht Khan succeeded for a time in improving the discipline of the army in Delhi and in turning aside the anger and jealousy of the princes, he did not prove himself an effective general in the field, and by the beginning of August the King had begun to lose patience with him. On 2 August he composed some verses which he dispatched to the General:

May all the enemies of the Faith be killed today;
The *Firinghis* be destroyed root and branch!

Celebrate the festival of the *'Id Kurban* by great slaughter
Put our enemies to the edge of the sword – spare not![31]

But, far from putting their enemies to the sword, Bakht Khan
reported that

in consequence of the heavy rains the troops that had gone out . . . had
found the whole country flooded and had returned. The King, on hearing
this became very angry and said, 'You will never capture the Ridge.' The
same day the King summoned all his officers to the Hall of Public
Audience in the evening, and addressed them, 'All the treasure that you
have brought me, you have expended. The Royal Treasury is empty . . .
I hear that day by day the soldiers are leaving for their homes. I have no
hopes of becoming victorious . . .' In answer to this address, the officers
tried to cheer His Majesty and exclaimed, 'By the help of God, we will
take the Ridge yet!'[32]

The King, however, was not convinced. The next day, on being
told that there were 6,000 *mujahideen* in Nasirabad who wanted to
come to Delhi, he gloomily dictated the reply: 'Tell them there are
60,000 men in Delhi, and they have not yet driven the English away
from the Ridge. What can their 6,000 do?' That evening Bakht Khan
came to the durbar and complained that the soldiers were no longer
obeying his orders. The King wearily replied, 'Tell them, then, to
leave the city . . . It is quite clear to me that the English will ultimately recapture Delhi, and will kill me.'[33]

The King continued to make his inspections of the forts and gun
emplacements, but they depressed rather than encouraged him. One
day he said to the gunners in the fort of Selimgarh, 'It is much to be
regretted that, far from silencing the British fire, I see their batteries
getting nearer every day.' The gunners answered, 'Never fear, your
Majesty. We are getting the better of them.' The King 'turned away'.[34]
One morning a few days later

before the King had come out of his apartments, thirty or forty of the
nobles were seated round the ornamental tank in the Palace Square,
waiting for his arrival. Just as the monarch emerged from his private
room three shells fell directly in front and behind him and burst, but
without injury to anyone. The King immediately retired and all the
others who had been seated then got up and left. That same evening the
King called up the chief officers of the army and thus addressed them:
'My brothers – there is no longer any safe place for you, or the citizens,
or even for me to sit . . . You say you came here to fight. Can you not do
so even so far as to stop this rain of shot and shell pouring into the
Palace?'[35]

He had tried to prevent it himself by entering into secret negotiations with the British.[36] Nor was he the only member of the royal household whose agents were in touch with the enemy. His physician, Hakim Ahsanullah Khan, who had endeavoured to persuade the King not to become involved with the mutineers, was also in touch with the British camp. So was his wife, Zinat Mahal, who feared that her son, Jiwan Bakht, would not inherit the throne if the rebels were victorious. But the British were not prepared to negotiate.[37]

There were reports that sepoys were now leaving Delhi by hundreds, some of them secretly, others quite openly; and their departure was followed by numerous civilians of all classes who were afraid of being forced to work in the batteries.[38] On 15 August 'nearly three hundred soldiers . . . disheartened at the result of the rebellion, brought their fire-arms to the King and left the city through the Calcutta Gate for their homes'. A week later 'several foot-soldiers attended the Durbar and complained that no opium could be purchased in the bazaars, and from this cause many were dying'.[39]

By the end of August the King, worried by the growing shortages in Delhi, seems to have finally given way to despair. He had lost all confidence in Bakht Khan, yet could not trust the princes who were constantly quarrelling with their rivals and with each other. According to the British spy, Fath Mohammed, the various factions of the army were in perpetual dispute: 'Each cavalry is now split up into "thokes" – confederacies comprising those who are residents of a particular area. For instance, Hansi fellows form one "thoke", the Kalanor men another, and so on through the whole body. No one agrees with another.'[40]

The army did agree, however, on their need of immediate pay. The King, now in deep financial difficulties, and faced with a monthly demand for pay of Rs. 573,000, was eventually driven to promising the officers all the jewels of his zenana; and, when even that did not appear to satisfy them,

rising from his chair he threw before them the embroidered cushion on which he had been sitting and bid them take that . . . [Then] the King went into his private apartments and brought out jewellery and gave it to the officers, saying, 'Take this and forget your hunger!' But the officers refused, saying, 'We cannot accept of your Crown Jewels, but we are satisfied that you are willing to give your property as well as your life to sustain us.'[41]

There were still in Delhi many men who were prepared to die for what was believed by most of their leaders to be a lost cause.

Fully five thousand men from various quarters poured into Delhi as Ghazis . . . dressed in blue tunics and green turbans [recorded Syed Mubarak Shah]. All these Ghazis received two annas a day from the King. They usually joined in the attacks on the British lines . . . Several of the fanatics engaged in hand to hand contact and great numbers were killed by the Europeans . . . and some Europeans were killed by them. The lower classes of the city people . . . who generally hung about the batteries in considerable numbers . . . rushed forward and beheaded some of the dead Europeans, and after fixing the heads on poles, took them into the city, followed by enormous crowds. The bearer of every head brought to the King received five rupees.[42]

Many soldiers offered their lives to the King. The 9th Infantry went in a body to him and declared, 'Fate has been fulfilled. Now we will issue from the Kashmir Gate and yield up our lives.' And others, equally conscious that the end was near, were determined to defend Delhi to the last shot. During the second week in September spies reported that the guards on the walls were stronger and more alert than usual, that 'guns were mounted on all sides . . . In the main streets every house is filled from top to bottom with sepoys . . . The *mujahideen* are collected in a body, ready for action . . . The rebels . . . now declare that if they had fought from the outset with the same spirit the affair would not have been so protracted.'[43]

On 12 September, so Jivanlal recorded in his diary:

a proclamation was issued by beat of drum that his Majesty would himself lead an attack on the English this night and would destroy them. It urged the whole city to rise and sweep through the English camp, and by force of numbers kill every European soldier. The proclamation invited both Hindus and Mahommedans to bind themselves by an oath to do so. In consequence of this proclamation upwards of 10,000 Mahommedans congregated near the Kashmir Gate and waited till midnight for the arrival of the King.[44]

But the King did not come. And soon afterwards it was the British who attacked.

15

The Ridge

· *The camp before Delhi* · *dissatisfaction with the commanders* ·
death of General Barnard, 5 July 1957 · *Wilson's problems –*
the 'steaming bog' · *arrival of John Nicholson, 14 August* ·

For many weeks now the British troops had been enduring a dreadful camp life on the Ridge above Delhi. From the beginning they had realized how much more difficult it would prove to recapture the city than the civilians in Calcutta had supposed. 'I don't think we shall take Delhi in a hurry with our small force,' Lieutenant Ewart of the 2nd Bengal Fusiliers had written shortly after his arrival on the Ridge in June. 'It is not the sort of thing I expected at all – much more serious.'[1] Brigadier Wilson agreed with him. 'I cannot see my way clearly, nor know how we can conduct this business to a successful termination,' he had told his wife that same week. 'The insurgents came out this afternoon and attacked our picquets on the Ridge. They were soon driven off. But it shows what determined rascals they are . . . In the field we can beat the wretches whenever we come upon them, but we have no means for a regular siege such as this strong place requires.'[2]

Several junior officers urged an immediate assault before the rebels received any further reinforcements and had time to strengthen their defences. General Barnard, anxious not to be considered less resolute than they, succumbed to their entreaties and authorized their drawing up detailed plans for a *coup de main*. This was on the point of being undertaken when Brigadier Graves persuaded him that it was a foolhardy idea and induced him to recall the leading columns, to the infinite disgust of the head of the Intelligence Department, Lieutenant William Hodson, one of the *coup de main's* most outspoken champions, who was 'confident it would have been successful. The rebels were . . . perfectly ignorant of any intention of so bold a stroke . . . The surprise would have done everything.'[3]

A revised plan for an immediate assault was then submitted by the engineers to General Barnard who seemed for a time inclined to favour it until the older, more cautious officers on his staff succeeded in changing his mind once again by persuading him that even if the assaulting columns managed to force their way into the city they might well be wiped out before reinforcements arrived to help them hold it. He had no more than two thousand infantry at his disposal whereas the enemy's force, growing daily, was already believed to be well over three times as strong; and since practically all his force would be needed for the assault, the camp would be exposed to the danger of being overrun. Besides, in the unlikely event of an assault being successful, the mutineers would merely be dispersed to cause trouble elsewhere.[4]

Wearily Barnard agreed: he would have to wait for reinforcements; an immediate assault was out of the question. Nevertheless the idea still found its advocates, and the arguments and counter-arguments continued at headquarters for weeks, throughout the day and long into the night.[5]

'We have too many talkers,' Brigadier Wilson lamented, 'and our General, though a kind, generous and brave fellow, has no decision.'[6] It was a common enough complaint. Lieutenant Thomas Cadell of the 2nd Bengal Fusiliers wrote home:

I don't see how we are ever to get inside Delhi under the choice collection of muffs we have at our head ... The mismanagement beats the Crimea almost ... The Enemy attack us in great numbers and the General sends two companies from one regiment and two from another to back them up and so on till men from all the regiments either get jumbled up together or else go at it perfectly independently. On such occasions we seldom see a field officer and everything is left to the captains and subalterns.[7]

Charles Ewart agreed with Cadell. The mismanagement was 'terrible'. The whole camp was 'crying out against the Commander-in-Chief'.[8]

'The great want in all our actions,' an Engineer officer confirmed, 'is the want of a head. Officers lead on their parties without any method or arrangement.'[9] An officer on the staff confessed that the mismanagement and incompetence were 'perfectly sickening'.[10] 'Oh for a *man* of command!' wrote Major Baird Smith, the Chief Engineer. 'We are perfectly – rather ignominiously – safe and there lies Delhi mosque'd, minaret-ed and inaccessible ... It is as clear as noonday that our sole chance of taking Delhi is by an assault which grows more and more difficult with every day's delay.'[11]

In almost every letter he wrote to his wife, Archdale Wilson gave examples of the incompetence of the Delhi Force:

The insurgents got in our rear again yesterday. They were attacked but without method, and we made a bungling business of it, in fact were nearly beaten back and very nearly lost some of our guns . . . There was no one to give any orders and after sending everywhere for General Barnard, I was at last told to do what I thought proper, so I took the command . . . There was another attack today. As usual we had no head . . . Some of our men, I am sorry to say, did not behave so well as they ought to have done for want of good leading (in fact, they refused to advance at all in face of an enemy far superior in numbers) . . . We have been making another mess of it today . . . It is a sad state of things in such a crisis not to have some one capable of leading and directing properly . . . We continue to fire at the insurgents at long shot distances with no credit to us and little or no loss to the enemy . . . Instead of being besiegers we are besieged, with a fair prospect of being starved out, for from utter recklessness or incapacity they allowed the Baghput Bridge, over which we draw our supplies, to be again destroyed by the enemy, not an attempt being made to keep open our lines of communication. I impressed upon the General the day before yesterday and again yesterday the necessity of preserving this bridge at all risks, to preserve our convoys and supplies, but nothing was done.[12]

It was hoped that the arrival of the dashing Brigadier Neville Chamberlain as Adjutant-General would lead to much needed reforms at headquarters. Wilson thought that he would prove 'a host in himself' and 'keep all things straight'. But he soon 'much disappointed' his admirers who were forced to conclude that 'he was no more fitted for his staff appointment than old Barnard himself', and that while he was 'of decided excellence as a man of action', he was 'but a poor man of business'.[13]

As the days went by old Barnard grew more and more indecisive, less and less able to cope with the appalling difficulties that faced him. One commanding officer received from him an order to occupy a group of buildings of whose exact location, it subsequently transpired, the 'old gentleman' had no idea.[14] Everyone was fond of Barnard. He was a 'dear gallant old gentleman, kind and courteous to all'.[15] Lieutenant William Hodson, who thought him a 'fine old man', if 'hardly up to his work', remembered waking up in the middle of the night to find 'the dear old boy' gently covering him with a blanket to protect him from a draught. Others recalled numerous similar kindnesses. But when, worn out by worry and lack of sleep, he died of cholera, no one supposed the army had lost a capable general. Nor did anyone expect to benefit much from his successor, General Reed, who being 'more fit for an invalid couch' than high command, had not yet been called upon to exercise his slender talents in the army's affairs. Indeed, he did not feel capable of exercising them now; and within a fortnight he handed over the command to Brigadier Wilson.

Ready as he had been to criticize his predecessors, Wilson was only too well aware of his own shortcomings. 'This is a fearful responsibility that has been thrown on my shoulders,' he told his wife, 'and knowing as I do my own weakness and incapacity I feel as if I should faint under the burden . . . I hope I am not breaking down, but . . . care and anxiety are fast ageing me into an old man.'[16]

The problems that faced him appeared insurmountable. As he looked down upon Delhi he doubted that he would ever be able to take it. His troops were so few that he could not possibly lay proper siege to it; he could merely cover the parts that could be seen from the Ridge and endeavour to keep open his lines of supply. Beyond the wide, deep ditch, a wall almost twenty-five feet high and seven miles in length completely surrounded the city. Its ten huge gates were commanded by strong bastions. The mutineers seemed to have vast stocks of ammunition even though the city magazine had been blown up by George Willoughby, its remaining undamaged contents subsequently plundered by the people of Delhi and a far larger magazine outside the city robbed by Goojurs. The rebels also had plenty of heavy guns which they handled so well that even the British artillery officers admitted that they were 'out-matched by the rascals in accuracy and rapidity of fire'.[17] The British, in contrast, were so short of ammunition that they were reduced to paying camp-followers to pick up the shot which the enemy fired at them, at the rate of two annas a piece.[18]

On one occasion I saw a party of native servants, carrying on their heads cooked provisions for the men on picket, wend their way up the slope from the camp [wrote Captain Griffiths of the 61st]. Two round-shot fired by the enemy struck the top of the Ridge and rolled down the declivity . . . The cooks, depositing the dishes on the ground, ran in all haste to seize the treasures. I watched the race with interest, and anticipated some fun, knowing that in their eagerness they would forget that the shots had not had time to cool. Two men in advance of the rest picked up the balls and, uttering a cry, dropped them quickly, rubbing and blowing their hands. The remainder stood patiently and then . . . two men placed the shot on their heads, and all in a body moved off towards the Commissariat quarters to rèceive and divide the reward.[19]

Reinforcements were constantly entering the city, while the troops that reached the British lines barely made up for the losses inflicted by gunfire, illness and the raiding parties that frequently issued from the city and crept through the no-man's-land of trees and tangled undergrowth, tombs, mosques, orange gardens, lemon groves and ruined walls, to fall upon unwary outposts. By the end of June, the 60th Rifles alone had lost a hundred and sixty-five men in the past month. And the 60th – commanded by Colonel Jones, 'a fine old gentleman who might have sat for a portrait of Falstaff, he was so fat and jolly' – was one of the few units in which Wilson felt able to place unqualified trust.[20]

Soon after his arrival on the Ridge a detachment of the Corps of Guides, tough horsemen and infantry from the Punjab, had entered the camp, cheering and shouting and crowding around William Hodson, their former leader, before whose horse they threw themselves to the ground 'with tears streaming down their faces'.[21] Under their new commander, Captain Henry Daly, they had marched 580 miles in just over twenty-one days, an average of over twenty-seven miles a day; yet on being asked by a staff officer how soon they would be ready for action, Daly cheerfully replied, 'In half an hour.'[22]

Wilson, however, was far more pleased to see the Gurkhas whose Sirmur Battalion, commanded by Major Charles Reid, was given the important task of defending a large mansion known as Hindu Rao's house on the far right of the British lines.[23] The Gurkhas, Wilson felt, were 'true as steel'; and their commander, unlike many of his other subordinates, he trusted implicitly. The trust was not misplaced.

Reid himself did not have much faith in the British regiments on the Ridge, apart from the 60th Rifles and the 9th Lancers; but his confidence in his own 'little fellows' was boundless. On the march to Delhi they had fallen in with some native sappers from Roorkee who were marching about with 'insolent looks and an air of defiance'. Reid saw some of these sappers talking to his men. He affected to take no notice at the time; but afterwards, so he recorded,

I called up a couple of my men and asked what the sappers had said to them. One little fellow replied, 'They wanted to know if we were going over to Meerut to eat the *otta* which was sent up specially for the Gurkhas by the Governor-General and was nothing but ground bullocks' bones!' 'And what was your reply?' 'I said the regiment was going wherever it was ordered. We obey the bugle call.'[24]

At Delhi they certainly did obey the bugle call. Hindu Rao's house was repeatedly attacked; and the attacks were repeatedly repulsed. 'Come on, Gurkhas! We won't fire on *you*,' the mutineers called out to them. 'Come and join us!' 'Oh, yes, we *are* coming,' the Gurkhas replied, running out with their kukris. 'My little fellows behaved splendidly,' Reid recorded with pride, 'and were cheered by every European regiment.'

The Pandies, as they are called, made their *twenty-first* attack on my position yesterday [Reid wrote in his diary a few days later]. They turned out of the city at half-past seven in the morning and kept us at it until dark. Not a thing had we to eat, and we all came home dead beat. I never was so completely done up before. The sun was something fearful . . . I had another orderly killed . . . I was handing out my telescope to him when a 24-pounder round shot took his head clean off and then passed through the body of a *peepawallah* who was carrying my serai of tea which was kept pretty warm by the heat of the sun! . . . Perfectly wonderful how I escaped. Round shot, shell and musket balls come phit, phit, phee, phish, past my old head, but still here it is, all safe on my shoulders.

Few of his men were as lucky. In a fortnight he lost over a hundred of them and at that rate began to doubt that he would have 'any left for *the* attack'.

The cheerfulness of the Gurkhas, despite their heavy losses, endeared them to all the British troops, particularly to the 60th Rifles. 'They called one another "brothers",' Reid wrote. 'They shared their grog with each other and smoked their pipes together. Often were the Rifles seen carrying a wounded Gurkha off the field and vice versa . . . My men used to speak of them as "Our Riffles", and the men of the 60th, when mentioning the Gurkhas, said, "Them Gurkhees of ours".'[25]

'Gurkhas and Europeans were often to be seen together,' another British officer confirmed. 'They would sit behind a breastwork nodding their heads and grinning at each other without a word being spoken on either side.'[26] The Sikhs were as popular with the 75th as were the Gurkhas with the 60th. Richard Barter wrote:

They were always together, and seemingly in close and amusing conversation which must have been curious as both were almost totally ignorant of each other's lingo . . . 'Liquor' seemed to go a long way. The Sikh, merely grinning and showing his magnificent teeth with little dots of gold in the centre of each, said, 'Hah!' Upon which Private Jones would slap Doll Sing on the shoulder and turning to his comrade, Smith, would remark, '*Be hanged!* But he's a good fellow!'[27]

Such comradeship between British troops and other natives was most uncommon. There were numerous native camp-followers and servants in the camp who daily risked their lives in the service of their British masters. Every day lines of them could be seen marching out to picquets and batteries carrying dishes, pots, skinfuls of water, braziers and camp-stools, doing their best to disregard the round-shot that came hurtling and bouncing towards them. Yet many of them were treated with contempt, if not with cruelty.

Lieutenant Cadell, whose own servants regularly brought him out beer and sandwiches 'under a very heavy fire', was grateful enough for their attentions. But he could not 'find language to express' how much he 'despised the brutish race' from which they came. His Uncle George, who had served in the Madras Army, objected to his calling them niggers; yet, really, he could scarcely look upon them as human beings. Why, several of his friends' servants had actually run off to join the rebels! 'What bosh the bigwigs at home are talking about this rebellion!' Cadell complained to his sister. 'Their ideas about treating the "Mild Hindoo" with kindness are simply ludicrous. The "Mild Hindoo", with his friend the Mussulman, is the lowest brute God ever gave a soul to . . . I fear you will think me a cruel wretch for using this language but I assure you I only share the feelings of everyone in camp.'[28]

One of Brigadier Wilson's first acts on assuming command was to announce that any inhumane treatment of the camp-followers, some of whom had been 'recklessly bayonetted and shot by European soldiers', would no longer be tolerated.[29] He also issued orders designed to tighten up the lax discipline that had begun to prevail in the camp, forbidding men to turn out in their shirt-sleeves and soiled blue dungaree trousers as they had taken to doing, providing for a more regular system of watch and relief, for officers to visit sentries more often and to submit written reports, for buglers to be attached to picquets so that the alarm could be sounded immediately.[30]

Yet as the days passed, as more reinforcements arrived in Delhi, as the enemy's attacks grew more frequent and their gunfire showed no signs of slackening, Wilson's depression deepened.

We are altogether in a false position here . . . We want 25,000 to 30,000 men to take such a strong position as Delhi . . . The enemy are wearing us out by their continual attacks which their numbers allow them to affect . . . They can always relieve one another . . . One party goes in and another comes out . . . If we advance upon them they bolt. When we retire they follow us, keeping a respectable distance, but there is such cover for them all round our position we can never get fairly near them . . . My force is too weak to go out and attack them properly. Our artillery men are worked night and day, and are getting knocked up . . . These rascals are so persevering and systematic in their attacks that we are getting in a precarious situation.[31]

When, at the beginning of August, his wife replied with some comment on the prevailing regret that the operations at Delhi were proving so protracted, Wilson came near to losing his temper:

> You are getting as unreasonable as other know-nothings who, acting on their own impatience, think a force under 2,000 bayonets (Europeans) can easily hop over the walls of Delhi covered with heavy guns and massacre with ease the 30,000 or 40,000 men defending it, as easy as toasting cheese. We here all think this force has done wonders in keeping these fellows at bay so long . . . I am suffering from one of my fits of weariness and prostration – very fagged – can't get more than four or five hours sleep at night . . . It is all very dreadful.[32]

It was also 'frightfully hot', the thermometers in the tents sometimes registering over one hundred and thirty degrees. At the end of June the rains had begun to pour down, flooding the camp, putting an end to the cricket matches, the pony races, the games of quoits and the fishing in the canal, drowning the music of the military bands but not stopping for long the enemy's attacks, alarms of which would repeatedly send officers splashing through the mud in their ragged shirts, shouting orders as they buckled on their swords.

It was difficult to tell one regiment from another by their uniforms any more. Despite the extreme heat, both the 60th Rifles and the Gurkhas had continued to wear their green cloth coats, believing that the material 'kept out the rays of the sun' far better than linen which reduced the wearer's skin to the appearance of 'raw beef'.[33] But most other units wore jackets and trousers of cotton died with khaki, a colour which had been adopted by the Corps of Guides and by the 75th, whose adjutant had persuaded his colonel that it was 'impossible for the men to turn out clean with only two sets of white uniform'.[34]

As the whole countryside became, in Hodson's words, 'a steaming bog', huge flies buzzed through the flaps of the tents, crawling between the lips of sleeping men, darkening the food like locusts, while black scorpions, 'like young lobsters', crawled about in the damp bedding, and snakes, 'dreaded almost [as much as] if not more than the enemy's missiles', made 'picquet duty a nightmare'.

The hearts of many failed them at this time, I know [wrote Captain Barter]. I heard several say that we should never take the city and that it was only a question of time before we should all perish . . . Worn out and knowing that there was no hope of relief some soldiers grew desperate and dashed at the enemy, getting killed on purpose to be rid of such existence as soon as possible . . . [But] no man died without leaving his mark by killing or wounding as many as he could before being killed himself.[35]

Below the tents, in the clumps of spear grass, beside the broken trees and beneath the tangled hedges of prickly pear and cactus, lay the bodies of mutineers rotting in the heat and giving off so fearful a smell that handkerchiefs soaked in eau de Cologne gave little protection from it. 'The day before yesterday I had a most wretched picquet of it,' Charles Ewart complained in a letter to his mother. 'There were about fifteen dead Pandies within ten yards in a state of decay, and the stench was quite overpowering, inhaling it as we did for 38 hours.'[36]

Sanitary conditions in the camp itself were appalling. Cases of cholera and other bacterial diseases were common; and by the beginning of September Wilson, complaining that his force was 'sadly reduced by all this dreadful sickness', feared that he would lose even more men from heat-stroke and 'sheer fatigue'.[37]

The fourteen hospitals were crowded to the doors. The Rev John Rotton, visiting one of them in the unclerical but practical attire of jackboots and *choga* which he had adopted, found it most melancholy

to see nearly every man in the three wards languishing from that terrible disease cholera . . . It required strong nerves to withstand the sickening sights of these infirmaries. The patients constantly retching made the place very offensive. The flies, almost as innumerable as the sand on the sea-shore, alighted on your face and head, and crawled down your back, through the openings of the shirt collar and occasionally flew even into your throat.[38]

Life had its small compensations, though. The water, which was drawn from the canal where the servants washed clothes and the elephants drank and splashed their backs, was atrocious: Harriet Tytler, whose baby had been born in a tumbril on the Ridge in the early hours of 21 June, said that 'were it not for the flavour it might have passed for pea-soup'.[39] But food was good and plentiful. A large flock of fat sheep had been brought in from Ferozepore; and Messrs. Peake and Allen of Ambala had set up a branch shop on the

36. Advance of the siege train to Delhi

37. John Nicholson

38. William Hodson

39. The storming of Delhi
from the painting by W. S. Morgan

40. Ruins of the Kashmir Gate

41. Ruins of Metcalfe House

42. Humayun's tomb and gateway

43. Prize agents at work

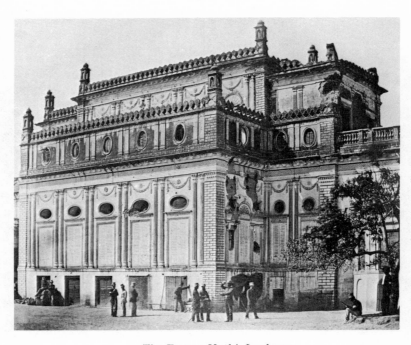

44. The Begum Kothi, Lucknow

45. The Dilkusha Palace, Lucknow

46. Sir Colin Campbell

47. Jung Bahadur

48. Listening for miners in Lucknow
from C. H. Mecham's *Sketches and Incidents of the Siege of Lucknow*

49. Charles Kavanagh and his daughter, Blanche

50. Site of the Massacre at Jhansi

51. Sir James Hope Grant

52. The Rani of Jhansi,
a posthumous portrait on ivory

53. Officers of Hodson's Horse

54. and 55. Captured rebel leaders

Ridge where they offered a variety of goods from pocket-books to tooth powder, pins and paper, tobacco and soap. Bottled beer was plentiful, too, and, if brandy was expensive at eight rupees a bottle, it was a good deal cheaper than it was in Lucknow.[40]

Some men actually appeared to be enjoying themselves. One of these was William Hodson, the blue-eyed, spruce and fresh-looking officer who combined his duties as head of the Intelligence Department with command of a body of horsemen who wore scarlet turbans and shoulder sashes over dust-coloured tunics. Hodson aroused more awe than affection except in animals, to which he seemed peculiarly attractive, horses immediately yielding to the sound of his voice, kittens, shy and timid with everyone else, jumping on to his knee without a care. 'A tallish man with yellow hair, a pale, smooth face, heavy moustache, and large, restless, rather unforgiving eyes,' as J. W. Sherer described him, Hodson had left the Guide Corps four years before under suspicion of having misappropriated the regimental funds. Since then he had killed a native officer whom he accused of being a mutineer, though it was believed a more likely motive was that Hodson owed him money. Thirty-six years old, the son of a clergyman, he had been at Rugby under Thomas Arnold; and according to his brother, also a clergyman, he might have devoted himself to an academic life after he had taken his degree at Trinity College, Cambridge, had not 'a constitutional tendency to headache very much stood in the way of any close application to books'. Some of his fellow officers thought him rather mad; others agreed with Surgeon Edward Hare that he was 'fit only to lead Italian banditti'. But he was a brilliant and intrepid horseman with a remarkable capacity for going to sleep in the saddle for an hour or so, then waking up 'fresh as a lark'. 'As a cavalry soldier he was perfection,' Hugh Gough thought, 'a strong seat on horseback (though an ugly rider), a perfect swordsman, nerves like iron, and a quick, intelligent eye.'[41]

Hodson obviously delighted in fighting. 'It was beautiful to see him riding a little in front and in the centre of his troopers,' thought Lieutenant Fairweather of the 4th Punjab Infantry, 'and to see how quietly he controlled their eagerness to press on by motioning them back, first on the right, then on the left, by a mere wave of the hand, as he passed the hog-spear (the weapon he always used) from one hand to the other while he rolled up his sleeves preparatory to action.'[42] Then, when it was time to charge, he would shout, 'Come along, lads, the fun's begun!' waving his spear in the air, tormenting his opponents with a stream of abuse and mockery, sometimes in his own language, sometimes in theirs. 'I fancy I see him now,' one of his officers recalled, 'laughing, parrying most fearful blows, as calmly as if he were brushing off flies, calling out all the time, "Why, try again now!" "What's that!" "Do you call yourself a swordsman?" etc.'[43] He was a brilliant linguist, another officer said, 'a thorough master of all the various idioms, phrases and accents peculiar to the different districts through which we were campaigning'.[44]

Hodson's team of spies, who regularly succeeded in gaining access to the city and reporting back to him, enabled him to keep the British headquarters accurately informed of events in Delhi, of troop movements and the damage done by British guns. It was estimated that there were 30,000 mutineers in the city in the middle of July, but that by the end of the second week in August casualties and desertions had reduced this number to 20,000. Guided perhaps by a wish to provide their paymasters with the kind of news they wished to hear, the spies reported that though they greatly outnumbered the Europeans, the morale of the mutineers was low, that the citizens were angered by the princes' alleged embezzlement of funds levied as taxes, that the troops were 'much disturbed and distressed from lack of pay', that it had been necessary for the *mahajums* to be 'well kicked and thrashed' before they agreed to supply the troops with food on credit.

Yesterday a great number of the mutineers were killed and wounded and they are therefore discouraged . . . The citizens are in great dismay and perpetually praying for your arrival [were the sort of comments frequently occurring in these intelligence reports]. The King has forbidden the killing of cows; but there is bad feeling between the Mohammedans and Hindoos . . . Both cavalry are asking for leave to return to their homes on the plea that the English are threatening danger to them. Some have gone already . . . The supply of powder is failing . . . Yesterday the troops made a great clamour about pay . . . the King replied that he had not summoned them to Delhi, that they came without permission and had caused great misery to his subjects . . . The rebel troops are daily decreasing in numbers.[45]

It was such reports as these that prompted Hodson to continue to press for an early assault, though he well knew that the losses incurred by the small British force made it 'less likely than ever' that the 'rulers would decide on a bold course'. Others were convinced, as was Major Reid, that to mount an assault before reinforcements came was now a 'mad idea'. Harvey Greathed, representative at Delhi of the Lieutenant-Governor of the North-Western Provinces and earlier a strong advocate of a *coup de main*, felt sure that the time had now gone by for such a venture.⁶ 'All the men in military command [were] in favour of waiting for reinforcements.'⁴⁶ Baird Smith, though formerly – like his able assistant Captain Alexander Taylor – also a warm advocate of immediate assault, agreed that now the losses 'would be too great'. He told Wilson that they could do nothing but hang on to Delhi 'like grim death' until reinforcements arrived.⁴⁷

Wilson himself by now had even begun to doubt the wisdom of trying to hold on at Delhi at all. He was considering the possibility of withdrawal, of abandoning Delhi which he could not possibly take, and using his small force to bring order to other parts of the country. There were officers on his staff who supported his view that this would be the more sensible course. But Baird Smith was convinced that to abandon Delhi and its communications with the Punjab would be an unforgivable error; it would lead all India to suppose that we 'retreated because we were beaten'. Certainly more heavy guns were needed, Baird Smith agreed, more ordnance and musket powder, more engineering supplies, and more men, too, though surely not as many as the 25,000 to 30,000 which Wilson thought he needed. But it would be folly to retreat now when the means to take Delhi would soon be on the way. Baird Smith earnestly pressed his case; and though attacked by diarrhoea and scurvy and wounded by a shell-splinter, he continued to press it, keeping up his spirits with port and peppermint, cherry brandy and calomel, and 'pitching into' opium pills with a regularity that would have done credit to his father-in-law, Thomas de Quincey.⁴⁸

In the end Baird Smith gained his point: the Delhi Force remained in position; and on 14 August it was reinforced by a large body of troops from the Punjab at the head of which was a man who was dramatically to transform the gloomy mood of the troops on the Ridge, Brigadier John Nicholson.

16

The Assault

Soon after his arrival on the Ridge, Nicholson went across the lines to
inspect the position at Hindu Rao's house.

I had never seen him before in my life [Major Reid recorded]. And I
thought I had never seen a man I disliked so much at first sight. His
haughty manner and peculiar sneer I could not stand. He asked several
questions relative to the enemy's position and then moved on. Baird
Smith was with me at the time . . . I complained of Nicholson's overbearing manner. He replied, 'Yes, but that wears off. I'm sure you'll like
him when you have seen more of him.'[1]

At headquarters the officers who met him for the first time doubted
that they would ever get to like him. He did not smile; he scarcely
spoke; the dark grey eyes in the pale, black-bearded face seemed at
once disapproving, accusatory and remote. An immense Pathan
orderly, as silent as his master, stood behind his chair at the mess-
table, a cocked revolver in one hand, serving the dishes with the other.
In his presence jokes and banter died away: war was a serious business.

The eldest of five sons of an Irish doctor who had died when he
was eight, John Nicholson had been brought up in straitened circumstances in Ulster by his impoverished mother, to whom he was, and
always remained, utterly devoted. When he was fifteen he had been
grateful to accept a cadetship in the Bengal Infantry provided for him
by an uncle who had made a fortune at the Calcutta Bar and had been
made a Director of the East India Company.

Nicholson had arrived in India in July 1839 and had served as a
young infantry officer in the Afghan War. Since then, however, most
of his time had been spent in civil appointments, principally in the
Punjab where he stamped out lawlessness in the districts under his

control with the utmost severity, pursuing criminals personally and displaying their severed heads upon his desk. His strange and forceful personality so impressed the natives that numbers of them worshipped him as their spiritual guide and deity, falling down at his feet in reverent submission.

They used to be admitted into his tent in bodies of a dozen at a time [wrote Ensign R. G. Wilberforce of the 52nd Light Infantry]. Once in his presence, they seated themselves on the ground, and fixed their eyes on the object of their admiration, who all the while went steadfastly on with whatever work he was engaged in, never even lifting his eyes to the faces of his mute worshippers. Sometimes . . . one of them would prostrate himself in prayer. This was an offence, against the committal of which warning had been given, and the penalty never varied: three dozen lashes with the cat-o'-nine tails on the bare back. This they did not mind, but on the contrary rejoiced in the punishment.[2]

Nicholson's own religion was tortured by persistent doubts, just as he seems to have been tortured by homosexual desires that shamed and horrified him. He did not like India, or Indians, detesting sepoys, so Ensign Wilberforce said, 'with a hatred no words could describe'; and when the mutiny broke out he responded to tales of massacre with predictable ferocity.[3]

Let us propose a Bill for the flaying alive, impalement, or burning of the murderers of the women and children at Delhi [he wrote to Herbert Edwardes, Commissioner at Peshawar]. The idea of simply hanging the perpetrators of such atrocities is maddening. I wish that I were in that part of the world, that if necessary I might take the law into my own hands . . . We are told in the Bible that stripes shall be meted out according to faults . . . If I had . . . [the wretches] . . . in my power today and knew that I were to die tomorrow, I would inflict the most excruciating tortures I could think of on them with a perfectly easy conscience.[4]

Certainly he did not hesitate to hang any mutineers he came across. Requested by the civil authorities on his march to Delhi to furnish 'a return of courts-martial, held upon insurgent natives, with a list of the various punishments inflicted', he returned the letter inscribed on the back: 'The punishment of mutiny is death.' 'Few courts-martial were held by Nicholson; his dictum "the punishment of mutiny is death" obviated any necessity for trial . . . Nicholson issued an order that no native should pass a white man riding, without dismounting and salaaming.'[5]

At the time of his arrival in Delhi, Nicholson was thirty-four years old, 'a man cast in a giant mould', according to an officer who saw his tall figure 'visiting all the pickets, examining everything, and making most searching inquiries about their strength and history'.

He had a massive chest and powerful limbs, and an expression ardent and commanding, with a dash of roughness; features of stern beauty [bearing a 'striking resemblance' to those of the young Benjamin Disraeli], a long, black beard, and deep, sonorous voice. There was something of immense strength, talent, and resolution in his whole frame and manner, and a power of ruling men on high occasions which no one could escape noticing. His imperial air never left him.[6]

Baird Smith was right, though. Intimidating, brusque and curtly sarcastic as he appeared on first acquaintance, most men did find him more likeable the longer they knew him. They were initially surprised, then disarmed, to discover that he was innately shy, that the overbearing manner was undermined by inner doubts and insecurities. Even those who could not bring themselves to like him, who could never get used to 'his disagreeable manners, his overbearing and violent language', could not but admire his industry and determination, and could not but be impressed by the power of his personality.[7] Lieutenant Frederick Roberts, who told his mother that Nicholson was then 'about the best man in India', wrote over half a century later that he impressed him 'more profoundly' than any man he had ever met before or had ever met since; he had 'never seen anyone like him'.[8]

Nicholson, who immediately settled down to examine every facet of the problem facing the Delhi Force, found Wilson intolerably indecisive and exasperatingly forlorn. 'Wilson says that we will assume the offensive on the arrival of the heavy guns,' he wrote to John Lawrence. 'But he says it in an undecided kind of way which makes me doubt if he will do so if he is not kept up to the mark . . . He is not at all equal to the crisis, and I believe he feels it himself . . .' 'He will take no responsibility on himself,' Nicholson complained a few days later. 'And it seems to me that he is becoming jealous of me, lest I should earn more than my share of *kudos*.'[9] There were far harsher criticisms yet to come.

While their commanders planned and argued, the bitter fighting went on. Hodson continued to enjoy it all, and recounted 'an amusing story' for the entertainment of his wife:

A rascally Pandy, thinking all was over [after a counter-attack],put his head out of the window of a house in the shade of which a few Europeans and Goorkhas were resting. One of the latter jumped up, laid hold of the rebel by his hair, and with one chop of his 'kookrie' took his head clean off. Atkinson should make a sketch of this for the *Illustrated London News*.[10]

Men with nerves less strong than Hodson's found such sights less amusing than sickening. 'You have no idea what nasty fighting we have,' Thomas Cadell told his father. 'No quarter is given on either side. We bayonet all their wounded, and they cut up ours with their tulwars.'[11]

'We took a Pandy prisoner,' another officer confessed, 'and my men amused themselves by making him eat greased cartridges, but we are to take no prisoners in future . . . It is impossible to feel the slightest pity for these black beasts . . . Some men of the 9th Lancers at a village on the way down found two baby's feet with little socks on them and a well near was full of dead bodies.'[12]

No prisoners were ever taken after this. When a sepoy surrendered he was killed, then carefully searched for any loot he might have secreted in his clothes. 'The Kammerbund was quickly torn off and the money snatched up,' recorded Captain Charles Griffiths of the 61st, 'a wrangle often ensuing among the men as to the division of the booty. In this manner many soldiers succeeded, to my knowledge, in securing large sums of money; one in particular, a Grenadier of my regiment, after killing a sepoy, rifled the body, and, returning in great glee to where I was standing, showed me twenty gold mohurs.'[13]

Despite their heavy losses and the spies' reports of desertions and unrest in the city, the mutineers maintained their attacks on the outposts, issuing from the gates of the city, frequently, so it seems, 'banged up to the eyes' with drugs, fighting bravely though rarely able to overcome their dread of the bayonet which Richard Barter described as 'quite ludicrous'. 'Often it used to happen when a door was broken open that the fellows inside fired their muskets and then, knowing that their time had come, they would drop on their knees and putting aside our men's bayonets, beg, "Nahu, sahib. Golee, sahib, golee." "No, sir. The bullet, sir. The bullet." '[14]

Sometimes the rebels attacked in native dress with dhoties instead of trousers, at others in their British uniforms, wearing their British medals and responding to words of command given in English. The bugle calls, too, were those they had been taught by their former masters to obey; and, to the constant irritation of the British soldiers, their bands continued to play familiar British tunes, 'Cheer, Boys, Cheer', 'The British Grenadiers' and 'The Girls We Left Behind Us'.[15]

On occasions a woman came out on horseback with the men, a peculiarly ugly woman known as 'The Fair Maid of Delhi', who 'fought against us like a fiend'. Her valiant exploits were sometimes watched, as were those of several of the larger fighting patrols, by various ladies of the city, for whom seats were erected beside the sunken batteries, and by the King's sons and grandsons who were dressed 'in green velvet suits, covered with gold'.[16]

Frequently 'two old withered Muslim women from Rampur' also led the rebels, according to Syed Mubarak Shah.

They went far in advance with naked swords, bitterly taunting the sepoys when they held back, calling them cowards and shouting to them to see how women went in front where they dared not follow ... The sepoys would excuse themselves, saying, 'We go to fetch ammunition.' But the women would reply, 'You stop and fight and we will get your ammunition for you.' These women frequently did bring cartridges to the men in the batteries and walked fearlessly in perfect showers of grape.[17]

While the enemy infantry continued to attack, their artillery also kept up their fire, the gunners clearly visible on the walls 'stripped to the waist, sponging and firing with great rapidity'. At night-time they laid their guns in the general direction of the picquets, sending 'the round shot whistling through the trees and shells bursting around us', Captain Griffiths recorded. 'The din and roar were deafening ... Nothing can be grander than the sight of live shells cleaving the air on a dark night. They seemed like so many brilliant meteors rushing through the heavens, or like lightning-flashes during a storm.'[18]

Towards the end of August it was evident that the rebels had used up all their powder, for they had taken to making their own, 'a very good thing for us,' Lieutenant Hugh Chichester of the Royal Bengal Artillery thought, 'as the powder is not strong enough to burst the shells ... But it is not such a bad powder for a Pandy to make,' he felt compelled to add. 'And they certainly send their shot with great velocity.'[19]

The ingenuity of the sepoys, in fact, could not be denied. They had, so spies reported, 'prepared rocket tubes in the city and learned the use of them'.[20] They had also succeeded in making mortars from the cast-iron sockets in which the bases of telegraph poles were encased.[21] For a time several British guns were put out of action. 'Sometimes our guns carried too far, while at others the shot fell very short of the proper range,' Rotton, the chaplain, explained. 'Moreover the guns would sometimes flash as often as three or four times, and once I heard of a piece of artillery flashing as many as seven times before it would discharge. We were at a loss to account for this phenomenon.' At length it was discovered that the 'gun lascars had been sympathizing with the rebels' who had taught them 'an ingenious method of tampering with the ordnance charges and a means of filling the vent of the guns with powdered glass . . . By this last means, the enemy having the benefit of the signal flash had ample time to escape'.[22]

Traitors such as the gun lascars were hanged on the spot. So were scores of camp-followers who were suspected, on no very certain evidence, of being spies. But this in no way deterred those who really were spies. Hodson's agents repeatedly reported that there were traitors on the Ridge who supplied the mutineers with accurate intelligence about British movements, supplies and intentions. 'Full information of everything going on in your camp reaches the mutineers,' one of Hodson's agents reported on 8 August; and, for the rest of the month, this flow of information from the Ridge to Delhi was maintained. The arrival of the British siege-train at the British camp, for instance, was known in the city within a few hours.[23]

The news that the siege-train had at last arrived caused the greatest excitement all along the Ridge.

I believe we are to escalade [Charles Ewart told his mother]. You know what that will be – rush up a ladder with men trying to push you down, bayonet and shoot you from above. But you must wave your sword and think it capital fun, bring your men up as fast as you can and jump down on top of men ready with fixed bayonets to receive you. All this is not very pleasant to think coolly of, but when the moment comes excitement and the knowledge that your men are looking to you to lead them on and bring them up with a cheer makes you feel as happy as possible . . . It will be fearfully exciting work. I hope it won't make me swear, though that is almost allowable for you are mad with excitement and know not what you are saying. But I will strive against it with all my might.[24]

The prospect of an imminent escalade filled Brigadier Wilson with dismay rather than excitement and made him feel more ill and tired than ever. His insomnia grew worse; he suffered from 'dreadful cramps' in his feet and legs; he found the 'frightful heat' intolerable. 'I get so exhausted,' he confessed, 'and my head gets so confused that I at times almost despair.' He was constantly at loggerheads with Hodson, who gave him 'great anxiety by exceeding his orders'; with Baird Smith, who proposed the 'most impracticable plans' which he could 'not possibly carry out'; and with Nicholson, whose evident belief in his Messianic mission exasperated other senior officers as much as it did Wilson himself.[25]

In their turn, Baird Smith, Hodson and Nicholson all found Wilson increasingly exasperating. 'We sadly want a head over us,' Hodson commented the day after the siege-train arrived. Nicholson, who thought he himself ought to have been that head, admitted to John Lawrence that if Wilson did not take the necessary measures to go ahead with the bombardment and assault he 'was quite prepared to appeal to the army to set him aside and elect a successor'. He confessed this also to his staff, though he added, 'I shall make it perfectly clear that, under the circumstances, I could not possibly accept the command myself, and I shall propose that it be given to Campbell of the 52nd. I am prepared to serve under him for the time being, so no one can ever accuse me of being influenced by personal motives.'[26]

Baird Smith, who had initially welcomed Wilson's appointment, was now more irritated by him than anyone. For a time it had been 'rather amusing taking care of the old gentleman' when he got into 'one of his fidgetty fits'; it was like 'patting a child on the back . . . to comfort it'. Baird Smith could 'scarcely avoid laughing sometimes' when he discovered himself 'doing monthly nurse in this fashion'. But by now 'the old general' had become 'a terrible bore'. He was 'so peevish and positively so childish' that Baird Smith had 'great difficulty' in keeping his temper with him. 'He combines a wondrous amount of ignorance and obstinacy,' Baird Smith told his wife. 'He is the most obstructive being ever created . . . and gets in a towering rage with me because I keep harping on' about the necessity for an assault.[27]

Eventually Wilson refused to speak to Baird Smith any more, notifying him that he would in future communicate with him only through the staff. In the end, though, Wilson was obliged to agree that the assault could no longer be delayed. So the engineers drew up plans for the construction of heavy siege batteries below the Ridge with light batteries to cover them on the higher ground above.

The main heavy battery was to be constructed below Hindu Rao's house less than half a mile from a fortification known as the Mori Bastion which commanded part of the northern wall of Delhi between the Kabul and Kashmir Gates. Construction of this battery began after dark on 7 September. The men digging into the hard earth were 'in a fever of anxiety' that the noise they made would at any moment bring down upon them a storm of shot and shell from the enemy guns. The incessant groaning of the strings of camels that carried down the fascines and gabions was ' enough to wake the dead ', while the row made by the bullock carts dragging down first the ammunition, then the siege guns, seemed 'loud enough to be heard in Simla '. Yet Lieutenant Coghill on the Ridge above heard nothing but the occasional dead thud of a pick. 'Fortunately,' as he explained, 'a strong wind blowing from the city towards our trenches prevented the rebels hearing the noise, though we could distinctly hear *their* voices, talking and singing as if nothing was about to happen.'[28]

Throughout the night the work continued, but as dawn approached not a single gun had been dragged into its allotted position. And, while bullocks bellowed under the whips of their frantic drivers, while engineers hammered at the platforms, and artillerymen stored shot and shell into the magazines, the sun came up. Soon afterwards the first gun was dragged on to its platform as the enemy in the Mori Bastion, aware at last of what had been happening in the night, opened so fierce fire on the battery that Wilson wondered whether the guns ought to be withdrawn before it was destroyed. In command of the battery, however, was a resourceful, experienced officer, Major Brind, whose coolness under fire had already excited the admiration of the army.

Before the siege-train arrived we could always tell when old Brind was Field Officer of the day by the constant fire he kept up from the Ridge [the Adjutant of the 75th recorded]. There was an order that there was to be no unnecessary firing and Brind never fired the first shot, but once let the enemy commence and he was ready for him. He used to lie reading his Bible in the battery at Hindu Rao's house, and, quiet as a lamb, suddenly the look-out man would cry, 'Shot from the Mori!' or 'Shell from the Kashmir!' or whatever it was, and then, first carefully marking the passage he had been reading, and putting his Bible under his pillow, the fine old soldier jumped on the parapet of the battery – no dodging behind walls with him – and, straight as a ramrod, he paced up and down within full view of friend and foe. But woe be to you if you presumed to show even a head above the work, he was down on you like a shot, and soon let you know that he was the only one there who had a right to put himself in danger. Quietly, without the least show of excitement, he'd give the order, 'No. 1 gun, are you ready?' The answer would come, 'All ready, sir!' Then, 'Fire!' And up went the glass to note the effects of the shot.[29]

Brind was equally calm and determined now: there was no need to withdraw the guns, he assured Wilson. They would soon be in position; the enemy's fire could be endured until they were. And so it was endured. Gradually the guns were mounted; by midday nearly all had opened fire, 'bucket after bucket of water being drenched over them and wet blankets laid on them to try to cool the metal'. Before nightfall the masonry of the Mori Bastion had begun to crumble, and the enemy's artillery there had ceased to fire.[30]

The other two heavy batteries, which were being constructed opposite the Kashmir Gate and close to the fortification on the north-eastern corner of the wall known as the Water Bastion, were not yet ready.

The fact is [Wilson complained to his wife], my Engineers, although very zealous, have little or no experience, and attempted to perform more in a certain time than was possible with the means at their disposal. There is also a sad want of arrangement amongst them. I told them all this before we commenced, but they would not believe me. Fortunately there is no great harm done beyond loss of time.[31]

There was great loss, though, among the camp-followers, thirty-nine of whom were killed on 10 September while helping to construct the batteries. 'They were merely the unarmed native pioneers, and not meant to be fighting men,' wrote Captain J. G. Medley, paying them a rare tribute. 'With the passive courage so common to natives, as man after man was knocked over, they would stop a moment, weep a little over their fallen friend, pop his body in a row along with the rest, and then work on as before.'[32]

It had been hoped that the assault would be made on 11 September. But by dawn that day neither of the two batteries on the left had begun to fire. When they did so, however, the cannonade was of devastating effect. It was like some unimaginably powerful thunderstorm, thought an officer of the Punjab Infantry as he watched the flashes and smoke and listened to 'the deadly roar of the guns'. 'The rain of shells on the city and the stream of musketry fire from the walls all seemed a dream of something I had read about rather than reality.'[33] Major Reid had 'never seen such plucky gunners' in his life as those of the Bengal Artillery: 'Fight it out they will, and every gunner will be killed at his post.'[34] Within a few hours both the Kashmir and Water Bastions were crumbling into ruins and wide breaches were being made for the assaulting infantry columns.

At ten o'clock on the night of 13 September the firing suddenly stopped while two engineer officers crept forward to inspect the damage that had been done to the Kashmir Bastion. One of them,

Lieutenant Arthur Lang, had already dashed to the top of the glacis by the Bastion that afternoon, and, having lain for a few minutes on the crest inspecting the breach, had rushed back through fierce fire from the snipers on the walls. Now he set out again with Captain Medley who confirmed that the breach was a practicable one, the slope possible to climb.[35]

The plan of assault, drawn up by Baird Smith and Wilson, provided for the Delhi Force, now numbering about eight thousand men, to be divided into four attacking columns and a reserve. The main column under Nicholson was to make for the breach near the Kashmir Bastion, to escalade the shattered wall and clamber down into the main-guard by St James's Church. On its left, the second column under Colonel Jones was to storm the breach by the Water Bastion; while the third, commanded by Colonel Campbell of the 52nd, was to advance towards the Kashmir Gate, blow it in, and then join Nicholson's column by the main-guard. The fourth column, under Major Reid, was to attack the suburbs outside the Kabul and Lahore Gates, clear the enemy out of them, then enter the city through the Kabul Gate which was to be opened for it by men of the other columns. The reserves were to follow Nicholson who was appointed to the overall command of the various columns once the assault was under way.[36]

All this was explained to the commanding officers, second-in-commands and adjutants of the various regiments who assembled in Nicholson's tent to receive their detailed orders. Richard Barter vividly remembered Nicholson standing there, tall and broad and 'rather bald', his right foot on a chair, a map of the city on a table before him, as he explained 'in a clear and lucid manner' what each column was to do and how he himself 'would be distinguished by his standard', a green flag which would be held aloft by one of his Afghan followers. Nicholson then took the officers out to the trenches to show them the exact positions which their regiments were to take up before the assault.

There was not much sleep that night in our camp [Barter continued]. I dropped off now and then but never for long and whenever I woke I could see that there was a light in more than one of the officers' tents and talking was going on in a low tone amongst the men, the snapping of a lock or springing of a ramrod sounding far in the still air . . . Each of us looked carefully to the loading of our pistols, the filling of flasks and getting as good protection as possible for our heads which would be exposed so much in going up the ladders. I wound two turbans round my old forage cap with my last letter from the hills in the top.[37]

The regiments fell in shortly after midnight when, by the lights of horn-lanterns, the orders were read out to the men. They were told to abandon the wounded where they fell: if the assault were successful they would be picked up later and carried back to the rear on litters by the hospital coolies; if the assault failed they must be prepared to bear the worst. There was to be no plundering: all the treasure which might eventually be taken would be placed in a common stock for fair division when the city was captured. No prisoners would be taken; but no women or children were to be injured. On hearing this last injunction the men of the 75th answered at once, 'No fear, sir!'[38]

The orders having been read, the officers pledged their honour on their swords to abide by them, while the men promised to follow their example. The march for the rendezvous was then just about to begin when, wearing his vestments, up came a French priest, Father Bertrand, 'a noble old fellow' who had been appointed Roman Catholic chaplain. 'We may differ some of us in matters of religion,' Father Bertrand said to Colonel Charles Herbert. 'But the blessings of an old man and a clergyman can do nothing but good.'

Already the men had heard a long sermon from the Protestant chaplain who had reminded them that the Old Testament lesson for the day foretold the doom of 'the bloody city' of Nineveh, 'full of lies and robbery'. 'Draw thee waters for the siege, fortify thy strongholds,' the chaplain had quoted from the Book of Nahum, 'then shall the fire devour thee; the sword shall cut thee off; it shall eat thee up like the canker-worm . . . There is a multitude of slain, and a great number of carcasses . . . They stumble upon their corpses.' Hoping that Father Bertrand's sermon would be less disturbingly apocalyptic, Colonel Herbert granted him permission to say a few words. The old priest then lifted his hands to heaven, blessed the men 'in a most impressive manner', offering up at the same time a prayer for their success and 'for mercy on the souls of those so soon to die'.[39]

Some of their number comforted by these words, others more frightened than ever, the men moved slowly down towards the road that led from the Flagstaff Tower towards the Kashmir Gate. Soon, however, they were halted again. It was discovered that within the past few hours the enemy had filled the breaches with fascines, gabions and broken masonry, and that a further bombardment by the heavy guns would be needed to tear a path through the debris. So the batteries again opened fire 'with a terrific roar' to which the enemy's guns immediately responded; and for half an hour the darkness before day was illuminated by the constant flashes of shell-bursts and rockets. While the troops waited Brigadier Wilson rode down, looking ill and apprehensive, worrying, as he confessed, that with so much illness in the camp only four thousand five hundred men were available for the assault and that many of these were Sikhs intent mainly on plunder.[40]

Suddenly the guns ceased and the signal for the attack was given.

We had been watching anxiously for it [Richard Barter recorded], and now in columns of fours we rushed at the double through a high archway into a garden of roses and through this to the foot of the glacis. Small birds were twittering amongst the trees as we dashed on, and the perfume of the roses was quite apparent in spite of the sulphur smell of powder. The dark forms of the 60th Rifles seemed to spring out of the earth as they lined the bank at the side of the garden, keeping up a galling fire on the walls and breach. Day had broken and the sun was just showing like a large red ball in the east as, passing through the line of the 60th who cheered us loudly, we emerged on the glacis and there, straight before us, was the breach. It was a huge gap in the wall, full of men whose heads showed just over the edges of it. Along the walls they swarmed thick as bees, the sun shining full upon the white turbans and the black faces, sparkling brightly on their swords and bayonets.

Our men cheered madly as they rushed on. The enemy, whose fire had slackened when ours ceased, at first seemed perfectly taken aback by our sudden appearance, but recovering from their surprise they now began firing again in earnest. Round shot came screaming from the guns far on our right, while grape and shells whistled from those nearer, and the walls seemed one line of fire all along our front. Bullets whipped through the air and tore up the ground about our feet and men fell fast. Amongst the first was Colonel Herbert, with a ball through his leg . . . Three times the ladder parties were swept away, and three times the ladders were snatched from the shoulders of the dead and wounded.[41]

To the left of the 75th a party of Engineers was trying to blow in the Kashmir Gate. The planks of the bridge leading towards it across the ditch were no longer there, but the beams that had supported them remained. Across these, followed by a bugler of the 52nd, ran the officer in command of the party who managed to place a bag of powder beside the gate before jumping down into the ditch in a storm of musketry fire. A sergeant followed him but was shot before he reached the gate. Another sergeant, Smith of the Bengal Engineers, snatched up his bag and, planting it together with his own by the gate, prepared the fuses, while a second officer held a slow match waiting to fire the charge. Before he could do so the officer was shot dead; and a sergeant who took the slow match from him was also shot and fell over with the match into the ditch. Then Sergeant Smith pressed himself as close as he could against the powder bags, so that the enemy could not deflect their muskets sufficiently to fire at him, struck a light and was just about to apply it when one of the fuses in the powder-bags exploded in his face. He was thrown back into the ditch as a cascade of shattered masonry flew into the air and the timbers of the gate splintered and broke.[42]

Lieutenant Coghill, who had been waiting impatiently for the explosion, felt 'a species of wildness or madness' come over him as the sound of it – followed by the order to charge and the call of the bugle – reached his ears.

I took a bit of a pistol bullet in my mouth and with a devil's yell rushed from under cover, knowing that the quicker the rush the nearer the enemy and the earlier the revenge [he told his father]. The musketry and jingalls poured in like rain and men kept falling on every side of me, but I thought my life charmed and they could not touch me. The groans and execrations of the wounded and dying, cursing their fate at being left outside and not able to revenge themselves, was pitiable in the extreme. They rolled and writhed in agony . . . I felt like a drunken man. I just remember putting my sword back and seizing the ladders and throwing them down the ditch. They were only eight feet long and the ditch we found twenty feet deep. In the excitement we just dropped down and then rushed up [the other side]. The brutes fought till we regularly cut and hacked our way through them with sword and bayonet. Unfortunately the first thing my sword stuck in was the body of a colour sergeant of mine who was shot and fell on to it. But the next moment it was skivering through a Pandy and then another. All orders and formation was over and we cut and hacked wherever we could. I never thought of drawing my pistol but poked, thrust and hacked till my arm was tired.[43]

On either side of him men were clambering up the ditches and through the breaches, holding their weapons in their right hands, grabbing hold of the rungs of the ladders or handfuls of slipping earth with their left. Some of the officers contrived to fire their pistols while gripping their swords under their arms, for they carried no scabbards. The troops of the 2nd Punjab Infantry, unable to get a footing on the ladders, scrambled up over one another's shoulders. All the time the enemy maintained their musketry fire and hurled huge blocks of masonry down on the heads of the masses of bodies climbing up towards them, yelling curses and defiance.

Lieutenant Gerald Money of the Bengal Fusiliers, having taken the place of a ladder-man who had been killed and having thrown the ladder into the ditch, slid to the bottom with his men who 'scrambled up the other side like flies up a wall'. He caught hold of a man in front of him, put one foot on his pouch, climbed up on to his shoulder, and claimed to be one of the first three men to reach the top.[44] Several other officers made similar claims. Captain Barter caught a subaltern by the arm and, claiming a right to precede him as his senior officer, pulled him back so as to reach the gabions at the crest of the breach. Another captain, who arrived there at the same time, shook hands with Barter, then ran down inside the walls where he was immediately killed by a discharge of grape.[45]

The rebels had now retreated from the Kashmir and Water Bastions to take up defensive positions deeper in the city. Followed by a bugler, Barter rushed along the parapet down towards the Kashmir Gate – on his way killing with a back-stroke of his sword a rebel gunner who was running away into the city – and, on arrival at the Gate, 'where numbers of enemy bodies were lying about', ordered the bugler to sound the regimental call of the 75th. But so many men from other regiments came crowding in amongst his own that, despairing of bringing order out of such confusion, he called on the men to follow him as best they could towards the Mori Bastion. Shot at from the windows of the tall house and from behind garden walls, they ran through archways and down narrow alleys, charging and bayoneting any sepoys who attempted to bar their path, sheltering in recesses when they saw port-fires being put to enemy guns, then rushing out to slaughter the gunners after the first discharge, entering houses where numbers of rebels appeared to have concentrated, shooting their way up from storey to storey, rushing out on to the flat roofs and hurling the defenders, dead and wounded alike, over the balustrades. Many of them were killed; but they were joined by men of other regiments, Bengal Fusiliers, Sikhs and troops of the 61st; and eventually they reached the Mori Bastion from which those defenders who had not already fled were soon evicted and their bodies pitched down over the parapet into the ditch.[46]

While Barter and his men were fighting their way across to the Mori Bastion, Gerald Money and the leading men of the Bengal Fusiliers were making for the Kabul Gate.

While the regiment was forming up inside the city I asked the Adjutant where we had to go [recorded Money]. He showed me a narrow lane, saying we were to keep down this and along under the wall. I went up to the lane and found some of the Queen's 75th and 60th Rifles firing down it at a lot of niggers. I called out, 'Come along boys. We've got to go down there.' But they hesitated, saying it was full of men. So I said, 'Well, you won't let me go alone, I know,' and jumped over the barricade of boughs and ran down. Before I had gone ten yards a lot of men were alongside, and we charged along and took a battery of about six heavy guns . . . After this I went ahead of the men, and turning down a narrow place found myself in the Mori Bastion among about thirty Pandies. They bolted at first; but, seeing I was alone, came at me and I was obliged to retreat, calling out to the men who soon came up and we polished them nearly all off. But one of them proved more than a match for me and would have finished me if a man of my company had not rushed up with his bayonet . . . I then saw another man hiding under a gun, and went towards him. The moment he saw me he jumped out and came at me. I warded off his blow and gave him a point, and the first resistance I felt was the hilt of my sword coming bump up against his breast while the warm blood spurted over my hand. There were only about seven or eight men with me now, and we had gone so far ahead that the Pandies had closed all round us. I got a 6-pounder which was there, and, loading it with grape, turned it on the entrance to the battery . . . I then jumped on the parapet, and cheered as loud as I could, and was rather disgusted at being answered by a shower of grape from our advanced batteries. Luckily I wasn't hit and, jumping down, I tied a blue and white turban together and, fastening it to the end of a musket and bayonet, I jumped up and waved it. This brought a cheer from our batteries and a storm of shot from a line of Pandies which I then saw for the first time lining a breastwork between the Mori and our advanced troops. I got down and loaded a 24-pounder with grape, laid it and fired it. It knocked down a lot of them and the rest bolted . . .

Colonel Greathed of the 8th Queen's was now in the battery and seeing that I had lost my sword which had been stolen by a Sikh while I was laying the gun, he took a sword that had belonged to an officer of his regiment who had been killed just before, and he gave it to me, saying, 'Here, Money, this is one of our swords. If you use it as I saw you using your own a little while ago, you will not disgrace it.' . . .

When our regiment came up, I joined them and went on to the Kabul Gate, and from there we made three charges at the Lahore Gate and Bastion. But we were driven back . . . Anything I had been in before was child's play. I was hit by about a dozen spent balls and bruised all over by them and by splinters, etc . . . It was here that I saw about twelve officers knocked out in five minutes.[47]

Brigadier Nicholson himself was leading the attack on the Lahore Gate. So far the assault had not gone as smoothly as he had hoped. Far too many units had been split up in the confusion of the storming and it had proved impossible to reorganize them properly once the walls had been crossed. Many of his best officers were already dead or wounded; his green standard had, as one young officer at least had expected, proved 'perfectly invisible' through the smoke. He now appeared to be both indignant and over-excited as he pointed the way down the narrow lane which led to the Lahore Gate and which was covered both by guns and by sharpshooters in the buildings on either side. The surviving officers pleaded with him to abandon an impossible task which had already cost so many valuable lives. He would not listen to them. Another attempt was made. Once more it failed with heavy losses. Undeterred, Nicholson waved his sword above his head as he jumped out into the lane with his back to the enemy, shouting at the men to come forward yet again. At that moment a shot struck him in the back. He reeled round and fell to the ground. At first he refused assistance saying that men who would not follow him should not lift him from the ground, that he would die where he had fallen. But then, catching sight of an officer, Captain Hay, with whom he had recently quarrelled, 'he gasped out "I will make up my difference with you, Hay. I will let you take me back."' So, under Hay's direction, Nicholson was carried back to the Kabul Gate.[48]

Lieutenant Coghill had also by now reached the Kabul Gate where he found both officers and men 'fatigued to death'. There were only about two hundred of them, for not only had casualties been excessively severe, but detachments had been left to hold all the bastions and gateways between there and the breach by the Kashmir Gate. They were divided into three parties, the larger party remaining by the gateway, the two smaller being sent to line the roofs of the highest houses down the adjoining streets.

The enemy regularly mobbed us [Coghill said], but if we had made a charge they could have attacked us in flank and retaken the gateway, so we had to lie down flat and let their guns fire over us until they came near and then [we stood up and charged] and our bayonets always told. This work continued until four o'clock in the afternoon, and we were being picked off from a distance without hope of retaliation or assistance coming to us, and we did not know what was going on to our left or in the rear.[49]

In the rear, Major Reid's column, which had been instructed to support the troops at the Kabul Gate, was, in fact, in serious difficulties. Its advance had been delayed by Reid who did not want to move off without three guns which had been promised him but who had been obliged to start without them when part of his force, the Jammu Contingent commanded by Major R. C. Lawrence, had engaged the enemy prematurely. Soon afterwards Reid had been wounded on a bridge beneath the walls of the suburb of Kishengaji; and his Gurkhas, deprived of his leadership, had faltered, seeming for once to lose their nerve. The 1st Bengal Fusiliers and the 61st had charged past them across the bridge; but in Kishengaji the men of these two regiments had become so entangled and confused as a storm of musketry descended upon them from the loopholed walls that their officers had completely lost control of them. And when the Jammu Contingent, falling back in panic before the enemy whom they had foolhardily engaged, had poured into the disorderly ranks, Captain Muter, assuming command, had withdrawn what troops he could muster to Hindu Rao's house. As an enemy force had gathered to follow up the rebel success, the Cavalry Brigade, commanded by Brigadier Hope Grant, had moved to the support of Reid's shattered column only to come under so heavy a fire that Tombs's troop of horse artillery had had to be brought down to extricate them. This had no sooner been effected than both cavalry and horse artillery had been ferociously bombarded with grape from the Lahore Bastion and had suffered fearful casualties.[50]

The wounded were carried away to the field hospital, a large yellow building beyond the racquet-court. Dr Wise, a young Scottish surgeon, was there and thought that of all the awful sights he had so far witnessed in India the scenes in that hospital were

certainly the worst. Hundreds of wounded men were brought in, also many killed . . . Amputations were going on in all directions. The noise was incessant. Strong men groaning in their agony; men with mortal wounds shouting for water; and the grating of the saw, as some poor fellow's limb was removed, gave one no bad idea of hell.[51]

Denied the reinforcements which they had expected, the troops at the Kabul Gate had to abandon all hope of making further headway into the city; and, as the afternoon wore on, they began to wonder whether, indeed, they would be able to hold on to the ground which they had won at the cost of so many of their comrades' lives.

The position at the Mori Bastion was rather more secure and the troops there less apprehensive and forlorn. Seeing the Union Jack, which during the entire siege had flown from the Flagstaff Tower, being hoisted on the Kashmir Bastion, the men began to cheer and laugh and dance about as though the battle were already over. That afternoon, however, the Mori Bastion came under heavy fire and several officers and men were hit, while others collapsed with heatstroke, their faces turning black.

Various sudden deaths in the 75th gave Captain Barter command of the regiment; and as its senior surviving officer he presented himself at the army headquarters which had been established in Skinner's House near St James's Church. Here he found Brigadier Wilson 'pacing up and down a large room in a troubled manner'. Deeply concerned by the day's casualties which already amounted to over sixty officers and more than a thousand men, Wilson evidently had 'serious thoughts of retiring to the camp'. The walls between the Water Bastion and the Kabul Gate were temporarily in his hands and the positions occupied were being slowly strengthened. But the failure of Reid's column left him open to attack from the south, while a force of sepoys far stronger than his own still held most of the city to the east. As he mournfully elaborated his difficulties, a note was handed to him from that stern old Puritan, Major Brind: 'God has given you a great victory. See that you do not throw it away.'[52]

'This decided the General who was himself an old Bengal artilleryman,' Barter commented, 'and the recall, which I feel sure would not have been obeyed, was never sounded.'[53] During the next few days, however, Wilson seemed on several occasions about to change his mind as he talked of his difficulties in a manner that suggested he was on the verge of mental collapse. 'I am satisfied,' Baird Smith bluntly told his wife, 'that poor old Wilson has gone mad.'[54] He spent much of his time sitting in the hall of the house, 'balancing himself in a chair, with his face to the wall, on which his feet rested'. Most of his staff did not dare go near him.[55] Nevertheless, he listened to the advice of his Chief Engineer on whom, despite their incompatibility, he had learned it wise to rely; and, whenever he spoke of withdrawing from the city, Baird Smith prevailed upon him not to give way to his fears.[56]

When told of Wilson's inclination to retire, Nicholson, slowly dying in his tent, cried out in fury, 'Thank God, I have strength yet to shoot that man, if necessary.'[57] He then dictated a letter to John Lawrence urging him, on his own authority, to dismiss the poltroon and to appoint Neville Chamberlain in his place.[58] The change was not necessary though. Wilson continued to be guided by Baird Smith: the advance into Delhi was to continue.[59]

17

The Captured City

· *Incompetent advance into Delhi – looting and murder · last rebel strongholds captured, 20 September 1857 · flight of King – Hodson captures him, 21 September · and murders the princes, 22 September hanging of captured rebels – looting · Greathed's column, pursuing mutineers, reaches Agra · defeat of rebels there, 10 October ·*

The advance through Delhi was a slow and painful operation, directed with the utmost incompetence. Junior officers bitterly complained of the 'most wretched' manner in which the street fighting was conducted, of the incapacity of most of the senior officers who had survived, particularly Colonel Greathed of the 8th, a 'regular muff' who knew nothing, who was 'certainly *not* the right man in the right place', being 'not only a perfect fool' but ' a "funk stick"', whose reputation at home was 'just a lot of blether'.[1]

I have not a Queen's Officer under me worth a pin, or who can preserve any sort of discipline except Jones of the 60th Rifles [Wilson complained to his wife]. In fact the men are so badly officered that they will and can do nothing ... All we can expect to do is to get on gradually, but this street fighting is frightful work; and Pandy is as good a soldier at that as our men ... We have to gain our way inch by inch, and, of the force we have, unfortunately there is a large portion besides the [native] troops upon whom I can place no confidence ... I do not suppose any Commanding Officer had such wretched tools to work with, as I have. The only good officers I had are killed or wounded, and *such* a set left, no head, no control over their men ... An attempt was made this morning [18 September] to take the Lahore Gate, but failed from the refusal of the European soldiers to follow their officers. One rush and it could have been done easily but they would not make it. The fact is our men have a great dislike of street fighting. They do not see their enemy, and find their comrades falling ... and get in a panic and will not advance ... I have always been of the opinion that to be successful perfectly the assault on Delhi should not have taken place until the force from Cawnpore could come up to support us, but their inability to move forward, and the pressure from Government and Sir John Lawrence, forced me to make the attempt . . . We are and always have been too weak for the work to be performed. It has been a hard task imposed upon me, dearest, harder than I can bear. Both mind and body are giving way . . . I am knocked up . . . cannot sleep . . . and unequal to any exertion.[2]

Wilson's worst trouble, so he added, 'even worse than the enemy', was the 'immense quantity of wines, spirits and beer' which the men had got hold of, 'making beasts of themselves and incapable of doing their duty'. Gallons of liquor were destroyed on Wilson's orders. But further supplies were constantly being found; and although some officers afterwards denied it, the sight of hopelessly drunken men in the streets was not at all uncommon. 'The fact is,' Hodson wrote, 'the troops are utterly demoralized by hard work and hard drink. For the first time in my life I have had to see English soldiers refusing repeatedly to follow their officers.'[3] 'It is a really lamentable state of affairs,' Dr Wise thought. 'We cannot advance on account of the drunkenness of our men . . . The 52nd are the disgrace of the army. They make a point of running away, and it is said the officers show them the way . . . A nice state . . . that we cannot advance on account of our men getting drunk!'[4]

Barter and Coghill came across two British soldiers brandishing their bayonets in the face of a captain, not of their regiment, who had had the temerity to confiscate a bottle which they were carrying through the streets. They had seized the captain's bridle and would, Barter fully expected, have pulled him from his horse and stabbed him with their bayonets had not he and Coghill chanced to pass by.[5]

As well as drunkenness there was much indiscriminate violence. Unwary citizens who showed their faces in the streets were as likely to be murdered as captured sepoys. Those suspected of being or of harbouring rebels were hanged, bayoneted or shot. 'Already intent on vengeance, the soldiers were more than ever determined to exact it when they came across the mutilated corpses of comrades murdered in side streets and alleys to which they had been enticed by the female accomplices of badmashes and fanatics.'[6] The revenge was appalling. Old men were shot without a second thought; groups of younger men endeavouring to escape from the city were rounded up and executed in the ditch outside the gates. 'No one with a coloured skin could feel himself safe.' The murders were committed quite without compunction or regret. A soldier of the 75th, after shooting a butcher whose distaste for the British troops was apparent in his expression, 'came down the lane laughing and reloading his firelock'; and, when asked if he had committed what his officer described as an act of 'simple murder', replied airily, 'Yes, sir. I was seeing if my firelock would go off all right after being loaded so long. But, faith, it didn't miss and I bowled him over up there in the lane.'[7]

Captain Barter described how 'a native gentleman, in a dreadful state of funk', ran up to him out of the cellar of a big house, seized hold of his feet and gasped out that 'his honour was gone and that the European soldiers were in his zenana'.

> I asked him to show me the way [Barter recorded], and followed him down to a large house covered with carpets. Sitting on some silk cushions were a number of veiled women who set up a shrill kind of howl on our appearance. To our right, leaning on his firelock and gazing at them with a most stolid expression of countenance, stood a stalwart grenadier of the 75th who came to attention on my entrance and looked at me with a half puzzled, half amused air. I asked him what all the row was about and how he came to be frightening the women there. He grinned and said, 'Why, Lord bless you, Mr Barter. I done nothing to 'em. While ransacking the house I comes across this lot 'ere, and the moment I shows my nose they sets to squealin' like blazes.' . . . Seeing that there was no harm done, and rather angry at the fuss our host had made about our getting a glimpse of his veiled beauties when I remembered how his brethren had treated our poor helpless creatures, I said, 'Let's have a look at the ladies. They must be very beautiful I suppose.' So, commencing at the right we lifted the veil from each houri and I certainly never saw a more abominably ugly and dirty looking set of females anywhere.

Assuring their master that he need not be in the least alarmed about his females as the British fought only with soldiers, Barter returned upstairs, followed by the owner of the house; he was still 'in a blue funk', and, now that his hiding-place had been discovered, refused to leave the officer's side. He kept close to Barter until they reached the roof where, terrified by the gestures that the soldiers made at him behind their captain's back, he jumped into the branches of a tall tree growing in the street and began to scramble down the trunk. 'There were two or three Sikh soldiers in the doorway below; and one of these, seeing the man come down in this extraordinary fashion, darted out and quietly held his firelock with fixed bayonet underneath him. He came down full swing and was in an instant impaled on the bayonet, to the great delight of the Sikhs who in a few seconds put him out of his pain.'[8]

If many other male citizens of Delhi met a similar fate, the women were generally spared. And, relying on the reluctance of most British soldiers to shoot at women, sepoys often used them as cover when escaping from a house, or even disguised themselves as women to escape. But several women in Delhi were killed, inadvertently or intentionally, all the same. Some 'came out of their houses along with their children and killed themselves by jumping into the wells'.[9] Others were killed by their husbands or father. 'We found fourteen women with their throats cut from ear to ear by their own husbands, and laid out on shawls,' one officer recorded. 'We caught a man there who said he saw them killed, for fear they should fall into our hands; and showed us their husbands who had done the best they could afterwards and killed themselves.'[10]

The husbands' dread of their wives falling into British hands was not always unjustified. The women and children who were brought into headquarters were spared, so Henry Ouvry assured his wife, but he was 'sorry to say a great many were shot in the shops and streets'.[11] Some, too, were shot in their own homes. Captain Griffiths of the 61st related the story of an old school-friend of his, an Assistant Collector in the Bengal Civil Service, whose sister had been murdered – and, so the brother was convinced, violated – by the rebels. This young civilian was in the habit of attaching himself to any regiment with whom he might have an opportunity of glutting his desire for vengeance. Griffiths met him one day in the streets of Delhi. 'He shook my hand,' Griffiths wrote, 'saying that he had put to death all he had come across, not excepting women and children, and from his excited manner and the appearance of his dress – which was covered with bloodstains – I quite believe he told me the truth. One would imagine he must have tired of slaughter during the six days of fighting in the city, but it was not so.'[12]

After the sixth day of fighting, the last of the rebel strongholds in Delhi, the Lahore Gate, the Jama Masjid and the fort of Solimgarh, all fell at last. The gates of the palace were blown in; the remaining Ghazis were killed in the courtyards or by the gates where they stood 'grim and immovable, prepared for [their] doom'; and the conquerors' flag was unfurled from the highest pinnacle.[13]

The King, his family and entourage had fled two days before. He had been urged to make a stand.

But, afraid for his life, his Majesty hesitated [wrote Syed Mubarak Shah] on which they more earnestly entreated him saying: 'Your end is now approaching – you will be captured. Why die a shameful, dishonourable death? Why not die fighting and leave an unperishable name?' The King replied that he would place himself at the head of the troops at 12 o'clock that day.

As soon as the royal intention of leading the army to battle was known, masses of mutineers, Ghazis and townsmen collected in front of the Palace, not less than 70,000 men. Presently [the royal sedan chair] was seen slowly issuing forth from the great gate . . . But then Hakim Ahsanullah Khan, forcing his way to his royal master, told him that if he went any further he would to a certainty be shot as European riflemen were concealed in the different houses. 'Moreover,' added the Hakim, 'if you go out with the army to fight how can I possibly explain your conduct tomorrow to the British? What excuse can I advance for you after you have joined the mutineers in battle?' On hearing these words the King left the procession and re-entered the Palace on the plea of going to evening prayers. The mass of the people and the troops now became confused, then alarmed, and eventually dispersed.[14]

The King had not gone far in his flight from the city. Rejecting Bakht Khan's plea that he should remain with the army, he had preferred the advice of Mirza Ilahi Baksh, the father-in-law of one of his sons, and of Hakim Ahsanullah Khan, who continued to advise him to dissociate himself from the rebel cause. 'Recollect you are the King,' Hakim Ahsanullah Khan is believed to have said to him. 'It is not right for you to go. The army of the English mutinied against their masters, fought with them and have been utterly routed and dispersed. What has your Majesty to do with them . . . The English will not regard you as guilty.'[15] The King had accordingly retreated no farther than the tomb of the Emperor Humayun five miles south of the palace on the road to Muttra.

Learning of his presence there from a spy, William Hodson, who had already come to profitable terms with the King's wife, Zinat Mahal, offered to go out to capture him and to bring him back to Delhi for trial. After some hesitation Wilson agreed. So Hodson set out with fifty of his troopers; and, halting at the gateway of the tomb, sent in two emissaries to say that if the King surrendered, his life – together with the lives of his wife and young son who were both with him – would be spared. Two hours later the emissaries returned to the gateway: the King would surrender if Hodson himself came forward to repeat the Government's guarantee of safety.

Hodson walked out to the middle of the road in front of the gateway and, sword in hand, facing the white domes of the tomb, he called out that if the King came forward he would repeat the promise. A few moments later the Begum came out, followed by the King in a *palka-ghari*; and, the guarantee reaffirmed, the procession of horsemen escorted the royal family back to Delhi with thousands of people walking in their wake.[16]

The next morning Hodson determined to bring in the King's sons as well. He sent a note to his second-in-command, Lieutenant Macdowell: 'Come sharp. Bring one hundred men.'

We started at eight o'clock [Macdowell recorded], and halted half a mile from the tomb where the Princes were. Close by were about 3,000 of their Mussulman followers, so it was rather a ticklish bit of work. We sent in to say the Princes must give themselves up unconditionally, or take the consequences. A long half hour elapsed, when a messenger came out to say the Princes wished to know if their lives would be promised them if they came out. 'Unconditional surrender,' was the answer. Again we waited. It was a most anxious time . . . We heard the shouts of fanatics (as we found they were afterwards) begging the Princes to lead them on against us. And we had only one hundred men and were six miles from Delhi. At length, I suppose imagining that sooner or later they would be taken and fancying that as we had spared the King we would spare them, they resolved to give themselves up . . . We sent ten men to meet them, and by Hodson's order I drew the troops up across the road . . . Soon the Princes [two of the King's sons, Mirza Moghul and Mirza Khizr Sultan, and his grandson, Mirza Abu Bakr] appeared in a cart. Behind them thronged about 2,000 or 3,000 Mussulmans (I am not exaggerating).

Hodson rode up to meet them, leaving his men where they were, and ordered the driver of the bullock cart to move on to Delhi. The princes' followers surged forward as if intending to follow the cart; but Hodson waved them back with a commanding gesture, while Macdowell formed up his troop on either side of the road between the crowd and the cart.

Meanwhile Hodson galloped back and told the ten sowars of the escort to hurry the Princes along the road while we kept back the mob [Macdowell continued his report]. They retired on Humayoon's tomb, and step by step we followed them. They went up the steps and formed up in the immense garden inside. Leaving the men outside, Hodson and myself with four men rode up the steps and through the archway.

Hodson pointed his carbine at the crowd and said, 'The first man that moves is dead.'

He then called out to them to lay down their arms. There was a murmur. He reiterated the command and (God knows why, I never can understand it) they commenced doing so. Now, you see, we didn't want their arms, and under ordinary circumstances would not have risked our lives in so rash a way, but what we wanted was time to get the Princes away . . . Well there we stayed for two hours collecting their arms, and every moment I thought they would rush at us. I said nothing but smoked all the time to show I was unconcerned.

When all the weapons had been collected and thrown into a cart, Hodson turned to Macdowell, calmly said, 'We'll go now', and, followed by the crowd, rode quietly back towards Delhi, overtaking the princes' cart about a mile from the walls. Affecting now to believe that the crowd would prevent him getting his captives any further, Hodson turned to Macdowell and said, 'What shall we do with them? I think we had better shoot them here. We shall never get them in.'

He ordered his troopers to surround the cart, told the captives to strip off their clothes, and, calling out that the princes had massacred British women and children and that the Government had now sent him to punish them, took a carbine from one of his men and shot all three princes dead.

The effect was marvellous [Macdowell thought]. The Mussulmans seemed struck with a wholesome idea of retribution, and the Sikhs shouted with delight, while the mass moved off slowly and silently. One of the sowars pointed out to me a man running across a piece of cultivated ground with arms gleaming in the sunlight. I and the sowar rode after him when I discovered it was the King's favourite eunuch of whose atrocities we had heard so much. The sowar cut him down instantly . . . It was now four o'clock . . . The cart containing the bodies was driven to the most public street where all might see them. Side by side they lay, where four months earlier, on the same spot, they had outraged and murdered our women.[17]

Hodson went to bed 'very tired but very much satisfied with [his] day's work'. 'I cannot help being pleased with the warm congratulations I received on all sides for my success in destroying the enemies of our race,' he wrote. 'The whole nation will rejoice.'[18] He had taken a turquoise armlet and some signet rings from the 'rascally princes' as well as their swords, thinking it would be 'quite something hereafter to wear a sword taken from the last of the House of Timour'. 'If I ever part with it,' he added, having had to hand over the jewellery he had appropriated, 'it shall be to . . . our good Queen. She ought to give me her own Cross for it, and that's a fact, though I say it myself . . . Tombs declares I shall get a C.B. . . . and, between ourselves, I *ought* to have anything they can give me, for it was a fearful risk.'[19]

Hodson's execution of the princes was later condemned by several of his contemporaries, but at the time few were either surprised or shocked, or, indeed, other than gratified by what he had done. Contemplating the princes' corpses in the Chandni Chowk, naked but for a cloth covering part of their loins, Captain Griffiths and his companions could not feel any pity in their 'hearts for the wretches on whom had fallen a most righteous retribution for their crimes'.[20] Henry Ouvry, though 'sick of blood', grimly accepted the fact that many others would have to be dealt with in the same way. 'We shall,' he said, 'have to execute a vast number before we are done.'[21]

No time was lost in the fulfilment of this aim. Gallows were immediately erected in the city, and the hangings began. Natives suspected of complicity with the mutineers were brought forward to be tried by military or special commissions, all of which were granted plenary powers. If an officer more tender-hearted than most pleaded for restraint he was sure to be overruled by such stern and masterful avengers as Sir Theophilus Metcalfe whose victims were hanged from the charred beams of his house.[22]

John Lawrence's was one of the few voices raised in condemnation of the vengeance perpetrated under martial law in Delhi. 'I do hope that your Lordship will put an end to martial law and looting in Delhi,' Lawrence wrote to Canning on 4 December. 'I am a strong advocate of prompt and severe punishment when such has been deserved. But the systematic spoliation which I understand goes on at Delhi cannot fail to exasperate the natives, and render more wide and lasting the breach which has taken place between them and us.'[23] When the spoliation nevertheless continued, Lawrence wrote to General Penny, Commander in Delhi, who had not intervened to stop it:

I wish I could induce you to interfere in this matter. I believe we shall lastingly, and, indeed, justly be abused for the way in which we have despoiled all classes without distinction . . . I have even heard, though it seems incredible, that officers have gone about and murdered natives in cold blood. You may depend upon it we cannot allow such acts to pass unnoticed. If we have no higher motives, the common dictates of policy should make us refrain from such outrages . . . Unless we endeavour to distinguish friend from foe, we shall unite all classes against us.[24]

It was not, however, until February 1858 that Lawrence had his way and the administration of the city was transferred to the Punjab Government. By then hundreds of natives had been shot or hanged while British officers sat by puffing contentedly on their cigars and soldiers evidently bribed the executioners to keep the condemned men 'a long time hanging, as they liked to see the criminals dance a "Pandies' hornpipe" as they termed the dying struggles of the wretches'.[25] 'Lots of blackguards are hanged every morning,' Thomas Cadell, who had won the Victoria Cross during the siege, wrote home to his sister with satisfaction. 'The more the merrier . . . I am delighted to see that the good folks at home hate the Pandies almost as much as we do . . . You say Delhi ought to be thoroughly destroyed. We all say the same.'[26]

There has been nothing but shooting these villains for the past three days [wrote Hugh Chichester in the same vein]. Some 300 or 400 were shot yesterday . . . There are several mosques in the city most beautiful to look at. But I should like to see them all destroyed. The rascally brutes desecrated our churches and graveyards, and I do not think we ought to have any regard for their stinking religion. One was always supposed to take off one's shoes on going to visit one of these mosques, or to have an interview with the King. But these little affairs we drop now. I have seen the old Pig of a King. He is a very old man and just like an old *Khitmugar*.[27]

Kendal Coghill, who 'had the satisfaction of receiving him over as a prisoner', also 'could not help' calling the King a pig, though he knew 'it was not a manly thing to do'. 'I would have shot him dead,' Coghill added, 'if he had only looked up, the brute.'[28] Others, though, when they saw the old man lying quietly on his charpoy, his 'mild countenance displaying no signs of cruelty', felt an unexpected compassion.[29] He looked so hopeless and helpless, his white beard unbrushed, his white conical-shaped turban none too clean, 'rambling on about his dreams and quoting verses of his own composition' or gazing at the floor while, as though in mockery of his former greatness, two attendants stood at his back waving over his head large peacock-feather fans, emblems of sovereignty.[30]

He seemed very miserable [wrote one visitor]. He was lying on his charpoy with his knees up, smoking a hookah which was supplied with rose water. He is a lean and slippered old man with a large Roman nose and a rather stupid expression, probably from his constant smoking. He has his favourite Queen in another room and eight or ten female slaves . . . the officer in charge showed us the square where the harem was which was very filthy as were most of the beauties. Many of them were also very old and ugly. My romantic notions respecting an Eastern harem were quite dissipated.[31]

The palace had by then been thoroughly ransacked and looted. When Mrs Muter, who claimed to be the first woman to enter Delhi after the siege, came to inspect it, she was horrified by its dilapidated state, 'the dirt that overlaid everything', dulling the paint and sullying the marble.[32]

The Sikhs, masters of plunder, had been amongst the first to break into it. Richard Barter, who had seen them at work, marvelled at their greed and destructiveness:

I never saw such fellows for loot, nothing escaped them, and they were sure to destroy what they could not take away. I have walked up to my knees in tea which they had thrown out into the street, shouting the while with mischief and laughter like a lot of schoolboys. And I have seen a fellow admire himself and after arranging his moustache at a huge mirror walk to the end of the room and deliberately fire at his own reflection in it. I saw them on another occasion busily engaged with clubs and muskets smashing magnificent chandeliers.[33]

By the time the Sikhs had worked their way through the palace, there was, as Dr Wise sadly noted, 'little of value left amidst the piles of old clothes and bottles of medicines'. Wise himself found nothing but a Persian book. Hugh Chichester discovered only a few pairs of silk pyjamas; and Stewart Lithgow 'one or two Hindostanee books, two little bottles of scent . . . and a pair of *Ladies unmentionables* in lace or silk!'[34]

Elsewhere the amount of loot collected by both native and European troops was enormous. Captain Griffiths, who saw a heap of plunder many feet high at the Kashmir Gate on 20 September, said that arguments ending in fights and even in bloodshed often took place in houses where soldiers were dividing their spoil, and that

each street was filled with a mass of debris, all lying in inextricable confusion . . . We entered several of the large houses belonging to the wealthier class of natives and found every one in the same condition, turned inside out, their ornaments torn to pieces, costly articles, too heavy to remove, battered into fragments . . . We saw parties of Europeans and native soldiers, all eager in pursuit of plunder, going from house to house, or diving down courts and alleys when they saw us approaching. Interference or remonstrance with these men would have been useless, if not dangerous; in their excited state they were no respecters of persons, and we deemed it the better judgement to take no notice of their actions . . . To my certain knowledge many soldiers of the English regiments got possession of jewellery and gold ornaments taken from the bodies of the slain city inhabitants, and I was shown by men of my regiment strings of pearls and gold *mohurs* which had fallen into their hands . . . That many of the private soldiers of my regiment succeeded in acquiring a great quantity of valuable plunder was fully demonstrated soon after our return to England. An unusual number of non-commissioned officers and men bought their discharge, having kept possession of the plunder acquired at Delhi awaiting a favourable opportunity for the sale of the articles.[35]

The officers were quite as avaricious as the men. 'I fancy every officer present at the siege might be able to retire at once,' a surgeon wrote. 'The plunder daily being found in the city is more than enormous. It is almost incredible.'[36] Captain Griffiths admitted that he was as greedy for plunder as anyone, and that he often went about in search of loot, meeting other officers on the same errand who, after 'interrogations and many jokes', would affirm 'that looting was not the object of their perambulations but that they were only inspecting the houses out of a feeling of curiosity'.[37]

After some sort of order had been restored in Delhi prize agents were appointed; and thereafter the search for plunder could only be carried out by those who obtained official digging tickets. Armed with these tickets, with guides, coolies, pickaxes, shovels, tape-measures, crowbars, and iron sounding-rods, officers, civilians and their wives went out on treasure-hunts all over the city, into houses and Hindu temples, shops and offices, pouring water over the floors, as the Sikhs did, to 'observe where it sank through fastest'. Many searched for days without finding anything of value or interest. Others were amply rewarded. Captain Muter, setting out one morning with a troop of coolies after an early breakfast, found by careful measurement a concealed space in a house and returned with thirteen wagonloads of treasure including 80,000 rupees.[38] Captain Griffiths and a friend, with the help of a mason who had sealed it up behind a wall for one of his rich employers, discovered an earthenware jar containing jewellery and precious stones worth over £7,000.[39] Mrs Tytler unearthed several beautiful ornaments as well as a wonderful silken garment with passages from the Koran worked into the fabric which the King was supposed to have worn during the siege.[40] The Wagentreibers, after long and fruitless searches, were led by their guide to a 'wretched little place' in the heart of the city where, to their astonishment, in a dark and poky room, behind a pile of onions in a niche in the wall, they uncovered seven bags filled with gold and silver coins. Later they discovered jewellery and silver boxes, ancient coins, an exquisite lizard cut from a single emerald and so many other treasures that when they rebuilt their house outside Delhi they were able to fill it 'from floor to ceiling with all the wonderful things collected in those eventful days'.[41]

Although much, perhaps most, of the treasure unearthed was appropriated by those who discovered it, an enormous quantity was handed over to the prize agents who seem to have added to their collections by the most ruthless methods.

They caught a very nice fat sleek-looking Hindoo who they felt assured was a man of property [wrote Lieutenant A. H. Lindsay of the Bengal Horse Artillery]. He refused for a long time to confess where his money was concealed, so they shut him up in a dark cellar and fired pistols over his head until he got into such a state of alarm that he told them where they could find Rs. 50,000 of his own and Rs. 40,000 of a friend of his, who he was determined should not get off scot free. The next day they got hold of another corpulent nigger, who however was up to the dodge of the pistols, and did not even care [about] knives being thrown all round him, after the manner of the Chinese jugglers, so they loaded a pistol before his eyes, and sent the bullet through his turban, which he thought was getting beyond a joke, so he divulged the whereabouts of Rs. 40,000. What would Bright and Cobden & Co say if they knew this.[42]

The more valuable articles discovered by these means were offered for sale in a marquee on the roof of a house overlooking the *Diwan-i-Khas*. Here, in chests and iron strong boxes, displayed on tables and draped over chairs, were hundreds of Cashmere shawls and silks, kincobs and fans, swords, daggers and fowling-pieces, pearls and emeralds, rings and bracelets, gold bangles and exquisite filigree ornaments.

For many disappointed men their opportunities of sharing in the further plunder of Delhi came to an end on 24 September when a column, over 2,500 strong, was dispatched from Delhi under the command of Colonel Edward Greathed to pursue the mutineers who were now pouring across the Doab into Oudh. These men could never forget their march across Delhi down the Chandni Chowk to the Grand Trunk Road.

It was simply awful [Richard Barter recalled]. Our advance guard, consisting of cavalry and artillery, had burst and squashed the dead bodies which lay swelled to an enormous size, and the stench was fearful. Men and officers were sick all round and I thought we were never to get through the city. Anticipating something of this kind I had stowed away in my holster pipes a bottle of Eau de Cologne which I had looted out of a shop in the city and this I have to thank for not having suffered so much as the rest; all the same it was a ride I don't care to have to take again. The horse felt it as much as I did, for he snorted and shook as he slid rather than walked over the abominations which covered the street, and was continually starting for fear, or stumbling against a dead body in the dark. At length we reached the bridge of boats and crossed the Jumna to the open country beyond, sniffing with delight the pure atmosphere after what we had gone through.[43]

To those left in Delhi the city now seemed like a deserted charnel house. Since there was no means of feeding them, thousands of inhabitants had been expelled and escorted out into the country, many of them being forced to give up their bundles of possessions to the soldiers at the gates.[44] 'It was a melancholy sight seeing them trooping out of the town,' Captain Griffiths thought, 'hundreds passing through the Lahore Gate every day for a whole week. We were told that provisions had been collected for their use at a place some miles distant, and it is to be hoped the poor creatures were saved from starvation; but we had our doubts on the subject, and, knowing how callous with regard to human suffering the authorities had become, I fear that many perished from want and exposure.'[45]

Those too ill or old to leave, huddled, half-starved, in cellars, so that the streets were silent and empty apart from the parties of marauders and looters, the cats on the roofs of the houses, the tame monkeys chattering with fear, the pet birds dying in their cages, and the rotting corpses of men and camels which lay where they had fallen, poisoning the air and making Kendal Coghill think that the sanitary arrangements of the city could not have been worse managed even if they had been entrusted to an Irish District Council.[46]

Walking these streets at night, officers and men found themselves talking in whispers as though afraid of disturbing the dead.

There was something so strange and weird in every sound made in those silent streets, which echoed to our footfalls like a city of the dead [an officer recorded]. Here and there a dog lay crouching at a body, or a vulture, completely gorged and unable to rise, flapped aside at our approach with outspread wings and head dabbled and matted with blood. And some bodies lay with arms lifted as if beckoning in such a strangely life-like manner that we walked up and examined them to see if they really were corpses. When we stood still the silence became really awful, and we all breathed more freely as we returned to our quarters in the mosque.[47]

Greathed's column, thankful to be out in the clearer air beyond the Jumna, marched up the Grand Trunk Road through villages which had been plundered by the Goojurs or which, having escaped destruction, were now burned by British soldiers in revenge for their inhabitants having 'befriended the enemy and kept them in supplies'.[48] 'Our cavalry surround the place,' Lieutenant Coghill explained, 'and we walk in, turn the women and children out, sack the place and fire it – any that try to escape the flames get cut up. Sometimes by forced marches we have the luck to get two villages in a night . . . You should see the wholesome funk we have established over the country.'[49]

As he advanced in pursuit of the fleeing rebels, Greathed was himself pursued by a succession of urgent letters, 'written in every language, living and dead . . . beseeching, commanding him to hasten at his utmost speed' to the help of the garrison at Agra.[50] The European families there, incarcerated in the fort for the past few months, were in terror of attack from a huge force of rebels from Central India, reinforced by mutineers from Delhi and Gwalior. Greathed felt sure that the people at Agra were in no such danger as they claimed to be, but he decided to respond to their urgent pleas.[51] So, turning aside, the column headed for Agra, marching forty-four miles in twenty-eight hours and reaching the bridge beneath the walls of the fort on the morning of 10 October. Who were these 'dreadful-looking men?' a lady in the fort wanted to know as she looked down upon the dirty figures of the sunburned, unshaven men of the 8th Queen's. Surely they 'must be Afghans'? Captain Barter overheard another lady remark disapprovingly in by no means whispered accents... ' "Did you ever see such a dirty-looking lot?" '[52]

A few weeks before, Greathed's column would not have been accorded so disparaging a welcome. News of the fall of Delhi had been greeted in the fort by cheers and flag waving. Bands had played celebratory airs; and a salute of guns had sent such a shower of stone chips and fragments of mortar hurtling from the walls that the engineers were thankful that the embrasures had not been put to a test of their strength in the face of the enemy.[53] But since then there had seemed little cause for celebration. The native inhabitants of Agra refused to believe that Delhi had fallen; the Rajah of Dholpore, on being told why the guns at Agra were firing a salute, laughed and said that that sort of device would not delude *him*; and when the mutineers in flight from Delhi arrived at Muttra to announce that they had left the city only because the English there had all been destroyed ('apart from a handful not worth bothering about'), they were given a most flattering reception by the townspeople who went out to meet them, 'carrying offerings of flowers and sweetmeats, preceded by Brahmins singing hymns'.[54]

In Agra the Europeans heard of the mutineers' arrival at Muttra with terror. Mark Thornhill had spent the day at the Taj Mahal and had arrived back at the gateway to the fort at sunset.

There [so he recorded], we found the greatest confusion. For nearly a quarter of a mile the road was completely blocked by a mass of men, carts and animals. The crowd was so dense that it was hopeless to attempt to get through it in the carriage. We alighted, and even then, surrounded by our servants, it was with the greatest difficulty that we managed to force our way to the drawbridge. There the confusion and struggling baffled description. The crowd, which was nearly entirely composed of natives, were half frantic with terror and excitement. Each time the gates swung open they surged in, in such a mass as several times actually carrying away the sentry with them. I saw him more than once lifted completely off the ground, and forced back some yards before he could extricate himself. The crowd seemed to think that the mutineers were close behind them.[55]

When Greathed arrived in Agra the panic had subsided. Most of the mutineers who had arrived at Muttra from Delhi had dispersed to their homes. The others, whose reported approach upon Agra had been responsible for the flood of letters handed to Greathed during his march up the Great Trunk Road, were now said to have retired nine miles. The column was 'not really needed', after all. Thus it was that the ladies, looking down upon it from the walls of the fort, watched it pass with expressions of disgust at its dirtiness rather than of gratitude for its prompt arrival. Greathed took his men to the parade-ground south of the fort where some went immediately to sleep while others had their breakfast, bargained with native vendors of drinks and sweetmeats, or talked to the soldiers of the garrison who had strolled down from the fort.[56] Most of the civilians in the fort had also wandered down to the parade-ground; so had thousands of the inhabitants of the city who had come out 'to watch the camp being pitched, and to see what was going on'.[57] It seemed 'like a fair more than anything else'.[58]

No picquets were posted, no patrols sent out into the surrounding fields where high crops stood beneath the morning sun. The night before, one of the civilian so-called volunteers from the fort unwillingly acting as sentry had twice reported to the officer on duty the sound of tramping feet, as of a large column on the march. He had been told that he must have imagined it: there were no troops anywhere near Agra.[59]

On the parade-ground a party of Sikhs and 9th Lancers sat watching a group of jugglers who came towards them 'throwing balls and doing tricks' when 'all of a sudden' the jugglers threw off their costumes and, drawing swords, revealed themselves as Muslim fanatics.[60] They rushed upon the cavalrymen and Sikhs slashing to right and left, as two troops of rebel cavalry galloped out from the crops and heavy guns began firing on the camp. At the noise of the firing, the people from the fort, the inhabitants of the city and the tradesmen from the bazaar all turned and fled for their lives.

Instantly, elephants, camels, horses, *doolie*-bearers carrying the sick and wounded, bullocks yoked to heavily-laden carts, all becoming panic-stricken, turned round and joined in the stampede [Frederick Roberts recalled]. Elephants, as terrified as their mahouts, shuffled along, screaming and trumpeting; drivers twisted the tails of their long-suffering bullocks with more than usual energy and heartlessness, in the vain hope of goading them into a gallop; and camels had their nostrils rent asunder by the men in charge of them, in their unsuccessful endeavours to urge their phlegmatic animals into something faster than their ordinary stately pace.[61]

Although taken so completely by surprise, the British troops reacted with a promptness and energy that one observer described as 'simply astonishing'. An officer galloped off to the fort to fetch Greathed who had gone there for breakfast; the infantry rushed to seize their arms; the cavalry to saddle their horses. The Bengal Artillery, though in quarters 'never the most amiable or the best disciplined' of troops, demonstrated once more that on service they were 'certainly inferior to none'.[62] 'The round shot were coming in pretty fast,' Captain Barter wrote, 'and it was really beautiful to see the artillery prepare for service. Their guns were all in park and horses unharnessed and yet it was perfectly marvellous the rapidity with which they got into action, the enemy shot all the time rattling amongst the guns and limbers.'[63]

Within minutes the British force was ready to repel the attack, many of the 75th in their shirt-sleeves, some of the 9th Lancers still in their stockinged feet. The troops in the fort marched out to support them, wearing 'bright new uniforms', fifes playing, drums beating, bayonets gleaming in the sunlight, making the walls 're-echo with the tramp of the footsteps as they fell to the time of the music'.[64] But their help was not needed. By the time they reached the parade-ground the rebels had broken and fled, losing all their guns and ammunition, chased away through the crops of *bajra* whose tall shattered stalks indicated the path of their flight. Stewart Lithgow of the 75th, who had mistaken the enemy's first shots for Sikhs potting at pigeons, wrote:

It was really a very pretty sight ... We advanced through the crops which reached over our heads. We were in the centre, a Regiment of Seikhs on our left, the bright scarlet jackets and white cap covers of the 3rd Europeans on our right, with skirmishers thrown out in front, all pressing forward ... I have never seen so many dead pandies as I did on that day, the road being perfectly strewed with bodies.[65]

The Sikhs dismounted to strip and plunder the dead Muslim fanatics whom they detested for they had a far longer and fiercer tradition of hostility to Muslim rule than they had to the British. They rolled the bodies over on to their backs and slashed at their faces as they shouted, 'Take this for the Prophet, and this, and this, and this for the three Imaums!'[66]

Elsewhere in the countryside around Delhi other rebel forces had also been driven off by British troops. General Van Cortland had carried out successful operations in the districts to the north-west, Brigadier Showers in the west and south-west. Colonel Gerrard, though mortally wounded as he sat resplendent in red coat covered with medals on a snow-white Arab horse, had defeated the mutineers of the Jodhpur Legion at Narnul. By the end of November the whole of the Delhi area – over which tens of thousands of Indians wandered homeless and hungry – had been freed of mutineers, if not yet of violence and disorder. There were, though, hard battles still to be fought to the west in Oudh.

18

Scorched Earth

*· Looting in Lucknow · Havelock and Outram still surrounded there –
the second siege · and savage fighting, 25 September to end of
October 1857 · Kavanagh's escape through the enemy lines, 9 November ·
Sir Colin Campbell's army marches from Cawnpore
to relief of Lucknow · second relief of Lucknow, 17 November ·*

As in Delhi so in Lucknow, victory was followed by looting. The troops who had followed Havelock and Outram into the Residency spent most of their first days there plundering the surrounding palaces. Beds and palanquins loaded with piles of silk, looking-glasses, gilded furniture, brocaded turbans, damascened swords and velvet saddles kept passing in an apparently endless stream through the Baillie Guard Gate.

Everywhere might be seen people helping themselves to whatever they pleased [wrote L. E. R. Rees]. Plunder was the order of the day. Jewels, shawls, dresses, pieces of satin, broadcloths ... the most magnificent divan carpets studded with pearls ... books, pictures, European clocks, English clothes, full-dress officers' uniforms, epaulettes, aiguillettes, manuscripts, charms; vehicles of the most grotesque forms, shaped like fish, dragons and sea horses; representations of the prophet's hands; cups, saucers, cooking utensils, chinaware enough to set up fifty merchants in Lombard Street; scientific instruments, ivory, telescopes, pistols ...[1]

The sight of all this plunder passing into the compound, together with camels, bullocks, wounded men on *doolies* and baggage of all description, struck Brigadier Inglis's orderly as 'more like Donnybrook fair than anything else'.[2]

Officers joined in the search with their men. George Blake of the 84th got hold of 'eleven very fair pearls', but he had to sell them 'to a native for £5 in order to buy necessities'. His men endeavoured to make up for this, however, by presenting him with the milk of a goat they had stolen together with 'twenty yards of very fine silk'.[3]

Although the amount of plunder collected was immense, provisions were in very short supply. Apart from a few pounds of tea, a small store of grain, some rice, spices and vegetables, 'and one or two bales of that much-prized article, tobacco', there was very little else to be found.[4] And what there was did not last long, even though some items fetched enormous prices, bacon selling for over two pounds a pound, sugar fetching thirty-two shillings a pound and penny cheroots going for eight shillings each.[5] Men took to following Outram about, ready to pounce on his cigar butts the moment he dropped them.[6]

A few days after the relieving force entered Lucknow it was discovered that the stores of grain were not nearly as bad as Inglis had supposed, for an enormous pile was discovered in the swimming-bath. Yet all the Lucknow diarists continued to lament the scarcity of rations. Mrs Inglis still had a better store than most of beef, rice, dhal and chupatties. Guests at Martin Gubbins's table never had cause for complaint. They still enjoyed tinned salmon and carrots at dinner, as well as rice puddings, with one glass of sherry and two of champagne or claret for each man, rather less for the ladies. Tea was served by Mrs Gubbins' English maid, Chivers, three times a day with not only sugar but also milk, which was provided by the host's surviving goats.[7] Gubbins' seemingly inexhaustible stocks caused much resentment in other houses. Dr Hadow recorded:

Mr Gubbins is not at all liked in the garrison . . . He was not popular in Lucknow, even before the siege . . . Though I was latterly consistently in his house, attending Adair and L'Estrange, and was almost starving, at least ravenous for food, I never even had a chupatti offered to me – and in their compound was a swimming bath that I bathed in at first but very soon I was given to understand that they would rather I gave up my daily bathe there as I was not one of *their* garrison. [However] . . . I think it unfair to cry Gubbins down because he did not supply us all with luxuries of which he certainly had plenty for his own garrison . . . They would not have gone far if given out [to everyone] . . . He very wisely lay in supplies for the siege and fortunate indeed were those whom he received into his house.[8]

In other houses also there were occasional treats: Dr Fayrer once shot one hundred and fifty sparrows which were made into a curry. Captain Barrow was pursued one day by a little boy screaming at the top of his voice, 'Come to dinner, we've got a pudding!'[9] For a time excellent biscuits could be bought at six rupees a seer from a man who set up a bakery stocked with wheat plundered from the palaces and stolen from the garrison commissariat; but his stocks were soon exhausted.[10]

So, with very few exceptions, everyone within the Residency compound had cause to lament the poor fare to which the advent of so many more mouths to feed had reduced them. Rations of dhal had eventually to be stopped; the 'modicum of salt' was reduced to one and a half ounces; allowances of ground wheat to one pound, and of rice to four ounces; the ration of plain coarse beef from slaughtered gun-bullocks had also to be reduced from twelve to six ounces a day; 'those eternal chupatties' remained the staple food.[11] Both women and sepoys received less than British soldiers, and the camp-followers less than either. Even so, not everyone received even the meagre rations to which they were entitled. Mrs Case, who had to content herself with one chupatty a day and 'make do for the rest with grain', said that some soldiers were so hungry that they would 'do anything to obtain food'. Whenever they saw 'cooking going on' they would 'seize on a chupatti and leave a rupee in its place'.[12] Rees admitted that on going to call on a friend who was not at home he found a bone on an empty plate, picked it up and gnawed at it.[13]

Many soldiers risked their lives for food. Arthur Owen of the Madras Fusiliers, seeing a man carrying a sack of wheat-meal back to his quarters under fire, ran out to bargain with him for part of its contents. During the discussion the man was shot full in the chest; so Owen grabbed the whole sack and ran back to his gun emplacement with it.[14] One heavily-built officer's constant readiness to volunteer for sorties beyond the defences was supposed to be due solely to his hope of finding food in houses to be wrested from the enemy.[15] Certainly the enemy exasperated the British by jeering at them and flaunting chickens and chupatties on the ends of long poles while their bands played, 'God Save the Queen' and 'The Girl I Left Behind Me'.[16]

Havelock had never supposed that provisioning his force would present any problems. But this was now Outram's responsibility, for within hours of their arrival in Lucknow he had taken over command, leaving Havelock free to read his Bible and the military episodes in Macaulay's *History of England* and to enjoy for his health's sake the occasional 'excellent bottle of sherry' presented to him by Martin Gubbins.[17] Outram had not expected to be long in Lucknow. He had hoped that, once he had got his wounded and the rearguard in, the army would be able to set out again, escorting the former garrison to Cawnpore. But although the casualties incurred in the final assault on the city were not as heavy as he had at first feared, they had reduced the numbers of the relieving force by well over five hundred; and many of the mutineers who had fled from the city during the night of 25 September were gradually coming back, encouraged to do so by the sight of the severed heads of British soldiers who had had to be left behind in the city when a party, sent out to bring in the wounded, came under such heavy fire that not all of them could be saved. Joined by hundreds of mutineers from Delhi, the Lucknow rebels, so Outram calculated, soon numbered over one hundred thousand men. Indeed, at the end of the first week of October he was forced to conclude that not only was his force too small in comparison with that of the enemy for him to escape from Lucknow – even if transport could be found for the women, children and wounded – his position was actually 'more untenable than that of the previous garrison'. For he had been 'obliged to occupy the neighbouring palaces outside the entrenchment to accommodate the Europeans; and the enemy were able to mine these palaces from the cover of nearby buildings'. Moreover, there was 'little prospect of procuring provisions', the sorties sent out for them having returned empty-handed 'at much cost of life'. Outram's concern was obvious to all. One night, when his private secretary came into his room, he found him kneeling on his bed, his head on the pillow, deep in prayer.[18]

For a time Outram considered the possibility of leaving the 90th Regiment in Lucknow and marching to Cawnpore with the remainder of his force. But after the discovery of the grain in the swimming-bath which – provided they ate the artillery bullocks as well – would ensure at least that the garrison would not starve, he decided to remain.

So, placing Havelock in command of the new posts and leaving Inglis in control of the old, Outram contented himself with repairing the defences and with extending his perimeter, which was pushed out to the river on the north and to the Tehri Koti, Farhat Buksh and Chattar Manzil in the east. Yet while these extensions ensured that some houses, like Fayrer's and Gubbins's, became relatively secure, the danger from enemy shelling increased. When the rebel guns had been close, many if not most of their shells had passed over their target; but now a far higher proportion landed on it. Thus it was, as Martin Gubbins noted, 'that upon many days which appeared to be the quietest, when neither the enemy attacked, nor we had made a sortie, severe casualties would occur'. One morning at the beginning of November, for example, when danger seemed far away, an ensign lost both his legs while sketching in what he had supposed to be a peaceful spot; and four soldiers were wounded, two of them mortally.[19]

Steady casualties were also incurred during the frequent sorties on enemy gun emplacements and houses used by snipers, particularly amongst the men of the 32nd who, in spite of Inglis's protestations, were sent out regularly by Outram, being 'best acquainted with the ground'.[20] So it was that, week by week, the numbers of wounded in the hospitals mounted, while medical supplies dwindled and chloroform eventually became unobtainable. 'None who are badly wounded', commented Mrs Brydon, 'ever seem to come out of hospital', amputations being invariably followed by gangrene or necrosis of the bone.[21] 'The scenes of this hospital are past belief,' wrote John Blick Spurgin. 'Two hundred and upward lying side by side, sick and wounded, and our poor good ladies walking about, bathing the heads, and soothing the dying.'[22]

The fighting was more savage than ever, all prisoners being slaughtered out of hand. 'I proceeded to deal with the prisoners, marching them down to where my guard was stationed,' recorded George Blake of one wholesale execution. 'I told the guard that any man who wanted to fire off his musket (in case of damp) might come and shoot a sepoy. Several men at once came forward and I told them to march the prisoners down to the river bank to avoid having to carry the bodies there. Only one prisoner – a low-caste man – fell at my feet and asked for mercy. I told him that the only mercy I'd give him was to have him shot first. All the rest died bravely and their bodies were hove into the river.'[23]

Another sepoy 'tried hard to be spared, but a soldier said to him, "You black rascal, do you think we are going to carry your ugly face all over the face of the blessed earth?" Saying this, he ran him through with his bayonet.'[24] So indiscriminate in killing natives did the British become, in fact, that the loyal sepoys of the garrison who were sent out on sorties had to be given special bright red armbands so that there could be no excuse for men who claimed that they had shot them in error. There was none of the camaraderie between Indian and European soldiers that there had been on the Delhi Ridge. When native soldiers and pensioners were rewarded for their continuing loyalty and 'returned from the General's presence with joyful countenances', the European soldiers – whose recompense was left to the future orders of the Government of India – cried out, 'Damn those black fellows! There they go – as usual, petted and rewarded while we get nothing.'[25]

Most of the fighting during these weeks in Lucknow was done underground. Stocks of gunpowder were not considered sufficient to allow the blowing up of every mine detected, so it became common practice to dig shafts and tunnels, then break through into the enemy's mine and drive the occupants out of it, endeavouring to shoot or capture the enemy miners.[26] This kind of fighting most British soldiers disliked even more than street-fighting, for, as one of them put it, 'down below is very different from up above'.[27]

One man who did not appear to share the general fear of counter-mining was Thomas Kavanagh, a tall, muscular, talkative and ludicrously vain Irishman of thirty-six who was appointed assistant to Captain Crommelin, the Field Engineer. Before the siege he had been a disgruntled, impoverished junior clerk who had narrowly escaped dismissal on landing himself heavily in debt to various native money-lenders. The siege seemed to him, as he confessed himself, the only opportunity he would ever have of showing the world that he was worthy of higher regard than his past career had accorded him.

Wearing a specially constructed suit of coarse canvas, Kavanagh would sit at the end of tunnels for hours, pistol in hand, listening for the sound of spades and picks, waiting for the wall of earth to crumble, and then firing at the rebel miners as it collapsed. On one occasion, having fired, he dashed through the hole between the two mines and ran to grab the tools which lay near the bottom of the enemy shaft. At the top of the shaft he could hear the voices of excited sepoys. As one of them appeared, he shot him in the stomach. The others clustered round the top of the shaft where Kavanagh taunted them with cowardice until a volley of musket balls drove him back to his own tunnel. He soon returned, however, with two Sikhs, shouting more abuse at the sepoys and warning them that their faithlessness and cruelty had ensured their ruin. The sepoys tried to argue with him, but one of their officers appeared and they opened fire again. After this fresh volley Kavanagh dashed forward once more and seized the tools. As he carried them back, the mutineers hastily filled in their shaft with earth.[28]

When reports reached the Residency that a relieving force under command of Sir Colin Campbell was approaching Lucknow, Kavanagh decided that he could achieve wider fame and honour by acting as messenger than as Assistant Field Engineer. He approached Sir James Outram with the suggestion that he should disguise himself as a native and slip out through the enemy lines with dispatches for Sir Colin whom he could then guide back to the Residency. Outram was at first reluctant to accept the Irishman's offer. He reminded him of the dangers, and of the fate that would overtake him were he to be caught. But Kavanagh was insistent, and it was agreed that he should go.

On the evening of 9 November, he crept out of the Residency lines accompanied by a cunning native spy, Kanauji Lal, who had formerly been employed in a court of law as a *nazir*. Kavanagh was wearing native clothes, his hair tucked into a turban and his face darkened with oil and lampblack. A pistol was secured in his belt so that he could shoot himself if captured. He and his companion passed silently through Lucknow, keeping to the shadows; but beyond the canal they lost their way in the Dilkusha park, and wandered about in the darkness until they came upon a peasant whom they asked to guide them to the Alambagh. The peasant, however, said that he was lame and could not help them, so they went on until they found themselves in a small village. Here Kavanagh crawled into one of the huts, feeling his way on hands and knees until his fingers closed upon a woman's thigh. Begging her not to be alarmed, he whispered that he and his companion were lost and that they were looking for someone to show them the way; so the woman woke her mother and together the two women pointed out the road.

As they proceeded the moon came up; but although it enabled them to pick their way more easily across the rough countryside, they themselves were now more clearly visible. Suddenly, in a mango grove, they ran into a patrol of sepoys. Kanauji Lal, terrified, threw away his copy of the dispatches, but Kavanagh managed to keep his nerve. They were, he said, poor travellers on their way to a village near Bani to report the death of a friend's brother. This story was believed, and the sepoys allowed them to pass. An hour later, after crossing a swamp whose muddy waters reached their waists, they finally stumbled into an outlying picquet of Sir Colin Campbell's force.[29]

Sir Colin Campbell had arrived in Calcutta to take up his duties as Commander-in-Chief three months before. He had struck Lady Canning as being much more companionable than Sir James Outram. 'Very amiable and cheerful', she thought him, if 'an endless talker and *raconteur*'.[30] Officers who met him for the first time, though warned of his ferocious temper, found him 'a very nice old fellow indeed . . . just the man to do the thing properly'. He was certainly 'a tough old buck'.[31] The son of a Glasgow carpenter named John Macliver, Sir Colin, who had adopted the name Campbell as a *nom de guerre*, had been in the Army for nearly fifty years, and had served in Spain as a young officer under Wellington and more recently as commander of the 1st Division in the Crimea. Promotion to high rank had not come quickly: it was only after thirty years' service that he had become a colonel. But Sir Colin had always been more noted for thoroughness and care than for dispatch. This was surprising, one of his officers thought, for his quick movements, his sharp, pink, lively face with its crop of curly, crisp grey hair led one to suppose that he would prove 'dashing rather than prudent'. But so cautious did he prove to be that he was to become known in the Army as 'Sir Crawling Camel'. 'He was utterly devoid of dash,' Captain Barter wrote, expressing a rather unjust but widespread opinion. 'His whole thoughts were centred on a peerage and he'd risk nothing for fear of losing it, nay more he'd sacrifice all and anybody for its attainment . . . A brave man undoubtedly, but too cautious for India, and too selfish for any place.'[32]

It was not Sir Colin's fault, however, that the reinforcements from the Cape and elsewhere that arrived at intervals in the muddy, corpse-strewn waters of the Hugli River at Calcutta should have been so slow in reaching Cawnpore. Soon after docking they were sent up by rail to Raniganj, one hundred and twenty miles from Calcutta; but the rest of the journey to Allahabad had to be made in those clumsy, creaking, lumbering bullock-wagons so execrated by generations of British soldiers.

The railway journey was tedious but not otherwise unpleasant. Looking out of the windows of his carriage and thankful to escape from the damp, oppressive atmosphere of Calcutta, Lieutenant Robert Biddulph, one of the many young English officers now arriving in India for the first time, could almost fancy himself at home again. Everything was so green; even the trees looked English; only the parrots sitting on the telegraph wires, and the natives lying in the pools of water to keep cool, with 'nothing but their brown heads poking out, like buffaloes', made him realize how far he was from home. Then he thought of 'the dreadful heat', and of how unpleasant life was going to be unless the army could find more honest servants.[33] So far, there had been 'the greatest difficulty' in getting hold of any servants at all, other than the 'kind of small, bandy-legged, ugly-faced villain' that Lieutenant Nicholl of the Rifle Brigade picked up in Calcutta.[34]

They are all afraid to come [Biddulph explained to a friend], and it is a very serious inconvenience in a country where no Europeans can go out in the sun between 8 a.m. and 4 p.m. And one is obliged to have so many of them . . . They are so slow, but beat them with a big stick for their slowness and stupidity, they would only immediately run away . . . They are thorough savages in spite of the number of years that the Europeans have been with them. Nearly all the women have large rings through their noses, from one to two inches in diameter, hanging down right over their mouths. The men nearly all daub their faces with clay and paint and the height of dandyism seems to be to stick a red wafer in the middle of their noses. They are very humble in speaking to a superior, salaaming down to the ground, pressing their foreheads with their hands at the same time; yet all the time they profess this humility they are endeavouring to rob or cheat you as much as possible. One of my grooms comes to me with great respect and says, 'Your Highness, there is no corn for the horses. The money you gave me is all spent.' And I generally find he has only spent half. And he tries the same trick about twice a week. That is the worst of it. One can never trust them in the smallest degree. No native has the smallest idea of truth or honesty.[35]

Biddulph preferred the elephants, 'the nicest creatures in the world . . . so strong, so sagacious and yet so very gentle'. They followed their mahouts about everywhere, waddling along like faithful fat old gentlemen, taking up bunches of rice grass with their trunks, twisting them up, then beating the dust out of them with their feet before eating some and throwing the rest over their backs. They sometimes tore a branch off a tree with their trunks to use it, so a soldier said, as a fly whisk 'just like a Christian'.[36]

Some mahouts treated their animals roughly, goading them along with stout iron bars sharpened into spikes which were 'unmercifully dug into the base of the creatures' ears from which they sometimes returned with bits of fat and blood on them'.[37] But the elephants appeared not to resent such treatment. They remained patient, obedient and so trustworthy that the mahouts' wives would unhesitatingly leave their babies under an elephant's charge while they were cooking. 'The big nurse is on the careful watch all the time, and when you would suppose [one of the babies] has crawled so far as to be quite out of its reach, out goes the nurse's trunk and the little brat is lifted up and quietly placed between the monster's forelegs.'[38]

Watching the passing scene, talking about elephants and grumbling about servants, the officers found that the railway journey to Raniganj passed agreeably enough. The bullock-train, though, was quite another matter. It was not only 'hideously uncomfortable, without the faintest attempt to springs', but extremely slow, the wagons, which carried four men each, continually breaking down and the oxen, which were uniformly small, having to be changed every eighth mile or so. Moreover, the drivers were 'always going to sleep and falling off their perches and getting run over'.[39] This, however, never seemed 'to hurt them much in general', though Lieutenant Nicholl noted laconically in his diary one day, 'Ran over a driver's head and squashed it this morning.'[40]

Sir Colin Campbell and his staff arrived in Allahabad on 1 November, and two days later were at Cawnpore. Here they discovered that the Gwalior Contingent, which up till now the pro-British Maharajah Jyagi Rao Sindhia – much influenced by the Political Agent, Major Macpherson – had succeeded in keeping at Gwalior, were marching towards Kalpi with the presumed intention of joining forces with Nana Sahib and the mutineers from Dinapore. Sir James Outram unselfishly suggested that, in view of this, Campbell should consider Lucknow a secondary objective since it was 'so obviously to the advantage of the state that the Gwalior rebels should be first effectually destroyed'. But Sir Colin rejected the advice, left some five hundred Europeans and a few Sikhs to protect Cawnpore under command of General Windham, and then – with a caution which several of his officers considered absurd – moved on himself towards the Alambagh outside Lucknow where five hundred of his men had already arrived with a convoy of provisions.

On approaching the Alambagh, Campbell heard that Kavanagh had escaped from Lucknow with an important message for him. He sent a brigadier ahead of him with an escort of cavalry to fetch it. But Major MacIntyre, the officer in command, refused to part with it unless Sir Colin came to claim it in person. On hearing this Sir Colin flew into one of his wild rages; and by the time he arrived at the Alambagh, his face, so Captain Garnet Wolseley of the 90th noticed, was 'contorted with anger'. He advanced upon MacIntyre, 'his face blazing and his frame quivering', and 'began a sort of war-dance. Round and round he went, shaking his fist and screaming at the top of his voice.'[41]

The message, which he read as soon as he was calm enough to do so, advised Sir Colin not to enter the city by the canal bridge as Outram and Havelock had done, but to strike across country southeast of Lucknow to the Dilkusha, cross the canal north of the Dilkusha by the Martinière, and then advance through the palace area south of the Gumti to the Residency. Sir Colin agreed that this was probably the best route and issued his preliminary orders accordingly.

The next day he inspected his army which was drawn up for his approval on the plain beside the Alambagh. Apart from Hope Grant's 9th Lancers, immaculate as always in their blue uniforms and white turbans, and the Sikh cavalry – their silky beards carefully combed, their silver-mounted firearms and gleaming scimitars resting easily against the clean cloth of their loose, fawn-coloured robes – the ranks did not look very imposing. A lieutenant in the 84th confessed:

I had no uniform to speak of. I had been served out a tunic of scarlet cloth wadded with wool which was supposed to be bullet-proof, but as, out of three of us in the brigade who wore one, one was killed and one badly wounded, I was told to take it off, and wear instead a grey flannel coat and trousers and a sowar's belt and pouch I had picked up.[42]

The commanding officer of the 75th, whose men's khaki uniforms were now 'sadly patched and worn', was wearing on his head

a kind of thing shaped like a basin and made out of an old shako with a brass ventilation at the top . . . His jacket was khaki in colour, but was not according to the regulation of the regiment, being decorated by a row of small brass buttons, while his shoulder displayed a pair of faded gold cords of the very shabbiest description. He had on his nether man a pair of khaki trousers thrust into jack boots . . . the heels of which were armed with a pair of huge brass hunting spurs which, like the rest of his accoutrements, were guiltless of any attempt at being clean. A Cawnpore leather sling belt sustained an enormous cavalry sabre to which by way of sword knot was attached a pijama string of green yellow and pink silk. The finishing touch to this martial costume being given by a pair of old what had been white military gloves but now were all colours from filth and age.

This raggedly bearded figure of 'most peculiar countenance' – 'dirty Gordon' as he was known in the 75th – 'a queer and eccentric fellow, perfectly useless as a parade officer but a most gallant soldier – sat on a reddish brown brute of a native horse'.[43]

Beside him the 2nd and 4th Punjab Infantry seemed smart enough. So did the 53rd Queen's. But some of the Madras Fusiliers had patched their uniforms with 'curtains and other draperies', while others were actually wearing pyjamas of coloured silks or jackets of green baize. As for the 8th and 75th Queen's, who had fought at Delhi, 'they both looked most weary, even dispirited' in their patched, ill-cut cloth uniforms; and neither they nor the proud, aloof-looking Punjabis made the slightest response to the few words which the General addressed to them as he rode down the line. They listened to him 'in solemn silence'. As a Scotchman, however, Sir Colin got a better reception from the 93rd, the only complete regiment on parade, who cheered him loudly as he approached their ranks which were dressed in full Highland costume with feather bonnets and dark waving plumes. 'A solid mass of brawny-limbed men', over half of them were wearing Crimean medals on their chests. And, at the sight of them, the General's former 'worn and haggard expression' gave way to a broad and genial smile before he delivered a stirring address, in the manner of General Havelock, on their duty to rescue helpless women and children from a fate worse than death, ending with the words, carefully enunciated in a strong Scots accent: 'When we make an attack you must come to close quarters as quickly as possible. Keep well together and use the bayonet. Remember that the cowardly sepoys, who are eager to murder women and children, cannot look a European soldier in the face when it is accompanied by cold steel. 93rd! You are my own lads. I rely on you to do the work!'[44]

That was 'just the trouble', one of the soldiers of the English regiments thought. Campbell's propensity for the Highlanders was notorious. They were always sure 'to get the benefit of his favours'. He 'far preferred them to the 90th', or indeed, to any of the other regiments in the whole army.[45]

The 90th were not on parade that afternoon, having not yet come up; and at least one of their officers considered this a fortunate escape, since they did not even have the baggy uniforms which the tailors of Cawnpore had hastily stitched together for the men of the 8th and 75th. The uniforms which they had brought out from the Cape had been lost in the wreck of their troopship in the Strait of Banrea; the replacements issued to them in India had been left behind at Cawnpore. So, apart from their helmets and yellow leather boots, 'no two men or officers were clothed alike'.[46]

The Naval Brigade, two hundred and fifty sailors and marines under command of Captain William Peel of H.M.S. *Shannon*, looked quite as odd. They wore their own versions of naval uniform and sat athwart their heavy ships' guns, for which they had made special carriages, with all manner of pets, monkeys and parrots, guinea-pigs and mongooses, jumping from shoulder to shoulder.[47]

Leaving three hundred men to garrison the Alambagh, Sir Colin Campbell led his motley army off towards the Dilkusha park on the morning of 14 November. At his approach the rebels evacuated both the Dilkusha and the Martinière beyond it; so the army marched in without having had to fire more than a few shots, picking up rows of 'beautiful carrots' on the way and eating them raw.

There was roast venison for dinner the next day, as the Dilkusha park 'swarmed with deer, both black buck and spotted'. And after a solid early breakfast of three pounds of salt beef, twelve biscuits and a canteenful of tea, the troops moved off again on the morning of 16 November.They had spent the night firing and reconnoitering in a contrary direction so as to deceive the enemy as to their intended route, and the deception proved effective: the army crossed the canal without opposition, reached the river and, turning west, approached the large building known as the Sikandar Bagh. On their way the 93rd passed 'a naked wretch', his head closely shaved except for the usual tuft on his crown, his face 'all streaked in a hideous manner with red paint, his body smeared with ashes. He was sitting on a leopard's skin counting a rosary of beads'. One of the men declared that he would like to try his bayonet on the hide of the painted scoundrel, but was checked by a young staff officer who said, 'Oh, don't touch him. These fellows are harmless Hindu *jogees*, and won't hurt us. It is the Mahommedans who are to blame for the horrors of this mutiny.' The words had 'scarcely been uttered when the scoundrel stopped counting the beads, slipped a hand under the leopard skin, and quick as lightning brought out a short, brass, bell-mouthed blunderbuss and fired the contents of it into [the staff officer's] chest'.[48]

Soon afterwards the firing from the Sikandar Bagh became so intense that the leading units were thrown into confusion and the cavalry became so closely packed in the narrow lane down which they had been moving that neither the artillery nor the infantry could get forward. At length the artillery and the sailors managed to drag the heavy guns into position and open fire on the solid brick walls of the Sikandar Bagh while Sir Colin Campbell, bruised by a spent musket ball that had passed through the body of a gunner, called out to the infantry to lie down, shouting repeatedly to the 93rd, 'Lie down, 93rd, lie down! Every man of you is worth his weight in gold today!'[49]

After about three-quarters of an hour the holes pounded in the walls became wide gaps as huge blocks of brick and mortar crashed into the surrounding garden.

Thereupon [a man of the 93rd recalled] a sergeant of the 53rd who had served under Sir Colin in the Punjab, presuming on old acquaintance, called out: 'Sir Colin, your Excellency, let the infantry storm; let the two

"Thirds" at them (meaning the 53rd and 93rd) and we'll soon make short work of the murderous villains!' The sergeant who called to Sir Colin was a Welshman and I recognised him thirty-five years afterwards as old Joe Lee, proprietor of the Railway Hotel in Cawnpore. He was always known as Dobbin, in his regiment; and Sir Colin, who had a most wonderful memory for names and places, turning to General Mansfield [his Chief of Staff] who had formerly served in the 53rd, said, 'Isn't that Sergeant Dobbin?' [Assured that it was], Sir Colin said, 'Do you think the breach is wide enough, Dobbin?' Lee replied, 'Part of us can get through and hold it till the pioneers widen it with their crowbars to allow the rest to get in.' The word was then passed to the 4th Punjabis to prepare to lead the assault, and after a few more rounds were fired, the charge was ordered. The Punjabis dashed over the mud wall shouting the war-cry of the Sikhs, '*Jai Khâlsa Jee!*' [Victory to the *Khalsa*!] led by two of their European officers who were both shot down before they had gone a few yards. This staggered the Sikhs, and they halted. As soon as Sir Colin saw them waver, he turned to Colonel Ewart . . . of the 93rd . . . and said, 'Colonel Ewart, bring on the tartan! Let my own lads at them!' Before the command could be repeated or the buglers had time to sound the advance, the whole seven companies, like one man, leaped over the wall, with such a yell of pent-up rage as I had never heard before or since. It was not a cheer but a concentrated yell of rage and ferocity.[50]

Joined by the Sikhs, the Highlanders dashed forward towards the breach. A Sikh got there first, and fell back dead. A Highlander jumped over him and was also killed. Three others were also shot, before a lieutenant, followed by Colonel Ewart and ten to fifteen Sikhs and Highlanders, managed to get through and attack the swarms of rebels on the far side. At the same time several other Highlanders together with some men of the 53rd clambered through battered-down doors and windows.

The slaughter inside was appalling. Colonel Ewart, his feather bonnet blown off his head, shot six rebels with six successive shots of his revolver. A taciturn, well-educated Highlander known in the regiment as 'Quaker' Wallace was believed to have killed twenty, driving his bayonet through their bodies as he chanted verses from the 116th Psalm. Other soldiers shouted, 'Cawnpore! You bloody murderers!' as they lunged forward against the mutineers who 'fought back like devils'. The mutineers were armed with tulwars as well as muskets. And, having fired their last shots, some of them hurled the muskets at the *Firinghis'* bayonets like javelins; then, shouting '*Deen! Deen!*' they 'actually threw themselves under the bayonets', slashing with their tulwars at their enemies' legs.[51]

Before long the ground was covered with the dead and writhing bodies of sepoys. The piles, five feet high in places, were so densely entangled that the wounded could not extricate themselves from the squirming mass, but lay there struggling and hissing curses at the British soldiers who strewed flowers from the garden over them 'as if in derision'. Lieutenant Roberts had never seen 'such a sight'. The bodies 'were literally in heaps . . . some dead, but most wounded and unable to get up from the crush'.[52]

The fight continued from room to room as the Scottish pipers played their remorseless accompaniment to the shouts and screams and the crackling sound of a fire which had broken out, burning to death scores of mutineers who had so far escaped the fury of the British soldiers. Slowly the sepoys fell back, some of them retreating into the towers at the corners of the building, still discharging their muskets and slashing out with their tulwars, until the last of them were killed and their bodies, hurled through the windows, landed with sickening thuds on the hard ground below.

The scene inside the building was 'the most horrible' that Lieutenant Cubitt of the 5th Fusiliers had 'ever witnessed'.

There were hundreds of sepoys dead and dying, many on fire [he recorded in his journal]. Piled around the entrance and in every court and garden of the place, they lay in heaps, three and four deep, a suffocating, burning, smouldering mass while many a Highlander, Sikh, 50th and a few of ours lay among them. Now and then a stray shot came from some wretch yet able to pull his trigger. While there I saw 64 collected, drawn up and bayonetted with yells of 'Cawnpore'. God forgive us . . .[53]

The scene was 'terrible', Lieutenant Fairweather agreed.

But at the same time it gave a feeling of gratified revenge. You may think me a savage but I gloated over the sights of this charnel house. Who did not who saw the slaughter at Cawnpore? . . . Among the corpses were those of several women . . . I saw the body of a woman lying with a cross-belt upon her and by her a dead baby also shot with two bullet wounds in it. The poor mother had tied the wounds round with a rag . . . McQueen [Ensign J. W. McQueen of the 27th Native Infantry] told me he had seen a Highlander bayonet another woman and on his upbraiding him for such a brutal act, he said the man turned upon him like a madman and for a minute he almost expected to be run through with his bayonet himself.[54]

Colonel Ewart rushed out of the building, badly bruised and severely wounded in his right arm, carrying a colour that he had captured from two rebel officers both of whom he had killed. 'Covered with blood and powder smoke, his eyes still flashing with the excitement of the fight', and of so wild an appearance as to seem incapably drunk, he ran off with it to where Sir Colin Campbell was sitting on his grey charger outside the gate.

'I have killed the last two of the enemy with my own hand,' he announced breathlessly. 'And here is one of their colours.'

'Damn your colours, sir,' shouted Sir Colin, beside himself with rage at Ewart's irregular behaviour. 'It's not your place to be taking colours. Go back to your regiment this instant, sir!'[55]

Chastened and 'apparently very much upset', Ewart returned to the regiment where he found that nine officers and ninety men had been killed or wounded. Later, elephants began to drag the corpses out of the Sikandar Bagh; and as they were tossed into pits dug beside the main road, an observer counted them. There were 1,857.[56]

Exhausted by the savage fighting in a heat which was felt all the more intensely by men in thick red coats and heavy kilts, the Highlanders sat in groups in the shade of a huge pipal tree, gratefully drinking water from large jars and washing the taste of powder from their parched tongues. Around them lay the bodies of many men of their own regiment and of the 53rd. An officer, struck by the wounds which all these dead bodies bore, called out to 'Quaker' Wallace to look up to

see if he could see anyone in the top of the tree, because all the dead under it had apparently been shot from above. Wallace had his rifle loaded, and stepping back he carefully scanned the top of the tree. He almost immediately called out, 'I see him, sir!' and cocking his rifle he repeated aloud:

> 'I'll pay my vows now to the Lord
> Before His people all.'

[He fired and down fell a body dressed] in a tight-fitting red jacket and tight-fitting rose-coloured silk trousers; and the breast of the jacket bursting open with the fall, showed that the wearer was a woman. She was armed with a pair of heavy old-pattern cavalry pistols . . . When Wallace saw that the person whom he had shot was a woman, he burst into tears.[57]

Wallace was not left to grieve nor his comrades to rest for long. West of the Sikandar Bagh was a large, white-domed tomb, surrounded by a tangled garden and a strong high wall, the burial place of the first King of Oudh. This tomb, the Shah Najaf, which was occupied by the enemy in great force, commanded the route to the Residency; and Sir Colin Campbell determined to take it before nightfall. So strong and well defended a position was it, however, that neither artillery nor infantry could at first make much headway against it. So Sir Colin called up his Highlanders once more. He had not intended to use them again that day, he told them, but if the Lucknow garrison were not to perish the Shah Najaf must be taken. One of the men called back, 'Will we get a medal for this, Sir Colin?'

'Well, my lads,' Sir Colin replied. 'I can't say what her Majesty's Government may do; but if you don't get a medal, all I can say is you have deserved one better than any troops I have ever seen under fire.'[58]

The order was then given to man the drag ropes for Peel's guns; and Captain Middleton's battery of Royal Artillery 'dashed forward with loud cheers, the drivers waving their whips and the gunners their caps' as they passed Peel's guns at the gallop. One of the sailors

had his leg carried clean off above the knee by a round shot, and although knocked head over heels by the force of the shot, he sat bolt upright on the grass, with the blood spouting from the stump of the limb like water from the hose of a fire-engine, and shouted, 'Here goes a shilling a day, a shilling a day. Pitch into them boys, pitch into them! Remember Cawnpore, 93rd, remember Cawnpore! Go at them my hearties!' until he fell back . . . dead.[59]

But the 93rd could not get at the enemy who, from loopholes, windows, trees and bushes, maintained their fierce fire and even shot arrows from the walls 'with great force and precision', piercing one soldier through the brain so that the shaft projected more than a foot out at the back of his head, transfixing another through the heart and passing clean through his back. 'Boys, this is no joke,' a sergeant said. 'We must pay them off.'[60]

There seemed no hope of doing so. Men were falling on all sides. Several of the staff were hit. Peel was told to fire rockets to cover the withdrawal of the heavy guns. The infantry, too, were about to withdraw when a narrow gap was discovered in a distant corner of the wall surrounding the tomb. The infantry poured through it and rushed across the garden only to see the white figures of the sepoys running for their lives. They had been terrified by the rockets which had come hissing over the wall, veering to right and left, sinking and rising, as though guided by devils, before exploding with a shuddering roar against the wall. As the sepoys fled Sir Colin rode into the tomb. Here he set up his headquarters for the night, ordering the pipers to play 'The Campbells Are Coming' to give encouragement to Outram's people now less than a mile away.[61]

Awakening next morning to the smell of burning flesh, Captain Garnet Wolseley of the 90th looked up to see a sepoy's body crackling and smoking on top of the wall of the Sikandar Bagh. Getting up and walking away from the sickening smell, he came upon a party of Sikhs cutting off the heads of some snipers they had persuaded to surrender. The bells in the city were ringing loudly and the enemy's drums beating, but the attack which these insistent sounds seemed to presage did not materialize. It was the British who attacked again, and Wolseley who led them.[62]

There were two large buildings still to be taken before the relieving force could break through to the Residency defences, the Khoorsheyd Munzil, a battlemented and turreted palace like a castle which had been used as a mess house by the 32nd Regiment, and the Moti Mahal, a palace surrounded by orange and lemon trees and a high brick wall. Ordered to lead the assault on the Khoorsheyd Munzil, after its defenders had been battered into silence by Peel's guns, Wolseley dashed forward to find the 'niggers bolting' from it. Suspecting that if he did not now go forward to the Moti Mahal, Sir Colin would give his darling Highlanders the honour of capturing it, Wolseley made up his mind to exceed his orders. In this he was strongly encouraged by his men who, 'in very explicit Saxon English', resolved that 'no breeches-less Highlanders should get in front of them that day'. So Wolseley charged on, under heavy fire from the Kaiser Bagh.

All went off well, though we had some nasty work [Wolseley told his brother]. I got to the palace gate and found it built up by a thick masonry wall, well loopholed. The fools had forgotten to dig a ditch outside, so after they gave us the first volley I manned the loopholes on my side, and there we stood, the enemy on one side and we on the other, both striving for the holes. I sent back for tools and in a short time we had a hole big enough for a man to get through, so in we went, one after the other, the niggers bolting to the river and trying to swim across . . . I had capital practice at them in the water. But I lost a number of my men at those infernal loopholes.[63]

While Wolseley was firing at the sepoys in the river, there was a loud explosion and part of the wall of the courtyard fell in. Through the gap appeared an officer with a party of men sent out from the Residency defences to make contact with the relieving army.

Although bullets were still flying through the air, both Havelock and Outram set out to welcome the Commander-in-Chief. 'Worn and pale', Havelock was walking through a narrow passage with high buildings on both sides when a shell came through the wall on his right, rebounded from the wall on his left and, after lying for a few seconds on the ground, burst at his feet. He was knocked over flat on his back as his cap came flying off; but, to his companions' astonishment, he got up again unharmed and walked on down the passageway.[64] Beyond a broken wall at the end of it he came across some men of his own regiment, the 53rd, who 'immediately flocked around him and gave him three hearty cheers'.

This was too much for the fine old General [wrote Hope Grant who witnessed the meeting]. His breast heaved with emotion, and his eyes filled with tears. He turned to the men and said, 'Soldiers, I am happy to see you. Soldiers, I am happy to think you have got into this place with a smaller loss than I had.' Hearing this I asked him what he supposed our loss amounted to. He answered that he had heard it estimated at 80, and was much surprised and grieved when I told him we had lost about 43 officers and 450 men killed and wounded.[65]

Several members of Havelock's and Outram's staffs were wounded as they ran with Hope Grant across the dusty, broken ground to the Khoorsheyd Munzil where Sir Colin Campbell had established his headquarters. Both Generals arrived unhurt, however, and Sir Colin walked forward to greet them, raising his cap and holding out his hand, 'How do you do, Sir James?' he said. Then turning to Havelock he welcomed him with words conveying news of an honour that was received with obvious delight, 'And how do you do, *Sir* Henry?'[66]

Sir Colin Campbell was in a far more agreeable mood than he had been earlier when Captain Wolseley's independent action in attacking the Moti Mahal had made him so furious that he felt he had 'never been so enraged by any man in his life'. Warned by Brigadier Adrian Hope – who had never seen 'the Lord Sahib' so angry – to stay well clear of him, Wolseley had gone to bed in an apprehensive and disgruntled mood which was aggravated when some 'beastly nigger' stumbled over his recumbent form in the dark. Wolseley was even more disturbed when he woke up next morning to discover that the 'beastly nigger' was the Commander-in-Chief. Waking up at the same time, Sir Colin immediately recognized Wolseley and shook his fist at him, shouting, 'How dared you attack the Moti Mahal without instructions?' But there was no real anger in the words. The General was actually smiling. His success in relieving the Residency had quite overcome his bad temper; and Wolseley was eventually congratulated on his bravery and upon the ability that was one day to lead to his becoming a commander-in-chief himself.[67]

Satisfied as he was by his success, Sir Colin well understood how limited it was. The city of Lucknow still swarmed with rebels; his losses had been severe; he had over 1,000 sick and wounded as well as 500 women and children on his hands, and he was worried about Cawnpore which Windham had been left to protect with a force that might well prove inadequate. Once he had secured a safe escape for the women and children and the men in hospital, he knew that he would have to withdraw from Lucknow. Several officers urged him not to do so, but instead to attack the Kaiser Bagh while the rebels were so dispirited and drive them out of the city. Brigadier Inglis insisted that he could still hold on to the Residency with six hundred men. But Campbell had always thought the Residency a false position, and argued firmly that far more men than that would be needed to hold the defences there. In any case, he would need every available man to defeat the rebels at Cawnpore. He would brook no opposition. Lucknow must be evacuated as soon as possible.[68]

19

The Fall of Lucknow

· Evacuation of women and children from Lucknow, 19 November 1857 ·
withdrawal of the troops, 22–23 November · death of Havelock,
24 November · Campbell returns to Cawnpore – Windham
defeated there · in second battle of Cawnpore, 28 November ·
Campbell defeats Tatya Tope in third battle of Cawnpore,
6 December – and reoccupies Fatehgarh, 6 January 1858 ·
Campbell marches to Lucknow – the city falls · the last of the rebels
are dislodged, 21 March 1858 · the looting of Lucknow ·

When told that they were to leave Lucknow the next day, Mrs Inglis and Mrs Case looked at each other 'in the most complete bewilderment'. 'How all the wounded and sick people, and women and children [were] to be got off in such a hurried manner, at only a few hours' notice,' Mrs Case could not imagine.[1] As it happened it did prove impossible to get the women and children off on 18 November, so they were given another day in which to prepare themselves for the journey. They spent it hurriedly packing as many of their possessions as they believed it would be possible to carry with them, sewing big pockets on to their dresses, folding linen into pillowcases, cramming valuables into boxes, leaving out their best clothes which they intended to take with them by wearing them all, one garment on top of another.

I put on four flannel waistcoats, three pairs of stockings, three chemises, three drawers, one flannel and four white petticoats, my pink flannel dressing-gown, skirt, plaid jacket, and over all my cloth dress and jacket that I had made out of my habit [Mrs Germon recorded]. Then I tied my cashmere shawl sash-fashion round my waist and also Charlie's [her husband, Captain Germon's] silver mug, and put on a worsted cap and hat ... I forgot to say I had sewed dear mother's fish-knife and fork in my pink skirt and had put a lot of things in the pocket of it. I had also two under-pockets, one filled with jewellery ... the other with my journal and valuable papers. I then filled my cloth skirt pocket with pencil, knife, pin-cushion, handkerchief, etc. All my lace was sewn up in a bag which I wore also.[2]

Thus encumbered, the ladies prepared to leave Lucknow on the morning of 19 November. Sir Colin Campbell came to wish them a safe journey, smiling and calling them 'dear creatures', though Mrs Inglis felt sure he was really wishing them 'very far away – and no wonder!'[3]

The exodus began at ten o'clock, some of the women and children riding in hackeries, others on ponies; a few were carried on *doolies*, one or two in carriages drawn by coolies; the rest were on foot, with a camel unexpectedly provided for each lady's belongings. Part of the route was exposed to the fire of snipers and artillery on the far bank of the Gumti. But British sharpshooters in the Shah Najaf and guns at the Moti Mahal kept the enemy at a distance; and hurrying in their laden, cumbersome garments as fast as they could past the dangerous places, the fugitives were all escorted across to the Sikandar Bagh unharmed.

Mrs Boileau was one of the first to get away. The soldiers along the route greeted her with friendly looks and cheery cries of 'God bless you, Mum!'[4] Mrs Brydon also met 'with so much kindness and attention on the way', being offered a biscuit by one soldier, a piece of bread by another.[5] But other ladies, though reluctantly admired for the calm way in which they had long since grown accustomed to walk about under fire, caused great offence by their gloomy, even surly expressions, seeming to be much upset at having to leave at such short notice the place which had been their home for so long.[6]

Although they looked, so Francis Collins thought, much better than the 'haggard, worn men' and the 'pale, blanched' children, they were overwhelmed, perhaps, by the 'scenes of ruin, devastation and misery' which met the eye on every side, scenes which Mrs Case felt she would 'never, *never* forget'.[7] Certainly there 'was not a happy face among them', declared one officer who watched them depart, 'nor a kind word for the soldiers who had rescued them'.[8] A group of them who complained of the transport provided for them were sternly rebuked by Sir Colin Campbell with the words, 'Ladies – women I mean – you ought to be thankful that you have got out with your lives, for I do not know how it might have been in two hours more with you.'[9]

All the same, when they reached the Sikandar Bagh, they were treated with great kindness by officers and men alike who brought them wine and biscuits and sat them down on charpoys until the time came for them to be taken down to the Dilkusha. After many delays, false starts and halts, they reached the Dilkusha about midnight;

and here all was confusion. There seemed no one there to tell them where to go or what to do. Some were offered tents by good-natured officers who moved out into the open; others were ushered into quarters from which they were suddenly ejected without explanation; Mrs Boileau was told to get ready to move on, then told she could go to sleep again; Mrs Case utterly worn out, too tired to undress, lay down under a *rezais* at two o'clock in the morning. After waiting about for an hour in the cold – then being turned back from a building where she was told there were already 1,100 sick – Mrs Germon 'seized a gentleman with a lantern who was passing' and asked him where to go. 'He pointed to some tents a long way off,' she recorded in her journal. 'After tumbling over a lot of tent-pegs and ropes we reached them and lay down on the ground for the night. It was utterly impossible to find my pony with my bedding, but we got a *duree* to lie upon and I put my head on my basket – the tents were so open that I of course got a cold – however, daylight soon appeared.'[10]

With daylight all the mismanagement of the previous night was forgiven, for breakfast was served by the 9th Lancers under the trees, and it was such a breakfast that the fugitives from Lucknow had not seen for months – cold beef and mutton, tea with milk and sugar, biscuits and jam, coffee and, most welcome of all, 'to the children's intense delight, nice fresh bread and butter'.[11] 'Oh, Mamma!' cried one little girl, overcome with excitement at the sight of it. 'There is a loaf of bread on the table. I am certain of it. I saw it with my own eyes.'[12]

At midnight three days later, after Peel's guns had submitted the Kaiser Bagh to a continuous and ferocious bombardment, the last of the troops were silently withdrawn from the Residency defences, not 'looking anything like soldiers in a British army, so bedraggled and strangely dressed'. One regimental surgeon, his hair 'in elf locks' and with 'a long pointed beard, four inches below his chin', was wearing 'thirty yards of muslin in the shape of a turban for a hat, a dark flannel shirt with red spots, a shooting coat several sizes too large [for which he had paid 120 rupees], a pair of private's regimental trousers . . . and a great clumsy pair of ammunition boots'.[13]

When what appeared to be the last man had filed out in the darkness, Captain Birch was sent back to ensure that no one had been left behind. 'The utter stillness and solitude of the deserted position' struck coldly on his nerves as he walked across to the farthest post, past the shattered buildings and the spiked dismounted guns, meeting 'not a living soul'.[14] He reported the position empty. There was a man still there, though, Captain Waterman of the 13th Native Infantry who had fallen asleep and who, so shocked by waking up to find himself alone, 'went off his head for a time'.[15]

Though Waterman would willingly have foregone the distinction of being the last man to withdraw from the Lucknow Residency, Outram and Inglis almost quarrelled over the order in which they were to leave it. Outram waved his hand to indicate that, as he was the senior officer, he wished Inglis to precede him. Inglis held back, feeling that as he had commanded the garrison from the beginning it was his privilege to go out last. At length Outram held out his hand, smiled and said, 'Let us go out together'.

Outram's aide-de-camp was not prepared to make a similar concession. But Birch was ready to deal with his protests and, disdaining argument, made a charge at him. 'And weak from all the hardships and privations he had undergone,' so Birch said, 'he could not stand the trick of shoulder to shoulder learned in the Harrow playing fields. Prone on the earth he lay, till he rolled down the hill, and I was the last of the staff to leave the Baillie Guard Gate.'

The two aides-de-camp then walked on together down to the Dilkusha.[16]

At the Dilkusha, General Havelock was dying. He had contracted dysentery in Lucknow and had been carried out of the city in a *doolie* to a private soldier's tent, the only one available. He was 'still able to stand with assistance', but when Dr Fayrer called to see him he found him 'very ill'; and he knew himself, so he told his son, that he was dying. He would allow no one to help him except Harry whose painfully wounded left arm was in a sling. He could no longer make out the print in his Bible but Harry read him passages and verses from his hymn book which seemed to comfort him. He appeared to have no regrets and kept murmuring, 'I die happy and contented.' To Outram he said, 'For forty years I have endeavoured so to rule my life that when death came I might face it without fear.'

For most of the night of 23 November he lay awake, occasionally asking Harry for a drink of water. Soon after dawn he called for his son again. 'Harry,' he said, looking up at him smiling. 'See how a Christian can die.' Harry held him in his arms; and he died without a sound.[17]

. . . . .

Leaving Outram with rather more than 4,000 men to hold the Alambagh until he could return, Sir Colin Campbell marched for Cawnpore on 27 November with an army less than 3,000 strong encumbered by a straggling convoy of women, children and sick and wounded men. For the women the march was 'truly a nightmare'. The dust thrown up by the winding, nine-mile-long procession of hackeries, buggies, carriages, *doolies*, elephants, bullocks and camels was 'something fearful', so thick at times that it was impossible 'even to see the children in your arms'. There were constant halts, and perpetual alarms that the enemy were about to attack. When the cavalcade halted each night upon its designated camping-ground, the muddle was 'indescribable', as servants rushed about looking for their mistresses, and women called for their children, searched for their luggage and tried to find somewhere to sleep and something to eat. 'No one could tell us where to go,' wrote Mrs Brydon who, with the help of four coolies, had managed to bring her harp out of Lucknow and to have it put on a grain cart. 'And it was in vain to look for a servant in such a crowd and in the dark.' She was lucky enough to be given a tent the first night by a sergeant of the 9th Lancers; but other ladies, most of whom had bad colds now, had to sleep in the open air or in carts. The next morning they were roused early, and another day's journey began after 'a hurried bite of bread and a drink of water'. There was no food to be purchased on the way, for all the villages were deserted. One day Mrs Brydon could find nothing for the children to eat but 'some carrots and a little sugar candy'. She was 'never so thankful' as she was on the sixth day of the march when she was told that they would soon reach the river at Cawnpore, even though she could hear the sound of firing and 'see smoke rising in many places'.[18]

Sir Colin Campbell had already reached the river. Handed a letter on the march by a native messenger who had sprung out at the staff from beneath a hedge, he had learned that Cawnpore had already been attacked. Hearing later that Windham, hard-pressed by the rebels, had been obliged to fall back on the entrenchment which had been constructed four months before, Campbell had increased the pace of the army, beset by the fear that the bridge over the Ganges might have been captured, leaving him isolated in hostile country. But the convoy had not been able to maintain the pace he had set it; the *doolie*-bearers, gasping for breath, had lagged behind with their heavy loads; the bullock-drivers, flailing their whips, had urged on their animals to faster speeds in vain. The General, in a self-confessed 'agony of suspense', had hurried on ahead of them with the cavalry and horse artillery. Then at Mangalwar he had galloped on, escorted only by his staff, towards the Ganges. Just before dark he had approached the river bank and had seen with profound relief that the bridge still stood.[19]

Beyond it, though, Cawnpore was in flames and although the entrenchment was still in Windham's hands the battle had been lost. Faced by the superior forces of Tatya Tope – whose army, including the followers of Nana Sahib, numbered 25,000 men – Windham had been overwhelmed. Guilty of mistakes and miscalculations, and let down by a subordinate officer who had retreated without orders, Windham had also been dismayed by the behaviour of some of his troops who, 'throwing away their arms to accelerate their flight', had fallen back in panic to the entrenchment where they had broken open the stores, got drunk on the wine intended for the sick and smashed open their officers' trunks. Their commander, 'blamed by everyone', reported his humiliation to the Commander-in-Chief.[20]

Early in the morning of 29 November, Tatya Tope's guns opened up on the bridge beyond which the rebels could see the white tents of the foreign army newly arrived from Lucknow. But Peel's heavy guns and all the British siege batteries replied with such effect that Tatya Tope's artillery was silenced; and Sir Colin's army, together with the convoy of women, children and wounded men, crossed over the bridge in safety to encamp near the entrenchment from which so many of their friends had been escorted to their death in June.[21]

The entrenchment and its surroundings were a melancholy sight, arousing 'the most painful thoughts'. Burned bungalows, blackened walls, charred timbers, broken gates, trees lying on the ground stripped of leaves and branches, made the women, in Mrs Inglis's words, 'feel thoroughly miserable'. They were all deeply relieved when, four days later, their escort, bearers, animals and carts were ready to move off again for Allahabad and Calcutta.[22]

Sir Colin was 'more than thankful' to see them go. He could now concentrate on the enemy without the worry of their safety constantly at the back of his mind. Studying the position adopted by Tatya Tope, whose left was protected by the Ganges and whose centre was in Cawnpore, he realized at once that he must attack their right, crossing the canal and the road to Kalpi so as to cut off the retreat of the Gwalior Contingent, the enemy's best troops, whose camp was astride the road on the Kalpi side of the main highway between Delhi and Allahabad.

His army, now strengthened by five thousand infantry, six hundred cavalry and thirty-five guns, recently arrived from England, launched the attack on 6 December. It was immediately successful. Distracted by a furious bombardment of Cawnpore and of their positions between the city and the Ganges, the rebel leaders drew reinforcements towards the centre while four British brigades worked round their right. For a time the attack faltered as the enemy held on tenaciously amidst the brick kilns south of the canal; but then Peel's sailors came dashing up, dragging their 24-pounders, and as they opened fire from the canal bridge, the infantry rushed across the canal and sent the Gwalior Contingent flying beyond the Kalpi road.

I can't tell you how jolly it was seeing the brutes run [a young officer in the Naval Brigade, Edmund Verney, wrote home excitedly]. I could hardly believe my eyes. I felt perfectly mad, and our men got on top of the guns, waving their hats and yelling . . . It was most awfully exciting. We pursued them to their camp, found it all deserted, tents, horses, ponies, baggage, bedding, swords, muskets, everything lying about, hackeries loaded with all manner of treasure, all left . . .

On we went still, right through the camp and after them across the fields and roads at a tremendous pace . . . We chased them for about ten miles . . . We took seventeen guns, loads upon loads of ammunition, all their luggage, treasure and everything – there's for you! . . . The panic was taken up by those who were in the town and they all hooked up as fast as they could go, so we got the place quite clean of them.[23]

If General Mansfield, given the task of preventing the rebel centre and left from escaping, had proved himself as capable in the field as he was on the staff, Sir Colin's success would have been complete. But Mansfield's hesitations allowed thousands of the rebels to escape. Hope Grant was sent in pursuit of them, but although he managed to bring them to bay at a river crossing farther north, he had to satisfy himself with scattering them up the bank and capturing fifteen more guns.[24]

Left without transport, which was all being used for the conveyance of the refugees to Allahabad, Sir Colin could not follow up his success immediately. So the next few days were spent preparing for the reconquest of the Doab and the reoccupation of Fatehgarh, the only important town in the province still in rebel hands. Several converging columns were to advance on Fatehgarh where he himself hoped to join them at the beginning of the next month.

The operations were as satisfactorily conducted as the defeat of Tatya Tope at Cawnpore; and by 6 January, Sir Colin had reoccupied Fatehgarh and had given orders for the outlying districts to be brought back under British control. These orders, admitted Robert Biddulph, one of the officers involved, were 'performed in a summary and somewhat brigand-like manner'. Villages were burned without too scrupulous an inquiry as to the behaviour of the people who lived or had lived in them, their inhabitants often killed on the mere suspicion of being rebels.[25] In one village, wrote Arthur Ewen of the 38th, 'some villagers were found by our men up to their necks in holes to escape detection so we shot them without asking any questions'.[26]

Perhaps burning villages is not such a grave punishment after all [Biddulph wrote home to a friend in England], seeing that the inhabitants had generally fled with their most valuable articles, and that a Hindoo's house is built of mud and therefore rather improved than otherwise by burning. However on the third day of our triumphant progress the head men of the villages began to come out and present the receipts for the revenue that they had just gone and paid. We were however too just to let them off, and you will, I have no doubt, be glad to learn that they were all punished with the utmost impartiality . . . We approach a village. Out comes the head man with several attendants. He presses his head on his hands and salaams to the ground several times, then, placing his hands together in a supplicatory attitude, he says, 'Lord of the East, your slave has brought you some presents. The sight of your face fills him with joy at the prospect of your just rule.' The reply probably is, 'You rascal, where are the sepoys who were here yesterday? And where are all the rupees they stole from the Treasury?'
'Protector of the poor,' responds our friend. 'Those wicked men went away last week. They plundered your slave of all that he possessed.' And with that he bursts into a torrent of tears . . . Well the probabilities are that this gentleman has got some of the money buried in his house, that he is in league with the sepoys and probably a spy. You investigate his presents and find them to consist of bowls of sour milk, of yams, and other vegetables worth in all about 6d. and as for the exalted and laudatory ejaculations he made us of, why every native you meet addresses you either as Lord of the Earth or Protector of the Poor. The fact is they are all impostors or rogues.[27]

If the head men of the villages were considered rogues who were lucky to escape with their lives after being flogged, captured sepoys were universally condemned as 'brutes who deserved no mercy'. Few received any. 'I cannot consider these sepoys as human beings,' wrote Captain J. M. Wade of the 90th, voicing the general opinion; 'and it is only common practice to destroy them as reptiles.'[28]

'Nobody means to leave a sepoy *alive*, much less *wounded*,' Emma Nicholl was assured by her brother, Lieutenant Nicholl of the Rifle Brigade, who later told their mother that while out shooting deer and peacock, his fellow-officers did not neglect the 'runaway sepoys' but bagged them too, then 'hanged them up "on the trees for to dry"'.[29]

Nicholl, a perfectly ordinary young officer, devoted to his family and rather homesick, was no more cruel or heartless than anyone else in the army. Not long out of Eton, he had recently sailed from England in the steamship, *Lady Jocelyn*, swearing 'to avenge the deaths of the poor women and children in Delhi', and having plenty of time during the three-month voyage to 'dream of women hanging by their hair, children with throats cut and other horrors'. On arrival at Calcutta he was told of 'a lady who escaped the murders up-country but who was shockingly mutilated' and was 'now perfectly mad'; and this made him more inclined than ever to think of these 'damned niggers as lower than the brutes'. When there was a divisional parade 'to jaw the 38th about murdering niggers', his sympathies were with the soldiers rather than their victims. He did not become a murderer himself, but he could understand the feelings of those who did.[30]

Apart from the exhausting cross-country marches in pursuit of sepoys, picket-duty in the rain, and the white ants that devoured his boots, Nicholl found life at Fatehgarh quite tolerable. The camp was in a garden on the banks of the Ganges in which he could enjoy 'a stunning bathe'. It was 'such a nice place' with a 'splendid view of Oude', stretching for miles on the other side of the river in which elephants and oxen disported themselves, the elephants flapping their large ungainly ears and squirting water over their enormous backs, the oxen with nothing but their mouths above water. He walked into town one day and bought some chickens on which thereafter he spent a great deal of time and energy. His diary entries reveal the sort of life the army was then leading:

January 15th, 1858: Did nothing all day but read [Charles Reade's novel, *The Course of True Love Never Did Run Smooth*, published the previous year]. The Colonel still getting the boats up but very slowly, and making rifle pits in a most curious fashion, when he has half finished one leaving it to make another and so on . . . He is said to be very excited . . . When we fired a few shots at the sepoys who we found riding about at a distance of about 1000 yards, he came and fired a shot bang up in the air . . . Two of our men were slightly touched, but we knocked the enemy over very well. They had some guns down and so had we. Young Baillie knocked one nigger over. Very hot day . . .

January 18th: Ettridge tried and flogged, and he made a tremendous noise. Walker flogged at the same time . . . A great battle fought with clods of earth between our tent and other tents . . . *January 20th* . . . Bought 8 more chickens. Nothing going on in any way . . . *January 22nd:* Bought two kids who made a tremendous noise at night, crying out for their ma, and kept everybody awake. Consequently one had his throat cut in the morning. *January 23rd:* Nothing going on. Ate the kid which was very good indeed. We now have 10 chickens and they have laid by their mutual exertions the enormous quantity of one egg in 5 days! . . . *January 25th:* Rain, rain, rain, a dreary and wet day . . . Dog hunts going on . . . *January 28th:*Went out shooting, got some snipe and pigeons, etc. . . . made a better chicken domicile . . . *January 31st:* . . . Shot a dog at twenty yards with my revolver . . . splendid sunrise . . . *February 2nd:* . . . Bought a Hubble Bubble with a well trap bottom . . . *February 4th:* 5 eggs! . . . *February 5th:* Marched at six . . . Very dusty indeed and a very high wind. My eyes brimfull of mud . . . *February 7th:* Splendid day for marching, fine and cold, got along at a fine pace. Encamped in a large rice field . . . Mended the coop . . . Picked lots of peas which we found growing amongst the rice . . . Lost 116 rupees at loo . . . Stoned the natives. Church service at 4 p.m. . . . Some papers from England, not much news in them, all there *was* about India.[31]

Having reoccupied Fatehgarh and brought the surrounding districts once more under British control, Campbell turned his attention to the next stage in his campaign. He personally would have preferred to concentrate on the reduction of Rohilkhand; but Lord Canning was insistent that Oudh, where the rebels were more united and better led than anywhere else, ought not to be allowed the respite that a campaign in Rohilkhand would afford them. So Sir Colin gave way to the firmly expressed view of the Governor-General and began to make preparations for his return to Lucknow where the rebel leader known as the Maulvi of Faizabad had collected together an enormous army for its defence and was constantly attacking Sir James Outram's earthworks around the Alambagh.[32]

By the end of February 1858 Sir Colin Campbell's army was also of considerable size, comprising by now seventeen battalions of infantry, twenty-eight squadrons of cavalry and a hundred and thirty-four guns and mortars. Indeed, so large a British army had never before been seen in India; and although the defences of Lucknow had been greatly strengthened since he had relieved Outram and Havelock there in November, Campbell believed that – by operating from the north where the rebels had not been attacked before, and consequently appeared to consider they would not be attacked in future – the powerful British army would not find them insuperable.

Throughout the last two weeks of February Sir Colin Campbell's immense army of soldiers and camp followers had been marching, detachment after detachment, across the Ganges towards Banthira in Oudh. Rows of white canvas tents, erected only a few days before, would disappear and a long line of soldiers, trailed by animals, carts, guns and native servants, would make for the bridge of boats which swayed, creaked and groaned as the feet stamped and the wheels rumbled across it. The British soldiers marched along in a variety of uniforms and 'astounding cap covers', their fixed bayonets glinting in the sun, puffing away at their short black cutties which were 'filled with the nastiest tobacco in the world', keeping in step to the sound of the bands that sometimes seemed so far away that they half fancied the familiar notes were wafted to them 'straight from home across the wide sea'. There were riflemen in green coats; Bengal Fusiliers and artillerymen in blue; line regiments in khaki and red; Highlanders in kilts and stockings; sailors in the baggiest of trousers, chewing wads of quid; cavalrymen, their harness clinking and their steel scabbards jingling against their stirrup-irons; big-whiskered, stalwart Sikhs of the irregular cavalry, 'each one a picture down to the waist, but with something wrong about their legs – which are decidedly of the broomstick order'. And behind them, mile after mile along the dusty track, there straggled that enormous procession of men, women and animals, indispensable to an army in India: *doolie* bearers, six to each bed, six hundred for each regiment; *khalassis* for the hospital tents; cooks and *bhistis; bildahs* and sweepers; syces and grass-cutters; hackery-drivers; legions of dealers in food and liquor; officers' servants; milk-sellers; baboos and functionaries employed by the commissariat department; coolies and bearers attached to the fifteen-mile-long siege train; lookers-on; hangers-on; wives and children; mahouts on patient elephants; drivers of sulky groaning camels that grumbled in deep bubbling tones as they emitted blasts of noxious breath through yellow teeth; bullocks, driven by means of rope-reins passed through the cartilage of the nose, bellowing in protest as the friction of their wooden yolks galled their necks.

The progress, of course, was extremely slow. It was bedevilled by constant breakdowns as bullocks, dragging wagons laden high with ammunition, howitzers and mortars, 'somehow contrived never to have less than five hundred carts stuck in ditches or inextricably jammed'; as mutinous camels either refused to stand up or, having got up, dashed about in wild confusion, discarding tables, beds, baggage and portmanteaux from their overladen backs; or as an independent elephant lumbered off to sample the waters of a nearby pond.

At Banthira the army halted and encamped; and there Sir Colin Campbell joined them. He was anxious to lose no time in moving on to Lucknow, but he had been promised the help of a force of Gurkhas by Jang Bahadur, the *de facto* ruler of Nepal, who had been convinced by a visit to England of the vast resources of British power which he wished to see maintained in India.[33] These Gurkhas had not yet arrived, and Campbell decided to wait at Banthira for a day or two rather than proceed without their valuable support. One morning at Banthira when all was 'silent as the grave in camp', apart from the clanging of the *ghurrees* that announced the passing of each hour, there were sudden shouts of 'Get up! Get up! The sepoys is a-coming!' These cries were followed by 'a hideous clatter, a running of men, shouting, neighing of horses', calls of 'Stand to your arms! The enemy are coming!' Lieutenant Vivian Majendie, in pyjamas and shirt-sleeves, rushed out of his tent, buckling on his sword. Other officers, also in their shirt-sleeves, were rushing off to mount their horses, swearing and fastening their belts 'in the very hottest of hot haste'. Through a tent flap Majendie caught sight of a naked officer who had been having a bath and was 'now engaged in an attempt to perform the impossible feat of getting into a pair of trousers hindside before and fastening a revolver round his waist at one and the same moment, vociferating madly for his bearer and, of course, swearing desperately'. Another officer, very red in the face and 'using exceedingly strong language', was trying to get on a boot unaided, 'tumbling and hopping about on one leg in a manner stupendous to behold'. Everybody swore the enemy were coming; some swore they could see them 'or very nearly'; but they were 'not quite sure' in what direction. Sir Colin on his white Arab started off across country 'with the intention of judging for himself'; while another officer, perfectly justified in 'feeling quite sure that the whole affair was a false alarm', wondered what on earth this inexperienced army would do when the enemy really did appear.[34]

He did not have long to wait before he found out. On 2 March the advance towards Lucknow was resumed. The troops marched through the well cultivated countryside, passing dark topes of mango trees in whose branches scrambled innumerable monkeys, chattering and screeching, hanging now by one leg, now by their tails. And as they approached the Dilkusha, the troops came upon the skeletons of rebels killed by Outram's force from the Alambagh, lying in 'all sorts of unnatural and distorted positions, with their fleshless limbs contorted, and the white teeth imparting a horrid grin to the ghastly skulls. Some of their old rags yet clung to them, the mouldy remains of their red coats and uniforms as decayed as themselves'.[35]

After capturing the Dilkusha, the army was to split in two. One column, under Outram, was to turn right, cross the Gumti, then move north to the village of Ismailganj before advancing down the Fyzabad road to a yellow building known as the Chakar Kothi and the iron and stone bridges leading into the city from the north. The other column under Sir Colin was to cross the canal above the Martinière, then advance into the city and against its main citadel, the Kaiser Bagh, from the west.

By the morning of 9 March, Outram's force was in position to begin his attack through the jungle towards the Chakar Kothi. For many of his men this was their first battle, and they remembered it afterwards in vivid detail: the still hour before the action began when – surrounded by horses with heads deep in nose-bags and officers handing round cigar-cases and brandy flasks – the men ate what for many of them was to be their last meal, carving out hunks of bread and lumps of meat with pocket knives which, being used also for cutting tobacco, imparted to the food a particularly racy flavour. Then came the enemy's opening shots, whirring and rattling through the mango trees, bringing down showers of green leaves and shattered branches, or whooshing and bounding across open ground, tearing up turf and stones, then bounding up, perhaps, to pass overhead with a sort of scream or land with a thud in a bank. The attack began and sepoys were soon seen flitting away between the trees with British soldiers running after them. The soldiers paused to fire before running on again, their rifles smoking, their lips black with powder, biting cartridges as they hurried after fresh quarry, scarcely glancing at the men they killed who lay bleeding in the long grass. They cheered as the main body of sepoys ran from a village from which they had been driven by the shells of well-aimed howitzers, then chased the sepoys across mud walls, through the smoke of burning houses and the smell of sulphur, mad with excitement now as they lunged forward with their bayonets, then lifted them up, red with blood, for another thrust.

There were scenes, too, that those who witnessed them did not care to dwell upon: captured sepoys being stripped, tied to the ground and 'branded over every part of their bodies with red-hot' irons;[36] a crowd of Sikhs, assisted by some English soldiers, seizing a sepoy by his legs and attempting to tear him in two; and, failing in this, dragging him along the ground as they stabbed him in the face with their bayonets before holding him over a fire to roast his lacerated flesh in the flames.[37] Nor was it only sepoys who suffered in this way. 'Sepoy or Oude villager, it mattered not – no questions were asked. His skin was black and did not that suffice? A piece of rope and the branch of a tree, or a rifle bullet through his brain, soon terminated the poor devil's existence.'[38]

While Outram's troops were chasing the sepoys from the Chakar Kothi and down to the banks of the river, Campbell's men captured the Martinière which Dr Gilbert Hadow, so he told his sister, was disappointed to find deserted by the enemy. 'For though I have shot some,' he explained, 'I want to put my sword through some . . . I want more of their blood, and I'll have it yet, too.'[39]

Having taken the Martinière, Campbell crossed the canal and on the morning of 11 March prepared to attack the Begum Kothi. The sailors of the Naval Brigade pushed two of their heaviest guns to within fifty yards of the walls; and after about four hours' steady battering with eight-inch shot, a practicable breach was made. The storming party of eight hundred men waited in silence behind some ruined buildings.

Each man stood leaning on his rifle, wrapt in his own thoughts [recorded Dr Munro, surgeon to the 93rd Highlanders] . . . Suddenly there was a slight movement in the ranks, just enough to break the previous stillness. Officers moved quietly to their places, men stood erect, pressed their bonnets firmly down upon their heads, stretched their arms and limbs and then, grasping their rifles tightly, stood firm and steady. Thus they remained for a second or two, when the tall form of their favourite leader, Adrian Hope, appeared and his right hand waved the signal for the assault. Then a cry burst from their ranks. It was not a cheer, which has a pleasant ring in it, but a short, sharp, piercing cry which had an angry sound which almost made one tremble.[40]

After two hours' savage fighting the Begum Kothi was taken. Sir Colin Campbell 'could not conceal his delight'. He jumped up and down, clapping his hands, crying out, 'I knew it! I knew it! I knew they'd do it! I knew my Highlanders would take it!'[41] Over 860 rebels were killed in the central courtyard alone, most of them bayoneted by soldiers of the 93rd who had adopted the device of pitching bags of powder, with slow-matches fixed in them, into rooms occupied by the enemy. 'Two or three bags very soon brought the enemy out,' a soldier of the 93rd remarked, 'and they were bayoneted down without mercy.'[42] One tough old officer, a former Inverness-shire ploughman who had risen from the ranks to become adjutant of the regiment, killed eleven of them, a havildar, a *naik* and nine sepoys, one after the other with his sword. Another much younger officer, a mere boy who looked like a girl, had gone up to the surgeon before the assault and had handed him a rose with the words, 'Goodbye, old friend, keep this for my sake.' He was shot through the throat as he led his men through the breach, cheering them on and waving his claymore. His soldier-servant knelt down beside his body and burst into tears as he looked upon the unlined, pretty face, crying, 'Oh! But it was a shame to kill him!'[43]

William Hodson was also killed at the Begum Kothi, having joined in the assault without orders and, so it was alleged, in the hope of loot, he being 'the most notorious looter in the whole army'.[44] Refusing to wait for the powder-bags, he had dashed into a room, sabre in hand, and had staggered back, shot through the liver.

About twenty or thirty women were found in the Begum Kothi. A staff officer and Robert Biddulph were told to 'take them away some distance for safety'. This they did, the staff officer leading, Biddulph following with the women, all of whom 'talked and cackled like a flock of geese' except one who fainted with fright and had to be carried.

> They seemed to think they were going to be shot at once [Biddulph recorded], for in vain we begged them to hold their tongues, that they need not be afraid ... Chiefly they bewailed the loss of their jewellery, £100,000 worth they told us ... I certainly pitied the poor creatures ... We deposited them safely in a house, and on our return found that the sentry had been wounded and all their remaining magnificent jewellery, their ornaments and embroidered dresses and everything was gone.[45]

The Englishwomen held prisoner in Lucknow for five months, Madeline Jackson, Mrs Orr and Mrs Orr's daughter, had also been saved. When the Residency had been relieved in November, Madeline's brother and Mrs Orr's husband had been taken out of the Kaiser Bagh with Lieutenant Burnes and Sergeant-Major Morton; and they had all been shot. Little Sophy Christian had since died.

> I was heartbroken [Madeline Jackson confessed]. I now had no one to do anything for and I suppose I did not eat, for one day Mrs Orr came to me and said that the men said they must see me eat or they would

make me. So I had to sit in front of the open door with the subahdar sitting in front of me with all his swords and guns on, and ate rice which seemed like dry hay ... My tears were streaming down ... Our guards seemed to look on us as hostages for them if the English did come back.

The two women and Mrs Orr's daughter were removed from the Kaiser Bagh to a smaller building where they were given native clothes, veils and glass bangles and told to rim their eyes with the pencil that native women used. They were provided with pots and instructed to do their own cooking which they found very difficult as the wood smoke got in their eyes and the monkeys kept upsetting the pans. A man named Wajid Ali befriended them, and when Sir Colin Campbell's army approached Lucknow he arranged for Mrs Orr's daughter to be carried to the British camp 'like a bundle of clothes' on a woman's back with her face, feet and hands all stained brown. Wajid Ali then brought stain for Mrs Orr and Madeline Jackson who were carried out in a *doolie*. Madeline knew that other *doolies* were being searched, and that if she were asked to show her hands all would be lost for, although she had stained the skin the right colour, the nails were too pink. But her *doolie* was stopped only once, and then Wajid Ali said that the ladies inside were court ladies and could not show their hands. So they were allowed to pass on, and soon reached their own people.[46]

During the course of the next few days the rest of the palaces and large buildings south of the river were captured from the enemy, first the Sikandar Bagh, the Shah Najaf and the Kaddum Rasul, then the Moti Mahal, the Tehri Koti and the Chattar Manzil. To the annoyance of Campbell, Major Harry Havelock placed himself at the head of the 90th Light Infantry, just as he had led on the 64th at Cawnpore, and it was 'partly through him', so Private Charles Wickins of the 90th thought, 'that each place was taken so rapid. He led on our men with some of Brayser's Sikhs ... and at every [building] he came to he would say to [Colonel] Purnell [the commanding officer of the 90th], "Here is another little place. We may as well have it." '[47]

Outram sought permission to go out to attack the rebels who had fled in confusion from these buildings. But, receiving the astonishing order that he was not to do so if he thought he might lose a single man, he stayed where he was, allowing the enemy to escape. And it was not until 16 March that Outram crossed the river, attacked and captured the Residency, then pushed on to take the Machi Bhawan, the Hussainabad Imambara, the Daulatkhana and the Musa Bagh.[48]

Throughout northern Lucknow the ground was now strewn with dead bodies, matchlocks, brass pots, clothes and bits of uniforms, powder horns and tulwars; and over the debris British soldiers ran in search of hiding sepoys who were dragged from cellars and cupboards, and lined up against walls to be shot, bayoneted or have their throats cut. Unarmed men suffered with the rest. Two men discovered hiding in a house were brought before an officer who shot them both with his revolver 'in a cold-blooded, deliberate way which was most repulsive' to the young lieutenant who had brought them in for questioning. This same lieutenant recorded the discovery in a building near the iron bridge of a decrepit old man, severely wounded in the thigh by a sentry whose challenge he had failed to answer:

He was brought out and soon surrounded by a noisy, gaping crowd of soldiers, who clamoured loudly for his immediate execution . . . ''Ave his "nut" off,' cried one. 'Hang the brute,' cried another. 'Put him out of mess,' said a third. 'Give him a "Cawnpore dinner",' shouted a fourth . . . (the soldiers called six inches of steel a 'Cawnpore dinner') . . . The only person of the group who appeared unmoved and indifferent to what was going on was . . . the old man himself whose stoicism one could not but admire . . . He must have read his fate a hundred times over in the angry gestures and looks of his captors but never once did he open his lips to supplicate for mercy or betray either agitation or emotion . . . He was given over to two men who received orders to 'destroy him' (the expression usually employed on these occasions), and they led him away . . . The soldiers returned to their games of cards and their pipes and seemed to feel no further interest in the matter except when the executioners returned and one of their comrades carelessly asked, 'Well, Bill, what did yer do to him?' 'Oh,' said the man as he wiped the blood off an old tulwar, with an air of cool and horrible indifference which no words can convey. 'Oh, sliced his 'ed off', resuming his rubber, and dropping the subject, much as a man might who had drowned a litter of puppies.[49]

Nor did native servants escape the soldiers' heartless derision, even though many of them, like Major Olpherts's *khidmatgar* who followed him everywhere with a leather bottle of rum, had risked their lives in the service of their masters.[50] 'These poor devils when bringing down their masters' dinners, or employed in similar duties, were unable to keep entirely under cover, but were forced to run the gauntlet of the enemy's fire, exhibiting during this trying period an amount of terror very entertaining to behold.' To increase their fright, officers would throw handfuls of stones between their feet to make them believe they were hit by showers of grape. Against cooler, more dignified or fatter servants and baboos who walked rather than ran, black wooden pipe bowls resembling cannon-shot were used. 'It may be remarked that the amusement was considerably heightened if the missile was made actually to strike the shins of the victim, when he of course concluded he was mortally wounded.'[51]

Most soldiers, however, had little time to spare for such pranks, being occupied in the serious business of looting. Despite the heat and the numberless festering corpses which polluted the air, risking death in houses where armed men lay concealed behind doors and beneath bales of cloth, they broke into buildings through shattered windows to drag out into the streets a marvellous variety of plunder, from parrots, goats and chickens to a leopard shot for the sake of its skin. Much of the plunder was worthless; but 'some men found hundreds of pounds' worth of things, diamonds, pearls, etc.[52] On his way to the Kaiser Bagh, William Howard Russell saw soldiers rushing along laden with loot, past white statues reddened with blood, through corpse-strewn orange groves, ignoring a comrade shot through the neck, 'leaning against a smiling Venus, gasping and, at every gasp, bleeding to death'.

These men were wild with fury and lust of gold – literally drunk with plunder [Russell wrote in his diary]. Some come out with china vases or mirrors, dash them to pieces on the ground, and return to seek more valuable booty. Others are busy gouging out the precious stones from the stems of pipes, from saddle-cloths or the hilts of swords . . . Some swathe their bodies in stuffs crusted with precious metals and gems; others carry off useless lumber . . . One fellow, having burst open a leaden-looking lid, which was in reality of solid silver, drew out an armlet of emeralds and diamonds and pearls so large that I really believed they were not real stones and that they formed part of a chandelier chain. 'What will your honour give me for these?' said he. 'I'll take a hundred rupees on chance.'

Russell, not having that amount of money on him, offered a promissory note. But the soldier wanted cash. He would take two *mohurs*, he said, 'and a bottle of rum on the spot'.[53]

Although the troops, their faces black with powder, their eyes glittering in excitement, usually paid no attention to their officers as they hurried about in search of further treasures, occasionally a man 'out of whose head *all* ideas of discipline had not been driven would make a desperate effort to salute from beneath his plunder, struggling to free a hand for the purpose, or in happy forgetfulness bringing a cackling hen to his cap with military precision'.[54]

The officers themselves did not refrain from looting, though few admitted to having come across anything as valuable as the diamond star on the dome lid of a golden *tazia* which some men of the 93rd found in the mosque near the Bara Imambara and presented to a poor, well-liked young lieutenant who had to remit half his pay to support a widowed mother and could not afford to purchase a captaincy. The lid was eventually sold in London where it was said to have fetched £80,000.[55] If this officer was uniquely lucky, most others acquired at least one or two items of plunder worth taking home. Concentrating on military trophies, Edmund Verney, for instance, collected

a helmet of Damascus steel inlaid with gold and having Persian characters worked on various parts of it . . . a powder horn of inlaid mother-of-pearl . . . a red standard with the King of Oudh's arms embroidered on it in gold . . . a long straight sword of very curious workmanship . . . three scimitars, one with an iron hilt inlaid with gold . . . and a most valuable fowling-piece, beautifully inlaid with gold and silver.[56]

As the last of the rebels in Lucknow surrendered and were killed, and as thousands of others fled across the river – permitted to escape partly through Sir Colin Campbell's reluctance to risk life and partly through the incompetence of some of his subordinates – the officers of his army wandered about the ruined city. They walked up to the Residency to gaze upon its ruined walls and crumbling ceilings, at the haggard skeleton of the now famous Baillie Guard Gate, pitted by bullet marks and with lumps of plaster still falling from its sides. They looked down upon the tangles of bloated corpses caught up in bends of the river and by the arches of the bridges, and upon the vultures tearing away hunks of sodden, putrid flesh. They heard the occasional explosion of a hidden mine and, as the reverberations of the sound rolled and echoed through the air, watched the dense white columns of smoke rise above the towers and domes and minarets. They went to inspect the Kaiser Bagh past buildings on whose battered walls, drawn in charcoal and scratched with bayonet points, were the graffiti of hundreds of soldiers, names and slogans, caricatures, dates, obscenities, and those arcane statements, beloved by the wall defacer, whose meaning is usually known only to the *cognoscenti* and not always even to them. In the Kaiser Bagh which, like all the other large buildings in this part of Lucknow, had been fortified with great care and skill, there were scenes of appalling havoc. Decomposing corpses lay covered with fractured spear staves, bits of howdahs from which the silver had been prized, shattered crystal goblets and splinters of marble tables.

Most of the State Rooms had had very handsome chandeliers hanging from the ceilings and splendid mirrors on the walls [wrote Francis Collins]. Not one of these was left intact ... All the furniture was smashed to pieces ... The pictures ... without exception had been ripped up by the soldiers' bayonets, and I did not see one that was not torn across the face ... I went into a room full of boxes of china. I saw soldiers here, simply for mischief's sake, stepping from one box into another and smashing their contents ... The great delight seems to have been to fire a rifle into the centre of a mirror, thereby creating a beautiful star. Some, however, clubbed their rifles so as to make the destruction of the offending object more complete and in this way most of the furniture must have been destroyed and the handsome doors to the cabinets smashed up.[57]

Witnessing this wholesale destruction of valuable booty and looking at the shambles that Lucknow had become, many officers began to fear that their share of prize-money would not amount to nearly as much as they had hoped. 'They say we shall get a good lump of prize money for Lucknow,' Lieutenant Ashton Cromwell Warner wrote home, 'but I fear it is too good to be true. Some people say a captain's share will be £400, but where it is to come from is a mystery to me ... Lucknow used to be the finest city in India and beat Delhi into fits. Some of the buildings are the finest I saw in any part of the world ... But it is a most miserable looking city now.'[58] Ensign Richard Stairforth thought so too. 'Lucknow, once one of the most magnificent cities in India, is now in ruins almost,' he told his sister. 'Houses are being pulled down in all directions so as to render an enemy's approach without being seen impossible.'[59]

Even so the plunder accumulated by the prize-agents was estimated by The Times at over £600,000 before the army left Lucknow; and within a week it had 'reached a million and a quarter sterling'. But 'what became of it all?' Corporal Forbes-Mitchell wanted to know.

Each private soldier who served throughout the relief and capture of Lucknow got prize money [of less than 18 rupees, and] I could myself name over a dozen men who served throughout every engagement, two of whom gained the Victoria Cross, who have died in the almshouses of their native parishes, and several in the almshouses of the Calcutta District Charitable Society![60]

20

The Last of the Rebels

· Continued resistance of the talukdars *· Walpole's campaign
in Rohilkhand · his defeat at Ruiya, 15 April 1858 – Campbell's
victory over Khan Bahadur Khan outside Bareilly, 5 May 1858 ·
death of the Maulvi, 5 June · the mutiny at Indore, 1 July 1857 – the
Rani of Jhansi · massacre at Jhansi, 8 June 1857 · Sir Hugh Rose
arrives at Jhansi, 21 March 1858 · Jhansi captured, 3 April 1858 ·
Rose enters Kalpi, 23 May – Rani killed, 17 June · Tatya Tope
executed, 18 April 1859 · King of Delhi tried and found guilty
on all charges, 29 March 1859 ·*

On entering Lucknow one of Sir Colin Campbell's aides-de-camp – in
imitation of Sir Charles Napier's message, '*Peccavi*' ('I have sinned'),
announcing the annexation of the province of Sind – issued in his
master's name the proclamation, '*Nunc fortunatus sum*' ('I am in luck
now').[1] But although Lucknow was certainly in British hands again,
the rebellion was far from being suppressed.

Sir James Outram believed that the time had come to treat the
talukdars as honourable enemies rather than as rebels, to guarantee to
them the continued possession of their lands so that they might be
persuaded to exert their considerable influence in helping the
Government restore order. They had been treated badly in the past,
Outram argued; yet most of them had remained loyal to the British at
the outset of the mutinies and, if more recently they had given way to
the rebel leaders' demands for the services of their armed retainers,
they had otherwise contrived to keep out of the conflict. John Lawrence and George Campbell, the Second Civil Commissioner of
Oudh, were both inclined to agree with Outram. George Campbell,
who had been employed by Canning to write an official account of the
mutiny for the home authorities, argued that, for the sake of a peaceful future, the *talukdars* 'must be assured that bygones would be considered bygones'.[2] John Lawrence's views were expressed in a letter to
Lord Stanley, Secretary for the Colonies:

With the majority of Englishmen the cry has been 'War to the Knife!' totally forgetting that such a policy requires proportionate power. Now, it seems to me that, setting aside all considerations of mercy and humanity, we have not the means of enforcing such a policy. If every insurgent, or even every mutineer, is to be put to death, or transported beyond the seas, we shall require 200,000 European soldiers, and, even then, we shall not put down all opposition in half a dozen years. Is England prepared to send out from 20,000 to 30,000 troops annually to supply casualties? If she is not it behoves you all to meet the difficulty fairly, and to decide what ought to be done. Our prestige is gone! Our power is literally slipping away. In attempting to compass an impracticable policy we are endangering our very empire in the East. I am no advocate of forgiving the murderers of our women and children. I would hunt all such wretches down. But, to do this effectually, we must discriminate between the mutineers. At present every man who is caught is hanged or shot. Who will surrender under such circumstances? Thus all classes of mutineers or insurgents are bound together by the very desperation of their position.[3]

But Lord Canning and his advisers believed that the *talukdars* – who had been more active in their opposition to the British in the later stages of the struggle than Outram at first supposed – must be treated with severity. So a proclamation to be addressed to the people of Oudh was sent to Outram as Commissioner for the province. This proclamation declared that, since the mutineers had received much assistance from the people of Oudh, the lands of the province, with certain exceptions, were to be confiscated by the British Government. Outram's objections led to a small concession: that the Governor-General would be 'willing to view liberally' claims for the restitution of their former rights submitted by *talukdars* who came forward promptly to offer help in the restoration of order. But the concession carried little weight with the *talukdars* most of whom now determined to fight for what the Government seemed bent on taking from them.[4]

The *talukdars* had no recognized leader, however. They had their forts surrounded by jungles which their ancestors had specially grown or preserved as a means of defence. They had numerous armed retainers. They had the support of a few of the zemindars, though most of these remained neutral as did many of the peasants who continued to farm their land as in peaceful times, either indifferent to the change of ruler, or, if deriving pleasure from the spectacle of fallen masters, unwilling to leave the land to assist in their destruction. Yet the *talukdars* never combined their resources, never joined forces with those other rebels who did have leaders.

It was against one of these leaders, Khan Bahadur Khan, who had been proclaimed the rebels' Viceroy at Bareilly in Rohilkhand, that Sir Colin Campbell was now required to march. Campbell himself would have preferred to spend the next few months bringing the countryside around Lucknow securely under British rule: it seemed to him that as he had invaded Oudh and occupied the capital, the whole province ought to be completely pacified before the reconquest of another began. But it was Canning's view that, since most of the Hindus in Rohilkhand were still quite kindly disposed towards the British and looked to them for release from the tyranny of Khan Bahadur Khan, political considerations gave Rohilkhand priority over Oudh. So, giving way to the Governor-General's views, Campbell sent a strong column, including three Highland regiments, from Lucknow into Rohilkhand under command of Brigadier Walpole.[5]

The choice of Walpole to lead Campbell's beloved Highlanders astonished every officer in Lucknow. For, though a brave man, he was almost universally acknowledged to be an obstinate blunderer. Dr Hadow, who thought the man 'a great dolt', said that the whole army was 'horribly disgusted' by his appointment.[6] And the low opinion entertained of him was soon justified. His march into Rohilkhand was unopposed until, on the ninth day, he approached the fort of Ruiya. Here he was told by a trooper who had been taken prisoner in a previous encounter and held in the fort, that the *talukdar* in command of it had no intention of opposing him but would merely put up a show of resistance to save his honour. Walpole not only refused to believe this information but declined to make a reconnaissance of the fort whose wall, high and thick in front, was so low on the far side that 'a child would have had no trouble in climbing over it'. Without the least reflection he sent his infantry forward in a frontal attack; and the *talukdar*, presented with so tempting a target, decided to make a determined stand after all. Over a hundred men were killed when the defenders opened fire; several more, all Highlanders, were killed by splinters from the exploding shells of their own artillery. One of the dead was Brigadier Adrian Hope, the talented and popular Highlander who was believed to be on the point of relieving Walpole of the command. At length Walpole ordered a retreat from what became known in his army as 'Walpole's Folly', so savagely cursed by the men of the Highland regiments that their officers thought they might murder him.[7]

I was walking about our camp that evening [Private Potiphar recorded], and . . . it was all in an uproar . . . Small gangs of men might be seen all over it discussing the events of the day and the loss of their comrades and Brigadier Hope . . . Some of the men proposed to start off and take [the fort] by themselves, and others to go and set fire to the Commander's tent and hoot him for a coward. I even saw tears in many a soldier's eyes . . . What Sir Colin will say when he hears of it I cannot tell . . . Our infantry are almost mad.[8]

The subsequent engagements were not so appallingly mishandled, yet the officers under his command continued to complain of Walpole's 'utter inadequacy', his 'doing his best to make a mess of the whole affair'. It was reported that 'two officers of the 92nd broke their claymores and swore that they would never fight anymore under Walpole'.[9]

Sir Colin Campbell's march was, of course, more efficiently conducted. On 5 May he defeated Khan Bahadur Khan outside Bareilly and occupied the city. But although he was now able to end the rule in Rohilkhand of Khan Bahadur Khan of whom nothing more was heard, there was another, more formidable enemy still in the field – the Maulvi of Faizabad.

No one was sure, or ever afterwards discovered, who the Maulvi was. It seems that he had been known to the British authorities for several years as Ahmed Ahmadullah Shah, 'an inspired prophet or fakir . . . a tall, lean, muscular man, with thin jaw, long thin lips, high aquiline nose; deep-set, large dark eyes, beetle brows, long beard, and coarse black hair, falling in masses over his shoulders'.[10] He was believed to have travelled widely over the country in the months before the outbreak at Meerut, preaching sedition and calling for a holy war against the *Firinghis*. He had made 'a stay of considerable duration at Agra' where he became 'remarkable for the influence he appeared to exercise over the Mohammedan natives'. Ultimately he had been arrested at Faizabad; and, when released from prison there by the mutineers, had made his way to Lucknow.[11]

At Lucknow he had played a leading role in the siege, and had evidently endeavoured to persuade the various groups of rebels to cooperate more closely together; to induce the mutinous sepoys – who insisted upon electing their own leaders and rarely chose the most suitable – to work with the *talukdars*' men; and to get both these groups to work with the soldiers of the disbanded state army and with those other rebels from various classes who had given the uprising in Oudh the appearance of a civil as well as a military rebellion. Well aware of the rebels' need of a leader at Lucknow he had urged the acceptance as *Wali* of Birjis Qadr, the ten-year-old son of the ex-King of Oudh by one of his minor wives, Hazrat Mahal, a young woman of powerful personality. Hazrat Mahal was a courtesan by profession who had been taken into the royal harem as a *khawasin*, had been promoted to *pari*, then become a *begum* after being accepted as one of the King's concubines, and acknowledged as *mahal* after the birth of her child. As the mother of the *Wali*, she had become one of the most influential members of his Council of State in which a man supposed to be her lover had been appointed Chief Justice. Of the other officers appointed to the Council, half were Hindus, the other half Muslims. The military appointments had not, however, been given to experienced soldiers. No place had been found for Barhat Ahmad who had distinguished himself at the battle of Chinhat but who had apparently since been relieved of his command for proposing the selection of one of Birjis Qadr's brothers as *Wali* rather than Birjis Qadr himself. Nor had any post been found for the Maulvi.[12]

The Maulvi had, however, been permitted to lead an attack on Outram's defences at the Alambagh; and although this attack had failed and the Maulvi had for a time been disgraced, he had recovered his position as an influential rebel leader and had managed to escape from the city when Sir Colin Campbell's army moved in. He had retreated with his followers into Rohilkhand where he had since proved a most irksome enemy to the British, seizing Shajahanpur and shelling the entrenchment which the small British garrison had constructed there. Brigadier William Jones had been sent to help the garrison; but, although he had been able to get into the entrenchment, the enemy forces were too strong for him to move out to attack them, as the Maulvi had now been reinforced by the followers of both Hazrat Mahal and Firuz Shah, a Moghul prince who, being out of the country at the time of the uprising in Delhi, had escaped Hodson's vengeance. Jones was therefore obliged to ask Sir Colin Campbell to help him attack the Maulvi who was driven back into Oudh.[13]

In Oudh – where he called himself King of Hindustan and *Khalifat – Ullah*, the Deputy of God – the Maulvi was as troublesome to the British as he had been in Rohilkhand. The Governor-General offered a reward of 50,000 rupees for his capture; but he was as elusive as he had always been, reported in one place only to appear in another. He attacked Rohamdi where he destroyed the fort; he made a raid on the station of Pali; he then moved against Pawayan whose Rajah had so far declined to offer help to the rebels.

The Maulvi approached the fort at Pawayan on a war elephant; and, when the Rajah refused to open the gate, he ordered the mahout to charge. The elephant with lowered head lumbered forward and crashed into the gate which creaked on its hinges and seemed about to give way when the Rajah's retainers opened fire with their match-locks and shot the Maulvi dead. As the Maulvi's companions ran away, the Rajah's brothers came down from the walls of the fort and cut off the corpse's head. The Rajah, wrapping the head in a cloth, took it at once to the British Magistrate at Shajahanpur to claim the 50,000 rupees reward. He found the Magistrate in the dining-room with some friends, but, too impatient to consider that he might spoil their meal, he opened his bundle to let the head roll out on the floor. He received his reward; and the head was prominently displayed next day on the roof of the *Kotwali*.[14]

With the death of the Maulvi the fire of rebellion died down in Rohilkhand and north-western Oudh. Elsewhere in Oudh, however, it was some months before order was restored and the last of the rebels laid down their arms. During these months, British officers found the military operations utterly exasperating. 'It is only a very small portion of any rebel army that ever gets killed or wounded,' Lieutenant Nowell complained. 'The rest run away, join another party and again begin to commit all sorts of depredations.'[15]

Those who did not manage to escape were almost invariably slaughtered. William Howard Russell recorded in his journal the fate of one particular group of sepoys who agreed to surrender to a British officer. One by one they came out into the open where they were told to take off their belts and pouches and to lay them down with their bayonets on the ground. 'I then fell them in against the wall,' the officer informed Russell, 'and told some Sikhs who were handy to polish them off. This they did immediately, shooting and bayoneting [all fifty-seven of them] so that they were disposed of in a couple of minutes.'[16]

'Altogether I am thoroughly tired of this life,' Garnet Wolseley told his brother. 'As long as any honour or glory was attached to it, of course I liked it, but now that the row or whatever it should be called has degenerated down into pursuing small bodies of rebels without cannon and annihilating not fighting them, I take no interest whatever in the work as I consider it quite derogatory to a soldier's profession.' Only very rarely was there the kind of fight which Wolseley enjoyed; but when there was, he had to admit that he

saw some of the noblest examples of bravery [he] ever witnessed among the niggers; the fellows were shot down and bayoneted at their guns . . . The greater portion of the men we killed were Gaxees or fanatics and I must own that I do not care much if I never have to encounter any more of them. The first fellow I came up to roared, 'Come on with your tulwar!' not in English, of course.

The only cowards on the field were Hodson's Horse.

They would not charge. Over and over again their officers rushed to the front and tried to get them to go on, but they never did anything. At one place where the enemy had two guns in the open field and stood splendidly to them, firing grape at us until the last moment, we advanced with them. I was with the General [Hope Grant] at the time . . . when he told me to get these damned cowards to charge. So I ordered them on and charged with them; but to my horror upon coming up to the guns a devil [not] a sowar would go at these fellows; the officer who led them and myself went at them by ourselves . . . Do not say a word about my having told you of Hodson's Horse behaving badly, for owing to the pluck of their late commander they have acquired a great name [out here].[17]

Yet these operations in Oudh, tiresome as Wolseley found them, were for the most part patiently and conscientiously conducted by Sir Colin Campbell and Hope Grant. And, combined with promises to the rebel leaders that surrender would not necessarily be followed by confiscation of their lands, they eventually resulted in *vakils* being sent to the British headquarters to ask for terms. The rebels had been reluctant to surrender at first, even when there was no longer any hope of victory, disbelieving British promises of mercy. But Campbell had proved himself to be an honourable man who kept his word. So had Hope Grant who had been known to have his own soldiers, as well as native camp-followers, tied up and flogged for plundering villages.[18]

Those rebels who refused to surrender were driven across the frontier into Nepal where they would have chosen to remain had not Jang Bahadur, who had consistently refused to listen to their pleas for help, asked Lord Canning to send in troops to root them out. Jang Bahadur now learned with satisfaction that his request for British soldiers to drive away the unwelcome intruders from the foothills of the Himalayas had been granted, and that the rebels had been forced to flee before General Hope Grant's columns and had either returned to their homes or had perished in the hills above the pestilential jungles of the Terai.[19]

When Hazrat Mahal, who crossed the Nepalese frontier with her son at the end of 1858, appealed to Jang Bahadur for assistance, he replied sternly,

Be it known that an intimate friendship exists between the British Government and the Nepal State . . . I therefore inform you that if you should remain within my territory the Gurkha troops will most certainly . . . attack . . . you . . . Be it also known that the Nepal State will neither assist, show mercy to, nor permit to remain in its territories, those who have been so faithless and ungrateful as to do mischief, and raise animosity and insurrection against their masters, of whose salt they have partaken, to whom they owe their change for the better, and by whom they have been fostered.[20]

The need to concentrate as many troops as possible at Lucknow had dangerously weakened British garrisons elsewhere. There had been serious disturbances in Bihar where Kunwar Singh blockaded the garrison at Azamgarh, and having been driven from Azamgarh by Lord Mark Kerr, maintained a guerrilla warfare against British troops in the jungles of Jagdishpur. Here he was joined by thousands of peasants raised by his brother, Ammar Singh, who, on the old Rajput's death, succeeded to the command of his forces. These forces, fearing that to submit meant death, fought with great skill, first against General Sir Edward Lugard who, worn out by the hardships and anxieties of the campaign, had to be sent home; then against Brigadier Douglas whose force was increased to over seven thousand men.[21] But even a much larger force would have been no match for the rebels who sensibly avoided battles which they knew they could not win, yet wore out the unwieldy European columns by ambushes and quick night attacks followed by immediate retreats into the fastnesses of the jungle, obeying the rules for guerrilla warfare laid down by Khan Bahadur Khan:

Do not attempt to meet the regular columns of the infidels because they are superior to you in discipline and organisation, and have big guns. But watch their movements, guard all the ghauts on the rivers, intercept their communications; stop their supplies, cut up their daks and posts; keep constantly hanging about their camps; give them no rest.[22]

Time and again, after periods of relative quiet, it was hoped that the spirit of the guerrillas had been broken; but then would come another attack and another swift withdrawal. Major Havelock, who had inherited his father's baronetcy, suggested pursuing the rebels with squadrons of mounted infantry armed with Enfield rifles. This method of fighting the rebels proved successful. But it was not until the end of 1858 that they were finally dispersed in Bihar; and by then there had been trouble farther east. Infantry regiments at Chittagong and Dacca had mutinied in November 1857, cavalry detachments at

Madariganj and Jalpaiguri the next month. And the mutineers from these regiments, running off, then doubling backwards and forwards like hares, caused as much trouble to the British in that part of Bengal as the guerrillas had done in Bihar.

There had been trouble, too, in the Bombay Presidency; and in Bombay itself there had been a panic when terrified families fled aboard boats or into the fort. But the risings in that part of India had been quickly suppressed by the prompt disarming of mutinous regiments and the execution of ringleaders, while other threatened outbreaks had been checked before the affected regiments got out of hand. In Hyderabad – where the Nizam had no sympathy with those of his Muslim subjects who supported the restoration of the Moghul empire – a threatened uprising had been checked with equal promptness by the Resident, Major Cuthbert Davidson, whose guns, manned by the Madras Artillery, dispersed a mob about to attack the Residency. In Central India, however, a mutiny at Indore had serious consequences. The acting Agent there was Colonel Henry Marion Durand, a tall, commanding, outspoken and unimaginative man of forty-four. Durand was ostensibly supported by the Maratha prince, the Holkar, Tukoji Rao II, whose palace was at Indore. But the troops which the Holkar sent to protect the Residency were of doubtful loyalty; and Durand was constantly badgered by various members of the British community in Indore to withdraw to a place of greater security.

I was infinitely more plagued and worried by the cowardly fear of some of our guests, and of more than one officer, than I was by any idea of actual danger [wrote Durand's brave and resourceful wife]. We had one or two terrible alarmists. Among the worst was a Captain Magniac and his wife. They both *bored* me beyond expression with daily and hourly histories of what was going to happen ... Mrs M. was a perfect torment till at last I almost ceased either listening or speaking to her. Of course, the sole idea in her mind, and her husband's too, was the madness of trying to hold Indore (before anything had occurred) and the hopelessness of our escape when the attack should come ... Both Captain M. and one of Henry's adjutants wanted him to retire before any outbreak occurred, but of course he would never have heard of such a thing, and I was glad he would not. I had no idea of our giving the natives such a satisfaction and triumph.[23]

When the Holkar's artillery turned their guns on the Indore Residency, however, and the native troops who had been called in to help protect it refused to obey their officers' orders, Colonel Durand had to accept the inevitability of retreat. Mrs Durand, who did not long survive the hardships of their subsequent flight, described in a letter to a friend what happened when the Holkar's soldiers began their attack on the Residency:

The panic among our people was excessive . . . Henry called for our gunners to stand to their guns and urged all the officers to get their men together as quickly as possible, but it was an impossibility. The cavalry saddled and mounted as fast as they could, but were *wild* with the sudden surprise, and kept careering hither and thither in small knots utterly unmanageable. Meantime Holkar's guns kept up their fire and our two replied but no infantry could be assembled to support them . . . Colonel Travers, the officer in command, in vain endeavoured to make his cavalry of some use, but finding they were not to be collected as a body he charged Holkar's guns followed by *five* men, in hopes more would follow, but they did not and he was, of course, obliged to come back . . . Meanwhile [the infantry of the garrison] wandered about in the most apathetic looking manner . . . Henry posted them in windows and behind pillars, [but they refused to stay in these exposed positions] and assembled in the centre of the room . . . Everyone who could came over to the Residency but many unfortunate Europeans, even women and *children* were massacred. The wretches fired one of the guns into a covered cart in which 2 women and a little child of 5 years were going off and killed all. One of Henry's clerks and *six* children were murdered and many others. Officers and ladies all reached the Residency in safety and we were congregated, 7 ladies, 3 young children, 2 European women, 3 doctors, etc. . . . It was curious to see the difference in the behaviour of the various ladies who were collected in the Residency, two or three calm and quiet, others looking the picture of despair and weeping quietly, one *wild* with terror and excitement . . . You would almost have laughed had you seen Mrs Magniac (whose name should have been spelled without a g) rush up from her own room below, half dressed with her hair streaming about her face, and that the image of despair and terror. I cannot comprehend any woman with half a grain of sense *exhibiting* such desperate alarm . . .

What also *disgusted* me beyond measure was the dastardly conduct of our troops, *soldiers* they did not deserve the name of, and I was almost equally provoked at two of the *officers* whose one idea seemed not to hold out to the last, but to be off and save their wives and themselves with all possible speed . . . We had no time to think of saving anything and left the house by the back verandah while Holkar's artillery were raking the front . . . Henry was most bitterly mortified and I must say I felt far less rejoiced at getting out of danger than I should have done had our miserable *rabble* of troops done *something* to show themselves soldiers . . . The bungalows were burning as we left and the lower windows of the Residency all shattered. Being a stone building they could not set fire to it but after we left the whole contents were plundered ... We lost *everything* ... I had somehow got my wits about me enough to prepare a few needfuls to carry off, unlike a lady in another place who had to fly while the regiment were in open mutiny and shooting the officers down, she carried off her jewel box, *and marriage certificate*!

Holkar assures Henry that all his troops mutinied and that he himself was totally at their mercy, having nothing to do with their attack upon us, and this I believe.[24]

The ejection of the British from Indore had been followed by mutinies at Mhow and Agar. And it was several months before the rebels, besieged in Dhar, were forced to abandon the fort and were defeated in the open field at Goraria after a grim campaign in Malwa. This campaign in Malwa was a peculiarly brutal one. At the siege of Dhar – where the 'British generalship', in Dr Sylvester's opinion, was 'atrocious'

the men off duty, and even some native soldiers, but chiefly the 86th and artillery were frightfully drunk. Having seized on the native liquor shops, they then commenced looting and killed everything black, old men and young, women and children ... They shouted 'Cawnpore!' and 'Delhi!' and down they went. Streete says he saw a room full of dead women with children sucking at their breasts. Other women brought out dead children supplicating for mercy. Officers rushed down with the Provost Marshall and some dragoons and put a stop to it and destroyed all the liquor.[25]

Having taken Dhar, Durand – who had made 'a strange guy of himself by putting on a black cap cover for his wife's death' – led his column on towards the Chambal, capturing numerous prisoners who were shot with their hands tied behind their backs. 'Then we burned some houses near a village,' Dr Sylvester's account continued. 'The men in them ran out all on fire, their hair in a blaze and were killed by the infantry muskets. Whilst we were attacking the escaping villagers, I saw a man in a tree and shot him with my revolver.'[26]

Neither the fighting in Malwa nor in Bengal was as fierce or costly, though, as the battles in Bundelkhand where the sepoys at Jhansi had mutinied, murdered all but one of their officers, released the convicts from the gaol and marched upon the town fort where the rest of the Europeans in Jhansi had taken refuge. The Europeans, after firing the fort guns at their assailants, had decided to surrender on condition that the mutineers allowed them a safe conduct to a place of safety, trusting that the Rani of Jhansi would ensure there was no treachery.[27]

The Rani, Lakshmi Bai, a 'very civil, polite and clever young lady', in the opinion of Sir Robert Hamilton, Agent in Central India, was then in her early thirties.[28] She was a good-looking woman, 'rather stout but not too stout', so another Englishman who knew her said. Her face

> must have been very handsome when she was younger, and even now it had many charms . . . The expression also was . . . very intelligent. The eyes were particularly fine and the nose very delicately shaped. She was not very fair, though she was far from black . . . Her dress was plain white muslin, so fine in texture and drawn about her in such a way that the outline of her figure was plainly discernible – and a remarkably fine figure she had. What spoilt her was her voice.[29]

She was to acquire amongst British officers an undeserved reputation for excessive lasciviousness.[30] She had been married when she was fourteen to Gangadhar Rao, Rajah of Jhansi, a kindly, scholarly man much older than herself. She had had a child by him but the baby had died. So, shortly before his own death he had adopted a boy, expressing to the Governor-General the hope that the British would treat the child with kindness and allow the state to be governed by his adoptive mother 'during the length of her life'.

There was no doubt that she had the character and capacity to rule the state; but Lord Dalhousie, in accordance with his usual practice, had decided to reject the Rajah's plea and to annex Jhansi. The widow was treated quite generously. She was awarded a life pension of 60,000 rupees and allowed to keep the palace though she had to relinquish the fort. The adopted heir, on coming of age, was to be permitted to inherit the Rajah's personal estate. But the Rani was not so interested in money as in Jhansi. 'I shall not surrender my Jhansi,' she declared; and she issued an appeal to the Court of Directors in London. The appeal was rejected; and the Rani's resentment had been increased when she was told that she would be expected to pay her late husband's debts out of her own pension.[31]

In the three years that had passed since the annexation of Jhansi, the Rani had much impressed the Political Agent, Captain Alexander Skene, with the force and charm of her personality and with her evident wish to remain on friendly terms with her British masters. When the news reached Jhansi of the outbreak at Meerut, Skene had not hesitated in granting her request to raise an armed bodyguard for her personal protection. And when the sepoys at Jhansi mutinied he did not doubt that she would do what she could to save him and the other forty odd Europeans and Eurasians inside the city fort.

The Political Agent's *vakil* gave this account of what happened:

Early upon the morning of the 8th [June] the mutineers surrounded the fort and by the aid of their guns succeeded in effecting an entrance into it . . . when Captain Gordon [Deputy Superintendent of Jhansi], after making a most gallant resistance, finding the place was no longer defensible and preferring death to surrender, shot himself through the head, putting the muzzle under his chin and pulling the trigger with his toes. The mutineers then made prisoner all the European officers with their wives and children . . . took them . . . outside the city walls . . . and there brutally murdered every soul of them . . . The next day the mutineers left Jhansi, taking along with them the treasure and magazine.[32]

The Rani, either powerless or unwilling to help them, reported to Major W. C. Erskine, Commissioner of the Sagar Division:

The troops stationed at Jhansi through their faithlessness, cruelty and violence, killed all the European civil and military officers and the Rani . . . could render them no aid, which she very much regrets . . . The sepoys . . . sent her messages . . . to the effect that if she at all hesitated to comply with their requests [for money as a reward for liberating the state from British control] they would blow up her palace . . . She was obliged to consent to all the requests made . . . It is quite beyond her power to make any arrangements for the safety of the district and the measure would require funds which she does not possess . . .[33]

In response to her plea for help, Erskine agreed that until a new official arrived at Jhansi, she should 'manage the District for the British Government'. These instructions were disapproved of in Calcutta, where the Rani's protestations of innocence were generally discounted; and when Jhansi was invaded by troops of two neighbouring states, her appeal for help from the British was ignored. She turned, therefore, to the rebels who helped her drive out the invaders and who pressed her to fight for independence from the British too. Yet she seems still to have been unwilling to commit herself until a formidable British army appeared before the walls of Jhansi intent upon revenge for the massacre there; and then she determined to fight.[34]

The British army was commanded by Major-General Sir Hugh Rose, who had distinguished himself in various diplomatic appointments and had acted as British liaison officer at the French headquarters during the Crimean War. He had the reputation of being a brave, bright and dashing officer, but many of those who served under him did not at first regard his talents at all highly. He was 'laughed at and called a griff by a good many'.[35] To Dr Sylvester he appeared 'very effeminate, weak and I should think unable to rough it much'.[36] And for the first few weeks, the veterans' distrust seemed justified.

Rose began his march to Sehore on 6 January 1858, accompanied by Sir Robert Hamilton as political officer; and a slow and arduous march it proved to be. After a week's toiling through jungles and across rivers the army came upon their first obstacle, the fort of Rahatgarh. Rose laid siege to the town; but before a breach had been made in the walls, hordes of camp-followers came screaming into the batteries, for a large rebel force, commanded by the Rajah of Banpur – who had joined the rebel cause after a regiment of the Gwalior Contingent had mutinied at Lalitpur – had come to relieve the Rahatgarh garrison. Rose detached part of his force to deal with the new threat while continuing the siege operations. The Rajah's force was soon driven off. But most of his men escaped; and, during that night, the garrison also got away from the fort, eluding the levies of the Begum of Bhopal, and retreated to a defensive position at Barodia. Altogether, in the opinion of Captain J. G. Lightfoot, it was 'a very badly managed affair'.[37]

The rebels were forced out of Barodia without difficulty; but most of them escaped from there also. And although Sir Hugh entered Sagar in triumph on 3 February, when he marched out a few days later to capture the fort at Garhakota he returned to Sagar having once more failed to prevent the escape of the only partially invested garrison. Then, finding that it was quite impossible to collect supplies in the countryside around Sagar, he was obliged to remain there until the end of the month, giving the rebels time to occupy the mountain ranges that separated him from Jhansi.

When the march was resumed at the end of the month, Rose was warned that the Rajah of Banpur's men had occupied the pass of Narut. So he decided to make a feint against this pass and to take his men through the pass of Madanpur. This manoeuvre proved to be 'one of the most lamentably mismanaged affairs you ever saw', Captain Lightfoot recorded. The rebels fired into the British column from the heights on either side, inflicting many casualties, killing Rose's horse, and forcing the artillery to withdraw their guns. Then, after the column had been reorganized

the rebels were attacked in front, when they could have been taken in the rear and completely destroyed. It really is too bad that such incapable people should be sent out merely to serve some political ends at such a time as this [Lightfoot added]. I imagine [Rose] could never have held the command of even a company before . . . The whole force is crying out against him and his ridiculous proceedings. I imagine there never was a General who so little possessed the confidence of the men under him. The opinion of every man in the force is that he will turn out much worse than Wyndham.[38]

On the morning of 21 March, Rose arrived before Jhansi at last; and, determined not to repeat his mistakes at Rahatgarh and Garha-kota by allowing the rebels to escape, he immediately invested the city and fort. For the next ten days his heavy guns hurled shot and shell over the desolate granite crags while his infantry maintained a remorseless fire upon the figures of the sepoys who lined the massive walls and the women who could be seen carrying ammunition to the batteries. It was insufferably hot. The sun shone relentlessly down; blasts of hot wind swept across the plain 'as though from the jaws of hell'. The artillerymen worked their guns with wet towels wrapped round their heads, while the enemy kept up a fierce return fire which caused numerous casualties. On 30 March a breach was torn in the granite wall. The defenders, over eleven thousand strong, erected a stockade across the gap. But just when this had been destroyed by volleys of red-hot shot and an assault seemed practicable, a vast bon-fire on a nearby hill announced to the cheering rebels the arrival of Tatya Tope with a relieving force of over 20,000 men.

Rose kept his nerve. He decided to maintain the siege of Jhansi while withdrawing part of his small army towards the Betwa River to meet Tatya Tope's threat. It was a wise decision rewarded with suc-cess. Although Tatya Tope fought the ensuing engagements skilfully, he was sadly handicapped, as other rebel leaders were, by his lack of competent subordinate officers; and the British soon drove him back across the river and into the jungle beyond, killing hundreds of the rebel force. Tatya Tope set fire to the undergrowth to impede the pursuing cavalry, but the dragoons galloped through the flames, cutting down many stragglers and capturing some twenty guns. By 2 April, Rose, having won a brilliant victory at the cost of less than a hundred men, was back in front of Jhansi ready for the assault.

At three o'clock the next morning, in bright moonlight, the storm-ing parties moved forward in four columns into a savage fire of round-shot, musket balls and rockets. As bugles blared on the walls, 'the fire of the enemy waxed stronger', wrote Thomas Lowe, describ-ing the advance of the two columns which had been sent forward to assault one of the city gates, 'and amid the chaos of sounds; of volleys of musketry and roaring of cannon, and hissing and bursting of rockets, stink-pots, infernal machines, huge stones, blocks of wood and trees . . . the men wavered for a moment and sheltered themselves behind stones'.[39] But the engineers with the ladders reached the walls; and the infantry, reinforced, went forward through the fire and smoke to climb them. Three of the ladders broke, and the men on them fell into the ditch. The others held fast, though, and two officers managed to reach the ramparts. Both were killed; but their men followed them and soon scores of soldiers were clambering over the walls and running down the street that led towards the palace, joined by the men of the other two columns who had also now succeeded in getting into the city.

The houses on either side of the street were in flames; the musketry fire 'perfectly hellish'. Groups of sepoys stood their ground, slashing at the British soldiers with their tulwars. Others fled, jumping into wells from which they were dragged to be bayoneted in the by-lanes which were soon littered with corpses. The palace gateway was reached, and the storming parties rushed through, fighting their way from room to room. A store of gunpowder exploded, killing and wounding numbers of men. 'The whole place was a scene of quick ruin and confusion – windows, doors, boxes and furniture went to wreck like lightning.'[40] Forty *sowars* held out in a room near the stables. The building was set on fire; the sowars dashed out, their clothes on fire, and every one of them was killed.

All the next day the street fighting, looting, destruction and murder continued, the British soldiers eagerly exceeding their orders 'to spare nobody over sixteen years – except women, of course'.[41] The rebels 'who could not escape threw their women and babes down wells and then jumped down themselves'.[42] In all, about five thousand people were killed in Jhansi.

In the squares of the city . . . hundreds of corpses [were collected] in large heaps and covered with wood, floorboards and anything that came handy and set on fire. Now every square blazed with burning bodies and the city looked like one vast burning ground . . . It became difficult to breathe as the air stank with the odour of burning human flesh and the stench of rotting animals in the streets.[43]

Several of the richer families had long since left the city; others had sent their valuables to Gwalior where the fort, held in the name of the pro-British Sindhia, was believed to be impregnable. Yet most of the people of Jhansi had warmly supported the Rani from the beginning.

They had endorsed her decision to reject Sir Hugh Rose's demand for the city, and had responded enthusiastically to her proclamation: 'We fight for independence. In the words of Lord Krishna, we will, if we are victorious, enjoy the fruits of victory; if defeated and killed on the field of battle, we shall surely earn eternal glory and salvation.'[44] But now with Jhansi in ruins, most of the rebels who could escape fled from the city to join Tatya Tope at Kalpi. And the Rani rode away with them.

How or when or where she escaped [Cornet Combe of the 3rd Bombay Light Cavalry could not imagine] . . . We were sent all over the country in pursuit, and one of our troops overtook her at a place called Banda, 20 miles off. Her escort made a hard fight of it, and though our fellows did their utmost and killed every man she got away, her smart saddle falling into our hands. She is a wonderful woman, very brave and determined. It is fortunate for us that the men are not all like her.[45]

After spending three weeks in Jhansi collecting supplies and ammunition, Rose went in pursuit of the rebel forces. They were no longer in Kalpi, as Tatya Tope, intent upon wearing his enemies out in the heat, had taken up a defensive position at Kunch where Rose came upon them on 6 May. Rose's infantry, having made an exhausting flank march of fourteen miles, were overcome by heat and thirst and lack of sleep. They managed to drive Tatya Tope from Kunch; but they had no strength left for pursuit. Numbers of them fell dead from heat-stroke; others collapsed, sobbing, laughing hysterically, crying deliriously for water, and were carried to the rear in *doolies*. The cavalry and horse artillery chased the rebels along the Kalpi road for a little way; but they, too, were so worn out, and their horses so 'utterly knocked up', that the pursuit had to be abandoned.

This is most killing work [Cornet Combe recorded on 8 May]. We had nothing to eat from dinner on the 6th to this morning. We lost seven men of the 71st yesterday from sunstroke, three the day before, and four officers are not expected to live. It is almost impossible for Europeans to stand the heat. The glass registers 115° in the best tents so you can imagine what it is in the burning sun. My sword was so hot yesterday I really could hardly hold it. Everything is hot – even the water in the wells which, bye the bye, are very scarce . . . Sir H. Rose is suffering very much. He was lying in a dhoolie yesterday, covered with wet clothes [but] he insisted on getting up, and even joined in the pursuit, falling twice from his horse from the heat. He is a most determined, plucky fellow . . . Even the flying rebels gave in yesterday, after running for eight miles, begging for water.[46]

The rebels were much dispirited. They blamed Tatya Tope for retreating before he should have done; the infantry grumbled at the cavalry; the cavalry abused the infantry. It seemed for a time, indeed, that their army would break up completely. But then the Nawab of Banda arrived at Kalpi with a large retinue of retainers and rebel cavalry. He was joined there by the Rao Sahib, a nephew of the Nana. The Rani of Jhansi was also there. And Kalpi was one of the strongest forts in India, protected by formidable entrenchments, fortified buildings and chains of deep ravines. Gradually, therefore, the rebels returned to Kalpi, so encouraged by the Rani's promises to fight with them there to the end that on 22 May they marched out to the attack, having sworn on the sacred waters of the Jumna to defeat the *Firinghis* or die.

Their hopes of victory were not ill-founded. Rose's force was sadly weakened by illness and disease, tired out by the rebels' fighting patrols which, in response to a general order, fell upon his outposts when the sun was at its strongest after ten o'clock in the day. But the British fought well at Kalpi, and once more the rebels were forced to retreat.[47] On Queen Victoria's birthday the Union Jack was unfurled on the fort; and a week later Sir Hugh Rose, who had been suffering severely from heat-stroke, issued a farewell order to his troops and prepared to leave for a convalescent holiday in Poona. He had, it was thought, richly deserved it. There were still those who did not think much of him as a general, who, like Robert Poore, considered him 'a very lucky man', though certainly a brave one who was always prepared to 'go ahead which is the great thing with these fellows'.[48] Most officers, however, were less grudging and had now quite forgotten Rose's early mistakes. 'He is now the first man in India in most people's opinion here,' Henry Campion thought. 'Indeed he seems to have done more than any of them.'[49]

It seemed that the war was over at last. The Rani of Jhansi, the Rao Sahib and Tatya Tope were all at Gopalpur not far from Gwalior; but it was most unlikely now that they would ever again raise an army strong enough to oppose the British who had recently so often defeated them.

The rebel leaders, however, had conceived a bold plan: they had decided to march upon Gwalior in the hope that the army of the young Maharajah Sindhia – still over two thousand strong despite the defection of the British-officered Gwalior Contingent – could be persuaded to join them. The Maharajah himself was known to be still convinced that the British could never be defeated. But many of the leading nobles of Gwalior, as well as the officers of the army, were persuaded that if the rebels established themselves in Gwalior other Indian princes, who had so far remained neutral, would join in their cause. The rebel leaders accordingly marched on Gwalior with eleven thousand men and twelve guns. The Maharajah opposed them near Morar. But after firing one round his guns were captured; and this induced his army to go over to the rebels. His personal bodyguard stayed with him, but he and they were soon put to flight and forced to ride away for the safety of Agra.[50]

Rose had now to abandon all thoughts of leave in Poona. On 6 June he left Kalpi; and ten days later, by making forced marches at night, he reached and occupied Morar. The next day, at Kotah-ki-Serai, he attacked the rebels; and in the fighting the Rani of Jhansi, dressed as a man, 'using her sword with both hands and holding the reins of her horse in her mouth', was struck from her saddle and killed.[51] There were various conflicting reports of her death. The most credible, found among Lord Canning's papers, was that she was shot in the back by a trooper of the 8th Hussars 'who was never discovered'. She turned and fired back at the man who then ran her through with his sword. Canning's note continued:

She used to dress like a man (with a turban) and rode like one . . . Not pretty, & marked with smallpox, but beautiful eyes and figure. She used to wear gold anklets, and Sindia's pearl necklace, plundered from Gwalior (Sindia says its value is untold). These when dying she distributed among the soldiery when taken to die under the mango clump . . . The infantry attacked the cavalry for allowing her to be killed. The cavalry said she would ride too far in front. Her tent was very coquettish. Cheval Glass [Books and Pictures and Swing]. Two maids of honour rode with her. One was killed, and in her agony stripped off her clothes. Said to have been most beautiful.[52]

Although his men were utterly exhausted by their exertions and the heat of the sun – eighty-four men in a single regiment being incapacitated by heat-stroke – Rose again defeated the rebels at Gwalior. And while Tatya Tope and the Rao Sahib fled across the Chambal River into Rajputana, the Maharajah Sindhia returned to his capital.

For eight months, well supplied with money stolen from the Maharajah's treasury, Tatya Tope's small but disciplined army succeeded in eluding the British columns sent out to pursue him. Strong in cavalry, the last rebel army moved at great speed, helped by villagers who refused to betray them to their pursuers though tempted to do so by large rewards. Occasionally Tatya Tope's men stood their ground for a time before disappearing into the jungle, leading their pursuers on. Towards the end of October, Rao Sahib joined Tatya Tope once again; and the two rebel leaders took their men across the Narbada River into Nagpur, a former Maratha state whose people, they hoped, would rise up to welcome them. But the fires of revolt were dying now, and the end was near. During February 1859 the last of the rebels were gradually dispersed. Those still prepared to fight were defeated; the rest surrendered or wandered away to their homes. Tatya Tope was captured with the help of Man Singh, Rajah of Narwar, who, having quarrelled with his overlord, the Maharajah Sindhia, had rebelled against him and had in consequence found himself in conflict with the British. Hoping that if he led them to Tatya Tope, the British would help him regain some of the property which the Maharajah had confiscated, Man Singh agreed to betray the rebel leader. So under pretence of wishing to consult him about the advisability of his joining forces with Firuz Shah – the Moghul prince whom Campbell had driven out of Rohilkhand – Man Singh asked for an interview with Tatya Tope. Tatya Tope agreed to see him; and, as he lay down to sleep after a long talk with Man Singh, the native infantry who had been placed in ambush closed in silently and pounced upon him and his two attendants. Thus 'Tatya Tope was arrested and pinioned, his arms being secured by Man Singh himself'.[53]

His execution was announced to take place [at Sipri] at 4 p.m. on the 18 [April] . . . [wrote a man who witnessed it] . . . A considerable number of natives were scattered all over the plain; and any little elevation commanding a view of the scaffold was thickly studded with white clad spectators . . . He expressed the wish that, as they were about to take his life, the Government would see to his family in Gwalior. Major [Richard] Reade [who had persuaded Man Singh to betray him] read the charge . . . and the sentence, that he be hanged by the neck until he was dead. The *mistree* then knocked off the leg irons. He mounted the rickety ladder with as much firmness as handcuffs would allow him; was then pinioned and his legs tied, he remarking that there was no necessity for these operations; and he then deliberately put his head into the noose, which being drawn tight by the executioner, the fatal bolt was drawn. He struggled very slightly, and the *mehters* were called to drag him straight . . . After the troops left, a great scramble was made by officers and others to get a lock of hair.[54]

Rao Sahib was not captured until 1862 when he, too, was betrayed and hanged.[55] Firuz Shah died in poverty in Mecca in 1877.[56] Hazrat Mahal, despite Jang Bahadur's threats to send Gurkhas after her, was allowed to remain in Nepal with her son and small retinue.[57] Nana Sahib disappeared into oblivion, having pretended to commit suicide in the Ganges after his defeat at Cawnpore and leaving his seal with Tatya Tope who issued a number of proclamations in his name. After failing to enlist the help of the Emperor Napoleon III, Nana Sahib entered Nepal and was said to have died of fever there in September 1859.[58] Thereafter he was frequently reported to have been seen alive and sometimes to have been recaptured. But he was never identified with certainty. And so tired did the Government become of reports that men resembling the Nana had been apprehended that when a young officer excitedly telegraphed to Calcutta from a small town near Rajkot in 1895, 'Have arrested Nana Sahib Wire instruction', the reply was prompt, short and deflating: 'Release at once.'[59]

The King of Delhi was put on trial before a military court at the end of January 1859, accused of having abetted the mutineers in their crimes, of 'not regarding his allegiance' as a British subject, and of having allowed himself to be proclaimed 'the reigning King and sovereign of India'.[60]

While waiting for these charges to be considered the King continued to be displayed to European visitors as one of the curiosities of Delhi. One of those who inspected him was William Hodson's wife who found him, as most other spectators did, lying on the grass ropes of his bamboo charpoy smoking a hookah. His small room was divided into two by a screen of grass matting 'behind which was a woman cooking some atrocious compound'. Mrs Hodson was 'almost ashamed to say that a feeling of pity mingled with [her] disgust, at seeing a man recently Lord of an imperial city almost unparalleled for riches and magnificence, confined in a low, close, dirty room which the lowest slave in his household would scarcely have occupied'.[61]

William Howard Russell was also moved to pity at the sight of 'the dim-wandering-eyed, dreamy old man, with feeble hanging nether lip and toothless gums' who sat 'crouched on his haunches . . . dressed in an ordinary and rather dirty muslin tunic [and] small thin cambric skull-cap' He was being sick when Russell arrived, and was still gasping for breath when his visitor entered the room. He had, he said, evidently wishing to arouse sympathy rather than to convey exact information, filled twelve basins.[62]

Mrs Muter was present when he was carried in a palanquin into the Hall of Private Audience to face the military court.

He was accompanied by Jumna Buckt, the child of his old age. He rested on a pile of cushions on the floor . . . At first he appeared alarmed, and his face wore an anxious expression; but by degrees it became more vacant, and he assumed or felt indifference, remaining apparently in a state of lethargy, with his eyes closed during the greater part of the proceedings.

He declined to reply when asked to plead; so his silence was presumed to constitute a plea of 'not guilty'. 'The witness treated him with the greatest respect, bowing to the ground with hands clasped. They addressed him as "Ruler of the Universe", though the members of the Committee called him *tum*, a mode of address usually reserved for inferiors and servants.'[63]

The trial lasted more than two months; but the verdict was never in doubt. On 29 March he was found guilty on all charges and later sentenced to be transported for life to Rangoon.[64] He left Delhi in October accompanied by Jiwan Bakht, another young son whom he had had by a concubine, and by a most unwilling Zinat Mahal who, by now 'quite tired of him', described him as 'a troublesome, nasty, cross old fellow'.[65] He died on 7 November 1862 in Rangoon where the descendants of his son, Jiwan Bakht, are still living today.

Epilogue

In July 1859, calling for a day of thanksgiving, Lord Canning announced, 'War is at an end. Rebellion has been put down . . . The presence of large forces in the field has ceased to be necessary. Order is re-established; and peaceful pursuits have everywhere been resumed.'[1]

How to prevent another such outbreak had long been the subject of heated debate. There were those who believed that the British had been too lenient in India, that their mission was to rule, and *rule* they must, treating the natives with justice but as a subservient race upon whom civilized values must be imposed, if necessary by force. There were those, too, like Herbert Edwardes, who believed that the rebellion had come as a punishment from God, that the English had ignored the teachings of the Bible and Christianity, that the people of India had been provided with the material benefits of civilization at the expense of the spiritual benefits of Christianity. Caste, therefore, must be abolished; Hindu and Muslim law must be replaced by British law; the Christian religion must be taught in Government schools.[2] Then there were those who saw the problem in purely military terms: the rebellion would never have broken out had there been more European regiments in India, had there been more and better British officers with the Indian regiments. So the solution lay in remedying this imbalance.[3]

The authorities agreed that the native army must be radically reformed; steps were taken to reduce the number of Indian regiments in the Bengal Army, to increase the proportion of European troops so that in future they should be outnumbered by only two to one, and to place the artillery under exclusively European control.[4] But Lord

Canning and his supporters insisted that what was now required in India was a spirit of reconciliation not retribution, that the friendship of the Indian people was to be desired, not their enforced submission. They were comforted by the knowledge that the rebellion had, after all, affected only a small part of the country. Few princes had become involved; some had actively – and, in the case of the Maharajah Sindhia, indispensably – supported the British; a reassuring number of landholders had remained aloof. The mutiny in the army had been largely confined to various regiments in Bengal; many disarmed sepoys had returned quietly to their homes; thousands of Indian soldiers and camp-followers had fought with the British who could not have survived without their support. The rebellion had not prevented the establishment of universities at Madras, Bombay and Calcutta. 'It is sometimes forgotten,' Arthur Ewen commented, 'that most of India was not involved in all this. This should encourage the Government not to be too harsh.'[5]

Already the Government had, in fact, decided that harshness was not to inform their policy. On 1 November 1858, preceded by military salutes and followed by thanksgiving services and firework displays, a proclamation had been read out at every station in India. The document declared that the East India Company was abolished; that the British Government now ruled India directly; that the treaties made by the Company with native princes would be honoured and no extensions of territory would be required; that the Queen offered pardon to all rebels who had not taken part in the murder of Europeans; that religious toleration would be observed and ancient customs respected.[6]

In pursuit of his declared policy of bringing 'the influential classes into that condition and temper' in which, should a European war lead to a running down of troops in India, they could be entrusted with 'the keeping of internal peace and order', Canning implemented the spirit of the proclamation with vigour. Loyal princes were summoned to durbars, officially confirmed in their lands and titles, awarded further titles, given presents, assured they could now adopt any heir they wished. The *talukdars* of Oudh were told that their lands would be restored to them, that they would be granted unprecedented financial and judicial powers. Lesser men who had rebelled were quickly pardoned; even those convicted of murder were sentenced to imprisonment rather than to death.[7]

By April 1861 Canning could declare that the province of Oudh, so recently the centre of rebellion, was once more 'so thriving . . . so tranquil that an English child might travel from one end of it to the other in safety'.[8]

Not all was sweetness and light. The attitude of the average British soldier and civilian official towards the natives of India had not undergone any fundamental change. William Howard Russell was 'greatly amused' when he attended the ceremony at which Lord Canning read out the proclamation promising the people 'pardon, forgiveness, justice, respect to religious belief, and non-annexation', to hear a sergeant 'who was on duty at the foot of the platform staircase call to one of the men, "I am going away for a moment. Do you stay here and take care that no *nigger* goes up."'[9]

It was an attitude of mind that long persisted. Little less than twenty years later the Prince of Wales on a visit to India confessed himself deeply shocked by the 'rude and rough manner' with which English public servants treated the natives and by the 'disgraceful habit of officers . . . speaking of the inhabitants of India, many of them sprung from the great races, as "niggers"'.[10] 'If I were an Indian,' observed one of the prince's suite, Albert Grey, 'I would long to be free of such contemptuous masters.'[11]

In time, though, attitudes did change; the wounds did heal. And when, two generations later, India won her long struggle for national independence, the Indian people parted from their former masters with far less bitterness than anyone who had fought in the Great Mutiny could ever have imagined.

Whether or not the rebellion of 1857–8 was the beginning of this long struggle for national independence has long been a subject of scholarly debate. Certainly the rebellion was more momentous than the familiar English term 'Indian Mutiny' implies; yet there seems little justification for its being called the 'First Indian War of Independence', the title chosen for a book of essays by Marx and Engels published in Moscow in 1960. Many of those who later fought for India's independence were undoubtedly inspired by memories of the Mutiny, having lost faith in the belief that, as soon as India proved herself worthy of it, 'the countrymen of Hampden, Milton and Burke' would restore her people to their birthright.[12] But the followers of Gandhi, who rejected violence, had much more in common with earlier forward-looking intellectuals such as the Brahmin, Ram Mohan Roy, than with the reactionary rebels of 1857 whose methods they condemned.

In a book which appeared in 1909, Vinayak Damodar Savarkar insisted that the Mutiny was, indeed, a national revolt.[13] A more recent Indian historian, Dr B. S. Chaudhuri, has supported this theory, stressing the importance of *Civil Rebellion in the Indian Mutinies* (the title of one of his books) and the influence of 'their political and historical traditions' on the outlook of British writers on the subject.[14] Other Indian historians, however, have not found Dr Chaudhuri's arguments convincing. Dr R. C. Majumdar, for instance, in a refutation described by Professor Eric Stokes as 'Johnsonian', has roundly declared that the so-called First National War of Independence was neither first, nor national, nor a war of independence.[15] And, Dr Surendra Nath Sen – while admitting that areas ouside the main fields of conflict displayed 'signs of restlessness', and that, in spite of racial, religious and linguistic differences, the people of India felt that 'they had something in common as against Englishmen' – has emphasized that the concept of Indian nationality was then still in embryo. To the Punjabi the Hindustani was still a stranger; very few Bengalis 'realised that they belonged to the same nation as men from Maharashtra'; the people of Central India and Rajputana 'did not acknowledge any bond of kinship with the people of the south'. Outside Oudh and the neighbouring district of Shahabad 'there is no evidence of that general sympathy which would invest the Mutiny with the dignity of a national war'.[16]

Other Indian scholars have emphasized that it was mainly selfish motives and personal ambitions that impelled the people to revolt, that each group and individual leader fought for self-interest and had no allegiance to a common cause, and that from the very beginning the criminal elements of the population 'took a prominent part in the local risings. Even the ordinary people were animated more by subversive than constructive activities.'[17]

The leaders of the revolt, as Dr Percival Spear, the distinguished British historian of India, has concluded, were 'backward-looking men whose aims were incompatible. Nana Sahib hoped to revive the Peshwaship and the Delhi leaders the Moghul Empire. Success would have meant a further war between the two.' Their followers had 'no confidence in themselves or their cause', no 'ideas of creating anything new'.[18] Indeed, in 1857 it was their enemies, the British, who were considered the radicals and hated for their reforms by traditionalist Indians who supported the mutineers.

The Mutiny, in fact, was not so much a national revolt as the culmination of a period of unrest, 'a last passionate protest against the relentless penetration of the west'. And it was this which gave the rising its extreme emotional content, with sepoys 'professing loyalty one day and shooting their officers the next. They were torn to distraction between loyalty and affection on the one hand and the belief that their religion and way of life were threatened on the other. The Mutiny was the swan-song of the old India.'[19]

Glossary

This list is limited to words to be found in the text and to the sense in which they are used. Those printed in Roman *letters are in the* Oxford English Dictionary. *Alternative spellings given in the text are shown in brackets.*

Anna Coin, one-sixteenth part of a rupee.

Arrack Alcoholic spirit usually distilled from coco sap or rice.

Atta (attah, ottah) Ground corn with the husks unsifted.

Ayah Native nurse or maidservant.

Baba-logue (baba-log) Children. *Baba* was a term of respect for an old man as well as a fond word for a child; *logue* means people.

Baboo *(babu)* Title of respect, especially to Hindus; used derogatively of Indian clerks who wrote English.

Badmash *(budmash)* Rascal, hooligan.

Bagh Garden, also habitation.

Bajra One of the tall millets forming a dry crop.

Baniya (baniah, bunya) Grain dealer, moneylender; also anyone of the Hindu communities.

Bara Big.

Batta Additional allowance for soldiers or public servants, especially when on active service or posted to certain areas.

Beebee (bibi) Lady, wife.

Begum Muslim lady of high rank.

Bell of Arms Conical bell-shaped tent; in a cantonment a building of brick and plaster so shaped, used for storing weapons.

Bhainchute Insulting epithet (sister-violator).

Bhang An infusion of Indian hemp.

Bhisti (bheesty) Water-carrier.

Bildar (bildah) Digging labourer.

Boorao Insulting epithet (*boor* = cunt).

Brahmin (brahman) Member of Hindu priestly caste, the highest caste.

Brinjal Aubergine.

Cantonments (pronounced cantoonment) Military station.

Caste Hindu hereditary class, with members socially equal, united in religion and having no social intercourse with persons of other castes. The principal castes were the Brahmin (priestly caste), Kshetriya (military caste), Vaisha (trader caste), Sudra (cultivator and artisan caste). The untouchables were outside the caste system.

Cess Tax, rate.

Chaprassi Messenger or doorkeeper.

Charpoy Indian bedstead.

Chillum The part of the hookah which contains the tobacco and charcoal balls; sometimes loosely used for the pipe itself.

Chillumchee (chillumjee) Brass or tinned copper basin for washing hands.

Choga A long-sleeved garment like a dressing-gown.

Chowki (chowkee) Shed, also chair.

Chowkidar (Chokidar, chakidar) Watchman.

Chuddur (chudder) Sheet worn by women in North India.

Chupatti Small flat thin cake of coarse unleavened bread.

Coolie Unskilled labourer, the name of a tribe of Gujarat.

Coss Measure of distance which varied in different localities, usually about two miles.

Cossid Runner, courier.

Cutcherry Court house, office.

Dacoits Armed robbers.

Dak (dawk) Transport by relays of men and horses, hence mail.

Dasehra The nine nights, or ten days, Hindu festival in October.

Dhal (dal) Split pulse.

Dhobi (dhobee) Washerman.

Dhoti (dhootee) Loin-cloth worn tucked between legs and fastened at waist.

Din (Deen) The Faith of a Muslim; his party cry.

Diwan Royal court of council; principal officer of state.

Diwan-i-Am Hall of Public Audience in the Imperial Palace.

Diwan-i-Khas Hall of Private Audience in the Imperial Palace.

Doolie (dhoolee) Covered litter or stretcher.

Dudh Milk.

Durbar Royal court, levee; also synonym for government.

Duree Rug.

Dustoor Custom.

Eed ('Id) Muslim holy festival, in common application in India restricted to two, the *bari* and the *choti.*

Fakir (fakeer) Poor person, usually religious mendicant living on charity.

Firinghi (Feringhee) Derogatory term for European.

Ganga (ganja) Hashish.

Gharry Cart or carriage.

Ghat (ghaut) Quay or wharf, steps on bank of river.

Ghazee (Ghazi) Muslim fanatic who believes the slaughter of unbelievers will open the gates of paradise.

Ghee (ghi) Clarified butter.

Ghosulkhana Bathroom.

Ghurrah Clay water-pot.

Ghurry (Ghurree, gurree) A water instrument for measuring time; also the gong on which the time so indicated is struck.

Gingall (*jingall*) Heavy musket fired from a rest, swivel gun.

Godown Storeroom, warehouse.

Goojurs (gujars) Hindu group, notorious for predatory character.

Goonda Bad character, *budmash.*

Goor (gur) Coarse brown sugar.

Gram Pulse used as horse fodder.

Hackery Cart drawn by bullocks.

Hakim Muslim physician.

Havildar Indian non-commissioned officer with rank equivalent to sergeant.

Hookah Tobacco-pipe with long tube for smoking through water.

'Id see *Eed.*

Imambara Building in which the Shiah Muslim festival of *Mohurram* is celebrated and services in celebration of martyrs are performed.

Imaum (Imam) Leader, a title technically applied to the Caliph or Successor, the Head of Islam; also given to the heads of the four Orthodox sects.

Jats Indo-Aryan people of North-West India.

Jemadar Indian officer with rank equivalent to lieutenant.

Jingall See Gingall.
Jogee Hindu ascetic, also a conjuror.

Kaffir Infidel, applied derogatively by Muslims to Christians.
Karela Bitter gourd.
Khaki Dust-coloured, dull, brownish yellow; though it seems to have been more grey than yellow when first adopted in India. J. W. Sherer described it as 'ash-coloured'; Vivian Majendie as 'slaty'.
Khalassi (khalassee) Camp-follower, tent pitcher.
Khalsa The Sikh community.
Khansaman Cook, house steward, table servant.
Khawasin Attendant.
Khidmatgar (Khidmuttgar, kitmutgar, khitmutgar) Butler, waiter.
Kincob Rich Indian fabric embroidered with gold or silver.
Kotwal Police officer, Indian town magistrate.
Kotwali (kotwalee) Police station.
Kukri Curved knife, broadening towards point, used by Gurkhas.
Kunker (kunkar) Coarse limestone.
Kutcherry see Cutcherry.

Lahaf Coverlet, bedspread.
Lakh 100,000 units.
Lathi (lathee, lattee) Thick iron-bound stick or bludgeon.
Lota (lotah) Small metal pot.

Mahajan (mahajum) Moneylender, banker, merchant.
Mahal House, palace; queen.
Mahout Elephant-driver.
Mali (mally) Gardener.
Maratha (Mahratta) Member of warlike Hindu race, who gave their name to Maharashtra.
Maulvi (moulvi) Learned man; Moslem scholar or teacher, usually of religion.
Mehters Sweeper, scavenger.
Memsahib European married lady, from 'madam-sahib'.

Misree Sugar candy.
Mistree (mistri) Mason; any artisan.
Mohalla Quarter or ward of a town.
Mohur Gold coin of the value of about Rs. 16.
Mohurram (Mohurrum) Muslim festival; first month of Muslim year.
Mujahideen Muslims who take to the sword for a religious cause.
Mulligatawny Highly seasoned soup.
Munshi (moonshee) Writer or secretary.

Naik (naick) Indian non-commissioned officer, corporal.
Nautch Exhibition of professional dancing-girls.
Nautch-girl Dancing-girl.
Nawab Nobleman, governor.
Nazir A court official who serves processes, etc.
Nazrs Ceremonial gifts from inferior to superior.
Nizam Hereditary title of the rulers of Hyderabad.
Nullah Small stream or ditch.

Otta See *Atta*

Paddy Rice in the husk.
Paddy-field Field where rice grows.
Palanquin Covered litter for one person usually carried by four or six men.
Palka-ghari Covered wagon for woman in purdah.
Pan Leaf of the betel.
Pari Dancing-girl.
Pathans People of Afghan descent settled in India, especially Rohilkhand; also people on the North-West Frontier.
Patwari Village accountant and record-keeper.
Peepul (pipal) *Ficus religiosa*, large fig tree sacred to Hindus.
Pice Small coin, one quarter anna.
Pilao (pilau) Dish of rice or wheat with meat, spices, etc.

Puggree (puggaree) Light turban; thin scarf worn round hat and sometimes hanging down behind as protection against sun.

Pukka Proper, as in pukka roof, tiled rather than thatched.

Punkah Large swinging cloth fan on frame worked by pulling cord.

Purdah Curtain, especially one used to screen native women from sight of men or strangers; Indian system of secluding women of rank from public view.

Raj Rule, sovereignty.

Rajput (Rajpoot) Member of Hindu soldier caste claiming descent from Kshatriyas.

Rezais (Razai) Quilt.

Risaldar Indian officer commanding a troop of cavalry.

Rupee Coin, worth in 1857 about 2s.

Sadr Amin (Sadeer Ameen) Indian court official.

Sahib European or other presumed superior as spoken of or to by Indians.

Sahib-logue Europeans, *logue* meaning people as in *Baba-logue.*

Seer Measure of weight (about 2lb.–2½lb.), or liquid (about 1 litre).

Sepoy Private soldier in infantry.

Serai Place for the accommodation of travellers, also a long-necked earthenware flagon.

Sirdar Leader, commander.

Soour (suar) Insulting epithet (pig).

Sowar Private soldier in cavalry.

Subahdar *(Subedar)* Native officer of company of sepoys.

Subahdar-Major Senior native officer of an infantry regiment.

Sufi Muslim ascetic mystic.

Suttee (sati) Hindu widow who immolated herself on husband's funeral pyre; custom requiring such immolation.

Syce (sice) Groom.

Tahsil Revenue; a revenue district; revenue office.

Tahsildar Revenue officer, also cashier in business house.

Talukdar Holder of a taluk; a member of the landed gentry class in Oudh.

Tank Storage pond, artificial lake.

Tatty *(tatti)* Screen of sweet-scented grass *(khus)* used in doorways and windows in hot weather and kept wet to reduce temperature of winds passing through them.

Tazia (tazeea) Expression of sympathy, the mourning of the Shiahs for Husain and Hasan. The copy of the tomb at Kerbala which is carried in procession at *Mohurram.*

Thannadar Police officer in charge of a ward.

Tiffin Light meal, luncheon.

Tika Red mark on forehead worn by Hindu women who are not widows.

Tindal Labourer.

Tope Grove of trees, especially mangoes.

Tulwar Native sword.

Tykhana Underground room.

Vakil Agent, man of business.

Wahabis *(wahhabis)* 'Puritans of Islam'.

Wali Ruler, governor.

Zemindar (zamindar) Landholder.

Zenana Quarters of Muslim Indian house in which women of high-caste families are secluded.

Zomboruk (Zumbooruck) A small gun usually carried on a camel and mounted on a saddle.

Chronological Table

1857

January		Trouble over greased cartridges at Dum-Dum.
February		Mutinies at Barrackpore and Berhampore.
March		Mangal Pande affair at Barrackpore.
April		Unrest and incendiarism at Ambala.
		Uprising of the 48th Native Infantry at Lucknow.
		Firing-parade of the 3rd Light Cavalry at Meerut.
May	10	Outbreak and murders at Meerut.
	11	Massacre of Europeans in Delhi.
	23	Panic in Agra.
	30	Mutiny in Muttra, and of regiments at Lucknow.
	31	Mutiny of Bhurtpore army.
June	5	Mutiny of 2nd Cavalry at Cawnpore.
	6	Siege of Cawnpore entrenchment begins; mutiny of 6th Native Infantry at Allahabad.
	7	Wilson and Barnard join forces at Alipur.
	8	Battle of Badli-ki-Serai; massacre at Jhansi.
	11	Mutiny of Lucknow police; Neill arrives at Allahabad.
	25	Nana Sahib offers terms to Wheeler at Cawnpore.
	27	Massacre at Satichaura Ghat, Cawnpore.
	30	Disaster at Chinhat; Lucknow Residency surrounded.
July	1	Mutiny at Indore.
	2	Arrival of Bakht Khan at Delhi with Bareilly force.
	4	Death of Sir Henry Lawrence at Lucknow.
	5	Death of General Barnard.
	7	Havelock's force leaves Allahabad for Cawnpore.
	16	Nana Sahib defeated at first battle of Cawnpore.
	27	Siege of Arrah begins.
	29	Havelock's victory at Unao.
August	5	Havelock defeats rebels at Bashiratganj.
	13	Havelock withdraws to Cawnpore.
	14	Arrival of John Nicholson on Delhi Ridge with moveable column.
	16	Havelock defeats rebels at Bithur.

1857

September	5	Sir James Outram arrives at Cawnpore.
	14	Assault on Delhi.
	19	Havelock and Outram begin march on Lucknow.
	20	Last Delhi strongholds captured.
	21	William Hodson captures King.
	22	Hodson murders Princes.
	25	First relief of Lucknow by Havelock and Outram; siege resumed.
October	10	Greathed's column defeats mutineers at Agra. Siege of Lucknow continues.
November	9	Kavanagh escapes from Lucknow.
	17	Second relief of Lucknow by Sir Colin Campbell.
	19	Women and children evacuated from Lucknow.
	22–23	Withdrawal of British troops from Lucknow.
	24	Death of Havelock.
	28	Windham defeated in second battle of Cawnpore.
December	6	Campbell defeats Tatya Tope in third battle of Cawnpore.

1858

January	6	Campbell reoccupies Fatehgarh.
March	2	Campbell opens operations against Lucknow.
	21	Last of the rebels dislodged in Lucknow; Sir Hugh Rose arrives at Jhansi.
April	3	Jhansi captured and sacked.
	15	Walpole defeated at Ruiya.
	23	Rose enters Kalpi.
May	5	Campbell defeats Khan Bahadur Khan outside Bareilly.
June	5	Death of the Maulvi.
	17	Battle of Kotah-ki-Serai; death of Rani of Jhansi.
	19	Battle of Gwalior.
November	1	Royal Proclamation abolishes East India Company and places India under direct rule of British Government.

1859

| March | 29 | King of Delhi tried and found guilty on all charges. |
| April | 18 | Tatya Tope executed. |

Notes and References

For full bibliographical details of sources quoted, see pp. 434–50

Abbreviations used:
BPIR British Paramountcy and Indian Renaissance
FDPC (NAI) Foreign Department Political Consultations (National Archives of India)
FDPP (NAI) Foreign Department Political Proceedings (National Archives of India)
FDSC (NAI) Foreign Department Secret Consultations (National Archives of India)
JSAHR Journal of the Society for Army Historical Research
KMP (IOL) Sir John Kaye's Mutiny Papers (India Office Library)
MP (NAI) Mutiny Papers (National Archives of India)
MDP (NAI) Military Department Papers (National Archives of India)
PP Parliamentary Papers
PTBS Proceedings of the Trial of Bahadur Shah
RCSSAI Royal Commission on the Sanitary State of the Army in India
SLDSP Selections from Letters, Despatches and other State Papers (Forrest)

1. Sahibs and Memsahibs (*pages 23–39*)

1. Metcalfe Family Papers. Metcalfe House, which was extensively restored in 1913, is now the Ministry of Defence Science Laboratory.
2. Metcalfe Family Papers.
3. Oswell, *Sketches of Rulers of India*, i, 24.
4. q. Maclagan, '*Clemency*' *Canning*, 57.
5. ibid., 26.
6. Canning Papers; Maclagan, 37, 39; Surtees, *Charlotte Canning*, 203.
7. Maclagan, 20.
8. Surtees, 203, 206.
9. q. Surtees, 206.
10. Hodgson Papers, BM ADD. MSS 47469, q. Maclagan, 57.

11. q. Surtees, 218–19.
12. Canning Papers.
13. q. Maclagan, 46.
14. Cubitt Papers.
15. Trevelyan, *Cawnpore*, 9.
16. Kincaid, *British Social Life in India, 1608–1937*, 155, 176.
17. Trevelyan, op. cit., 5.
18. Cubitt Papers.
19. Hadow Papers.
20. Ouvry, *Cavalry Experiences*, 105.
21. Ludlow Papers.
22. Russell, *My Diary in India*, i, 190.
23. Monk Bretton MSS; Heneage MSS.
24. Poore MSS.
25. Nicholl MS letters.
26. Majendie, *Up Among the*

Pandies: A Year's Service in India, 264–5.
27. ibid., 266–7; Verney, *The Devil's Wind*, 116, 125.
28. Mountsteven MS letters.
29. Cubitt Papers.
30. Hadow Papers.
31. Wise, *The Diary of a Medical Officer*, 299.
32. Cubitt, Barter, Fairweather, Nicholl, Ewen MSS.
33. Nicholl MS diary.
34. Quevillart MS diaries.
35. q. Kincaid, 182.
36. Compton, *Indian Life in Town and Country*, q. Golant, *The Long Afternoon*, 23.
37. Kincaid, 181–2.
38. Hadow Papers. Many of the young ladies who arrived in India were extremely young. 'The Indian ladies generally have come out as almost children,' Lady Canning wrote, 'and have the most crude manners and no sort of observation or interest in anything.' (Canning Papers.) So were the pubescent girls inspected as possible brides at the Orphan Girls' School in Calcutta which was 'divided into two parts to preserve the social distinctions of the day, one for the children of officers and gentlemen and the other for the children of soldiers'. Balls were held each month, after which orphans of fourteen, thirteen, or even twelve years of age were taken off to be married. (Wilkinson, Theon, *Two Monsoons*, 105–7.)
39. Ewen MS letters. There were, of course, memsahibs who led more active lives, like Flora Annie Steel who wrote, amongst other books, *The Complete Indian Housekeeper and Cook*; and Honoria Lawrence, the conscientious, earnest though rather muddle-headed student of *Home Education*, whose daily time-tables provided for rising 'at four a.m., reading and prayer', arranging her husband's papers, copying his letters, going out with him, supervising the household affairs and learning Hindustani. (Barr, *The Memsahibs*, 44, 51, 152–3.) But these were exceptions. Most women, like Lady Canning, took 'strangely to dawdling' and allowed the time to slip by 'quite unmarked'. (Canning Papers.)
40. q. Kincaid, 194.
41. Russell, op. cit., ii, 243.
42. Kincaid, 194.
43. Parkes, *Wanderings of a Pilgrim*, ii, 17.
44. Kincaid, 193.
45. Acton, *Popular Account of the Manners . . . of India* (1847), q. Mudford, *Birds of a Different Plumage*, 143.
46. Russell, op. cit., ii, 255.
47. Jacob, *Views and Opinions* (1858), q. Mudford, 138.
48. Mudford, 153.
49. *Oakfield, or Fellowship in the East* by 'Punjabee', q. Edwardes, *Necessary Hell*, 147.
50. Blake, Ponsonby, Ewen MSS.
51. Brown MSS.
52. Verney, op. cit., 103–4.
53. Russell, op. cit., 51.

2. Soldiers and Sepoys (*pages* 40–58)

1. Gordon MS diary; Mowbray Thomson, *The Story of Cawnpore*, 19–20; Trevelyan, *Cawnpore*, 9–10; Barr, *The Memsahibs*, 145; Atkinson, *Curry and Rice*, 72.
2. Russell, op. cit., i, 180.
3. Quevillart MS Diaries.
4. ibid.
5. *RCSSAI*, q. Anglesey, *A History of the British Cavalry, 1816–1919*, ii, 339.
6. Quevillart MS Diaries.
7. Anglesey, 351–2. The incidence of syphilis amongst European troops was about six times greater than it was among the sepoys, which was

attributed to the majority of the native troops having their families with them. Sikhs, however, were said to be 'eaten up with syphilis. They do not carry their families with them; they are just as gregarious in their amours as the British soldier, and in that way one woman who is popular among them, may affect a whole company.' (*RCSSAI*, q. Anglesey, 352.)

8. Quevillart MS Diaries.
9. ibid.
10. W. G. Shelton, *JSAHR*, vol. LII, No. 209, Spring 1974.
11. Pearman, *Memoirs*, 27, 61–3. Most men would have preferred beer; 'and the only reason for their not using beer almost exclusively is their means being insufficient to procure it'. (*RCSSAI*, q. Anglesey, 350.)
12. Quevillart MS Diaries.
13. Pearman, 65.
14. q. Anglesey, 359.
15. Pearman, 65–6.
16. Lyttelton, *Eighty Years' Soldiering* (1927), q. Anglesey, 354.
17. Anglesey, 354.
18. Quevillart MS Diaries.
19. MS Notebook of Private Hyom, q. Anglesey, 358.
20. Pearman, 27.
21. Quevillart MS Diaries.
22. ibid.
23. ibid.
24. Anglesey, 345.
25. ibid., 335–7.
26. ibid., 361–2.
27. *RCSSAI*, q. Anglesey, 361–2.
28. Mason, *A Matter of Honour*, 125–6; Anglesey, 361–2; Gardner MSS; Ewen Papers. There was a far higher proportion of Muslims to Hindus in the cavalry than there was in the infantry.
29. *From Sepoy to Subedar*, 4; Anglesey, 361; Mason, 206; Rice Holmes, *A History of the Indian Mutiny*, 53.

30. Mason, 200; Anglesey, 362–3; Quevillart MS Diaries; Ewen MSS.
31. q. Rice Holmes, 62.
32. *From Sepoy to Subedar*, 23.
33. Wilson MS letters.
34. q. Ball, *The History of The India Mutiny*, i, 114.
35. q. Mudford, 164.
36. Mason, 259.
37. Thurburn, *Reminiscences of the Indian Rebellion*, 50; Edwardes and Merivale, *Life of Sir Henry Lawrence*, i, 169.
38. q. Edwardes, *Red Year*, 18.
39. Mason, 185; *From Sepoy to Subedar*, 160.
40. Mason, 258–9.
41. Kaye, *History of the Sepoy War in India*, i, 480–81.
42. q. Maclagan, 69.
43. Quevillart MS Diaries.
44. Mudford, 151.
45. Sneyd MSS.
46. q. Montgomery Martin, ii, 109; Kaye, i, 472.
47. Mason, 258.
48. ibid., 261.
49. q. Sen, *Eighteen Fifty-Seven*, 12.
50. q. Mudford, 151.
51. Mason, 243.
52. q. Sen, 7.
53. Sen, 17.
54. *From Sepoy to Subedar*, 24–5.
55. *The Rebellion in India, by a Resident in the North-Western Provinces*, q. Sen, 23.
56. Mason, 178.
57. q. Anglesey, 397.
58. *From Sepoy to Subedar*, 77.
59. ibid.
60. Mason, 168.
61. ibid., 186.
62. ibid., 175.

3. Chupatties and Lotus Flowers (*pages 59–74*)

1. Hadow Papers.
2. Thornhill, *Personal Adventures and Experiences of a Magistrate*, 2.

3. Harvey, *Narrative of Events*, q. Palmer, *The Mutiny Outbreak at Meerut*, 1.

4. Gardner M S letters.

5. *Mainuddin Hassan Khan's Narrative*, 39, 41. 'The fact is,' wrote Sayyid Ahmed, 'that even at the present day we do not know what caused the distribution of these chupatties' (Sayyid Ahmed, 3). Great trouble was taken at the subsequent trial of the King of Delhi to extract from Indian witnesses some explanation of the 'chupatty movement'. This is a typical extract from the proceedings:

Q. Did you ever hear of the circulation of chupatties about the country some months before the outbreak . . . ?

A. Yes, I did hear of the circumstance . . .

Q. Is sending such articles about the country a custom among the Hindoos or Mussulmans; and would the meaning be at once understood without any accompanying explanation?

A. No, it is not by any means a custom. I am fifty years of age and never heard of such a thing before.

Q. Did you hear that any message was ever sent with the chupatties?

A. No, I never heard of any.

Q. Were these chupatties chiefly circulated by Mahommedans or Hindoos?

A. They were circulated indiscriminately . . . (*PTBS*, 129–30).

6. Sneyd MSS; Edwardes, *Red Year*, 25; Bloomfield MSS; Gubbins, *An Account of the Mutinies in Oudh*, 99; Ewen MS letters.

7. Mason, 231–6; Kaye, i, 316–23, 328.

8. Mason, 237; Kaye, i, 202, 210.

9. Rice Holmes, 62, 65.

10. Danvers Papers; Case, *Day by Day at Lucknow*, 281; Rice Holmes, 65.

11. Sydney Cotton, *Indian and Home Memories*, 157.

12. ibid.

13. Montagu Hall MSS. 'Before the year 1856 had closed a singular circumstance was brought to my notice, which surprised me not a little,' wrote Captain J. S. Rawlins, adjutant of the 44th Native Infantry, then stationed at Agra. 'It had always been the ambition of native officers to invest their savings in what they called "Company's Kargus", or "Government Paper", and every native officer throughout the Army possessed Paper to the value of 3 or 4,000 Rs. and some as much as double . . . I found out that during the past year all my native officers had parted with their "Paper", and turned it into gold mohurs. I endeavoured to ascertain the cause of so extraordinary a proceeding, but got evasive answers and failed to do so . . . I reported the circumstance to the Colonel, who also seemed surprised, and considered the information so important that we at once repaired to Mr Colvin, the Lieutenant-Governor, and communicated the strange circumstance to him. He seemed much exercised at the communication, said it was most significant, and that he would set his secret agents to ascertain the cause – but as the Mutiny followed a couple of months later, the circumstance explained itself.' (Rawlins, 152.)

14. Wagentreiber, *Reminiscences of the Sepoy Rebellion*, 4.

15. Ouvry, *Cavalry Experiences*, 109.

16. Rice Holmes, 65; Mason, 192; Muir, *Records of the Intelligence Department*, i, 263.

17. *SLDSP*, i, 25; Palmer, 15; *Annals*, 8.

18. *SLDSP*, i, 3.
19. Surtees, 229.
20. *SLDSP*, i, 7–9.
21. ibid., i, 17.
22. ibid., i, 20.
23. ibid., i, 19, 24.
24. ibid., i, 15.
25. ibid., i, 27.
26. ibid., i, 40.
27. ibid., i, 27.
28. ibid., i, 46, 85; *PP*, 1857, 30, 271–8, 290.
29. Kaye, i, 502–4.
30. Sneyd MSS.
31. Peppé Papers.
32. *SLDSP*, i, 117.
33. ibid., i, 147–8.
34. ibid., 112.
35. ibid., i, 152.
36. ibid., i, 170, 172; *Annals*, XXIX.
37. *SLDSP*, i, 168, 167, 173.
38. Wood MS Diary; Chichester Papers; Ouvry, *Cavalry Experiences*, 109.
39. Dawson, *Squires and Sepoys*, 21.
40. Rice Holmes, 87, 94.
41. Monypenny and Buckle, *Life of Benjamin Disraeli*, iv, 1487; Anson, *With H.M. 9th Lancers*, 55–6; Beresford MSS; Kaye, i, 10, 393–4.
42. Canning Papers, q. Maclagan, 64.
43. KMP (IOL) (725), 35.
44. *PP*, 30, 1857, 7; *SLDSP*, i, 162.

4. Mutiny at Meerut (*pages 75–90*)

1. Wilson Letters.
2. *SLDSP*, i, 228.
3. Palmer, 44–6; Kaye, ii, 43–4; Richardson of Kirklands MS letters.
4. *Annals*, 23.
5. ibid., 24.
6. Gough, *Old Memories*, 26.
7. Cadell, 'The Outbreak of the Indian Mutiny', *JSAHR*, XXXIII (1955).
8. *SLDSP*, i, 131.
9. Cadell, 'The Outbreak of the Indian Mutiny', *JSAHR*, XXXIII (1955).
10. *SLDSP*, i, 230–37.
11. Palmer, 67; Kaye, ii, 48–9.
12. Gough, 17.
13. ibid., 21.
14. Cadell, 'The Outbreak of the Indian Mutiny', *JSAHR*, XXXIII (1955).
15. Palmer, 69.
16. ibid.
17. Gough, 22.
18. ibid., 28.
19. Palmer, 69.
20. ibid., 36.
21. Gardner MSS.
22. Wilson Letters.
23. ibid.
24. Gough, 24.
25. *Annals*, 30.
26. Gough, 26.
27. ibid., 34; *Annals*, 35; Kaye, ii, 59; Richardson of Kirklands MS letters.
28. Muter, *My Recollections of the Sepoy Revolt*, 29–31.
29. Palmer, 88–90; Williams, 92; Mackenzie, *Mutiny Memoirs*, 22–3; Kaye, ii, 69–70.
30. Palmer, 95.
31. Palmer, 105; Rice Holmes, 100–101; Williams, 97; *Annals*, 28–9.
32. Gough, 35; *Annals*, 30.
33. Williams, 119–27; Rice Holmes, 103.
34. *Annals*, 30–31.
35. Gough, 38.
36. Mackenzie, 'The Outbreak at Meerut', in Vibart, *The Sepoy Mutiny*, 227.
37. ibid., 238–9.
38. Palmer, 96; Kaye, ii, 66–72.
39. Wilson's claim that he had no reason to suppose that the mutineers would go to Delhi was not

unjustified. 'Before my escape from Delhi I happened to hear the conversation of two mutineers,' wrote Munshi Mohan Lal. 'They said that before they broke out and released their comrades and prisoners from the jail, they had no idea of coming to Delhi. It was only after they had burnt the houses of the *Sahib-logue* they all assembled on the south side of Meerut. Here the point of refuge was discussed.' (K M P 725 (10), 399.)

40. Palmer, 97–118; Anglesey, 143–4; Rice Holmes, 101–4; Kaye, ii, 65–7; F D S C (N A I), 40–42; M D P (N A I), 409.

5. Rebels and Fugitives (*pages 91–119*)

1. Sayyid Ahmed, 4; Husain, *Bahadur Shah II*, 42; Spear, *Twilight*, 73–4; Metcalfe Papers; Andrews, *Maulvi Zaka Ullah of Delhi*, 3, 41–3.

2. Husain, 50–59; Metcalfe Papers; Spear, op. cit., 74; Sen, 68–9.

3. Husain, 60–64; Spear, op. cit., 40–41. The King's son, Mirza Jiwan Bakht, is a shadowy figure about whom virtually nothing is known. Colonel Hogge, who caused great offence by taking him for a ride on an elephant after the mutineers had been defeated, described him as 'a very intelligent lad' about fifteen or sixteen years of age (F D S C (N A I) 514–15).

4. 'Account of Munshi Mohan Lal' and 'Narrative of Ahsannullah Khan' in K M P (725); Husain, 163–5; Spear, op. cit., 201.

5. Metcalfe Papers.

6. Wagentreiber, *Reminiscences of the Sepoy Rebellion*, 47. Mrs Leeson, who witnessed the murders, was protected and hidden by a young Afghan student after her baby had been shot and killed in her arms. (Wagentreiber, 47.) Three months later she escaped from Delhi disguised as an Afghan boy. 'She was in an awful condition and many of the soldiers shed tears of commiseration and pity, when they saw her sad case.' (*Annals*, 231.)

7. *Annals*, 95–6. The bodies were heaped into a cart and thrown into the Jumna. The executions were carried out in the King's name; but his guilt in having authorized them was never satisfactorily established. His son, Mirza Moghul, was said to have watched them from a neighbouring roof. (Kaye, ii, 100.)

8. *Annals*, 86–9.

9. ibid., 90–91.

10. ibid., 47; Harriet Tytler, 'Through the Sepoy Mutiny' (*Chambers's Journal*, XXI).

11. Vibart, 12–13; *Annals*, 45–8.

12. Kaye, ii, 93–4; Vibart, 14–15; Rice Holmes, 107–8.

13. Vibart, 16–18.

14. Rice Holmes, 108; Kaye, ii, 88; Gardner M S letters; M D P (N A I), 409.

15. q. Vibart, 42–3; *Annals*, 43-4.

16. Vibart, 45–7; M D P (N A I), 409.

17. Vibart, 49–52; Kaye, ii, 95.

18. Vibart, 52–6.

19. Wallace M S S.

20. *Annals*, 89–91.

21. Metcalfe Family Papers.

22. The almost legendary Lieutenant-Colonel James Skinner (1778–1841), known throughout India as 'Sikunder' or 'Sikander' (Alexander), was the son of a Scottish officer in the East India Company's army and a Rajput girl who committed suicide when her daughters were removed from her care and sent to school. James, whose irregular cavalry became known as Skinner's Horse, built St

James's Church in Delhi in fulfilment
of a vow he made when he feared
for his life in one of the campaigns
against the Mahrattas. He had
previously built a mosque for one of
his wives and a Hindu temple for his
mother. His children by his
numerous wives spoke English with
'extraordinary accents'. One of
them, Joseph Skinner, Mrs
Wagentreiber's eldest half-brother,
was 'a marvellous creation' in his
green coat with gilt buttons, his
claret-coloured trousers, patent
leather boots and white waistcoat.
He was fond of talking of his service
with Her Majesty's Guards though
he had never left India. (Bayley
Family Papers.)
23. Wagentreiber, 12–16.
24. [Colonel H. B.] Edwardes
Collection; Vibart, 247–62; Rice
Holmes, 106.
25. Wagentreiber, 18; Gardner
M S letters.
26. *Annals*, 81.
27. ibid., 60.
28. ibid., 49–51.
29. ibid., 66–7.
30. ibid., 51–7.
31. Wagentreiber, 18–20.
32. *Annals*, 69–70.
33. ibid., 70–78.
34. Sir Theophilus Metcalfe's
sister inspected the damage to the
house the next year. She found
Canova's bust of Napoleon had been
splintered, but two plaster
caricatures of Lords Sefton and
Brougham were retrieved intact from
a Hindu temple where they had been
revered as gods. (Metcalfe Family
Papers.)
35. Vibart, 57–77.
36. *Annals*, 60–62.
37. Vibart, 77–99; *Annals*, 63;
Gardner M S letters.
38. Gardner M S letters.
39. Vibart, 100–102; *Annals*, 63–
4; Gardner M S letters.

40. Gough, 55–60; *Annals*, 64;
Vibart, 111–14.
41. Vibart, 118–19; Gardner M S
letters; Gough, 61.

6. The Mutiny Spreads (*pages 120–42*)

1. Roberts, *Letters*, 56, 3, 6, 14,
12, 5.
2. Wilson M S letters.
3. Wise, 45; Barter M S memoirs;
Baird Smith, M S letters.
4. Coghill Papers.
5. Barter M S memoirs.
6. *History of the Siege of Delhi*,
59, 60; Rice Holmes, 120; Kaye, ii,
170.
7. Dunlop, *Service and Adventure
with the Khekee Ressalah*, 12.
8. Quevillart M S diaries.
9. Thurburn, 89.
10. Gordon M S diaries. Charles
Dickens's *Household Words*
explained the apparent stoicism of
the executed rebels: 'To men of keen
sensibilities the few minutes
preceding the execution must appear
like cycles of torture; but to brutes
like the savages of . . . Delhi – they
can have few terrors.'
11. Wade, Wolseley, Sylvester,
Ponsonby Papers.
12. Wolseley Papers.
13. Stansfield M SS.
14. Dunlop, 156–7.
15. ibid., 62.
16. Wallace M SS.
17. Fairweather M SS.
18. Sylvester M S diaries.
19. Potiphar Papers; Stansfield
Papers; Owen, *Recollections*, 29;
Maude and Sherer, *Memoirs of the
Mutiny*, iii.
20. *Blackwood's Magazine*,
November, 1857.
21. Hodson, *Twelve Years of a
Soldier's Life*, 87; Wilson M S letters.
22. Ewart Papers.
23. Chichester Papers.

24. Pearson, Poore, Chichester Papers.

25. Barter MS memoirs.

26. 'A special malignity appears to have been shown in destroying all educational buildings,' one British official reported (FDSC (NAI), 104–5). And since many rebels looked upon the uprising as a religious crusade (*Secret Letters from India*, Vol. 163, 434), churches were particularly marked out for destruction. Monsignor Persico, apostolic vicar of Agra, said that in his vicariate alone, the rebels had destroyed a cathedral, twenty-five churches and five nunneries. (Chaudhuri, *Civil Rebellion*, 260.) Mosques and Hindu temples were, if not often destroyed by the British troops and their allies, frequently looted and desecrated. The gates of a mosque at Fatehpur were blown open by guns which carried away part of the delicate stone feathering that ornamented the interior of the arch. Sikhs then plundered the inside of the mosque, tearing up the Koran, breaking to pieces some old sandalwood chests and prising the mother-of-pearl from a canopy (Thornhill, 319). 'I always smash all the images in the temples we come up to,' Dr Gilbert Hadow admitted. 'Before the mutiny no one was allowed to go inside one of these temples, but now we go where we like.' (Hadow Papers.)

27. q. Russell, op. cit., ii, 109. It was widely believed at the time – though no evidence has since come to light to support the view – that the mutinies in the Bengal Army were part of a preconceived plan. Lieutenant-Colonel Carmichael-Smyth claimed that his action at Meerut in insisting upon a firing parade had provoked a premature explosion and thus averted a far more serious threat to the empire.

'This mutiny has been planned since the taking of Oudh,' wrote Mrs Vansittart, the intelligent wife of an official at Agra, expressing a common opinion. 'It was settled about 20 May that every cantonment all down the country was to rise and murder all the Europeans, seize forts, magazines, treasures. But the confining of the 80 troopers of the 3rd Cavalry at Meerut, and putting them under the guard of their own brethren in arms, caused the plot to explode ten days too soon.' (Vansittart MSS.)

'It is likely that some secret negotiations were going on between the leading sepoys of different cantonments,' Dr R. C. Majumdar has commented, 'though the exact nature of these cannot be ascertained. It is probable that the object of these was to organize a general mutiny, but for this we have no definite evidence.' (Majumdar, *The Sepoy Mutiny*, 207, 218.)

28. q. Rice Holmes, 141.

29. *Annals*, 227.

30. Emma Young's MS narrative; Cave-Brown, *Incidents of Indian Life*, 142. There was a similar panic in Calcutta on Sunday 14 June when rumours spread throughout the city that the sepoys from Barrackpore were on their way to murder the inhabitants. Government secretaries and junior officials barricaded their doors or fled from their homes to take refuge on the ships in the river, and the streets were jammed with the carts, palanquins, horses and carriages of the fugitives. 'In the suburbs almost every house belonging to the Christian population was abandoned,' wrote a resident. 'Half a dozen determined fanatics could have burned down three parts of the town.' (Kaye, iii, 28–33; Malleson, *History of the Indian Mutiny*, i, 25.)

31. Shakespeare Papers.
32. Kaye, ii, 209, 366–7.
33. Edwards, *Personal Adventures*, *passim*.
34. Danvers MSS.
35. Roberts, *41 years*, 77.
36. Kaye, ii, 485.
37. Bailie Papers.
38. Lawrence MS letters, 29 August 1857.
39. Bailie Papers.
40. Kaye, ii, 481; Cooper, *Crisis in the Punjab*, 154–6; Rice Holmes, 362.
41. Cooper, op. cit., 167–9; Rice Holmes, 362–3; Cave-Brown, op. cit., ii, 101–3.
42. Kaye, iii, 91; Malleson, op. cit., i, 65; Christison MSS.
43. Christison MSS. A few sepoys of the 40th remained true to their colours. These, however, were attacked in their tents one night by a party of British soldiers with bayonets. None was killed but several were wounded. It was offered in excuse of the British soldiers that they themselves had been attacked by mutinous sepoys some nights before. (Kaye, iii, 122–3; Christison MSS.)
44. Halls, *Two Months in Arrah*, 31–3.
45. ibid., 44–5.
46. ibid., 32; *Brief Narrative of the Defence of the Arrah Garrison*, 17–20.
47. Mangles MS narrative.
48. ibid.
49. Kaye, iii, 115.
50. Malleson, op. cit., i, 126–45; Rice Holmes, 196–200; Sen, 260–61.
51. Kaye, iii, 459–60; Malleson, op. cit., i, 387; Sneyd MSS.
52. Blake MSS.
53. Esther Anne Nicholson's MS narrative.
54. Sarah Fagan's MS narrative.
55. *Our Escape in June, 1857*, *passim*.
56. Sheriff Papers.
57. ibid.
58. ibid.
59. q. Thornton, 34–6.
60. Carew Papers; FDSC (NAI), 122–4, 139–42; MDP (NAI), 453.

7. A Magistrate in Rajputana
(*pages 143–51*)

This chapter is based on Mark Thornhill's *Personal Adventures and Experiences of a Magistrate during the Rise, Progress and Suppression of the Indian Mutiny*.

8. Agra and Calcutta (*pages 152–67*)

1. Kaye, iii, 195–204. Colvin was censured by Canning for issuing a proclamation in which a free pardon was offered to all sepoys who laid down their arms, with the exception of 'evil-minded instigators' and those guilty of 'heinous crimes against private persons'. Since the mutineers might have interpreted this proclamation as an indication of the Government's fear of them, Canning made it clear that only sepoys from regiments which had merely deserted their posts could expect to be pardoned. (Maclagan, 92–3; Kaye, iii, 232–7; Malleson, *A History of the Indian Mutiny*, i, 164.)
2. Kaye, iii, 204–5; Rice Holmes, 129–30. 'Mr Drummond's activity and energy were admirable,' reported G. F. Harvey, Commissioner of the Agra Division. 'But, I have since learned, he allowed them to produce an overbearing manner, which engendered rather general dislike, and was very unfortunate at such a time.' (*Narrative of Events in the Agra Division*, 107.)
3. Kaye, iii, 206.

4. Henderson Papers.

5. Edith Sharpley's M S narrative.

6. Malleson, op. cit., i, 149; Rice Holmes, 133; Vansittart M S S; Henderson Papers. Robert Drummond was, however, profoundly grateful later when Lieutenant Henry Henderson brought two serviceable guns into the fort at Agra. 'Mr Robert Drummond met me at the gate,' Henderson recorded in amazement, 'and kissed me!' (Henderson Papers.)

7. Vansittart M S S.

8. Edith Sharpley's M S narrative.

9. Thornhill, 199.

10. Henderson Papers.

11. Thornhill, 203.

12. Rice Holmes, 158; Raikes, *Notes on the Revolt*, 192; Malleson, op. cit., i, 283.

13. Edith Sharpley's M S narrative.

14. Thornhill, 167.

15. ibid., 169.

16. ibid., 171.

17. Vansittart M S S.

18. ibid.; Thornhill, 184.

19. Rice Holmes, 157–9; Kaye, iii, 394–404; Malleson, op. cit., i, 283; Vansittart M S S.

20. Thornhill, 196–7; Henderson M S S; F D S C (N A I), 306–9, 640–43.

21. Thornhill, 198.

22. ibid.

23. ibid., 204–6.

24. Kaye, iii, 410; Malleson, op. cit., i, 285; Rice Holmes, 158.

25. Thornhill, 217. Not all Ghazis were rabid fanatics, as Dr Gilbert Hadow discovered. He saw one, 'a calm, quiet-looking man, neatly dressed in white', advance demurely from the rebel ranks, as though he wished to surrender. A soldier went out to meet him. He then fired at the soldier, drew his sword, and kept nine men at bay for nearly five minutes. (Hadow Papers.)

According to W. H. Russell they were 'grizzly-bearded, elderly men for the most part with green turbans and cummerbunds and every one of them had a silver signet ring with a long text of the Koran engraved on it'. (Russell, op. cit., ii, 65.)

26. Vansittart M S S; Henderson M S S.

27. Thornhill, 219.

28. Sharpley M S narrative; Vansittart M S S.

29. Gore-Lindsay M S S.

30. Thornhill, 220–22; F D S C (N A I), 306–9, 640–43.

31. Kaye, ii, 480.

32. Cunningham, *Earl Canning*, 122–4; F D S C (N A I), 27.

33. q. Bence-Jones, *Palaces of the Raj*, 60.

34. Kaye, ii, 119.

35. Elizabeth Sneyd M S S.

36. q. Bence-Jones, 61.

37. q. Maclagan, 86.

38. Canning Papers. To one of his correspondents, who demanded that the fiercest vengeance be inflicted on the sepoys, Canning replied, 'You are entirely and most dangerously wrong. The one difficulty, which of all the others it is the most difficult to meet, is that the regiments which have not yet fallen away are mad with fear – fear for their caste and religion, fear of disgrace in the eyes of their comrades, fear that the European troops are being collected to crush and decimate them as well as their already guilty comrades. Your bloody, off-hand measures are not the cure for this sort of disease . . . Don't mistake violence for vigour.' (Canning Papers.)

39. Bishop Gleig's M S S.

40. Mrs Juxon Henry Jones M S letters.

41. Berkeley M S S. Canning's orders were not as lenient as many of his critics protested. An Act of 6 June had made the waging of war

against the Government, or the instigation of persons to do so, punishable by death, transportation or imprisonment. And on 31 July a series of instructions was issued to explain to the Special Commissioners how this Act was to be administered: distinctions were to be made between mutineers from regiments whose officers had been murdered and those who were apprehended unarmed or who came from regiments that had not been guilty of bloodshed. But the sepoys accused of the lesser crimes, Lady Canning commented, would not, perhaps, find her husband's so-called clemency 'a virtue to their liking. For the best that can happen to them is to be imprisoned by a civil authority, and kept in prison until he can hand him over to a military authority; and this latter authority does what he pleases, and I should think will not be gentle . . . Canning is as much for strict and stern justice as the Duke of Cambridge and *The Times*, and it *is* a necessity.' (q. Maclagan, 136.)

42. q. Maclagan, 140. In an instruction to civil officers, dated 31 July 1857, Canning wrote, 'There is reason to believe that in some even of those native regiments whose revolt has been stained by the most sanguinary atrocities, some men may have distinguished themselves from the mass by protecting an officer. In some cases men of very guilty regiments possess certificates in their favour from officers of their regiment; but there may be others equally deserving of clemency who are without any such ready means of clearing themselves from the presumptive evidence of their deep guilt . . . It is understood that in regiments which mutinied . . . there were men who had no heart in this revolt . . . It is desirable to treat such men with all reasonable lenience . . . Another point to be noted . . . is the general burning of villages which the Governor-General in Council has reason to fear may have been carried too far . . . A severe measure of this sort is doubtless necessary, as an example, in some cases where the mass of the inhabitants of a village have committed a grave outrage, and the perpetrators cannot be punished in their persons, but any approach to a wholesale destruction of property by the officers of the Government, without due regard to guilt or innocence of those who are affected by it, must be strongly reprehended.' (Secret Department Consultations (N A I), 28 August 1857, 114.)

43. q. Surtees, 232. The Queen was not convinced, however, that the Government regarded the crisis in India with sufficient gravity. 'The Queen *must* repeat to Lord Palmerston,' she wrote to the Prime Minister on 22 August, 1857, 'that the measures taken by the Government are *not* commensurate with the magnitude of the crisis.' 'The details of the atrocious crimes committed by the sepoys in India which [the *Morning Advertiser*] gives are *most harrowing*,' the Prince Consort added on 27 November 1857, 'and must render it most difficult for our Commanders to restrain there [*sic*] troops in any degree from reprisals. The difficulty will be to bring the punishment home to the [real] offenders and it is to be expected that many an innocent person will suffer while many a culprit will escape.' (Broadlands Papers.)

9. Nana Sahib (*pages 168–97*)

1. *Parliamentary Papers* (1857), 308–9.

412

2. Thomson, *The Story of Cawnpore*, 141.

3. ibid., 33.

4. q. Gupta, *Nana Sahib*, 49.

5. Thomson, 20–21.

6. *Parliamentary Papers*, 308–9; Gupta, 50.

7. *SLDSP*, ii, 113–14; Gupta, 60.

8. Gupta, 49, 55.

9. Trevelyan, *Cawnpore*, 66.

10. ibid., 29.

11. Shepherd, *A Personal Narrative of the Outbreak and Massacre at Cawnpore*, 4.

12. Kaye, ii, 300–301.

13. Shepherd, 191; Gupta, 60; Trevelyan, op. cit., 71.

14. Trevelyan, op. cit., 62.

15. Thomson, 31; Shepherd, 36.

16. Roberts, *Letters*, 120. 'While searching over the Nana's Palaces at Bithur, 'Lieutenant Roberts told his sister, 'we found heaps of letters directed to that fiend "Azimula Khan" by ladies in England . . . written in the most lovable manner. Such rubbish I never read . . . How English ladies can be so infatuated . . . You would not believe them if I sent home the letters.'

17. Gupta, 1–27; Lang, *Wandering in India*, 118; Martin, *The Indian Empire*, ii, 249; FDSC (NAI), 541–44. 'According to European ideas the ruling [against Nana Sahib's claims] was perfectly just,' commented G. B. Malleson. 'It strictly carried out the agreement made . . . in 1818. But it was, nevertheless, totally repugnant to the ideas and opposed to the customs of the races of Hindustan. With them it was a point of honour to recognize in the son, whether begotten or adopted, the successor to the titles of his father. Whether the English recognized him or not, Nana Sahib was still Peshwa in the eyes of every true Maratha.'

(Malleson, *A History of the Indian Mutiny*, iii, 483.)

18. Trevelyan, op. cit., 47, 48.

19. Lang, 114.

20. Trevelyan, op. cit., 49.

21. Lang, 113; Martin, ii, 249; Gupta, 6, 8.

22. Lang, 116.

23. Maude and Sherer, i, 215; Shepherd, 85.

24. Gupta, 7–8; Trevelyan, op. cit., 48–9; *The Times*, 29 October 1874; Sen, 124–6.

25. Gubbins, 30–1.

26. Kaye, ii, 297–9.

27. *The Times*, 5 September 1857.

28. Gupta, 66–70; Sen, 138; Kaye, ii, 308–11.

29. Williams, *Synopsis of Evidence of Cawnpore Mutiny*, q. Gupta, 72; Rice Holmes, 228; Kaye, ii, 313; FDSC (NAI), 84–91, 139–40.

30. Shepherd, 28.

31. Gupta, 76; Trevelyan, op. cit., 100.

32. Shepherd, 31.

33. FDSC (NAI), 1361, 1362. Tatya Tope's origins were a mystery which various British officials endeavoured to solve. George Plowden, Commissioner at Nagpur, believed that he was 'the son of the ex Peshwa Baji Rao's Soobadhar Ramchunder Punt and that the Rao Sahib [was] his younger brother'. (FDPC (NAI), 173.) Sir James Outram had 'reason to think that he [was] Bhow Tambakar, the late Minister of Baroda'. (FDPC (NAI), 156–68.)

34. Lang, 410–11.

35. Gupta, 84; Shepherd, 135.

36. Gupta, 84–5; Sen, 143.

37. Gupta, 86.

38. Williams, *Synopsis of Evidence*, 4, q. Gupta, 87–8.

39. Thomson, 66; Sherer, 64, 102.

40. Thomson, 101, 108, 129; Hewitt, 98.

41. Shepherd, 44, 57, 61;

Trevelyan, op. cit., 137.
42. Shepherd, 42–3.
43. Trevelyan, op. cit., 94, 95.
44. Shepherd, 55.
45. ibid., 55–6.
46. Thomson, 76.
47. ibid., 27.
48. Shepherd, 62.
49. Thomson, 90.
50. Shepherd, 63.
51. Thomson, 87; Trevelyan, op. cit., 135.
52. Thomson, 78–83; Shepherd, 59.
53. Thomson, 68; Lieutenant Mowbray Thomson's MS report.
54. Trevelyan, op. cit., 105.
55. Thomson, 67, 71–4, 136–7; Trevelyan, op. cit., 111.
56. Mowbray Thomson's MS report.
57. Gupta, 81.
58. Shepherd, 60; Thomson, 129.
59. Thomson, 59, 77.
60. ibid., 103.
61. Amelia Horne's MS account.
62. Mowbray Thomson's MS report.
63. Trevelyan, op. cit., 134; Thomson, 107, 108.
64. Shepherd, 83–4.
65. Edwardes and Merivale, ii, 350–57; Gupta, 99; Shepherd, 83–4.
66. Kaye, ii, 320–32; Shepherd, 54, 76; Thomson, 105, 106, 141; Trevelyan, op. cit., 138; Gupta, 89–90.
67. Gupta, 76; Trevelyan, op. cit., 148; Forrest, *SLDSP*, ii, 117.
68. Kaye, ii, 333; Gupta, 103.
69. Amelia Horne's MS account.
70. ibid.
71. Thomson, 161.
72. Amelia Horne's MS account.
73. Thomson, 165.
74. q. Trevelyan, op. cit., 182.
75. Trevelyan, op. cit., 182.
76. Delafosse's MS report in KMP, 725 (41).
77. Mowbray Thomson said that he and his companions opened fire on the boatmen immediately they jumped overboard and that 'simultaneously' the mutineers opened fire on the Europeans (Thomson, 166). Michael Edwardes has suggested that 'it was one of those ghastly accidents that spatter the pages of history and on which any interpretation suitable to the needs of the occasion can be imposed. Probably a musket-shot was heard and the British, fearful of treachery and [with] nerves tattered by their weeks of constant siege, immediately opened fire.' (Edwardes, *Battles of the Indian Mutiny*, 66.)
78. Trevelyan, op. cit., 188–9; Kaye, ii, 336–43; Gupta, 108–10; Thomson, 166–7; Delafosse's MS report; FDSC (NAI), 450.
79. Amelia Horne's MS account.
80. Thomson, 168–9.
81. Hadow Papers; Thomson, 168–98.
82. q. Trevelyan, op. cit., 193.
83. Morrison Family Records.
84. Amelia Horne's MS account.
85. q. Trevelyan, op. cit., 213–14.
86. Gupta, 140; Kaye, ii, 353–4; Trevelyan, op. cit., 228–9; Forrest, *History*, i, 476.
87. *Parliamentary Papers*, 44, i, 120; Gupta, 129–30; Trevelyan, op. cit., 226–7; Kaye, ii, 352.
88. Gupta, 139–40; Kaye, ii, 354–5; Trevelyan, op. cit., 230–31; FDSC (NAI), 125; MDP (NAI), 445, 462–3.

10. Enter Henry Havelock (*pages 198–215*)

1. q. Pollock, *Way to Glory*, 153.
2. q. Maclagan, 46.
3. q. Surtees, 234.
4. Marshman, *Memoirs*, 279; Pollock, 151.
5. Dawson, 43.
6. Gordon MS diary.

7. Kaye, ii, 220–26, 129–32.
8. ibid., ii, 236.
9. ibid., ii, 236–7.
10. ibid., ii, 256–7; FDSC (NAI) 94–5.
11. *Annals*, 158.
12. Rice Holmes, 219; Malleson, *A History of the Indian Mutiny*, iii, 439. 'The finest champagnes of Clicquot and Perrier-Jouet, and the best brandies of Martel and Hennessey, were selling for 6d. a bottle. So a reign of intoxication commenced, which, for a while, subverted all military authority.' (Kaye, ii, 265.)
13. Thurburn, 35.
14. Pearson MS letters.
15. Chunder, *Travels of a Hindu*, i, 104.
16. Kaye, ii, 269.
17. Rice Holmes, 221.
18. Gupta, 127, Kaye, ii, 275.
19. Havelock was also blamed for taking too gloomy a view of his army's prospects. 'All such talk is certain to reach the ears of those against us,' he was warned by the acting Commander-in-Chief, Sir Patrick Grant. 'And it is equally certain that no possible good can come of it amongst our own people . . . Pray be careful, therefore. I tell you frankly that some things you have said . . . have been repeated and made their way down here.' The last sentence of this letter in the Havelock Papers is annotated, in Harry Havelock's hand, 'By Neill, of course.'
20. Pollock, 159; Forrest, *History*, i, 372.
21. Rice Holmes, 383–5; Pollock, 162–3.
22. Pollock, 163; Gordon MS diary; Kaye, ii, 360.
23. Gordon MS diary.
24. Pollock, 164.
25. ibid., Havelock Papers.
26. Havelock Papers.
27. Havelock Papers; Kaye, ii, 368–70.
28. Pollock, 176.
29. Kaye, ii, 353–5, 371–4; Rice Holmes, 241–2; *Depositions taken at Cawnpore* (Cawnpore Collectorate Records), 12–16, 35–9, 58, 107–14; Gupta, 140; FDPP (NAI), 666.
30. q. Gupta, 140.
31. q. Trevelyan, op. cit., 256.
32. FDPP, 666.
33. Pollock, 178.
34. ibid., 179–84; Kaye, ii, 374–82; Rice Holmes, 286–9.
35. Gordon MS diary.
36. Pollock, 191; Kaye, ii, 397.
37. Sherer, *Daily Life During the Indian Mutiny*, 89.
38. Gordon MS diary; Barter MS memoirs; Maclean, 'A Surgeon's Memoir', *SAR*.
39. Pearson MS letters.
40. Bingham Papers.
41. Kaye, ii, 388. Even so, in Neill's opinion, the steps taken to prevent plundering at Cawnpore were far from sufficient. 'There is great plundering going on by the troops – most disgraceful,' he wrote in his diary on 22 July. 'And on the part of commandants, more particularly the 64th, a disinclination to prevent their men misconducting themselves. I should have adopted very decided steps with all these regiments . . . but this has been neglected. All have taken to plundering and the example set by officers has been very bad indeed. The plundering of the merchants and shopkeepers in the city by bands of soldiers and Sikhs has been most outrageous, and there has been no check to it. Orders here seem to be unattended to. Pistols and guns fired off in camp. Colonel Tytler informs me the want of attention to orders by commandants and others is disgraceful, and I see it plainly. I suppose no force ever marched with

a set of so inferior commanding officers.' (Neill's MS diary.)

42. Kaye, ii, 399.
43. Bingham Papers.
44. Gordon MS diary.
45. Potiphar Papers.
46. Kaye, ii, 400.
47. Shepherd, 184; Case, 314. At the beginning of 1858 the walls of the Bibighar were whitewashed and the graffiti obliterated in order – so Lieutenant Ashton Warner thought – 'to prevent our inflicting punishment on any more sepoys'. (Warner MS letters.)
48. *JSAHR*, vol. XXXV, No. 143, September 1957.
49. Metcalfe, *Two Native Narratives*, 68.
50. Wolseley Papers.
51. Lehmann, *All Sir Garnet*, 51.
52. Gardner MS letters.
53. Poore Papers.
54. KMP, 725.
55. Canning Papers.
56. Lang Papers.
57. Bailie MS letters.
58. Dawson, 90.
59. Coghill Papers. It was true that at Shajahanpur Europeans had been attacked and killed in church. Here, on Sunday 31 May, mutineers from the 28th Native Infantry crowded round the church during morning service. The chaplain, who went to the door, was attacked and had his hand severed by a sword stroke. He was later murdered by some villagers. The magistrate was also wounded by a sword stroke, then killed as he fled for safety across the courtyard. A clerk was also killed; another clerk was wounded and murdered later. The rest of the male members of the congregation meanwhile barricaded the chancel doors while the ladies fled to safety in the church turret. On the appearance of an armed British officer, Captain Henry Sneyd, the mutineers, who were themselves armed only with swords and clubs, ran back to their lines for their muskets. No sooner had they departed than the Europeans' faithful servants arrived at the church with their masters' guns and rifles. The Europeans then ran out into the churchyard where they found their carriages and horses still standing outside, together with a party of about a hundred sepoys, mostly Sikhs, who had come down to offer the officers and the memsahibs their protection. Captain Sneyd, his sister, Anna, and brother-in-law, Captain Lysaght, thus managed to escape; but they and several other fugitives from Shahjahanpur were all murdered a week later near Aurangabad. As a child, so her mother, Elizabeth Sneyd, related, Anna had had a particularly vivid dream in which she saw herself and her brother being murdered in a church by men with black skins (MS reminiscences of Elizabeth Sneyd; Malleson, op. cit., i, 319–20; Kaye, iii, 459).
60. Wolseley Papers.
61. Ouvry, *Cavalry Experiences*, 150.
62. Wise, 37, 145.
63. Wade Papers.
64. Havelock Papers. Sir Patrick Grant himself wrote to Havelock on 8 July: 'Your first object should be to retake Cawnpore and utterly destroy all belonging to that Fiend the Nana Sahib . . . If the wretch falls into your clutches you will know how to deal with him – hanging by the hands of the lowest sweeper is much too good for him but our laws and practice allow no more severe or degrading punishment.' (Havelock Papers.)
65. Rotton, 123. Others were less sure that God's vengeance would fall only on the Indians. Major Anson

expressed a common opinion when he wrote, 'Yes, it would be most cruel to think that God was not on our side. But . . . I look upon this business as in the light of a heavy punishment for the ungodly, infidel lives the greater part of us have lived in India . . . God will grind the heathen to powder . . . but [not before] justly punishing *us* for our sins.' (Anson, 21, 31.) Karl Marx wrote of retribution: 'However infamous the conduct of the sepoys, it is only the reflex, in a concentrated form, of England's own conduct in India, not only during the epoch of the foundation of her Eastern Empire, but even during the last ten years of a long-settled rule. To characterize that rule it suffices to say that torture formed an organic institution of its financial policy. There is something in human history like retribution; and it is a rule of historical retribution that its instrument be forged not by the offended, but by the offender himself.' (Marx, 91.)

66. Sylvester MS diary.
67. Nowell Papers.
68. Sylvester MS diary.
69. Clifford Papers.
70. Trevelyan, *Competition Wallah*, 288.
71. Maclagan, 142. 'At each halting place Mr Power held a court of summary jurisdiction, and condemned to death scores of truculent traitors . . . Here at Mau nearly a hundred . . . rebels, caught hiding in the town and in the surrounding villages . . . were summarily tried and hanged upon the branches of a great pipul tree in the square in the centre of the town.' (Gordon-Alexander, 214.)
72. Ponsonby Papers.
73. Dunlop, 94.
74. Ricketts Papers.
75. Gordon MS diary.

11. Lawrence at Lucknow (*pages 216–34*)

1. Bence-Jones, 110; Rice Holmes, 248–9; Malleson, *A History of the Indian Mutiny*, ii, 365. Part of what remains of the ground floor of the Residency is now a rather decrepit museum. The surrounding buildings stand as ruins in a pleasant park.
2. *SLDSP*, 19, 20. Everyone referred to Lawrence as though he were an old man. Julia Inglis described him as 'a particularly nice old man'. (Inglis MS letters.)
3. Rice Holmes, 246.
4. q. Edwardes, *Necessary Hell*, 41.
5. ibid., 42, 136; Edwardes and Merivale, 197, 208–17; FDPC (NAI), 372.
6. Sen, 176–9; Malleson, op. cit., i, 348; Rice Holmes, 45, 71, 559.
7. q. Edwardes, *Red Year*, 97.
8. Morison, *Lawrence of Lucknow*, 299.
9. The palace was the Chattar Manzil. Jackson subsequently abandoned it. But further offence was caused by the appropriation of the Qudam Rasul, which contained a stone bearing the imprint of the Prophet's foot, as an ammunition store. (Sen, 177.)
10. q. Edwardes, *Necessary Hell*, 140.
11. Wells MS letters.
12. q. Edwardes, *Necessary Hell*, 140.
13. Lawrence's tactful and courteous treatment of the Indian gentry was in striking contrast to the hospitality offered to the Indians in the recent past. Dr Joseph Fayrer, on being appointed Residency Surgeon at Lucknow in 1853, was told by the then resident, Colonel William Sleeman, 'how necessary it was that native gentlemen should receive only that exact amount of

official recognition to which they were entitled, but of which they were constantly trying to obtain more than was their due . . . He explained that . . . for example, some native gentlemen were to have chairs, others *morahs* (stools), others were not permitted to sit in the presence of the Resident or of the officers of the Residency, whilst others again were not received as visitors at all.' (Fayrer, *Recollections*, 86.)

14. Edwardes, *Necessary Hell*, 140; Rice Holmes, 249–50.

15. Wells MS letters.

16. It was never established why the sepoys at Lucknow were required to bite their cartridges after the practice had been officially abandoned in favour of tearing them open. The Commander-in-Chief wrote of 'a presumption of any imaginable degree of perverse management'. And the Governor-General asked for an explanation; but none was forthcoming. (*Parliamentary Papers*, 30 (1857), 210–16.)

17. Gubbins, 120–24; Kaye, i, 592–4; Malleson, op. cit., i, 354; Rice Holmes, 250–52.

18. 'Almost insubordinate' in his personal encounters with Lawrence, Gubbins also complained of his superior's inability in letters to the Governor-General. 'Sir Henry Lawrence came to us attenuated and weak,' runs one of Gubbins' letters to Canning. 'And the severe mental anxiety which he has undergone has prostrated him greatly. Sir Henry Lawrence is no longer, I think, firm, nor his mental vision clear.' (Canning Papers, 2 June 1857.)

19. *Annals,* 26.

20. Brydon MS journal; Inglis, 21; Edwardes and Merivale, 580–81; Gubbins, 106; FDSC (NAI), 560–80.

21. Anderson, *Reminiscences*, 8–10.

22. Inglis, *The Siege of Lucknow*, 24.

23. Gubbins, 172; Bartrum, *A Widow's Reminiscences*, 21.

24. Anderson, 31.

25. Gubbins, 255.

26. Rees, *A Personal Narrative*, 115; Kaye, iii, 522.

27. Hadow Papers.

28. Rees, 109.

29. Hadow Papers.

30. Anderson, 29, 38.

31. Rees, 127; Inglis, op. cit., 80.

32. Rees, 38.

33. Wells MS letters.

34. Brydon MS journal.

35. Sherer, 153.

36. Rice Holmes, 261.

37. Case, 22.

38. Inglis, op. cit., 32; Case, 20.

39. Rees, 61.

40. Metcalfe, 45; Inglis, op. cit., 31; Brydon MS journal.

41. Inglis, op. cit., 33.

42. Bartrum, 16.

43. ibid., 12.

44. ibid.

45. Inglis, op. cit., 31; Rees, 51.

46. Madeline Jackson's MS account.

47. Kaye, iii, 502; Morison, *Lawrence of Lucknow*, 317; Rice Holmes, 260; Edwardes, *Red Year*, 168.

48. Rees, 76; Rice Holmes, 264; Kaye, iii, 669.

49. Metcalfe, 49.

50. Rice Holmes, 264.

51. Rees, 78; Kaye, iii, 507–9.

52. Rees, 75.

53. ibid., 73.

54. ibid., 75.

55. Metcalfe, 52.

56. Inglis, op. cit., 44.

57. Inglis, op. cit., 45; Case, 71.

58. Brydon MS journal; Gubbins, 184–8; Anderson, 52–3; Inglis, op. cit., 48–50.

59. Rees, 95; MDP (NAI), 339.

12. The Siege of Lucknow
(*pages 235–52*)

1. Hutchinson Papers.
2. Kaye, iii, 514.
3. Brydon MS journal.
4. Hadow Papers.
5. Anderson, 57; Rees, 121.
6. Hadow Papers; Fayrer, 165; Gubbins, 222; *Defence of Lucknow*, 45–6.
7. Edwardes and Merivale, 609–14; Malleson, *A History of the Indian Mutiny*, i, 433–4; Kaye, iii, 516–21; 'Remonstrance of M. R. Gubbins against appointment of Major Banks', FDSC (NAI), 267.
8. Rice Holmes, 270–71; Brydon MS journal; Hadow Papers; Germon, *Journal of the Siege of Lucknow*, 58–9; Boileau Papers; Gubbins, 224.
9. Innes, *Lucknow and Oude in the Mutiny*, 271.
10. Gubbins, 190, 435; Innes, 122; Rice Holmes, 271; Edwardes, *Season in Hell*, 73, 76.
11. Inglis, *The Siege of Lucknow*, 69; Rees, 135, 136; Brydon MS journal; *Defence of Lucknow*, 81.
12. Rees, 144.
13. ibid., 116.
14. Case, 118; Inglis, op. cit., 100–101, 116; Edwardes, *Season in Hell*, 76, 100; Inglis MS letters.
15. Bartrum, 28, 37, 38, 40.
16. Inglis, op. cit., 70, 74.
17. Boileau Papers.
18. Inglis, op. cit., 170.
19. *Defence of Lucknow*, 154; *Graphic*, 15 June 1907, q. *Annals*, 261.
20. Inglis, op. cit., 60, 107. At the end of August an unsatisfied craving for opium drove sixteen men, including several of the King of Oudh's musicians, to leave the Residency for the city. They left the excuse, inscribed in several places on the wall of their former quarters: 'Because I have no opium.' (Inglis, 137.)
21. Rees, 140, 137, 138.
22. Inglis, op. cit., 79, 149, 107; Bartrum, 39; Case, 168, 161, 178, 194; Brydon MS journal.
23. Gubbins, 278.
24. Rees, 162–3, 167, 168.
25. Anderson, 59.
26. Rees, 136.
27. Inglis, op. cit., 69; Edwardes, *Season in Hell*, 99; *Defence of Lucknow*, 135.
28. Inglis, op. cit., 71.
29. Rees, 175.
30. ibid., 114, 174, 142.
31. Inglis, op. cit., 117, 71; Case, 128, 129, 152.
32. Anderson, 61; Gubbins, 277; Rees, 71, 142.
33. Gubbins, 308; Rees, 205, 295, 296; Case, 125, 171, 185, 197, 198, 219, 221–2, 246; Brydon MS journal; Boileau Papers.
34. Rees, 88.
35. Inglis, op. cit., 101–2; Inglis MS letters.
36. Brydon MS journal; Case, 195; Bartrum, 42; Rees, 169, 170.
37. Case, 84; Rees, 170.
38. Inglis, op. cit., 111; Anderson, 58.
39. Metcalfe, 49.
40. Metcalfe, 50; Rees, 137, 149; Anderson, 66; Boileau Papers; Brydon MS journal. It has been suggested that the rebels never really tried for an outright victory at Lucknow as 'their soldiers felt that once they captured it [their services] would no longer be needed'. (Sen, 15.)
41. Anderson, 67.
42. Rees, 147.
43. Case, 147–9.
44. ibid., 114–15.
45. Boileau Papers.
46. Rees, 191.
47. Gubbins, 304.

48. Inglis, op. cit., 144; Anderson, 96; Inglis MS letters.
49. Inglis, op. cit., 81.
50. ibid., 98.
51. ibid., 146.
52. Hadow Papers.
53. Brydon MS journal.
54. Hadow Papers.
55. Brydon MS journal.
56. Boileau Papers.
57. ibid.
58. Inglis MS letters.
59. Rees, 114.
60. Inglis, op. cit., 134, 142; Inglis MS letters.
61. Anderson, 85.
62. Gubbins, 280, 303–4; Inglis, op. cit., 107, 115, 153; Case, 146; Anderson, 60.
63. Bartrum MS diary.
64. Rice Holmes, 278.
65. Hadow Papers.
66. MDP (NAI), 610.

13. The First Relief of Lucknow (*pages 253–66*)

1. North, *Journal of an English Officer in India*, 182.
2. q. Pollock, 193.
3. Pollock, 194–7; Malleson, *A History of the Indian Mutiny* i, 492–5.
4. Havelock Papers.
5. Malleson, op. cit., i, 495–6; Rice Holmes, 292–4.
6. Havelock Papers.
7. ibid.
8. Malleson, op. cit., ii, 502. Having delivered his reprimand, Havelock dispatched a telegram to Sir Patrick Grant: 'I regret to have to report to your Excellency that General Neill's conduct has turned out the very reverse of what I had expected. He vaunts and promises largely in his letters to me, but does nothing. Worse than this he impedes the public service by his factious opposition to my measures, and has at last begun to write to me in a style of censure and dictation which I have been compelled to reprove by threatening him with arrest.' (Havelock Papers.)
9. Groom, *With Havelock from Allahabad to Lucknow*, 123.
10. q. Pollock, 203.
11. Malleson, op. cit., i, 502–3; Pollock, 204–5; Rice Holmes, 295.
12. Havelock Papers.
13. q. Pollock, 214.
14. Havelock Papers.
15. Goldsmid, *James Outram*, i, 104–7.
16. q. Maclagan, 122.
17. Wade MS letters.
18. Barter MS memoirs.
19. Havelock Papers; Goldsmid, ii, 207; Rice Holmes, 302; Malleson, op. cit., i, 524.
20. Havelock Papers.
21. ibid.
22. ibid.
23. ibid.
24. ibid.
25. Gordon MS diary.
26. Maude and Sherer, i, 227.
27. Amongst the Havelock Papers there is a document in Harry Havelock's hand, in an envelope marked 'Important Historical Memorandum made 10 September 1874 10 a.m. before leaving for France'. It reads: 'This paper (attached) is the original on which I took down roughly Outram's order for the attack on Lucknow the next day. This was at 2.30 p.m. on the 24 September 1857 in the centre room of the house at the Alum Bagh. I took this rough then into the next room, drafted the order in full and then came back to Outram and read it out to him for his approval clause by clause. I write this to note what is the fact that Outram, though ostensibly leaving the command in my Father's hands (as he left him certainly all the

responsibility of nominal command), had in fact assumed it entirely himself. As he told Kaye in 1863 he only nominally resigned it so that he might get the Victoria Cross (he said this himself repeatedly) a strange fancy for a General officer of so high a reputation. When I went to my Father for orders at 2 p.m. he sent me "to take them from General Outram" – and I repeated to Outram that he had so sent me, in which he acquiesced without remark.'

28. Dawson, 43; Gordon MS diary; Pollock, 221–36; Rice Holmes, 303–7; Malleson, op. cit., i, 527–40; Marshman, 414–22; FDSC (NAI), 103–8.

29. Boileau Papers. Mrs Bartrum was amongst those who ran out to welcome the relieving force. She hoped that her husband would be one of them. She was told that he was with the heavy artillery and would be in next morning. 'So I went back to my own room,' she recorded in her diary. 'I could not sleep that night for joy at the thought of seeing him so soon . . . *September 26* – Was up with the daylight and dressed myself and baby in the one clean dress which I had kept for him throughout the siege until his papa should come. I took him out and met Mr Freeling who told me that dear Robert was just coming in, that they had been sharing the same tent on the march, and that he was in high spirits at the thought of seeing his wife and child again. I waited, expecting to see him, but he did not come, so I gave baby his breakfast and sat at the door to watch for him again full of happiness. I felt he was so near to me that at any moment we might be together again; and here I watched for him nearly all day. In the evening I took baby up to the top of the Residency, to look down the road, but I could not see him coming and returned back to my room disappointed. *September 27* – Still watching for my husband, and still he came not, and my heart was growing very sick with anxiety. That afternoon Dr Darby came to me: he looked so kindly and so sadly in my face, and I said to him, "How strange it is my husband is not come in!" "Yes," he said, "it *is* strange!" and turned round and went out of the room. Then the thought struck me: something has happened which they do not like to tell me.' Mrs Bartrum later learned that her husband had been shot through the head as he approached the Residency. Their baby died in February aboard the *Himalaya* at Calcutta on the day before she was due to sail home to England. (Bartrum, 43–8; Bartrum MS diary.)

30. Inglis, *The Siege of Lucknow*, 156.

31. Edwardes, *Season in Hell*, 183.

32. Inglis, op. cit., 158.

33. ibid.

34. Boileau Papers.

14. The King of Delhi (*pages 269–79*)

1. *PTBS*, 28, 17, 168; Muir, 36–9. The King's surprise at the mutineers' arrival was shared by the people of Delhi who believed at first that the Russians had come. (Spear, *Twilight*, 202.)

2. *PTBS*, 30, 94, 180.

3. A characteristic letter to the Rajah of Patiala ran in part: 'On account of your proud attachment to my family, you are directed as quickly as possible to repair here in person with all your army . . . Delay not.' (FDSC (NAI), 25). The Rajah of Patiala, like the Rajah of Jind and the Nawab of Kernal, decided, however, to remain loyal to the British to whom they offered

the resources of their states. (Sen, 78.)

4. Edwardes, *Red Year*, 46; MP (NAI), 57, 60–61.

5. Narrative of Syed Mubarak Shah, q. Edwardes, *Red Year*, 212.

6. *PTBS*, 39, 94; *Mainuddin's Narrative*, 86–7.

7. *Mainuddin's Narrative*, 87.

8. ibid.

9. KMP (IOL), 725 (10) 399; Spear, *Twilight*, 203.

10. *BPIR* q. Chaudhuri, *Theories*, 48–9; Husain, 66–7; Sen, 74–5; Spear, *Twilight*, 207.

11. Husain, 191.

12. ibid.

13. *PTBS*, 113; Husain, 195, 202, 203.

14. Narrative of Syed Mubarak Shah, q. Edwardes, *Red Year*, 214.

15. Husain, 203–4; *Mainuddin's Narrative*, 61–2.

16. Husain, 207.

17. MP (NAI), Boxes 15, 16.

18. Young, q. Norman, *Delhi 1857*, xiv.

19. Husain, 197.

20. passim *Jivanlal's Narrative*, 98–123.

21. ibid., 126.

22. ibid., 133–4; Narrative of Syed Mubarak Shah, q. Edwardes, *Red Year*, 208–9; Sen, 83–4. One of the European non-commissioned officers was later identified as the sergeant-major of the rebel 28th Native Infantry (Cooper, *The Crisis in the Punjab*, 197). Hugh Gough mentioned a British soldier named Gordon as fighting with the mutineers in Delhi (Gough, 110). There is a portrait of a Sergeant-Major Gordon in the museum at the Red Fort.

23. *Jivanlal's Narrative*, 134, 146.

24. Forrest, *History*, i, 96–7; Cooper, op. cit., 201; Bourchier, *Eight Months' Campaign*, 44; Sen, 84.

25. *Jivanlal's Narrative*, 146; Husain, 251.

26. *Jivanlal's Narrative*, 134–5.

27. Husain, 233–6.

28. *Jivanlal's Narrative*, 143.

29. ibid., 140. Within a few days of Bakht Khan's arrival the Military Committee, no doubt pressed to do so by Mirza Moghul, delivered this reprimand: 'The Kingdom of Delhi which has sprung up by the grace of God is in its infancy and resembles a child. We believe that God sent you to foster this child, and relying on God we hoped that you would manage the affairs of this infant kingdom in a satisfactory manner . . . But great tact and good policy is required to rear an infant Kingdom . . . We now write to protest that you have set at naught the troops that nobly braved the fire of the English, and they and their officers, who were the first to rush into the flames, have now been forgotten by you . . . Here in the first fierce struggle everything was managed by the Commander-in-Chief, Mirza Moghul . . . He is a Prince of high dignity and superior to all . . . In every respect he is your superior. Nevertheless [you have disregarded his commands]. If you will not obey your superior, how can you expect your inferiors to obey you?' (FDSC (NAI), 20–21.)

30. ibid., 161.

31. ibid., 177.

32. ibid., 177–8.

33. ibid., 179–80.

34. ibid., 203.

35. Narrative of Syed Mubarak Shah, q. Edwardes, *Red Year*, 221.

36. Sen, 96. On learning of these overtures the Governor-General 'wished it to be understood that any concession to the King, of which the King's restoration to his former position should be the basis, [was]

one to which the Government . . . [could] not for a moment give its consent'. (FDSC (NAI), 342.)

37. Greathed, *Letters*, 217. 'There was a hollow pretence of negotiation entered into by the King of Delhi,' wrote James Neill. 'It was noticed in the Lieutenant-Governor's letter to the Governor-General in these words . . . "accommodation is now out of the question". Nothing further has been heard of any overtures from the palace until a letter came from Mr Greathed this morning [4 September]. In it he says yesterday an emissary came in from the chief lady of the palace offering her good offices. She was told we were anxious for her person's safety but that no communications would be received from inmates of the palace.' (FDSC (NAI), 236.)

38. Chaudhuri, *Civil Rebellion*, 74; Sen, 102–3.

39. *Jivanlal's Narrative*, 195, 205.

40. Husain, 263–4.

41. *Jivanlal's Narrative*, 207. Bankers and businessmen of all sorts had been called upon to contribute to the expenses of maintaining an army in Delhi; but the response had been very disappointing. Some of those subject to the levy could not be found when the tax inspectors called; others actually refused payment or bribed the officials appointed to supervise the collection. (MP (NAI), 153 (11), 16 (8), 111 (71).)

42. Narrative of Syed Mubarak Shah, q. Edwardes, *Red Year*, 220. 'On several occasions his Majesty rewarded the mutineers for bringing in the heads of British officers killed in the action,' confirmed Mohan Lal. 'At other times he gave presents to the wounded sepoys and graced the dressing of their wounds by his presence.' (Account of Munshi Mohan Lal, KMP, 725(10) 399.)

43. Husain, 274, 275; Delhi Force Intelligence Reports.

44. *Jivanlal's Narrative*, 229.

15. The Ridge (*pages 280–91*)

1. Ewart MS letters.

2. Wilson MS letters.

3. Hodson, 204.

4. MDP (NAI), 387–94.

5. Wilson MS letters; Rice Holmes, 341–2; Kaye, ii, 526–33.

6. Wilson MS letters.

7. Cadell MS letters.

8. Ewart MS letters.

9. Baird Smith MS letters.

10. Hodson, 216.

11. Baird Smith MS letters.

12. Wilson MS letters.

13. Hodson, 226; Wilson MS letters.

14. Reid, 27.

15. Baird Smith MS letters.

16. Wilson MS letters.

17. Hodson, 205.

18. Rotton, *The Chaplain's Narrative*, 66.

19. Griffiths, *The Narrative of the Siege of Delhi*, 84.

20. Wilson MS letters.

21. Hodson, 199.

22. Younghusband, *The Story of the Guides*, 67, 73.

23. Hindu Rao was a Mahratta nobleman, 'of frank, bluff manners and genial temperament'. His house, 'an Anglo-Indian mansion of the better class', had been built probably by Sir Edward Colebroke who sold it to William Fraser. It was sold to Hindu Rao in 1835; but since his death in 1855 it had been left empty. (Kaye, ii, 517; Spear, *Twilight*, 191–2.) It is now a hospital.

24. Reid, 34.

25. ibid., 38–41.

26. Cadell MS letters.

27. Barter MS memoirs.

28. Cadell MS letters.

29. Shakespeare Papers.
30. Wilson MS letters; Barter MS memoirs; Rice Holmes, 348–9; Kaye, ii, 586–7.
31. Wilson MS letters.
32. ibid.
33. Reid, *Extracts from Letters and Notes*, 55.
34. Griffiths, 115; Barter MS memoirs.
35. Barter MS memoirs.
36. Ewart MS letters.
37. Wilson MS letters.
38. Rotton, 135.
39. Harriet Tytler's 'Through the Sepoy Mutiny' in *Chambers's Journal*.
40. Cadell MS letters; Ewart MS letters; Barter MS memoirs. 'There are two Parsee merchants also in camp, Jehangeer and Cowasjee, with lots of supplies . . . Beer they wanted twenty-four rupees a dozen for at first; but they came down to fifteen rupees for their best English bottle, and the Headquarters' Mess took a hundred dozen from them at this price.' (Young, 347.)
41. Gough; 190, 220–21; Hodson, 318; Sherer, 139.
42. Hare Papers; Fairweather MS letters.
43. Hodson, 318.
44. Gough, 190.
45. Delhi Force Intelligence Reports.
46. Reid, 20; Greathed, 50; Young, 61.
47. Baird Smith MS letters.
48. ibid.

16. The Assault (*pages 292–303*)

1. Reid, 47.
2. Wilberforce, *An Unrecorded Chapter*, 152.
3. ibid., 153; Edwardes, *Red Year*, 49.
4. Kaye, ii, 401.
5. Wilberforce, 154.
6. Trotter, *Life of John Nicholson*, 256; Malleson, *A History of the Indian Mutiny*, ii, 83.
7. Ouvry, *Cavalry Experiences*, 183a.
8. Roberts, *41 Years*, 33.
9. Trotter, op. cit., 275.
10. Hodson, 215.
11. Cadell MS letters.
12. Hare MS letters.
13. Griffiths, 107.
14. Barter MS memoirs.
15. Griffiths, 63, 85; Hodson, 213; Reid, 41.
16. Hodson, 259; Reid, 51.
17. Narrative of Syed Mubarak Shah, q. Edwardes, *Red Year*, 221.
18. Griffiths, 73.
19. Chichester MS letters; Lithgow MS letters.
20. Delhi Force Intelligence Reports.
21. Dunlop, 125.
22. Rotton, 193; Young, 212.
23. Delhi Force Intelligence Reports.
24. Ewart MS letters.
25. Wilson MS letters.
26. Hodson, 282; Rice Holmes, 369; Roberts, *41 Years*, 118.
27. Baird Smith MS letters.
28. Coghill MS letters.
29. Barter MS memoirs.
30. Coghill MS letters.
31. Wilson MS letters.
32. Medley, *A Year's Campaign in India*, 82–3.
33. Fairweather MS letters.
34. Reid, 53.
35. Malleson, op. cit., ii, 25; Rice Holmes, 373.
36. MDP (NA I), 387–94.
37. Barter MS memoirs.
38. Malleson, op. cit., ii, 9–12; Barter MS memoirs.
39. Barter MS memoirs; Rotton, 259–60; Cave-Brown, *The Punjab and Delhi in 1857*, ii, 156–7.
40. Wilson MS letters.

41. Barter MS memoirs.

42. Malleson, op. cit., ii, 36–7; Rice Holmes, 379–80; Cave-Brown, op. cit., ii, 173.

43. Coghill MS letters.

44. Money MS letters.

45. Barter MS memoirs; Lithgow MS letters.

46. ibid.

47. Money MS letters.

48. Trotter, op. cit., 93–4; Barter MS memoirs; Kaye, iii, 599.

49. Coghill MS letters.

50. Kaye, iii, 579–608; Rice Holmes, 377–8.

51. Wise, 103.

52. Barter MS memoirs.

53. ibid.

54. Baird Smith MS letters.

55. Kaye, iii, 617.

56. Baird Smith MS letters; Rice Holmes, 381, 590; Malleson, op. cit., ii, 10.

57. Roberts, *Letters*, 69; Roberts, *41 Years*, 132; Kaye, iii, 657.

58. Trotter, op. cit., 283; Lawrence MS letters.

59. The bearers carrying Nicholson back to the hospital had put the *doolie* down and gone off to join in the plundering. Frederick Roberts found him lying by the road outside the Kashmir Gate. 'He was lying on his back,' Roberts recalled, 'no wound was visible, and but for the pallor of his face, always colourless, there was no sign of the agony he must have been enduring. On my expressing a hope that he was not seriously wounded, he said "I am dying . . ." The sight of that great man lying helpless and on the point of death was almost more than I could bear. Other men had died daily round me . . . but I never felt as I felt then – to lose Nicholson seemed to me at that moment to lose everything.' (Roberts, *41 Years*, 130.)

At Nicholson's funeral a few days later, ' the men of the Multani Horse gave way,' R. G. Wilberforce wrote. ' Throwing themselves on the ground, they sobbed and wept as if their very hearts were breaking . . . Probably not one of these men had ever shed a tear before; but for them Nicholson was everything. For him they had left their frontier homes, for him they had forsaken their beloved hills to come down to the detested plains; they acknowledged none but him, they served none but him . . . When, a few days after the funeral, an order was received by them from headquarters to march somewhere – they returned for answer that they owed no allegiance to the English Government; that they had come down to protect and save Nicholson, and to loot Delhi . . . And when they had collected as much plunder as they could, they marched back again, up-country, to their own homes, carrying their plunder with them.' (Wilberforce, 201.)

17. The Captured City (*pages 310–26*)

1. Chichester MS letters; Cadell MS letters.

2. Wilson MS letters.

3. Hodson, 296.

4. Wise, 108, 109.

5. Barter MS memoirs.

6. ibid.; Sen, 116.

7. Barter MS memoirs.

8. ibid.

9. Krishna Lal, *The Sack of Delhi as witnessed by Ghalib*, q. Sen, 116; Wilberforce, 178.

10. Griffiths, 161.

11. Ouvry, *Cavalry Experiences*, 179a.

12. Griffiths, 97–8.

13. Kaye, iii, 633; Sen, 108.

14. Narrative of Syed Mubarak Shah, q. Edwardes, *Red Year*, 233.

15. KMP (IOL), 755 (10); Kaye, iii, 644.
16. Hodson, 306–9.
17. ibid., 310–14.
18. ibid., 297, 303.
19. ibid., 322, 329.
20. Griffiths, 205.
21. Ouvry, op. cit., 182a. Among the victims were twenty-one princes of the imperial family, all of whom were hanged together with the Rajah of Ballabhgarh and the Nawab of Jajjar both of whom, while maintaining friendly contacts with the British, had tendered their homage to the King. (KMP, 726; Sen, 111.)
22. Metcalfe was held in particular dread by Indians. According to a letter published in *The Times* in January 1858 he was 'every day trying and hanging all he can catch'. 'One day a native jeweller came to offer his wares to Mrs Garstin who, thinking he charged too much, said "I will send you to Metcalfe Sahib"; on which the man bolted in such a hurry that he left his treasures behind and never again showed his face.' (Coopland, *A Lady's Escape*, 212.)
23. q. Edwardes, *Necessary Hell*, 173–4.
24. ibid., 174. Long after the wholesale executions had been discontinued the citizens of Delhi continued to be insulted and occasionally robbed by British troops and officers. At the end of November a native Christian employed by the Prize Agents had cause to complain to the Military Governor of being hit on the head with a stick by an officer who required him to salaam. 'I made many salaams instead of one,' the complainant continued, 'and cried I was a Christian, Sir . . . and after this he proceeded towards the Dewan Khas abusing me and saying

that I was black as jet. Being much hurt, almost stunned and grieved I stopped a little . . . seeing which the gentleman who struck me returned towards me galloping and alighting from his horse inflicted many severe blows on my left arm and back with his stick . . . As I was passing on the road . . . I saw some English officers throwing clay balls . . . at the native passengers . . . Yesterday evening a Hindoo acquaintance was bringing [me] two new *lahafs* . . . An English officer on horseback with two syces met him in the way, forcibly took one of these *lahafs* . . . and went away galloping.' FDSC (NAI), 524.)
25. Rice Holmes, 398; Edwardes, *Necessary Hell*, 60.
26. Cadell MS letters.
27. Chichester MS letters.
28. Coghill MS letters.
29. Wise, 115.
30. Griffiths, 202; Raikes, 81.
31. Gordon MS diaries.
32. Muter, 112, 117.
33. Barter MS memoirs.
34. Wise, 115; Chichester MS letters; Lithgow MS letters.
35. Griffiths, 196–8, 208, 232–3.
36. Muir, i, 239.
37. Griffiths, 234–5.
38. Muter, 137.
39. Griffiths, 240–42.
40. Wagentreiber, 45.
41. ibid., 41–2.
42. *JSAHR*, Vol. L, No. 204, 215. C. B. Saunders, who became the representative of the Lieutenant-Governor of the North-Western Provinces at Delhi after the death from cholera of Harvey Greathed, protested to Cecil Beadon, Secretary in the Home Department at Calcutta, about the activities of the Prize Agents: 'With regard to the difficulty of distinguishing the evil from the well affected citizens, I confess that the difficulty has been a great one and no very great trouble

has been taken to discriminate between the two by either the Prize Agents or the military authorities. General Wilson ordered that no protection tickets should be held to be valid unless countersigned by him and the consequence was that few obtained anything like protection for their property. No guards could be furnished and before two or three days had expired there was not a house which had not been ransacked and plundered of its contents, friends and foe suffering to an equal extent. The chief wealth of the citizens, however, has been carefully buried and secreted in closets which have been ingeniously bricked and plastered over. The Sikhs and others with the force very soon learned the artifice and a very considerable amount of plunder has been carried off which will not enrich the prize fund. The Prize Agents have since been busily engaged in ransacking the houses of those . . . who have enjoyed a reputation for wealth . . . It has been considered by the Prize Agents that . . . all must be considered enemies who cannot satisfactorily prove that they . . . are our friends.' (FDSC (NAI), 524, 18 November 1857.)

43. Barter MS memoirs. Wilson had wanted to evacuate Delhi, leaving a few troops to hold the city walls and blowing up 'the several bastions and portions of the palace'. But he had been advised by the Chief Commissioner at Lahore: 'The palace at Delhi would make a splendid and safe magazine . . . You must leave some troops at Delhi. Those you do leave could hardly, in my mind, be better placed than in the palace . . . The occupation of the palace would do as much good politically as its destruction. I would not destroy anything pending the orders of government. We can always destroy. We cannot so easily construct. It will take years to build such a magazine.' (FDSC (NAI), 439.) After the palace had been designated for use as a barracks, instructions were given to preserve 'buildings of architectural or historic interest'. Parts of these buildings were, nevertheless, demolished for the convenience of the troops. In 1860 permission was given for the demolition of all buildings within 448 yards of the fort walls. The Jama Masjid was also occupied by troops; and it was not for five years that it was handed back to a Muslim committee. Part of the next largest mosque, the Fatehpuri Masjid, was sold by auction and was not restored to the Muslims for almost twenty years. (Spear, *Twilight*, 220–22.)

44. Hewitt, 71.

45. Griffiths, 200. 'The wretched inhabitants have been driven out to starve [a surgeon reported] . . . And I cannot help thinking they have been rather cruelly treated.' (Muir, i, 239.)

46. Coghill MS letters.

47. Barter MS memoirs.

48. Coghill MS letters.

49. ibid.

50. Rice Holmes, 392.

51. Malleson, *A History of the Indian Mutiny*, ii, 93, 97. 'From having been so long shut out from all communication with other places,' Frederick Roberts wrote to his mother of the people in the fort at Agra, 'many have become most terribly selfish and fancy Agra is the one place in India.' (Roberts, *Letters*, 82.)

52. Barter MS memoirs.

53. Thornhill, 280.

54. ibid., 285.

55. ibid.

56. Malleson, op. cit., ii, 98–100.

57. Roberts, *41 Years*, 150.

58. Barter MS memoirs.
59. Sharpley Papers.
60. Thornhill, 302.
61. Roberts, *41 Years*, 150–51.
62. Barter MS memoirs.
63. ibid.
64. Thornhill, 287.
65. Lithgow MS letters.
66. Ouvry, op. cit., 144–5;
Thornhill, 302, 306.

18. Scorched Earth (*pages 327–46*)

1. Rees, 252–3.
2. Inglis, *The Siege of Lucknow*, 166.
3. Dawson, 72–3.
4. Gubbins, 399; Rees, 253.
5. Hadow Papers.
6. Owen, *Recollections of a Veteran*, 57.
7. Gubbins, 229–30.
8. Hadow Papers.
9. Inglis, op. cit., 195; Edwardes, *Season in Hell*, 241.
10. Rees, 256.
11. ibid., 254–5.
12. Case, 268.
13. Rees, 256.
14. Owen, 64.
15. Edwardes, *Season in Hell*, 235.
16. Owen, 54.
17. Pollock, 239–41; Marshman, 327; Havelock Papers; Edwardes, *Season in Hell*, 247.
18. Rice Holmes, 402; Malleson, *A History of the Indian Mutiny*, ii, 151–60; Edwardes, *Season in Hell*, 225.
19. Gubbins, 224.
20. Inglis, op. cit., 172.
21. Brydon MS journal.
22. Spurgin Papers.
23. Dawson, 77.
24. Anderson, 106.
25. Gubbins, 399.
26. Innes, *Lucknow and Oude in the Mutiny*, 175.
27. Edwardes, *Season in Hell*, 248.
28. Kavanagh, *How I Won the Victoria Cross*, 68–72.
29. ibid., 75–87.
30. q. Maclagan, 123.
31. Warner Papers; Monk Bretton MSS.
32. Barter MS memoirs.
33. Biddulph MS letters.
34. Nicholl MS diaries.
35. Biddulph MS letters.
36. ibid.
37. Russell, *My Diary in India*, i, 235.
38. Collins Papers.
39. Quevillart MS diaries; Nicholl MS diaries.
40. Nicholl MS diaries.
41. q. Lehmann, 56.
42. Hardy Papers.
43. Barter MS memoirs.
44. Forbes-Mitchell, 33–4; Owen, 68.
45. Barter MS memoirs.
46. Lehmann, 59.
47. Nicholl MS letters.
48. Forbes-Mitchell 44–5.
49. Forbes-Mitchell, *Reminiscences*, 46.
50. ibid., 47–8.
51. ibid., 54–8; Barter MS memoirs.
52. Roberts, *Letters*, 103.
53. Cubitt Papers.
54. Fairweather Papers.
55. Forbes-Mitchell, 65–6.
56. Lehmann, 61.
57. Forbes-Mitchell, 58.
58. ibid., 72.
59. ibid., 63.
60. ibid., 76–8.
61. Wolseley Papers; Lehmann, 63.
62. Wolseley Papers; Lehmann, 63–4.
63. Wolseley Papers.
64. Pollock, 246–7.
65. Hope Grant, *Incidents in the Sepoy War*, 179.
66. Pollock, 247.

428

67. Wolseley Papers; Lehmann, 67–8.
68. Malleson, op. cit., ii, 214; Inglis Papers; Rice Holmes, 415.

19. The Fall of Lucknow (*pages 347–66*)

1. Case, 284.
2. Germon, 120–21.
3. Inglis, *The Siege of Lucknow*, 290.
4. Boileau Papers.
5. Brydon MS journal.
6. Wolseley Papers.
7. Collins Papers; Case, 285.
8. Lehmann, 69.
9. Campbell, *Narrative*, 113; Wolseley Papers. 'They were a singular party,' wrote Matilda Spry of the Lucknow refugees when she saw them at the end of their journey, 'and the troubles and sorrow and horrors they had gone through appeared, in most cases, to have made them unnaturally cold-hearted. With *few* exceptions, you saw no real sorrowing for husbands and children. They seem latterly to have had no fear, indeed young delicate looking widows have told me so themselves. They were all a most cheerful party, and, with few exceptions, you could hardly find out the widows and childless. We must not blame them, poor creatures, for their apparent heartlessness, for perhaps such continued exposure to such fearful scenes caused their feelings to be blunted.' (Spry MS letters.) According to Lady Canning, Mrs Gubbins was 'the only person who [looked] much shaken and nervous'. (Canning Papers.)
10. Germon, 125.
11. Boileau Papers.
12. Hope Grant, 193.
13. Hadow Papers.
14. Inglis, op. cit., 206.

15. ibid.
16. ibid.
17. Pollock, 250–52; Marshman, 444–6.
18. Brydon MS journal; Boileau Papers; Germon, 122–30.
19. Rice Holmes, 423; Malleson, *A History of the Indian Mutiny*, ii, 224; Shadwell, *Life of Colin Campbell*, ii, 79.
20. Malleson, op. cit., ii, 238–45; Wise, 183; Barter MS memoirs.
21. Malleson, op. cit., ii, 259–61.
22. Inglis, op. cit., 214; Case, 308.
23. Verney, *The Devil's Wind*, 98–9.
24. Mansfield, *Confidential Notes*. ii, 275; Rice Holmes, 427–8.
25. Biddulph Papers.
26. Ewen MS letters.
27. Biddulph Papers.
28. Wade Papers.
29. Nicholl MS letters.
30. Nicholl MS diaries.
31. ibid.
32. Malleson, op. cit., ii, 309; Canning Papers.
33. When he arrived with his Gurkhas, Jang Bahadur told Campbell 'had he not visited England he would now have been fighting against us instead of with us'. (Traill-Burroughs MS journal.)
34. Majendie, 138–40.
35. ibid., 146.
36. Cotton, *Indian and Home Memories*, 143.
37. Majendie, 196.
38. ibid.
39. Hadow Papers.
40. Munro, *Reminiscences of Military Service*, 123.
41. Cubitt Papers.
42. Forbes-Mitchell, 210.
43. ibid., 207–8.
44. Rice Holmes, 611.
45. Biddulph MS letters; FDSC (NAI), 465–9.
46. Madeline Jackson's MS narrative.

47. *JSAHR*, Vol. XXXVI, No. 145, 21.

48. Malleson, op. cit., ii, 397–404. 'In the camp,' Malleson comments, 'the order [given by Campbell to Outram] was attributed to the counsels of Mansfield; but the responsibility rested, and still rests, with Sir Colin.'

49. Majendie, 223–4.

50. Owen, 60. Olpherts was the 'most daring individual' Private Wickins 'ever saw'. (*JSAHR*, Vol. XXXVI, No. 145, 19.)

51. Majendie, 211.

52. Wolseley Papers.

53. Russell, *My Diary in India*, ii, 133.

54. Majendie, 231–2.

55. Forbes-Mitchell, 226–7.

56. Verney, op. cit., 138. Looting was still going on in Lucknow in the middle of April 1858. On 7 April orders were issued designed to put a stop to 'indiscriminate ransacking' by the furnishing of tickets of protection to all citizens who were not known criminals. But on 15 April Captain Forster, one of the Prize Agents, and a party of British soldiers surrounded the house of Wajid Ali, who had helped Madeline Jackson and Mrs Orr to escape, on the pretext that he was allowing his house to be used to shelter the property of other citizens not so well regarded by the government as himself.

'As his Excellency the Commander-in-Chief has not yet thought fit to put a stop to the search for prize,' the Secretary to the Chief Commissioner of Oudh wrote to Calcutta, 'the Chief Commissioner feels it beyond his competency to prohibit the proceedings of the Prize Agents. The Deputy Commissioner has therefore been instructed to try and settle the matter for the present by persuading Meer Wazid Ali to deposit with him any valuable property . . . pending special orders . . . It is now a month since the British Army obtained a footing in the city of Lucknow and 25 days since it was completely in possession. For the first few days and even weeks whilst a place which has been taken by storm is essentially held by military force, all property found may be looked upon as found in course of capture. But now that the invading army has been broken up, a garrison settled in the town, and the civil power introduced, the essentially military occupation may be considered at an end and when once a proclamation [is] issued to the people [on 15 March] inviting all peaceable and loyal citizens to return to their homes and occupations, there is surely a guarantee implied that all who comply with the invitation shall be free from molestation. It were in vain to talk of restoring confidence and re-populating a town if the citizens are only enticed back to be plundered.' (FDSC (NAI), 109–11.)

57. Collins Papers.

58. Warner Papers.

59. Stairforth MS letters.

60. Forbes-Mitchell, 228–9.

20. The Last of the Rebels (*pages 367–88*)

1. Lehmann, 74.

2. Campbell, *Memoirs*, ii, 14; Canning Papers.

3. Bosworth Smith, *Life of Lord Lawrence*, 432–3.

4. Chaudhuri, *Theories*, 104; Malleson, *A History of the Indian Mutiny*, iii, 247–50; Sen, 243–4; Rice Holmes, 446–9. 'In the celebrated controversy over the

Oudh proclamation,' Professor Eric Stokes has commented, 'Canning was quick to refute Outram's assertion that the rebellion of the taluqdars sprang from the injustice of the land revenue settlement of 1856. He was able to point to a number of taluqdars who in a material sense had demonstrably benefited from British rule but who were proving most inveterate in resistance ... Canning was acute enough to see that the source of their hostility lay in the loss of their powers of military lordship and jurisdiction.' (Stokes, 'The Context of the 1857 Mutiny Rebellion in India', *Past and Present*, 48, 111–12.)

5. Malleson, op. cit., ii, 502–3.
6. Hadow Papers.
7. ibid.
8. Potiphar Papers.
9. Hadow Papers; Wise, 174; Nicholl MS diaries.
10. Ball, ii, 337.
11. ibid.; Rice Holmes, 72; Edwardes, *Red Year*, 102; Malleson, op. cit., ii, 261, 541–2.
12. Edwardes, *Red Year*, 103–4; Sen, 209–10.
13. Malleson, op. cit., ii, 534.
14. ibid., ii, 543–4; Sen, 355.
15. Nowell MSS.
16. Russell, ii, 295–6.
17. Wolseley Papers. The General to whom Wolseley refers was James Hope Grant, one of the most popular and admired of all the senior officers in India. He was 'a dear old man, so good and kind' in Wolseley's opinion and a 'dear old fellow' in Frederick Roberts's. He had a 'quick, quaint way' of talking, was 'deeply religious and talented as a musician'. On this campaign, as on nearly all others, he was accompanied by 'an enormous violoncello, carried on a camel. Natives ran away from it

whenever it appeared, calling it "shaitan" (the devil)'. (Wolseley Papers; Roberts, *41 Years*, 165; Burne, *Memories*, 29.)

Few other senior officers were as widely respected. Indeed, several were condemned for utter incompetence. Lieutenant Clowes, for example, had the lowest possible opinion of Colonel Holmes who received much official praise for surprising a body of rebels encamped at Sikar and 'by merely firing a few rounds', throwing them 'into the utmost confusion'. Clowes's view was that Holmes was really an utter 'humbug'. It was 'very evident' from what Clowes saw that he was 'in a thundering funk on finding he had come upon the rebels so suddenly'. He was, Clowes concluded 'a shocking old man, very like Aunt Sophy'. (Clowes Papers.) Dr Wrench entertained an equally low opinion of General Whitlock whose 'military arrangements' were 'miserable'. (Wrench MSS.)

18. Potiphar Papers.
19. Sen, 359, 367–8; Malleson, op. cit., ii, 498; Rice Holmes, 533.
20. q. Sen, 367–8.
21. Malleson, op. cit., ii, 479–82, 490–92.
22. q. Russell, *My Diary in India*, ii, 86.
23. Durand Papers.
24. ibid.; FDSC (NAI), 31–2.
25. Sylvester MS diary.
26. ibid.
27. MDP (NAI), 408–9; FDSC (NAI), 545–6.
28. Shakespeare Papers.
29. Lang, 93–4.
30. Sylvester, 109.
31. Sen, 270; Kaye, i, 91; Durand Papers.
32. FDSC (NAI), 343–5.
33. FDSC (NAI), 354. The Political Agent's *vakil* who evidently believed – or affected to

believe – the Rani's version of events was afterwards questioned about the Jhansi massacre:

Q. Where was the Ranee of Jhansi living when the massacre occurred?

A. She was in her own *Bara.*

Q. What native Government officials were at Jhansi at the time?

A. All the native Government officials were there.

Q. Did they make no exertions to save the lives of the officers in the fort?

A. It was as much as they could do to save their own.

Q. Did none of them go to the Ranee and beg her to use her influence in saving them?

A. They could do nothing. If they came out of their houses they were immediately made prisoner and carried away by the mutineers . . .

Q. Did you hear how much money the mutineers took away from the Ranee?

A. I did not hear how much but I heard that she paid them a large sum of money before they would leave the city.

(FDSC (NAI), 343–5.)

34. FDSC (NAI), 602–4. Major Erskine subsequently decided that he had been wrong to believe the Rani's protestations that she had been forced to comply with the mutineers' demands for money. 'It is the general impression,' he reported on 21 August, 'that the mutineers, after killing some of their own officers and plundering the town, were going off, and it was only at the instigation of the Jhansi Ranee, with the object of obtaining possession of the Jhansi state, that they attacked the fort the next day together with other armed men furnished by her . . . The mutineers are said to have received Rs. 35,000 in cash, 2 elephants and 5 horses from the Ranee.' (FDSC (NAI), 602–4.)

In a book published in 1894 a letter – which cannot now be traced – was quoted as having been sent to the Rani's adopted son in 1889 by an Englishman called Martin. 'Your poor mother was very unjustly and cruelly dealt with,' this letter is alleged to have run, 'and no one knows her true case as I do. The poor thing took no part whatever in the massacre of the European residents of Jhansi in June 1857. On the contrary she supplied them with food for 2 days after they had gone into the Fort.' (Parasnis, *Maharani Lakshmi Bai Saheb Hyanche Charita*, q. Sen, 279–80.)

35. Lowe, *Central India during the Rebellion of 1857*, 154.

36. Sylvester MS diary.

37. Lightfoot MSS.

38. ibid.

39. Lowe, 200.

40. Sylvester MS diary.

41. Combe MSS; Lowe, 204; Sylvester, 107–8.

42. Sylvester MS diary.

43. Godse, *Majha Pravas*, q. Edwardes, *Red Year*, 122.

44. ibid., q. Edwardes, op. cit., 119.

45. Combe, 40, q. Anglesey, *History of British Cavalry*, 190.

46. Combe, 8 May 1858. Sir Hugh Rose got used to the heat in the end, Dr Wrench said. 'His remedy was to be followed by a *bheestee* who poured water over him.' (Wrench MS diary.)

47. Malleson, op. cit., iii, 185.

48. Poore MSS.

49. Monk Bretton MSS.

50. Malleson, op. cit., iii, 205–9.

51. Malleson, op. cit., iii, 221; Sen, 294–5; Rice Holmes, 538; FDPC (NAI), 4293.

52. Canning Papers. Lord Canning's Notebook.

432

53. FDPC (NAI), 156–68.

54. Ball, ii, 602; FDSC (NAI), 157–68.

55. Sen, 378–9.

56. ibid., 380.

57. ibid., 370.

58. Gupta, 158, 176. 'Some months ago I offered £10,000 for the Nana's person,' runs an undated entry in Lord Canning's notebook. 'He has now offered £20,000 for my head.' (Canning Papers.)

59. Gupta, 202. The Commissioner of Police at Poona was informed that Nana Sahib had 'for some time collected round him as many as six or twelve people having a great personal resemblance to himself so that in the event of a reverse his escape [might] be more easy.' (FDSC (NAI), 542.)

60. *Parliamentary Papers* (1859), i, 18.

61. Ball, ii, 169.

62. Russell, op. cit., ii, 60.

63. Muter, 148–9.

64. *PTBS*; Malleson, op. cit., iii, 387; Sen, 113.

65. Russell, op. cit., ii, 60.

Epilogue (*pages 389–93*)

1. q. Maclagan, 232.

2. *Memorial of the Life and Letters of Sir Herbert Edwardes*, ii, 90, q. Edwardes, *Red Year*, 149.

3. Ewen MSS; Poore Papers; Wolseley Papers.

4. Mason, 318–20, 326; Edwardes, *Red Year*, 150.

5. Ewen MSS.

6. Sen, 356–7. The Begum Hazrat Mahal immediately issued a counter-proclamation in the name of her son urging the people of Oudh not to trust in the offer of pardon for it was 'the unvarying custom of the English never to forgive a fault'. 'Why does Her Majesty not restore our country to us when our people wish it?' the counter-proclamation continued. 'The English . . . have promised no better employment for Hindoostanies than making roads and digging canals. If people cannot see clearly what this means there is no help for them . . . The rebellion began with religion, and for it millions of men have been killed. Let not our subjects be deceived.' (FDPC (NAI), 3022, q. Sen, 357–8.) Syed Muhammad Hasan Khan, who had been Nazim of Gorakhpur in Oudh before the annexation, shared the Begum's distrust of the proclamation. 'Her Majesty's Proclamation is somewhat obscure and indefinite,' he replied in answer to a demand that he should surrender. 'The Government having committed every description of oppression, it [would be] foolish of me to have any hope . . . I do not consider my submission would be lawful but criminal . . . We servants and dependants of the King of Oudh consider it essential to our prosperity in both worlds to display devotion in protecting the Kingdom and opposing the efforts of invaders who seek to gain a footing in it. If we fail in doing so we are traitors and will have our faces blackened in both worlds.' (FDPC (NAI), 7–9, q. Sen, 365–6.) Despite these defiant words, Syed Muhammad Hasan Khan was subsequently persuaded to surrender to the British authorities. But other leaders who shared his views, including Beni Madho of Shankarpur, Devi Baksh of Gonda and Golab Singh of Biswah, refused to do so and died in the jungles of Nepal.

7. Edwardes, *Red Year*, 150–51.

8. *Parliamentary Papers* (47), 1861, 579, q. Edwardes, *Red Year*, 151.

9. Russell, *My Diary in India*, ii, 282.

10. Lee, *King Edward VII*, i, 399.
11. Grey Papers.
12. Sen, 418.
13. Savarkar, *The Indian War of Independence, 1857*, 542.
14. Chaudhuri, *Civil Rebellion*, and *Theories*, 82.
15. Majumdar, *Sepoy Mutiny*, 297; Stokes, 'The Context of the 1857 Mutiny Rebellion in India'.
16. Sen, 410, 411.
17. *BPIR*, 498–9, 613.
18. Spear, *India*, 269.
19. ibid., 270.

Bibliography

MANUSCRIPTS

*(For privately owned MSS see
Author's Note and Acknowledgements,
pages 11–15)*

National Archives of India, Delhi
  Military Department Papers
  Mutiny Papers
  Foreign Department Political
    Consultations
  Foreign Department Political
    Proceedings
  Foreign Department Secret
    Consultations
Regional Archives, Allahabad
  Cawnpore Collectorate Records
  Meerut and Bareilly
    Commissioner's Office Mutiny
    Records
*Uttar Pradesh State Archives,
Lucknow*
  Daily bulletins issued by E. A.
    Reade
  Proceedings of the Foreign,
    Political, General, Judicial and
    Military Departments of the
    North-Western Provinces
  Telegrams sent to E. A. Reade
  These archives also contain the
    printed 'Narrative of Events'
    for the Districts and Divisions
    of the North-Western Provinces
India Office Library
  Ahsanullah (transl. H. S. Reid).
    Account of the Mutiny (KMP).
  Baird Smith, Colonel Richard.
    Letters.
  Bartrum, Mrs Katherine. Diary,
    Letters.

Beams, John. Memoirs.
Beresford, General Marcus. Diary.
Biddulph, Major Robert. Letters.
Blake, General Henry William.
  Letters.
Campbell, Sir Colin. Papers.
Carrington, Samuel. Letters.
Carter, Sergeant-Major George.
  Diary.
Chief of Staff. Memoranda.
Clifford, R. H. Diary.
Clowes, Major G. R. Letters.
Coldstream Collection.
Collins, Brigadier-Surgeon
  Francis. Letters.
Cust, R. N. Letters.
Dearlove, Corporal Charles.
  Letters.
Delafosse, Lieutenant. Narrative
  (KMP).
Edwardes, Sir Herbert. Papers.
Edwards, Robert. Diary.
Edwards, R. M. Papers.
Ewart, Mrs J. A. Letters.
Fraser, Lieutenant-Colonel
  Charles. Letters.
Goldney, Lieutenant-Colonel
  Philip. Letters.
Gonne, Henry. Diary.
Grant Collection.
Havelock, Sir Henry. Papers.
Hutchinson Collection.
Hutchinson, Lieutenant George.
  Letters.
Kaye, Sir John. Mutiny Papers
  (KMP).
Kirk, Dr K. W. Letters.
Lawrence (Henry) Collection.
Lawrence (John) Collection.

Lawrence, Lieutenant-General Sir
George. Letters.
Littledale, Arthur. Letters.
Lyall Collection.
Mansfield, General W. R.
Confidential Notes (K M P).
Marsden, Colonel. Diary.
Mawe, Thomas. Letters.
Moorsom, Lieutenant-Colonel
H. M. Letters.
Moorsom, Captain W. R. Letters.
Munshi Mohan Lal. Account
(K M P).
Neill, Brigadier-General James.
Diary (K M P).
Nicholson, Brigadier-General John.
Letters.
Oliver, Major-General J. R.
Memoirs.
Outram, Sir James. Papers.
Palmer, T. S. M. Memoirs.
Pearson, Colonel Hugh Pearce.
Letters.
Poore, Major Robert. Letters.
Porter, Corporal Joseph. Memoirs.
Saunders, Charles Burslem.
Correspondence.
Shakespeare, Major W. Diary.
Sneyd, Mrs Elizabeth. Memoirs.
Spurgin, Sir John Blick. Diary.
Strachey Collection.
Sturt, John Venables. Memoirs.
Syed Mubarak Shah (transl. R. M.
Edwards). 'The City of Delhi
during the Siege'.
Sylvester, Dr John Henry. Diary.
Timbrell, Mrs Agnes. Memoirs.
Vansittart, Mrs Henry. Diary.
Vibart Collection.
Vibart, E. C. Letters.
Warner, Lieutenant A. C. Letters.
Warner, Ensign W. H. Letters.
Wilkie, William. Memoirs.
Wood, J. A. Diary.
National Army Museum
Bingham, General G. W. Diary.
Blake, Colonel Pilkington. Diary.
Borthwick, Colonel John.
Letters.
Bradshaw, Dr A. P. Letters.

Cadell, Lieutenant Thomas.
Letters.
Carmichael, Lieutenant-Colonel
G. L. Diary.
Clowes, Colonel P. L. Letters.
Delhi Force Intelligence Reports.
Dixon, Dr Edward Livesey.
Diary.
Ewart, C. H. Letters.
Ewen, A. A. Letters.
Fairweather, Surgeon-General
James. 'Through the Mutiny
with the 4th Punjab Infantry'.
Greathed, William. Wilberforce
Harris, Major-General. Letters.
Hargood, Lieutenant William.
Letters.
Hargood, Lieutenant William.
Reminiscences.
Holditch, Edward Alan. Diary.
Huxham, Mrs G. Reminiscences.
Jackson, Miss Madeline.
Reminiscences.
Lawrence, Sir Henry. Letters.
Lawrence, Sir John. Letters.
Lewes, Ensign W. L. P. Diary.
Ludlow Smith, Lieutenant-
General O. Diary.
Maxwell, Thomas. Diary.
Mills, Arthur. Letters.
Mills, Dr John. Diary.
Nash, Major Edward. Letters.
Powlett, Lieutenant P. W.
Diary.
Rean, Surgeon W. H. Letters.
Simpson, John. Diary.
Stansfeld, Lieutenant H. H.
Letters.
Taylor, Sir Alexander. Letters.
Wilson, Captain T. F. Diary.
Wood, Private Thomas. Letters.
*Centre for South Asian Studies,
Cambridge*
Baynes. Family Papers.
Berners. Family Papers.
Boileau. Family Papers.
Christison. Family Papers.
Erskine. Family Papers.
Gore Lindsay. Family Papers.
Hare. Family Papers.

Kenyon. Family Papers.
Laughton. Family Papers.
Lenox-Conyngham. Family
Papers.
Monckton. Family Papers.
'Narrative of occurrences at
Delhi, written by a native
residing within the walls of the
city of Delhi commencing from
11 May 1857.'
Peppé. Family Papers.
Pollard. Family Papers.
Showers. Family Papers.
Stansfield. Family Papers.
Waller. Family Papers.
British Museum
Hands, Lieutenant J. S. Diary
(Add. MSS 37151–3).
Hearsey, General Sir John.
Letters (Add. MSS 41488,
41489).
Holmes, Major James Garner.
Letters (Add. MSS 41488,
41489).
Horne, Miss Amelia. Narrative
(Add. MSS 41488).
Lang, Lieutenant Arthur. Diary
(Add. MSS 37151–3).
Layard. Papers (Add. MSS
38985–6, 38989, 40027).
Moore, Rev Thomas. Diary (Add.
MSS 37151–3).
Mutiny Papers, miscellaneous
(Add. MSS 41996).
Napier. Papers (Add. MSS
38985–6, 38989, 40027).
County Record Offices
Berkshire
Dundas. Papers.
Ewen. Papers.
Cambridgeshire
Brown, William Tod. Diary.
Gloucestershire
Hyett. Papers.
Wemyss, Lieutenant. Journals.
Wemyss, Mrs Francis. Journals.
Hampshire
Burton, Lieutenant W. H. Letters.
Hertfordshire
Leake, Martin. Papers.

Kent
Ashburnham, Cromer. Letters.
Best, Mawdistley Gaussen.
Papers.
Garrett, Sir Robert. Letters.
Woodgate, Francis Henry.
Letters.
Lincolnshire
The Fane Collections.
Norfolk
Cubitt, Major Frank Astley.
Journals.
Norman, Sir Henry Wylie.
Letters.
Quevillart, Private Charles
William. Journals.
Northamptonshire
Longden, Major-General Charles.
Diary and Papers.
Northumberland
The Ridley MSS.
Suffolk
Fraser, Sir Charles. Letters.
Smith, Colonel Thomas.
Letters.
Wade, Captain J. H. Letters.
Sussex (West)
Lennox, Sir Wilbraham Oates.
Papers.
Warwickshire
Dormer, J. C. Letters.
Newdigate, Henry. Letters.
Yorkshire (North)
The Havelock Papers.
Bodleian Library
Durand, Sir Henry Marion.
Papers.
Monk Bretton. Papers.
Cambridge University Library
Berkeley, Lionel. Papers.
Ludlow, J. M. Papers.
Stoneyhurst College
'Captain Mowbray Thomson's
Narrative.'
Ryan, James. Papers.
Worcester College, Oxford
Hadow, Dr Gilbert. Letters.
*Royal Commission on Historical
Manuscripts*
The Broadlands Papers.

Sheffield City Library
  Blake, Major W. G. Letters
    (Stephenson of Hassop
    Collection).
Leeds City Library
  Canning, Lord. Papers.
Nottingham University Library
  Wrench, Dr E. M. Diaries and
    Letters.
*Durham University, Department of
Palaeography and Diplomatic*
  Grey, Earl. Papers.
National Library of Scotland
  Brown, General Sir George.
    Letters.
  Campbell, Sir Colin. Letters.
  Gleig, George Robert. Letters.
  Halkett, Colonel James. Diary.
  Lithgow, Major-General Stewart.
    Letters.
  Pasley, Sir Charles. Diary.
  Richardson, John. Letters.
  Traill-Burroughs, Sir Frederick.
    Diary.
*Merseyside County Museum,
Liverpool*
  Greathed, Major-General E. H.
    Papers.
Wolseley Library, Hove
  Wolseley Papers.

PRIVATELY PRINTED WORKS

Bayley, John. *Reminiscences of School
  and Army Life* (London, 1875).
'C.C.' [Charles Combe]. *Letters from
  Persia and India 1856–1859* (n.d.).
Cooper, John Spencer. *Rough Notes
  of Seven Campaigns* (Carlisle, 1914).
Danvers, Robert William. *Letters
  from India and China During the
  Years 1854–58* (London, 1898).
De Salis, Rachel Elizabeth Francis
  Fane. *De Salis Family: English
  Branch* (1934).
D'Oyly, Major-General Sir Charles.
  *Eight Months' Experience During
  the Sepoy Revolt in 1857* (Bland-
  ford, 1891).

Halls, John James. *Arrah in 1857*
  (Dover, 1893).
Hearsey, Captain J. B. *Narrative of
  the Outbreak at Seetapore* (Seeta-
  pore, 1858).
Inglis, Hon. Julia. *Letters Containing
  Extracts from a Journal Kept during
  the Siege of Lucknow* (London,
  1858).
*Journal of Lieutenant-General Sir
  Bryan Milman* (Dover, 1899).
*Letters of the late Major-General R.
  H. Hall ... while serving under
  General Sir Hugh Rose* (Hitchin,
  1881).
*Memoirs of Jeremiah Brayser: Per-
  sonal Reminiscences of an Indian
  Mutiny Veteran* (Brighton, 1911).
Muir, W. *Mutiny in Agra* (Edinburgh,
  1890).
*Mutinies in India: Extracts of Letters
  from an Assistant Surgeon in the ...
  Hyderabad Contingent* (1857).
My Journal ... by a Volunteer [Now
  Major-General Swanston] (Ux-
  bridge, 1896).
Our Escape in June, 1857 (Dundalk,
  1862).
Ouvry, Colonel H. A. *Cavalry
  Experiences and Leaves from my
  Journal* (Lymington, 1892).
Ouvry, Mrs Matilda. *A Lady's Diary
  before and during the Indian Mutiny*
  (Lymington, 1892).
Rawlins, Major-General J. S. *The
  Autobiography of an Old Soldier*
  (Weston-super-Mare, 1883).
Reid, General Sir Charles. *Extracts
  from Letters and Notes Written
  during the Siege of Delhi in 1857*
  (London, 1957).
Ricketts, G. H. M. *Extracts from
  the Diary of a Bengal Civilian*
  (1893).
Sayyid Ahmed Khan. *Rissalah Asbab-
  e-Bhgawat-i-Hind* (transl. Graham
  and Colvin, Benares, 1873).
Spencer, Margaret. *Personal Remin-
  iscences of the Indian Mutiny*
  (Clifton, 1905).

438

Steuart, Mary E. (ed.). *Reminiscences of Lieutenant-Colonel Thomas Ruddiman Steuart* (1900).

Thackeray, Colonel E. T. *Two Indian Campaigns in 1857–58* (Chatham, 1896).

Thurburn, Lieutenant-Colonel F. A. V. *Reminiscences of the Indian Rebellion of 1857–1858 by a Staff Officer* (London, 1889).

Turnbull, Lieutenant-Colonel John. *Letters during the Siege of Delhi* (Torquay, 1881).

Ward, Beatrice (ed.). *Letters of Edwin Utterton from the . . . Indian Mutiny* (Gibraltar, n.d.).

Watson, E. S. *Journal . . . India with H. M. S. Shannon* (Kettering, 1858).

Yule, H. (ed.). *Life and Service of Major-General W. H. Greathed* (London, 1879).

JOURNALS

ABBREVIATIONS USED:

AQ	*Army Quarterly*
BM	*Blackwood's Magazine*
BPP	*Bengal Past and Present*
CR	*Calcutta Review*
IAQR	*Imperial and Asiatic Quarterly Review*
IHQ	*Indian Historical Quarterly*
IHRCP	*Indian Historical Records, Proceedings*
JBRS	*Journal of the Bihar Record Society*
JRUSI	*Journal of the Royal United Services Institute*
JSAHR	*Journal of the Society of Army Historical Research*
JUSII	*Journal of the United Services Institute of India*
PUHSJ	*Punjab University Historical Society Journal*
RAJ	*Royal Artillery Journal*
REJ	*Royal Engineers' Journal*
RHST	*Royal Historical Society Transactions*
SAR	*South Asia Review*

Addington, Hon. Mrs Hiley. 'The Crimean and Indian Mutiny Letters of the Hon. Charles John Addington, 38th Regiment' (*JSAHR*, Vol. XLVI, 1968).

Alison, Archibald. 'Lord Clyde's Campaign in India' (*BM*, October 1858).

— 'The Pursuit of Tantia Topee' (*BM*, August 1860).

Annand, Major A. McK. 'Captain Henry Thurburn (1826–1897) 42nd Madras Native Infantry' (*JSAHR*, Vol. XLV, 1967).

— 'Indian Mutiny Letters of Lieutenant William Harwood, 1st Madras Fusiliers' (*JSAHR*, Vol. LIII, 1975).

— '"Lucknow" Cavanagh and the 1st European Bengal Fusiliers, Lucknow, 1858' (*JSAHR*, Vol. XLIV, 1966).

Bagley, F. R. 'A Small Boy in the Indian Mutiny' (*BM*, October 1930).

Bennett, Mrs Amelia. 'Ten Months' Captivity after the Massacre at Cawnpore' (*Nineteenth Century*, June 1913).

Bhargava, K. D. 'A Note on Tantia Topi' (*IHRCP*, Vol. XXIV, 1948).

Bishop, Anthony. 'John Nicholson in

the Indian Mutiny' (*Irish Sword,* Winter, 1968).

Bradshaw, Lieutenant J. H. 'Letters on the Delhi Campaign' (*The Oxfordshire and Buckinghamshire Light Infantry Chronicle*, Vol. XVIII, 1909).

Buckler, F. W. 'The Political Theory of the Indian Mutiny' (*RHST*, Series 4, Vol. V, 1932).

Cadell, Colonel Sir Patrick. 'The Outbreak of the Indian Mutiny' (*JSAHR*, Vol. XXXIII, 1955).

Chattopadhyaya, H. P. 'The Sepoy Army, its Strength, Composition and Recruitment' (*CR*, May, July, August, September 1956).

— 'Mutiny in Bihar' (*BPP*, Vols. LXXIV–LXXV).

Cust, R. N. 'A District During the Rebellion' (*CR*, September 1858).

Das, Manmatha Nath. 'Western Innovations and the Rising of 1857' (*BPP*, Vol. 76, 1957).

Datta, K. K. 'Some Unpublished Papers relating to the Mutiny' (*IHQ*, March, 1936).

— 'Nature of the Indian Revolt of 1857–9' (*BPP*, Vol. 73, 1954).

— 'Some Newly Discovered Records relating to the Bihar phase of the Indian Movement' (*PUHSJ*, Vol. 8, 1954).

— 'Popular Discontent in Bihar' (*BPP*, Vol. 74, 1955).

— 'Some Original Documents Relating to the Indian Mutiny' (*IHRCP* Vol. 30, 1954).

— 'Contemporary Account of the Indian Movement of 1857' (*JBRS*, Vol. 36, 1950).

Daunt, W. D. 'The Operations of Sir Hugh Rose in Central India, January–June, 1858' (*JUSII*, Vol. 40, 1911).

Garrett, H. L. O. 'The Trial of Bahadur Shah II' (*PUHSJ*, April 1932).

Gray, Lieutenant W. J. 'Journal of

the Siege Train from Ferozepore to Delhi' (*JSAHR*, Vol. X, 1931). *See* Leslie.

Innes, Lieutenant-General McLeod. 'The Defence of the Lucknow Residency' (*JUSII*, No. 56, 1883).

Keene, H. G. 'The Literature of the Rebellion' (*CR*, March 1859).

Lang, Lieutenant Arthur Moffat. 'Diary and Letters' (*JSAHR*, Vols. IX–XI, 1930–32).

Laws, Colonel M. E. S. 'A Contemporary Account of the Battle of Banda, 1858' (*JSAHR*, Vol. XXXII, 1954).

Lee-Warner, W. 'Archdale Wilson, the Captor of Delhi' (*Fortnightly Review*, 555, March 1913).

Leslie, Lieutenant-Colonel J. H. (ed.). 'The March of the Siege Train from Ferozepore to Delhi ... The Journal of 1st Lieutenant W. J. Gray' (*JSAHR*, Vol. X, January 1931).

Lindsay, Lieutenant-Colonel Sir Martin. 'The Indian Mutiny Letters of Lieutenant Alexander Hadden Lindsay' (*JSAHR*, Vol. L, No. 204, 1972).

Mackenzie, Mrs Colin. 'English Women in the Rebellion' (*CR*, September 1859).

Maclean, James N. M. 'A Surgeon's Memoir of Cawnpore, 1957' (*SAR*, Vol. 6, No. 2).

Macmunn, Lieutenant-General Sir George. 'Some New Light on the Indian Mutiny' (*BM*, Vol. 224, 1928).

Macpherson, A. G. 'The Siege of Lucknow' (*CR*, September 1858).

Maunsell, General Sir F. R. 'A Few Notes on the Siege of Delhi' (*REJ.*, July 1911).

Medley, Colonel Julius George. 'The Siege of Delhi' (*JUSII*, No. 56, 1883).

'Military Family at the Wars, the Lindsays of Downhill' (*AQ*, Vol. c, No. 1, April 1970).

440

Nicholson, Esther Anne. 'An Irish-woman's Account of the Indian Mutiny' (*Irish Sword*, Vol. IX, No. 34).

Nilsson, Sten. 'Egron Lundgren: Reporter of the Indian Mutiny' (*Apollo*, August 1970).

Samaddar, J. N. 'Two Forgotten Mutiny Heroes' (*IHRCP*, Vol. X, 1927).

Seton, Captain Sir James. 'Outram's Division Watching Lucknow' (*JRUSI*, Vol. XXVII).

— 'The Indian Mutiny: The Last Phase' (*BM*, May 1912).

Shackleton, Robert. 'A Soldier of Delhi' (*Harper's*, October 1909).

Shelton, W. G. 'A Soldier's Life in Burma and India, 1854–1874' [Based on MS *Biography of Soldier's Life for Twenty-two Years in the Army*, by Sergeant-Major Alexander Morton] (*JSAHR*, Vol. LII, 1974).

'The Siege of Delhi. A Reminder from one who was Present' (*Nineteenth Century and After*, October 1911).

Stokes, Eric. 'Rural Revolt in the Great Rebellion of 1857' (*Historical Journal*, XI, 1969).

— 'The Context of the 1857 Mutiny Rebellion in India' (*Past and Present*, 46, August 1970).

Sumner, Percy (ed.). 'Indian Mutiny Recollections of Bugler Johnson' (*JSAHR*, Vol. XX, Autumn 1941).

Taimuri, M. H. R. 'Some Unpublished Documents on the Death of the Rani of Jhansi' (*IHRCP*, Vol. 29, 1953).

Thackeray, Colonel Sir Edward. 'Two Indian Campaigns, 1857–8' (Royal Engineers Institute, 1896).

— 'A Subaltern in the Indian Mutiny' (*REJ*, 1930).

—'Recollections of the Siege of Delhi' (*CM*, July–December 1913).

Thicknesse, H. J. A. 'The Indian Mutiny at Mhow and Indore' (*RAJ*, Vol. LXI, 1934).

Thornton, Lieutenant-Colonel L. H. 'Some Lucknow Memories' (*AQ*, Vol. 25, 1932).

Tweedie, Major General W. 'A Memory and A Study of the Indian Mutiny' (*BM*, December 1904).

— 'Two Unpublished Proclamations of Nana Sahib' (*IHRCP*, Vol. XXV, 1948).

Tyrrell, Lieutenant-General F. H. 'In Piam Memoriam: The Services of the Madras Native Troops in the Suppression of the Mutiny' (*IAQR*, July 1908).

Tytler, Harriet C. 'Through the Sepoy Mutiny and the Siege of Delhi' (*Chambers's Journal*, Vol. XXI, 1936).

Waine, Harry. 'Memoirs of a Fighting Man during the Indian Mutiny: Being Extracts from the Diary of the late Sergeant Thomas Anderson (*AQ*, July and October 1936).

Whitton, F. E. 'The Last of the Paladins: Sir Hugh Rose and the Indian Mutiny' (*BM*, June 1934).

Wickins, Peter (ed.). 'The Indian Mutiny Journal of Private Charles Wickins of the 90th Light Infantry' (*JSAHR*, Vols. XXXV, XXXVI, 1957–8).

PUBLICATIONS

Addison, Lieutenant-Colonel. *Traits and Stories of Anglo-Indian Life* (London, 1858).

Adye, Lieutenant-Colonel John. *The Defence of Cawnpore by the Troops under the Orders of Major General Charles A. Windham in November 1857* (London, 1858).

— *Recollections of a Military Life* (London, 1895).

Aitchison, Sir Charles. *Lord Lawrence* (Oxford, 1892).

Anderson, H. S. *Reminiscences during*

Forty-five Years' Service in India (Horsham, 1903).

Anderson, Captain R. P. *A Personal Journal of the Siege of Lucknow* (ed. T. C. Anderson, London, 1858).

Andrews, C. F. *Maulvi Zaka Ullah of Delhi* (London, 1928).

Anglesey, the Marquess of. *A History of the British Cavalry, 1816–1919.* Vol. 2 (London, 1975).

— (ed.) *Sergeant Pearman's Memoirs* (London, 1968).

Annals. See Chick.

Annand, A. McKenzie (ed.). *Cavalry Surgeon: the Recollections of J. H. Sylvester* (London, 1971).

Anson, Brevet Major O. H. S. G. *With H.M. 9th Lancers during the Indian Mutiny* ed. Harcourt S. Anson (London, 1896).

Atkinson, G. F. *The Campaign in India, 1857–8* (London, 1859).

— *Curry and Rice* (London, 1859).

At the Front: A Soldier's Experiences in the . . . Indian Mutiny (Paisley, 1916).

Baird, J. A. (ed.). *Private Letters of the Marquess of Dalhousie* (London, 1910).

Ball, Charles. *The History of the India Mutiny* 2 vols. (London, n.d.).

Barker, G. D. *Letters from Persia and India in 1857–9* (London, 1915).

Barr, Pat. *The Memsahibs* (London, 1976).

Bartrum, Mrs Katherine. *A Widow's Reminiscences of the Siege of Lucknow* (London, 1858).

Bayley, John. *The Assault of Delhi* (London, 1858).

Beames, John. *Memoirs of a Bengal Civilian* (London, 1861).

Becher, Mrs Augusta. *Personal Reminiscences in India and Europe* (London, 1930).

Bell, Major Evans. *The English in India: Letters from Nagpore 1857–8* (London, 1859).

Bence-Jones, Mark. *Palaces of the Raj* (London, 1973).

Benson, A. C. and Viscount Esher (eds.). *The Letters of Queen Victoria* (London, 1908).

Bhargava. *See* Rizvi.

Blanchard, Sidney. *Yesterday and Today in India* (London, 1867).

Bonham, Colonel John. *Oudh in 1857: Some memories of the Indian Mutiny* (London, 1928).

Bora, Mahendra. *1857 in Assam* (Assam, 1957).

Bosworth Smith. *See* Smith.

Bourchier, Colonel George. *Eight Months' Campaign against the Bengal Sepoy Army during the Mutiny of 1857* (London, 1858).

Brief Narrative of the Defence of the Arrah Garrison (London, 1858).

British Paramountcy and Indian Renaissance. Vol. IX of *The History and Culture of the Indian People*, Gen. Ed. R. C. Majumdar (Calcutta).

Bruce, Henry (ed.). *The Story of My Life by the Late Colonel Philip Meadows Taylor* (London, 1920).

Buckle. *See* Monypenny.

Burne, Sir Owen Tudor. *Clyde and Strathnairn* (London, 1895).

— *Memories* (London, 1907).

Campbell, Sir Colin. *A Narrative of the Indian Revolt* (London, 1858).

Campbell, Sir George. *Memoirs of My Indian Career* 2 vols. (London, 1893).

Campbell, Robert. *The Indian Mutiny: Its Causes and Remedies* (London, 1857).

Cardew, Major F. G. *Hodson's Horse, 1857–1922* (London, 1928).

Case, Mrs [Adelaide]. *Day by Day at Lucknow: A Journal of the Siege of Lucknow* (London, 1858).

Cave-Browne, The Rev. John. *The Punjab and Delhi in 1857: Being a Narrative of the Measures by which the Punjab was saved and Delhi Recovered during the Indian Mutiny* 2 vols. (Edinburgh, 1861).

442

— *Incidents of Indian Life* (Maidstone, 1895).

Cavenagh, Sir Orfeur. *Reminiscences of an Indian Official* (London, 1884).

Chalmers, Colonel John. *Letters from India during the Mutiny* (Edinburgh, 1904).

Chaudhuri, S. B. *Civil Rebellion in the Indian Mutinies, 1857–1859* (Calcutta, 1957).

— *Theories of the Indian Mutiny 1857–1859* (Calcutta, 1965).

Chick, N. A. *Annals of the Indian Rebellion*, ed. David Hutchinson (London, 1974).

Cholmeley, Johnstone Montague. *The Jullundur Mutineers: A Vindication* (London, 1858).

Chunder, Bholananth. *Travels of a Hindu* 2 vols. (London, 1869).

Churcher, E. J. *Some Reminiscences of Three Quarters of a Century in India by a Mutiny Veteran* (London, 1909).

Collier, Richard. *The Sound and Fury: An Account of the Indian Mutiny* (London, 1963).

Colvin, Sir Auckland. *Life of J. R. Colvin* (Oxford, 1895).

Cooper, Frederic. *The Crisis in the Punjab from the 10th of May until the Fall of Delhi* (London, 1858).

Cooper, Leonard. *Havelock* (London, 1957).

Coopland, Mrs R. M. *A Lady's Escape from Gwalior . . . in . . . 1857* (London, 1859).

Cotton, E. S. *Indian and Home Memories* (London, 1907).

Crommelin, N. A. *Memorandum of three Passages of the River Ganges in . . . 1857* (Calcutta, 1858).

Cunningham, Sir H. S. *Earl Canning* (Oxford, 1891).

Cust, R. N. *Pictures of Indian Life* (London, 1881).

Daly, Major H. *Memoirs of General Sir Henry Dermot Daly* (London, 1905).

Dangerfield, George. *Bengal Mutiny:*

The Story of the Sepoy Rebellion (London, 1933).

Dawson, Captain Lionel. *Squires and Sepoys, 1857–1958* (London, 1960).

Defence of Lucknow: A Diary recording the Daily Events During the Siege of the European Residency by a Staff Officer [Captain Thomas F. Wilson] (London, 1858).

De Kantzow, Colonel C. A. *Record of Services in India* (Brighton, 1898).

Duberley, Mrs Henry. *Campaigning Experiences in Rajpootana and Central India during the Suppression of the Mutiny* (London, 1859).

Duff, Alexander. *The Indian Rebellion: Its Causes and Results in a Series of Letters* (London, 1858).

Dunlop, Robert Henry Wallace. *Service and Adventure with the Khekee Ressalah or Meerut Volunteer Force during the Mutinies of 1857–58* (London, 1858).

Durand, Henry Marion. *Central India in 1857* (London, 1859).

Durand, H. M. *The Life of Major General Sir Henry Durand* 2 vols. (London, 1883).

Edwardes, Emma. *Memorials of the Life and Letters of Major-General Sir Herbert Edwardes* (London, 1886).

Edwardes, H. B. and Merivale, H. *Life of Sir Henry Lawrence* 2 vols. (London, 1873).

Edwardes, Michael. *Battles of the Indian Mutiny* (London, 1963).

— *The Necessary Hell: John and Henry Lawrence and the Indian Empire* (London, 1958).

— *British India, 1792–1942: A Survey of the Nature and Effects of Alien Rule* (London, 1967).

— *Red Year: The Indian Rebellion of 1857* (London, 1973).

— *A Season in Hell: The Defence of the Lucknow Residency* (London, 1973).

— *Bound to Exile: The Victorians in India* (London, 1969).

Edwards, William. *Personal Adventures during the Indian Rebellion in Rohilcund, Futtenghur and Oude* (London, 1858).

Embree, Ainslie T. *1857 in India: Mutiny or War of Independence* (Lexington, Mass., 1963).

Esher. *See* Benson.

Ewart, Lieutenant-General J. A. *Story of a Soldier's Life* 2 vols. (London, 1881).

Fayrer, Surgeon-General Sir Joseph. *Recollections of My Life* (London, 1900).

Forbes, Archibald. *Havelock* (London, 1891).

— *Colin Campbell, Lord Clyde* (London, 1895).

Forbes-Mitchell, William. *Reminiscences of the Great Mutiny, 1857–59, including the Relief, Siege and Capture of Lucknow, and the Campaigns in Rohilcund and Oude* (London, 1894).

Forrest, George W. *Selection from the Letters, Despatches and other State Papers preserved in the Military Department of the Government of India, 1857–1858* 3 vols. (Calcutta, 1893–1912).

— *History of the Indian Mutiny* 3 vols. (Edinburgh, 1904–1912).

— *Life of Field Marshal Sir Neville Chamberlain* (Edinburgh, 1909).

Forsyth, Sir Douglas. *Autobiography and Reminiscences* (London, 1887).

Fortescue, J. W. *A History of the British Army* Vol. XIII (London, 1930).

From Sepoy to Subedar. See Lunt.

Further Papers Relative to the Mutinies in the East 2 vols. (Calcutta, 1901).

Gardiner, General Sir Robert. *Military Analysis of the Remote and Proximate Causes of the Indian Rebellion* (London, 1858).

Garret, H. L. O. *The Trial of Muhammed Bahudar Shah, ex-King of Delhi* (Punjab Government Record Office, 1932).

Germon, Maria. *Journal of the Siege of Lucknow* ed. Michael Edwardes, (London, n.d.).

Gibney, Robert D. *My Escape from the Mutineers in Oudh* (London, 1858).

Gimlette, Lieutenant-Colonel G. H. D. *A Postscript to the Records of the Indian Mutiny . . . 1857–58* (London, 1927).

Golant, William. *The Long Afternoon: British India, 1601–1947* (London, 1975).

Goldsmid, Major-General Sir F. J. *James Outram: A Biography* 2 vols. (London, 1881).

Gordon, C. A. *Recollections of Thirty-nine Years in the Army* (London, 1898).

Gordon-Alexander, Lieutenant-Colonel W. *Recollections of a Highland Subaltern in India . . . in 1857–1859* (London, 1898).

Gough, General Sir Hugh. *Old Memories* (Edinburgh, 1897).

Graham, G. F. *Life and Work of Sir Syed Ahmed Khan* (London, 1909).

Grant, General Sir Hope and Sir H. Knollys (ed.). *Incidents in the Sepoy War 1857–1858* (Edinburgh, 1873).

Gray, Robert. *Reminiscences of India* (London, 1913).

Greathed, H. H. *Letters Written During the Siege of Delhi. Edited by His Widow* (London, 1858).

Griffiths, Charles John. *The Narrative of the Siege of Delhi with an Account of the Mutiny at Ferozepore in 1857* ed. Henry John Yonge (London, 1910).

Groom, W. T. *With Havelock from Allahabad to Lucknow* (London, 1894).

Gubbins, Martin Richard. *An Account of the Mutinies in Oudh and of the Siege of the Lucknow Residency . . . with some observations . . . on*

444

the Causes of the Mutiny (London, 1858).

Gupta, Pratul Chandra. *Nana Sahib and the Rising at Cawnpore* (Oxford, 1963).

Halls, John James. *Two Months in Arrah in 1857* (London, 1860).

Hancock, Colonel A. G. *A Short Account of the Siege of Delhi* (Simla, 1892).

Hare, Augustus. *The Story of Two Noble Lives* 3 vols. (London, 1893).

Harris, Major J. T. *'China Jim': Being Adventures of an Indian Mutiny Veteran* (London, 1912).

Harris, Mrs. *A Lady's Diary of the Siege of Lucknow* (London, 1858).

Harrison, Richard. *Recollections of Life in the British Army During the Latter Half of the 19th Century* (London, 1908).

Herford, I. S. A. *Stirring Times Under Canvas* (London, 1862).

Hewitt, James (ed.). *Eye-Witnesses to the Indian Mutiny* (Reading, 1972).

Hilton, Major-General Richard. *The Indian Mutiny: A Centenary History* (London, 1957).

History of the Indian Mutiny . . . A Detailed Account of the Sepoy Insurrection in India (London, n.d.).

History of the Siege of Delhi by an Officer who Served There (Edinburgh, 1861).

Hodson, G. H. (ed.). *Twelve Years of a Soldier's Life in India: Being Extracts from the Letters of the late Major W. S. R. Hodson* (1859).

Holloway, John. *Essays on the Indian Mutiny* (London, 1863).

Holmes, T. Rice. *A History of the Indian Mutiny and of the Disturbances which accompanied it among the Civil Population* 5th ed. (London, 1898).

Home, Sir A. D. *Service Memories* (London, 1912).

Hope Grant. *See* Grant.

Hunter, Charles. *Personal Remini-scences by an Indian Mutiny Veteran* (Brighton, 1911).

Hunter, Sir William. *The Marquess of Dalhousie* (Oxford, 1890).

Husain, Mahdi. *Bahadur Shah II and the War of 1857 in Delhi* (Delhi, 1958).

Hutchinson, David (ed.). *See* Chick.

Hutchinson, Captain George. *Narratives of the Mutinies in Oude* (Calcutta, 1859).

The Indian Mutiny to the Recapture of Lucknow . . . Compiled by a Former Editor of the Delhi Gazette (London, 1858).

Inge, Lieutenant-Colonel D. M. *A Subaltern's Diary* (London, 1894).

Inglis, The Hon. Lady. *The Siege of Lucknow; A Diary* (London, 1892).

Innes, Lieutenant-General McLeod. *The Sepoy Revolt: A Critical Narrative* (London, 1897).

— *Lucknow and Oude in the Mutiny* (London, 1895).

[Ireland, William]. *See History of the Siege of Delhi by an Officer who Served There.*

Jacob, Major-General Sir George Le Grand. *Western India before and during the Mutinies* (London, 1871).

James, David. *Life of Lord Roberts* (London, 1954).

Jivan Lal's Narrative. See Metcalfe.

Jocelyn, Colonel J. R. J. *The History of the Royal and Indian Artillery in the Mutiny of 1857* (London, 1915).

Johnson, W. T. *Twelve Years of a Soldier's Life* (London, 1897).

Jones, Gavin. *My Escape from Fatehgarh* (Cawnpore, 1913).

Jones, Captain Oliver J. *Recollections of a Winter Campaign in India in 1857–1858* (London, 1859).

Jones-Parry, S. H. *An Old Soldier's Memories* (London, 1897).

Joshi, P. C. (ed.). *Rebellion, 1857. A Symposium* (Delhi, 1957).

Journal of the late General Sir Sam Browne (Edinburgh, 1937).

Joyce, Michael. *Ordeal at Lucknow: The Defence of the Residency* (London, 1938).

Kavanagh, T. Henry. *How I Won the Victoria Cross* (London, 1860).

Kaye, Sir John William. *History of the Sepoy War in India, 1857–1858* 9th edn. 3 vols. (London, 1880).

— *Lives of Indian Officers* 2 vols., (London, 1867).

Keene, Henry George. *Fifty-Seven: Some Account of the Administration of Indian Districts during the Revolt of the Bengal Army* (London, 1883).

Kennedy, The Rev. James. *Life and Work in Benares and Kumaon* (London, 1884).

Kincaid, Dennis. *British Social Life in India, 1608–1937* (London, 1973).

Knollys, Sir Henry (ed.). *Incidents in the Sepoy War, 1857–58, compiled from the Private Journals of General Sir Hope Grant* (Edinburgh, 1873).

— (ed.) *Life of General Sir Hope Grant* 2 vols. (1894).

Laird, Michael A. *Missionaries and Education in Bengal 1793–1837* (London, 1972).

Lale, Roderick Hamilton Burgoyne (ed.).*Historical Records of the 93rd Sutherland Highlanders* (London, 1892).

Lang, John. *Wanderings in India* (London, 1859).

Laurence, T. B. *Six Years in the North-West* (Calcutta, 1861).

Laverack, Sergeant Alfred. *A Methodist Soldier in the Indian Army* (London, n.d.).

Lawrence, Lieutenant-General Sir George. *Forty Years' Service in India* (London, 1874).

Leach, E. R. (ed. with S. N. Mukherjee). *Elites in South Asia* (Cambridge, 1970).

Leasor, James. *The Red Fort: An Account of the Siege of Delhi in 1857* (London, 1956).

Leckey, Edward. *Fictions Connected with the Indian Outbreak of 1857 Exposed* (Bombay, 1859).

Lee, Corporal J. *The Indian Mutiny: Events at Cawnpore in June and July 1857* (London, 1893).

Lee, Joseph 'Dobbin'. *The Indian Mutiny: A Narrative of the Events at Cawnpore* (Cawnpore, 1893).

Lee, Sir Sidney. *King Edward VII: A Biography* 2 vols. (London 1925–7).

Lee-Warner, Sir William. *Life of the Marquis of Dalhousie* (London, 1904).

Lehmann, Joseph. *All Sir Garnet: A Life of Field-Marshal Lord Wolseley* (London, 1968).

Letters from the Field During the Indian Mutiny (London, 1907).

Low, Ursula. *Fifty Years with John Company* (London, 1936).

Lowe, Thomas. *Central India during the Rebellion of 1857 and 1858: A Narrative of Operations ... from the Suppression of Mutiny in Aurungabad to the Capture of Gwalior ...* (London, 1860).

Luard, C. E. *Contemporary Newspaper Accounts of Events during the Mutiny in Central India 1857–1858* (Allahabad, 1912).

Lunt, James (ed.). *From Sepoy to Subedar: Being the Life and Adventures of Subedar Sita Ram ... related by Himself* (London, 1970).

Mackay, Rev. James. *From London to Lucknow* 2 vols. (London, 1860).

Mackenzie, Colonel A. R. D. *Mutiny Memoirs: Being Personal Reminiscences of the Great Sepoy Revolt of 1857* (Allahabad, 1891).

Mackenzie, Mrs Colin. *Life in the Mission, the Camp and the Zenana* 3 vols. (London, 1872).

Maclagan, Michael. '*Clemency*' *Canning* (London, 1962).

MacMunn, Lieutenant-General Sir George. *The Indian Mutiny in Perspective* (London, 1931).

Macpherson, William (ed.). *Memorial of Service in India* (London, 1865).

Mainuddin Hassan Khan's Narrative. See Metcalfe.

Majendie, Lieutenant Vivian Dering. *Up Among the Pandies: A Year's Service in India* (London, 1859).

Majumdar, R. C. *The Sepoy Mutiny and the Revolt of 1857* (2nd edition, Calcutta, 1963).

— *History of the Freedom Movement in India* (Vol. 1, Calcutta, 1962). (Gen. ed.) *British Paramountcy and Indian Renaissance,* Vol. IX of *The History and Culture of the Indian People* (Calcutta).

Malet, H. P. *Lost Links in the Indian Mutiny* (London, 1867).

Malleson, Colonel G. B. *A History of the Indian Mutiny 1857–1858 Commencing from the close of the second volume of . . . Sir John Kaye's History of the Sepoy War* 2nd edn. 3 vols. (London, 1878–80).

— *Recreations of an Indian Official* (London, 1872).

Mangin, Arthur. *La Révolte au Bengale 1857 et 1858: Souvenirs d'un officier Irlandais* (Tours, 1880).

Marshman, John Clark. *Memoirs of Major General Sir Henry Havelock K.C.B.* (London, 1860).

Martin, R. Montgomery. *The Indian Empire* 3 vols. (London, n.d.).

Marx, Karl and Frederic Engels. *The First Indian War of Independence* (Moscow, 1960).

Mason, Philip (*see also* Philip Woodruff). *A Matter of Honour: An Account of the Indian Army, its Officers and Men* (London, 1974).

Maude, Colonel Edwin. *Oriental Campaigns . . . Autobiography of a Veteran of the Indian Mutiny* (London, 1908).

Maude, Francis Cornwallis. *Memories of the Mutiny with which is Incorporated the Personal Narrative of John Walter Sherer* 2nd edn., 2 vols. (London, 1894).

Maunsell, General Sir F. R. *The Siege of Delhi* (London, 1912).

Mead, Henry. *The Sepoy Revolt: Its Causes and its Consequences* (London, 1857).

Medley, Julius George. *A Year's Campaign in India from 1857–1858* (London, 1858).

Meek, Rev. Robert. *The Martyr of Allahabad: Memorials of Ensign Arthur Marcus Hill Cheek* (London, 1857).

Memorials of the Life and Letters of General Sir Herbert Edwardes By His Wife 2 vols. (London, 1886).

Merivale, H. *See* Edwardes, H. B.

Metcalfe, Charles Theophilus (transl.). *Two Native Narratives of the Mutiny in Delhi* (London, 1898).

Monypenny, W. F. and C. E. Buckle. *Life of Benjamin Disraeli* Vol. IV (London, 1916).

Morison, J. L. *Lawrence of Lucknow* (London, 1934).

Mouat, Fred J. *The British Soldier in India* (London, 1859).

Mudford, Peter. *Birds of a Different Plumage: A Study of British Indian Relations from Akbar to Curzon* (London, 1974).

Muir, Sir William. *Records of the Intelligence Department of the Government of the North-West Provinces of India during the Mutiny of 1857* ed. William Coldstream, 2 vols. (Edinburgh, 1902).

Mukherjee, S. N. *See* Leach.

Munro, Surgeon-General William. *Reminiscences of Military Service with the 93rd Highlanders* (London, 1883).

Muter, Mrs. *My Recollections of the Sepoy Revolt (1857–1858)* (London, 1911).

Mutinies and the People or Statements of Native Fidelity Exhibited during the Outbreak of 1857–58 by a Hindu (Calcutta, 1859) .

Mutiny of the Bengal Army: An Historical Narrative by one who has served under Sir Charles Napier (London, 1857).

Narrative of Events Attending the Outbreak of Disturbances and the Restoration of Authority in All the Districts of the North-West Provinces in 1857-8 (Calcutta, 1881).

Narrative of an Escape from Gwalior (London, n.d.).

Narrative of the Indian Revolt from its Outbreak to the Capture of Lucknow (London, 1858).

Nash, John Tullock. *Volunteering in India or an Authentic Narrative of the . . . Bengal Yeoman Cavalry during the . . . Sepoy War* (London, 1893).

Norman, Sir Henry Wylie. *A Narrative of the Campaign of the Delhi Army* (London, 1858).

— *Delhi, 1857: The Siege, Assault and Capture as given in the Correspondence of the Late Colonel Keith Young* (London, 1902).

North, Major Charles. *Journal of an English Officer in India* (London, 1858).

Norton, John Bruce. *The Rebellion of India: How to Prevent Another* (London, 1857).

O'Callaghan, D[aniel]. *Scattered Chapters of the Indian Mutiny: The Fatal Falter at Meerut* (Calcutta, 1861).

Oswell, G. D. *Sketches of Rulers of India. Vol. I. The Mutiny Era and After* (Oxford, 1908).

Outram, Sir James. *The Campaign in India, 1857-58* (London, 1860).

Owen, Arthur. *Recollections of a Veteran of the Days of the Great Mutiny* (Lucknow, 1916).

Paget, Mrs Leopold. *Camp and Cantonments: A Journal of Life in India in 1857-1859* (London, 1865).

Palmer, Henry. *India Life Sketches* (Mussoorie, n.d.).

Palmer, J. A. B. *The Mutiny Outbreak at Meerut in 1857* (Cambridge, 1966).

Parker, N. T. *Memoirs of the Indian Mutiny in Meerut* (Meerut, 1914).

Parkes, Fanny. *Wanderings of a Pilgrim in Search of the Picturesque* 2 vols. (London, 1850).

Parliamentary. Reports: 1857 (Vols., 29, 30); 1857-8 (Vols., 42, 43, 44); 1859 (Vols., 11, 23, 25, 37). (London, 1857-60).

Parry, S. H. J. *An Old Soldier's Memories* (London, 1897).

[Parsons, Lieutenant-Colonel Richard]. *A Journal of Jugdespore, 1858* (London, 1904).

Pearman. *See* Anglesey.

Pearse, Colonel Hugh. *The Hearseys* (Edinburgh, 1905).

Pearson, Hesketh. *The Hero of Delhi. John Nicholson and His Wars* (London, 1939).

Peile, Mrs Fanny. *The Delhi Massacre* (Calcutta, 1870).

Pemble, John. *The Raj, The Indian Mutiny and the Princely State of Oudh, 1801-59* (Hassocks, 1976).

Phillips, Alfred. *Anecdotes and Reminiscences of Service in Bengal* (Inverness, 1878).

Pitt, F. W. (ed.). *Incidents in India and Memories of the Mutiny* (London, 1896).

Polehampton, Rev. Henry S. *A Memoir, Letters and Diary of the Rev. Henry S. Polehampton, Chaplain of Lucknow* ed. Revs. E. & T. S. Polehampton (London, 1858).

Pollock, J. C. *Way to Glory: The Life of Havelock of Lucknow* (London, 1957).

Prichard, Iltudus Thomas. *The Mutinies in Rajpootana: Being a Personal Narrative of the Mutiny at Nusseerabad* (London, 1864).

Raikes, Charles. *Notes on the Revolt in the North-Western Provinces of India* (London, 1858).

Ramsay, B. D. W. *Rough Recollections of Military Service* (Edinburgh, 1882).

448

The Rebellion in India. By a Resident of the North-Western Provinces of India (London, 1858).

Rees, L. E. Ruutz. *A Personal Narrative of the Siege of Lucknow* 2nd edn. (London, 1858).

Reeves, P. D. (ed.). *Sleeman in Oudh: An Abridgement of W. H. Sleeman's 'A Journey through the Kingdom of Oude in 1849–50'* (Cambridge, 1971).

Report of the Commissioners Appointed to Inquire into the Organization of the Indian Army (1859).

Revolt in Central India in 1857–9. Compiled in the Intelligence Branch Division of . . . Army Headquarters, India (Simla, 1908).

Rice Holmes. *See* Holmes, T. Rice.

Rich, Captain Gregory. *The Mutiny at Sialkot* (Sialkot, 1924).

Rivett-Carnac, Colonel H. *Many Memories of Life in India* (Edinburgh, 1910).

Rizvi, S. A. (ed. with M. I. Bhargava). *Freedom Struggle in Uttar Pradesh* 6 vols. (Lucknow, 1957–61).

Roberts, Field-Marshal Earl. *Forty-One Years in India* (London, 1911). *Letters written During the Indian Mutiny* (London, 1924).

Roberts, N. J. P. *Personal Adventures and Anecdotes of an Old Soldier* (London, 1906).

Robertson, H. Dundas. *District Duties during the Revolt in the North-West Provinces of India in 1857* (London, 1859).

Robertson, James P. *Personal Adventures* (London, 1906).

Rotton, Rev. John Edward Wharton. *The Chaplain's Narrative of the Siege of Delhi* (London, 1858).

Rowbotham, William (ed.). *The Naval Brigades in the Indian Mutiny* (London, 1947).

Royal Commission on the Sanitary State of the Army in India. Report of the Commissioners . . . (London, 1863).

Ruggles, John. *Recollections of a Lucknow Veteran* (London, 1906).

Russell, Ralph. *The Life of Ghalib* (London, 1952).

Russell, William Howard. *My Indian Mutiny Diary* (ed. Michael Edwardes, with an essay on 'The Mutiny and its consequences', London, 1957).

— *My Diary in India* 2 vols. (London, 1860).

Savarkar, Vinayak Damodar. *The Indian War of Independence, 1857* (Bombay, 1957).

Seaton, Major-General Sir Thomas. *From Cadet to Colonel* 2 vols. (London, 1866).

Sedgwick, F. R. *The Indian Mutiny of 1857* (London, 1909).

Sen, Surendra Nath. *Eighteen Fifty-Seven* (Delhi, 1958).

Services of the Kamptee Moveable Column During the Mutiny and Rebellion in Bengal (Madras, 1862).

Seymour, Charles Crossley. *How I Won the Indian Mutiny Medal* (Benares, 1888).

Shadwell, Lieutenant-General L. *The Life of Colin Campbell, Lord Clyde* 2 vols. (Edinburgh, 1881).

Sharar, Abdul Halim. *Lucknow: the Last Phase of an Oriental Culture* transl. and ed. E. S. Harcourt and Fakhir Hussain (London, 1975).

Shepherd, J. W. *A Personal Narrative of the Outbreak and Massacre at Cawnpore during the Sepoy Revolt of 1857.* 3rd edn. (Lucknow, 1886).

Sherer, J. W. *Daily Life During the Indian Mutiny. Personal Experiences of 1857* (London, 1898). *See also* Maude, F. C.

Showers, Lieutenant-General Charles Lionel. *A Missing Chapter of the Indian Mutiny* (London, 1888).

Sieveking, I. Giberne. *A Turning Point in the Indian Mutiny* (London, 1910).

Small, E. M. (ed.). *Told from the Ranks* (London, 1897).

Smith, H. Bosworth. *Life of Lord Lawrence* 2 vols. (London, 1883).

Smith, Sir John. *The Rebellious Rani* (London, 1966).

Source Material for a History of the Freedom Movement in India Vol. I (Bombay, 1957).

Spear, Percival. *India* (University of Michigan Press, 1961).

— *Twilight of the Mughuls* (Cambridge, 1951).

Spottiswoode, Colonel Robert. *Reminiscences* (Edinburgh, 1935).

Sprot, Lieutenant-General John. *Incidents and Anecdotes* 2 vols. (Edinburgh, 1906).

Srivastava, Khushhalial. *The Revolt of 1857 in Central India* (Delhi, 1966).

Stanford, J. K. *Ladies in the Sun: Memsahibs in India, 1790–1860* (London, 1962).

Stent, G. C. *Scraps from my Sabretache, being Personal Adventures while in the 14th (King's Light) Dragoons* (London, 1911).

Stewart, Charles E. *Through Persia in Disguise . . . with Reminiscences of the Indian Mutiny* (London, 1911).

Surtees, Virginia. *Charlotte Canning* (London, 1972).

Swanston, W. O. *My Journal by a Volunteer* (Calcutta, 1858).

Sylvester, Assistant Surgeon J. H. *Recollections of the Campaign in Malwa and Central India* (Bombay, 1860).

Tahmankar, D. V. *The Rani of Jhansi* (London, 1958).

Taylor, Bayard. *A Visit to India . . . in 1858* (Edinburgh, 1859).

Taylor, Meadows. *Letters During the Indian Rebellion* (London, 1857).

Temple, Sir Richard. *Men and Events of My Time in India* (London, 1882).

Thackeray, Colonel E. T. *Two Indian Campaigns in 1857–1858* (Chatham, 1896).

Thompson, Edward. *The Other Side of the Medal* (London, 1925).

Thomson, Captain Mowbray. *The Story of Cawnpore* (London, 1859).

Thornhill, Mark. *Personal Adventures and Experiences of a Magistrate during the Rise, Progress and Suppression of the Indian Mutiny* (London, 1884).

Thornton, J. H. *Memories of Seven Campaigns* (London, 1895).

Thornton, Thomas Henry. *General Sir Richard Meade and the Feudatory States of Central and Southern India* (London, 1898).

Thoughts of a Native of Northern India on the Rebellion (London, 1858).

Trevelyan, G. O. *Cawnpore* (London, 1865).

— *The Competition Wallah* (London, 1864).

Trial of Mohammed Bahadur Shah for Rebellion (Lahore, 1870).

Trotter, Captain Lionel J. *The Life of John Nicholson* (London, 1897).

— *The Bayard of India* (London, 1910).

Tucker, Henry. *A Letter to an Official Concerned in the Education of India* (London, 1858).

Tuker, Lieutenant-General Sir Francis (ed.). *The Chronicle of Private Henry Metcalfe, H.M. 32nd Regiment of Foot* (London, 1953).

Valvezen, E. de. *The English and India: New Sketches Translated from the French by A Diplomat* (London, 1883).

Vaughan, J. Luther. *My Service in the Indian Army and After* (London, 1904).

Verney, Edmund Hope. *The Shannon's Brigade in India: Being Some Account of Sir William Peel's Naval Brigade in the Indian Campaign of 1857–1858* (London, 1862).

Verney, Major-General G. L. *The Devil's wind: The Story of the Naval Brigade at Lucknow* (London, 1956).

Vibart, Colonel Edward. *The Sepoy Mutiny as seen by a subaltern from Delhi to Lucknow* (London, 1898).

450

Wagentreiber, Florence. *Reminiscences of the Sepoy Rebellion of 1857* (Lahore, 1911).

Walker, T. N. *Through the Mutiny: Reminiscences of Thirty Years ... in India* (London, 1907).

Waterfield, Robert. *The Memoirs of Private Waterfield, Soldier in H.M. 32nd Regiment of Foot, 1842–57.* ed. Arthur Swinson and Donald Scott (London, 1968).

White, S. Dewe. *Indian Reminiscences* (London, 1880).

Wilberforce, Reginald G. *An Unrecorded Chapter of the Indian Mutiny* (London, 1894).

Wilkinson, Theon. *Two Monsoons* (London, 1976).

Williams, G. W. *Memorandum and Depositions on the Outbreak at Meerut* (Allahabad, 1858).

Wilson, Captain T. F. *See Defence of Lucknow.*

Wise, James. *The Diary of a Medical Officer during the Great Indian Mutiny of 1857* (Cork, 1894).

With Havelock from Allahabad to Lucknow in 1857 (London, 1894).

Wolseley, Garnet. *The Story of a Soldier's Life* 2 vols. (London, 1903).

Wood, Field Marshal Sir Evelyn. *From Midshipman to Field Marshal* (London, 1906).

— *The Revolt in Hindustan, 1857–59* (London, 1908).

Woodruff, Philip (Philip Mason). *The Men Who Ruled India. Vol. I. The Founders* (London, 1953).

Wylie, M. (ed.). *The English Captives in Oudh: An Episode of the History of the Mutinies of 1857–58* (Calcutta, 1858).

Wylly, H. C. *Neill's Blue Caps* (Aldershot, 1925).

Yeoward, George. *An Episode of the Rebellion and Mutiny in Oudh* (Lucknow, 1871).

Young, Keith. *See* Norman.

Younghusband, Colonel G. J. *The Story of the Guides* (London, 1909).

Index

Abbott, Major H. E. S., 74th N.I., 99, 100

Abu Bakr, Mirza, 270, 272

Adam, Robert, 26

Afghanistan, 164

Afghan War, First, 54, 60

Agar, 377

Agra, 169; fugitives make for, 142; Muttra treasure to be sent to, 144; Kotah Contingent mutinies in, 151; Moghul architecture, 152; Colvin's handling of situation in, 152–3; panic in, 154–6, 324; conditions in fort, 156–60; incapacity of Colvin and Polwhele, 160–61; Cotton takes command of fort, 161; life at, 162–3; authorities at, 256; cool reception of Greathed's column, 323; and news of fall of Delhi, 323; surprise attack at, 324–5; Ahmed Ahmadullah Shah, 370; Maharajah Sindhia flees to, 385; destruction of churches, 408; Roberts on inhabitants of fort, 426

Ahmadullah Shad, see Maulvi of Faizabad

Ahsanullah Khan, Hakim, 270, 274, 278

Aislabie, Lt, 99, 100

Ajnala, 132

Akbar Shah, King of Delhi, 91–2

Akbar the Great, Moghul emperor, 17, 91, 152

Albert, Prince Consort, 411

Aldwell, Mrs, 94

Alexander, Capt., 240

Aligarh, 126, 162

Ali Khan, 194

Alipur, 125

Allahabad, 137; safe passage guaranteed to, 189; refugees make their way to, 194; 6th N.I. mutinies, 201; Neill restores order, 201–2; cholera, 202; Sikhs sent back to, 205; journey to, 334; Campbell at, 336; refugees sent to, 352, 353; alcohol, 414

Allen, Capt. A. S., 34th N.I., 65, 71

Alten, Major-Gen. Sir Charles von (1764–1840), 199

Ambala (Umbala): trouble at, 72–3, 77; firing practice suspended, 73; revised drill, 74; incendiarism, 74; John Lawrence urges disarmament of native regiments, 121

Ammar Singh, 374

Amritsar, 132

Anderson, Capt. R. F., 25th N.I.: fortifies his house, 224; and volunteers for defence of Lucknow, 225; on Barsatelli, 226; and wounded animals, 241; attacks on his house, 246; on steadfastness of sepoys, 251

Angad Tewari (Ungud; spy), 251–2, 256, 261

Anson, General the Hon. George (1797–1857): background, history, personality, 72; suspends firing practice, 73; Roberts on, 120; and news of massacres at Meerut and Delhi, 120–21; Lawrence's advice to, 121

Anson, Major, 415–16

Aong, 206

452

Army, *see* Bengal Army, Bengal Fusiliers, Corps of Guides, Gurkhas, Gwalior Contingent, Jammu Contingent, Jodhpur Legion, Kotah Contingent, Madras Fusiliers, Regiments *and* Sikhs
Arnold, Dr Thomas, 289
Arnold, Matthew, 38
Arnold, William Delafield (1828–59), 38
Arrah: officials remain at their posts, 133; siege of, 134–5; failure of first attempt to relieve, 135–7; Eyre relieves, 137
Astrologers, 275
Aubert, Capt., 34th N.I., 71
Aurangabad, 415
Aurangzeb, Moghul emperor, 17
Azamgarh, 126, 374
Azimullah Khan, 173, 177, 188–9, 412
Azizun, the courtesan, 188

Baba Bhat, 179
Babur, Moghul emperor, 17
Badli-ki-Serai, 126
Bahadur Shah II, King of Delhi (*d.* 1862), 18; history and interests, 91; British and, 92, 278; and mutineers, 92–3, 269, 271, 420, 422; murder of Christians by servants of, 95, 406; and Magazine in Delhi, 100; Nawab of Jugaur fears, 103; subversive letters from Muttra to, 149; appoints army commanders, 269–70, 272; and shopkeepers' fear of looting, 270; encourages rebellion, 271; financial problems, 272, 278; his letter to Mirza Moghul, 273; Jivanlal on, 274; and Bakht Khan, 275–6, 277, 279; inspects forts and gun emplacements, 277; in despair, 278; at capture of Delhi, 313–14; Chichester and others on, 318; displayed to European visitors, 387–8; tried and sentenced, 388; death of, 388;

extract from his trial about 'chupatty movement', 404; writes to Rajah of Patiala, 420; Canning on relations with, 421–2; Neill on negotiations with, 422
Bailie, Major James, 87th Fusiliers, 131, 213
Baji Rao II, Peshwa of Bithur, 172, 173, 177
Bakht Khan, 275–6, 277, 314
Ballabhgarh, Rajah of, 425
Banda, Nawab of, 384
Bandpur, Rajah of, 139, 380
Banks, Major John Sherbrooke (1811–57), 226, 236–7, 249
Banthira (Banthra), 357–8
Bareilly: mutiny at, 126, 128; Khan Bahadur Khan at, 138, 369; Bareilly force in Delhi, 275; treasury looted, 275–6; Campbell beats Bahadur Khan at, 370
Barhat Ahmad, 232, 233, 371
Barnard, Lt-Gen. Sir Henry William (1799–1857): personality, history, 122; to rendezvous with Hewitt and Wilson, 122; and Wilson join forces at Alipur, 126; and proposed assault on Delhi, 280, 281; Wilson on, 281, 282; general affection for, 282; death of, 283
Barodia, 380
Barrackpore: mutiny, 62; anxiety about cartridges, 64–5; Hearsey reassures sepoys, 67; 19th N.I. disbanded, 71; rumour about sepoys from, 408
Barrow, Capt., 328
Barsatelli, Signor, Lucknow merchant, 225–6
Barter, Capt. (*later* Lt-Gen.) Richard, 75th Highlanders: and execution of holy men, 122; on burning of villages, 122–3; on 75th and Gurkhas, 285; on soldiers in Delhi, 288; on mutineers' dread of bayonet, 295; on Nicholson, 301; on night before assault, 301–2; and assault on Delhi,

460

470

472

Whitlock, Gen., 430
Wickins, Private, 90th, 212, 362, 429
Widdowson, Bridget, 183
Wilberforce, Ensign R. G., 52nd, 293, 424
Williams, Col. *and* Mrs, 180, 190–91
Willoughby, Lt George, 99–100, 119, 283
Wilson, Capt. T. F., 222, 236, 239
Wilson, Lt-Gen. Sir Archdale (1803–74), 83; history and ambition, 75; Gough warns, 81; on Hewitt, 81, 121; and mutiny at Meerut, 89, 90, 405–6; and mutiny in Delhi, 121; on march to Delhi, 125–6; on difficulty of besieging Delhi, 280; on Barnard, 281; and Delhi Force, 282, 283; and reinforcements, 284; tightens discipline, 286; on situation in Delhi, 286–7; on illness and exhaustion in his army, 288; considers withdrawing from Delhi, 291, 309; Nicholson on, 294; ill, tired, at loggerheads with senior officers, 297–8; and proposed assault, 297, 298; on inexperience of Engineers, 300; and plan of assault, 301; apprehensive, 303; concerned by casualties, 309; complains of his officers, 310; and liquor problem, 311; and King of Delhi, 314; and prize agents, 426; takes advice from Chief Commissioner, Lahore, 426
Windham, Major-Gen. (*later* Lt-Gen. Sir) Charles Ash (1810–70), 336, 346, 351, 352
Wise, Dr, 214, 308, 311, 319
Wolseley, Capt. Garnet Joseph (*later*

Field Marshal Viscount Wolseley; 1833–1913); takes oath of vengeance, 212; outraged by stories of atrocities, 213; on Campbell's anger, 336; at second relief of Lucknow, 344; Campbell and, 345; on bravery of Indians, 372–3; on Hope Grant, 430
women, European: Lady Canning's social obligations, 27–8; normal daily life, 35–6; young unmarried, 36, 402; attitude to natives, 37; soldiers' widows, 44; evangelizing by, 45–6; murder of Englishwomen at Meerut, 84; and mutiny in Delhi, 94–5, 101–2, 105–6; Roberts on behaviour of, 120; acts of kindness by Indians to, 138–9; spared at Gwalior, 140–41; alleged atrocities against, 213; at Lucknow, 221, 227, 229, 238; ability to identify missiles, 247; evacuated from Lucknow, 347–9; on march to Cawnpore, 351, 352; at Indore, 376; Lucknow widows, 428
women, native: Hindu widows, 53; in Delhi, 296, 312–13; woman at Sikandar Bagh, Lucknow, 342; in Begum Kothi, Lucknow, 361
Wood, Dr *and* Mrs, 38th N.I., 111, 114
Wrench, Dr, 430, 431
Wright, Capt. J. A., 63–4
Wyatt, James, 26

Young, Miss Emma, 127

Zea-ood-deen Khan, Nawab, 108, 109
Zinat Mahal, 92, 278, 314, 388